A Measure of Wealth

A Measure of Wealth

The English Land Tax in Historical Analysis

DONALD E. GINTER

The Hambledon Press

Published in the United Kingdom by
The Hambledon Press, 1992
102 Gloucester Avenue, London NW1 8HX
ISBN 1 85285 075 2

British Library Cataloguing in Publication Data

Ginter, Donald E.
A measure of wealth: the English land
tax in historical analysis.
I. Title
336.2220942

Published simultaneously in Canada by McGill-Queen's University Press

Printed in Canada on acid-free paper

This book has been published with the help of a grant from the Social Science Federation of Canada, using funds provided by the Social Sciences and Humanities Research Council of Canada.

For Jessica and Adam

Contents

List of Tables

List of Maps

List of Appendices

Abbreviations

NYCRO	North Yorkshire County Record Office
PP	Parliamentary Papers

Preface

For the last twenty years I have been involved, in portions of my research, with the analysis of land tax duplicates. As has so often been the experience of those who first encounter the returns, I was initially full of grandiose projects on how to fully exploit them. But these nasty little documents, which at the outset seemed so simple, proved treacherous. Like others before me, and after years of struggling, I learned to interpret them with the utmost caution. A 1981 article on wealth distributions by Professor Soltow provoked me into publishing a few critical comments on the valuational basis of the tax. The resulting controversy, which coincided with a conference on the interpretation of the tax, suggested that the time was ripe for me to present my views in a more general essay. What began as a brief essay has grown into a large book, and I must confess that even I have been surprised by how much more I have learned about the tax as I have delved ever more deeply into it during the last eight years.

Some topics have been either avoided or skirted in this study. Although I have a number of important and new things to say about the tax in the later seventeenth and early eighteenth centuries, I have not undertaken new research on the political origins of the tax or on the details of most aspects of its early administration. In particular, I have omitted any discussion of the voluminous pamphlet literature on the tax, partly because of its political nature, and partly because I am not in a good position to verify the many unsubstantiated allegations contained therein. My analysis is primarily confined to the years 1780 to 1832, the period where my expertise is greatest and for which documentation on the valuational basis and administration of the tax is abundant. It is unfortunate that the Public Record Office was closed for repairs during the critical period of this research, but an earlier inspection of its holdings leads me to believe that they would in no way have altered my conclusions.

I must apologize to the reader for the poor quality of the maps included in this volume. They are my own crude drawings, and I am no cartographer. I had asked that they be professionally redrawn and presented in colour, but financial constraints have unfortunately made professional redrawing impossible. However, given the spatial nature of many of my arguments, I felt that their inclusion, even in their present format, was important. I hope the reader will find the resulting maps readable; they are not as easily interpretable as I would have wished.

All dates in the book are given in the New Style. Place names have been standardized in their spelling and are based on Bartholomew's *Gazetteer of the British Isles* (ninth edition, 1966). Readers will notice that I tend to employ the term *township* rather than the more familiar *parish*. Much of my evidence comes from Yorkshire, and the discussion in this book is often national in scope. Applied to northern counties, the term *parish* is both ambiguous and misleading, as it is to a lesser degree in some other regions. Indeed the choice of regional terms is a wide one, and I have thought it unwise to introduce *tithings* and other such terms into general discussions. I especially hope southern specialists, who deal almost exclusively with parishes, will be patient with my decision to employ *township* when I am referring in a general way to the lowest units of local civil government. When references are geographically specific, I have tried to employ locally appropriate language.

I would like to thank Michael Ashcroft of the North Yorkshire County Record Office for walks across moors and intellectual companionship, unstinted assistance in my research, and a smiling tolerance of my professorial ways. My deepest sense of gratitude, however, is to Gordon Mingay, whose friendship and advice have both sustained and enlightened me. The more deeply I have delved into the land tax, the more I have come to appreciate the wisdom and penetration of his earlier insights.

Concordia University
Montreal
May 1988

Illustration 1 Page 11 from the Land Tax Register for Birdforth wapentake, North Riding (NYCRO), showing copies of the land tax returns for Dalton and East Harlsey townships in 1693 (n.s.). These are examples of "single-column" duplicates in which both owners and occupiers are intermixed in the first column (see chapter 3). Note in the East Harlsey return that proprietors are listed for at least parts of their holdings (the baronets and perhaps George Lawson) but the return also lists Thomas Fossicke "& other Tennants."

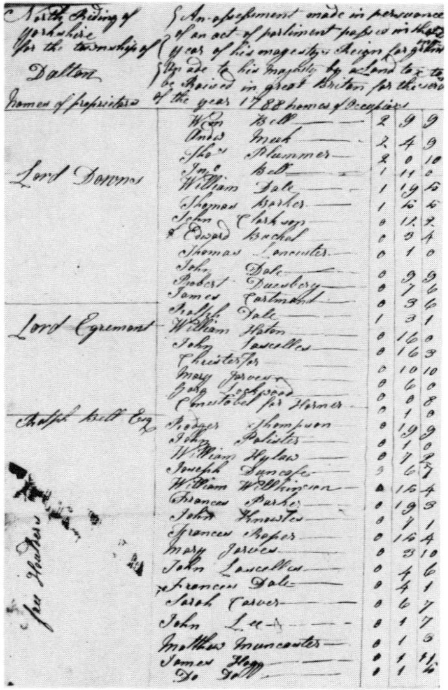

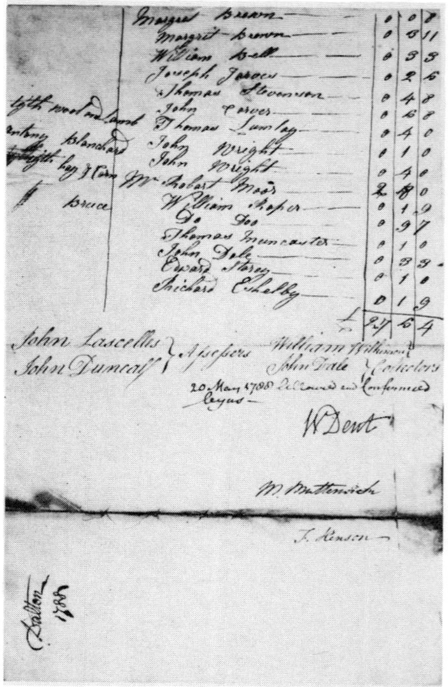

Illustrations 2a and 2b Verso and recto of a 1788 land tax duplicate for Dalton township, Birdforth wapentake (NYCRO). This is an example of the ''two-column'' format common to most duplicates during the 1780s and 1790s prior to the Redemption Act. Notice that in this case it is difficult to distinguish the precise relationships between ''proprietors'' (who appear in the first column) and the ''occupiers'' (who appear in the second column), despite the lines drawn in the proprietor column. It is particularly difficult to discern how many occupiers and tax entries should be assigned to Ralph Bell and which of the occupiers begins the list of ''free Holders.'' Not all of the freeholders are owner-occupiers, as they appear to be (see Illustration 3). Problems such as these can usually be resolved by consulting duplicates for adjacent years. The signatures of Dent, Butterwick, and Henson at the bottom of the duplicate are those of the land tax commissioners.

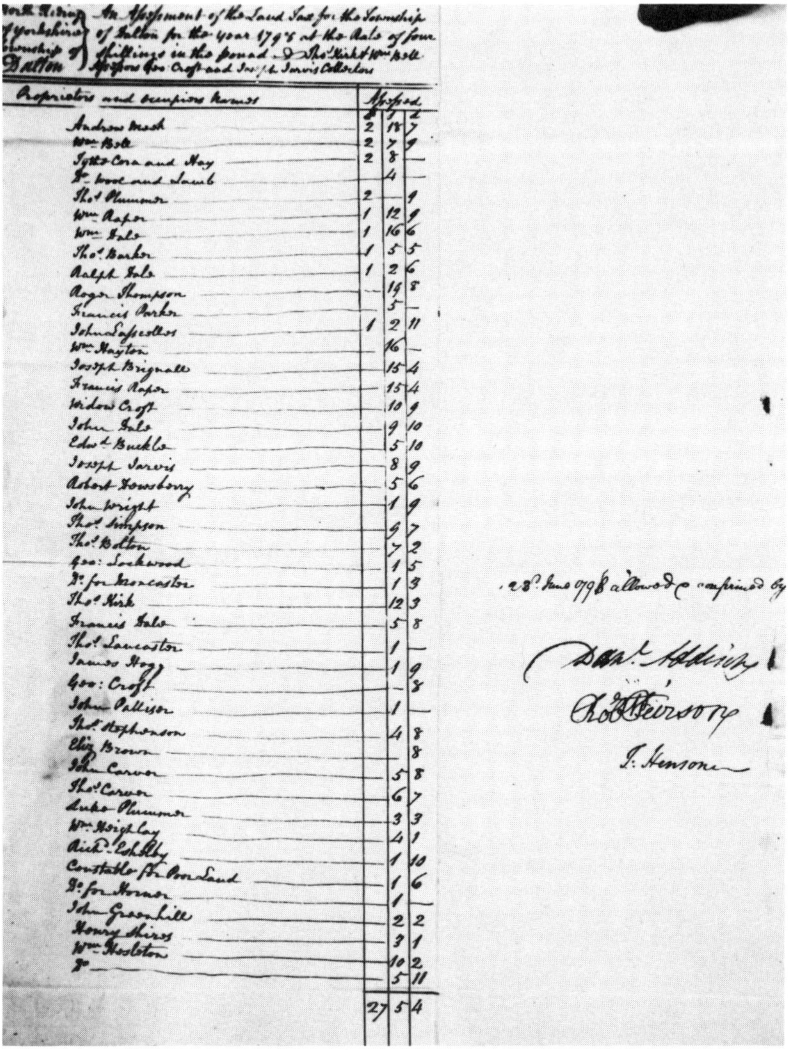

North Riding of Yorkshire Township of Dalton — An Assessment of the Land Tax for the Township of Dalton for the year 1798 at the Rate of four shillings in the pound — Thos. Kirk & Wm. Bell Assessors Geo. Croft and Joseph Jarvis Collectors

Proprietors and occupiers Names	Assessed £	s	d
Andrew Mash	2	18	7
Wm. Bell	2	7	9
Tythe Corn and Hay	2	8	—
Do. wool and Lamb		4	—
Thos. Plummer	2	—	9
Wm. Raper	1	12	9
Wm. Dale	1	16	6
Thos. Barker	1	5	5
Ralph Dale	1	2	6
Roger Thompson	—	14	8
Francis Parker		5	—
John Lascelles	1	2	11
Wm. Hayton		16	—
Joseph Brignall		15	4
Francis Raper		15	4
Widow Croft		10	9
John Dale		9	10
Edwd. Buckle		5	10
Joseph Jarvis		8	9
Robert Towsbury		5	6
John Wright		1	9
Thos. Simpson		9	7
Thos. Bolton		7	2
Geo: Lockwood		1	5
Do. for Moncaster		1	3
Thos. Kirk		12	3
Francis Dale		5	8
Thos. Lancaster		1	—
James Hogg		1	9
Geo: Croft		—	8
John Pallison		1	—
Thos. Stephenson		4	8
Eliz. Brown			8
John Carver		5	8
Thos. Carver		6	7
Luke Plummer		3	3
Wm. Heighley		4	1
Richd. Ashby		1	10
Constable for Poor Land		1	6
Do. for Horner		1	
John Greenhill		2	2
Henry Shires		3	1
Wm. Heslton		10	2
Do.		5	11
	27	5	4

28th June 1798 allowed & confirmed by

Danl. Addison

Robt. Peirson

J. Hensone

Illustration 3 1798 land tax duplicate for Dalton township, Birdforth wapentake (NYCRO). The quotas listed in the returns of this year were those which were fixed permanently by the Redemption Act. Dalton has now temporarily returned to the single-column format, intermixing "Proprietors and Occupiers" in the column of names. The major proprietors, Lords Downe and Egremont and Ralph Bell, are not listed since they are in "occupation" of none of their holdings (see illustrations 4a & 4b and the discussion in chapter 3). Some absentee freeholders are listed (e.g., William Heslington and Luke Plumber), but in some cases their tenants are listed (e.g., Joseph Brignall and Thomas Kirk).

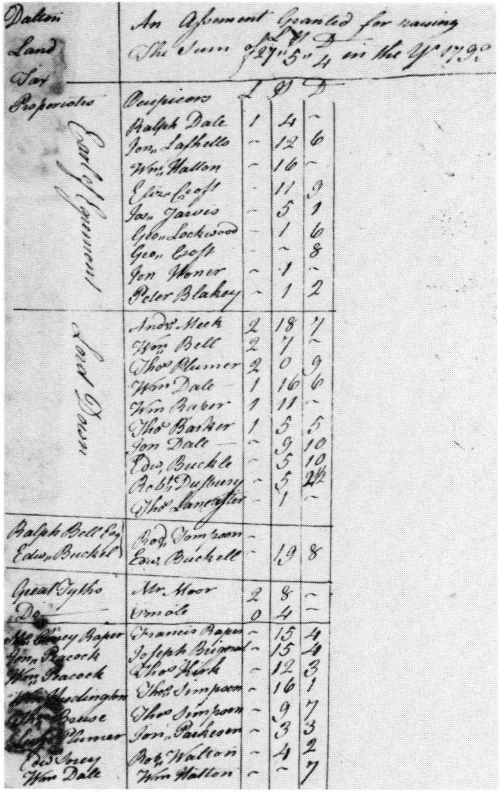

Dalton Land Tax Proprietors	An Assessment Granted for raising The Sum of £27 5 4 in the Yr 1799. Occupiers	L	S	D
Earl of Egremont	Ralph Dale	1	4	–
	Jon. Lashells	–	12	6
	Wm. Walton	–	16	–
	Elin Croft	–	11	9
	Jos. Jarvis	–	5	1
	Geo. Lockwood	–	1	6
	Geo. Croft	–	–	8
	Jon Wener	–	1	–
	Peter Blakey	–	1	2
Lord Down	Andw. Meek	2	18	7
	Wm. Bell	2	7	–
	Thos. Plumer	2	0	9
	Wm. Dale	1	16	6
	Wm. Baker	1	11	–
	Thos. Barker	1	5	5
	Jon Dale	–	9	10
	Edw. Buckle	–	5	10
	Robt. Dusbury	–	5	2½
	Thos. Lancaster	–	1	–
Ralph Bell Esq.	Rob. Tomson	–		
Edw. Buckell	Edw. Buckell	–	19	8
Great Tythe	Mr. Moor	2	8	–
Do.	Ornole	0	4	–
[illegible] Baper	Francis Baper	–	15	4
Wm. Peacock	Joseph Birnal	–	15	4
Wm. Peacock	Thos. Kirk	–	12	3
[illegible]	Thos. Simpson	–	16	1
[illegible]	Thos. Simpson	–	9	7
[illegible] Plumer	Jon. Parkeson	–	3	3
Edw. [illegible]	Robt. Walton	–	4	2
Wm. Dale	Wm. Walton	–	–	7

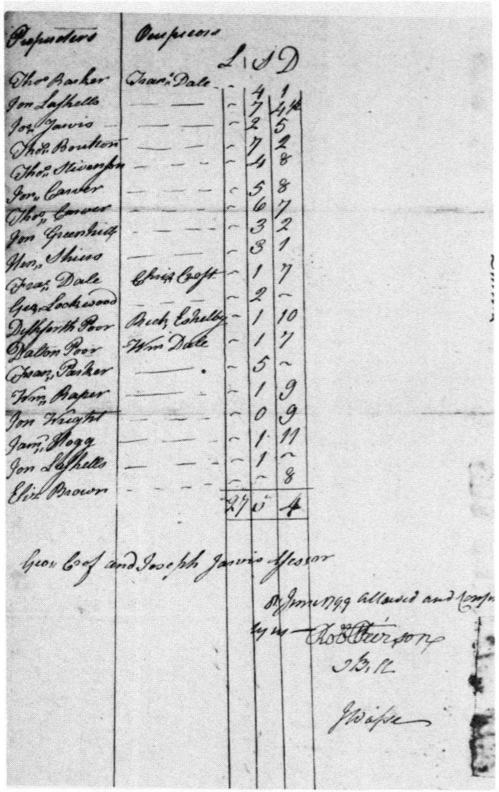

Proprietors	Occupiers	L	S	D
Thos. Barker	Chars. Dale	–	4	1
Jon Lashells	—	–	7	4½
Jos. Jarvis	—	–	2	5
Thos. Boulton	—	–	7	2
Thos. Stevenson	—	–	4	8
Jon. Carver	—	–	5	8
Thos. Carver	—	–	6	7
Jon Greenhill	—	–	3	2
Wm. Shires	—	–	3	1
Fras. Dale	Chris. Croft	–	1	7
Geo. Lockwood	—	–	2	–
Birdforth Poor	Rich. Eshelby	–	1	10
Dalton Poor	Wm. Dale	–	1	7
Fran. Parker	—	–	5	–
Wm. Baper	—	–	1	9
Jon Wright	—	–	0	9
Jam. Hogg	—	–	1	11
Jon Lashells	—	–	1	–
Eliz. Brown	—	–	–	8
		27	5	4

Geo. Croft and Joseph Jarvis Assessors

8 June 1799 allowed and Confirmed by us — [illegible]

Illustrations 4a and 4b 1799 land tax duplicate for Dalton township, Birdforth wapentake (NYCRO). The two-column format has now been resumed. A comparison with adjacent years will confirm that blanks in the occupancy column imply occupancy by the proprietor listed to the left.

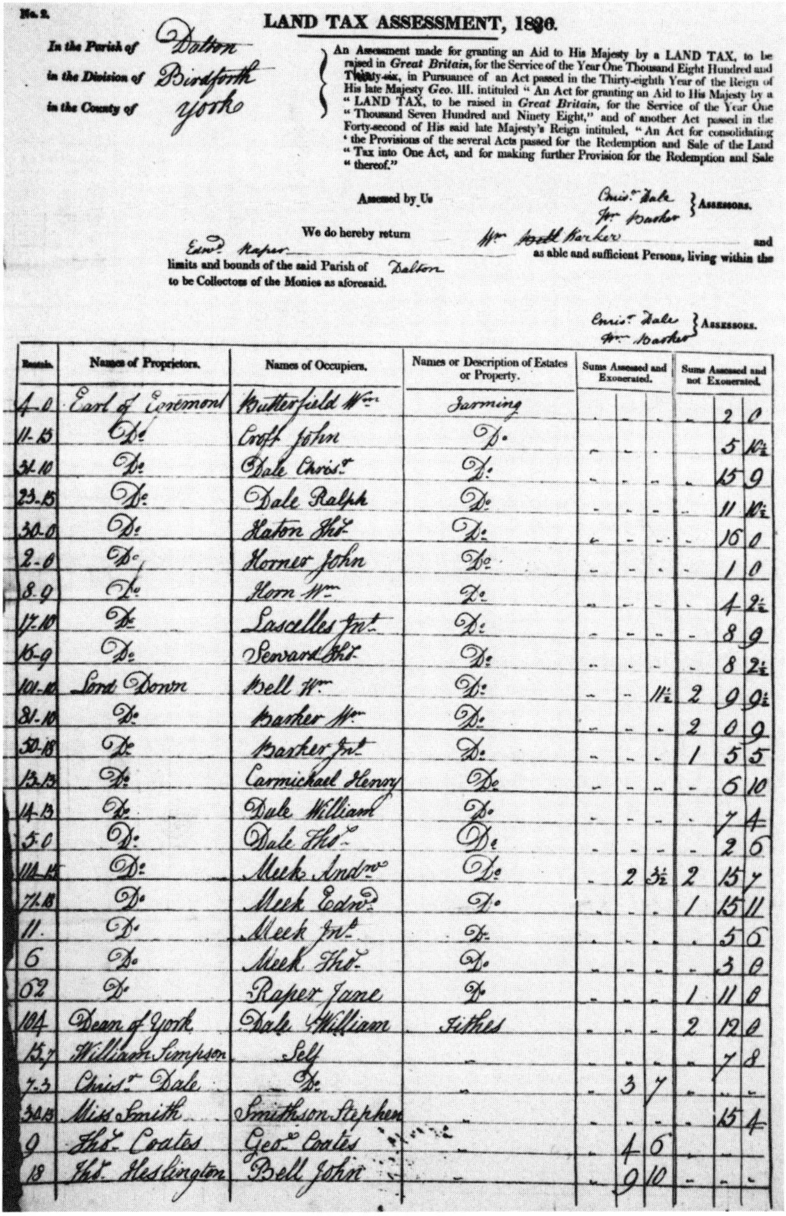
No. 2.

LAND TAX ASSESSMENT, 1830.

In the Parish of Dalton
in the Division of Birdforth
in the County of York

An Assessment made for granting an Aid to His Majesty by a LAND TAX, to be raised in *Great Britain*, for the Service of the Year One Thousand Eight Hundred and Thirty-six, in Pursuance of an Act passed in the Thirty-eighth Year of the Reign of His late Majesty *Geo. III.* intituled "An Act for granting an Aid to His Majesty by a "LAND TAX, to be raised in *Great Britain*, for the Service of the Year One "Thousand Seven Hundred and Ninety Eight," and of another Act passed in the Forty-second of His said late Majesty's Reign intituled, "An Act for consolidating 'the Provisions of the several Acts passed for the Redemption and Sale of the Land "Tax into One Act, and for making further Provision for the Redemption and Sale "thereof."

Assessed by Us — Christr Dale, Wm Barker } Assessors.

We do hereby return Wm Bell Barker and Edwd Raper as able and sufficient Persons, living within the limits and bounds of the said Parish of Dalton to be Collectors of the Monies as aforesaid.

Christr Dale, Wm Barker } Assessors.

Rentals.	Names of Proprietors.	Names of Occupiers.	Names or Description of Estates or Property.	Sums Assessed and Exonerated.			Sums Assessed and not Exonerated.		
4-0	Earl of Egremont	Butterfield Wm	Farming	-	-	-	-	2	0
11-15	Do	Croft John	Do	-	-	-		5	10½
31-10	Do	Dale Christr	Do	-	-	-	-	15	9
23-15	Do	Dale Ralph	Do	-	-	-	-	11	10½
30-0	Do	Haton Thos	Do	-	-	-	-	16	0
2-0	Do	Horner John	Do	-	-	-	-	1	0
8-9	Do	Horn Wm	Do	-	-	-	-	4	2½
17-10	Do	Lascelles Jnt	Do	-	-	-	-	8	9
16-9	Do	Seward Thos	Do	-	-	-	-	8	2½
101-10	Lord Downe	Bell Wm	Do	-	-	11½	2	9	9½
81-10	Do	Barker Wm	Do	-	-	-	2	0	9
50-18	Do	Barker Jnt	Do	-	-	-	1	5	5
13-13	Do	Carmichael Henry	Do	-	-	-	-	6	10
14-13	Do	Dale William	Do	-	-	-	-	7	4
5-0	Do	Dale Thos	Do	-	-	-	-	2	6
114-15	Do	Meek Andw	Do	-	2	3½	2	15	7
71-18	Do	Meek Edwd	Do	-	-	-	1	15	11
11-	Do	Meek Jnt	Do	-	-	-	-	5	6
6	Do	Meek Thos	Do	-	-	-	-	3	0
62	Do	Raper Jane	Do	-	-	-	1	11	0
104	Dean of York	Dale William	Tithes	-	-	-	2	12	0
15-7	William Simpson	Self	-	-	-	-	-	7	8
7-3	Christr Dale	Do	-	-	3	7	-	-	-
30-15	Miss Smith	Smithson Stephen		-	-	-	-	15	4
9	Thos Coates	Geo. Coates	-	-	4	6	-	-	
18	Thos Heslington	Bell John	-	-	9	10	-	-	-

Illustrations 5a and 5b 1830 land tax duplicate for Dalton township, Birdforth wapentake (NYCRO). Most duplicates appear in this format by the later 1820s, although not always on printed forms. The valuational rents appear in the first column, although not all parishes and townships fill them in. The fourth column lists nothing very useful in this case, except tithes, which can now be more firmly identified in Dalton's earlier duplicates. Tithe identification is not usually so easy, however (see chapter 2). Following the Redemption Act of 1798 tax entries appear in separate "exonerated" and "not exonerated" columns. But notice that Dalton and some other North Riding townships "split" tax amounts (cont.)

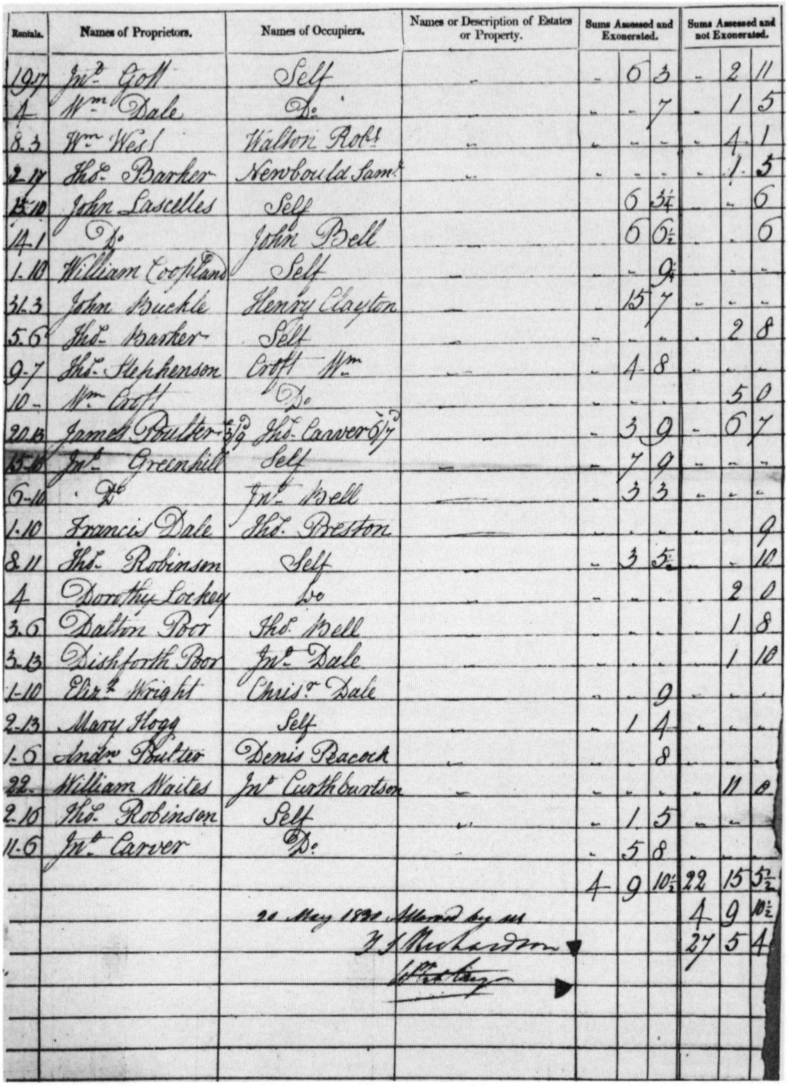

Rentals.	Names of Proprietors.	Names of Occupiers.	Names or Description of Estates or Property.	Sums Assessed and Exonerated.			Sums Assessed and not Exonerated.		
19.7	Jno Goll	Self	–	-	6	3	-	2	11
4	Wm Dale	Do		-	-	7	-	1	5
8.3	Wm West	Walton Robt		-	-	-	-	4	1
2.17	Thos Barker	Newbould Saml		-	-	-	-	1	5
15.10	John Lascelles	Self			6	3¼		-	6
14.1	Do	John Bell			6	6½		.	6
1.10	William Coopland	Self	–		-	9¼		-	-
31.3	John Buckle	Henry Clayton		-	15	7	-	-	-
5.6	Thos Barker	Self	–	-		-	.	2	8
9.7	Thos Stephenson	Croft Wm		-	4	8	-	-	-
10.-	Wm Croft	Do		-	-	-		5	0
20.13	James Boulter 3/9	Thos Carver 6/7		-	3	9	-	6	7
15.16	Jno Greenhill	Self		-	7	9		-	-
6.16	Do	Jno Bell		-	3	3	-	-	-
1.10	Francis Dale	Thos Preston							9
8.11	Thos Robinson	Self		-	3	5¼		-	10
4	Dorothy Lockey	Do		-	-	-	-	2	0
3.6	Dalton Poor	Thos Bell			-	-		1	8
3.13	Dishforth Poor	Jno Dale			-	-		1	10
1.10	Elizth Wright	Chrisr Dale			-	9	-	-	-
2.13	Mary Hogg	Self	–	-	1	4	-	-	-
1.6	Andw Boulter	Denis Peacock	–			8			
22	William Waites	Jno Cuthbertson	–					11	0
2.10	Thos Robinson	Self		-	1	5	-		
11.6	Jno Carver	Do		.	5	8			
				4	9	10½	22	15	5½
		20 May 1830 Allowed by us					4	9	10½
		T. J. Richardson					27	5	4
		W. Lockey							

between both columns on a single line of the return (e.g., the first line of Lord Downe's holdings). Such entries are undoubtedly lumping multiple holdings into a single line entry, but how many holdings are thus lumped cannot be determined. Other types of entries, such as those which appear in the ''Description'' column of other townships, also indicate widespread lumping of multiple holdings into a single line entry (see chapter 3). In addition, proportionate shares of the valuational rent entered in the first column cannot be assigned to either of the tax entries on that line, since redeemed and unredeemed tax entries are not comparable (see chapter 8 and Appendix J).

PART ONE

Introduction

CHAPTER ONE

The Role of the Land Tax in Historical Analysis

In 1981 Lee Soltow reported on a study of wealth inequalities in England and Wales which had made a staggeringly arduous and novel use of the land tax duplicates, and one which is certain never to be duplicated. He sampled the entire range of 1798 duplicates housed in the Public Record Office, compiling a file of 1,073,000 property entries from all counties. This exquisite display of energy was thanklessly attacked by myself and G.J. Wilson in the pages of the *Economic History Review*.[1] What had impressed me most about the Soltow project was the extent to which a careful and widely respected historical economist could misuse the land tax. Clearly those of us with the most experience in using the land tax had failed in our responsibilities to explain fully and in sufficient detail the enormous dangers which are entailed in its use. It had also become apparent within the last few years that new applications of the land tax were rapidly proliferating and that the old abuses, which had never been fully set to rest, were now taking their places beside a growing number of new ones. The magnitudes of error, which had been incorporated within virtually all land tax based studies from the beginning, were now expanding. They had never really been fully appreciated. I therefore began gathering materials for a comprehensive article, which, as I began to write, grew into a small book and then into this larger volume as the topics I undertook to cover proliferated ineluctably.

As documentation on landed society, the land tax is both daunting and seductive. It was first imposed in 1693 (N.S.) in the form of a national poundage rate on both personal and real property. By 1698 land tax collections had begun to experience those sharp declines in revenues which had always tended to plague such taxes, and in that year the decline was checked by replacing the direct poundage rate with a system of county quotas. These county quotas were further subdivided into hundred and parish, or township level, quotas by the local commissioners of the tax.

During the later years of Queen Anne these quotas had in practice become unchangeable. In 1798 they became unalterable by statute, and they remained unchanged until the land tax was abolished in 1963. During the early eighteenth century the government had found, as had prior seventeenth century governments, that impositions of this type on personal property were unenforceable, and the tax evolved, with minor exceptions, into a true land tax assessing land, buildings, and various forms of rents. The most important documents produced by the tax are the annual copies, or "duplicates," of the assessments owed by each owner of real property and, quite often after 1780, by each of his tenants. The original returns and the duplicates were compiled at the township level. Relatively few duplicates survive prior to 1780, but in that year Parliament required that duplicates be retained annually by clerks of the peace for all townships within their jurisdictions as a basis for establishing the qualifications of county voters. Thus from 1780 to 1832 there accumulated within the quarter sessions records of each county a formidable body of information on the landholders and landed relations of the kingdom. It survives, largely intact, in most county record offices and is the most important systematic documentation, both in its geographical and chronological coverage, which we have on landed society in the years between the Domesday of the Conqueror and the New Domesday of the late Victorian era. Its central role in the interpretation of some of our most important historical questions is therefore not surprising. But it is, perhaps, surprising that the reliability of the land tax duplicates in pursuing those questions has never, until now, been thoroughly explored.

The historical use of the land tax duplicates was born amidst the political controversies of the later nineteenth and early twentieth centuries. By the 1870s, and for some fifty years thereafter, English radicals and many of those whose political persuasions were of a more moderate tone were deeply vexed – if not obsessed – by alterations in the distribution of agricultural lands. Most believed that fundamental alterations had occurred in this distribution within the last one hundred years, culminating a longer historical process. In particular, an entire peasant culture based on small, independent family-owned farms and open commons was thought to have given way to an agricultural society characterized by large, capitalist market-oriented farmers and, consequently, that most of the land had become concentrated to an unprecedented degree into the hands of a landed elite and their larger dependent tenantry. These fears, it was believed, had been dramatically confirmed by the New Domesday survey of landed property in 1873 and by the findings of John Bateman, as well as by every parliamentary investigation of the next few decades. In the process, something had passed out of the fibre of the British personality and the structure of British society. Non-Marxist historians such as Arthur

Johnson at Oxford drew parallels with the structure of contemporary agricultural society in France, where the small peasant proprietor was still characteristic. Johnson sought to trace the origins of this catastrophic decline in small proprietorship within England by establishing its chronology since the fifteenth century. He sought the mechanisms of that decline, as had most of his predecessors, within agriculture itself and especially in the process and consequences of enclosure.[2]

Johnson's contemporaries reacted to evidence of the disappearance of the small yeomanry in a variety of ways. Their discussions of this disappearance, or decline, formed only one aspect of a much larger debate on the social and economic merits of the industrial and agricultural revolutions. Those revolutions were analytically the creations of the liberal social reformer and Oxford historian, Arnold Toynbee. In his famous set of university lectures, Toynbee had coined the terms and set (seemingly forever) the boundaries of the debate. The "essence" of the industrial revolution for Toynbee was "the substitution of competition for the medieval regulations which had previously controlled the production and distribution of wealth." "The all-prominent fact" of the industrial revolution was the substitution of a factory for a domestic system of production. The "factory system," which had begun in England around 1785 (though he dates the broader revolution from 1760), was the result of a series of new technological inventions. The system was greatly expanded in the early nineteenth century as canal, road, and railroad infrastructures improved. New scales of demand created further incentives for centralization of production in factories. Structural change was thereby self-sustaining.

Toynbee's treatment of the industrial revolution, in the form it has descended to us (as the posthumously published lecture notes of his students, and we all know how inadequate those can be), was essentially descriptive rather than analytical. The causes and features of the revolution tended to be presented as mere lists, without order and clear inter-relationships. But the elements of more sophisticated analysis were fully present, and they have comprised the content of all future debate. "Coming to the facts of the Industrial Revolution," he says, "the first thing that strikes us is" the unprecedented rate of demographic growth experienced by England from 1760. Toynbee associated this growth with the economic changes he was describing. He also pointed to shifts in the geographical and sectoral distributions of the population and to the declining share of the population held by the Irish. Industrial change was further accompanied by revolutionary changes in the structure of English society. The agricultural population was deeply and permanently affected by rising rents and prices and decreasing wages. Farmers and the *rentier* class of proprietors prospered as agricultural labourers sank deeply into unprecedented levels of poverty. The abandonment of traditional paternalism and the spread of a "cash nexus" created new conditions of class alienation between farmers and those who created their profits by their labour. These same conditions also occurred within the factories of the industrial economy. The nation had fundamentally and systematically become a different sort of place. All forms of significant structural change that occurred in England during the century following the accession of George III were analytically a subset, an aspect, of a sweeping transformation of traditional society. Industrial change was merely the leading edge of that revolution.

Toynbee specifically included an agricultural revolution within that larger context of change and linked it to the processes of industrialization. He described the agricultural revolution as a function of the introduction of new techniques, just as he had seen the introduction of factories and production techniques as triggering the forces of change in the industrial sector. The techniques that he cited were managerial as well as technological and prominently included the dissolution of the common fields through enclosure and the engrossment and consolidation of farms. But note the way he defined his revolution in the countryside: "An agrarian [not agricultural] revolution plays as large a part in the great industrial change of the end of the eighteenth century as does the revolution in manufacturing industries." The revolution in the countryside was more than a technical one. It was more than economic. It was social, and as such it was susceptible to moral judgment. Toynbee was not reluctant to make that judgment in the most categorical terms: "The effects of the Industrial Revolution [and of the Agricultural Revolution with which it was now forever to be associated] prove that free competition [which was its hallmark] may produce wealth without producing well-being. We all know the horrors that ensued in England before it was restrained by legislation and combination." The decline of the small yeoman and the impoverishment of a landless and alienated agricultural labour force were equally the products of a spirit of unfettered market forces, technical innovation and unrestrained greed. The transformation was long in the making, but reached its critical stage during the later eighteenth and nineteenth centuries. Within agricultural society and with respect to the decline of the small landowner, enclosure was its leading instrument. Toynbee's concerns, like his life, were more than academic. Like that of Marx, with whom he had so much in common, his was a historiography of ideological indignation.[3]

But there was more than ideology or indignation underlying the debates that ensued over the timing and causes of the decline of the small landowner. Historians of a more conservative bent could find themselves concerned about the economic efficiency and welfare implications of an agriculture in which self-sustaining family farms had been driven virtually out of existence by more efficient and profitable, but less socially effective, larger units. Historians and politicians of this ilk had more in common with eighteenth century analysts of national wealth than they did with men like Toynbee or the Fabians of Victorian and Edwardian England. There was an additional strain which ran through the writing on the agricultural revolution during these formative years, however; and it was to be of the greatest importance in bringing the decline or disappearance of the small landowner into the forefront of the debate. That strain, and the emotional tone which is its essence, was perhaps best expressed by the French historian, Paul Mantoux. Like Toynbee, Mantoux treated agricultural change as no more than an aspect of the emergence of a larger "factory system," a term which applied equally to agricultural and industrial society after 1760. And like the generality of late Victorian and Edwardian radicals to whom he was indebted, Mantoux focused his indignation and analysis principally on the fortunes of the *smaller* yeomanry, "men whose annual income did not exceed £80 and who compared fairly well with the landowning peasants on the Continent" (echoing the concerns of Arthur Johnson). The tumultuous changes of the industrial and agricultural revolutions had swept away an entire peasant culture based on small holdings and open commons, and in the process the very roots of English society had been undermined. Mantoux described those consequences in thundering tones.

up to a comparatively recent date England possessed a considerable class of small landowners and of customary tenants who were almost as strongly attached to the soil as if it had actually belonged to them. They were the *yeomanry*, whose almost total disappearance it became, in the nineteenth century, a kind of ritual to lament. John Stuart Mill wrote with respect of that hard-working, independent peasantry "who were vaunted as the glory of England while they existed, and have been so much mourned over since they disappeared." They were, in Macaulay's words, a manly and a true breed. Wordsworth, describing the Lake District, praised its former inhabitants and wrote: "Till within the last sixty years, towards the head of these dales was found a perfect republic of shepherds and agriculturalists, among whom the plough of each man was confined to the maintenance of his own family or to the occasional accommodation of his neighbour. Two or three cows furnished each family with milk and cheese ... Neither high-born nobleman, knight, nor esquire, was here, but many of these humble sons of the hills had a consciousness that the lands which they walked over and tilled had for more than five hundred years been possessed by men of their name and blood. ..." That which made the yeoman different [than the squire above him or the tenant beneath him] was his independence. To it he chiefly owed his stalwart character, and the part he played in the ancient days of English history. Out of the yeomanry came, in the

Middle Ages, those dreaded archers and pikemen who won the day at Crécy, at Poitiers and at Agincourt. Later, the yeomen became Protestants and Puritans; they were the staunchest supporters of the Reformation and fought in the armies of Fairfax and Cromwell. Their importance may have somewhat diminished in the course of the seventeenth century. Yet, even after the Revolution of 1688, they still formed a large section of the community. ... Today the yeomanry no longer exist as a class.[4]

The yeomanry, like the glories of Britannia, had gone the way of the good roast beef of old England. This was a historiography of nostalgia.

Academic concern with the fortunes of the small landowner was therefore born within the context of a larger debate about the nature and moral consequences of a revolutionary change in the structure of traditional society. The tone of that debate was ideological, often jingoistic, romantically nostalgic and intensely emotional. The framework and terms of later discussion had thus been set from an early date. Though the early impetus has largely disappeared, the framework has not. The decline of the small landowner and the role of enclosure in that decline remain central issues among those who study the consequences of industrial change and the "modernization" of society – or, as others would have it, the spread of a capitalist mode of production. Arthur Johnson and H.L. Gray, who were the first to make a historical use of the land tax duplicates, wedded the pursuit of such questions to an exploitation of those duplicates.[5] This was the first use of the duplicates for academic purposes. It remains their most important use. What could be more suitable to the study of the declining fortunes of the yeomanry of old England than a documentation which ostensibly provides a complete year-by-year inventory of all proprietors and all occupiers, with the amounts of tax each owed, for every township of the kingdom? And what could be more serendipitous than this systematic documentation covering precisely the period when virtually all moral critics of the decline claimed this decline occurred, namely, during the years 1780 to 1832, when the "factory system" was most intensively penetrating the countryside and parliamentary enclosure, the nefarious instrument of that exploitation, was at its height? The land tax as a source of historical investigation has thus remained throughout this century the most important documentation on questions that are at the heart of our most heated and sophisticated academic and political debates. This book will undertake the first systematic critique ever made of the land tax duplicates as historical documentation. I will suggest that the documentation is wholly inadequate to the study of the fortunes of the small yeoman, and that the literature on this most important subject must be fundamentally reconsidered and perhaps set aside.

The land tax has more recently been employed to investigate other important effects of the transition to a modern industrial society. Lee Soltow is a leading student of the historical development and comparative differences in wealth inequalities. In 1981, on the basis of a gigantic machine-readable national sample of tax entries from the 1798 land tax duplicates, Soltow attempted to establish a firm statistical base-line from which to measure the development of wealth inequalities in England before and after industrialization. If allowed to stand unchallenged, that study would have permanently coloured the interpretation of industrialization within England – and elsewhere by implication – and the uses to which this extraordinarily attractive documentation might properly be put. The use of the land tax employed in that study was challenged in the pages of the *Economic History Review*. The challenge will be expanded and made more categorical here.[6]

The analytical use of the land tax has generally been restricted to the study of rural and agricultural townships, due to distortions which were believed to exist in the tax values of urban properties. Within the last decade, however, pioneering applications of the duplicates have been made in the study of urbanization, more particularly in the development of morphological patterns among small market towns. The progress of development on industrial coalfields has also been studied using the land tax. I shall suggest that such uses of the duplicates are promising but should be pursued under certain restrictive conditions.[7]

A more slowly expanding but exceedingly important application of the land tax documentation has been in the study of the unreformed English electorate. The eighteenth and early nineteenth centuries are now widely perceived as the germination period for the emergence of modern forms of political society, as well as for the industrial and agricultural revolutions. It may be, in fact, that modern political systems are only one more form in which the "factory system" and all it implies manifested itself in the English countryside. The political history of later Stuart and Georgian England has come to focus – generating a good deal of heat – on the emergence of modern political parties. Over the last three decades, three schools of thought have predominated. One school tends to view modern political parties as having first emerged in the later seventeenth century and surviving thereafter continuously but with varying intensity.[8] A second school of thought finds political parties emerging for the first time during the 1780s and early 1790s, only to lapse thereafter until the 1830s. This second view tends to rely on conceptual definitions and to strongly emphasize the importance of altering structural differences in the economics and infrastructure of the countryside.[9] A third school of historians has for almost a century viewed party as emerging for the first time in the 1830s in the wake of the first Reform Bill and as a function of an expanding electorate.[10] The differences between these three schools of interpretation are fragmented, with the specialists of each chronological period arguing for the importance of their own period. Or, perhaps one should say that at least the argument has now begun.[11] Until the early 1980s, the specialists of each period simply ignored one another. There has always been a queer parochialism among English historians, a parochialism which is more than geographical.

An important part of the search for political parties has, within the last decade, come to focus on the behaviour of the unreformed electorate. Was that electorate ideologically alert and issue-oriented, as Professor Rudé has suggested? Was the urban politics of the later eighteenth century a politics of class?[12] Or was it a politics that was fundamentally aligned on a basis of religious affiliation, as John Phillips has suggested? Did party aligned behaviour emerge in urban constituencies during the 1780s, coinciding with the emergence (according to some of us) of party at the national level? Phillips has offered evidence that it did.[13] All such research, which is growing in quality and sophistication, is largely dependent on a massive development of data bases derived (for its economic analysis) from the land tax and poor rate documentation. I shall suggest that this particular use of the land tax duplicates and poor rate books is ill-advised and fundamentally flawed – a most unfortunate conclusion, since I shall thereby undermine views which strongly support my own interpretations.

But in the end I shall attempt to lift the veil of gloom and usher in a brighter and more promising day. There is a method which can reliably exploit the land tax duplicates as a systematic documentation covering every township in the kingdom. Provided the duplicates are used within a narrow span of years, they are amenable to studies incorporating the widest range of variables – whether they be economic, social, demographic or political – and in a manner which is suitable either to qualitative or to the full range of mathematical and statistical analyses. The full potential for studies based centrally on the land tax has scarcely begun to be explored. If my conclusions are acceptable, then the land tax duplicates will remain what they have always been since the days of Johnson and Gray: Along with the Domesday Survey of 1086 and the New Domesday and Bateman surveys of the 1870s, and the more fragmentary tithe surveys, they are one of the premier sources of systematic documentation on landholding in Britain.

PART TWO

Interpreting the Structure of the Land Tax Duplicates

CHAPTER TWO

Minor Problems

The land tax duplicates have an appearance of clarity and simplicity. Basically they contain three categories of data, each arranged in a separate column: the name of each proprietor within the township; the names of the occupiers, sometimes described in the duplicates as "tenants," of each property; and the amount of tax assessed, sometimes broken down only at the level of each proprietor entry, but most often distributed at the level of each occupier. A sizeable proportion of duplicates may contain one or more additional categories of information. For example, a value called "rent" is widely reported in duplicates throughout England after 1826. Scattered reportings of so-called rents are found at much earlier dates, and in some counties they are commonly reported as early as the 1780s. After 1826 most land tax printed forms also call for the "Names or Descriptions of Estates or Property." Local officials variously interpreted this instruction, some reporting the nature of tenure for each property. Field and place names were normally reported in Cornwall and sometimes elsewhere. Occasionally land use or farming regime was entered in the column. But the majority of assessors responded to the instruction by indicating whether the property was land, building, tithes, or some combination thereof. As in the case of the value "rent," property descriptions are also found in scattered duplicates at earlier dates, and quite frequently in some counties. In some townships, and particularly in market and commercial towns, it is not unusual to encounter separate tax entries, sometimes occupying separate columns, for "stock in trade" and income from offices, the latter most often representing the salaries of excise and customs officers. And, finally, in 1798 the government permitted proprietors to buy out or "redeem" their land tax assessment in perpetuity. Beginning in 1799 or 1800 the tax entries in the duplicates are therefore separately entered in redeemed and unredeemed columns.

MINOR AMBIGUITIES

Despite its appearance of clarity and simplicity, the land tax is as hazardous as a mine field for the historian. Very little in the duplicates is quite what it appears to be, nor do the duplicates say precisely what they appear to say to the uninitiated. Some of their defects, which have long been recognized by historians, quickly become evident even to the novice user. Horizontal matchings of proprietors, occupiers, and assessments are often written ambiguously and are sometimes out of sequence in the duplicate being examined. Handwriting can be execrable. Owner-occupiers are commonly indicated in the duplicates by entries of ''himself'' in the occupier column; but, when the returning officer enters ''ditto'' in that column, as he so frequently does, it is not always evident whether the ditto refers to the occupier above or to the proprietor to the left, since clear instances of both practices are commonly encountered. Proprietor entries will sometimes contain a name followed by a generalized entry such as ''& Co.'' It is often difficult if not impossible to determine whether such an entry refers simply to additional unidentified proprietors or to a business firm. The former interpretation is supported for some proportion of cases by the frequent incidence of such entries as ''sundry persons'' or ''his tenants'' in the occupier column. On some duplicates the tax entries represent only quarterly or half-yearly rather than yearly amounts. In rare cases a duplicate will report only valuational rents in the tax column, without identifying them as such. Redeemed entries, which no longer required collection, are sometimes quietly omitted. Quite frequently the individual assessments will not add up to the total for the township recorded at the bottom of the duplicate. Such deficiencies are commonplace in the land tax duplicates, and there is a broad consensus among experienced users that, if ignored, they are capable of producing errors of considerable magnitude. There is a further consensus of opinion, however, that such hazards are substantially avoidable. Most of the deficiencies can be identified and the ambiguities resolved if one takes the trouble to consult duplicates for a series of years immediately surrounding the duplicate being analysed. More intractable problems can be avoided by treating offending duplicates as defective and turning to alternative townships. Such defects will thus not be given much attention in the discussion that follows.[1]

NOMINAL RECORD LINKAGE

More difficult problems arise when personal names appear more than once in the proprietor or occupier columns. In many townships the names of the proprietors are encountered only once and, especially when such entries list multiple occupiers, it would appear that the assessor has aggregated all holdings of each proprietor into a single line entry or uninterrupted sequence of entries. But, in a large proportion of duplicates, the names of various proprietors are entered many times within the proprietor column, apparently for different pieces of property held within the township. For example, the 1806 duplicate for New Malton St Michael's in the North Riding of Yorkshire lists Lord Fitzwilliam in 109 proprietor entries scattered throughout the duplicate. Since it can easily be established that there was only one peerage creation of that title in 1806, the various Fitzwilliam entries can be linked with a perfect assurance of accuracy. Moreover, in such cases nominal linkages can also be made between townships and even between counties. Other titles conferred formally by the Crown can similarly be used with confidence for broad geographical linkage.

More informally ascribed ranks, such as esquire or gentleman, can also be useful, but within more circumscribed geographical areas, and their employment for linkages must be supported by a substantial knowledge of major landholdings in the region. Within the North Riding wapentakes of Ryedale and Pickering Lythe, any entries of "Charles Duncombe, Esq." almost certainly pertain to a single individual, Charles Duncombe of Duncombe Park. But what if the name "Charles Duncombe" is entered without the rank? A reference to duplicates for other years would normally clarify such a problem, especially for large properties; and, in any case, the linkage is more certain when the property in question is a large one within the region of a largeholder of that name. But often the name of a large proprietor within the region, lacking any rank ascription, is entered on the duplicate of a township only once and for a small piece of property. What then? Estate records would help, of course, but they are not always available. One could simply dismiss such an entry as an improbable linkage, on the assumption that large landowners would not acquire, or if acquired would not retain, very small holdings detached from their principal possessions. But unfortunately such an assumption is not warranted. There are innumerable clear instances in the land tax duplicates of small and well-detached parcels held by persons who are baronets and peers of the realm and who are therefore firmly identifiable. Nor do all great landowners have names so relatively rare as Duncombe. There are considerable difficulties, then, in identifying all of the properties even of major landholders of a region.[2]

But it is in moving further down the social scale that the most severe problems in nominal record linkage arise. The remaining names in the duplicates do not normally have additional ascriptions that might be employed in identifying them. Sometimes individuals sharing a common name are identifiable as separate individuals by the addition of "Sr" or

"Jr," or by a place of residence or an occupation, but such auxiliary designations are found only in a small minority of cases. Thus nominal record linkage is a hazardous undertaking even within individual townships for the great majority of proprietors and occupiers, and it should be attempted between townships only for persons with ascribed status or title.

Nominal record linkage cannot be dismissed as a trivial problem. The incidence of multiple name entry in the duplicates is very high, and it is difficult to think of a study based on the land tax whose results would not have been significantly affected by the choice of procedures in handling such cases. In studying the disappearance of the small landowner, for example, surely it is sensible first to aggregate the holdings owned by each proprietor within the township. *Smallness* is thus measured in terms of the total owned holdings of each proprietor – within that township at least. If a proprietor bears no title or ascribed status, then he may have unidentified (and unidentifiable) holdings in adjacent or more distant townships. Indeed he may be "small" in township A but "large" in township B. Where spuriously *small* holders can be identified, as they can in those numerous cases where persons of title or status are reported only with small holdings, they should receive special analytical treatment and not be merely lumped in with yeomen and cottagers. To some incalculable extent smallness is a function of the structure of the land tax returns, which fail to report and link across township boundaries and thus fundamentally distort the real structure of landholding by administratively fragmenting it.[3]

On the other hand nominal record linkage can exploit one of the principal strengths of the land tax duplicates. Landholding studies have tended to categorize holders as absentee proprietors, owner-occupiers, and tenants. But in fact, as some critics have noted, these three categories fall far short of portraying the complexity of English landholding. Persons who owned some of their properties often held others on lease, and some of those properties they owned might themselves even have been leased to another farmer. Such persons cannot in any simple fashion be placed in any one of the three traditional landholding categories, and it is difficult to know how they have traditionally been treated in studies which traced the decline of owner-occupiers, for example. Such procedures are never explained. Similarly, it is striking how often the largest tenants in a township are also entered in the duplicates as small owner-occupiers. Such tenants owned and occupied their own house and garth, or sometimes a small home farm which constituted the core of their holdings, and this is information which the estate records of their large landlord would not normally reveal. Nominal record linkage within the land tax duplicate will inform us that this small owner-occupying cottager was actually a major tenant farmer and a man of considerable substance and standing in his community.[4] It is questionable whether such large tenant farmers should find their way into counts of declining owner-occupiers. Owner-occupation was not their primary characteristic. Nor were they *small* holders, except (misleadingly) as proprietors. It is inevitable that landholding categories be employed in such studies, but the categories must be filled by line entry counts that take fully into account the complexities of the farming community. Too mechanical an interpretation of the land tax duplicates will destroy the rich textures in landholding which they so uniquely reveal.[5]

Without elaborating any further examples, it is perhaps sufficiently clear that linking names within or between land tax duplicates poses procedural problems which are severe and which bear substantial consequences. To choose a procedure is unavoidable. Even a decision never to link names constitutes a choice. The dilemma lies in selecting a procedure which optimally supports research objectives while minimizing bias. The critical literature on nominal record linkage has generally focused on unifying entries between separate records of different provenance.[6] The rigorous logic employed in such studies applies somewhat to linkages between the land tax duplicates of separate townships, then, but it does not really apply to linkages within a single duplicate. Unless assistance can be found through supplementary data sources, linkages within a land tax duplicate must be based wholly on procedures rooted in experience and common sense assumptions. To most scholars common sense will probably suggest that assessors, being often semi-literate and generally uninstructed, were quite capable of listing two separate individuals of the same name on the duplicate without distinguishing between them. If one concedes such an assumption (as we should), and further assumes that shared names are not unusual in the countryside (a certainty) *and* that assessors failed to distinguish them with significant frequency (a more dubious assumption), then it may be wise to adopt a procedure which resists all linkages when titles or ascribed ranks or other supplementary indicators are not present. Such a procedure would fail to identify a large tenant as also being a small owner-occupying cottager and would result in a large number of inappropriate and highly distorting classifications. An analysis based on such a procedure would produce a highly distinctive picture of landholding society.

An alternative procedure, and a rather different and less fragmented view of landholding society, would result if a different set of assumptions governed the analysis. It is important to remember, I think, that land tax duplicates were not constructed for purposes of historical research. They were practical instruments of local government, designed for the assessment and collection of national taxes at a particular point in time. They were subject to local review and appeal, and a copy of the return was attached to the church door. The return therefore should have been interpretable to the local community – or that at least would have been the intention of a conscientious assessor. The document should also have been sufficiently free of ambiguity to enable the collector to identify the person responsible for payment of the tax. Even if the assessor and collector were the same person, as they most often were, it would have been helpful to serve clear notice against whom the collector intended to proceed. If this practical aspect of the document is assumed, then it may be possible to assume further that persons bearing the same name without further designations were indeed the same person. The occasional employment of "Sr" or "Jr" or other supplementary designators serve to confirm that distinctions were often made where confusion could arise. It is therefore possible to make assumptions regarding the practical nature of the documents, assumptions which enable systematic linkages to be made within townships. Occasional careless entries may be rectified to some extent by consulting duplicates for adjacent series of years.[7] Some errors will remain, but they will be relatively few and have small statistical impact.

But whatever the assumptions, it is essential that the procedures adopted and the reasons for their adoption be clearly and fully specified when the research is reported. A failure to report all procedures has been a leading deficiency in land tax studies to date and has almost certainly contributed to a lack of comparability. The problem is so severe that comparability often cannot be judged from the reports alone. It is usually easy to see whether class intervals are comparably constructed, for example; but how the counts were achieved which fill each interval is an important mystery to which we are seldom introduced.

TITHES

As a unit of analysis, tithes pose a special problem, one which is worth considering separately. Some historians have wished to exclude tithes. Gray wished to count only owner-occupying yeomen and therefore, so he claimed, he excluded all entries of tithes. Hunt felt it was "often possible to deduce the payments on tithes when the payer was described as 'Rev.' or 'expropriator.' " In some cases he consulted the 1825–32 duplicates where descriptions of property were given, and "sometimes" he was able thus to trace tithe entries back to much earlier duplicates. He argued that tithe entries should be excluded from landownership distribution counts before enclosure, when tithe was payable on crops and not on land, but he included tithe entries after enclosure, when payments were based on landownership.[8]

Hunt's argument is an important one, but it is not equally important for all studies. Those studies which attempt to measure the size of holdings as acreage are compelled to take the argument very seriously indeed. Tithes prior to enclosure are not real property, if one means acreage by that term. Nor are buildings, for that matter. Again the problem is not a trivial one. In most agricultural townships where tithes are identifiable they probably constituted between 5 and 10 percent of the taxable value by the end of the eighteenth century. Higher proportions were not unusual. In the North Riding lowland mixed-husbandry wapentake of Hallikeld, they generally comprised 10 to 15 percent of taxable value (table 2.1). In counting acres, then, it is clear that tithes should somehow be excluded. But can they be? Certainly they cannot be excluded systematically in all townships. It is simply incorrect to suggest, as Hunt does, that all clerical proprietor entries represent tithes. Some clergymen were also independently wealthy and held vast estates, and innumberable small holdings, as many duplicates make abundantly clear. Nor is it possible to resolve all such residual problems by tracing tithe entries back from the duplicates of the later 1820s, as Hunt himself concedes. The simple fact is that tithes cannot be systematically excluded.[9] To exclude them from some townships, where they can be identified, but not from others, will only introduce incomparabilities into data which is already replete with such problems.

Alternative solutions are possible. One may give up the hoary old procedure of converting tax entries into acreage equivalents, for example. One may go even further and give up thinking of "large" and "small" in acreage terms at all. It is possible instead to think of the tax entries as representing proportionate shares of the real wealth of the township, including the income directly produced by real property.[10] Tithes, like rents, constitute such income. This treatment is not unreasonable, provided suitable adjustments are made in explanatory objectives. Moreover, field books and valuations show that tithes owed by a property often, and perhaps normally, formed part of a landlord's calculation in imposing rents on his tenants. In short, there is every reason to include tithes when measuring the distribution of real property values within a township, providing real property is considered as one type of wealth rather than as acres. I have systematically included tithes and buildings in my calculations for this study. Only salaries and stock-in-trade have been excluded. The latter two categories have the virtue of being more systematically identifiable, in no way constitute income or direct outputs of real property, and are thus inappropriate to calculations of real wealth.

QUOTAS

It has always been said that the land tax quotas, after having been imposed on the counties by statute in 1698 and further distributed in that year among the hundred divisions and parishes, were never again altered until

Table 2.1
Tithe (excluding glebe) as a percentage of total reported value, all townships separately reporting tithe, Hallikeld wapentake, North Riding, 1824

Township	1824 County rate (%)	1824 Land tax (%)
Asenby	13.2	11.1[a]
Baldersby	10.3	13.8
Burneston	10.6	9.2
Carthorpe	12.1	NE
Dishforth	12.5	NE
East Tanfield	13.6	18.8
Exelby, Leeming and Newton	3.4	2.6[a]
Gatenby	3.9	3.0
Howe	14.0	11.0
Humburton and Milby	15.2	6.9
Marton le Moor	1.2[b]	0.6[b]
Melmerby	NE	8.8
Pickhill and Roxby	12.7	4.5
Rainton and Newby	0.3[b]	def.
Sinderby	11.1	14.4
Sutton Howgrave	14.9	10.1
Swainby and Allerthorpe	10.1	4.8
Wath	NE	11.5
West Tanfield	9.8	11.7

Notes: Glebe may have been included in some townships where "tithes" were lumped into a single entry.
NE = not separately entered; lumped with landed property
def. = defective
[a] Tithes were not identified as such on the land tax duplicate. The correct entries were inferred by matching the county rate valuations.
[b] Only wool and lamb tithes were reported. Most townships reporting tithes include the tithes on corn and hay, which are much larger, and sometimes vicarial tithes as well. The nature of the tithes in Exelby and Gatenby was not specified.
Sources: 1824 valuations for the county rate, QFR 1/5; 1824 land tax duplicates, NYCRO.

the tax was abolished in 1963. This generalization is substantially correct, and most studies, including this one, correctly refer to the parish and township quotas as ossified. But strictly speaking this generalization is not correct. During the first decade or so of the administration of the land tax following the statute of 1698, the amounts imposed by the land tax commissioners on many townships varied sharply. Only towards the end of the reign of Queen Anne did parish and township quotas begin to conform more uniformly to those employed throughout the subsequent history of the tax and imposed by statute in 1798. We shall examine these early fluctuations in more detail in chapter 4, where we shall see that they were largely due to variations in double assessment among Roman Catholics.

The variability of these early quotas should be taken into account by those who wish to compare landholding structures in the early and later periods. Subsequent chapters in this book will raise numerous objections to comparing landholders *between* townships on the basis of the amount of tax paid – for example, by grouping together landholders from a sample of townships who owed £10 to £19 tax. Since the tax values are not comparable between townships in the wealth and acres they represent, as we shall see, the landholders placed within such an interval will not comprise a statistically homogeneous group. A similar objection, though not always so insuperable a one, must here be raised to chronological comparisons by class interval *within* townships when significant variations occur in the total amount of tax imposed. Two types of distortion may occur: double assessment, if not accurately recalculated (and it is clear that simply halving such tax entries is often not an appropriate procedure), will cause those Catholic properties which were subject to such penalties to be inappropriately classed; and significant variations in quota will alter the proportional relationship which a (for example) £20 entry bears to the total tax owed for the township in each of the two years being compared. The denominator employed in calculating percentage (the quota) has altered. Even if we assume comparable valuation procedures, £20 of tax simply cannot represent the same proportion of the township's property or wealth in the two years under study.[11]

Although the imposition and cessation of double assessment caused fluctuations in township and parish quotas during the early years of the century, the same result did not occur during the 1790s when double assessment was widely discontinued. During the 1790s, as shall be shown in chapter 4, quotas remained unaltered as double assessment ceased. Adjustments were made within the township to redistribute the tax. By the end of the century quotas apparently had, as has so often been claimed, generally become unalterable in practice, and in 1798 the Redemption Act fixed them permanently – or so it would seem if only the statutory and legal evidence and those practices associated with double assessment were examined. When we look more broadly at what actually happened to quotas in the late eighteenth and early nineteenth centuries, a slightly different story emerges. The great majority of quotas remained unaltered, but not all. Quotas seem to have been reduced during the first two decades of the nineteenth century throughout the North Riding of Yorkshire in all of those townships which had customarily imposed the land tax on government offices.

The "land tax" was not at its inception designed to be only a tax on land. Throughout the eighteenth century the statutes required that the tax be levied on personal property and on income from government offices in addition to landed wealth. But in practice the impositions on personal property became generally impossible to assess because personal property could not be properly valued. Valuations of landed property were popularly acceptable because land could be seen. It was open to public view, and there was much accurate local knowledge regarding its relative (if not its absolute or marketable) value. But to place a valuation on personal and moveable wealth required an inquisitional structure which smacked of French despotism, intruded on the rights of private enjoyment of property, and was abhorrent to the instincts of freeborn Englishmen. Nevertheless there were many notable exceptions to the evasion of personal property from land tax assessment. Every county in which I examined duplicates from the late eighteenth and early nineteenth centuries contains some number of townships which taxed what was generally termed "stock in trade." The practice is most commonly found in market towns. Since the practice was not a universal one even among market towns, it was clearly self-imposed by community agreement. The device was undoubtedly useful in partially redistributing the tax within those towns where real wealth was reflected poorly in the commercial wealth on which the prosperity of the town was essentially based. But even where assessments on personal wealth occur, they have every appearance of having been very lightly imposed.

Direct evidence of the tax burden imposed on personal property in the early years of the land tax is difficult to find. It has widely been accepted, following the seminal article by Professor Habakkuk,[12] that the impositions of that period on land were fully at the statutory rate, which in most years was set at 4s. in the pound rental. But an entry in the 1695 register for Sutton under Whitestonecliffe in the North Riding suggests that the landed estates in Bedfordshire and Northamptonshire, where Habakkuk derived his evidence, may not properly represent the general burden of the tax, at least with respect to personal property, even in those years when the mounting expenses of warfare were straining the finances of the state. The Sutton register has Sir William Ashworth down for £6 of tax on a personal estate whose valuation is there recorded at £500. The ratio of valuation to tax is therefore no more than 83:1, which is hardly the onerous burden commonly associated with that period. By the late eighteenth century, the sheer magnitudes of the tax entries on stock-in-trade, being uniformly very small, unavoidably convey an impression of severe underassessment.

The total amount of tax imposed on the personal property of a township may collectively comprise a considerable proportion of the quota owed, however. Where the personal property was assessed, it must be assumed that the burden of tax was proportionately lightened on real properties. The tax values on real properties in such townships will therefore depart from full potential assessment levels (even though the relative departure of each entry may be equivalent), thus introducing further distortions into inter-township comparisons based on absolute tax values. Taxes on stock-in-trade are rare in Yorkshire, unlike most other counties, and I have been unable to trace systematically their persistence in the nineteenth century. They are not uncommon in Lincolnshire in 1830, however; and they continue at that date to comprise 20 percent of the quota of New Malton in the North Riding. But there is reason to believe that many townships had by then stopped assessing for stock-in-trade. It is not known whether the cessation of such assessments affected the quota for such townships, or whether the burden of the full quota was simply shifted onto landed properties. If the burden shifted, then tax values on landed properties would be inflated (assuming they had previously been fully assessed) and lose full comparability with earlier years. Students should not be lulled by the mere absence of such tax entries, especially when working on market towns in the early nineteenth century.

Unlike stock-in-trade, which is encountered more erratically in the duplicates of the later eighteenth century, the land tax seems to have fallen almost universally – albeit with some irregularity – on certain classes of government salaries. It should not be surprising that those who were most commonly singled out were the excise and customs officers whose functions were so odious to their countrymen. Moreover, these men were heavily taxed. Indeed it is not too much to say that by the later eighteenth century these men were almost (though not completely) alone in experiencing severe burdens under the land tax. The land tax may well have been assessed on the full salaries (though not the fees) of such officers at the statutory rate. A typical tax assessment on such a salary in the later eighteenth century would range from £6 to £10. Amounts of this size could make a considerable impact on the tax collections of individual townships and they often comprise a considerable proportion of the township quota.

There are several reasons, then, for deleting salary entries and deducting their amounts from quotas when undertaking analyses from the land tax. An obvious reason is to maintain comparability when the object of analysis is landed property. Unless deleted, or specially identified, "proprietors" of salaries may inadvertantly appear in analyses as major landowners. But it should also be noted that comparability may also be impaired due to the irregularity with which the tax on such salaries was collected in some townships and the widespread tendency for the amount to fluctuate annually. And finally, in some counties at least, assessments on salary ceased at some point in the early nineteenth century and, in the North Riding, quotas were reduced proportionately.

Table 2.2 identifies all North Riding townships which taxed salaries in 1790 and then traces the history of such tax entries at varying intervals to 1830. The total amount of tax levied on salaries and the total amount of tax due, as recorded at the bottom of the duplicate, is given for each year.

Table 2.2

(1) The total amount (£. s. d.) of tax for salaries and (2) the total tax (£. s. d.) recorded at the bottom of the duplicate; all North Riding townships taxing for salaries; 1790–1830

Wapentake Township		1790	1798	1806	1810	1815	1820	1825	1830
Allertonshire									
Northallerton	(1)	20.00.00	def.	12.04.08	NR	NR	–	–	–
	(2)	167.07.02		170.03.03 3/4			NT	NT	154.18.08 3/4
Birdforth									
Coxwold etc.	(1)	–	–	10.00.00	–	NR	–	–	–
	(2)	57.13.00	57.13.00	57.13.00	57.13.00		47.13.00	47.13.00	47.13.00
Sand Hutton	(1)	9.04.00	9.04.00	–	–	NR	–	–	–
	(2)	39.12.08	41.13.08 1/2	39.12.08	35.15.04 1/2		39.13.01 3/4	39.12.07 3/4	39.12.08 1/2
Thirkleby	(1)	10.00.00	10.00.00	–	–	NR	–	–	–
	(2)	51.02.00	51.02.00	51.02.00	51.02.00		51.02.00	51.02.00	51.02.00
Thirsk	(1)	35.04.00	36.00.00	NR	10.00.00	NR	–	–	–
	(2)	102.02.07	102.02.07		NT		NT	69.10.05 3/4	69.07.03 3/4
Bulmer									
Easingwold	(1)	6.00.00	6.00.00	22.00.00	22.00.00	–	–	–	-
	(2)	257.05.10	257.05.09	273.05.09	273.05.09	251.05.09	251.05.09	251.05.09	251.05.09
Helmsley, Gate	(1)	–	8.00.00	8.00.00	8.00.00	–	–	–	–
	(2)	25.06.08	25.06.08	25.06.08	25.06.08	17.06.08	17.06.08	17.06.08	17.06.08
Helperby	(1)	5.10.00	6.00.00	6.00.00	6.00.00	crossed off	NR	–	–
	(2)	55.06.08	55.06.08	55.06.08	55.06.08	49.06.08		49.06.08	49.06.08
Stillington	(1)	5.03.10 1/2	5.00.00	5.00.00	5.00.00	NR	–	–	–
	(2)	INC.	52.14.01	52.14.01	52.14.01		47.14.01	47.14.01	47.14.01
Gilling West									
Aldbrough	(1)	–	9.07.06	NR	9.07.06	NR	–	–	–
	(2)	70.18.08	70.18.08		70.18.08		NT	72.11.07 1/4	62.07.11 1/2

Table 2.2 continued

Wapentake Township		1790	1798	1806	1810	1815	1820	1825	1830
Gilling West continued									
Gailes	(1)	3.18.02	9.15.00	9.15.00	9.15.00	NR	9.15.00 Redeemed	9.15.00 Redeemed	9.15.00 Redeemed
	(2)	49.00.00	49.00.00	49.00.00	49.05.08		NT	NT	NT
Hang East									
Aiskew	(1)	–	14.00.00	14.00.00	–	–	–	–	–
	(2)	75.15.08	75.15.08	75.15.08	61.15.08	61.15.08	61.15.08	61.18.06	61.16.06
Bedale and Firby	(1)	21.00.00	–	7.00.00	21.00.00	–	–	–	–
	(2)	156.08.03	156.08.03	156.08.03	170.08.03	149.08.03	149.08.03	149.05.08½	NT
Catterick and Killerby	(1)	4.00.00	4.00.00	4.00.00	4.00.00	–	–	–	–
	(2)	129.06.11	129.06.11	129.06.11	129.07.11	125.06.02	125.06.02	125.06.11	125.07.10
Masham	(1)	7.00.00	8.00.00	8.00.00	8.00.00	–	–	–	–
	(2)	66.17.07	66.17.07	66.17.08	66.17.07	58.17.07	58.17.07	58.17.07	58.17.08½
Hang West									
Askrigg	(1)	7.00.00	7.00.00	7.00.00	Crossed off	NR	–	–	–
	(2)	48.07.04	48.07.04	48.04.00	48.04.00		41.04.06	41.02.08	41.03.00
Leyburn	(1)	6.10.00	9.00.00	9.00.00	NR	NR	–	–	–
	(2)	48.10.08	48.10.08	48.10.08			NT	39.10.10¾	39.10.08
Middleham	(1)	9.15.01	9.15.01	NR	9.15.01	NR	9.15.01 Redeemed	Crossed off	-
	(2)	45.14.05½	45.14.05½		46.04.04		46.04.02	35.19.04½	35.19.04½
Witton, West	(1)	5.05.00	5.05.00	5.00.00	Crossed off	NR	5.05.00 Redeemed	Crossed off	-
	(2)	43.10.00	43.10.08	43.10.08	43.10.08		NT	38.05.08	38.13.04¾
Langbaurgh									
Ayton, Great	(1)	6.06.07	6.06.07	NR	NR	NR	–	–	–
	(2)	84.07.01	84.07.01				78.00.06	78.00.06	78.00.06

Table 2.2 continued

Wapentake Township		1790	1798	1806	1810	1815	1820	1825	1830
Lanbaurgh continued									
Egton	(1)	6.00.00	6.00.00	6.00.00	NR	NR	–	–	-
	(2)	183.04.08	183.04.08	183.04.08			177.05.10	177.05.10	177.05.10
Guisborough	(1)	8.00.00	8.00.00	8.00.00	NR	NR	8.00.00	8.00.00	–
	(2)	155.13.11	155.13.11	155.13.11			155.13.01½	155.13.01½	147.13.11
Lofthouse	(1)	4.14.02	4.14.02	4.14.02	NR	NR	–	–	–
	(2)	71.15.05½	71.15.05	71.15.09½			67.01.09½	67.01.09½	67.01.09½
Marske	(1)	def.	–	4.00.00	NR	NR	–	–	-
	(2)	121.02.06	121.02.06	121.02.06			117.02.06	117.02.06	117.02.06
Stokesley	(1)	7.07.00	7.07.00	7.07.00	NR	NR	–	–	-
	(2)	141.00.06	141.00.06	141.00.07¾			NT	NT	NT
Yarm	(1)	5.12.00	5.12.00	NR	NR	NR	–	–	-
	(2)	97.01.00	97.01.00				92.03.10½	91.06.01½	91.09.00
Pickering Lythe									
Brompton, Sawdon and Troutsdale	(1)	8.00.00¾	8.00.00	8.00.00	8.00.00	–	–	–	–
	(2)	94.04.04	94.04.04	94.04.04	94.04.04	86.03.07	86.13.07¼	86.03.07	NT
Cloughton	(1)	8.00.00	8.00.00	8.00.00	8.00.00	–	–	–	-
	(2)	33.02.10	33.02.10	33.02.10	33.02.10	25.02.10	25.02.10	25.02.10	25.02.10
Pickering	(1)	14.00.00	14.00.00	14.00.00	14.00.00	–	–	–	-
	(2)	116.03.02	116.03.02	116.03.02	116.03.03	102.03.02	102.03.02	102.03.02	102.03.02
Ryedale									
Helmsley Blackmoor[a]	(1)	5.00.00	5.00.00	5.00.00	5.00.00	5.00.00	5.00.00	5.00.00	5.00.00
	(2)	115.10.10	115.10.10	115.10.10	115.10.10	115.10.10	115.17.07	115.17.07	115.17.07
Hovingham	(1)	6.00.00	6.00.00	6.00.00	6.00.00	–	–	–	–
	(2)	57.04.08	57.04.08	57.04.08	57.04.08	51.04.08	51.04.08	51.04.08	51.04.08

Table 2.2 continued

Wapentake Township		1790	1798	1806	1810	1815	1820	1825	1830
Ryedale continued									
Kirby Moorside	(1)	5.00.00	5.00.00	NR	5.00.00	–	–	–	-
	(2)	96.16.00	96.18.00		96.18.00	91.18.00	91.18.00	91.18.00	92.02.10 3/4
Malton, New, St Leonard's[b]	(1)	12.00.00	INC	4.10.06	4.10.06	–	–	–	-
	(2)	33.10.03		33.10.06	33.10.06	29.00.00	29.00.00	29.00.00	29.00.00
Malton, New, St Michael's[c]	(1)	6.00.00	6.00.00	10.00.00	10.00.00	–	–	–	-
	(2)	65.10.00	65.10.00	65.10.00	65.10.00	55.07.00	55.07.00	53.06.00	53.06.00
Malton, Old	(1)	–	6.00.00	–	–	–	–	–	-
	(2)	98.10.04	98.10.04	92.10.04	92.10.04	92.10.04	92.10.04	92.10.04	92.10.04
Whitby Strand									
Fylingdales	(1)	6.00.00	6.00.00	6.00.00	NR	NR	–	–	-
	(2)	113.06.10	NT	113.15.00			110.00.06	NT	NT
Whitby	(1)	91.00.00	86.00.00	64.00.00	NR	NR	–	–	-
	(2)	NT	NT	NT			NT	NT	NT

Notes: NR = no return. NT = no total recorded at the bottom of return. INC. = incomplete data on return. def. = defective return. Dash indicates no salaries are taxed.
[a]On the duplicates of 1806–30 the £5 for salary is entered in a separate ''Offices'' column. It is therefore not certain that it was actually collected after 1810. Like redeemed entries, it may have been included in the duplicate as a bookkeeping measure to account for the full quota.
[b]Assessments for stock-in-trade are also dropped by 1830.
[c]Assessments for stock-in-trade are retained through 1830, though recorded in separate columns as always.
Source: Land tax duplicates, NYCRO.

It can be seen that the amounts levied on salaries could vary significantly over short spans of time, and in many townships the total assessments on salary comprised a large percentage of the total tax due. Only three of those thirty-five townships failed to tax salaries in 1798, and it was the amounts reported in the returns of that year which statutorily determined all future quotas. The widespread inclusion of salaries in that year may not have been accidental, since it seems to have laid the groundwork for later adjustments in quotas. With the sole exception of Guisborough, all North Riding townships had ceased the assessment of salaries by the end of the Napoleonic wars. Before those assessments ceased permanently, fluctuations in the incidence or amounts of assessment on salaries failed to affect the quotas. But in each of the thirty-five townships, when the assessment for salaries did permanently cease, the quota for that township was permanently lowered, most commonly by the amount assessed on salary in 1798. The precise legal basis for these alterations in quotas remains something of a mystery. Nor is it clear from this research that quotas were altered on such a basis in other counties. Salaries were still being widely taxed in Lincolnshire as late as 1830. But it is clear that quotas at the township level were not in practice unalterable, even after 1798. At least they were not unalterable in those townships which had included a tax on salaries in their returns for that year. It is fortunate that, with the possible exception of stock-in-trade, only salaries seem to have provided a basis for such alterations in the nineteenth century.

The problems associated with varying quotas, then, are significant but they are probably in most cases not insurmountable. If properties within a township are found to be held by Roman Catholics, or if they had formerly been held by Roman Catholics in the time of William and Mary or Queen Anne, then one should satisfy oneself that (a) they were not being double assessed in the year under investigation and (b) earlier cessations of double assessment did not result in undue compensatory inflation of the remaining non-Catholic properties in the township. If reasonable assurances cannot be achieved, then it might be better to omit such townships from analysis. When double assessments occur and are identifiable, such entries may be recalculated and made comparable with other entries in the same township. But in undertaking such recalculations it cannot be assumed that halving the Catholic assessment (and deducting that amount from the quota) will necessarily be the appropriate procedure. An examination of later duplicates, which record the cessation of double assessment, will reveal that many such properties were relieved of less than half of their assessment, probably reflecting valuational adjustments for propertied improvements. Analysts will therefore enhance comparability if they do not undertake adjustments which exceed those eventually made by the township itself. Salaries and stock-in-trade pose fewer problems for adjustment. Normally they are both easily identifiable in the duplicates. Salary is occasionally not labelled as such, but an examination of duplicates for adjacent years will normally complete such identifications. Such entries can simply be deleted from the analysis, and their amounts deducted from the quotas. Finally, it is prudent as a general rule to refer to the 1798 quotas, which are recorded as totals at the bottom of the 1798 duplicates. Such a precaution can prevent innumerable errors which are otherwise difficult to detect. For example, not all duplicates record individual tax entries which add up to the total recorded at the bottom of the final column. Although the differences are usually insignificant, they are not always so. In some cases, as in many West Riding townships during the 1780s, the individual entries record (without so indicating) an aggregate of the total amount due from local rates as well as from the land tax. After the turn of the century, as the process of redemption settled in, a small proportion of townships throughout England lazily, and again without warning, began to record only the unredeemed properties on the duplicate and in the total, thus omitting a large proportion of the township. The 1798 quotas, when used as a checklist, can quickly alert the researcher to these and a host of other grievous problems.

CHAPTER THREE

Major Problems

Let us now shift our attention to defects or limitations in the land tax duplicates which have seldom been recognized by historians or, if recognized, have been insufficiently discussed and rather pushed to one side. These limitations and ambiguities are, like the defects rehearsed above, to a considerable extent inherent to the structural arrangements for reporting land tax assessments. But unlike the defects cited above, the problems posed by the limitations which we shall now examine are for the most part unresolvable.[1] Only in those isolated instances when supplementary documentation such as estate records are available can the problems even be identified, let alone solved. It must be emphasized as well that these limitations can be fatal for many – though not all – forms of analysis. It is thus essential that such limitations be well understood.

THE UNIT OF ANALYSIS

There has been an understandable tendency among some analysts to treat each individual line entry within the duplicates as a single and separate "farm" – or at least to do so when it is not designated or judged to be merely a cottage, tithe, or non-agricultural property.[2] Such a treatment of line entries constitutes a fundamental and significant error. An individual line entry may be a true farm, but it need not be. Indeed it need not even be a "holding," such as a meadow, which is geographically detached but nevertheless associated with a true farm. Such modes of classification do not reflect the actual complexity of the line entries encountered in these duplicates.

Let us consider an actual case. The Earl of Ailesbury had vast holdings scattered through many townships of the mixed husbandry lowlands and pastoral uplands of the wapentakes of Hang East and Hang West in the North Riding of Yorkshire. In 1804 the estates of the earl were newly surveyed and a fresh valuation and system of rents were imposed, effective Lady Day 1805. The data from the valuation and field books and from the 1805 land tax duplicates have been brought together in appendix A for the earl's holdings in two townships, Thornton Steward and Rookwith, the latter being civilly united and jointly reported for tax purposes with Thirn and Clifton on Ure. The new survey and valuation had been undertaken partly in order to increase rentals, but a more long-range objective had been to create more efficient farm units through consolidation. Thus a considerable acreage had been taken away from one of the earl's tenants, Christopher Firbank, who had been accustomed to subletting a "great part" of his earlier holding. The surveyor reported that the new reduced holding would be "sufficiently large for the present Tenant's capital, and he is more likely to succeed now than he could have done with the occupation of the whole." The farming units reported with each tenant entry in appendix A are thus to an unusual degree real and consolidated working farms. No large pieces are detached, except for a few meadows held principally by cottagers.

The important thing to note is that six of the consolidated Ailesbury farms (or fully 50 percent of the holdings of more than 10 acres) spilled over the boundaries of more than one township. Portions of each of those six farms were reported separately as individual line entries in the land tax duplicates of differing townships. The farm of William Mitchell, for example, was a highly compact and wholly contiguous unit with the farm house set in the midst of the Thornton Steward fields. But the farm spilled over into the adjacent townships of Rookwith and Newton le Willows and was separately assessed in each of those three townships. It would thus be quite erroneous to identify the line entry for William Mitchell in any one of those townships as an individual real farming unit. They referred not to "farms" but to parts of a single farm. Moreover, if the Ailesbury survey were not extant and available, there would be no means for determining that the three Mitchell entries together constituted a single working farm. Nor, without parish registers and a bit of luck, could one even infer that each of the Mitchell entries, being in different townships and lacking title or status ascriptions, referred to the same man. Anyone searching for the decline of the small landholder might wrongly count three "small" William Mitchells in three different townships.

The Ailesbury entries in these few townships are a model of clarity when compared with entries commonly encountered in other land tax duplicates. As noted, the name of an individual will often appear several times in a scattered fashion within a single duplicate, sometimes as a proprietor and sometimes as an occupier or as both. A researcher may decide that each entry refers to the same person, as I have recommended. But there is nothing within the duplicate that will indicate whether such entries collectively constituted a single farming unit, or whether they constituted a series of separate and independent farming units owned or tenanted by one person but which in no way functioned within a single interactive system. There is no indication whether they were even contiguous or dispersed from one another. Spatial distribution should not be inferred from placement within the duplicate. In short, land tax duplicates are inherently incapable of uniformly identifying all real farming units, or the size of all such units, or even the regional population of genuine farmers, with any degree of confidence. Any attempt at such identification would inevitably result in error which was significant in magnitude and incapable of estimation.

Conversely, individual line entries within the duplicate sometimes mask multiple units of property. Some duplicates fail to list all tenants. But even when all tenants are listed, serious problems may remain. When the tax assessment of tenanted property is only given at the level of the proprietor, it is impossible to estimate the relative proportion of the property held by each tenant. If size of holding forms part of the investigation, then the entire analysis must shift to the proprietors, or the duplicate for that township must be discarded as defective. But this type of problem is quite apparent and easily accommodated. The problem is more serious when the tax is given at the appropriate level, the propietor and tenant are clearly named, and the entry seems entirely normal. Can we be certain even under these circumstances that a single unit of property is being reported?

There is clear evidence that we cannot be certain a single property unit is being reported when the assessment is relatively small in magnitude. Some of the traditional work on the decline of the small landowner and the impact of enclosure has deleted assessment entries below a certain value on the assumption that they represent cottages and urban properties. Gray, who employed such a procedure, seems to have assumed that each cottage and building, when not combined with agricultural land, is separately reported in the duplicates.[3] Such an assumption may introduce serious errors. If buildings were not reported separately, but were instead sometimes reported in clusters within single line entries, then the upward range of urban and cottager assessments might be erratically extended, and the arbitrary cutoff rendered less useful. Class intervals would similarly become less homogeneous.

After 1826 the duplicates tend to provide data which identify such problems, since properties are often described. Unfortunately these later duplicates do include within single line entries such descriptors as "cottages" in the plural. These plural descriptors do not occur in the majority of cases, but neither are they rare. Nor is there anything within the duplicates themselves to suggest whether the cottages in question are contiguous or scattered. For that matter, the duplicates do not inform us whether the cottages so reported, or any one of the building entries, are within the precincts of any urban nucleation which might lie within the township. In some towns the attachment of farm land to farm houses, which themselves lie within the village, may further distort urban/rural boundaries. While the severity of many of these problems is eased in the duplicates of the later 1820s, in most other cases the researcher must make a careful use of supplementary sources – and hope such sources are available. Duplicates for earlier years, when appropriate property descriptions are not often included, pose particular hazards. It would be wrong to suggest that these hazards are invariably fatal to any single form of analysis. Indeed one of the difficulties is precisely that the incidence and magnitude of the problems here described cannot be estimated on most duplicates. But an awareness of such sources of error should encourage users of the duplicates to proceed with caution and restraint. Only large differences should be considered statistically significant when measurements include a discreet use of small tax values.

Considering the ambiguities inherent in the line entries of the land tax duplicates, it seems wise to employ a special terminology which retains an appropriate ambiguity and avoids the misleading connotations of such words as *holding* or – even worse – *farm.* In the following pages the term *property bundle* will be employed when it is necessary to refer to individual line entries in a technically precise manner. A property bundle is based on a single tax-assessment entry. Thus a property bundle occurs at the level of each tenant when the assessments are also reported at that level. Alternatively, property bundles are defined at the level of proprietor when the tax assessment is reported only at that level.

ARE ALL PROPERTIES INCLUDED?

In recent years there has been a growing concern whether all properties are assessed and reported in the land tax duplicates. Quite apart from debates concerning the nature of the unit of analysis, or whether some units are lumped into single line entries, a few scholars have begun to debate whether the land tax duplicates provide a complete inventory of property units or whether some units are exempted from taxation and are thus excluded. In his 1964 article, Mingay suggested that many of the smallest cottagers, who are known to have first come on to the land tax rolls when awarded small allotments following enclosure, might have then disappeared from the land tax duplicates following the passage of the Redemption Act in 1798, since that act exempted persons whose estates were valued at less than £1 annual rental. Such exemptions might account for many ''disappearances'' of smallholders. Martin, in his reply to Mingay, acknowledged the sudden disappearance of cottagers from the duplicates following the Redemption Act as a "well known" phenomenon, but he summarily dismissed it as a problem and suggested it "is commonly taken into account by students." How it was taken into account, or by whom, was not explained. More recently, Wilson has noted that the exemption of properties valued at less than £1 rental was not unique to the 1798 act. It was also included in the act of 1693 and had in fact been a feature of the seventeenth century hearth tax. He found little evidence of such exemptions occurring suddenly in West Derby hundred and therefore concluded that the 1798 clause was not an innovation and "should not in itself have had any marked influence upon the operation of the tax."[4]

If the problem of omissions involved no more than substantial disappearances of very small holdings of a definable size or value, all occurring suddenly at one point in time due to statutory exemption, the difficulties posed for analysis would be identifiable and manageable – though distressing. But evidence has begun to emerge that the problem affecting the inclusion or exemption of small holdings goes much deeper and is far more serious in nature. Wilson reported in 1980 that he had found it

frequently difficult to match [estate] surveys and land tax returns which were made very close to each other. A Miss Tatlock holding four and half acres, and a Mr. Travis owning eight and half acres on the Roby survey made in 1790, are absent from both the 1790 and 1791 land tax returns which were made either side of it. In Netherton a partial survey of the Sefton Estates made in 1800 reveals that several properties were apparently not mentioned on the returns. At least five life leaseholders: James Hallwood with two properties of total yearly value £65 4s. 7d; Thomas Shaw with one property £2 10s. yearly value; Samuel Warren with one property yearly value £6; James Travers with one property yearly value £16; John Glover with two small properties yearly value £3 15s.; were all missing from the 1799, 1800, and 1801 returns.

Wilson speculated that such omissions may have been common among life leasehold and rack rented holdings or were perhaps related to the operation of the poor rate. But, whatever the cause, he concluded that

In some cases it seems fairly clear that properties were being simply omitted. The Ince Blundell survey [of 1793] indicates that at least seven dwellings, some with gardens and land varying in value from £1 5s. to £4 annually were not on the 1793 return. In addition four rack rented holdings and one leasehold tenure were not specifically mentioned. That these omissions were a compound of error and deliberate policy seems to be substantiated by the 1795 return for the township. By this time two of the large rack rented holdings in the hands of Francis Morley and James Goore were being entered, as was the leasehold of William South. Three of

> the higher value dwellings held by Richard Hewett, James Tyrer and Edmund Cockshoot had also been added but Margery Blundell's cottage £1 5s., Sarah Hunter's £1, John Almond's £4 and Richard Pye's £1 were still missing.... Similarly at Knowsley at least two small properties, probably cottages and gardens, do not appear on the returns though they were valued at £2 and £3. ... All in all omission of at least some of the cottagers does not seem unusual even though the properties were worth more than 20s. annually.[5]

These findings constitute new charges against the land tax as a complete inventory of real property. The data presented by Wilson do not relate to statutory alterations connected with the Land Tax Redemption Act of 1798. Nor do they relate to enclosure. The parishes under observation appear to have been operating under normal conditions of taxation, except for the process of revaluation which made the observations possible. Moreover, the values being omitted exceed the £1 level stipulated in the statutes. Indeed the pattern of omissions seems essentially random and unrelated to any general rule, though it clearly affects principally the small holdings. What is missing from Wilson's analysis is a clear specification of the statistical impact of his findings. If it can be shown that such omissions were widely distributed among townships, and that they were statistically significant within townships, then the implications are very grave indeed for many of the traditional applications of the land tax. Those applications that employ the total number of occupiers as a part of their computations will be peculiarly affected. By contrast, methods which focus more centrally on total assessed value may not be so severely affected if it can be shown that omissions or exemptions are common only among small properties (provided, of course, the study does not specially focus on the fortunes of the smallholder). The number of such omissions may be large, but their collective value may constitute only a small percentage of the total value of their township. Finally, it must be shown that such omissions were characteristic not only of predominantly (though not wholly) industrial and commercial areas, such as West Derby hundred, but were also common among the mixed husbandry townships of the rural lowlands.

Further evidence of omissions of small entries has emerged from the work of Margaret Noble, who has focused especially on such entries in her highly innovative studies of urban growth, alterations in the urban hierarchy, and the development of urban morphology among several small country towns in the East Riding of Yorkshire. Noble made careful comparisons between the numbers of buildings reported in the land tax duplicates for decennial years between 1801 and 1831 and compared these figures with total buildings reported in the aggregate census and, where possible, in poor rate assessments. The results are sobering. In four out of six towns examined Noble was able to find less than half the number of buildings in the 1832 land tax as were reported in the 1831 census. In the best case, Market Weighton, Noble identified 257 buildings in the land tax. The census reported 371. In the worst case, Great Driffield, she counted 123 buildings in the land tax, while the 1831 census reported 541. The poor rate assessments tended to yield totals between these two extremes. While there was a secular deterioration between 1801 and 1831, the discrepancies in 1801 were comparably large.[6]

In part these findings lend strong support to fears that lumping of properties among small tax entries is frequent in its incidence and severe in its statistical implications. Noble herself tends to attribute the discrepancies to lumping, and perhaps to the omission of new buildings, dismally concluding that "the role of the Land Tax Assessments must remain that of an aggregate sample indicating the general nature of development and change in both urban and rural communities, but incapable of being used for precise quantitative measurement." Unless her sample can be shown to be highly unrepresentative, her conclusions seem inescapable for the types of urban studies on which she has been engaged. They are also serious for any computations from the land tax relying on total numbers of occupiers, and probably even of owners. Her missing houses are far too proportionately numerous to be considered less than statistically catastrophic – provided the *entire* population of occupiers is required in the computation. Houses are peculiarly a feature of towns, however. Urban townships have always been known to be peculiarly hazardous for land tax studies – albeit for other reasons having principally to do with higher urban land values – and students have generally been advised to avoid them. It is not equally clear from Noble's findings that rural communities, where buildings need not play so statistically central a role, should be included in her strictures. Nor is it clear that the discrepancies she attributes to lumping are wholly or even principally due to this, or whether they are instead the result of genuine omissions or exemptions. If the former, then the tax values may be correct but the numbers of occupiers (or the distribution of those values) are flawed. But if the latter, then it must be concluded that the land tax is to some degree deficient in both occupiers (and probably proprietors) and in tax values. A further test of these conclusions under non-industrialized and minimally urbanized conditions, and utilizing documents which can clearly identify genuine omissions or exemptions, is therefore urgently needed.

Appendix B presents such a test for the twenty-seven townships of the wapentake of Hallikeld in the North Riding of Yorkshire. Hallikeld is generally a lowland region of mixed husbandry with numerous large aristocratic estates extending some sixteen miles along both sides of the Great North Road (A1) in the lower Vale of Mowbray from Boroughbridge to Leeming. Its villages were wholly agricultural and small, and there was no significant industrial activity either in or immediately near its boundaries. The wapentake did not even contain a market town, the farmers of the region having to travel or send by common carrier principally to Boroughbridge, Ripon, Masham or Bedale – all in adjacent wapentakes – to find outlets for their products or their needs. Virtually all of Hallikeld wapentake had been enclosed early. A few additional enclosures occurred in the eighteenth and early nineteenth centuries, but all were minor and none took place between 1815 and 1836.[7] This wapentake thus provides a suitable alternative – though still northern – region in which to test the findings of Wilson, who had focused on a generally industrialized and commercialized south Lancashire, and of Noble, whose East Riding country towns bore more pronounced marketing and urbanized characteristics.

Appendix B utilizes three types of sources: the land tax duplicates for 1824 and 1831, the aggregate census columns for total houses in 1821 and 1831, and detailed valuations for the county rate which were required to be submitted to justices in 1824. In appendix B.1 comparisons are made between the total number of buildings (identifying overtly lumped entries separately) counted in the 1831 land tax duplicates and reported in the 1831 census, thereby replicating one of the procedures employed by Noble. Noble additionally used rate books in two of her eight towns in order to compile totals for the number of taxable properties. The difficulty in using rate books is that they do not survive for most townships. Nor are they randomly distributed. They are thus incapable of providing a systematic test for a region. The valuations for the county rate, while confined to a single year, enjoy the considerable advantage of being complete in their geographical coverage. They are also fully appropriate for a test of the land tax in the properties they assess. The basis for the county rate was precisely that of the poor rate, that is, it was levied on ''every inhabitant, parson, vicar, and other, and [on] every occupier of lands, houses, tithes, coal mines, or saleable underwoods.'' It should therefore have included, and only have included, every person rateable to the land tax as an occupier – plus perhaps those excluded from the land tax as occupiers of properties valued at less than £1 annual rental, if such exclusions in fact occurred.[8]

A pattern of widespread omission or exemption emerges from column 3 of this table. In eight out of twenty-five townships the land tax reported less than 80 percent of the occupiers listed in the county rate. In Pickhill only 28 percent of the occupiers listed for the county rate appeared in the land tax. In only four townships was there a perfect match of occupiers between the two lists, and it is notable that these four were townships with very small numbers of occupiers who each held properties with large valuations. In general those townships which held small numbers of occupiers tended to be less characterized by omissions. Middleton Quernhow is unusual in this group in having excluded from the land tax duplicates all four of its £2 occupiers (appendix B.2), the eight remaining all being sizeable holders. Middleton thus seems to have engaged in a deliberate policy of exempting houses unconnected with farmland from the land tax. Other instances of such a practice can be found among townships with larger numbers of occupiers. Kirklington failed to include on the land tax 40 percent of its fifty rateable occupiers, while Pickhill, as we have noted, excluded an astonishing 72 percent of its eighty occupiers. But while it is possible to discern a policy of exemption for houses and very small landed properties in these three townships, the policy was not a perfect one even there. Kirklington exempted one piece of landed property valued at £12 and several houses valued as high as £8 to £10, while retaining in the land tax three houses valued at £2, £5, and £6. The pattern for Pickhill was similarly erratic. Exclusions ran as high as £9, but at least one "cottage and land" valued at £4 17s. was retained.

In fact one searches the townships of Hallikeld in vain trying to detect within the wapentake as a whole some general pattern or principle of exclusion based on assigned property values. Even within most individual townships the exclusions seem erratic. Exclusions in Exelby and Melmerby were numerous and were distributed almost randomly among all classes of small and even middle-sized holders. Indeed these two townships, along with Rainton, retained properties in the land tax which were valued at rentals of less than £1. There would therefore appear to be no basis for assuming the statutory exemption clause was being observed in these townships. Local administrators of the land tax obviously interpreted this clause as they saw fit, and in accordance with local traditions, as they did all clauses of the statute. Nor was there any general tendency within the wapentake for exclusions to occur at a specific level of valuation – even granting erratic implementations. While some townships such as Ainderby Quernhow appear to have exempted all entries valued at less than £5, others such as West Tanfield undertook almost no exemptions, and many retained some proportion of their smallest properties. In short, there are no real patterns to be found among the data, except for the undoubted fact that exclusions from the land tax were overwhelmingly confined to smaller properties and principally – but by no means exclusively – to cottages and houses standing alone or attached to no more than a garden or garth. Moreover, this pattern of erratic exclusions cannot be attributed to differing eccentricities among assessors and valuation officers. In fourteen out of twenty-three townships, the assessor for the land tax was also the valuer for the county rate.

The problem of exclusions of both houses and small landed properties appears to be a sufficiently serious one if we base our conclusions only on a comparison of the land tax duplicates with the valuations for the county rate. But if we further introduce comparisons with the numbers of houses reported in the aggregate census for 1821 (appendix B.2, col. 6) and 1831 (col. 7), and compare them with the total number of houses reported in the 1824 county rate (cols. 4–5) and in the 1831 land tax duplicates (cols. 8–9), the full potential magnitude of the problem begins to emerge. Both the county rate and the land tax were severely underreporting buildings, even in this relatively non-urbanized agricultural wapentake. In only eleven out of twenty-four townships does the count of buildings from either the county rate or the land tax reach even 50 percent of the total for either census. Lumping clearly accounts for some of the "unreported" houses and can be specifically identified in columns 5 and 9. Additional houses may have been silently lumped into what are reported on the land tax and county rate as being no more than one house and farm. There has perhaps been too little critical attention to what census enumerators counted as a "house," particularly among the early census returns. Were detached dwellings of farm labourers counted separately? They may have been so counted by census enumerators but not so listed by tax assessors. Students of later manuscript census returns are familiar with confusions regarding "house" numbering, especially in more urban environments.[9] But no matter how much we speculate in this fashion, the numbers of unreported houses in the tax documents of this period are simply too large to be accommodated by any such explanations. It is impossible to escape the conclusion that very frequently some large proportion of houses, and less frequently some smaller proportion of small farming properties, were wholly excluded from the land tax and, to a lesser degree, from the county and other local rates.

How can such exclusions be explained? Numerous land tax duplicates can be found which explicitly state that the occupiers of a few specified properties were being exempted as "too poor." The scattered returns of this type suggest the possibility that occupiers in some townships may have been exempted from the land tax on the basis of their *personal* financial circumstances and in such a manner which correlates poorly with the specific rental value of their holding. Such practices would explain the erratic patterns noted in Hallikeld. If any such considerations were operating in the local administration of taxes, however, it will be impossible to detect them systematically since there is no direct evidence with which to confirm them.[10] It may also be that favouritism was at work; but the evidence from the county rate valuations suggests that omissions of occupiers from the land tax were just as likely – but no more likely – to occur on the estates of large holders as on those of middling and small proprietors. It is also possible, as Wilson suggests, that some omissions were related to long-term leaseholding; but no general pattern of such omissions, or any direct evidence for their occurrence, has appeared in the Yorkshire evidence I have examined. On the contrary, there is abundant evidence that long leaseholders, copyholders, and tenants at rack rent were all frequently included in the land tax. The tenants of the King in Rosedale East Side were all stipulated as at rack rent. The twenty omissions in Kirklington were all identified in the duplicates of the later 1820s as freehold. And as will be shown, both copyhold and leasehold were widely reported in the duplicates of the North Riding and elsewhere. I have been unable to determine that any of the omitted properties in Hallikeld fell into any tenurial category other than freehold.

While there appears to be no explanation for the erratic omissions from the land tax, or any consistency in the pattern of such omissions among the townships of a region, it must also be said that there is no assurance that the rate – or even the basis for such omissions – was constant through time. It is well known that the modes of entering names and properties in the duplicates sometimes altered. Certainly one has the impression that many assessors essentially copied the duplicate of the previous year, making only those minimal alterations that landed transactions required. But variations in name sequence, status ascription, and spelling are commonplace. Occasionally an assessor will radically break with the practices of his predecessors and create an alphabetized list, for example, such alphabetization usually necessitating a new and unusual degree of lumping. The point is that local assessors for the land tax were prone to vary their procedures. Little prevented them from doing so; they were bound by no regulations, guided by no general instructions, and demonstrably were bound to the practices of their predecessors only to the extent of their own convenience or of the customs and current wishes of their own community. There is abundant internal evidence in the duplicates that the commissioners of the land tax never interfered in such matters, except when appeals were brought before them. The royal courts, for their part, had always refused to interfere in who was or was not to be included in a rate.[11] There is reason to assume, then, that the rate at which properties were omitted varied temporally within a single township as well as spatially among the townships of a region. Or at least it would be prudent to make such an assumption. It would follow as a corollary that the determination of land tax omission rates at a given point in time does not provide a firm basis for estimating the rates on duplicates for other years, even within the same township. The estimation of omissions poses problems which would seem to be insoluble.

Let us suppose a student wished to minimize some of these difficulties and to ignore others by attempting to delete systematically all entries below an arbitrarily set valuation. The student decides to ignore any possibility of significant temporal variations in the bases for inclusion and instead focuses on enhancing the comparability of the data base by systematically deleting small-tax-value properties throughout his population of townships. The problem will then lie principally in identifying a cutoff tax value in each township which represents the same *valuational* worth as the selected tax value of all other townships. Appendix B.2 presents for each township in Hallikeld the ratio of its total valuation to its total land tax assessment (col. 4). Table 3.1 converts these ratios to a tax entry whose valuational rent was established at £1. The range of variation among townships is high. The tax entries representing £1 gross annual rental in Gatenby would be almost 4 times those in Kirklington. Variations of 100 percent or more are not unusual. Moreover, Hallikeld is a relatively homogeneous wapentake within the North Riding. Appendices M, P, and Q present evidence of much wider ratio variations. Table 3.1 also masks the alterations in ratios which occur between redeemed and unredeemed properties within the land tax duplicates. Nor does it take into account the considerable secular variation which occurs in ratios, or the fact that such variation is unpredictable since it tends to occur in both directions. These are matters which will be discussed more fully in subsequent chapters, but it is important to note them here lest anyone believe that the development of standardizing procedures can overcome the problems posed by omissions.

If the problem of omissions cannot be satisfactorily overcome, it then becomes proportionately more important to estimate its statistical significance. Analyses which focus principally on the total value of the township, such as those which calculate the tax of each proprietor on a duplicate as a percentage of the total tax owed by the township, are likely to incur relatively little error. Column 1 of appendix B.2 calculates the cumulative omissions of each township as a percentage of its total valuation according to the county rate. In only three townships do the omissions account for more than 5 percent of total valuation. In Dishforth the omissions amount to a devastating 21.7 percent, but that percentage is almost wholly accounted for by one omission of tithe (£269) and one omission of "Land" (£184 17s.). If these two omissions (which are unusual in their nature) had been included in the duplicate, the remaining omissions would have comprised 6.1 percent of the total value. In Carthorpe the 9.8 percent omissions would have been reduced to 5.2 percent if one "Farm" entry of £103 had been included. One entry of "House and Land" at £125 entirely accounted for the 10.3 percent omission at Theakston. If one were to accept the county rate valuation as a full accounting of properties within these townships, then we could conclude that the great majority of land tax duplicates – in Hallikeld some twenty-two out of twenty-five non-defective duplicates – are sufficiently complete to allow statistically reliable percentage computations of individual tax values against the total tax of each township.[12]

Table 3.1
Ratios of total valuation to total tax applied to tax entries reported at £1 rental value, all townships, Hallikeld wapentake, North Riding, 1824

Townships	Ratio	Tax entry of £1 reported value
Ainderby Quernhow	36	61/2d.
Asenby	48	5d.
Baldersby	45	51/4d.
Burneston	34	7d.
Carthorpe	44	51/2d.
Cundall etc.	41	53/4d.
Dishforth	def.	def.
East Tanfield	39	6d.
Exelby	37	61/2d.
Gatenby	19	1s. 01/2d.
Howe	38	61/4d.
Humburton etc.	37	61/2d.
Kirby Hill etc.	def.	def.
Kirklington etc.	73	31/4d.
Langthorne	22	11d.
Marton le Moor	62	33/4d.
Melmerby	55	41/4d.
Middleton Quernhow	56	41/4d.
Norton le Clay	60	4d.
Pickhill etc.	40	6d.
Rainton etc.	43	51/2d.
Sinderby	29	81/4d.
Sutton Howgrave	49	5d.
Swainby etc.	26	91/4d.
Theakston	46	51/4d.
Wath	42	53/4d.
West Tanfield	48	5d.

Note: def. = defective return.
Source: Appendix B.2.

But we have seen that the county rate valuations are not a complete accounting of properties within the townships of Hallikeld. It is impossible to know if further landed properties are generally omitted, even from the county rate, because further systematic documentation is lacking. But comparisons with numbers of houses reported in the census confirms that substantial numbers of houses are indeed missing from the land tax. It may therefore be prudent to double the "percent omitted" figures in column 5 of appendix B.2 in order to estimate more fully the extent of potential statistical error. The number of townships with omissions exceeding 5 percent of total valuation now rises to eight, or fully one-third of the townships. But the omissions of these five additional townships still account for less than 10 percent of their total valuations. The potential error estimated at a reasonably maximum level can therefore be judged to be significant, but not catastrophic, for valuations. A few cases of any sample population of townships may be expected to emerge as outliers, having unusual values due either to unique empirical conditions or to faults in the data – a result which is hardly unusual in economic and social analysis. A further sizeable minority of townships should be affected by deflations of their valuation totals, producing error of plus or minus 10 percent. But the land tax duplicates for the majority of townships – if Hallikeld proves to be at all typical – should provide tax totals which are sufficiently error free (plus or minus 5 percent or less) for use in statistical computations that are internal to the township.

The same optimistic view cannot be taken of statistical computations that include the total number of occupiers as a denominator (or in any other arithmetic role). The land tax duplicates in fully one-third of the townships of Hallikeld reported less than 80 percent of the occupiers listed in the valuation for the county rate. But once again the additional missing houses reported by the census suggest that these estimates of omissions utilizing the county rate are no more than minimal. There is little likelihood that the additional missing houses, not being the principal houses of farms, were occupied by persons already appearing in the county rate. It would therefore once again seem prudent to estimate the maximal extent of error by doubling omissions, which means halving the percentages reported in column 3 of appendix B.1. In more than half the townships, the number of occupiers reported in the land tax now comprise less than 50 percent of those estimated. Precise comparisons cannot uniformly be made due to the lumping of entries in both the land tax and the county rate. In some cases halving the percentage clearly exaggerates the error. The county rate for Pickhill, for example, seems to have reported approximately three-quarters of the census houses. Even so the adjusted percentage for Pickhill would drop from 28 percent to perhaps 20 percent. In other cases halving the percentage would appear to underestimate error. Burneston listed only three houses in its county rate (out of thirty-one total entries) but reported sixty-four and sixty-eight houses respectively in its 1821 and 1831 census returns.

There seems little escaping the cruel statistical fact that occupiers, and presumably their properties, were catastrophically underenumerated in the land tax duplicates. We have also seen that omissions in the duplicates were not confined to houses, nor were all houses eliminated. There were no consistent cutoffs based on valuation, even within most individual townships. It is therefore impossible to stipulate that calculations from the land tax are based on a consistent, if incomplete, population of occupiers and properties. Variations in rate of occupation can very plausibly be attributed merely to variations in rate of inclusion, both in comparisons between townships and in estimations of secular trends. Since it is plausible to assume that some of the missing small properties are owned by their occupiers or by other absentee proprietors who also fail to appear on the land tax, it must be concluded that apparent variations in numbers of land tax proprietors may similarly be illusory. It is indeed unfortunate that so large a proportion of land tax studies have employed total numbers of occupiers or of proprietors as variables in their analyses.

TENURIAL STATUS

The land tax duplicates contain a number of further ambiguities which pose problems of interpretation that once again cannot be resolved in a systematic fashion. One of the more important of these concerns the tenurial status of each property bundle. The duplicates of the later 1820s sometimes enter tenurial status in the column calling for a description of the property. The frequency of tenurial ascriptions is not great. In 1830 only thirty-nine (8 percent) North Riding townships interpreted the instruction in this manner. In other counties, and even at much earlier dates, such ascriptions are more frequently encountered. I found them to be quite numerous in some of the western counties, for example. But whatever the incidence might be, such ascriptions appear with sufficient frequency for an important conclusion to emerge: both copyhold and leasehold were widely scattered throughout the countryside and were taxed and reported in that form in a significant proportion of land tax duplicates.[13] This phenomenon appears to be more widespread in the west and north, but instances are found even in the home counties.

The implication of such ascriptions is that not all persons listed in the duplicates as "proprietors" are indeed owners in the most commonly accepted meaning of that term, that is, they do not hold their property in freehold. An ascription of leasehold and copyhold can most often only apply to the proprietor column, it must be remembered; otherwise the even more frequently encountered ascription of "freehold" would be nonsense, since it cannot apply to tenants. The term "leasehold" in particular can only make sense if it is understood as applying to the proprietor; otherwise the term "freehold," when found within the same duplicate next to tenanted property, would be uninterpretable. "Proprietors" of "leasehold" must therefore be tenants on a lease of years. An ascription of "copyhold" may perhaps be subject to a more flexible interpretation. There do appear to be instances when copyhold is specified and the lord of the manor appears as proprietor. But in the township of Muker in Swaledale, the 1830 duplicate identified almost every property bundle in the township as copyhold. If that ascription had not been present, one would have classified the "proprietors" of this township as being entirely composed of small independent freeholders. The Lyell family, as lords of the manor, appear nowhere in the duplicate. The "proprietors" were in fact copyholders, while the "occupiers" (when not the proprietor) were sub-tenants. A similar ambiguity can be found in the 1830 duplicate of the adjoining moorland parish of Arkengarthdale. All of the property bundles described as land in that parish were recorded as leasehold. Buildings are curiously lacking a tenurial ascription. The Bathursts, as lords of the manor, had entered into agreements in 1658 to rent the land on long-term leasehold, some leases extending to as much as two thousand years. The leases were subject to fixed annual rents and fines on renewal and succession. Tenure would appear to have been unusually secure, some of the families residing in the parish during the early twentieth century having occupied their farms for more than three centuries. As in Muker, the "proprietors" listed in the Arkengarthdale land tax duplicate were not owners of the land. In this case they were long-term leaseholders, the "occupiers" being their sub-tenants.[14]

The ambiguities surrounding tenurial status may be more serious for some forms of analysis than they need be for others. There is no doubt that the problem is widespread. It cannot be assumed that a failure to ascribe tenure when property descriptions are entered is somehow an indication that only freehold was present. The majority of townships in the North Riding which ascribed tenure contained only freehold. The frequency with which copyhold and leasehold is found in the duplicates must therefore be taken as a minimum indicator of their real occurrence. If the objectives of an analysis require the identification of freehold ownership, then the land tax duplicates may well contain ambiguities which will introduce error of fatal magnitude. And yet in some districts the magnitude may not be great. The problem lies in the fact that the error cannot be estimated from the land tax duplicates alone. On the other hand, if the objectives of the analysis do not strictly require the identification of freehold proprietorship, then the information which the duplicates provide may be sufficient. For example, it may be possible to assume that leasehold "proprietors" were generally on very long leases and therefore held effective control of their property bundles. Such an interpretation would explain why they are found in the proprietor column. Similarly, one might assume that copyholders widely enjoyed a secure tenure and, like long-term leaseholders, were in effective control of their holdings. If one is prepared to live with such assumptions, and if the effective control of one's holding sufficiently meets the objectives of the analysis, then tenurial ambiguities need not be unduly vexing.

RESIDENCE

Users of land tax duplicates may also be misled if they interpret "occupation" to mean "residence." An "occupier" of a property bundle does not necessarily reside on that property; nor does he necessarily reside in that township. Occupation in this sense merely means having the property in hand and fully at one's personal disposal or use. Such errors are most easily detected when they occur among the titled gentry or peerage. The tendency to equate occupation with residence operates more subtly when middling to small holders are being examined. It is perhaps not unfair to suggest that there is often an implication of residence assigned to small owner-occupiers by historians tracing the decline of the yeoman farmer and the impact of enclosure. The implication arises partly because smallholders cannot be linked between the duplicates of differing townships. Thus it is impossible to place them residentially in any township except the one in which they are recorded, and the recording in each township must be treated as referring to a unique person. And yet we know from poll books and estate surveys that sizeable proportions of middling to small holders either owned or rented properties which lay in more than one township. It would therefore seem imprudent to attribute residence indiscriminately and on the basis of land tax evidence alone to untitled middling and small holders, any more than we would to titled gentry and the peerage. As a corollary, we must resist the inference that persons whose names drop out of a land tax duplicate must also have dropped out of landholding society – an inference implicit in most small landowner studies. The areal fragmentation of the duplicates into townships or parishes renders them wholly unsuitable for drawing such conclusions.

WHO PAID THE TAX

The tax assessment entries, as already noted, are inconsistently entered in the duplicates, sometimes at the level of the tenant and sometimes at the level of the proprietor. Why should this be so? There is reason to believe the practice was not merely inconsistent but was in conformity with a practical purpose. Bear in mind that the land tax duplicates were not created as artifacts for the use of historians but as working documents for the collection of revenue. Their central purpose was to specify the amount owed for each individual property bundle and, further, to identify the person responsible for payment of that tax. Apart from acting as a basis for determining county electoral qualifications, at no point in their history were land tax duplicates drawn up for any other than tax purposes.

Assuming the practical nature of the duplicates, then, it is possible to infer that those line entries in which the tax was assigned only at the level of the proprietor refer to properties where the landlord assumed direct responsibility for the payment of the tax. There is no alternative to such an assumption, unless we are prepared to believe that a large proportion of the land tax duplicates were devised in a fashion that would have been quite impractical and inconvenient for the collectors themselves or in a manner so careless as to be quite extraordinary. If the occupiers rather than the landlords were responsible for payment, then duplicates embodying such entries would fail to record the proportionate responsibility of each tenant. Each tenant would have no knowledge of his obligation and no basis for appeal to the commissioners. Nor would the commissioners have a basis for judging an appeal. The collectors themselves would lack written guidance.

It is not equally clear that tax entries broken down at the level of the tenant indicate that the responsibility for the payment of the tax belonged to the tenants. It may be that, for whatever reason, a more complete enumeration of property bundles was deemed desirable. It is possible to aduce practical reasons for listing occupiers with their tax amounts even when the whole of their tax is to be paid by the proprietor. Buying and selling of small properties was almost continuous in most townships, and sometimes the properties in question were subtracted or added to the holdings of large proprietors. Under such circumstances a more complete annual bookkeeping of alterations in tax assessment and collection would be effected by recording the tax at the level of each occupier, regardless of who was to pay the tax. The possibility of this more complete form of accounting must prevent any easy assumption regarding payment when the tax is assigned to occupiers.[15] It seems safer to reach conclusions for an individual property bundle when the tax is assigned to a proprietor, but it seems unsafe to conclude that only such proprietors paid the tax. These suggestions do not resolve systematically, or even in most cases, who paid the land tax. That old and classic problem remains.[16] But the evidence does seem to suggest quite clearly that there was no uniform practice among landlords – not within counties, not within farming regions, not even within many townships where mixed practices may be observed. The assignment of assessments to proprietors was too widespread to permit any assumption of uniform practice. In their tax collection, as in so much else, English agriculturalists were incorrigibly idiosyncratic.

OCCUPANCY

We have seen that it is hazardous to infer residence from the "occupier" column of a duplicate. I can offer no direct evidence on the following point, but I am increasingly convinced that inclusion in the occupier column also does not invariably mean that person is "in occupation" of that holding in the sense of working it himself or through hired employees (if land) or physically occupying it (if a house or cottage). It is disturbing to find in so many townships throughout Yorkshire persons owning and "in occupation" of tiny holdings who in other distant parts of the county are very large landowners. Perhaps these aristocrats are genuinely in occupation of such tiny detached properties, but surely they are not. Frequently these holdings are no more than a cottage. I believe the answer lies with the occasional entries on the great consolidated estates where the owner is temporarily listed in the occupier column for farms which are currently not tenanted. Under these conditions the owner assumes responsibility for the tax and is accordingly entered in the occupier column. Since the duplicates are bookkeeping systems for the collection of taxes, the practical requirements of collection may often be expected to override the nature of tenured relations. Such problems are relatively detectable among the tenants of large consolidated estates. One can only wonder how often smallholders who are apparently "owner-occupiers" in the duplicates are no more than owners who pay the tax.

DUPLICATES THAT FAIL TO DISTINGUISH BETWEEN PROPRIETORS AND OCCUPIERS

The land tax duplicates of the later eighteenth and early nineteenth centuries normally list the names of both the proprietor and the occupier of each property bundle assessed, the proprietors and occupiers being entered in separate parallel columns. But not all duplicates are completed in this format. The majority of duplicates which have survived for years prior to 1780, and a smaller but significant proportion of those for the 1780s and 1790s, record only a single column of names, without specifying whether each name is that of a proprietor or of an occupier. The ability to make this distinction is of the utmost importance. Anyone attempting to follow the decline of the small landholder, for example, must be able to distinguish and compute separately small land owners, occupiers, and owner-occupiers. If such distinctions are not possible, then the degree and incidence of "smallness" becomes to some (almost certainly significant) extent a function of intermixing the tenurial categories. The inclusion of some proportion of tenants will by definition redistribute size categories of holdings downwards, since multiple tenancies on single estates are, after all, fractions of those estates.[17] Similarly, studies of land ownership, or political and economic studies which depend on either the size or tenurial nature of holdings or on the identification of major proprietors, may entirely miss some proportion of the larger landlords and mistake tenants for yeomen when tenants rather than proprietors are listed. These considerations are by no means trivial.

The difficulties presented by these single-column duplicates have been well understood by specialists, and it is perhaps for this reason more than any other that land tax duplicates prior to 1780 have hitherto only rarely been studied. Two specialists, Dennis Mills and Richard Grover, recently urged that major attention be shifted to such duplicates, however, and it seems likely that many others will take up their study. Mills offers grounds which he believes justify an indiscriminate use of the early duplicates. He suggests, with stunning ease, that "historians should, for the time being at least, regard the names of taxpayers [on single-column duplicates] as those of owners, unless there is evidence to the contrary." This is in my opinion a rash and dangerous recommendation. Let us examine the grounds Mills offers for justifying such a procedure.[18]

Mills finds two types of single-column lists in a 1712 land tax register for the county of Rutland. The duplicates for eleven of his fifty-five parishes (his first type of list) do make explicit distinctions between occupiers and proprietors for some proportion of their entries. Mills therefore concedes that in these eleven parishes both tenants and proprietors are intermixed in single-column lists. What he fails to note, in addition, is that each of these lists, being single-column, may also list persons designated as proprietors whose properties are tenanted. In such cases it may be the proprietor who pays the tax and thus only his name is listed. If that inference seems likely, then one should not *infer* owner-occupancy, even in those parishes which list some number of tenants.[19]

Mills further identifies a second type of single-column duplicate in which no direct attributions of either tenancy or proprietorship are recorded. Though he concedes that such duplicates may in fact include some mixture of tenants and proprietors, it is precisely in these lists that he urges us to assume that all names are those of proprietors. Here are his reasons. First, he presents the surprising argument that some duplicates offer internal stylistic evidence that no less than "minor gentry" are present, since every name (with the exception of one baronet and one doctor in the example he gives in table 1) is prefixed by "Mr." How Mills concludes that the status designation of mister is one appropriate to, much less exclusive to, minor gentry is a mystery into which we are not introduced, and perhaps no more should be said about it. He further contends that the smallest tax entry on such duplicates, which in the example he presents is £1 0s. 8d., is far in excess of the 4s. entries which he finds to be the smallest normally found in the county. He fails to note that several of his explicitly designated tenants on a type-one list (reproduced in the very next table) held for tax amounts ranging from £1 1s. to £17 4s. On his own evidence, then, tenants may indeed be expected on properties reporting taxes of a few pounds. Nor can one imagine that tenancies of far larger tax values were uncommon in that or any other county. To infer tenancy from tax magnitudes is an impossibility.

His third and final set of evidence for the overwhelming incidence of proprietorship in such lists is equally irrelevant and unconvincing. He divides the total number of taxpayers in each of his forty-four type-two duplicates into the total tax of each parish and into its total acres. He then examines the distribution of the mean tax and mean acreage computations among these parishes and, without explaining his grounds, concludes that such distributions are "hardly credible if one assumed that all [sic] the names were those of occupiers." On the contrary, he wishes to infer that "most of these taxpayers were owners." Perhaps "most" were. Given normal distributions of owner- occupancy, it would surely be silly to argue that "all" were the names of mere tenant occupiers. The question – and it is a statistically crucial one – is simply whether there are grounds for believing or disbelieving that such lists do, or may often, include in statistically significant proportions the names of *both* owners and non-owning tenants. There is nothing in the mean-tax and mean-acreage distributions of Mills' forty-four parishes which can assist us in this question. Even if we accept the size of tax payments or the acreage of holdings as an indication of tenurial status, which I cannot, the distributions do not suggest that these parishes are characterized by large holdings (whether tenanted or not). Fifteen parishes have a mean tax of less than £3. An additional fourteen parishes have a mean tax of less than £6. Since a considerable proportion of holders in each parish must also fall below the mean – and the means themselves are not high – it is difficult indeed to see any evidence of a preponderance of large holdings. It should be remembered, too, that one or two very large holdings would have a much stronger upward effect on small means such as these than would a similar number of very small holdings. If anything, the means are biased upwards. The distribution of mean acreages is also unconvincing for Mills' argument, and for the same reasons. Surely no one would wish to suggest that holdings of less than 50 acres are large. Yet seventeen of his parishes produce acreage *means* in this range. An additional seventeen parishes fall between 50 and 99 mean acres. Holdings of these sizes can not exclude a high incidence of tenancy. In the real world of the English countryside, it is quite easy to find entire parishes held by one or two large tenant farmers, and it is a commonplace to find one or more very large tenants among a larger group of farmers holding on a single large estate within the parish. Tenants are not invariably – or even typically – small, or large. They come in all sizes and shapes. Evidence such as that presented by Mills is therefore perfectly meaningless in resolving questions of tenure on single-column duplicates.[20]

I would suggest instead that we think about the single-column pre-1780 duplicates in the light of what we *know* about assessor practices in the post-1780 period when double-column duplicates and more complete modes of accounting are widely available. I have argued in a preceding section that those property bundles which aggregate the tax at the level of the proprietor (while still listing tenants or indicating that multiple tenants are present) were entered in that form because the proprietor, not the tenant, was liable by agreement for the payment of the tax. If that argument is persuasive, then there are certain further conclusions which may be inferred regarding single-column formats. The evidence of the double-column duplicates shows that proprietors were commonly, though probably not in most instances, responsible for the payment of the tax. The responsibility for payment seems to have been most often a private matter between a landlord and his tenants; it was not governed by the custom of the local community, as evidenced by the mixing of aggregation levels within the duplicate of a single township.[21] On the other hand, post-1780 evidence also shows that *some* townships, when they periodically adopt the single-column format, exclusively list *either* proprietors or owners. Some North Riding townships employing the single-column format list only proprietors. Others list only tenants and owners in occupation. Some West Riding townships, because their individual tax entries aggregate land and local taxes, are constrained to list only occupiers, since local taxes fall only on the latter. But all three types of instances occur: double-column formats with mixed levels of aggregation, and single-column formats with either proprietors or occupiers exclusively included in the list, and single-column formats which intermix proprietors and occupiers. The presence of all three forms reinforces my suggestion that the land tax duplicates must be interpreted as practical documents designed for the requirements of tax collectors. If only one name is listed, we must conclude that it is that of the person owing the tax. While sometimes considerations extraneous to the requirements of the land tax might override other considerations, such as in the West Riding, it should be assumed that variations in who is listed – whether the proprietor or his occupiers – is purely a function of variations in individual rental agreements as to who is liable for actual payment of the tax.

The evidence shows that such rental practices varied widely. If one practice was preponderant, it was probably (judging from the double-column duplicates, occasional notations, and the law[22]) that the tenant paid. Unless it can be shown that assessors behaved differently prior to 1780, or that early eighteenth-century rental agreements placed the responsibility for the tax more uniformly on either proprietors or tenants than they clearly did later in the century, we cannot assume that earlier single-column duplicates are unmixed in the names they list. Least of all can it be assumed they uniformly, or even mostly, list proprietors. The truth is, however irritating it might be, that there is no basis whatsoever for assuming tenurial status on the single-column duplicates of earlier years, except on those isolated line entries where tenure is stipulated or can be confirmed from other sources. These conclusions hold little hope for more than the most restricted uses of these early duplicates.

CHAPTER FOUR

Roman Catholic Double Assessment

There are few problems associated with the land tax which are more perplexing or, when they occur, more statistically important than Roman Catholic double assessment. The 1693 act establishing the land tax, and the annual acts for a century thereafter, provided that Catholics be assessed at double the normal rate on their rack rents. Whether Catholics were in fact double assessed throughout the countryside, and what the consequences of double assessment might have been for the non-Catholic properties of the township and county, are questions which have never been systematically investigated. G.J. Wilson is the first modern scholar to have seriously called our attention to the problems posed by double assessment for interpreting the land tax. Wilson's area of study was West Derby hundred in south Lancashire, where an unusually large proportion of Catholics were located in the eighteenth century. His findings were inconclusive for other regions of the country, but they broadly confirmed the impressions of historians who have encountered this problem. He found no general pattern to the incidence of double assessment. Some of the townships seem to have double assessed their Catholics, but other townships did not. Some appear to have ceased double assessments early, while others continued the practice into the 1790s. When double assessments ceased, the tax on some Catholic properties dropped dramatically, as might be expected. But the tax actually increased on some other Catholic properties. Perhaps more importantly, Wilson speculated that double assessments imposed in the 1690s, when anti-Catholic sentiment ran high, probably caused many townships to be assigned original tax quotas which were high with respect to real rents and acres. Maximally, a township wholly owned by a Catholic family might have had its quota doubled. Since the reduction of quotas was an exceedingly difficult process, and had probably become impossible by mid-century, Wilson's findings suggest that the land tax quotas of townships with significant Catholic properties in the 1690s may be expected to have been unusually high when compared to real rental values and to acres. Quotas in such townships will therefore to a peculiar degree "provide an unreliable guide to the comparative economic importance of the townships" of their region in the early eighteenth century and, if unrevised, in later decades as well.[1]

There is no doubt that double assessments occurred – or that they were recorded in the duplicates as occurring – in widely scattered parts of the country and even in regions where Catholics were not numerous. They also occurred at very late dates. Notations of double assessment may be found in townships of each of the three ridings of Yorkshire well into the nineteenth century, for example, although less commonly after the 1790s.[2] I have new and systematic evidence to offer on this important phenomenon. But many historians will not have such evidence for the regions they are studying. Rather than go directly to the evidence and to my final conclusions, it may therefore be worthwhile to proceed in two preliminary stages.

First, I propose to explore systematically and in some detail the logical implications of double assessment for interpreting the land tax duplicates. In this first stage I shall consider principally the evidence for a single township, Welwick, which is in the South Holderness division of the East Riding. Some supplementary data will be derived from the duplicates of other townships in its region, but all data will be post-1780. This is precisely the situation in which most historians find themselves, since pre-1780 duplicates are seldom available. A good deal about the logical implications of double assessment will be learned in this manner, but in the end it will become evident that our ability to draw reliable and unambiguous conclusions has been severely hampered by lack of a fuller range of evidence.

In the second section of this chapter, I shall turn to a more traditional literary source, an 1828 report from a select committee of the House of Commons, that provides a long chronological perspective on the legal basis and operation of the double assessment clauses, as that history was understood by the Catholic community at that time. As subsequent evidence will suggest, some of the implications of that valuable report are misleading.

In the final section I shall turn to more direct and systematic evidence for the operation of the double assessment clauses in the forty-seven townships of Birdforth wapentake in the North Riding of Yorkshire during the later seventeenth and early eighteenth centuries and during the 1790s. On the basis of that evidence, a fairly reliable general history of double assessment to the end of the eighteenth century will emerge.

Double assessment creates two associated but distinguishable sets of problems, one having to do with the tax quota assigned to the township and the other having to do with the internal distribution of the tax burden within a township. I shall pursue each of these two sets of problems, beginning with those associated with quotas, by first drawing evidence from the mixed husbandry township of Welwick in the South Holderness division of the East Riding of Yorkshire. The Crathornes of Crathorne, a Catholic gentry family based in the North Riding, had extensive holdings here throughout the later seventeenth and eighteenth centuries. The Welwick duplicates of the early 1790s specifically describe the family's holdings at that time as double assessed. Both Wilson and the 1828 select committee surmised that the quotas assigned some townships in the 1690s were unnaturally high due to double assessments. There are procedures which, in northern counties where reliable township acreages are available, make it possible to test the plausibility of such an inference. Dividing the Welwick land tax quota into the total acres of the parish gives a figure of eighteen acres per pound of tax.[3] That figure is approximately half that of the similarly alluvial, adjacent Humberside parishes and is below the divisional mean of 24. Welwick was, that is to say, strikingly more heavily taxed than adjacent parishes with similar soils – if acres (even when accurately known) are accepted as a sufficient test. One is tempted to conclude that Welwick was heavily taxed as a direct result of double assessments on the Crathorne properties. But lacking further verification, such a conclusion would be imprudent. Not all townships within the riding which are known to have had large Catholic holdings show up on such a test as heavily taxed. Nor can it be shown that all heavily taxed townships contained Catholic estates at the end of the seventeenth century.

When confined to post-1780 evidence, there is nothing indicating in a reliable and systematic fashion whether quotas were affected by double assessment. But there are two ways in which the effects on the quotas of a sample of townships can be indirectly gauged. The results, though hardly conclusive, are at least suggestive. Table 4.1 identifies townships in the East Riding of Yorkshire where Catholic estates of more than £100 rental were registered in 1715. Two ratios are then given for each township, along with the divisional or wapentake mean: the number of acres per pound of land tax quota, and the pounds of valuational rent (according to schedule A of the 1815 property tax) per pound of land tax.[4] The first ratio measures the relative burden of the tax quotas per acre at the time the quota was imposed in the late seventeenth century, while the second estimates the relative burden of the land tax on real land values at a time when the Napoleonic rise in rentals had peaked.

The table offers some evidence which could support an argument that quotas were adjusted significantly upward due to the presence of large

Catholic estates. Everingham and Hayton, where the Constables held estates, or Brigham and Dunnington, containing the Brigham estates, and the Cutler estate at Westow provide the best examples. In these townships the quotas per acre are significantly heavier, and the later tax burdens are more onerous, than their divisional means. But most of the townships do not support an argument that the land tax quotas of townships with large Catholic estates were always high within their divisional context. Most of the ratios of acres to quota do not significantly depart from the mean, and several of the rent-to-tax ratios rise considerably above it. Indeed many of the lowest acres-per-quota ratios of each division occur in townships which contained no Catholic estates (appendix P.l).

It becomes impossible therefore to argue with confidence that low acres-per-quota ratios were in fact caused by the double assessment of Catholic estates. Clearly other factors were at work in those other low ratio townships where only Protestant estates were to be found. Such factors may equally have been at work in Catholic townships. On the other hand it is equally difficult to argue that land tax quotas were adjusted upward in those Catholic townships where the acres-per-quota ratio was at or near (or, in Thornton, even well above) the mean. This evidence for the non-adjustment of quotas is inherently more persuasive. On the basis of this evidence it may be concluded that upward adjustments of quotas *may* have occurred within some townships, but that such adjustments were certainly, if they occurred at all, not universal. It is also clear, as in the case of Pocklington, that initially heavy quotas did not always prevent a thriving market town from significantly lightening its burden over the years; nor did a normal quota ensure a continuing normal tax burden for a declining center such as North Cliffe.

Certainly it is wrong to *assume* that double assessment affected quotas as such, either in the 1690s or at any other time. There are good reasons why the pattern of quota adjustment, if any adjustments in fact occurred, should have been a mixed one. An increased quota would have reduced the quotas of all other townships within the county (the level at which the parliamentary quotas were actually imposed), or perhaps the division, but only marginally. An unadjusted quota, on the other hand, would have dramatically reduced the taxes of each of the non-Catholic properties within the township. The latter would have been a most satisfying form of bigotry indeed, and it would certainly be interesting if no unadjusted quotas had been imposed. Since quotas were distributed within the counties and the divisions by the local commissioners, the pattern of imposition, as always in such matters, was probably a mixed one and the result of local circumstances. There is every reason to agree with Wilson that the quotas provide a highly imprecise guide to the comparative economic importance of townships within a region, but it does not necessarily follow

Table 4.1
Land tax burdens in townships containing larger Roman Catholic estates, East Riding

Wapentake division	Family	Township	Ratio: acres / land tax quota	Ratio: 1815 property tax value / land tax quota
Buckrose			58	61
	Nandyke	Norton, Sutton, Welham	40	87
	Hansbie	Thixendale, Raisthorpe	68	56
	Cutler	Westow	25	34
Dickering			69	70
	Brigham	Brigham	27	40
Harthill, Holme Beacon			47	44
	Constable	Everingham	27	24
	Vavasour	Gribthorpe, Willitoft	41	43
	Constable	Hayton	18	27
	Langdale	Holme on Spalding Moor	55	42
Harthill, Hunsley Beacon			33	63
	Metham	North Cave	32	69
	Langdale	North Cliffe	33	18
	Langdale	Sancton and Houghton	42	30
Harthill, Wilton Beacon			40	36
	Dolman	Pocklington	20	51
	Metham	Thornton	70	36
Holderness, Middle			26	48
	Metham	Burton Pidsea	30	40
	Brigham	Wyton	24	54
Holderness, North			41	52
	Brigham	Dunnington	25	30

Table 4.1 continued

Wapentake division	Family	Township	Ratio: acres / land tax quota	Ratio: 1815 property tax value / land tax quota
Holderness, South			24	38
	Dunbar	Burstwick, Skeckling	26	34
	Dunbar	Halsham	25	42
	Crathorne	Welwick	18	28
Howdenshire			30	40
	Metham	Saltmarsh, Metham	29	34
Ouse and Derwent			35	40
	Palmes	Naburn	22	29
	Middleton	North Duffield	26	33

Sources: Appendix P.1; Estcourt and Payne, eds., *The English Catholic Nonjurors of 1715*.

that double assessment often or significantly played a role in creating that imprecision. The different ratios between quotas and acres or rentals which are found throughout the countryside would have been sufficiently striking even if double assessment had never occurred.[5]

A second set of problems arising from double assessment concerns the internal distribution of the tax burden within a township in which such an assessment occurred. As noted, if the quota was adjusted upward to accommodate the double assessment, then the tax burden on the non-Catholic properties of the township would have remained normal. But if the quota was not adjusted, then each of the non-Catholic properties would have had its tax assessment reduced in proportion to the double assessment. This observation is important for two reasons. First, the tax entries of the non-Catholic properties would bear radically different relationships to both acres and rentals in the two cases; in the second case, when the quota was unadjusted, the tax entries would significantly underestimate the proportion of acres (assuming acreage equivalents could in principle be accurately applied) and rentals represented by the holdings of the non-Catholic proprietors. The quota system demands arithmetically that such distortions occur, since the quota is a constant. Second, if for any reason the double assessments were to cease, the tax assessments of all or some of the non-Catholic properties would necessarily rise sharply in order to meet the newly created shortfall in the quota.[6] Such a rise in the tax burden of non-Catholic properties would occur whether or not the quota had originally been adjusted upward; but if the quota had been upwardly adjusted, then the new non-Catholic tax burden would be above that which Protestants within the township might normally have been expected to bear. When these considerations are brought sharply into focus, it becomes sufficiently clear why so many townships persisted in practising double assessment long after the seventeenth-century anti-papist passions had largely subsided. Intolerance was rooted in hard economics and may not easily have been overcome by the sentiments of what was perhaps in some times and in some places a more enlightened age.

The consequences of double assessment, and of the cessation of double assessment, can be very serious for those wishing to use the land tax duplicates for analysis. The nature and possible range of those consequences, and their causes, can also be specified, since they follow logically from the structure of the tax itself. This much is clear. But the precise nature of the consequences may vary from case to case. Detecting the specific set of consequences pertaining to a specific township is not always achievable from a scrutiny of the land tax duplicates alone, and particularly when only post-1780 duplicates are available.

Returning to the case of Welwick and examining it in more detail, it becomes clear how important the consequences of double assessment can be and how difficult it is to interpret the evidence of the late eighteenth century duplicates. Welwick appears to have ceased double assessing its principal proprietor, H.R. Crathorne, in 1794 or 1795. Table 4.2 traces the effect of that cessation on the tax burdens within the parish. The effect is measured by calculating the ratio of valuational rent (which is annually reported in the Welwick duplicates) to tax for the Roman Catholic property and for the township as a whole. The effect of cessation on the land market is measured by counting the number of proprietors reported in the duplicates each year and by specifying the number of names which have annually been dropped or added. The number of property bundles reveals any structural alterations in the mode of reporting which might affect the number of names included. The final column gives the Roman Catholic rent as a percentage of the total rent of the township, thus tracking significant alterations in the physical size or relative worth of the Catholic holding. Each series spans a period of five years on either side of the cessation.

An interesting story appears to emerge. The Roman Catholic family of Crathorne had held the manors of Ploughland, Welwick Provost, and Welwick Thorpe within the parish of Welwick since 1664. By the end of the eighteenth century, they appear to have been disposing of their properties. The land tax duplicates for the North Riding show that by 1788 they had already sold their current seat at East Ness to their principal tenant there. In the early 1790s they were once again preparing to dispose of a large holding, this time in Welwick. Between 1793 and 1796 the duplicates show that they progressively sold off more than two-thirds the value of their property within the township. It was also in 1794 or 1795 that double assessments on their property ceased. One might reasonably infer, then, that double assessment was halted in order to make the Crathorne property more attractive to prospective buyers. In Welwick the purchasers were, once again, two of the principal Crathorne tenants, who by 1796 collectively held 24.5 percent of the township rental. The large addition of new small to middling proprietors in the 1795 duplicate and the further differentiation of property bundles suggest that the remainder of the Crathorne properties had been sold in small separate allotments.[7]

The story of the Crathorne properties, as I have delineated it, is indeed a tempting one. It conforms well with the more important features of the statistics derivable from the land tax, and it fulfills logical assumptions. But should we accept it? Table 4.2 shows that the Crathorne property was in fact double assessed prior to the sale. The ratio of its valuational rent to tax before 1795 had been half that of the remainder of the township. The land tax quota for the township, when compared against total acres, appears to be high, suggesting that the quota may have been adjusted upward during the 1690s. The case appears to form a neat basis for further

Table 4.2

The impact of double assessment on landholding, valuation, and tax burden in Welwick township, South Holderness, East Riding, 1790–99

Year	No. of Proprietors	No. of Property Bundles	No. of Proprietors Dropped	No. of Proprietors Added	Total Rent	Total Tax	Rent of R.C. Property	Tax of R.C. Property	Ratio of Total Rent to Total Tax	Ratio of R.C. Rent to R.C. Tax	R.C. Rent as % of Total Rent
1790	42	47	NA	NA	652.00.00	189.06.00	294.10.00	117.16.00[a]	3.4[b]	2.5	45.2
1791	42	47	3	3	655.10.00	190.00.00	294.10.00	117.16.00[a]	3.4[b]	2.5	44.9
1792	42	47	2	2	654.10.00	189.16.00	294.10.00	117.16.00[a]	3.4[b]	2.5	45.0
1793	41	47	2	1	654.10.00	189.16.00	294.10.00	117.16.00[a]	3.4[b]	2.5	45.0
1794	NO DUPLICATE										
1795	52	54	2	13	939.03.03	186.13.09	331.18.09	66.04.09	5.0[c]	5.0	35.4
1796	52	56	5	5	961.16.01 3/4	189.19.10 1/4	127.07.08	25.06.11	5.1	5.0	13.2
1797	51	56	1	0	2,270.00.00	193.19.05 1/2	308.00.00	25.06.11	11.7	12.1	13.6
1798	48	59	7[d]	4	1,200.00.00	189.09.07	158.00.00	25.00.04	6.3	6.3	13.2
1799	50	63	2	4	2,326.00.00	190.11.00	(316.00.00	(26.00.01	12.4	(12.2	(13.6
							(25.00.00)[e]	(2.01.00 3/4)[e]		(12.2)[e]	(1.1)[e]

Notes: [a]Specified in duplicate as double assessed.
[b]All property bundles except R.C. properties are at 5:1 ratio.
[c]All property bundles including R.C. properties are at 5:1 ratio.
[d]Includes five smallholders added in 1794–95.
[e]Tithes.
Source: Land tax duplicates, Humberside County Record Office.

generalization regarding quotas. If the quota had been adjusted upward, the end of double assessment should indeed have caused the non-Catholic proprietors to assume tax burdens above those which should have been normal within the township.

And yet, as we have seen, the township offers no evidence that quotas in such townships were *generally* adjusted upward. East Ness, where the Crathornes had their seat, was not double assessed by the 1780s – or at least no such ascription appears in the duplicates – and a calculation of quota against acres does not suggest that any upward adjustment of quota had ever been made there. The East Ness quota conforms well with those of neighbouring townships. Similar inconsistencies may be found on the properties of one of the largest Catholic landholders of the region, the Constables of Burton Constable, some of whose properties appear to have produced upward quota adjustments, while their other properties in adjacent townships did not. Table 4.1 provides other examples of inconsistent treatment among the properties of a single family. In short, when confined to land tax duplicates and restricted to evidence from the later eighteenth century, no consistent pattern of either double assessment or of quota adjustment can be detected among the Catholic properties of the county, not even among those of the same family lying in adjacent townships. The patterns are so erratic, in fact, that one might almost be inclined from such evidence to doubt the importance of double assessment in the original assignment of quotas.

Similarly, while it is plausible that the imminent sale of the Crathorne properties precipitated the ending of double assessment, there are grounds for doubting such a conclusion. Certainly such an interpretation leaves many important questions unanswered. For one thing, the ending of double assessment on the Crathorne properties in Welwick coincided with the statutory changes of 1794, which will be discussed in the next section. While the dropping of the double assessment clause in the land tax bill of that year, and the adding of a statement of intent towards the relief of Catholics in the preamble of the appeals clause, did not in fact provide sufficient mechanisms to Catholics for enforcing an end to double assessment, nevertheless the actions of Parliament undoubtedly contributed moral force to arguments made locally. A judicious person might therefore offer a more complex explanation for the ending of double assessment in Welwick. The sale of the Crathorne property in East Ness as early as 1788, well before the enactment of Catholic relief, suggests that the family had already formed an intention to dispose of further holdings prior to 1794 and that the act of 1794 may merely have facilitated this intention. But the puzzle remains. The role of the 1794 act in Welwick is not precisely traceable.

There is some reason to believe that the Crathorne tenants themselves may have been instrumental in persuading the township to end double assessment. The Crathorne property in East Ness is reported in the duplicates as separate property bundles broken down at the level of the tenant. This mode of reporting suggests, though not conclusively, that the East Ness tenants were paying the tax. In Welwick the Crathorne property was reported as a single property bundle with various tenants, strongly suggesting that there the tax was paid by Crathorne himself. Peter Roebuck, in his study of the Yorkshire baronetage, has found that earlier in the century Catholic proprietors had experienced considerable difficulty in persuading their tenants on double assessed property to assume full responsibility for the tax, and those tenants who did so often fell into arrears. Some Catholic landlords agreed to pay half the tax, leaving the tenants to pay only the normal rate. In some instances a failure by tenants to pay the full tax, even when doubled, caused some upward pressure on their rents.[8] It is not unreasonable to assume, then, that the Crathorne tenants, and especially those two large tenants who in 1796 purchased the bulk of the Crathorne holdings, would have been active in lending their support to ending double assessment, even if Crathorne had traditionally borne the direct burden of the tax.

But if it were so economically advantageous to the Crathornes and their tenantry to end double assessment, why had they not succeeded in doing so years earlier? Ostensibly they enjoyed an overwhelming influence within the township. No other proprietors within Welwick were of a size to contest that influence. The Askews, who were the next largest holders in the township in 1793, held only 10 percent of the total rental against the 45 percent of the Crathornes. Of course, not all large proprietors were skilled in exercising their natural interest, and non-resident landlords were particularly restricted in doing so. Perhaps the Crathornes lacked such skills or the inclination to use them. But one should not push such a conclusion too far. Double assessment in Welwick did end in 1794–95, and it ended without the assistance of statutory remedy. Parliament had provided only its moral authority, and the Crathornes' sole ostensible weapons were persuasion. Must we assume that the newly imposed moral authority of Parliament was decisive?

Perhaps it was. The Crathornes could hardly have enjoyed the cordial support of the remaining proprietors and their tenants, either in 1794 or at any other time. The end of double assessment was extraordinarily severe in its effects on the non-Catholic properties. While the Crathornes enjoyed a 43.8 percent decline in their tax between 1793 and 1795, the tax owed by the remainder of the township rose by 67.3 percent. Virtually all of the non-Catholic proprietors in Welwick were smallholders. In 1793 two-thirds of them held rent valuations of less than £10, and it was among this group that the largest increases occurred. Over a third of this group experienced tax increases of 100 to more than 200 percent. Indeed the entire township was thrown into flux. The size and distribution of holdings altered sharply at all levels during those years, and the township began a series of general revaluations for tax purposes. The old valuation level, which had remained at just over £650 for the township as a whole throughout the 1780s and early 1790s, rose sharply in stages following the end of double assessment. By 1799, and for several years thereafter, it appears to have stabilized at approximately rack rent.[9] Rather than be surprised that the Crathornes had failed to end double assessment earlier, perhaps we should wonder that it was possible for a non-resident Catholic gentry family, in the years of its decline, to produce an effect which was so strikingly beneficial for themselves and so decidedly harmful to their neighbours.[10] Important pieces of the Welwick puzzle, which the land tax duplicates do not supply, are missing, and explanations based on the duplicates alone, while suggestive, cannot be accepted with confidence.

One can go farther. It is not certain that the thirteen new proprietors appearing for the first time in the 1795 duplicate (table 4.2) were owners of estates alienated by the Crathornes, or that they were even genuinely new to the township. As noted in the preceding chapter, small occupiers and proprietors were not fully reported in most land tax duplicates. It is quite possible that some number of small proprietors (and their properties) who had simply been omitted in previous years were added to the duplicate in 1795. Such additions would assist in meeting the shortfall in the quota created by the end of double assessment. This possibility cannot be verified, because the imposition of the general revaluation makes it impossible to compare the total valuational rental for 1793 and 1795. Even the rank order and proportional relationships between individual properties altered considerably between the two years due to the general nature of the revaluation. But the fact that five of the smallholders added in 1794–95 were dropped in 1798 should not be ignored. Erratic inclusion on the duplicates of 1795 to 1799 also occurred among a few other small properties. Though it is reasonably certain that the bulk of the Crathorne estate was acquired by two of its principal tenants, it would be rash to conclude from the land tax duplicates alone that the remainder was sold to small proprietors who were new to the township. The "new" proprietors need not have been new; both they and their properties may simply have previously been omitted from the tax. The general revaluation may mask such a phenomenon and prevent our perceiving that the redistribution of the remainder of the Crathorne property occurred only among the previous proprietors and tenants of the township.[11]

In 1828 a select committee of the House of Commons conducted hearings on the history and operation of double assessment. Its report often conveys only the impressions and inferences of contemporary Catholic landlords and their agents on the early history of the land tax acts, and some of the testimony must be treated as misleading and as no more than informed hearsay. But the report also contains direct testimony on the later operation of the acts which is of great value, and the report as a whole delineates a history of the operation of the Roman Catholic clauses of the land tax and other penal statutes which is probably correct in its broad outlines and invaluable in its detail. The following few paragraphs on the history of double assessment are based principally on the committee's findings.[12] In the concluding section of this chapter, I shall modify and extend these findings by examining direct evidence for the administration of the penal provisions during the first century of their operation in one wapentake of the North Riding of Yorkshire.

The land tax acts were passed annually, and the statutory authority for double assessment was contained in a separate clause in each of those acts from the inception of the tax in 1693 until 1794. Following the rebellion of 1715, the pressure on Catholic estates increased significantly and resulted in the passage of the Catholic Registry Act (1 Geo. I, st. 2, c. 55). That statute required that Roman Catholics register their estates with the clerk of the peace in the county in which the estates lay, stipulating their location, occupancy, and annual rental. The penalty for failing to register was forfeiture of two-thirds of the estate, or its equivalent, to the Crown and forfeiture of one-third to whomever might sue for the same at the common law or in chancery.[13] The select committee inferred, and with some apparent justification, that the penalties for non-registration were so severe that few Catholics could be expected not to have complied. The registration of Catholic estates, which continued until the statute was repealed in 1790, must have greatly facilitated and further encouraged the imposition of the double assessments.

As shown in the preceding section, double assessment could have consequences, sometimes unfortunate ones, for the non-Catholics of a district as well as for Catholics. The report of the select committee delineates further penalties that non-Catholics might suffer when a property passed out of the hands of a Catholic owner. Once a double assessment was imposed on a property, it could not be lifted without legal process. The penalty was in fact (though not technically in law) on the property and not on the person. If an owner conformed to the Church of England or took the oaths, if an heir or the tenantry were Protestant, or if the estate was purchased by a non-Catholic, the property remained subject to double assessment unless a process at law lifted that penalty.

By the early years of the reign of Anne it had become evident to Parliament that inequities had emerged in the administration of the land tax, particularly in the way double assessment affected non-Catholics. A clause came to be annually included in the acts whereby an owner could appeal an assessment which he claimed was in excess of the statutory rate (most often set at 4s. in the pound). Such an appeal would be heard by two or more of the land tax commissioners for the division, who would then certify to the Barons of the Exchequer that the statutory rate was in fact exceeded on that property. The Barons, after confirming the facts through witnesses, were granted discretionary power to discharge the overplus exceeding the statutory rate. The process sounds like a fair one, and it was open to Roman Catholic as well as Protestant landlords. But there was a rub. Only the overplus exceeding the 4s. (or statutory) rate on fully improved rack rent was dischargable. As rents rose in the eighteenth century, the burden of double assessments declined until, in the end, no statutory overpluses actually occurred. By providing only for excesses above the statutory rate, the act increasingly failed to relieve inequalities in the real rate. Although the clause providing for appeal was included annually in the land tax statutes until 1794, it had long since become wholly nugatory.

By the 1770s there was a growing sentiment among the governing classes that Roman Catholics should be substantially relieved of their disabilities. Acts granting various forms of relief were passed in 1778 (leading to the Gordon Riots) and in 1791. In the latter year William Pitt promised Charles Butler and the members of the Catholic Committee that a separate bill repealing double assessment would be introduced following passage of the Catholic Relief Bill (31 Geo. III c. 32). But the Catholic Bill was passed by the House late in the session and the Catholic Committee, having been given assurances of future action, was dissolved the following year. Pitt seems to have become persuaded that a general bill for the repeal of double assessment was unnecessary, since the only legal basis for such assessments were the clauses contained in the annual land tax bills. In 1794 the government took action. The land tax act for that year (34 Geo. III c. 8) omitted the double assessment clause for the first time. A preamble was also added to the Queen Anne clause providing for appeal of assessments in excess of 4s. on the rack rent. The preamble explicitly stipulated that it was no longer the intention of Parliament or of the act to impose double assessments, thus identifying the Queen Anne clause as a remedy for ending the fiscal penalty.

This was an unfortunate choice of remedies. According to testimony before the select committee, no one within the government or in the House at the time seems to have realized or noted that this appeals clause had become nugatory. Thus, between 1794 and 1798, Catholics enjoyed the advantage of having the government and Parliament on record as wishing double assessment to end, but the statutory mechanism provided for ending the practice was inoperable. Some Catholics sought relief from yet another clause in the annual land tax acts providing for appeal against internally unequal assessments within a township, and according to the 1828 report some few succeeded. But that clause was designed for non-Catholics and required that the remitted portion of the tax be redistributed either within the township (without altering the quota) or within the division (by altering all other quotas). It is hardly surprising, the 1828 committee concluded, that few such appeals were successful. On this point the 1828 report is surely midleading, however. Those Catholics who obtained an end to double assessment during the mid-1790s, while enjoying the moral authority of the new preamble to the Queen Anne clause, must have used the more general clause on unequal assessment as their technical grounds, and, as shall be shown, many did so successfully.

The Land Tax Redemption Act of 1798 (38 Geo. III c. 60) further impeded the relief of Catholic or formerly Catholic properties from double assessment, making even the former avenues for appeal impossible. The Redemption Act fixed the quotas in perpetuity. It also fixed the tax amounts on redeemed properties, so that any abatement arising from an end to double assessment would necessarily be borne only by those properties within the township that were unredeemed. Such a procedure was clearly inequitable. But the fixed quota could be met in no other way. Testimony before the select committee indicated, and quite understandably, that neither local land tax commissioners nor the Tax Board nor the Barons of the Exchequer were prepared, without further statutory authorization, to approve or endorse an end to double assessments after passage of the 1798 act.[14]

I shall now turn to more direct and systematic evidence for the local administration of double assessments. The evidence is derived from a virtually complete register of early returns for the forty-seven townships of Birdforth wapentake in the North Riding during the years 1693–95, 1699, and 1712–18, and from later duplicates during the 1790s. The evidence for the early period, with which I shall begin, is presented in appendix D.1, where the total amount owed by each township in every year reported by the register is given, along with the official quota eventually established by statute in 1798. The apparent cause of significant fluctuations in the quota, or the amount owed, are in each case delineated in the notes.[15]

The first thing to notice is that the amount of land tax owed at the township level, in this wapentake at least, was by no means ossified or stable during the first ten or twenty years of land tax administration, even after the establishment of quotas in 1698. Amounts owed fluctuated widely, and no township in the wapentake had settled into its 1798 quota (or within 12d. of that amount) before 1700. By 1712, when the register resumes, thirty-seven out of the forty-seven townships within the wapentake had permanently stabilized their quotas at that level. Four of the remaining ten townships achieved the 1798 quota in 1713, two in 1714 and one in 1717. Only three townships had continued to vary from the 1798 quota by the latter year. One of those, Thirlby, was short by only 2s. 4d. A second township, Gueldable with Borrowby, experienced significant boundary changes later in the century. The third township, Kepwick, was wholly owned by the third Viscount Fauconberg, a Catholic recusant. Since the Kepwick quota had increased from £33 4s. to £38 14s. 3d. between 1699 and 1713, and was again to increase after 1717 to £43 19s. 3d., it is possible that the properties of that township were coming progressively under some degree of double assessment, even after other townships had stabilized their quotas.

Virtually all major variations in quota during these years may be explained by the imposition or lifting of double assessment on Roman Catholic properties. It is further evident that the imposition of double assessment did not at that time reduce non-Catholic properties within the township below the tax levels which would normally have been imposed on them. Double assessment during these early years uniformly inflated quotas. When double assessment was lifted, the quotas were then brought down to what was to be henceforth an invariable level, and one that was fixed as such by statute in 1798. A calculation of the total tax owed by the wapentake in 1693, 1695, 1699, and 1713 further shows that significant fluctuations in township totals and quotas had virtually no effect on the amount owed by the division as a whole. This lack of variation at the divisional level confirms an impression that the imposition or lifting of double assessments in some townships caused the commissioners to proportionately either reduce or increase the quotas in other townships within the wapentake. The land tax acts empowered them to do so, and this is apparently precisely what they did – in Birdforth at least. The commissioners do not appear to have undertaken general revaluations of quotas within the division, however. In years when double assessments were imposed or were lifted, the quotas of some townships within the division remained stable. The evidence suggests that the more significant shiftings of the divisional burden were among those townships holding Catholic properties, the more purely Protestant townships remaining relatively untouched. But the patterns are not sufficiently clear to be fully confident that such was the conscious policy.

A few minor points are also worth noting. Boundary changes among townships could affect quotas in this early period. The commissioners in at least one case adjusted two quotas after reassigning a small portion of a township to its neighbour. Before the imposition of quotas in 1698, the total amount owed could easily be adjusted when assessments were either levied or lifted on the salaries of excise officers, as in Topcliffe, or on personal property, as in Sutton under Whitestonecliffe. Moreover, not all alterations relating to double assessment were impositions. Relief could also be granted. The quota of Nether Silton was reduced in 1713 when a major Catholic proprietor, John Pinkney, sold his previously double assessed properties to two non-Catholic gentry. Similarly, Sir Hugh Smithson appears to have been relieved of double assessment on his properties in Breckenbrough when he conformed to the Church of England. Though the 1828 report seems correct in its assertions that such sales and changes in religious persuasion generally did not result in the ending of double assessment later in the century, in these early years the flexibility of quotas would seem to have made such adjustments comparatively easy.[16]

Although a sprinkling of Catholic or formerly Catholic properties in Birdforth wapentake had been relieved from double assessment by the Hanoverian accession, or shortly thereafter, such a policy was by no means the dominant one. A comparison of the Queen Anne quotas within the wapentake to those established by statute in 1798 will show that the process of imposing double assessment was virtually complete, even before the greatly increased fear of Jacobitism following the 1715 rebellion. The quotas of 1798 also show that Catholic properties, within this division at least, were to experience no further relief during that century, at least not in the form of quota revision. Some major Catholic proprietors were severely hit by abrupt tax increases. Lord Fauconberg and his tenants were forced to absorb sharp tax increases on his properties in Old Byland, Coxwold, Newburgh, Over Silton, and Thornton – townships where he owned all or most of the land.

And yet, curiously, not all of the Fauconberg properties experienced severe double assessment. In Dale Town, Oulston, and Yearsley, where his holdings were similarly dominant, the quotas remained stable or varied only marginally. Similarly, the township of Thornborough, where the Catholic Philip Saltmarshe held for about two-thirds of the tax, and Upsall, which was wholly owned by Lord Dunbar, experienced no significant alteration in their quotas. A decision to impose double assessment on a township which was wholly owned – or virtually so – by a single proprietor could only have come from the commissioners for the division. But why the same body of men would decide to levy such impositions on some Catholics and not on others or – even more unlikely – on some properties of a Catholic earl but not on all must remain a mystery. There is some evidence apart from quota stability to confirm that Fauconberg in Dale Town and Dunbar in Upsall were not double assessed. By the 1780s the Dunbar properties in Upsall had passed to the Protestant Turtons, while Fauconberg had sold Dale Town to Lord Pelham, a Protestant of impeccable Whig lineage. The quotas of these single-proprietor townships remained unaltered. Perhaps these estates were saleable to Protestants partly because they had never been double assessed. But it is not wholly clear that townships with stable quotas were in fact escaping double assessment. The Pelhams and Turtons, or their tenants, may have been forced to suffer the ancient penalties without relief. It is possible that some Catholic properties had been double assessed earlier in the seventeenth century and that the totals assessed in 1693, and the quotas that followed, had all been assigned accordingly, silently following local tradition. The possibility of hidden double assessments is one to which I shall return shortly.

Double assessment, once it was imposed in the early eighteenth century, seems to have persisted well into the 1790s. Appendix D.2 presents evidence for all properties in the North Riding which were actually labelled as double assessed in the duplicates of 1789 or 1790. The appendix identifies the Catholic proprietor and then reports the township quota and (in parentheses below) the amount of tax assessed on the Catholic property bundles for each year from 1790 to 1795 and for 1798. The tax amount is underscored each time double assessment for a Catholic is explicitly ascribed in the duplicate. It is fully evident from this appendix that double assessment was widespread in the North Riding during the 1790s, albeit ascriptions were erratic and intermittant. But it is also evident that, on properties which were at any time explicitly labelled as double assessed, those penalties were almost invariably lifted by the middle of the decade. Moreover, with a few minor exceptions, the cessation of double assessment overwhelmingly occurred in either 1794 or 1795. Despite the impression conveyed by the 1828 report, which was clearly misleading on this point, the legislation of 1794 did have a widespread impact on ending tax penalties on Roman Catholic properties.

The ending of double assessment in the 1790s, unlike the earlier period, was not accomplished by altering township tax quotas. The quotas remained at those traditional levels which were to become fixed by statute in 1798. Instead the commissioners, or perhaps the township community itself by private agreement, redistributed the burden of the affected quota among the non-Catholic holders within the township. Most non-Catholic properties experienced a sharp rise in tax as double assessment ceased, usually in rough proportion to the newly created shortfall on Catholic properties. But very few Catholic properties had their assessment precisely halved. In most cases the tax on Catholic properties was significantly reduced, but by less than half. In some cases the amounts were phased down over two or three years, which suggests countervailing economic pressures and perhaps real hardship among Protestant holders. But most often the end of double assessment was achieved by a process of general or limited revaluation within the township. Such a process could suggest that most Catholic properties may not in fact have been fully double assessed immediately prior to 1794. When the possibility of improvements is taken into account, such an argument is not implausible. Alternatively, and more correctly I think, we must remember that the imposition of double assessments in the late seventeenth or early eighteenth centuries had been accomplished by adjusting quotas upwards. If the amounts on Catholic properties had been merely halved in the 1790s, and if it is assumed that halving would achieve the rate previously imposed on non-Catholics, non-Catholic properties would necessarily have risen above their previous rates (with respect to valuation) in order to meet the shortfall in the quota, thus reversing the old inequalities between the Catholic and non-Catholic properties. Whichever view is taken of the matter – and both may well be true – it seems reasonable to assume that the revaluations that accompanied the end of double assessment in the mid-1790s genuinely brought the tax values of that township into correct proportional relations to assessed valuations.

Since, as shown in appendix D.2, all identifiably double assessed estates were relieved of such penalties during the 1790s, how should one understand the evidence presented before the 1828 select committee that many Catholic estates continued to be double assessed well into the nineteenth century? It may be noted that a sprinkling of very small properties listed in the appendix were ostensibly not relieved. Some actually found their taxes rise. But properties of that size may have been unusually affected by the resulting revaluation. More puzzling are townships such as Hutton Longvillers, where the tax of the Tunstalls amounted to 98 percent of the quota, or Lartington, where the Maires paid about 84 percent. In those townships the estates of both families were labelled as double assessed. But though other Catholic estates within the division sought and found relief, neither of these estates was relieved of the penalty during this decade.

The evidence of the 1828 report did suggest that resistance to ending double assessment was greatest in those townships where Catholics owned the principal proportion of holdings. And it is understandable why resistance should have been strongest in such places and adjustments sometimes impossible to undertake. So long as quotas themselves could not be adjusted – and it has been shown that they were not adjusted in the 1790s – townships wholly owned by a Catholic could not end double assessment without jeopardizing the divisional quota. Similarly, if one or more Catholics owned not all but a large proportion of a township, the end of double assessment could only shift the entire (and in such cases very heavy) shortfall in the township's quota entirely onto the remaining smaller

Protestant holders. Such sudden and onerous shifts in tax burden would be difficult to bear, however much they might be required in correcting an ancient injustice. It might come as no surprise, then, that unusually large estates, such as those of the Tunstalls and Maires in Hutton Longvillers and Lartington, even though acknowledged in the duplicates to be double assessed, would not be successful in seeking an end to the penalty. Table 4.3 offers statistical evidence to support such a conclusion. This table lists all townships reported in appendix D.2 in which at least 33 percent of the 1790 tax quota was paid by Catholics. Catholic properties in all of these townships were relieved during the 1790s. With the striking exception of Gatenby, these Catholic properties at double assessed rates never paid more than 75 percent of the quota in their townships, and in most cases they paid considerably less. The full burden of the quota shortfalls in these townships fell fully on the remaining Protestant holders. But the evidence suggests the burdens, though heavy, were tolerable, so long as the proportion of the township in Catholic hands was not more than two-thirds to three-quarters of the whole.

More about the incidence of double assessment is revealed though an examination of the estates of Catholics in townships that never recorded annotations of double assessment in their late eighteenth century duplicates. For one thing, some townships throughout the North Riding appear to have ended double assessment on Catholic properties in the mid-1790s, despite their never having explicitly identified those properties in their duplicates as being double assessed. The tax on the Witham properties in St John Stanwick, where the Withams had paid 14 percent of the tax, suddenly dropped in 1794 from £8 17s. 9d. to £4 15s. 4d. All other taxes in the township rose proportionately. The same pattern occurred during that year in East and West Appleton, where the Charltons had owed 45 percent and the Lawsons 16 percent of the tax, and in Burrell and Cowling, where Thomas Stapleton had owed 28 percent.

Other estates, by contrast, continued to be double assessed but were not labelled as such. The Fauconberg estates in Old Byland, Coxwold, Newburgh, Over Silton, and Thornton, which experienced severe double assessment early in the century and continued to be owned by that family to the end of the century, were never labelled as double assessed during the 1780s and 1790s. Since the quotas remained unchanged, the double assessment must have persisted. When all of those townships passed into the hands of the Protestant Wombwells in the early nineteenth century, the quotas remained intact. They were still unchanged in 1830, following Catholic emancipation. There is little basis for believing that in townships such as these, which had been wholly owned by Catholic families (or virtually so), double assessment ever ceased until the land tax itself was abolished.[17]

Table 4.3
Tax quota burdens (acres/£) on Roman Catholic townships relieved of double assessment in the 1790s, North Riding

Wapentake	Township	Acres/£	% tax (double assessed) paid by R.C.s 1790
Allertonshire		28	
	Thornton le Street	24	35.2
Gilling East		30	
	Cowton, East	27	41.3
	Cowton, South	20	64.4
	Manfield	19	62.2
	Thrintoft	23	58.3
Gilling West		83	
	Dalton	41	75.1
	Ovington	26	46.5
	Thorp	14	68.1
Hallikeld		34	
	Gatenby	13	90.2
	Pickhill and Roxby	31	38.1
Hang East		39	
	Bedale and Firby	16	51.5
	Colburn	26	54.0
Hang West		120	
	Thornton Steward	61	46.8

Note: Only townships with at least 33 percent Catholic proprietorship have been included.
Source: Appendices D.2 and M.

Other townships containing Catholic estates also failed to label those estates as double assessed during the 1790s, and the end of double assessment there cannot be confirmed by any evidence in the duplicates. Some of these are listed in table 4.4. Is it possible that, instead of continuing to be double assessed beyond the 1790s, some of these estates had never in fact been double assessed? Or that double assessment had ceased early in the century? These are most difficult questions to answer. One way to test these assumptions, though it is most unsatisfactory, is to examine the land tax quotas for each township in relation to its total acres, as was done earlier for the East Riding. It can be seen in table 4.3, and from three townships listed in table 4.4, that double assessments do often seem to have caused a higher than normal tax burden in respect to acres. Most of these townships have acres-to-tax ratios that are strikingly lower than their wapentake mean, reflecting a higher burden of tax per acre. Can the remaining entries in table 4.4 be examined to infer whether their properties were to any degree double assessed during the 1790s? Unfor-

Table 4.4
Tax quota burdens (acres/£) on Roman Catholic townships apparently not relieved of double assessment in the 1790s, North Riding

Wapentake	Township	Acres/£	% tax (double assessed) paid by R.C.s 1790
Allertonshire		28	
	North Kilvington	10	97.7
Birdforth		43	
	Coxwold[a]	51	100.0
	Dale Town	94	100.0[c]
	Newburgh[a]	42	100.0
	Old Byland[a]	48	100.0
	Oulston	40	100.0
	Over Silton[a]	45	96.1
	Thornborough	16	93.2
	Thornton and Baxby[a]	19	77.4
	Yearsley	109	93.8
Gilling West		83	
	Cliffe[b]	16	100.0
	Hutton Longvillers[b]	21	98.1
	Lartington[b]	86	83.7
	Scargill	46	100.0
Hang East		39	
	Brough	13	100.0
	Catterick and Killerby	19	80.2

Source: Land tax duplicates, NYCRO; appendix M.
Notes: [a]Double assessed during the early eighteenth century and thereafter, though not labelled as such.
[b]Labelled as double assessed during the 1790s. Other townships in this table were never so labelled.
[c]Early in the century Dale Town was wholly owned by Lord Fauconberg, a Catholic recusant. By 1790 it was wholly owned by Lord Pelham.

tunately, any such inference would not be reliable. Even if we were to accept acres as a satisfactory indicator of tax burden, which perhaps we should not do except in the most gross terms, the series is too inconsistent to inspire full confidence. Four of the Fauconberg townships in Birdforth known to have been double assessed have ratios which hover around the wapentake mean. Only one of those townships, Thornton, seems strikingly low. Another Fauconberg township, Oulston, which never significantly altered its ratio and where double assessment is not certain, also produces a ratio near the mean. But Yearsley, an adjacent township in the same parish with a similar tax history, produces a ratio which is far too high for its wapentake and its entire region. On the other hand, Thornborough and North Kilvington, two townships which are adjacent across the wapentake boundary, along with Upsall, present a contiguous pattern of markedly low ratios. In the duplicates there is no indication that these three townships had ever been double assessed or experienced quota alteration. In short, known cases of double assessment will often produce strikingly low ratios of acres to tax, suggesting heavier than normal burdens of tax-to-land value. But such ratios are not always low. They are an unreliable indicator of double assessment in those townships where Catholic ownership is evident but where no early alterations in quota occurred and no ascriptions of double assessment were entered in the duplicates.

Having dismissed this method as a general solution to the problem of identifying hidden double assessments, let me now trot it back into the arena in support of some cautionary statements. The townships listed in table 4.4 were almost wholly owned by single Catholic families. Several were the seats of those families. Although not all of their ratios are markedly low, enough are significantly so to raise doubts regarding the normality of their quotas. Edward Meynell, for example, had his seat at North Kilvington in Allertonshire, where he paid 98 percent of the tax. North Kilvington duplicates never indicated double assessment, and the quotas never changed. Meynell was widely relieved of double assessments in other townships (appendix D.2). Was he not double assessed at his seat? Or did he possess sufficient influence to secure relief elsewhere but not here? Remember once more that, once quotas had become stable following the Hanoverian accession, those townships that were almost wholly in the hands of one family had virtually no chance of relief from double assessment. Internal readjustment of the burden was impossible, and external relief could only jeapordize the divisional quota – short of a revaluation of the division, which all evidence shows was not in the cards during the later years. Hugh Aveling has reminded us that the principle of double taxation on Catholics was first established by a Subsidy Act of 1625 and was simply transferred to the land tax during the 1690s.[18] If in some cases the transference was precisely that – a continuance of earlier patterns of taxation within that division and township – then double assessment may well have been present from the inception of the land tax and, reflecting what would by then have been perceived as ancient practice, never have been ascribed or commented upon in the duplicates. Testimony brought before the select committee in 1828 indeed shows that some Catholic landlords at that time could not directly prove their properties were double assessed but were compelled to infer it from acreage comparisons with their neighbours. It seems prudent for historians to assume, therefore, that many townships which held Catholic, especially large Catholic, properties in the late seventeenth and early eighteenth centuries were in fact double assessed throughout their later history, even when no direct evidence indicating double assessment has survived.

The problems associated with double assessment are serious. What is worse, they are probably more widespread than the evidence of the post-1780 duplicates would suggest. But where a suspected double assessment occurs within a township which is wholly owned by one family, analytical problems should not arise so long as derived statistics are confined to that township. One may still conclude, for example, that the entire township is in the hands of a single proprietor. However, the possibility of double assessment places yet one more obstacle in the way of those who would wish to compare absolute tax values between townships.[19] And even internal analyses may to some degree be affected, though perhaps not seriously, when the major proprietor owns almost all, but not quite all, of the acres and tithe.

CHAPTER FIVE

Converting Tax Values to Acres

The causes and consequences of the decline of the small owner-occupying farmer were at the centre of one of the great political debates of the later nineteenth century, and the land tax studies of the first half of the twentieth century were the intellectual offspring of that discussion. The debate had always tended to conceptualize the "smallness" of small owner-occupiers in terms of the numbers of acres they had farmed. The pioneers in the use of the land tax – Johnson, Gray, and Davies – inherited the terminology of this debate and formulated their questions in the manner of their predecessors. It was only natural that, in using land tax duplicates to trace the decline of the small landowner, they felt inclined to convert individual land tax entries into acres by means of conversion factors called "acreage equivalents." Gray and some of his successors further tied themselves to the use of equivalents by their development of long chronological perspectives through the combined use of land tax duplicates and enclosure awards. If awards were to be used, and especially for the period before 1780 when land tax duplicates are not generally available, then the tax amounts must be made to conform to the acres reported in the awards. In addition, conversions to acres permitted the inter-parish grouping of landowners by size of holding, thereby facilitating regional analyses. It has always been known that the burden of the land tax was to some degree unequally distributed among the counties. More recently it has also been acknowledged that the distributions of the quotas were similarly unequal among the parishes of individual counties. The conversion of tax values to acres has thus acted as a standardization procedure in some studies, enabling students to overcome the deficiencies in comparability embedded in the tax entries of different parishes and permitting the grouping of properties by size across parish boundaries. While differing methods are employed, the conversion of tax entries to acres continues to be one of the most common and important features of land tax studies. And since the understanding of the reliability of such conversions has undergone a considerable and highly technical evolution, it is necessary to review that debate in some detail.

Johnson assigned acreage equivalents to his land tax entries, but he never revealed how he did so.[1] Gray, writing one year later, obviously fretted over the problem a good deal, and he was more candid in revealing his methods. First, he compared his land tax duplicates with contemporary enclosure awards and concluded that, while "accuracy in the exact size of holdings cannot, of course, be attained," nevertheless the tax entries within his county of Oxfordshire varied between 1s. 6d. and 2s. per acre. He in fact appears only to have employed the lower conversion figure, thus quietly accepting an underestimation error range of up to one-third. Second, he estimated secular trends in owner-occupation by size category by calculating the percentage of total tax reported for various size groupings of such holders and then assuming that variations in percentage were proportional to variations in acreage. This method was applied indiscriminately to all parishes within the county.[2] Almost two decades later, Davies adopted a strikingly different, and far simpler, procedure. He achieved the acreage equivalent for each of his seven counties by simply dividing the total assigned land tax of the county by its total acreage. The resulting tax per acre for each county was then applied to the tax entries of each of its parishes.[3] None of these early students of the land tax made any allowance for variations in soil quality or land values within a county.

The methods of Gray and Davies were variously followed for the next thirty years. Chambers worried about doing so, but adopted Davies' equivalent for Lindsey in order to maintain comparability.[4] In the late 1950s, Hunt openly rehearsed the deficiencies of acreage equivalents more fully than anyone had attempted previously, but then he proceeded to apply Davies' county level formula to "those parishes where all payments were made on land and, in some instances, a small number of houses." The acreage equivalent he derived for Leicestershire by this approach was precisely that of Davies for the same county: 1s. 4d. He then applied that conversion figure indiscriminately to all parishes within the county.[5]

It is only in the 1960s that a more sustained and practical concern with the reliability of acreage equivalents began to produce significant variations in the methods of Gray and Davies. That decade also witnessed the first publicly expressed doubts that such methods could ever reliably be employed. Grigg was the first to sound the alarm. He accepted the *principle* of acreage equivalents, and he conceded that variations in the amount of tax paid should reflect variations in the number of acres held *within* individual parishes. But Grigg rejected the county level equivalents of Davies on the grounds of soil variability. He equally rejected equivalents for soil regions, insisting that even such regions contain varieties of soils which are sufficiently divergent in value and distributed in location as to render any single conversion figure spurious. Grigg was prepared to accept equivalents only when they were derived on a parish-by-parish basis, and even then only when they were computed for parishes which were fairly homogeneous with respect to soil. In his own work, and in a manner similar to Gray, he computed the total combined tax of all owner-occupiers for each individual parish and computed that total as a percentage of the total tax owed by the parish. He concluded that any secular variation in that percentage would reliably reflect variations in the acreage held by his owner-occupiers, since he assumed that they were randomly distributed among the various soils of the parish, thus avoiding any distortions that might occur in any single holding. Since he showed that differences in acreage equivalents within a single parish could vary greatly, even when the soils were relatively homogeneous, the latter assumption remains peculiarly crucial to the acceptability of his method.[6]

A more sweeping assault on acreage equivalents was launched three years later by Professor Mingay. Mingay's attack focused explicitly on the county level equivalents of Davies, but the implications of his findings were critical of all the methods that had previously been employed. Like Grigg, he rejected county equivalents on grounds of soil variability. But he went further than Grigg in suggesting that differences in land values, and inequalities in assessment levels of individual holdings within a single parish (with large holders often being more lightly assessed), had been present from the beginning in the way the burden of the land tax had been distributed. He further doubted that regular and accurate revaluations had occurred. If not, he suggested that further distortions had accumulated in the proportional distributions of the tax both within and among parishes by the end of the eighteenth century, since no corrections had been made for changes in land use and value. He therefore concluded that "there was, even early in the century, no consistency in the relationship of assessment to acreage." The land tax duplicates of the later eighteenth century may be able to reveal the larger contours of what happened to smaller owner-occupiers. But "certainly, the returns cannot tell us anything very useful about the acreages actually owned and occupied by small owners at any time." He offered detailed evidence from estate records in several counties to demonstrate that acreage equivalents for specific holdings departed sharply from Davies' estimates and varied widely even on the estates of a single landowner within individual parishes. Again unlike Grigg, who had rejected the notion that small holdings might be disproportionately distributed on the *poorer* lands of a parish, Mingay found it plausible that inequitable assessment rates might be due to small holdings being placed more uniformly on more valuable lands. As shall be seen when considering more fully the problem of inequalities, smaller properties were indeed often (though not invariably) assessed more lightly by the later eighteenth century, a pattern which conforms well with other suggestions that village and urban properties enjoyed higher values than did the generality of agricultural lands. Grigg's crucial assumption regarding the equitable distribution of small holdings on the soils of the parish seemed then, and now seems to be even more clearly, thoroughly undermined.[7]

Martin, in his response to Mingay, vigorously reaffirmed that acreage equivalents which were sufficiently reliable for statistical purposes could be achieved, provided they were calculated on a parish-by-parish basis and restricted to places relatively unaffected by industrialization and urbanization. He questioned the distribution of the sample estate data presented by Mingay, and instead he offered evidence from sixty-three holdings in five regionally distributed parishes of Warwickshire. He suggested that a comparison of acreages derived from contemporary enclosure awards with tax entries in the duplicates reveal margins of error or variability in tax per acre which are quite acceptable. He concluded that the more serious departures tended to occur on small holdings, perhaps due to the proportion of the tax applied to the house, or perhaps because small holdings were being assessed at a higher rate. So long as one avoided industrial and urban areas, such problems could be held to acceptable levels.[8]

It has been widely accepted that Martin's reply was sufficient. But Mingay did respond, and this response was not much heeded, to judge by subsequent practice. It should have been. "It does not appear to me very reassuring that in Warwickshire, after excluding parishes of contrasting soil and cultivation, and excluding also the semi-industrialized and semi-urban parishes, Dr. Martin still finds in some instances errors ranging up to 36 per cent, and that 4s. of tax may represent anything from 2.7 acres to 6.6 acres."[9] Mingay could have been even more severe. Martin presents 4s. equivalents[10] from eight holdings, all described as "farms" ranging from 36 to 272 acres, on the old-enclosed manor and parish of Claverdon. These are "real" equivalents based on comparisons with the enclosure award. The equivalents varied, Martin notes, "only" between 2.5 and 3.7 acres, but this is a variation of 68 percent. The heaviest tax rates were on the two largest properties *and* on the smallest. There was no pattern in the distribution of the burden. In three of his five parishes the variation was even greater. In the arable parish of Cubbington the 4s. equivalent variation was from 3.6 to 6.6 acres, a difference of 83 percent. Both the lightest and the heaviest burden fell on the two smallest properties. In the pasture parish of Harbury the variation was again at 85 percent, ranging from 2.7 to 5.0 acres, with the smaller properties departing from the mean in both directions and constituting the principal source of error. In Cubbington and Harbury he also reported the actual acres derived from the enclosure award and the estimated acres computed from the land tax.

Three entries reported as "negligible" in the percentage error column run as high as 10 and 11 percent. The seventeen numerically reported percentages range from 12 to 36. Ten of the thirty-four holdings in these two parishes (38 percent in Cubbington and 27 percent in Harbury) either exceeded or fell short of their actual acreage by more than 20 percent when estimated by the acreage equivalent.

If the magnitude of error could be this great in parishes so carefully selected for their relative agricultural purity and their typological qualities, then Mingay was quite right not to be reassured. Martin may indeed have found, as he contended, that his class interval distributions were not much disturbed by such error, but then much depends upon how these arbitrarily constructed intervals are formed. Smaller sized intervals are obviously more subject to the effects of error. As noted in a previous chapter, when considering the problem of missing properties, even the most purely agricultural regions are likely to be replete with small properties variously described (but not usually so described in the land tax duplicates) as "house and garden" or "cottage." The "urban" problem which Martin believed capable of invalidating acreage equivalents is also a problem which lurks in what often appear to be the purest of agrarian landscapes. Nor should it be comforting to anyone interested principally in the fortunes of small holdings to learn, as Martin did, that it is precisely those holdings which constitute the principal source of error.

Within the last few years, Sarah Banks has undertaken further tests of Martin's conclusions through an analysis of eighty-nine parishes in three non-industrial hundreds of northwest Norfolk, an area also characterized by relatively homogeneous soils. Her documentation included the 1831 land tax duplicates, the total acres per parish reported in the 1831 census, and the tithe apportionment surveys of c. 1840 for each selected parish. Her purpose was to compare the statistical differences arising from computations of estate size when employing each of these documentary sources. In her first test she computed the percentage of land owned in each parish by the largest owner, first by means of the tithe survey, which gives reliable acreages for each holding, and second by means of the land tax duplicate, after converting its tax entries to acres by means of parish level acreage equivalents. The same computations were made for the combined holdings of the four largest owners of each parish. The percentages resulting from the two modes of computation were not significantly different when estimating the combined holdings of the four largest owners (three percentage points difference at the mean and two at the median). Because these holdings constituted over 90 percent of the property and all of the major holdings under observation, the result is not surprising, and the test is not convincing. But the percentages for the largest single owner did diverge significantly (though the rank orders were not much disturbed), the land tax estimates being nine points lower at the mean and twelve points lower at the median than those computed from the tithe awards.[11]

Banks and others have recently constructed typologies of "open" and "close" parishes based on estimates of concentration or dispersal of landholding, as calculated from the land tax, employing acreage equivalents.[12] Banks therefore sought to confirm the reliability of this particular method of using the tax by examining the classificatory impact of the estimating differences she detected. Unfortunately she chose to do so by offering Spearman rank order correlation coefficients. Rank order tests do not directly address error in orders of magnitude. Banks did not indicate the Spearman tests were undertaken on grouped data. It must therefore be assumed they were applied to individual cases. It is thus impossible to use the Spearman coefficients to judge directly the impact of these findings on class interval analysis and upon groupings suitable to typological constructs. Since the Spearman coefficients are quite high (.89 for the largest owner and .92 for the largest four owners), they could generously be interpreted as lending some support for her conclusion that the typological method is reliable. Further doubts about her conclusion arise from deficiencies in her data, however. The tithe surveys, though reliable, are generally eight years removed from her land tax duplicates and, as she rightly notes, many substantial differences in landholding may be expected to have occurred in the interim, though perhaps not in all parishes or among all sizes of property. Her use of parish acreages as reported in the 1831 census for the computation of acreage equivalents poses further serious problems which we shall shortly examine in more detail.

When Banks turned to a direct examination of the impact of the two modes of estimating estate size on class interval analyses, the differences which emerged were more serious in their magnitudes. She grouped all proprietors within her eighty-nine parishes into six class intervals based on acres owned per parish, the largest class comprising estates of one thousand or more acres and the smallest being holdings of less than one acre. The two modes of estimation produced strikingly different hierarchies, when the figure for the combined acres of each class is expressed as a percentage of total acres. The number of proprietors per class were also strikingly different.[13] Only the largest interval, comprising owners of one thousand or more acres, produced numbers which were significantly identical. A second major source of disturbance lies in the smallest properties classed at less than one acre, which were both overestimated in their acres (due to the value of houses, Banks thinks) and severely underreported and omitted in the land tax. The land tax duplicates collectively reported 25 percent fewer proprietors than did the tithe surveys, almost all of the omitted proprietors being small. Their exclusion underscores once again the findings of chapter 3 regarding smallholders. The land tax omits them in large proportions. But even putting missing proprietors to one side, Banks' test of interval placements based on acreage conversions from the land tax strongly suggests that all but the largest of interval categories would be subject to very large and significant error. Some caution is advisable, however, due to the eight-year difference in her documentation and her use of 1831 census acreages.[14]

Martin had gone beyond aggregate statistics and had offered direct evidence for individual properties in three of his five parishes. Banks sought to meet him directly on these grounds. She directly compared the results of differing methods of estimation – by tithe and by land tax acreage equivalents – on fifty-seven proprietary holdings in eight parishes. Since she limited herself to those holdings which could be clearly linked between the land tax and the tithe surveys, she also sought to overcome objections related to the eight year interval and the incomplete inclusion of properties in the land tax. When she examined the percent of total acres held by the largest single owner in each of the eight parishes, she found that in half of those parishes the percentage estimated by the tithe exceeded that estimated by the land tax by more than 10 points (11, 16, 19, and 24 points respectively). In all eight parishes the land tax estimates were low. She suggested that acres estimated from the land tax tend to be "more accurate in parishes where the land is more equally distributed amongst its owners, and above all where there is no single dominant owner." But that generalization held in only six of her eight parishes, and her sample is far too small, even for this limited region of Norfolk, to reach any reliable conclusions of this nature.

If one examines her fifty-seven cases more closely than she attempted to do, her findings continue to be disturbing in their implications for any class interval analysis utilizing the land tax in conjunction with acreage equivalents. Compiling the two differently estimated sets of acreages into the six class intervals she proposed, only twenty-four (or 42 percent) of the fifty-seven cases are grouped into the same class interval by both the tithe and land tax methods (table 5.1). Twenty-eight cases (49 percent) shift into a higher interval when estimated by the land tax; five shift into a lower interval. More importantly, the class interval disturbance is not confined to smaller properties. Examining only those holdings reported (reliably) in the tithe survey at fifty acres or more, only eleven (58 percent) out of nineteen remain stable. Three (16 percent) shift upward, and five (26 percent) shift downward. It must be emphasized that this sample of fifty-seven property groupings has no representative qualities and satisfies no statistical requirements for reliable sampling. But neither is there any indication that the sample was drawn in a manner which would directly bias the result. From a statistical standpoint, it shares the weaknesses and deficiencies of that of Martin. Its findings are given enhanced credibility when they are placed beside Banks' fuller regional sample of eighty-nine Norfolk parishes, however. Though it is doubtful that Banks has confirmed her case that the land tax is reliable in estimating the relative concentration and dispersion of ownership between parishes – at least through the use of acreage conversions – she has, by contrast, been able to cast considerable new doubt on the ability of such procedures either to predict accurately the acreages of individual holdings reported in the duplicates or, having made the acreage conversions, to group such holdings reliably into reasonably constructed, acreage-based class intervals.

Michael Turner replied to Banks in the same volume of essays in which her findings were published, and his reply ushered in an entirely new stage in the debate. Turner defended the use of acreage equivalents, with the now usual provisos that they be constructed parish by parish in regions relatively free from industrialization and urbanization and on soils that are relatively homogeneous. But he considered the old centre of the debate, which focused on whether acreage equivalents could accurately predict the acres of individual holdings, to have been unfortunate and misleading. He agreed that the acreages of individual properties when computed from the land tax are subject to considerable error. He instead sought, like Banks, to shift the debate on errors arising from acreage equivalents to measurements of their impact on class interval frequencies. He presented evidence from 304 landowners in those twelve parishes of Buckinghamshire where enclosure awards for the entire parish can be compared against land tax duplicates for the same and adjacent years. He first tested the land-tax-derived acreages against the enclosure acres for the reliability of their placement in class intervals. He then went on to test their rank order stability.[15]

Turner noted that the estimation errors detected by Martin had largely disappeared when his data was grouped, for the simple reason that error had been produced by both over- and under-estimations, which had tended to cancel out. He found this to be "not a conclusion which would inspire confidence in the continued use of the Land Tax in this way," however. Turner was able to demonstrate a tight hierarchical conformity between his own two sets of landowning estimates, one set derived from enclosure awards and another from the land tax, and which he grouped into nine class intervals. He readily agreed that such conformity could be interpreted as resulting from counterbalancing estimation errors. He showed that such was substantially not the case, however. When he reduced his classification scheme to eight intervals,[16] 232 (76 percent) of his 304 cases did not depart from their true interval (as determined by the enclosure awards) when estimated by the land tax (table 5.1). Only 3 cases departed by more than

Table 5.1
A comparison of changes in class interval assignments due to estimation error, using the Turner and Banks samples and different interval schemes

	8 Turner intervals: Turner sample (N=304)	6 Banks intervals: Banks sample (N=57)		8 Turner intervals: Banks sample (N=57)	
		50+ acres	All acres	50+ acres	All acres
% shift upward (n)	8	16 (3)	49 (28)	16 (3)	68 (39)
% no change (n)	76	58 (11)	42 (24)	79 (15)	30 (17)
% shift downward (n)	15	26 (5)	9 (5)	5 (1)	2 (1)

Sources: Turner and Mills, *Land and Property*, chapters 2 and 3.

one interval. Of the remaining 69 cases, 45 (15 percent) dropped one interval and 24 (8 percent) rose one interval. Errors derived from the land tax, he concluded, are more likely to inflate holdings than to underestimate their size; but the error will proceed in both directions. He argued that the error is not really very serious for class interval analysis, however, because it is "predominantly" associated with very small landowners. Eighty percent of his errors occurred among properties estimated at ten acres or less, and 60 percent among those estimated at five acres or less. As noted, problems in estimating acreages among small properties has been a constant theme with every scholar who has closely investigated the reliability of the land tax. Turner reached a conclusion which in itself is quite reasonable.

> does it matter whether in absolute specific terms a landowner was estimated to own four acres but actually owned six acres, or whether he was estimated to own six acres but actually owned four acres? He is, by any stretch of analysis and imagination, no more nor less than a very small landowner. Such examples abound ... and mainly, though not exclusively, highlight the problems of the disproportionate influence of buildings in the Land Tax Assessments of these small estates.

Provided all things are reasonably equal – one would not wish to have one "small" estate under market gardening and another under corn, for example – Turner's argument is well taken. Further, he reached the important conclusion that, in addition to error being principally confined to small estates, "*gross* distortions of an individual's position on the agricultural ladder are rare" when employing acreage equivalents. He ended with the more sweeping judgment that the land tax may be used "with confidence" in constructing grouped distributions of landholding.

Turner next examined his twelve parishes to demonstrate that land tax acreage estimates can reliably establish rank order distributions for all owners within individual parishes. Thirty-eight percent of his 304 cases were placed in the correct rank order of acreage by the land tax estimate. A further 31 percent departed by one position from their correct rank. Only 21 cases (7 percent) departed by more than four positions, and only 4 of these were estimated at more than ten acres. Indeed, in ten of the twelve sample parishes, a large majority of the errors in rank order assignment occurred on estates estimated at ten acres or less. The pattern was not a perfect one, however. The instability in Little Kimble parish occurred principally among estates estimated at approximately one hundred acres, while Marsworth parish displayed marked instability throughout virtually its entire range of holdings below fifty acres. Nine of the 21 cases departing by more than four positions were located in this latter parish.

The debate over the reliability of acreage equivalents has gained considerably in focus and sophistication within the last few years, then.

But the results of that debate remain inconclusive. It is relatively simple to point out why this is so. First, none of the samplings employed by Martin or Banks or Turner were genuine statistical samples, even for the regions from which they were drawn. Nor could they have been, since they were limited to those few parishes in which land tax duplicates could be matched against either tithe or complete parish enclosure surveys. Such samplings cannot bear the weight of generalizations pertaining to all of England, or even to all of the regions or counties from which they were drawn. It is also apparent that the range of error estimation varied significantly between the three samplings. Table 5.1 summarizes the percentage distributions of upward and downward shifts in class intervals, presenting first the results of the twelve-parish Buckinghamshire sample of Turner grouped into his eight intervals, then my calculations from Banks' eight-parish Norfolk sample grouped into her six intervals, and finally my calculations of Banks' sample grouped into Turner's eight intervals. The latter two columns separately report cases of fifty or more acres and give the number of cases in parentheses. The proportion of cases subject to upward or downward shifts within a class interval scheme is clearly substantially greater in Banks' sampling. While Banks' sample is smaller than Turner's, the magnitude of the differences suggest real variations in regional characteristics affecting acreage conversions (although the unrepresentative nature of the two samplings prevents our reliably measuring the extent of those differences). Additional samplings of these types drawn by other scholars would likely reveal still further permutations and would only deepen the debate without resolving it. So long as we proceed in this direction, the debate seems destined to remain in deadlock.

A second reason why the debate has remained inconclusive concerns the use of arbitrarily constructed class intervals. Table 5.1 demonstrates that the proportion of cases which shift upward or downward in Banks' sample alter markedly when the class interval scheme is changed. Turner's scheme is far more differentiated in its categories of less than one hundred acres, making it easier for the frequently offending smaller cases to cross interval boundaries. On the other hand Banks' scheme is more differentiated for properties of more than one hundred acres. Indeed, since Turner's scheme places all properties of 300 or more acres in a single category (in contrast with Banks' top interval which begins at 1,000 acres), a substantial proportion of the major variations in large properties under Turner's scheme did not entail crossing interval boundaries. In short, the impact of acreage conversion error is to a significant degree a function of the size (and therefore the number) of intervals being employed. If the intervals are unequal in size, as they would most likely be in schemes displaying landowning patterns, then the impact of error in estimation will, substantially, be a function of where within the hierarchy the finer differentiation occurs. These observations are hardly novel and should surprise no one. But since the debate has developed employing these methods, it is worth noting that the participants are playing a game without rules (since the constructs are arbitrarily derived) and one which threatens to become commensurately endless.

Similarly, additional observations may be made regarding the inordinate proportions of error found among smallholders. This error has generally been attributed to houses, which presumably constitute a large valuational share of these small holdings and which, or so it has frequently been assumed, are rated higher than other forms of real property. Small tax values on the duplicates would thus tend to produce overestimations of acreage. These conclusions are objectionable on several grounds. First, it is not at all clear that *all* buildings were more heavily rated than lands, or that they were valued at levels which were disproportionate to the acres on which they stood. Many estate valuations and field books make it clear that houses and buildings in agricultural districts were often (though not invariably on all estates) not included in the valuations of real property for rental except on the smallest of tofts; and since the land and other taxes were supposedly based on rental values, it is not unreasonable to assume that the tax entries for *moderately* small properties in the land tax duplicates (those representing properties which were actually larger than one or two acres, for example) reflected only acreage values. Such a conclusion still permits analysts to attribute error to higher levels of valuation per acre among the generality of small properties.

But while houses may cause overestimations on the *very* smallest holdings, it is also well known that even substantial agricultural properties in the immediate neighbourhood of market towns enjoyed values which were considerably higher than those of the region. If agricultural lands were generally renting at £1 per acre in the region, those near a thriving market town would characteristically rent at £2 or £3 per acre.[17] There is every reason to assume, and much evidence to support the conclusion, that village and town *lands*, and not merely buildings, were valued at levels significantly above those of agricultural properties. If so, then it might be expected that some proportion of small holdings, being in or near towns or villages, would be highly valued for their lands and thus overestimated for their acres. And since not all small properties are located in or near towns or villages, not all small entries in the land tax duplicates will produce overestimations. The mixed locational nature of such holdings will go far in explaining (though it will not completely explain) the erratic patterns of error found by Banks and Turner, as well as their predecessors.

A further source of error among small holdings lies in the small magnitude of their tax values. While some duplicates resort to farthings in attempting fine distinctions among small properties, most assessors have almost certainly engaged in rounding their smallest tax entries. Such practices are apparent in many duplicates which record both valuational "rent" and tax, where the smallest tax value sometimes corresponds to a range of small rents. Undoubtedly rounding was encouraged by the arithmetic complexity of applying a constantly varying annual rate. Small values are peculiarly affected by rounding, since a larger proportion of the total value is lost or gained. The effects of such losses or gains would be significant for acreage conversions and would cause seemingly erratic error of noticeable magnitudes.

Perhaps more importantly, the valuational process itself was arguably more prone to error or to generalized conclusions when the properties were small and were not principally agricultural. Agricultural lands, after all, had observable outputs. Houses, inns, and shops, even if lying in conjunction with garths or garden plots, did not have outputs that were observable by the local community or easily evaluated. Variations in valuation of such properties may therefore be expected, particularly in proportional relation to the numbers of acres on which they stood. But again, when minor variations occur in the absolute level of valuation, the impact on large properties may not greatly affect statistical analysis, since the percentage change in value may itself not be great. Percentage changes in small values are relatively easy to achieve, however; and when they are achieved they are disproportionately large in their effects. In short, it should surprise no one that small values, being inherently more error prone and more sensitive to the consequences of such errors, are found to be the principal locus of error in acreage conversion exercises.

The tests that have been performed so far to estimate the reliability of acreage equivalents have not been able to establish that error is sufficiently confined to the entries of smallholders, however (table 5.1). Turner's scheme of class intervals, as has been shown, utilizes a very broad upper interval which masks a good deal of variation in estimation among the largest holdings in Banks' sample – and undoubtedly in his own. In one of his twelve parishes the disturbances in rank order were principally at the 100-acre level. Large errors can occur among such properties without disturbing rank order, especially when rank order is examined parish by parish (as Turner does) and the sample size is small. Nor can it be ascertained what proportion of parishes in Buckinghamshire or any other county is comparably disturbed at the upper levels of their distribution, since a truly representative sample cannot be drawn. But enough evidence of disturbance among large properties has emerged to cause the problem to remain open. It does not help matters to point to estimation error among small holdings as being the "principal" source of error in compiling class intervals or in assigning rank order. The reliability of estimates among larger properties poses statistical problems which are sufficiently important and hazardous in themselves to deserve special attention.

There is in fact something disquieting about acreage conversions that goes beyond the specific procedures employed by Turner and Martin and their predecessors. Assuming it is possible to reliably convert the tax entries of middling and large holdings into acres – or at least to do so in non-industrialized rural parishes with relatively homogeneous soils – then would it not logically follow that one could aggregate acreages of holdings across parish boundaries and establish (where nominal record linkage based on rank and status ascriptions permit) combined regional holdings estimates for major proprietors? Such a procedure would violate the hoary old proscription against aggregating across parish and county boundaries, and no one has thus far attempted such a procedure. But the proscription has been repeatedly violated to this extent: After admitting the lack of comparability among land tax quotas, several scholars have nevertheless converted to acres and then grouped holdings by size across parish boundaries. Indeed the most compelling attraction of acreage equivalents – more powerful than the need for comparability with statistics derived from enclosure awards and other documentation – is that they remain the only surviving hope for undertaking the detailed comparison of sized individual holdings across parish boundaries. Such comparisons have been central to traditional studies of the decline of the small landowner and the impact of enclosure. Perhaps enough has been said to show that small-holder studies are peculiarly ill-served by acreage conversions in any case. But if the reliability of acreage conversions can in general be impeached, then the vestigial remains of inter-parish sized comparisons of individual holdings is also impeached. However reluctantly, we may be forced to come to the conclusion that some of our most important literature on landholding is empirically flawed and that some questions, no matter how urgently they need to be addressed or how important a role they have played in the past, cannot be answered satisfactorily by means of inter-parish grouped analyses of the land tax.

The reliability of acreage equivalents has always been critically examined by comparing the results of such conversions against "actual" acreages for individual cases, the latter being derived variously from enclosure awards, tithe surveys, or estate valuations. These tests have been indirect, in that they have not directly and systematically tested the intrinsic quality of the data – the acres per parish and the tax quotas – which are employed in the conversion. Nor have they been regionally comprehensive, since comprehensive matchings of land tax duplicates and other appropriate documentation is never possible. A more direct and more comprehensive estimate of the reliability of the procedure can be undertaken, however. The application of acreage equivalents rests on two assumptions, which are related to the two elements employed in the conversion equation. First, their use assumes that the relationship between the land tax assessment for each property within a parish and the acreage on which it stands is a consistent ratio. If it is not, then the computed acres of each property will inconsistently depart from the actual acres, and this departure will likely be in both directions, since the acreage equivalent employed in the computation is a constant based on the mean ratio. This assumption has long been recognized by students employing equivalents, and the acknowledgement of its importance has led to the consensus that equivalents should only be employed in non-industrialized rural parishes with relatively homogeneous soils. A second assumption is implicit in those procedures which group individual properties into acreage class intervals across parish boundaries. While the first assumption requires that the ratio of tax to acres remain sufficiently constant within parish boundaries, this second assumption requires that the ratio remain equivalently constant across parish boundaries so that regional groupings of individual properties may be made. As an alternative to this second assumption, more recent scholars have urged that conversions be made on a parish-by-parish basis; but this alternative procedure in turn assumes that the error produced for each parish (due to variability in the underlying quota values and total acreage estimates) will itself remain at comparable levels throughout the region under study.

Let us begin with the second assumption, which concerns the comparison or compiling of acres across parish boundaries. What is missing in the debate is a detailed and systematic evaluation of the inherent reliability of the two elements in the conversion equation: the tax quotas and the total acreage estimates for each parish. It has long been recognized that the tax quotas, for individual parishes as well as for counties, were unequally distributed in their relationship to rental values. The inequalities were probably present from the earliest period of the tax in the late seventeenth century, but certainly scholars have expected that such inequalities would only have worsened as improvements occurred and as rents increased to varying degrees in different places throughout the eighteenth century. As will be shown in the remaining chapters of this study, where the complexities of the valuational basis of the tax will be pursued, variations in the burden of the tax occurred throughout the countryside, and even among adjacent townships, to a degree that far surpasses all previous expectations. But such variations in the valuational basis of the quotas need not adversely affect the reliability of acreage conversions if, and only if, one condition is met: The estimate of total acres for each parish must be sufficiently accurate. The parish-by-parish development of acreage equivalents, in effect, standardizes the size relationship of all properties (provided the internal ratios of tax to acres are also consistent). Much can be said to rest on the reliability of total acreage estimates, then, and it is curious that no one except Sarah Banks has so much as questioned them.

Those who have employed acreage equivalents have rarely revealed their source for total parish acres, but there is reason to believe that the acres reported in the 1831 census are those which have been most commonly used. Sarah Banks used them for her Norfolk parishes, noting, quite correctly, that there was no systematic alternative to their use. In those eight parishes where she was able to make direct comparisons with the tithe surveys, she computed acreage equivalents by means of two sets of acreage totals, those reported in the 1831 census and those actually surveyed by the tithe commissioners. She then compared the two resulting acreage estimates for each property and found, in her opinion, that the two estimates were not "markedly different." She therefore concluded that any error she detected in acreage conversions from the land tax was not due to an inherent unreliability in the 1831 census acres. Unfortunately her statistics, apart from the smallness and unrepresentative qualities of the sample from which they were derived, do not support her conclusion. In the eight parishes she examined, the census-derived estimates ranged from 70 percent to 108 percent of those derived from the tithe surveys. While the results were hardly conclusive, they could not be said to be reassuring.[18] Could we expect an even wider range of variation, and at what frequencies, if a larger and more representative sample were available?

A larger sample can be drawn by extending the number of parishes in which matches can be made against contemporary enclosure awards or tithe surveys, but the representative nature of any such sample would still be in question. Data which is fully reliable and which is more systematic in its geographical coverage is needed. The only early acreage series which is both accurately surveyed and systematic in its coverage is that produced by the Ordnance Office and found on its six-inch series of maps. These maps report in full the acreage of every parish and township in the kingdom. But they pose one severe problem for comparisons against 1831 census acres: The Ordnance surveys, apart from those in Lancashire and Yorkshire, were conducted after the mid-1850s. After that date the pace of alterations in parish and township boundaries was too accelerated and widespread to permit reliable comparisons or applications to the unreformed units. The traditional regions for land tax studies, the Midlands and East Anglia, have no reliable and systematic acreage reports to which students can turn. But in parts of the North the six-inch map series is both reliable and available, and we shall now turn to it to test the acres reported for Yorkshire townships in the 1831 census.

Table 5.2 presents a frequency distribution of 1831 census acres as a percentage of ordnance acres for every township of the North Riding of Yorkshire. The results are displayed on map 4, and the details for each of

Table 5.2

Frequency distribution, census acres as a percentage of ordnance acres, all townships, North Riding

Numbered columns: 1 = Allertonshire wapentake; 2 = Birdforth wapentake; 3 = Bulmer wapentake; 4 = Gilling East wapentake; 5 = Gilling West wapentake; 6 = Hallikeld wapentake; 7 = Hang East wapentake; 8 = Hang West wapentake; 9 = Langbaurgh wapentake; 10 = Pickering Lythe wapentake; 11 = Ryedale wapentake; 12 = Whitby Strand wapentake

%	1	2	3	4	5	6	7	8	9	10	11	12	All cases N	All cases %	Summary Range	Summary % of cases[a]
< 50				1	1		2	1		1	1	1	8	1.7		
50–54							1				2		3	0.6		
55–59				1		1	2				1		5	1.1		
60–64	1	1		1	1	1		1	2		1	1	10	2.1	< 80	20.9
65–69		4	2	1	2	2	1	1	3	4	2		22	4.7		
70–74	2	3		1	1	1	1	1	5		1		16	3.4		
75–79	3	3	2	4	1	2	2	6	3	2	5	1	34	7.2		
80–84	2	3	5	4	1	2	2	2	9	1	5	2	38	8.1	80–89	19.9
85–89	3	3	10	2	4	4	3	2	14	4	4	2	55	11.7		
90–94	4	8	11	5	8	7	4	6	4	9	4		70	14.9	90–94	15.0
95–99	2	4	7	2	7	2	1	2	18	4	3		52	11.1		
100	1	1	3			1	1	1	1	1	1	1	12	2.6	95–105	21.4
101–105	1	2	7	3	5	1	2	5	3	2	4	1	36	7.7		
106–110	2	1	7		4		1		3	1	1		20	4.3	106–110	4.3
111–115	3	1	1		1		3	2	2	1	2		16	3.4		
116–120	1	2			2			2	2		2		11	2.4	111–120	5.8
121–125		1	1	1		1		3	2	1	2	1	13	2.8		
126–130	4	1	1		1	1					1		9	1.9		
131–135		1	2	1	1	1		1	2			1	10	2.1		
136–140	1	2			1				2	2	1		9	1.9		

Table 5.2 continued

%	1	2	3	4	5	6	7	8	9	10	11	12	All cases N	All cases %	Summary Range	Summary % of cases[a]
141–145		1											1	0.2		
146–150										1	1		2	0.4		
151–200	1	1		1			1	2	2	1			9	1.9		
201–250									1		1	1	3	0.6		
251–300		1					1						2	0.4		
301–350											1		1	0.2		
351–400																
> 400					1								1	0.2	> 120	12.8
NR									1				1	0.2		
N	31	44	59	28	42	27	28	38	79	35	46	12	469	100.0		
Mean	98	99	94	88	96	90	93	99	97	95	92	102	96			
Minimum	64	62	65	34	41	56	31	35	60	48	41	46	31			
Maximum	155	292	133	155	489	135	260	188	220	161	338	214	489			

Note: [a]The no return (NR) case is excluded from the denominator.
Source: Appendix C.

the 469 townships are given in appendix C. It is readily apparent that the census acres are not generally reliable for statistical purposes, either within the riding as a whole or within the various regions of the riding. No one can expect perfection in historical statistics, and an error of plus or minus 5 percent would be quite acceptable. But only just over one-fifth of the cases fall within this range. Only just over 40 percent fall within an error range of plus or minus 10 percent, and fully a third of the cases vary from their true acreage by more than plus or minus 20 percent. Indeed the full range of possible error within the riding is extraordinary, the census acres falling as low as 31 percent below and rising as high as 489 percent above true acreage.[19] In no wapentake is the range of variation small. Nor is the problem marked by differences in topography or farming regions. The variation is not explicable by some visible tendency to count only arable or non-waste. Though townships are more frequently underestimated, over-estimations are commonplace under all topographical conditions, even when waste is abundantly present. Analysis at the parish level (map 5) makes it quite clear that acres in the Dales as a whole, where upland waste abounded, were being fully accounted for, though often misassigned at the township level. Neither is the variation wholly explicable by misreadings of township boundaries among those making the estimates. Although the total acreage reported in the census for each wapentake (with some exceptions) approaches the total real acreage, the frequent patterns of underreporting among groups of contiguous townships suggests that the variation is often due to genuine ignorance and to faulty modes of estimation rather than to differing information regarding boundaries.

The Census Office and its local informants were quite simply unable to construct reliable acreages, as they themselves acknowledged. If one ponders the method by which the Census Office compiled acreages, it becomes fully apparent that the error displayed by table 5.2 is, to a large degree, genuinely erratic in nature and is likely to occur in the returns of every county in the kingdom.

> the present Abstract attempts to give the AREA of every Parish in England; for which purpose those County Maps which profess to mark the limits of each Parish were sedulously corrected wherever error or defect was discoverable; not less than 3,000 Letters of local enquiry (inclosing explanatory Tracings) having been despatched for this purpose. After correction thus obtained the Area of each Parish was computed by means of Glass plates marked in Squares of 40 Acres; and although reliance for any accurate purpose would be misplaced on the Result thus obtained, it may be deemed usually correct within one-tenth part, seldom erroneous beyond one-fifth part.[20]

It may be that Census Office computations were more accurate in more southerly regions of England, where parishes were generally smaller and less frequently subdivided into townships. The county maps to which reference is made – such as those of Greenwood – seldom trace boundaries below the parish level. But we shall never know with certainty whether better results were achieved elsewhere, since tests can only be conducted in the North. In the North Riding it is clear that even the cautious and rather gloomy conclusions of the Census Office were overly sanguine.

There are a number of objections which might be raised to these conclusions, however, and it is worth examining them in some detail. First, it is important to take seriously the possibility that the problems of estimation experienced among North Riding townships were due substantially to boundary confusions. One could argue that the restriction of studies to regions where such confusions tend not to occur might significantly – and sufficiently – reduce estimation error. If successful, such an argument would reinstate the usefulness of the census acres for the non-northern counties, since most such counties were overwhelmingly composed of undivided parishes. Table 5.3, derived from appendix C.2 and illustrated by map 5, tests such an argument by aggregating all North Riding acreages at the parish level. Detached townships, being separately delineated on contemporary maps, are treated separately in this series, along with the parish units. Table 5.4 summarizes these findings by reporting the percentage of cases falling within each of three ranges of error, first by estimating at the township level, and second by estimating at the level of the parish and detached unit.

Calculating at the parish level does substantially improve the performance of the census estimates. A large proportion of the most seriously incorrect estimates among the townships, those incorporating errors greater than 20 percent, have collapsed on map 5 into parishes which fall well within an acceptable range. One need only point to such parishes as Aysgarth (now 99 percent at the parish level) or Kirby Misperton (102 percent) to find illustrations of severe, township-level estimation errors arising apparently from confusions regarding township boundaries. Such confusions, and the errors to which they gave rise, largely disappeared when the unit being estimated was the parish. There can be little doubt that boundary systems below the level of the parish posed peculiar hazards for the Census Office and that their estimates for the northern counties must be unusually suspect. It could therefore be argued that an analysis of northern townships exaggerates estimation error to be found among parishes and that findings for the North Riding, when conducted at the township level, do not constitute an adequate test for the reliability of census acres in more southern regions of the country.

Table 5.3
Frequency distribution, census acres as a percentage of ordnance acres, all parishes, North Riding

Numbered columns: 1 = Allertonshire wapentake; 2 = Birdforth wapentake; 3 = Bulmer wapentake; 4 = Gilling East wapentake; 5 = Gilling West wapentake; 6 = Hallikeld wapentake; 7 = Hang East wapentake; 8 = Hang West wapentake; 9 = Langbaurgh wapentake; 10 = Pickering Lythe wapentake; 11 = Ryedale wapentake; 12 = Whitby Strand wapentake

%	1	2	3	4	5	6	7	8	9	10	11	12	All cases N	All cases %	Summary Range	Summary % of cases[a]
< 50																
50–54					1								1	0.5		
55–59																
60–64	1								1				2	1.0		
65–69		1	2							1			4	2.0		
70–74		1		1		1			1				4	2.0		
75–79		1	1	1	1				2	1	2		9	4.4	< 80	9.8
80–84		3	1	2	1		1	1	3		3	1	16	7.8		
85–89	2	3	6	2		1	1	2	5	2		1	25	12.2	80–89	20.1
90–94	3	2	10	4	6	3	4		7	6	2		47	23.0	90–94	23.0
95–99	2	2	1	2	5	3	2	3	8	3	4		35	17.2		
100			1		1				1				3	1.5		
101–105	4	1	4		1				2	3	4		19	9.3	95–105	27.9
106–110	1		4		2			2	3	1	1	1	15	7.4	106–110	7.4
111–115		2	2					1		1			6	2.9	111–120	4.9
116–120	1	1			1			1					4	2.0	> 120	6.9
121–125		1							1				2	1.0		
126–130	1	1				1					1		4	2.0		
131–135		1	1				1	1				1	5	2.4		
136–140											1		1	0.5		

Table 5.3 continued

													All cases		Summary	
%	1	2	3	4	5	6	7	8	9	10	11	12	N	%	Range	% of cases[a]
141–145																
146–150																
151–200									1				1	0.5		
201–250											1		1	0.5		
251–300																
301–350																
351–400																
> 400																
NR																
N	15	20	33	12	19	9	9	11	35	18	19	4	204	100.0		
Mean	99	97	94	88	95	93	94	100	97	95	92	102	96			
Minimum	64	67	65	70	54	71	81	84	61	69	75	83	54			
Maximum	126	132	133	99	116	128	134	133	197	115	224	132	224			

Source: Appendix C.

Table 5.4
A comparison of the range of error when calculating acreage at the township and parish levels

Range of error	% of cases within range Areal unit: township	 Areal unit: parish
± 5%	21.4	27.9
±10%	40.6	58.3
±20%	66.2	83.3

Source: Tables 5.2 and 5.3.

Before examining such an argument more closely, it should be noted that the result at the parish level is not in itself a reassuring one, even in the North Riding. While estimation error is significantly reduced at the parish level, it is not sufficiently reduced to restore our confidence in census acres among southern counties, assuming the error among southern parishes would be comparable. It must be remembered that error in estimating total parish acreages compounds errors that are already present within each parish. We have noted earlier that an inconstant ratio of tax to actual acres must be expected internally within most parishes, and it is precisely to reduce such inequalities, or their more severe instances, that historians have generally tried to avoid parishes with urban and industrial characteristics or which lie on soils of highly varying quality. But try as we may, some proportion of the properties of most parishes will depart in their actual ratios from the parish mean established by the acreage equivalent; and, as noted, the departures may be expected to occur in both directions. Additional error occurring in the acreage equivalent itself, while affecting absolute values, will not disturb the proportional distribution of acres within the parish, since the equivalent is applied as a constant. But errors in the estimations of total parish acres, and thereby in calculations of equivalents, may seriously affect inter-parish groupings and rankings, since the calculation of acreage conversions across parish boundaries is not itself based on a single constant but is the product of multiple applications of individually calculated equivalents. The individual parish acreage equivalents will thus introduce additional error into regional analyses, compounding those already present internally within each parish. Since the rates of additional error will be differentially distributed within the region, and will proceed in both directions, the direction and magnitude of the error cannot be estimated. Error in estimating the total acres for each parish or township is of more consequence than may at first appear, then. A range of plus or minus 10 percent is, or can be, serious in itself; but it becomes even more serious when it differentially compounds further error underlying it.

Bearing these considerations in mind, one can say with some assurance that the record of error established by the Census Office in estimating acres in the North Riding, even at the parish level, is a poor one for statistical purposes. Almost one out of five of the North Riding parishes was incorrectly estimated by the Census Office by more than 20 percent (tables 5.3 and 5.4). Two out of five parishes were incorrectly estimated by more than 10 percent. Such margins of error in themselves introduce substantial incomparabilities for analyses that attempt to group entries or establish rank orders across parish boundaries. When such error compounds additional intra-parish error, the adequacy of the data series for statistical analysis must be questioned. Moreover, the offending parishes, like the offending townships, display no predictable patterns in their areal distribution (map 5). Poorly estimated parishes are found under all topographical and agrarian conditions. It is thus impossible to minimize error by selecting cases from regions with restricted characteristics. The traditional restrictions to rural non-industrial parishes lying on relatively homogeneous soils will not suffice. A regional examination of the distribution of error in fact serves to raise doubts about the extent to which parishes were more reliable areal units for Census Office estimates. Individual regional patterns of error can to some extent be detected within the North Riding, but inter-regional comparisons are topographically inconsistent. The Dales were relatively well estimated at the parish level, for example, but the North Yorkshire Moors tend to remain, even at the parish level, a hodgepodge of incorrect estimation. The differences between these two upland moorland areas cannot be explained by relative differences in boundary confusion. The parishes on the North Yorkshire Moors which were most poorly estimated by the Census Office tend to be defined by wapentake boundaries, especially along the boundary of probable error, and wapentake boundaries would be unusually clearly delineated on contemporary maps. Upland parishes in the Dales, which were also large and sprawling, often enjoyed the advantage of riding and county boundaries but were seldom assisted internally by wapentake demarcations. If boundary confusions arising from a misreading of maps sufficiently explained estimation error, then the Moors should have been more accurately estimated than the Dales. This was not the case. It is understandable how the Census Office could have gone terribly wrong regarding township boundaries, since the contemporary maps which they employed most often failed to delineate them. But such maps did generally incorporate parish boundaries. The Census Office's failure to achieve reasonable estimates in large and well defined parishes on the Moors undermines confidence in its efforts among the more southerly parishes of the country. Error was no doubt substantially reduced when parishes, rather than townships, constituted the unit to be measured, but the evidence suggests that the parish posed its own sufficient obstacles to accurate estimation, obstacles which were seemingly inherent in the methods employed.

The Yorkshire findings presented in table 5.4 poorly support the general conclusion of the Census Office itself, that its estimations of total acreages, even when they are undertaken at the parish level, "may be deemed usually correct within one-tenth part, seldom erroneous beyond one-fifth part ... " But, may one conclude that a less extended range of error is likely to be found in the more southerly counties, where parishes were more universally the smallest reporting unit? Or that the wider ranges of error found among the townships of the North Riding genuinely exaggerate the unreliability of southern census estimates? To some degree an examination of townships does undoubtedly exaggerate the problem due to boundary confusions which are peculiar to such units. One may surmise that it was precisely such boundaries which provoked a considerable proportion of the three thousand letters of local enquiry sent out by the Census Office. The information it received was obviously less than satisfactory in many instances. But before leaping to the conclusion that error margins among the *parishes* of the North Riding sufficiently reflect error margins among parishes in other parts of the country, it would be well to examine these cases by size category. The extensive uplands of Yorkshire afford an unusually high proportion of immensely large and intermediate-sized parishes. Such parishes are quite uncharacteristic of the lowland zone, where acreages seldom exceeded 5,000 per parish and perhaps more normally fell within a range of 1,000 to 3,000. If it can be shown that estimation error among the parishes of the North Riding is unevenly distributed by size category, such findings would be significant for census acres in other parts of the country.

Table 5.5 presents the townships and parishes of the North Riding separately and by size category and reports the number and percent of each category falling within each of four error ranges. The patterns are striking. The most serious estimation errors, those exceeding 20 percent, are well above the mean in their incidence among parishes with less than 4,000 acres. Errors falling between 10 and 20 percent, when examined separately, are less clearly distributed; but a combination of all errors exceeding 10 percent shows parishes of 1,000–1,999 acres (53 percent) and 2,000–2,999 acres (54 percent) producing by far the highest incidences of serious estimation error, performing well above the mean of 41 percent. Conversely, those parishes containing less than 3,000 acres produce proportionately few cases whose error margins fall within plus or minus 5 percent. Patterns of error distribution among townships are similar, but less striking. These results suggest that estimations of total acres by the Census Office in the

Table 5.5

A comparison of total acreage estimation error in parishes and townships by size category, North Riding

Ordnance acres	No. of cases		± 5%				± 10%				± 20%				>± 20%				>± 10%	
	Parish	Township	Parish		Township		Parish		Township		Parish		Township		Parish		Township		Parish	Township
			N	%	N	%	N	%	N	%	N	%	N	%	N	%	N	%	%	%
< 1,000	7	67	2	28	13	19	2	28	10	15	1	14	14	21	2	28	30	45	43	66
1,000–1,999	32	163	7	22	30	18	9	28	29	18	6	19	44	27	10	31	60	37	50	64
2,000–2,999	41	106	9	22	22	21	10	24	23	22	14	34	29	27	8	20	32	30	54	58
3,000–3,999	30	53	11	37	16	30	7	23	12	23	5	17	13	24	7	23	12	23	40	47
4,000–4,999	15	25	6	40	8	32	4	27	3	12	4	27	6	24	1	7	8	32	33	56
5,000–5,999	14	11	3	21	2	18	5	36	4	36	6	43	3	27			2	18	43	45
6,000–6,999	8	15	2	25	4	27	2	25	4	27	3	38	1	7	1	12	6	40	50	47
7,000–7,999	10	6	3	30			4	40	1	17	3	30	4	67			1	17	30	83
8,000–8,999	8	5	5	62	1	20	1	12	1	20	1	12	1	20	1	12	2	40	25	60
9,000–9,999	5	4	1	20			1	20			2	40	2	50	1	20	2	50	60	100
≥ 10,000	34	13	8	24	4	31	17	50	3	23	6	18	3	23	3	9	3	23	26	46
Total	204	468	57	28	100	21	62	30	90	19	51	25	120	26	34	17	158	34	42	59

Note: The table is not cumulative. Size category is determined by ordnance acres.
Source: Appendix C.

more southerly counties, where parishes were characteristically small, should produce error ranges which fall somewhere between those estimated separately for parishes and townships in the North Riding. The general conclusion of the Census Office, that more than half the error falls within plus or minus 10 percent and seldom exceeds 20 percent, is probably an underestimate for regions in the lowland zone.

It seems impossible to escape the conclusion that, except in those northern counties where the six-inch Ordnance Survey was conducted prior to the mid-1850s, there presently exists no reasonably reliable series of acreage totals for the unreformed parishes – although it may be possible to reconstruct such a series by exceedingly laborious means.[21] If a user of acreage equivalents wishes to maintain that the range and frequency of error in his particular county or region is less than that depicted in tables 5.2 or 5.4, then surely the burden of proof must rest on him. He must demonstrate that claim. No systematic or statistically representative means will be available to him if his study lies outside the northern counties. Without reliable acreage totals, tax entries cannot reliably be converted and standardized; and if standardization to acres cannot be achieved, then inter-parish tablulations of large and small properties will be subject to the vicissitudes of the quotas. To varying degrees, acres and untreated tax entries both lead to unacceptable error when they are aggregated across parish and township boundaries. Acreage equivalents solve no problems; they merely raise new ones.

There is some danger that a few eyes might light up at these remarks and that there will be a rush of students to the northern counties where more reliable acreages are available. Any such impetus to northern studies may perhaps be slowed if we turn our attention to acreage problems that are internal to individual parishes.[22] There is now general agreement that, if acreage equivalents are to be employed, they should be calculated only for those parishes that are non-industrial and little urbanized, and which lie on soils that are relatively homogeneous. The reason for this caution lies in the first assumption noted above, that internal ratios of tax to acres must be consistent, and is related to the belief that industrial and urban buildings, being unusually valuable, cause differing ratios to occur between tax entries and the acres on which such buildings lie. But the caution also stems from the recognition that some acreages as such are more valuable than others. Assuming that land tax entries are somehow consistently related to property valuations, as they were supposed to have been according to statute, then one must also assume that a consistent relation of tax entry to acres will only be maintained if the values per acre of land remain fairly constant within the parish. Gross variations in the value of land will cause gross variations in estimations of acres when the acreage equivalent (which is no more than a derived mean) is applied to individual entries. It is therefore important to consider whether – in the real world of the English countryside – one can normally expect to find parishes in which the rental values of the soils are reasonably unvarying in their range, even when the parishes under examination appear from drift maps to contain soils that are relatively homogeneous and lack striking topographical variation.

The estates of the Earl of Ailesbury detailed in appendix A are agricultural properties lying on soils that, from the maps, appear to be relatively homogeneous. These are mixed husbandry farms which lie contiguous to one another among fertile vale lowlands at the foot of the western North Yorkshire Dales. The final columns of the appendix give the range of shillings-per-acre values reported in the field book for each field of each farm. A separate range is reported for each type of land use – arable, meadow, pasture, and fallow – and the mean shillings per acre for each farm has been calculated. The range of mean variation per farm is considerable, extending from 14s. to 33s. per acre. The highest mean values are found on the smaller holdings, not because houses and buildings are highly valued and make up a larger proportion of the holding (buildings are not separately valued for rental purposes on this estate), but rather because small holdings are disproportionately made up of meadow and pasture, which are valued much more dearly as a group than are arable fields. The range of variation in value is even more striking when one examines the internal distributions of these highly consolidated and compact lowland farms. The value of the best fields of a single farm – under the same land use – commonly varied from the value of the poorest field by 25 to 100 percent or more. In reality there was nothing approximating homogeneity among the soils of this relatively homogeneous group of townships.

The differences to be found even within the boundaries of a single field have been vividly recounted by modern geographers. S.E.J. Best related his experiences in the field while studying the relatively homogeneous regions of the East Riding during the 1920s.

> a preliminary six weeks, spent in personal study in the field, was quite sufficient to indicate the magnitude of the task of preparing a soil map of the East Riding. It is possible to pass over different types of soil on one farm, even in one field. An instance was taken from a field on a farm near Halsham in Holderness. Here, within a distance of 50 yards, specimens taken showed a thick unctuous clay, a clay not so thick, and then a much lighter sand and gravel. The field was divided into three parts for the purposes of cultivation. The heavy clay was laid down to permanent grass (3 acres), the lighter clay and gravel to clover (12½ acres), and in the top corner of the field, about 20 feet higher than the permanent grass, were 1½ acres of potatoes. This is far from being an isolated example, for many similar fields and farms could be noted.[23]

The homogeneity of parishes is an illusion fostered by generalized drift maps and by the broad observations of contemporary agricultural writers like Young and Marshall. But most users of acreage equivalents are aware that variations in land values are present, even in relatively homogeneous parishes. The point to be disputed concerns the degree of variation. The evidence on the Ailesbury estates – and comparable findings can easily be produced from other localities – suggests that the magnitude of the variation is likely, in a sizeable proportion of the cases, to be large and statistically significant. Since field books are not generally available, the extent of the error cannot normally be estimated. The application of acreage equivalents under these conditions seems a dubious exercise at best.

There is a further reason why acreage equivalents should no longer be employed, and it is perhaps the best reason of all. Acres are an appalling measure of "largeness" or "smallness" among agricultural holdings. It is simply quite wrong to treat a 10-acre farm under corn as though it were either socially or economically equivalent to ten acres of prime meadow or pasture, or to treat ten acres given to dairying as though it were the equal in "size" to ten acres employed in breeding and rearing. It is only necessary to add market gardening to the list of our 10-acre holdings in order to grasp the enormous differences encompassed by a single measure based on acres. The same observation can be made for large holdings. Are two landowners equally "large," equally dominant, or equally wealthy when one owns 1,000 acres of moorland waste and the other holds his 1,000 acres entirely in rich mixed-husbandry lowlands? Surely considerations of "size" ought to be related to potentials for output and income, to implications of financial independence, capital formation and status. When studying the decline of the smallholder, are historians not interested in persons whose economic and character traits are those associated with the yeomanry of old England? Questions of economic and political independence, of productivity and economies of scale, form the impetus of many of these studies, and properly so. Such questions bear no consistent relationship to the number of acres held. They do bear a more consistent relationship to the rental value of such holdings, however. From every possible perspective the assessed value of holdings is a more satisfactory surrogate for measuring "size" than is acres. The land tax entries are supposedly based on rental values. If their reliability as measures of rental value can be established, then we have the measures we require. It is perhaps not too much to suggest in fact that if the land tax had only reported acres rather than representations of rental values, then we ought all to have been applying our ingenuity to devising conversion formulas for transforming those relatively useless acres into a series of values which are analytically more appropriate to the questions we seek to address.

PART THREE

The Valuational Basis of the Land Tax within Townships

The valuational basis of the land tax has never been systematically examined. It is curious that those working with the tax must be reminded that the tax was by statute based on rack rents. If the tax entries have any meaning, it is presumably in relation to rents, not acres. But much of the debate on the meaning of the tax has focused on the problems of acreage conversion. Inequalities in the regional burdens of the tax and in the relationships between land tax quotas and changing property values have been noted, but the full extent and causes of those inequalities or their precise nature have never been fully explored. The remainder of this volume will undertake such an exploration. Part 3 will begin with an explication of the mechanisms and terminology of rating. Chapters 7–10 will then examine the process of valuation and the interpretation of tax entries within single townships. Part 4 will develop a method for estimating the real land tax burden borne by each township and will then apply that method in establishing the regional distributions of that burden among all the townships of the East, North and West Ridings of Yorkshire and of fourteen additional English counties. The real national distribution of the burden of the tax by the end of the Napoleonic wars will emerge with some clarity. That disparities in both the local and national distribution of the tax burden existed should suprise no one who is familiar with land tax studies. But the extent of those disparities and their impact on the interpretation of land tax entries may be found to be more severe than anyone might reasonably have expected.

CHAPTER SIX

The Mechanisms and Terminology of Rating

The land tax, along with the local rates which it resembled, employed a number of mechanisms that enabled assessors to adjust the burden of the tax. The first, and one which the land tax shared with the county and some earlier national rates, was the assignment of local quotas. County quotas for the land tax had been assigned by statute in 1698, on the basis of valuations employed and purportedly current for the year 1693, and these county quotas remained unchanged through the eighteenth, nineteenth and early twentieth centuries.[1] Quotas were further assigned below the county level – to each hundred division and to each township – by the land tax commissioners for the county. These local quotas also became quickly ossified and remained unchanged after the early years of the eighteenth century. Thus the amount of land tax due to the government from each local unit of administration remained unchanged throughout a long period of the most fundamental alterations in agricultural land values, industrialization, and urbanization.

By placing a cap on the total amounts of tax each township was to contribute, the system of quotas unavoidably caused the land tax to become increasingly divorced from the proportionate distribution of real land values, not only between counties but also between regions within counties and even among adjacent townships. Any distortions which might have existed in the original distribution of the quotas could only have increased as the eighteenth century progressed. The inter-regional distribution of the tax could not reflect agricultural improvements or changes in land use, because no adjustments could be made to the quotas. But within the townships themselves two mechanisms were available to the land tax assessors, as they were to the assessors of local rates, enabling assessors continuously to adjust the incidence of the tax within the township in an equitable manner, if they wished to do so. First, the annual statutes required that the land tax be assessed on a valuation based on gross rack rent. Such valuations, however they might in fact be based (which was certainly not invariably on rack rent), unavoidably formed a part of the taxation process of each township and were in principle subject to revisions that could redistribute the land tax burden within the township. A second mechanism, the local poundage rate, further enabled the valuation totals for each township to slide upward or downward.[2] Without downward poundage rate adjustments, for example, any increase in the total valuation of a township would have increased the total amount of tax collected. While increases or decreases in receipts might be acceptable, or even desired, for some local rates, the land tax quotas required that total receipts for each township remain static. Inversely sliding scales for valuations and poundage rates thus met the collection limitations imposed by the land tax quota system.[3]

It is clear, then, that no structural features were embedded in the system for assessing the land tax or other quota-based rates which *required* that inequalities be tolerated in the distribution of the burden of the tax *within* individual townships. If research indicates that such inequalities were in fact permitted to develop through a failure to revise valuations or to adopt a suitable array of mechanisms, then we may only conclude that such a failure was volitional at the township or division level. By contrast, inequalities *between* townships were destined to grow unavoidably, since an unaltered system of quotas was allowed to persist.

There are any number of reasons why pressures for internal revaluation should have grown within townships during the eighteenth century, forcing the assessors to utilize the mechanisms available to them. Inequalities could result when one landlord improved his property while others failed to do so. Natural disasters or neglect might cause some properties to decline. In some townships entirely new taxation units might be created, such as new tofts or houses, or even new agricultural properties through the enclosure of commons and wastes; such new properties should, under a system of quotas, have lightened the burden of tax on each of the older properties within the township, but could only do so if a general revaluation were to take place. Similarly any diminution in taxation units, such as would occur if cottages were torn down, would require a general revaluation in order to reallocate to the remaining old properties whatever proportion of the tax was required in order to continue to meet the quota. Other taxation units might in time have become difficult to identify under the terms of a very old valuation, as bundles of property became split up or aggregated in kaleidoscopic fashion in an active land market. Any perusal of land tax duplicates will quickly assure one that such complex patterns of engrossing and splitting did commonly occur over time and throughout the countryside. Only a limited or general revaluation could correct such problems.[4]

The creation or diminution of tax units, and the impact of improvements or deterioration of properties, might create pressure for internal revaluation and for the adjustment of individual assessments, but these changes need not impel an alteration in the combined total value of township "rent." The inequalities resulting from shifts in tax units and land values could all be adjusted within the framework of a constant total value for the township. After all, the quota system required a constant amount of tax revenue; assessors could therefore ensure equitability in the tax burden if they merely ensured that the proportionate share of each contribution to the quota bore a constant relation to rack rent or some other appropriate standard of value. Revaluations might thus occur, but individual "rents" would be recorded for tax purposes at levels substantially, and in most instances increasingly, below their rack rent values. Under such circumstances equitability would be maintained while the total valuational rent as well as the local poundage rate would remain unchanged.

The evidence presented below will demonstrate that many townships, while readjusting individual assessments, did not alter their total valuational rentals for long periods of years. Other townships did allow their total rents to increase or diminish, however; and it is worth enquiring why in general such alterations in total rentals might have been found desirable. The most obvious answer seems to be that a large proportion of townships throughout the country – although how such practice was regionally distributed is not at all clear – were in the habit of utilizing a single valuation for both the land tax and for some or all of the local parish and county rates. John Beckett has taught us how the "purvey" was utilized in this fashion in Cumberland and, in all probability, the Book of Rates was similarly employed in Westmorland.[5] Other counties also employed ancient, ossified valuations – at least for some tax purposes.[6] But not all systems of common valuation were so centralized at the county level, nor so ancient in their basis. For most townships the utilization of a single, multi-purpose valuation simply constituted an *ad hoc* and eminently practical way to deal with a vexatious and expensive problem. Why undertake several valuations when one will suffice for all purposes? Wherever single valuations were thus utilized, local rates not subject to quota restrictions would tend to push valuational totals upward, or downward, reflecting pressures on those local rates for expenditure. An alteration in valuational totals was not an inevitable consequence of such pressures, however. Local rates could generate larger receipts merely by levying multiple rates per year, as the purvey did in Cumberland and as was widespread throughout the kingdom. Still other townships could simply increase the poundage rate for local assessments. But not every township took these routes, and some others did but not completely. The evidence will show that rises in valuational totals were widespread.[7] Wherever such rises did occur, the quota system would require that the local land tax poundage rate for those townships be lowered proportionately.

There is, as can be seen, a certain logic to be found in the mechanisms that governed the levying of assessments for the land tax and the local rates, however imperfectly or incompletely that logic may have been outlined here. So long as one remains at a very high level of generalization, this logic probably fairly describes the processes of local administration that governed the assessment of rates within townships in England and Wales in the eighteenth and early nineteenth centuries. But, even within the framework of the description given here, the possibilities for variation in practice were enormous. No seasoned student of social or economic history will be surprised to learn that procedures in the countryside were in fact almost infinitely varied and that they did not conform to any simply described system. A letter written by Lord Fitzwilliam in December 1798 to French Laurence, a Member of Parliament who acted as his spokesman in the Commons, is most illuminating about the permutations to be found in the West Riding of Yorkshire.

Having this evening seen Baldwin,[8] I fear from his report of the amended Redemption Landtax bill, which I believe is still in the H of Commons, that cases in which I feel an Individual Interest, but which will affect vast numbers as well as myself, are not likely to be corrected. The first is one, which if left uncorrected, is a crying injustice. The scale of the Landtax being that, upon which other local rates have been levied, it occurs most frequently, that a Landtax rate levies a sum considerably beyond the sum payable to Government as the Landtax of the district. This has arisen from various causes, but principally from new property arising within the district; as for instance, a House is built. The House immediately becomes liable to bear its proportion in the Landtax of the district. The Assessors rate it, regulating the sum, we suppose, by the known Standard of some antient house of equal size. To keep the levy down to the precise demand of Government upon the district, every article of taxed property within the district ought to be relieved in its just proportion on such an occasion: but this has not been the practice, for other district rates being to be raised upon the scale of the Landtax rate, & generally by the very same persons though in other characters, to save the trouble of apportioning the reduction, the levy upon the new subject of taxation, has become an increase to the general levy. Government however never profited by the circumstance: They had no right to do so: their claim was for a definite sum: This sum, & *no more*, they received, & the excess was carried to the relief of the other occasional rates. Here then arises a serious grievance in this business. A whole district pays 100£ & no more: but from circumstances, the nominal levy for the Landtax now amounts to 150£ – Consequently A whose just proportion is 1/100th part only of the whole has been rated 30 shillings – The Act of last year directed the sale to be made to the Individual, *according to his last years* rate:

When A therefore proposes to buy of the Commissioners, They tell him he must pay for *30* sh: finding him rated at that sum, when they inspect the detail of the rate – This case occurring almost universally in parts of the West Riding, this was one, amongst other causes, for the Comrs suspending their proceedings; intending to make, & I believe actually making representations to Government, in order that by the new Act, They might be enabled to order a general proportionate reduction, where the case had arisen – but I collect from Baldwin, that no powers are given in the new Act: it remains as it was – Without the alteration redemption is out of the question wherever this has happened.[9]

The comments of Fitzwilliam, who is no mean authority, should not be taken to represent assessment procedures in every township of the West Riding, although they may apply to most. Aspects of his description certainly do not apply to the North Riding. For example, the total tax recorded at the foot of the land tax duplicates of the North Riding commonly does not equal the sum of the individual assessments, but such a sum only rarely departs from the township quota by more than one pound and only occasionally by as much as five. While evidence will be presented below that many North Riding townships employed a common valuation for the land tax and the local rates, the land tax does not seem to have produced significant levels of excess revenue for local purposes – although the poor rates themselves may have produced excess revenues to be applied for other local purposes, a practice which seems to have been far more common throughout the kingdom. If significant land tax surpluses were not being produced in the North Riding, and if new tax units such as houses or enclosed waste were being created, then either revaluation was not occurring, and the new units were not being absorbed into the land tax rolls, or such units were being absorbed through revaluation within the terms of the quota. Under these latter conditions it might be expected that local poundage rates would diminish in order to maintain quota levels; whereas the practices described by Lord Fitzwilliam in the West Riding, by in effect lifting the restrictions on total tax imposed by the quotas, would tend to stabilize the apparent[10] poundage rates (depending upon the degree of alteration in valuational rents) which would otherwise experience severe upward pressures in a region so heavily characterized by housing construction.

The complexity which is inherent in the mechanisms of rate assessment is further enhanced by the extraordinary latitude of meaning which could be assigned, both by modern scholars and by contemporaries, to one of the key terms employed in valuation: rent. After 1825, and in some townships from an even earlier date, the land tax duplicates commonly reported "rent" as well as the tax for each property bundle. Such reportings of *valuational* rent beg for analysis, since they may reveal much about the nature and process of land tax valuations – and chapters 12 and 13 will undertake such an analysis. But how are scholars to understand the meaning of these "rents"? What do they represent?

We can quickly conclude that they almost certainly do not represent the full potential rental value of the property. William Marshall warned prospective buyers of land that its full rental value would be exceedingly difficult to determine.

> the *real* rental value ... cannot easily be obtained. Speaking generally of the lands of England, it is what very few men are able to set down. It is true, that, in every district, almost every township, there are men who tolerably well know the rate at which the lands of their respective neighbourhoods are usually let. But interchange them, reciprocally, into each others districts, and their errors would be egregious ... Nor can a mere provincialist ... be aware of the value, even of his own farm, under the best course of management of which it may be capable: nor can he see, through the double veil of ignorance and prejudice, the more permanent improvements that may be made upon it, so evidently as one who has a more general knowledge of rural subjects, and is in the habit of detecting and prosecuting such improvements. ... These facts being evident, it follows that, before an offer be made, especially for a large purchase, it is no more than common prudence, in a man who is not himself a judge, to call in twofold assistance: a provincial valuer, to estimate its fair market price, to the tenants of the neighbourhood in which it lies; and a man of more general knowledge, to check his valuation, and to estimate the improvements of which the lands are evidently capable.[11]

The full rental values of all land tax entries are clearly not determinable, if full value includes the potential for improvement, as recommended by Marshall. The evidence for such determinations is not generally available, and "wealth" in that sense cannot be measured by the land tax or by any other systematic documentation. Surely it is safe to assume, in any case, that the valuational rents upon which land tax assessments were based were in the nature of those made by Marshall's "provincial valuer" and that at best they reflect local conditions and perceptions in the land market. If so, then the valuations may lack objective comparability in terms of potential income, as Marshall suggests, but they may perhaps reasonably reflect expectations of actual income – provided each valuer or assessor in each township consistently applied the same meaning to the term rent. Unfortunately, such an assumption of consistency seems to be excessively hazardous.

The problem lies in the wide variety of meanings, and therefore in the wide range of values, that may be conveyed by the term rent. Ideally one would wish the rents recorded in the land tax duplicates to be based on gross improved rack rents in fee simple, which would constitute the maximal, annual gross rental of the land under optimal management and current local market conditions, when held in ordinary freehold. The land tax statutes in fact required that valuations be based on the gross rack rent. Unfortunately, as the evidence presented in subsequent chapters will make clear, eighteenth century valuations for tax purposes were very occasionally, but not normally, based on rack rent, and it is by no means certain what adjustments, if any, were made for tenure. Realizing that the reported land tax valuational rents were not generally rack rents, a student might immediately be inclined to think of them as actual rents being paid to the landlord. But if the rents reported were consistently actual ones, then further problems would arise. Actual rents may not have constituted what contemporaries called the "full and fair" rental. Some landlords were notorious in underrenting their properties, while others pressed their tenants hard. The reporting of actual rents, even if consistent between townships, may thus still reduce the comparability and therefore the value of the land tax for some types of analysis. On the other hand, even if one were certain that actual rents were consistently being reported, one may not be equally certain whether those rents were consistently net or gross. It is simply not true that in general landlords paid the land tax, for example; nor is it clear that tenants invariably received rent abatements when they were forced to pay the tax. Practice varied widely, even within townships. Similarly, the "rentals" of owner-occupiers were not determinable in the same manner as the actual rents of tenants. The valuations of owner-occupiers may have been based on the rents of other comparable lands and buildings in the township. But there is evidence for the eighteenth century which suggests that in many (but not all) townships the properties of owner-occupiers were valued on the basis of very old purchase or construction prices, without any regard to subsequent improvements.[12] Such evasions were undoubtedly relatively easy for owner-occupiers, since no objective rents were actually being paid. The practice may therefore have been widespread, and it is not detectable by reference to the land tax duplicates alone. Indeed the full rental values of small and middling owner-occupiers, who have been so peculiarly the object of historical investigation, are the most unknowable of all rentals, since they cannot even be confirmed by the usual supplementary sources such as estate records.

The "rents" recorded in the land tax duplicates, and indeed those which underlay all assessment entries, should be treated as no more than nominal rents unless rack rent or some other standard can clearly be demonstrated. And the basis for establishing nominal rents undoubtedly varied widely. Many of the rents were in fact based on ancient systems of valuation. John Beckett has demonstrated that the eighteenth century township valuation totals of Cumberland, and perhaps those of Westmorland, date to 1617, and that they were seldom revised and never wholly abandoned until the early nineteenth century. Scattered evidence from throughout England at the end of the eighteenth century indicates that the levels at which nominal rents were placed in other counties were commonly, though not invariably, at two-thirds to three-quarters of what was locally understood to be "fair" or "full" values – whatever those terms may mean – even when based on new valuations.[13] There seems to have been no general inclination to assess on full values. One may go further: There seems to have been no general pattern whatever in the ways the mechanisms for assessment were employed – not within any county, not within any region, not even among the townships of any parish. Each township employed the mechanisms in whatever manner it found convenient. Once again grim conclusions appear inevitable. But before agreeing categorically with Professor Mingay "that detailed investigation of land tax assessments is simply not worth while,"[14] it is prudent to examine in more detail the evidence of actual assessment practice as it occurred in the countryside.

CHAPTER SEVEN

The Incidence and Level of Revaluation[1]

Those who wish to use the land tax for historical analysis must recognize and accept a number of constraints arising from the way in which the tax was assessed. The constraints normally mentioned in the literature are those which are due to the quota system described in the preceding chapter. As we have seen, in 1698 the government abandoned any further attempts to levy taxation on real and personal property by a national poundage rate and instead imposed a quota on each county. These county quotas never varied thereafter. The county land tax quotas were in turn subdivided by local authority into quotas for each individual parish or township. By the end of the reign of Queen Anne, these local quotas had also become traditional and ossified, and in 1798 the Redemption Act made them permanent.[2] Thus the total amount of land tax which each township owed to meet the annual county quota – barring a change in the national statutory rate[3] – never altered during two-and-a-half centuries of land tax administration. But land values did change, and quite dramatically by the later eighteenth century. Rents did not rise equally in all parts of the country, however, nor in all regions of a single county. The rental history of each township must in fact be considered as unique and as having pursued its own peculiar pattern of development. Thus by the years 1780 to 1832, when land tax duplicates are most generally available for analysis, the proportional distribution of township quotas no longer bore any consistent relationship to the distribution of real land values. They could not do so, since the quotas had become ossified and could not respond to fluctuations in any of the factors affecting land values.

In one sense, then, the land tax never underwent revaluation, since the quotas, and thus the proportional regional distribution of the burden of the tax and its relation to current land values, were never revised. And the failure to revalue by revising quotas imposes the most widely recognized constraint upon the use of the land tax: The tax quotas of the various parishes and townships are not equivalent departures from either rack rent or actual rent – or at least they are not so by the 1780s, after nearly a century of differential movements in rent – and thus individual tax entries in the later returns are not comparable in their absolute values across townships.[4] One cannot select, for example, a series of £10 tax entries in several different townships and expect them to represent equivalent land values. To some degree each tax entry, while appearing to represent the same property value, will represent holdings of quite different values, and precisely because the valuational base of the tax will have developed uniquely within each township. The lack of comparability among entries of different townships poses hazards of great seriousness for anyone wishing to undertake comparative analyses employing individual tax entries grouped by class interval. For some other and statistically more sophisticated forms of analysis the problems are surely fatal.[5]

But while no one doubts that all or most apparently equivalent tax entries in different townships represent different real property values, there persists a long-standing debate over the likely magnitudes and seriousness of such differences. This debate, which centres on only one aspect of the problem of revaluation, I shall engage at more length in part 4. Suffice it to say here that the magnitudes of differences in valuational base between townships is, by the early nineteenth century, far greater than any of us might have expected.[6] But, in the remainder of this chapter, I wish to turn to an equally important aspect of the topic, and one which has not hitherto been systematically studied, namely, the incidence and nature of revaluation within individual townships. If it could be shown that the townships themselves were failing to undertake continuous or at least reasonably periodic revaluations, or failing to accompany such revaluations with proportionate internal redistributions of the burden of the tax, then the land tax entries would indeed be perfectly useless to historians – except as exempla of a most remarkably inequitable and oppressive system of local government. Internal revaluation and reassessment had to occur if the tax entries were to maintain any relation whatever to actual land values or – given the continual parcelling off and engrossment of fields – to any real configuration of landed holdings within the community. Internal revaluation is thus an even more critical issue in estimating the reliability of the land tax than are those issues revolving around the consequences of the quota system.

The data base for the conclusions which follow are the valuational "rents"[7] and tax entries reported in the land tax duplicates of the twenty-nine townships of the wapentake of Gilling East in the North Riding of Yorkshire. Alterations in rent and tax entries have been examined for each township at five-year intervals from 1785 to 1830. Gilling East is an almost wholly agricultural wapentake lying just to the east of the Great

North Road in the Vale of Mowbray, and no significant enclosures occurred within these townships during that period. The wapentake thus offers a relatively normal and undisturbed rural area for testing the incidence of revaluation, one isolated from the processes of urbanization, industrialization, and enclosure, where the literature has taught us to expect revaluation might sometimes occur.

Internal revaluation and reassessment for the land tax may be expected to occur in one of four ways. The first mode would be a general revaluation in which every property bundle in the township would be reassigned its rental value and tax assessment. Such revaluations might be undertaken by professional valuers, in which case the expense to the township would be considerable, or they might be completed by local assessors on the basis of local knowledge. Such general revaluations should produce a rise in the aggregate total of valuational rent assigned within the township. A second mode of revaluation would also be one in which the total amount of assigned rent would rise, but in this case the rise would be wholly attributable to a restricted number of properties within the township. No general revaluation or reassessment would have occurred, and the rise in total rent would be a reflection of more limited adjustments in the distribution of the burden of the tax quota. A third mode of revaluation would similarly involve only a restricted number of property bundles, but in this case the adjustments would be made without altering the aggregate total of rent assigned within the township. A fourth mode, in which all property bundles would be revised without increasing the total rental, I have found to be quite rare.

The evidence from Gilling East suggests that internal revaluation was usually an intermittent but an almost universal process during the later eighteenth and early nineteenth centuries. General revaluations, in which the total rent rises and all properties are at risk, is a comparatively unusual phenomenon. The second mode of revaluation, in which total rent is allowed to rise while only a few properties are affected, is more commonly found within the wapentake. Only eight of the twenty-nine townships failed to alter their valuational rent totals significantly during the half century under observation (appendix E). The total rent to total tax ratios of some of those remaining eight townships[8] approach the wapentake mean, which suggests that they too had experienced substantial revaluation during the years prior to 1785.

In ten of the townships the valuational totals increased by more than 30 percent between 1785 and 1830. In the wapentake as a whole the increase following 1801 (when the series becomes fuller) was almost 22 percent, with virtually all of that increase (20.8 percent) occurring by 1815. By the end of the Napoleonic wars, overall growth in total rental values had virtually ceased in the wapentake as a whole. The pattern of valuational change is entirely plausible in the shape of its curve, then. But the magnitudes of change are all wrong. Evidence at the national level suggests that actual rents on large estates increased during the war years by 90 to 100 percent, falling off between 1815 and 1835 by 10 to 15 percent.[9] The records of some of the larger North Riding estates similarly suggest that the magnitude of rise in valuational rents in that region during the war years was substantially below that of actual rents.[10] If valuational rents were to any degree responding to movements in actual rents, as they appear to have been, the response was not a simple one. While it may be reasonable to conclude that revaluation for tax was widespread and was, to some degree, a response to changing land market values, it would clearly be unwise to estimate the magnitude of change in either series from the other.

The evidence from Gilling East also makes it clear that measurements of change in total valuational rents will substantially underestimate the incidence of revaluation. The third mode of internal revaluation, in which the values for a limited number of property bundles are altered without adjusting the total township rental, was common to all of the townships of the wapentake, even to those which on other occasions adjusted their total rentals upward or downward (appendix F). Revaluations of this type were almost invariably in response to transactions in the land market. Most land tax duplicates record some small number of alterations in their property bundles almost annually. Tenants come and go, giving occasion to adjustments in actual rents. Fields are transferred among tenants or are purchased by other proprietors, causing the total number of property bundles to fluctuate. Entire properties are sold. Cottages are built or torn down, thus altering the number of tax units.[11]

Innumerable illustrations could be given for more limited revaluations of this third type. To take just one example, the Gilling East township of Croft reported precisely the same total amount of valuational rent in 1825 and 1826. In both years rents were individually reported against the names of forty-six tenants, and the properties were listed in precisely the same order on both duplicates. But seven of the rental entries altered their values between the two years. In four of those seven cases the name of the tenant had changed; in only one had the proprietor changed. In the entire township the names recorded for five tenant and two proprietor entries had altered between the two years. Minor revaluations of the type described in Croft were virtually incessant throughout the wapentake, but more especially in those townships where the land was held by large numbers of proprietors or tenants and the land market was commensurately more active. Not all townships reported alterations in rentals from year to year. But then neither did all townships experience alterations in landholding personnel, and those which experienced changeovers in personnel did not always undergo alterations in the physical configuration of holdings.

These limited types of revaluation – when reallocations of valuational rent occurred without alteration in the total valuational rent of the township – did not constitute general revaluations in which every property was at risk and did not in general permit the valuation of the township to reflect or react directly to secular movements in the "fair and full" rental. The level of the valuation would continue to depart from rack rent as if the reallocations had not occurred. But such reallocations were of the greatest importance in maintaining the internal proportionality of the burden of the tax and the fiscal accountability of each tenant and proprietor. There is abundant evidence in the land tax duplicates that such adjustments within townships were universally made as land transactions occurred – albeit the duplicates as such provide no assurance that adjustments were made for all such transactions. Whether such adjustments also universally and perfectly preserved internal proportionality in the burden of the tax is also perhaps another question.

It nevertheless remains that the great majority of townships in Gilling East did alter their valuational rent totals between the years 1785 and 1830, and it is important to ask why they did so. While it is very tempting to conclude that such revaluations in total rental to some degree reflected and were caused by parallel movements in current actual rentals and land values, such a conclusion does not necessarily follow. Under the quota system it is in fact irrelevant to the administration of the tax whether the total valuational level of a township rises or remains constant. If the level rises, the only administrative consequence is that the general ratio of valuational rent to tax within the township also rises (as the local poundage rate decreases), and the individual tax assessment entries will depart proportionately further from current valuational rents. Such departures, while of considerable importance for historical analysis, had no consequences for the collection of the land tax as such, and there was nothing in the administration of the land tax which should either have inhibited or encouraged the rise of valuational totals whenever revaluation occurred.[12]

A rise in land values and actual rentals may take several forms. A general rise which is equally distributed within a township need not place any upward pressure whatsoever on total land tax valuation. So long as internal proportionality is maintained in distributing the tax burden within the township, the quota system will prevent any increase in individual tax burden. The relationship between total valuational rent and total rack rent is thus irrelevant, and especially to any tax based on quotas. So long as the valuation on each individual property bears the same proportion to its rack rent, no inequalities can arise.

But a general rise in current actual rental values is not what normally occurs in the countryside. Movements in commodity prices may move arable values ahead of pasture, or vice versa. Some properties will undergo improvement while others will not. Some landlords, when coming into a property, will tend to rack their tenants when their predecessors had indulged in abatements. Actions such as these cause actual land values and estimates of "full and fair" rentals to rise differentially within townships, and it is these differential movements in values which cause inequalities in valuation and tax burden to develop. Some adjustments to these inevitable inequalities might have been made in conjunction with individual land transactions, and particularly when such transactions entailed a physical reconfiguration of holdings rather than merely a change of ownership or tenancy. But significant general revaluations at such a moment seem unlikely, since the rateability of property constituted an important element of the value being conveyed in the sale or lease. A more general revaluation, unconnected in any direct way with any specific transaction or improvement, is thus more likely to have been acceptable to an agricultural community, and indeed to any urban one.

It seems highly probable, then, that periodic general revaluations for local and national rates did to some degree comprise attempts to reconstitute proportionality in the distribution of the tax burden by more closely representing current property values. The inequalities accumulating from numerous limited revaluations could thus be accommodated. But even so, a general revaluation did not require an increase in total valuational rent, any more than did a limited revaluation, and for the same reason. The quota system merely required the maintenance of proportionality; the absolute amount of individual or total valuation and its relationship to rack rent – so long as that relationship was constant – was irrelevant to the tax burden. In short, we may conclude that all significant alterations in total valuation signal that some degree of revaluation has occurred; but it does not follow that all revaluation, regardless of its extent, required an alteration in total valuational rents. Revaluation does seem to be more clearly attributable to activity in the land market than to any other factor; and indeed it is difficult to imagine how any society could either endure or operate a tax system that failed to reflect such propertied transactions. But other factors seem also to have been at work. The movements in valuational rent do seem to have mirrored movements in real rents, in direction if not in magnitude. But while secular trends in real rent may in broad terms have been influential, a more strict interpretation should perhaps view commodity prices as a constraint on movements in valuations, which were more directly being driven both by activity in the land market and by pressures from other local rates.

Direct evidence for the relationship between land tax valuations and those of other rates is difficult to find, but there is little doubt that throughout the country a large proportion of parishes and townships employed a common valuation in assessing the land tax and such local rates as the poor rate and constable's rate. Many townships in the industrial West Riding collected the land tax and constable's rate simultaneously and listed only the aggregate of the two assessments on the land tax duplicates. In other townships there is a clear statistical correlation between the valuational totals for the land tax and the poor rate, and Eden's *State of the Poor* offers abundant evidence that these two and other taxes shared valuational bases in many parishes throughout the countryside.[13] Moreover, most townships listing rent in the land tax duplicates after 1798 reported it for redeemed as well as unredeemed properties, and the redeemed rentals were revalued as well as the unredeemed. Since the redeemed tax entries had become permanently frozen by the very act of having them redeemed, there was no administrative purpose serviceable to the land tax in either recording or in revising the rentals of redeemed entries. The widespread recording and revision of redeemed rent entries can only be explained if the process of valuation for the land tax was itself part of a larger process of valuation for one or more local rates. If this hypothesis is correct, then land tax revaluations, and in particular the propensity to raise and lower the total valuation assigned to a township, must have been to some degree impelled by pressures from other forms of taxation than the land tax itself. A rise in valuational total would not result in an increase in the total land tax raised, because of the quota system. But if it were necessary to increase the amount to be raised for the poor rate, for example, then it would indeed be useful to permit the valuational total for the township to rise. Not that the total must rise to meet the full deficiency in the rate, since the local poundage rate can also be adjusted upward. Local patterns suggest that both of these mechanisms were being interactively employed in revaluations and, I strongly suspect, quite often to solve arithmetic complexities in computing assessments.[14]

A few final observations might be made about larger pressures for revision. None of the major fiscal events of the later eighteenth and early nineteenth centuries made a significant impact on the distribution of the burden of the tax or on the process of revaluation. The incidence of revaluation increased only marginally in Gilling East during the decade following redemption.[15] The publication of township valuations for the 1815 property tax, which were almost uniformly higher than land tax valuations throughout the North Riding, caused no embarrassment among local assessors of the land tax and no flurry of revaluations – on the contrary, the incidence of revaluation slackened at that point. When in

1824 the North Riding quarter sessions required that each overseer revalue his township so that the county rate quotas might be redistributed, the overseers were vexed to find that the valuations returned were generally higher than the land tax but still lower than the valuations for the 1814 property tax; and, even worse, the new valuations departed from the property tax in a disproportionate manner. The justices, after a year's efforts, were unable to secure a genuinely equitable system of new county rate valuations, and they gave up trying. They simply imposed the proportions of the property tax. All of this effort and fuss made not the slightest impact on the incidence of land tax revaluation. Nor was revaluation in any way a peculiar feature of the war years. It is clear from prewar examples, as well as from the rent to tax ratios found throughout the riding, that revaluation, and particularly in the third mode, was an almost continuous and intractable – and unflappable – feature of the local administration of the land tax.[16]

All of this is of course very good news to those who wish to use the land tax for historical analysis. Tax entries within townships were indeed being regularly revised and, to some degree, in a manner reflective of transactions in the land market. But is this all of the news? Unfortunately not. Lack of comparability between townships will continue to impose serious constraints on the use of the tax; and those constraints, as we shall see in part 4, arise from incompatabilities of greater magnitudes than any of us had previously realized. But there are other serious deficiencies which can now be identified internally within the duplicates of each individual township. Although reassessment may regularly occur, it may not necessarily result in an equitable distribution of the tax burden within the township. Even more importantly, the examination of reassessment procedures has revealed new and quite serious problems associated with the comparability of land tax entries, not only between townships but within the townships themselves, and all arising from – or at least associated with – the process of redemption. Let us now turn to these problems.

CHAPTER EIGHT

The Impact of Redemption

Everyone who worked with the land tax in the early years of this century noted that flaws had begun to enter the returns following the passage of the 1798 Redemption Act. An increasing number of parishes had, after that date, failed to report redeemed taxes at the level of the occupier. Thus those using the documents to trace secular trends in owner-occupation found their efforts frustrated. Davies put the problem most clearly in his 1927 article:

> In some instances the tax was redeemed and the land immediately disappeared from the returns. Generally speaking, however, all land was included, though in the case of exonerated land the assessors became indifferent as to who occupied the holdings, since the tenants, who previously – when they paid the tax – were of importance in the eyes of the assessors, no longer concerned them. With increasing frequency from 1798 onwards the tenants' names disappeared: with the result that it is no longer possible in many instances to distinguish between the occupying owners and proprietors generally.

More recently Professor Mingay repeated these concerns, citing Davies, and underscored their potential seriousness. It may be that in some midlands counties such as Oxfordshire, where the early work tended to focus, the problem of missing occupiers is a common one; where the problem is encountered, the miscreant parishes must simply be deleted from the analysis. The problem is annoying, but the solution is simple. It is questionable whether the problem is widespread, however. Martin did not encounter it in his thirty-four Warwickshire parishes, nor did Hunt in Leicestershire, or Turner in Buckinghamshire. The problem is only occasionally encountered in Yorkshire.[1]

It is perhaps odd that no one has expressed other or more serious apprehensions regarding the impact of redemption on the reliability of the land tax duplicates. The fault may lie partially in the comments of Davies, who was incorrect in his assumptions as well as misleading in his facts. The tax assessors were not indifferent as to who occupied exonerated holdings, any more than they could afford to be indifferent as to what happened to those holdings. Even exonerated holdings were subject to the permutations of the land market and to improvements. Davies was simply incorrect in treating the process of land tax assessment as though it were operating in isolation from a more general process of township valuation and assessment.

It is easy to understand why Davies assumed that land tax assessors would not concern themselves with entries for redeemed properties. The tax values for such properties were fixed by redemption and not subject to revision by local authority. The total amount of the tax that was redeemed was subtracted from the township quota, and only the remainder was then borne by the unredeemed properties in the township. It was thus not unreasonable for Davies to assume that the only task for the assessor was to distribute the unredeemed proportion of the township tax quota among those proprietors or tenants who were in possession of unredeemed properties. But, as was shown in the preceding chapter, valuational rents for the land tax were subject to substantial revision. Davies' assumption would lead us to infer that such revaluations would have been restricted to unredeemed properties, since only those properties were subject to revised land tax entries. If revaluation had been restricted in this manner, then both the rental and the tax entries for redeemed properties would have become increasingly incompatible with rentals and tax entries for unredeemed properties, since the latter underwent subsequent revaluation and reassessment.

Davies' assumption is not correct, however. Redeemed tax entries were of course ossified at redemption, and the rental values to which they were related were those current at the time of redemption. Redeemed tax values therefore became increasingly incompatible with those for unredeemed entries, since the latter were constantly subject to revision as their valuational rentals were themselves revised. But redeemed valuational rent was not ossified. The evidence shows quite clearly that redeemed rental entries reported on the land tax duplicates were fully subject to the same process of revaluation experienced by unredeemed properties. It is reasonable to conclude, then, that redeemed and unredeemed rental values – unlike tax values – remained compatible.

It should be noted, however, that each township where property had been redeemed now had two separate quota systems for tax: one redeemed quota and one unredeemed quota. Unless improving and unimproving properties were proportionately equally distributed between the redeemed and unredeemed groupings, the process of revaluation would have caused total rentals of each group to have increased or decreased at differing rates. Since both groups were governed by tax quota ceilings, the differing rates of adjustment in rental values should have caused their ratios of total rent to total tax increasingly to depart from one another. As we shall see, such departures did occur. All of the incompatibilities that, before the Redemption Act, had existed only between townships now began to develop rapidly between redeemed and unredeemed properties within townships – and for the same reasons: Differential movements in total valuation were linked to inflexible ceilings in total tax.[2]

Appendix F separately reports percentage changes in total redeemed and unredeemed rent in the townships of Gilling East at approximately five-year intervals from 1801 to 1830. It is immediately apparent that redeemed values were subject to revision. Since this appendix also reports the number of property bundles in each category for each year, it is equally apparent that percentage changes in total redeemed rental values were not normally attributable to the redemption of additional properties. In only one instance did a change in total valuation occur wholly among unredeemed properties; and even in this instance (Scorton-Uckerby 1806–10) the change in the number of redeemed properties suggests some adjustments in individual redeemed rentals. Noting in appendix E those townships which underwent major periodic revaluations and then noting the breakdowns of those revaluations in appendix F, it is clear that the process of revaluation almost universally affected both redeemed and unredeemed rentals. The magnitudes of change were never the same among redeemed and unredeemed properties, nor would one expect them to be. The distribution of improving and unimproving properties should have differed between the two tax groups. Each property within the township would have been uniquely affected by a general revaluation; and indeed not all revaluations need be general ones. Nor need the process of revaluation be incessant. But, when revaluation did occur in South Cowton, Dalton, Little Langton, Manfield, or Warlaby, it substantially altered the reported rentals of both redeemed and unredeemed properties. In Newby Wiske between 1806 and 1810 and Thrintoft between 1801 and 1806, the act of redemption itself seems to have stimulated widespread revaluation, but in general the revaluation of redeemed properties occurred independently of the process of redemption as such.

Appendix F reports percentage changes in total redeemed and unredeemed rents in 271 cases. In 86 (or almost one-third) of those cases the change reported is 0.0 percent. But a change did occur in the number of properties in 26 of those 86 cases, suggesting that rental values of individual properties had altered even if the total rental remained constant. Thus only 60 cases (or 22.1 percent of all cases in the wapentake for all years) reported no change in the number of properties and no change in total rental. Two-thirds of these unchanging rentals were redeemed, and their dominance of this category seems to stem from the small number of redeemed properties encountered in many townships. But, more broadly, cases of unchanging rental tend to be encountered simultaneously in both the redeemed and unredeemed rentals of a township and to reflect the periodic nature of the revaluation process. The remaining 185 cases reported some percentage of change in total rental, and in 59 (or 31.9 percent) of these cases the number of properties remained constant. Do these 59 cases necessarily indicate that factors other than the land market were stimulating revaluation? They do not. If we examine the 31 cases where the percentage change in total rental exceeded 10 percent, we find that in 4 cases changes had occurred in surnames of proprietors, in 6 cases in surnames of tenants, and in an additional 16 cases changes had occurred in the surnames of both proprietors and tenants.[3] Thus all of these cases lend support to a conclusion that activity in the land market was largely responsible for the process of revaluation among both redeemed and unredeemed properties.

That changes other than those attributable to the land market were at work also seems beyond doubt. The changes in rental which occurred in the townships of these 31 cases were not generally confined to the properties which reported new proprietors or tenants. Changes commonly occurred on other properties as well, though not usually on all other properties. Such additional changes in valuation may have been related to material alterations in properties, such as the construction or destruction of cottages or outbuildings, or the improvement of soils. The data suggests, then, that activity in the land market stimulated, or provided occasions for, limited periodic revaluations of both redeemed and unredeemed properties, but that such revaluations additionally took into account other alterations in land values, alterations which were themselves unrelated to land market transactions.

While it must be comforting to many of us that the land tax was not entirely ossified and inflexible, as it has so often been portrayed, there is no doubt that the Redemption Act, by creating separate quotas for redeemed and unredeemed tax values, created new and serious problems for anyone wishing to utilize the duplicates from 1798 to 1832 or later. For the majority of townships, these problems may be insurmountable, as they introduce errors of considerable magnitude. Table 8.1 delineates the problem for the townships of Gilling East by displaying the percentage differences between redeemed and unredeemed ratios of rent to tax at approximately five-year intervals from 1801 to 1830. It can easily be perceived that the departures between the two ratios are both progressive and, by 1830, quite large in many townships. Moreover, while the progression for each township is substantially a linear one, neither the direction nor the slope of the progression is uniformly distributed among the townships. In some townships the percentage differences between ratios become increasingly positive, indicating that unredeemed ratios are becoming increasingly higher than redeemed ratios. But in other townships the percentage differences become increasingly negative. The magnitude of the departures is also widely distributed. In some townships the two ratios are highly incompatible by 1830, while in others the ratios remain virtually identical. Unfortunately such a pattern of departures makes it impossible to estimate error in a manner which is reliable for individual townships; that is, if specific data on both redeemed and unredeemed rentals is lacking for any single township, it is unsafe by 1830 to form any assumptions regarding the differential relationships between redeemed and unredeemed tax and rental values in that township.[4]

The degree to which redeemed and unredeemed tax entries may progressively fail to represent equivalent rental values within the same township is more fully illustrated by table 8.2, where the percentage departures are presented in a frequency distribution, first for Gilling East and finally for the entire 1830 North Riding sample.[5] An almost perfect dispersal pattern emerges, offering striking confirmation of the progressive nature of the problem. Any reservations about the unrepresentative character of Gilling East are somewhat allayed by the match between the value distributions of the Gilling East townships and those of the larger North Riding sample. It is evident that by 1830 any assumption of a close relationship between redeemed and unredeemed ratios becomes hazardous. Only 47.3 percent of 131 townships in the North Riding sample reported ratios within plus or minus 10 percent of each other; and the remaining departures could be very great indeed and could proceed in both directions. Thus, if ratios of rent to tax could be determined for a township at one (and only one) point in time (such as 1826–32), such data would provide no basis for projecting either the direction or magnitude of such error in other earlier or later years. Since the margins of error are likely to be great in at least half the cases (probably without being able to identify which cases those might be), and since the error cannot be controlled for, any statistical analysis incorporating redeemed tax entries from the post-1798 duplicates seems destined to be hopelessly misleading, and to an extent that is unknowable. These are not heartening conclusions for most students of enclosure and the decline of the small landowner, or indeed for any studies utilizing the nineteenth century land tax.

Table 8.2 also shows that positive percentage differences between ratios strongly outnumber negative ones, indicating that in general there was a tendency for unredeemed ratios to be higher than redeemed ratios. It is unclear what such a pattern implies. If revaluation not only altered both redeemed and unredeemed rental values but also did so in a proportionate

Table 8.1
Percentage difference in ratios of rent to tax for redeemed and unredeemed properties, Gilling East, 1801–30

Township	1801	1806	1810	1815	1820	1826	1830
Ainderby Steeple	3.9	–2.8	1.6	0.8		–10.4	–10.4
Barton	–3.0	–10.4	–12.6	–1.2		–15.2	–28.6
Brompton on Swale	3.4	3.1	8.1	4.2	3.9	19.4	–2.7
Cleasby	0.0	0.0	0.0	0.0		2.8	2.8
Cowton, East	NA	NA	NA	NA		NA	NA
Cowton, North	–0.4	24.5	15.5	8.5		0.0	0.7
Cowton, South	3.6	2.2	2.2	3.6		19.1	18.3
Croft	NA	NA	NA	NA	NA	NA	NA
Dalton upon Tees	–0.8	14.3	32.6	40.2	24.3	32.3	33.8
Danby Wiske	4.6	–1.3	–1.3	0.9		NA	NA
Ellerton etc	NA	8.9	16.2	–48.8	–38.4	–30.9	–36.7
Eryholme	0.0	6.4	6.4	6.4	6.4	16.2	14.8
Kiplin	NA	NA	NA	NA	NA	NA	NA
Kirby Wiske	0.0	0.0	0.0	–9.0		0.0	0.0
Langton, Great	3.7	0.0	0.0	–2.2		–51.2	–18.3
Langton, Little	0.4	0.4	0.0	0.0		–5.5	–5.5
Manfield	–0.9	–3.3	0.0	–0.7		18.0	–3.1
Maunby	24.2	1.6	1.6	1.6	1.0	1.0	1.0
Middleton Tyas	–7.7	16.7	12.8	16.7		18.2	18.2
Morton upon Swale	0.0	0.0	–3.1	–10.5	–10.5	–18.8	–23.7
Moulton	2.1	2.9	2.0	–1.5			
Newby Wiske	0.0	0.0	27.9	30.1	33.0	30.7	30.7
Newton Morrell	NA	NA	NA	NA			
Scorton and Uckerby	6.7	6.3	52.5	52.0	51.7	37.8	48.3
Smeaton, Great	–5.0	0.0	0.0	–2.8			
Stapleton	1.1	2.8	2.8	2.8			

Table 8.1 continued

Township	1801	1806	1810	1815	1820	1826	1830
Thrintoft	0.5	17.1	17.1	21.2		–0.8	–0.8
Warlaby	2.5	0.0	1.2	–0.6		–21.3	–14.6
Yafforth	–3.9	–3.4	–3.4	–7.1		–7.0	–6.5
Total	–18.5	–8.2	–3.0	1.9	26.5	–4.2	–4.6

Note: Values are positive when the unredeemed ratio is higher than the redeemed. The ratios for wapentake totals include rents and taxes for those townships which had only unredeemed properties, thus allowing larger negative values to emerge than the individual column values would lead one to expect.
NA = not applicable.
Sources: Appendices J and K.

Table 8.2
Frequency distribution, percentage difference in ratios of rent to tax for redeemed and unredeemed properties, Gilling East 1801–30 and North Riding sample 1830

% difference in redeemed and unredeemed ratios		Gilling East cases							North Riding sample
		1801	1806	1810	1815	1820	1826	1830	1830
≤–100									
–99.9	–90.0								
–89.9	–80.0								
–79.9	–70.0								
–69.9	–60.0								1
–59.9	–50.0						1		
–49.9	–40.0				1				2
–39.9	–30.0					1	1	1	3
–29.9	–20.0						1	2	10
–19.9	–10.0		1	1	1	1	3	3	13
–9.9	–2.0	4	3	2	4		2	4	18
–1.9	1.9	11	10	10	9	1	4	4	25
2.0	9.9	8	7	5	5	2	1	1	19
10.0	19.9		3	4	1		5	3	16
20.0	29.9	1	1	1	1	1			11
30.0	39.9			1	1	1	3	2	6
40.0	49.9				1			1	2
50.0	59.9			1	1	1			2
60.0	69.9								1
70.0	79.9								
80.0	89.9								1
90.0	99.9								
≥100.0									1

Table 8.2 continued

% difference in redeemed and unredeemed ratios	Gilling East cases							North Riding sample
	1801	1806	1810	1815	1820	1826	1830	1830
NA	5	4	4	4	2	4	4	56
def.								11
N	29	29	29	29	10	25	25	198
% of cases <–1.9[a]	16.7	16.0	12.0	24.0	25.0	38.1	47.6	35.9
% of cases >1.9[a]	37.5	44.0	48.0	40.0	62.5	42.8	33.3	45.0

Note: [a]NA (not applicable) and def. (defective) cases are excluded from the denominator.
Source: Appendices J and K.

and equitable manner, then the differences in ratios must mean that in the majority of these North Riding townships, unredeemed land values were rising more steeply than redeemed land values. One should proceed with caution, however, because higher ratios also mean a lower burden of tax. It may be that some townships found incentives for valuing unredeemed properties at higher levels than redeemed properties. On the other hand it seems unlikely that differing levels of valuation would have been applied to the land tax – especially since such an exercise would produce no tax outputs for redeemed properties – if it can be demonstrated that the valuation for the land tax was also utilized for or influenced by the levying of other local rates. Since it does seem to be the case that common valuations were widespread – and why else would redeemed rentals be recorded and revised on the land tax duplicates? – it may well be true that unredeemed properties were rising in value more rapidly than redeemed properties in most townships and that, as a result, the real burden of the land tax for unredeemed properties was becoming proportionately lighter. If more steeply rising land values were a function of agricultural improvement, then it may be that improving properties tended to remain unredeemed. But however hypothetical these speculations must remain, it is at least clear that the system of tax quotas caused the rate of taxation to diminish as rents rose and thus provided significant incentives for improvement. Alternatively, and perhaps more plausibly, steeply rising wartime rents, and therefore rising ratios and steadily diminishing tax burdens, provided poor incentives for proprietors of the best lands to compound for the land tax through redemption.

CHAPTER NINE

The Equitability of Assessments within Townships

The most serious charge ever levelled against the land tax is that it was not equitably distributed among the properties of individual townships. Formal charges of internal inequitability have been infrequent. More attention has been given formally to possible inequities between townships, arising principally from the system of ossified quotas. But there has always been a widespread conviction among critics of the land tax, and fear among those who use it, that the land tax was often mismanaged within townships and that some properties were lightly taxed at the expense of others. Moreover, suspicion as to who was villainous by manipulating such inequalities has often fallen on the great landlord, who thus rewarded himself and his tenants at the expense of lesser freeholders or rival landlords, or who thereby brought pressure to bear on recalcitrant tenants or others among his neighbours who opposed his will or views. In more urban environments, where the elements of social control were more diffuse and less traditional, an upstart attorney or shopkeeper might find himself able to subvert both vestry and rates.[1] This study has little to say about urban environments. But the preponderantly rural North Riding offers an abundance of evidence regarding the administration of the land tax in agricultural communities and the role of great landowners in that administration.

It is unfortunate that the problem of inequalities cannot be definitively resolved by means of land tax duplicates, even when the duplicates report valuational rent. Even if one were to find townships in which all of the ratios of rent to tax were equal, it would still not be possible to conclude with full confidence that there was a genuine equitability in the distribution of the tax, for the simple reason that the reported rental values may themselves have variously been under- or over-valued. Nor on the other hand is it appropriate to conclude that those townships which reported values producing unequal ratios of rent to tax were necessarily engaging in inequitable distributions of the tax burden. It is possible that such townships were simply undertaking adjustments in tax values on the basis of outdated rentals, thus redressing inequalities rather than creating them. As shown in chapter 7, revaluation of rents, while widespread, was not universal and tended to be periodic. There is also direct evidence that some townships adjusted the tax for smaller holders in accordance with their ability to pay. Nevertheless, while bearing these reservations fully in mind, it is useful to examine whatever evidence for inequality might be found in the land tax duplicates. Appendix G.1 presents this evidence for all twenty-nine townships reporting rent in Gilling East in 1795, c. 1806 and c. 1830. The frequency distributions of all ratios of valuational rent to tax encountered within each township are separately given for redeemed and unredeemed entries. Property bundles reporting £10 or less rent and those reporting £100 or more rent are also separately presented as subsets of the total cases.

It is disturbing to find that apparent inequalities within townships are widespread within Gilling East and that the range of variation in ratios can be very great. Indeed, it is not difficult to find other townships with inequality problems in other regions of the North Riding. The problem should not be unduly exaggerated, however. Although the evidence is in some cases incomplete, seventeen of the twenty-nine townships never reveal a ratio spread of more than 10 percent. Table 9.1 summarizes the data by displaying the raw point spreads of ratios (i.e., the highest ratio minus the lowest ratio) for each of the townships in each year. Middleton Tyas serves to remind us that the point spreads can be alarmingly large and that such large spreads are not necessarily confined to redeemed properties. By and large, however, the inequalities are more typical of redeemed properties than they are of unredeemed ones , and precisely because ossified redeemed tax values, when set off against their revised rentals, tend to produce such inequalities. In any case inequalities in the ratios of redeemed properties, while vexing to the historical analyst who wishes to employ such values, produced no actual inequalities in the distribution of the land tax burden at the time the tax was levied. Redeemed tax values were no longer collected. It is the inequalities discernible among unredeemed entries which, if real, produced actual injustices at the time and which pose more difficult problems in explaining the local administration of the land tax.

Table 9.1 also reveals a remarkable inconsistency in the administration of the land tax within each township. In some townships the ratio spreads tend to diminish over time in both redeemed and unredeemed entries. Other townships tend to deteriorate in both categories. But in about fourteen of the townships the point spreads remain relatively static. It thus becomes impossible to classify a township for the reliability of its rent or

Table 9.1
The range of rent-to-tax ratio distributions (raw differences), Gilling East townships reporting rent, 1795, c. 1806, c. 1830

	Redeemed entries		Unredeemed entries		
	c.1806	c.1830	1795	c.1806	c.1830
Ainderby Steeple	7.6	1.3		11.8	2.7
Barton	25.6	94.7		0.0	19.0
Brompton on Swale	7.9	8.8	0.0	0.1	2.8
Cleasby	0.0	0.0	0.0	0.0	1.3
Cowton, East	NA	NA		0.0	0.7
Cowton, North	15.7	2.9		0.0	1.5
Cowton, South	1.0	2.5		0.4	10.4
Croft	NA	NA		0.2	4.4
Dalton upon Tees	6.9	def.	0.0	0.0	0.1
Danby Wiske	10.4	def.		0.1	0.4
Ellerton etc.	NA	35.2	2.0	2.2	11.1
Eryholme	15.6	11.7		26.1	12.0
Kiplin	NA	NA	0.1	0.2	1.3
Kirby Wiske	0.0	0.0	0.0	1.0	0.2
Langton, Great	0.0	8.5		1.6	0.0
Langton, Little	0.1	9.6		4.0	22.5
Manfield	0.0	NA		7.1	0.0
Maunby	2.3	2.3	0.3	0.0	1.6
Middleton Tyas	153.4	169.5		68.8	0.8
Morton on Swale	5.1	2.1		1.1	0.2
Moulton	1.6			0.1	
Newby Wiske	0.0	10.5	0.9	0.6	7.7
Newton Morrell	NA			0.0	
Scorton-Uckerby	18.0	18.6	1.0[a]	18.0	44.7
Smeaton, Great	7.5		0.2	1.3	
Stapleton	1.6			0.7	
Thrintoft	4.6	2.2		0.0	0.0
Warlaby	0.1	13.2		0.0	0.0
Yafforth	0.8	1.5	0.3	0.1	0.4

Notes: NA = not applicable. def. = defective.
[a]Uckerby not included.
Source: Appendix G.1

tax entries (assuming low point spreads reflect more reliable – or at least more consistent – entries) on the basis of a test conducted at any one point in time. This observation is especially important to bear in mind, since in most wapentakes of Yorkshire, and probably in most counties of England, rents are not commonly reported on the land tax duplicates until the later 1820s. Just as we found in the last chapter that we cannot backwardly estimate error arising from redemption, we must now similarly conclude that it is not safe to test those later duplicates and, on that basis, infer which townships have low inequalities fifty to twenty or even ten years earlier.

The importance of these apparent inequalities for historical analysis is brought more clearly into focus if the ratio spreads of property bundles reporting rents of £100 or more are separately examined. Table 9.2 examines all cases in Gilling East, whether among redeemed or unredeemed properties (usually reported at the level of the tenant), where the ratio difference among such entries equals or exceeds 2.0. While large ratio spreads may be a trivial matter for some statistical purposes when they are confined to small properties, large spreads among very large holdings can never be expected to be trivial in their impact – certainly not within the confines of a single township. Their impact within larger samplings will of course depend upon their frequency, which the Gilling East evidence suggests may well be great among both redeemed and unredeemed properties. The percentage differences displayed in table 9.2 are large in every case where they occur, rising to 373.9 percent in Middleton Tyas in 1805. Moreover, ratio differences among large holdings may be found among the tenanted entries of a single proprietor and not merely between the entries of different proprietors. Column 11 of table 9.2 tabulates the number of collective estates in each township which have large rent entries with significant ratio departures. The figures in column 10 indicate the number of estates with more than one large entry. Ten out of a possible twenty-three estates (43.5 percent) produced internal inequalities among their larger tenantry.

Inequitable tax burdens within estates are thus not unusual. It is true that many of these inequality problems are produced by redeemed properties. But redeemed properties can scarcely be excluded for most analytical purposes; and even if redeemed entries were excluded, a substantial amount of distortion would still remain among the larger unredeemed properties of several townships. It is clear, then, that inequalities among larger entries – and particularly among redeemed entries – can introduce distortions of considerable magnitude into most forms of quantitative analysis employing land tax duplicates at the level of the tenant.

A different sort of pitfall for the historical analyst is revealed by the township of Scorton-Uckerby, where the ratios range in 1806 from the mid-thirties to the mid-fifties and by 1830 from the mid-thirties to eighty. Scorton-Uckerby is actually an amalgam of two townships which for some local and national purposes (such as county rate valuations and the census) reported separately. In the later eighteenth century, they also reported separately for the land tax, although the total amount for Uckerby was normally entered at the bottom of the Scorton duplicate in order to register a combined total. By the nineteenth century property entries for Uckerby had come to be silently added to the Scorton duplicate as its final entries; nor was Uckerby normally mentioned in the heading of the duplicate.

Table 9.2
The magnitude of rent-to-tax ratio inequalities among property entries ≥£100 in rent (where raw ratio variation is ≥2.0), Gilling East townships reporting rent, 1795, c. 1806, c. 1830

Numbered columns:
1 Year of return
2 Township
3 Maximum % spread between entries with rents ≥£100, combining redeemed and unredeemed entries
4 Maximum % spread between entries with rents ≥£100, redeemed entries only
5 Maximum % spread between entries with rents ≥£100, unredeemed entries only
6 Total number of entries with rents ≥£100, combining redeemed and unredeemed entries
7 Number of entries with rents ≥£100, redeemed entries only
8 Number of entries with rents ≥£100, unredeemed entries only
9 Total number of estates with rent entries ≥£100
10 Number of estates with more than one entry ≥£100
11 Number of estates with rent entries ≥£100 where these large entries within a single estate are themselves unequal

1	2	3	4	5	6	7	8	9	10	11
1807	Barton	38.6	38.6	0.0	6	2	4	3	2	0
1806	Dalton upon Tees	47.8	NA	0.0	6	1	5	4	2	0
1806	Danby Wiske	9.8	NA	0.0	9	1	8	5	1	0
1806	Eryholme	27.0	NA	27.0	5	0	5	2	2	1
1806	Manfield	57.3	NA	57.3	8	1	7	4	2	2
1805	Middleton Tyas	373.9	373.9	1.2	16	13	3	5	1	1
1806	Smeaton, Great	19.0	19.0	4.8	7	4	3	5	1	1
1807	Thrintoft	21.8	21.8	NA	3	2	1	3	0	0
1830	Barton	24.5	NA	0.3	4	1	3	3	1	0
1830	Brompton on Swale	10.0	2.2	NA	3	2	1	3	0	0
1830	Cowton, South	41.7	24.3	16.8	7	2	5	3	2	1
1830	Croft	15.6	NA	15.6	15	0	15	3	2	1
1830	Ellerton, etc.	17.0	NA	17.0	16	1	15	5	2	0
1830	Eryholme	16.2	NA	16.2	5	0	5	2	2	1
1830	Langton, Great	22.2	22.2	NA	3	3	0	3	0	0
1830	Langton, Little	78.2	NA	78.2	3	1	2	3	0	0
1830	Middleton Tyas	84.3	84.3	0.2	14	12	2	4	1	1
1830	Morton on Swale	31.0	0.4	NA	7	6	1	3	1	0
1830	Scorton (without Uckerby)	51.2	1.9	5.8	9	4	5	7	1	1
1830	Warlaby	25.4	12.3	0.0	5	3	2	5	0	0

Source: Appendix G.1.

Unless the researcher had examined Scorton duplicates over a long span of years and with considerable care, and unless he had access to supplementary documentation (such as the valuations for the county rate), he might not detect the two-sector nature of the later Scorton duplicates or, if he had, be able to determine precisely where the division occurs. The consequences of such a failure would be considerable. The 1806 ratios with values in the thirties are wholly in Uckerby. All other ratios are in the fifties and in Scorton. By 1830 the two very large Uckerby farming properties (still at £327 and £210 rent as they had been in 1806) and two minor Uckerby redeemed properties (also with unaltered rents) still had ratios in the mid-thirties; but the six remaining Uckerby properties, all of them cottages reporting rents of less than £10, bore ratios of eighty. Scorton's redeemed properties in 1830 were all in the low fifties, while Scorton's unredeemed entries then varied from the low seventies to eighty. Scorton properties had undergone substantial revaluation between 1806 and 1810 (appendix E). In Uckerby the farming properties had never altered in rental values. Only six newly rated (either newly constructed or newly taxed) Uckerby cottages fell within the Scorton system in 1830. There is little doubt that this joint township did not employ a common system of valuation – though by 1830 it may have begun to evolve toward one – and that this poses internal problems which are characteristic of the problems normally associated with inter-township comparisons. It may be that jointly reporting townships commonly pose such problems.

CHAPTER TEN

The Explanation of Inequalities

While the land tax duplicates provide strong evidence that inequalities in assigning the burden of the tax within townships were widespread, they also afford considerable evidence on what classes of property were most affected. Certainly the administrative conditions for manipulation by the gentry were present. It is easy enough to conclude, for example, that the upper level of the land tax administration was wholly in the hands of great landed proprietors. The land tax commissioners, whose names were annually inserted in the statutes authorizing the tax, had come to be nominated by the county Members of Parliament. By 1830 the Board of Taxes was attempting to obtain more complete and up to date lists of all persons qualified to act as commissioners, and letters have survived among the North Riding land tax duplicates of that year, addressed by the clerks of wapentake divisions to the clerk of the peace for the riding, giving the names of those gentlemen resident within the division and qualified for nomination as well as those who had previously been nominated but were then deceased. The clerk of the peace was in turn expected to forward such lists to the county Members. An annual inspection of the names of those who signed the tax duplicates in the later eighteenth and early nineteenth centuries reveals that, though the duty circulated widely among the resident gentry and clergy, those who acted as land tax commissioners were, by and large, also those who were qualified by the size of their holdings to be nominated as justices of the peace. In short, the land tax was administered by the local resident magistracy and their peers. Even the geographical boundaries of the magistracy and land tax commissioners were coextensive.

The powers of the commissioners were very great indeed. While they could not alter the county quota, they had originally been responsible for distributing that quota to the townships. By the end of the eighteenth century, the township quotas had also become unalterable. But extensive powers of tax manipulation remained with the commissioners. It was they who were the overseers and court of last resort for any charge of unfair assessment which might come to their attention or be brought before them. It was undoubtedly they who decided that "rents" be reported in the returns; and once rents were reported, it was within their power – indeed it was their duty – to ensure that no apparent inequities existed in the rate of assessment within each township. Both rents and tax assessments could be questioned by them. If inequalities existed within the system, it was within their purview and authority to correct them. Since the duties of commissioner rotated among the gentry, one would think that the temptation to manipulate in one's self-interest would generally have been mitigated by fear of reprisal. But a more real danger to effective administration might lie in a tacit understanding to live and let live and not to meddle in the local manipulations of others, especially when those manipulations were occurring within a proper sphere of influence. Great property had its prerogatives as well as its responsibilities, perhaps even when those prerogatives were exercised in a questionable manner. There may well have been some reluctance on the commission to come between a gentleman and his tenants and lesser neighbours in this as in other matters.

Superficially there is every indication that the land tax commissioners were extraordinarily lax and casual in exercising their responsibilities. Everyone who has worked with the land tax duplicates will have noted the exasperating inconsistency and incomplete qualities of many of the returns. Nor are apparent "errors" difficult to identify. The tax columns seldom add to the total noted at the end of the return – though they rarely depart from the correct sum by more than £1 unless combined with another tax. Occasionally an individual tax entry is omitted without any explanation, including some entries of considerable magnitude. Most duplicates meticulously list all tenants and break down the tax at the level of the tenant; others will tend to refer only to "sundry tenants" or some such formula and then indicate the tax only at the level of the proprietor; while still other duplicates will reflect a mixture of such practices.[1] Even when commissioners of a division were clearly soliciting information on rents, not all townships were made to comply. The commissioners of Gilling East had a long-standing and unusual interest in rents, but non-compliance in reporting them was not unusual within the wapentake. One entire North Riding wapentake, Whitby Strand, refused to report rents even when the printed forms called for them, after 1826; in several other wapentakes only a paltry proportion of townships complied. Most seriously – and most inexplicably – there is no evidence that the commissioners acted to correct those apparent inequalities in ratios of rent to tax that must have been obvious to the most casual observer in many townships where rent was reported. Was the countryside so ill-governed as this evidence would suggest? There is a good deal of evidence in this and subsequent chapters to suggest that it was, and that the commissioners often acted in substantial and apparently invincible ignorance of valuational circumstances in the townships of their division. But as we proceed in this chapter we shall also find (as we have in earlier ones) that many of the laxities and inconsistencies are perhaps more apparent than real, while in other respects the commissioners were acting in as conscientious a manner as the deeply ingrained traditions of the countryside permitted.

But even if we are able to demonstrate that the land tax commissioners were reasonably conscientious in the performance of their duties, it nevertheless remains that they were members of the upper strata of landed society and that they had every opportunity to regulate or influence the individual incidence of the tax. But what of the process of assessment itself? Was the assessment process within each township also in the hands or under the direct influence of the larger landed estates? If so, then the hypothesis that large landowners manipulated the land tax to their own advantage is to this extent at least a plausible one. Appendix G.2 presents data on the size of holding (as measured by valuational rent) and the ratios of rent to tax of all assessors in each of the townships of the North Riding sample for 1830.[2] The percent of total rent within the township which these holdings represent, as well as the percent represented by the total holdings of their proprietors within the township, are also presented. The percentages may be utilized to measure the degree of control of taxable property within each township, as represented by the land tax assessors and by their proprietors. The percentages are aggregated for each township and separately presented for proprietors and for tenants as frequency distributions in table 10.1.

This evidence leaves no doubt that in the North Riding the process of assessment was overwhelmingly in the hands of large proprietors. The assessors themselves were almost all tenants – a minority were also proprietors of very small additional properties – and were typically farmers of considerable substance. Of the 357 assessors examined in the North Riding sample, 124 (34.7 percent) individually owned or occupied tenancies which collectively reported rents of £100 or more. If one were to make allowances for the substantial undervaluing of land tax rentals, that percentage would rise steeply.[3] In table 10.2 each individual holding or property bundle of each assessor is grouped in size categories. Again allowing for the deflated values of land tax rentals, it is clear that assessors tend to be men of substance who have probably invested substantial amounts of their own capital in their holdings. Table 10.1 similarly shows that the assessors' combined tenanted holdings often account for a sizeable proportion of the reported real wealth of their township. But table 10.1 is far more impressive when it displays the proportion of real wealth held

Table 10.1: Frequency distribution, percentage of control of taxable property held collectively by land tax assessors and by their proprietors, North Riding sample, c. 1830

% Control	Assessors and their Proprietors as Proprietors No. of Townships	%	Assessors as Tenants No. of Townships	%
100.0	12	9.4		
90.0 – 99.9	15	11.7		
80.0 – 89.9	15	11.7		
70.0 – 79.9	7	5.5		
60.0 – 69.9	7	5.5	1	0.8
50.0 – 59.9	9	7.0	3	2.4
40.0 – 49.9	12	9.4	4	3.1
30.0 – 39.9	10	7.8	10	7.9
20.0 – 29.9	7	5.5	18	14.2
10.0 – 19.9	13	10.2	40	31.5
0.0 – 9.9	21	16.4	51	40.2
N	128	100.0	127	100.0

Source: Appendix G.2.

collectively in each township by the proprietors of assessors. It is a commonplace to suggest that great landlords exerted their influence in the countryside most forcibly through their tenantry in matters ranging from estate management to politics. Those historians who believe that proprietors were able to influence the decisions of their substantial tenantry in such matters can also believe from the evidence here presented that in most townships of the North Riding the conditions for tax manipulation by large landowners were present. If one further believes that large tenant farmers were also likely to act in the interests of large holdings in general, then belief in the possibility of largeholder manipulation is further enhanced by the evidence of these tables. In over half the townships the collective holdings of the proprietors of assessors accounted for more than half the reported real wealth. In only one-quarter of the townships did the proprietors account for less than 20 percent of the wealth, and many of these townships fell into this category precisely because they were much divided in their landholding structures. Indeed it is true that the pattern of assessment control substantially mirrors the pattern of landholding structure within the riding. But it also remains true that the smaller owner-occupying farmer and the lesser tenant played little or no role in assessment in most townships. Largeholders could have penalized smallholders and favoured themselves if they had wished to do so – or if the political economy had been conducive to such actions.

Table 10.2
Percentage distribution, all separate property bundles (owned or tenanted) of assessors classified by rent size category, redeemed and unredeemed entries, North Riding sample, c. 1830

	≥£10		£11–49		£50–99		≥£100	
All Cases	No.	%	No.	%	No.	%	No.	%
385	82	21.3	116	30.1	77	20.0	110	28.6

Source: Appendix G.2.

Appendix G.1 provides some initial insight into the role of largeholders in the local administration of the land tax by revealing the relative burdens apparently borne by large and small holdings. Entries reporting rents of £100 or more tend, if anything, to produce lower ratios than the mode. Thus they reflect a heavier tax burden among such properties – provided one assumes the rentals are themselves equitably reported within the township. The exceptions are most commonly – though not exclusively – to be found among the larger redeemed properties, and these higher ratios are explicable on grounds other than tax manipulation, as was demonstrated when considering the impact of redemption (chapter 8). The more extreme ratio values among both redeemed and unredeemed properties are overwhelmingly to be found among the lower- to middle-range rental values, and especially among entries valued at £10 or less; and these extreme ratio values depart equally in the direction of heavier and lighter tax burdens. The data presented in appendix G.1 does not support a hypothesis that land tax burdens were widely manipulated in the interest of their own holdings by large landholders. The evidence suggests that, with relatively few exceptions, the larger unredeemed holdings were taxed at the mode or at a somewhat more onerous level. Any tax manipulation which occurred among unredeemed properties was principally applied to very small to middling properties, especially houses and cottages, and produced ratio deviations which proceed in both directions.

The evidence from the land tax duplicates further shows that those larger properties held by the assessors themselves were not generally favoured by the assessment procedures – provided once again one accepts the equitability of the rents themselves as reported in the returns. Table 10.3 displays the percentage by which each separate, redeemed property bundle of an assessor departs from the mean redeemed rent-to-tax ratio for its township. Table 10.4 presents the same percentage departures for each individual unredeemed property bundle. Just over two-thirds of all property bundles of assessors were unredeemed and were thus directly subject to the benefits or penalties of manipulation. Almost three-quarters of the largest

Table 10.3
Frequency distribution, percentage difference in rent-to-tax ratios for assessors' properties and the ratios for their townships, redeemed entries only, by rent size category, North Riding sample, c. 1830

% difference		All cases		≤£10		£11–49		£50–99		≥£100	
		No.	%	No.	%	No.	%	No.	%	No.	%
≤–100.0											
–99.9	–90.0										
–89.9	–80.0										
–79.9	–70.0										
–69.9	–60.0										
–59.9	–50.0	3	2.4	1	5.0	1	2.2			1	3.4
–49.9	–40.0	2	1.6			1	2.2	1	3.6		
–39.9	–30.0	3	2.4			1	2.2	1	3.6	1	3.4
–29.9	–20.0	7	5.7	1	5.0	2	4.4	1	3.6	3	10.3
–19.9	–10.0	10	8.2	1	5.0	4	8.9	3	10.7	2	6.9
–9.9	–2.0	16	13.1	2	10.0	7	15.6	5	17.8	2	6.9
–1.9	1.9	38	31.1	7	35.0	12	26.7	6	21.4	13	44.8
2.0	9.9	9	7.4	1	5.0	4	8.9	1	3.6	3	10.3
10.0	19.9	7	5.7	1	5.0	4	8.9	1	3.6	1	3.4
20.0	29.9	9	7.4	3	15.0	3	6.7	1	3.6	2	6.9
30.0	39.9	3	2.4			1	2.2	2	7.1		
40.0	49.9	6	4.9	2	10.0	2	4.4	2	7.1		
50.0	59.9	1	0.8					1	3.6		
60.0	69.9	1	0.8			1	2.2				
70.0	79.9	3	2.4			1	2.2	1	3.6	1	3.4
80.0	89.9										
90.0	99.9										
≥–100.0		4	3.3	1	5.0	1	2.2	2	7.1		

Table 10.3 continued

% difference	All cases No.	All cases %	≤£10 No.	≤£10 %	£11–49 No.	£11–49 %	£50–99 No.	£50–99 %	≥£100 No.	≥£100 %
N	122	100.0	20	100.0	45	100.0	28	100.0	29	100.0
% of all redeemed cases				16.4		36.9		23.0		23.8

Summary (percentages)

% difference	All cases	≤£10	£11–49	£50–99	≥£100
≤–10.0	20.5	15.0	20.0	21.4	24.1
±9.9	51.6	50.0	51.1	42.8	62.1
≥10.0	27.9	35.0	28.9	35.7	13.8

Note: Tables 10.3 and 10.4 are compiled for each individual property entry of each assessor. These tables are thus not comparable with statistics presented in appendix G.2, where ''rent'' is aggregated for each assessor and only unique ratios are reported.
Source: Land tax duplicates, NYCRO.

Table 10.4
Frequency distribution, percentage difference in rent-to-tax ratios for assessors' properties and the ratios for their townships, unredeemed entries only, by rent size category, North Riding, sample, c. 1830

% difference		All cases		≤£10		£11–49		£50–99		≥£100	
		No.	%	No.	%	No.	%	No.	%	No.	%
≤–100.0											
–99.9	–90.0										
–89.9	–80.0										
–79.9	–70.0										
-69.9	-60.0										
-59.9	-50.0	2	0.8	1	1.6	1	1.4				
-49.9	-40.0	2	0.8	1	1.6	1	1.4				
-39.9	-30.0	1	0.4			1	1.4				
-29.9	-20.0	5	1.9	1	1.6	1	1.4	1	2.0	2	2.5
-19.9	-10.0	11	4.2	3	4.8	3	4.2	2	4.1	3	3.7
-9.9	-2.0	28	10.6	3	4.8	11	15.5	6	12.2	8	9.9
-1.9	1.9	129	52.8	30	48.4	37	52.1	20	40.8	52	64.2
2.0	9.9	43	16.3	12	19.4	6	8.4	13	26.5	12	14.8
10.0	19.9	14	5.3	4	6.4	3	4.2	3	6.1	4	4.9
20.0	29.9	3	1.1	1	1.6	1	1.4	1	2.0		
30.0	39.9	1	0.4	1	1.6						
40.0	49.9	2	0.8			1	1.4	1	2.0		
50.0	59.9	1	0.4	1	1.6						
60.0	69.9	2	0.8	1	1.6	1	1.4				
70.0	79.9										
80.0	89.9	3	1.1	1	1.6	1	1.4	1	2.0		
90.0	99.9	2	0.8	1	1.6			1	2.0		
≥–100.0		4	1.5	1	1.6	3	4.2				

Table 10.4 continued

% difference	All cases		≤£10		£11–49		£50–99		≥£100	
	No.	%	No.	%	No.	%	No.	%	No.	%
N	263	100.0	62	100.0	71	100.0	49	100.0	81	100.0
% of all unredeemed cases				23.6		27.0		18.6		30.8

Summary (percentages)

% difference	All cases	≤£10	£11–49	£50–99	≥£100
≤–10.0	8.0	9.7	9.8	6.1	6.2
±9.9	79.8	72.6	76.0	79.6	88.9
≥10.0	12.2	17.7	14.1	14.3	4.9

Source: Land tax duplicates, NYCRO.

properties were unredeemed. Both tables show that properties reporting rents of £100 or more are strikingly overrepresented among those properties departing from the township mean by less than 2 percent. Indeed almost two-thirds of the larger unredeemed entries fall into this class interval. A grouping of the intervals under the summary sections of the tables brings the point home even more forcibly. Redeemed properties tend to depart from the mean more strongly than unredeemed properties, but stronger departures among redeeemed entries must be expected and are not necessarily due to manipulation. Both among redeemed and unredeemed entries, and particularly among the latter, the tendency for assessors' entries to remain within ten percentage points of the mean is a strong one. Moreover the tendency to conform to the mean increases sharply as the size of the property increases. Just as we found in appendix G.1 when examining all property bundles in Gilling East, the tendency for assessors' ratios to depart from the mean is most marked among those properties rated at £10 or less. The evidence does not warrant a conclusion that houses and cottages are wholly or even principally responsible for the overall dispersions, however. The decline in dispersions from the mean is not sharply defined until property size exceeds £100 rental.

If the land tax evidence can be accepted at face value, then, it becomes impossible to escape the conclusion that assessors in possession of very large properties did not unduly favour those properties in levying the tax. On the contrary, departures from the mean among the largest properties tended to be negative, implying a more onerous tax burden on them. It was the smallest properties which tended to depart preponderantly in a positive direction, implying their lighter tax burden. Manipulation, if it occurred, tended therefore to produce inequalities that favoured smaller properties at the expense of larger ones. Some tendency in this direction, with numerous exceptions among individual entries, may be found throughout the North Riding sample.

The evidence does not force us to conclude that the countryside was ruled preponderantly by a beneficent gentry who tended on the whole to favour smallholders at their own expense, however. Though it may be true, perhaps there are alternative explanations of the patterns of evidence found in the land tax. It has already been suggested that the rents themselves as reported in the land tax duplicates may not depart equitably from current rack rents. If this were true, the ratios could be fundamentally misleading. It is now time to approach such a suggestion in a more systematic manner. If the rent-to-tax ratio dispersions or apparent inequalities are not due to manipulations of the tax burden by the assessors or (through them) by their landlords, is it possible to explain these patterns in any other fashion? Table 10.5 delineates the logical possibilities under two sets of circumstances: first, when there is no ratio dispersion or apparent inequality of tax burden within a township; and, second, when there is such a dispersion.

Table 10.5
Conditions capable of producing or failing to produce rent-to-tax ratio dispersions, and the consequences of each condition for the reliability of rent and tax entries

	Condition	Reliability of Rent	Reliability of Taxes
A	If the township displays no dispersion of ratios		
1	The assessor accepts old "rents" from old tax records and assesses proportionately.	poor	poor
2	The assessor accepts actual rents being paid and assesses proportionately.	poor	poor
3	The assessor accepts and old and outdated professional valuation and assesses proportionately.	poor	poor
4	The assessor accepts a new professional general valuation and assesses proportionately.	good	good
5	The assessor determines actual or reputed rental values or some system of outdated rents, makes adjustments on what he takes to be the "full and fair" or rack rents (and perhaps reduces by a constant percentage), and assesses proportionately, recording his adjusted rental values on the return.	good	good
B.	If the township displays a dispersion of ratios		
1	The assessor accepts old "rents" from old tax records, recognizes their inequitable relationships to a "full and fair" or rack rental, and assesses proportionately on the basis of adjustments made to the old rental values, but reports only the old unadjusted rents on the return.	poor	good
2	The assessor accepts actual rents being paid, recognizes their inequitable relationships to a "full and fair" or rack rental, and assesses proportionately on the basis of adjustments made to the actual rental values, but reports only the unadjusted actual rentals on the return.	poor	good
3	The assessor accepts an old and outdated professional general valuation, recognizes the inequitable relationships among these values to a "full and fair" or rack rental, and assesses proportionately on the basis of adjustments made to the old rental values, but reports only the old unadjusted rents on the return.	poor	good
4	A "full and fair" or rack rent (or some constant percentage thereof) is reported uniformly on the return, but most tax assessments are ancient and unaltered	good	poor

There is nothing implausible about any of the conditions stipulated in table 10.5. There are several townships in Gilling East, for example, where the assessor seems year after year to have recorded both the rents and the tax entries from the duplicate of the preceding year, making only those minor adjustments required by current property transactions. Such townships would meet the first condition under section A. In such townships neither the reported rental values nor the tax values should be reliable in the sense of departing equally from their current "full and fair" or rack rental values – provided such a condition had obtained in the township for a number of years sufficient to allow the development of differential alterations in land values.

At first thought the most improbable condition is the final one in section B. It seems unlikely that an assessor would uniformly report rack rents and then unabashedly assign unrevised tax assessments which had clearly been levied at different rates. But there is a township in the North Riding which conforms precisely to this condition. The land tax duplicates of the late 1820s for Rosedale East Side, in the wapentake of Pickering Lythe, specify that the rents are "rack rents." Thirty-nine of the forty property bundles in 1826 were unredeemed, and their rent-to-tax ratios were evenly distributed from a low of 32.0 to a high of 74.7. Only two entries were valued at less than £10 rental, and none exceeded £89. That the rents were reported at rack rent is supported by comparing the total rent of the 1826 land tax duplicate with the values reported in the township for the property tax in 1814 and for the county rate in 1824. The land tax value exceeded the latter two valuations by 11.5 percent and 20.1 percent respectively. The dispersion of ratios was caused by a system of tax assessments that was severely out of date. A comparison of duplicates revealed that the assessments for most of the entries had not altered since at least the 1780s, the exceptions being adjustments for property transactions. There is little room for doubt, then, that real inequities were being practiced in the levying of land tax assessments in Rosedale East Side, and in a manner which was extraordinarily open and candid. Who was the landowner who dared to flaunt the law in this manner and under the explicit scrutiny of the land tax commissioners? Why, it was the King. The property of the township had formerly been in the hands of small to middling long-term leaseholders under the Crown. By the early nineteenth century it had passed wholly back into the hands of the King, and his former leaseholders were now his shorter-term tenants.

If the agents of the King could levy the tax on his tenantry in so extraordinary a manner, then surely almost any form of assessment practice was possible. But as shall be seen in chapter 13, not all of the conditions in table 10.5 were equally probable. Comparisons with other forms of valuation will show that land tax rentals only very rarely approached rack rents. It is likely, therefore, that townships displaying wide dispersions of ratios conform to conditions one to three and not to condition four of section B. Similarly, there is abundant evidence that new general valuations by professional land surveyors were also sufficiently rare and infrequent in the eighteenth and very early nineteenth centuries.[4] Townships displaying no dispersion of ratios are thus unlikely to conform to condition four in section A. The conditions specified in one to three and five are far more likely. It is not unreasonable to suggest that those townships which underwent significant assessor revaluation and yet developed no significant patterns of dispersion in their rent-to-tax ratios were conforming to condition five of section A. Those townships which failed to undergo assessor revaluation and also failed to develop patterns of dispersion in their ratios might be understood as conforming to conditions one to three. If these assumptions seem reasonable, then it would be well if those who employ the land tax resisted any temptation to base their calculations on rent, where rents are reported, and retained the traditional reliance on tax entries. Tax entries would seem to have a higher probability of reflecting a uniform relationship to rack rents than do the purported rentals encountered in the duplicates.[5]

It is difficult to escape the conclusion that local administrators of the land tax used a crazy quilt of discrepant practices in the levying of assessments. Indeed the assessors seem to have exhausted the logical possibilities in performing their duties; if patterns to their practices are found, it is probably because the possibilities for variation were finite. In fact the discrepancies in their practices should surprise no one; national rates such as the land tax were not really national in their administration, except at the upper levels of collection. The national government did not, and could not politically, have concerned itself directly in the details of local assessment. To have attempted to do so would have smacked of that dreadful engine of tyranny, a general excise, and have smelled of French despotism. National rates, like parish and county rates, were deeply embedded in the most ancient governmental traditions of the local community and were made sacrosanct by the strongest of prescriptions. To an extraordinary degree, the English countryside governed itself. National direct taxation such as excise and the income tax might penetrate and outflank the immemorial structures of the local community under the severe pressures of warfare, but in the early nineteenth century the day of modern governmental administration had not yet fully dawned, and for yet a decade or two the local community would continue to rule the countryside largely in the manner of its ancestors.

PART FOUR

The Regional and National Distribution of the Land Tax Burden

... Having of late received his maiesties commission to me and others directed for the ratinge and assessinge of the second entyre subsidy graunted unto his maiestie in the late parliament and with the said commission an especiall letter to the said commissioners from the lords of his maiesties most honourable privy councell that we should not take liberty to ourselves to keepe the assessments at such lowe rates as formerly they hadd beene laste sett att but that we must with all care and diligence make our present sessments more proportionable and nigher unto mens valewes both of ther lands and goods ... ... wherein I would not have youe Mr Bayliffe to be backward for that youe know that I knowe too much ...

Letter from Roger Wyvell, Osgodby, justice of the peace, to the bailiffs of Scarborough, John Farrer and Richard Peacocke, 29 March 1626, extracted in *Scarborough Records 1600–1640: A Calendar*, edited by M.Y. Ashcroft (Northallerton: North Yorkshire County Record Office Publications No. 47, 1991), 165.

CHAPTER ELEVEN

The National Distribution of the Land Tax Burden: The Traditional Evidence

It has always been believed, both by contemporaries and by recent economic historians, that the land tax quotas assigned to the counties in 1698 fell lightly on the North and West. In the early eighteenth century it was both publicly and privately asserted, even in Cumbria itself, that a 4s. statutory land tax rate probably generated a 9d. actual rate (or a ratio of rent to tax of 26.7:1) in the northwestern counties. Certainly it was then believed that the more western and northerly counties could not have been taxed at an actual rate of more than 1s. in the pound on the gross rental, which is a ratio of rent to tax of 20:1. By contrast Professor Habakkuk has confirmed that in Northamptonshire and Bedfordshire the assessment imposed by the 1698 quotas "was accurate and a tax of four shillings in the pound did really take one-fifth of a landowner's rental" during the war years of the early eighteenth century. W.R. Ward has further shown that the unequal incidence of the tax was not a new phenomenon, but that the burden of national taxation had been steadily decreasing in the northern and western counties since the civil war: "The imposition of land-tax quotas in 1698 came none too soon."[1]

The generalizations of recent historians on the regional and national distribution of the land tax burden can be tested in some detail by contemporary literary evidence. In particular, the evidence gleaned from the reports of Sir Frederick Morton Eden (appendix H) suggests that even the imposition of quotas failed to arrest, and in their way may have contributed to, a severely deteriorating situation. While it is true that governments in the late seventeenth century had found it impossible to impose taxes on a system of continuous reassessment, and would undoubtedly have found it equally impossible in the eighteenth century, nevertheless it also remains true that the system of ossified quotas made it impossible to adjust the increasingly inequitable national incidence of taxation, especially that caused by differentially rising land values, and in the northern industrial and commercial towns, by the creation of new taxation units such as houses, shops, factories, and mines.

Eden's enquiry into the state of the poor in England and Wales offers a unique literary opportunity to investigate the incidence and mechanisms of the land tax on a national scale, after a century of rising land prices and in the midst of the economic changes caused by war and industrial revolution. The results of his enquiry were published in 1797 and have become one of the classics of social and economic literature. During the winter of 1795-96, he secured the services of "a remarkably faithful and intelligent person, who has spent more than a year in travelling from place to place for the express purpose of obtaining exact information agreeably to a set of queries with which I furnished him." Included in those queries was information on the local poundage rate and the valuational basis for the land tax, as well as for the poor and other rates. Eden visited some of the parishes himself to gather information; for some other parishes he relied on communications from residents of his acquaintance. The results of his enquiries are published in some nine hundred pages of detailed reports which bear every mark of a critical and painstaking investigation.

Eden's reports have their difficulties, however. He and his agent found the inhabitants of most townships particularly reluctant to reveal the details of land tax assessment, above all in the northern counties – and for good reason, as we shall see. In many instances Eden's information seems unreliable or misleading. Moreover, while a large amount of nationally distributed information can be gleaned from the reports, the resulting sample can hardly be said to have statistically random or even representative qualities. Data on land tax rates is either provided or can be computed for more than 120 townships scattered throughout England and Wales. But industrial and heavily commercial or urbanizing townships are substantially overrepresented, undoubtedly because these were the townships where Eden felt the conditions of the poor and the pressures on the rates most deserved investigation. As a result, in Yorkshire for example, the larger towns of the West Riding are reported almost to the exclusion of agricultural regions. The southwestern counties are scarcely represented at all in the data. Given the striking nature of the information provided for Cumbria and Lancashire, one would have wished for more than a modicum of information about both rural and industrial Northumberland and Durham. Nevertheless, provided one bears these qualifications in mind, there is a great deal that can be learned about the national patterns of land tax administration from these reports.[2]

Because of its unrepresentative nature, the Eden sample does not permit the construction of county or regional means. An examination of his data does make it strikingly clear, however, that the margin of land tax burden had widened startlingly by the 1790s. The ratios of rent to tax reported by

Eden for parishes in most of the southeastern counties ranged below 10:1. In the midlands the ratios rose generally to the upper teens or lower twenties. It was in the industrial and commercial towns of the West Riding, however, that the ratios began to rise steeply, ranging from 30:1 in Skipton to as much as 120:1 in Sheffield. The ratios in Cumbria seem generally to have fallen between 50 and 99, but a cloth centre like Kendal registered a ratio of 295.6:1, while the highest ratio in the sample was recorded for Rickergate Quarter in Carlisle, at 320:1. The manufacturing towns of Lancashire which experienced the sharpest increases in building during the eighteenth century also registered ratios in excess of 150:1. The city of Bath in Somerset, which had also expanded sharply during the century, was reported as paying "under" one penny in the pound, producing a ratio in excess of 240:1.

If the early eighteenth century estimates reported by modern historians are correct, then, and the century did in fact begin with the northern and western counties enjoying a land tax burden approximately four to six times lighter than that in the southeast and midlands, by the 1790s the gap had widened enormously. Differences in rural rates are difficult to judge in Eden's data, especially in the North, but northwestern urban and industrial townships were by then enjoying a land tax burden perhaps ten or twenty times lighter than those of the south and east. In some instances the gap was very much larger. Of course, one may doubt the reliability of Eden's data. But its credibility may be enhanced if one recalls that those who provided Eden or his agent with the northern data had a vested interest in reporting more onerous land tax rates, not lighter ones; thus any bias in the reporting may be expected to understate rather than overstate the differences. Moreover, the reports are purportedly based on "net" or "fair" rentals, and not merely on nominal ones. Even so, given the unsystematic nature of the data, these conclusions cannot be considered definitive; but if they could be sustained by subsequent research, it would become evident that the industrial and commercial northwest was enjoying a sharply declining land tax burden precisely during those decades when rising capital formation was most crucial to the achievement of modern levels of economic growth.

Eden's data leads to one further important conclusion. In thirty-nine townships the reports provide two types of information: the amount of land tax paid and the local poundage rate at which it was paid, permitting the computation of total land tax rental; and the amount of poor rate assessments and the poundage rate of the assessment, permitting the computation of total poor rate rental. A calculation of poor rate rent as a percentage of land tax rent, as reported in appendix I and summarized in table 11.1, reveals a close relationship between the valuational bases of the land tax and the poor rate in the majority of this small sample of townships

Table 11.1
Poor tax valuation as a percentage of land tax valuation, Eden national sample

%	Cases	% of cases
≤49.9	3	7.7
50.0–69.9	3.5	9.0
70.0–79.9	4.5	11.5
80.0–89.9	5.5	14.1
90.0–99.9	11.5	29.5
100.0–109.9	7	17.9
110.0–119.9	3	7.7
≥120.0	1	2.6
N	39	100.0

Source:Sir Frederick Morton Eden, *The State of the Poor*, vols. 2 & 3 (London, 1797).

scattered throughout England. In over 47 percent of the cases, the poor rate valuation fell within 10 percent of the land tax valuation. More than 69 percent fell within 20 percent of the land tax. Certainly the sample is a small and unrepresentative one, and not all of the entries are comparable. Some of the poor rate rentals were only nominal, and the reports do not always specify the basis of the land tax valuation. In the case of Reigate, the land tax valuations were obviously nominal, since the nominal poor rate valuations so nearly equaled them. Some of the lower percentages may in fact be explained by such differences in nominal and net actual rentals. The low percentage in Preston was due to the low nominal valuation for the poor rate, where rentals for houses were assigned at one-half, and land at two-thirds, their actual rental values. The land tax valuation, which was nearly twice that of the poor rate, presumably represented actual rents.

The data therefore suggests that a common valuational basis (discounted differently for each rate, perhaps) for the land tax and the poor rate, while not invariable, was a widely employed procedure throughout England at the end of the eighteenth century. Evidence from the North Riding of Yorkshire, presented earlier and in chapter 12, lends further weight to such a conclusion. And the fact that the poor rate was widely collected in a manner which would provide sufficient surplus revenues to meet the requirements of other local rates – most commonly the county or constable's rates – lends additional credence to an argument that in the majority of townships a single valuational base, peculiar to the needs of that township, was employed to meet the demands imposed upon it by many (and sometimes perhaps by all) taxes which took the form of rates (and a few which did not), whether local or national.

The evidence employed by modern historians for the national distribution of the burden of the land tax has generally been concentrated in the early eighteenth century and has either been impressionistic in nature or, when statistical, unsystematic and undetailed in its geographical coverage. The data I have derived from Eden, while in some ways more extensive and pertaining to the 1790s, suffers from being unsystematic and unrepresentative. In the remaining chapters of part 4, I shall approach the problems of regional and national distribution in a manner based directly on a systematic statistical series that is broad in its geographical coverage, being in principle available for the whole of England and Wales at the parish or township level. In chapter 12 we shall first seek such a series by examining North Riding valuational rents reported in the land tax duplicates. I have utilized such rents myself in the past when estimating inequalities in the burden of the tax.[3] But we shall find that on closer examination the rents reported in the land tax duplicates do not in themselves tell us very much that is reliable about the distribution of the burden of the tax, principally because the land tax valuations of different townships depart from rack rent at differential rates. In chapter 13 we shall therefore select from among several available rental valuation series one which tends to report maximum total values for each township. Such a series presumably approaches rack rents more closely, thereby narrowing the possible range of departures, and thus tends to standardize our rental variable. In chapter 14 the spatial patterns produced by these maximum rental estimates will be examined for evidence of internal comparability. We shall then employ these rentals in constructing a new series of ratios of estimated actual rents to land tax at the parish or township level. Relatively reliable calculations of tax burden can then be undertaken in a series which is geographically systematic and which meets reasonable standards of internal comparability. This method, which will be developed in the North Riding of Yorkshire, will be further tested in the East and West Ridings and then, in chapter 15, applied to every parish in fourteen additional counties of England. What we shall learn is that, by the end of the Napoleonic wars, after more than a century of rising land values and regional redistributions of wealth, the burden of the land tax was far more unequally distributed, both within counties and nationally, than Eden's data and the earlier estimates of historians – myself included – have led us to believe.

CHAPTER TWELVE

Valuational Rent and Local Poundage Rates in the North Riding of Yorkshire c. 1830

Direct statistical evidence for the local administration of the land tax and for its valuational base may be found in the land tax duplicates in the form of valuational rents. This chapter will undertake a regional investigation of such evidence. The reporting of rents in the duplicates was both erratic and rare before 1826. In the North Riding of Yorkshire, where in this and the following chapter we shall again focus our attention, only a tiny minority of townships reported rents before that date, and they did so irregularly. An opportunity for a broad spatial analysis presents itself during the years 1826 to 1832, however. In 1826 a standard printed form for the land tax was adopted throughout the North Riding wapentakes. The first column of that form called for the listing of "rentals." Not all of the wapentakes adhered to the instructions of the new form; in some wapentakes only a small minority entered values in the rental column, and none did so in the wapentake of Whitby Strand, even though the town of Whitby itself had often reported rents during the 1780s. Nevertheless it will be seen from table 12.1 that over 41 percent of the townships of the North Riding reported rents c. 1830 in a form suitable for investigating the burden of the tax through the calculation of rent-to-tax ratios.

These townships are not evenly distributed throughout the agricultural regions of the riding, however. While the North Riding as a whole was preponderantly pastoral in the eighteenth and early nineteenth centuries, with some mixed husbandry in the lowlands, and breeding and rearing on the eastern and western moors, the riding was also notable for its resident great landlords whose seats and – to a lesser degree – whose holdings were heavily concentrated in the vales. Some of the upland townships were held substantially by large absentee landlords, but many were more typified by small freehold or copyhold estates. With the exceptions of the vale wapentakes of Birdforth and Hallikeld, the lowland townships are more regularly reported in the sample than are those in the Dales or the North

Table 12.1
North Riding townships reporting rent on land tax duplicates c. 1830, by wapentake

	Total townships	Reporting rent	%
Allertonshire	31	12	38.7
Birdforth	46	11	23.9
Bulmer	60	47	78.3
Gilling East	29	25	86.2
Gilling West*	40	18	45.0
Hallikeld	28	8	28.6
Hang East	30	10	33.3
Hang West*	38	7	18.4
Langbaurgh*	80	36	45.0
Pickering Lythe*	37	16	43.2
Ryedale*	51	8	15.7
Whitby Strand*	12	0	0.0
Total	482	198	41.1

Note: Wapentakes that are principally upland are asterisked. The total numbers of townships have been derived from a master list that aggregates or disaggregates a small number of duplicates in order to construct comparable data series for some townships which erratically reported separately or jointly for different administrative purposes. A few detached townships have also been assigned to the wapentakes in which they physically lay, rather than in those to which they were administratively assigned.
Source: Land tax duplicates, NYCRO.

Yorkshire Moors. An inspection of map 6 further confirms the impression that upland townships are underreported, especially when one notes the distribution of reporting townships within wapentakes. The 1830 sample is statistically neither random nor representative. But it is large and, with the above qualifications in mind, it seems clear that the land tax duplicates of c. 1830 provide an adequate basis for investigating the variety and spatial distribution of valuational rents and their relationship to tax entries in the North Riding.

The 1830 North Riding sample is presented in appendix J. In an earlier paper, drawing principally on a small number of land tax duplicates of the 1780s, I noted that a comparison of reported rents with corresponding tax entries in Yorkshire showed a wide range of variation in ratio of valuational rent to tax, some townships displaying the statutory rate of 5:1, but others yielding ratios as high as around 80:1. I suggested that such variations in ratio raised the most serious doubts about the comparability of individual tax entries between townships, even within the same county.[1] The 1830 sample enables us to examine this contention more systematically. The ratios of rent to tax found in appendix J are summarized in table

12.2 and are displayed on map 6. It would seem that my earlier doubts were amply justified. The variations in local poundage rate, which the ratios reflect, were indeed exceedingly great throughout the North Riding. The riding mean ratio in 1830 was 29:1, and the median similarly fell within the interval 25.0 to 29.9. But the range was widely distributed. Four townships in Ryedale produced ratios at the onerous statutory rate of 5:1, while in Old Malton (also in Ryedale) the ratio rose to a light 80.3:1. Almost one-third of the townships produced ratios in the 20.0 to 29.9 intervals, and over 70 percent of the ratios ranged from 15.0 to 39.9. An additional 20 percent of the ratios fell in even higher intervals. Judging from valuational base alone, it would seem that there was the most extraordinary variation in the burden of the land tax among the townships of the North Riding.

But appearances may be deceiving. It is important that the interactive nature of the land tax mechanisms not be forgotten. The variations in local poundage rate may merely reflect equivalent and compensatory variations in the levels of valuation adopted by each township. For example, valuational rents which approach rack rent should in general produce downward pressure on the local poundage rate and correspondingly higher ratios, while valuations which depart widely from rack rent should push poundage rates upward and ratios downward. Premature conclusions must again be avoided, however. One cannot simply conclude that townships with valuations most approaching rack rent will always have ratios that are higher than those of townships whose valuational rentals most depart from rack rent. In the Pickering Lythe township of Rosedale East Side, for example, the 1830 land tax duplicates identify the valuational basis as rack rent, but the ratio stands at only a moderately high 45.4:1.[2] Much depends on how land values had changed since the imposition of the quotas in 1698, or rather since the valuational base set in 1693 or earlier. Since land values altered differentially throughout the riding during that century or more, one might expect the quotas to have had equally differential effects on the interactions of valuational rents and local poundage rates, with the valuations having been further affected by the unique requirements of other forms of local taxation. No simple or precise conclusions should therefore be drawn from the magnitudes of ratios constructed in this manner, except perhaps for one: Individual tax assessments in townships were the products of highly variable combinations of mechanisms. There is no basis for concluding that the mechanisms worked similarly in different townships such that either comparable actual or rack rents would produce comparable tax assessments; indeed, wide variations in local poundage rates suggest the opposite conclusion. Because valuational procedures differed, the values of individual tax entries do not reflect comparable actual wealth or actual rental values across township boundaries and should not be used for

Table 12.2
Frequency distribution of ratios, total valuational rent to total tax, North Riding, c. 1830

Ratios	No. of townships	% of townships
0.0–4.9	0	0.0
5.0–9.9	5	2.5
10.0–14.9	14 (2)	7.1
15.0–19.9	25	12.6
20.0–24.9	38 (12)	19.2
25.0–29.9	27 (2)	13.6
30.0–34.9	30 (3)	15.2
35.0–39.9	20	10.1
40.0–44.9	11 (1)	5.6
45.0–49.9	4 (1)	2.0
50.0–54.9	10 (2)	5.0
55.0–59.9	7	3.5
60.0–64.9	3	1.5
65.0–69.9	1	0.5
70.0–74.9	1	0.5
75.0–79.9	1	0.5
80.0–84.9	1	0.5
Total	198 (23)	

Note: Ratios of unredeemed entries are included when ratios of total rent to tax was not available. Similarly, a ratio of only redeemed entries is included in one case when neither total nor unredeemed was available. The number of redeemed only and unredeemed only ratios included in each interval is indicated in parentheses.
Source: Appendix J.

comparative or cross-sectional analyses of real wealth which simply aggregate or group tax entries across such boundaries.

Some will justifiably find this reasoning too abstract to be wholly convincing. I would agree that it is worth proceeding cautiously before entirely dismissing any possibility that the valuational basis of the tax, and therefore its burden as measured by the ratios of table 12.2, was regionally distributed in a rational manner. If the valuational base of the tax was to any significant degree equal to or a consistent departure from either actual or rack rents, then the ratios of rent to tax calculated from such valuations should have been distributed in regional patterns which conform to farming regions and soil types – or at least that conclusion would follow if one believed that actual and rack rents were themselves to some degree rationally distributed across the agrarian landscape. There is in fact a marked tendency in the 1830 sample for higher ratios to occur in the more upland townships of the riding. The impression given in table 12.3 is even more strongly enforced by map 6, where the distributions within wapentakes are more clearly discernible. It may well be that upland townships experienced sufficient increases in land values, and comparatively lower pressures on the local rates, to permit a genuine lightening of the burden of taxation in comparison to the vale. But this is merely a clue worth pursuing, and the pattern should be considered as still uninterpreted.

Apart from the higher ratios found principally in upland townships, there are no significant patterns to be discerned from the 1830 sample in the spatial distribution of ratios. The highest ratio in the riding, found at Old Malton in Ryedale, occurs on soils which are almost entirely within the lower edge of a large area of sandstone, a condition not unlike that shared by numerous other townships with far lower ratios. Nor do the urban characteristics of the town explain the ratio. The more prosperous, wholly urban, and neighbouring parish of New Malton produced a nominal ratio on land of 5:1, doubtless reflecting an ancient level of valuation; but the 1803 poor returns reported New Malton at rack rent with a local poundage rate on land of 2s. 8d., which converts to a ratio of 7.5:1. There can be no doubt that the apparent differences between the neighbouring townships in relation to tax burden were real ones. The southeastern portions of the wapentake of Bulmer display a strikingly tight pattern of ratios which range in the thirties. But again the pattern bears no relationship to expected variations in land values. The pattern begins on large stretches of sand and gravel near the City of York, moves through boulder clays in Bossall parish and then on to the upland limestones of the Howardian Hills. Micro-level inspection simply comparing soils with ratios fails everywhere one looks.

But on comparing soils and reported actual rental values with valuational rents per acre as reported in the 1810 land tax duplicates, a more promising pattern emerges for explaining the distribution of ratios. Upland townships are unsatisfactory for such an analysis due to the distortions in rent per acre created by the presence of large amounts of waste. The returns for Gilling East wapentake in 1810 are therefore especially suitable in that valuational rents are fully reported at an early date, affording comparisons with average regional rentals reported by contemporaries; the townships all lie in the lowland zone and contain little waste or common; and there are no significant urban centres. Table 12.4 groups the townships into four soil types and summarizes the average valuational rent per acre for each soil region. The range of variation among the townships of soil type I is disturbingly wide, but the average value is surprisingly close – perhaps too close – to average rentals found on the boulder clays of the Vale of Cleveland and the upper Vale of Mowbray by Arthur Young during his 1770 tour. Young suggested an average rental per acre of 17s. 6d. in this region. Thirty years later John Tuke, a local land surveyor, still

Table 12.3:
Mean ratio of total valuational rent to total tax, by wapentake, North Riding, c. 1830

Wapentake	Ratio
Allertonshire	18.7
Birdforth	35.9
Bulmer	27.6
Gilling East	27.7
Gilling West*	26.6
Hallikeld	26.4
Hang East	28.5
Hang West*	46.1
Langbaurgh*	30.2
Pickering Lythe*	41.2
Ryedale*	38.7
Whitby Strand*	–
Riding	29.1

Note: Wapentakes which are principally upland are asterisked.
Source: Appendix J.

Table 12.4
Average valuational rent per acre of townships grouped by soil type, Gilling East, 1810

Soil type	Description	Cases	Mean	Range
I	Boulder clay.	17	£.86	£.62–1.16
II	Mostly sand and gravel but some lacustrine clay and a smaller amount of boulder clay.	8	.90	.50–1.30
III	Principally alluvium and river terraces.	3	1.04	.92–1.11
IV	Principally boulder clay but substantial magnesium limestone deposits.	1	1.23	

Source: Table 12.5.

found that "the average rent of farms of pretty good soil [in the riding as a whole] is from 15 to 21 shillings per acre."[3] These nearly contemporary estimates also conform well with those townships sharing soil type II, especially if one were to set aside the outlying values in Newby Wiske and Warlaby. The magnesium limestone and mining soils of Middleton Tyas produce suitably higher values. But the three townships in soil type III are puzzling. Arthur Young found lower values, ranging from 10s. to 12s. 6d. on the alluvium and river terraces. Yet the land tax produces a rise in values in this region.

Nevertheless, taking the wapentake as a whole, the evidence might incline one to the conclusion that the total valuational rent reported in the 1810 land tax in this particular portion of the riding, while somewhat low given the sharply rising secular trends in rents after 1800, did not depart widely from actual rents being paid. One cannot pronounce with equal confidence on the level of the valuation for any single township within the wapentake, however, since individual departures from the wapentake mean were substantial in 1810,[4] and in 1803 the valuations of townships for the land tax were often well below that for the poor rate (table 12.5). It is unlikely that many townships within the wapentake were reporting full actual rentals, much less rack rents, as valuations. Nor is it prudent to generalize too easily from Gilling East to the remainder of the riding, especially since Gilling East is peculiar in its inclination to report rent. It should be remembered, too, that any close analysis of valuational rents per acre employs data which is distorted to some degree by differential rates of revaluation and by the local pressures which cause such revaluations. Within Gilling East the per-acre rentals of Ellerton upon Swale, whose total valuational rentals steadily increased by over 98 percent during the years 1790 to 1830, are simply not comparable to those of Kirby Wiske, whose valuation seems to have remained unaltered throughout the same period (appendix D). On the whole it would not be entirely implausible, judging only from soil comparisons, to conclude that valuations in Gilling East were set at levels that approached but generally did not equal rack rent.[5]

But the evidence from soil comparisons and contemporary reports of regional average rentals is inherently vague and difficult to interpret. It would appear from such evidence that valuational rents within most townships fell short of both actual and rack rentals; but if comparative regional and national estimates of the land tax burden are to be undertaken, then it is important to determine how often, and in what magnitudes, such shortfalls occurred. The evidence we have been examining is too crude and inconsistent to provide such statistics.

Any remaining doubts that rack rent, at least, seldom provided a basis for land tax valuation may be further allayed by a perusal of the 1803 poor law report. In that report local poundage rates for the poor rate are given and rack rent, when it acted as a basis for the valuation, is indicated.[6] Table 12.6 indicates the number of townships reporting rack rent valuations for the poor rate in the three ridings of Yorkshire. If the county were typical, we would have to conclude the practice was rare indeed. Even in the East Riding, where thirty-one townships employed rack rent, twenty-two of those townships were within one wapentake division, Hunsley Beacon. But Yorkshire is not typical. Appendix L tabulates the evidence from the 1803 report from every county of England and Wales. Rack rent

Table 12.5
Total valuational rent per acre according to the land tax and the poor law report, Gilling East, 1803 and 1810

Township	Soil type	Poor rate 1803	Land tax 1803	Land tax 1810
Ainderby Steeple	II	.88	.83	.85
Barton	I	.99		1.10
Brompton on Swale	III	1.12		1.11
Cleasby	I	.70	.70	.70
Cowton, East	I	.91	.83	.99
Cowton, North	I	.80		.85
Cowton, South	I	.64	.65	.70
Croft	I	.58	.52	.70
Dalton upon Tees	I	.76	.68	1.16
Danby Wiske	I	.64	.62	.72
Ellerton upon Swale, Bolton on Swale and Whitwell	III	1.76	.94	1.10
Eryholme	I	.73		.82
Kiplin	I	.77	.79	1.04
Kirby Wiske	II	.94	.83	.83
Langton, Great	I	.63	.62	.62
Langton, Little	I	.87	.76	.76
Manfield	I	.84	.60	.78
Maunby	II	.93	.91	.84
Middleton Tyas	IV	1.04	1.12	1.23
Morton upon Swale	II	.92	.93	.92
Moulton	I	.63	.64	.64
Newby Wiske	II	.78	.46	.50
Newton Morrell	I	1.07	1.07	1.07
Scorton and Uckerby	III	.89	.75	.92
Smeaton, Great	I	1.08	.92	.92
Stapleton	I	.94	.98	.98
Thrintoft	II	1.06	.85	.96
Warlaby	II	.84	1.30	1.30
Yafforth	II	1.02	1.02	1.02

SUMMARY

	N	Mean	Stand. Dev
Poor rate 1803			
All cases	29	.89	.23
Cases reported in land tax	25	.88	.24
Excluding Newby Wiske and Warlaby	23	.89	.24
Land tax 1803			
All cases reported	25	.81	.20
Excluding Newby Wiske and Warlaby	23	.81	.16
Land tax 1810	29	.90	.19

Source: Geological Survey, drift maps (soil classifications); PP 1803–04 (175) XIII 610–12 (computed rents); Land tax duplicates, NYCRO; 6-inch Ordnance Survey of Yorkshire, (acreages).

Table 12.6

Townships reporting poor law valuations at rack rent, Yorkshire, 1803

Riding	No. of reporting townships	No. reporting at rack rent	% reporting at rack rent
East	422	31	7.4
North	532	8	1.5
West	644	33	5.1
COUNTY	1,598	72	4.5

Source: PP 1803–04 (175) XIII 586–656.

most commonly formed the basis for poor rate valuations in Norfolk, where it was reported for almost 22 percent of the parishes. In Radnor the proportion at rack was 12.7 percent, in Surrey and Middlesex 7.3 and 6.7 percent respectively. Between 5 and 6 percent of the parishes reported valuations at rack rent in Hertfordshire and Westmorland. No other counties achieved the totals of Yorkshire. The percentage for all of England was 2.8 percent and for Wales 0.9 percent. Clearly there was no general tendency to establish valuations for the poor rate at rack rent. Nor can it be assumed that rack rent formed a basis for land tax valuations.

An impression of how far townships normally departed from rack rents, and how erratic such departures were among the townships of a single county and among the counties themselves, may be gleaned from the observations pertaining to each county and appended to the 1803 report. The clerk of the peace of each county was asked to report "the usual Proportion of the Rated Rental to the Rack Rental in your County or District." The Yorkshire replies were not uncharacteristic. The clerk of the peace for the East Riding reported that the relationship in his wapentakes was "irregular; but I believe it will, on an average, be about Three-Fourths." In the North Riding the clerk of the peace was "not able to state any Thing satisfactory" on the subject; while in the West Riding the clerk of the peace, from the best information he could collect, reported the proportion to be "One-third, or somewhat higher." The evidence from the clerks throughout England and Wales (appendix L) generally confirms the reports in Eden (appendix H), that most valuations were set at levels which departed by three-quarters to one-half from what was locally understood to be rack rent. Variations in practice within counties was so great that twenty-one clerks from England and Wales could return no satisfactory answer to the query. There is no doubt whatever that contemporaries, and very well informed ones, believed the proportion to be highly variable within their counties, but they were substantially ignorant of the precise nature of the relationship. It behooves modern historians to be commensurately cautious.

What does this regional investigation of patterns of valuational rent as reported in the land tax demonstrate? Perhaps most importantly it demonstrates that the land tax valuational rents as such cannot provide the basis for any firm conclusions regarding the burden of the tax. Ratios of rent to tax appear to be generally higher in upland regions of the riding, but there is nothing in this evidence which reveals why this should be so. When looking for patterns at more micro levels, no convincing ones can be found. Ratios fail to reveal any patterns of correlation with soil type; and while most urban townships tend to have higher ratios, many are lower than one would expect. Indeed the small, wholly urban and thriving township of New Malton produced one of the lowest ratios in the riding while its more rural neighbour, Old Malton, produced the highest.

The relationship between the valuational levels for the land tax and some constant measure (such as rack rent) of full rental value differed among the townships, and therein lies the problem. Contemporary evidence of average actual rents per acre on a regional basis suggests that land tax valuations were in general not wildly different than actual rents; but land tax rents were almost certainly at considerably lower levels in most townships. They were rarely set at rack rent. How much lower they were set than actual rents is not apparent in the evidence examined here. What we can conclude with more certainty is that land tax valuational rents generally departed erratically and substantially from rack rents (probably by 25 to 50 percent or more), and probably to a lesser degree from actual rents, and that the ratios based on valuational rents themselves varied over a wide range throughout the riding, even among contiguous townships. Such a wide range of variation in ratio strongly suggests that the burden of the land tax was distributed in a most unequal fashion among the townships of the riding.

But these ratios based on valuational rents for the land tax cannot reveal precisely what the degree of inequality might have been. The ratios are deficient in two important respects. First, such ratios, by departing significantly and erratically from full rents (whether rack or actual), must substantially underestimate the inequality among townships. If we are to be more precise, then a fuller series must be utilized. But we must also know how the valuations of each township departed from a constant standard of measurement such as rack rent, and therein lies the second problem: the internal comparability of the series. Ratios of rent to tax are only comparable if the departures in valuational totals from a constant standard are themselves comparable. Neither a series based on full rental value nor a fully comparable series can be achieved, of course, because the data for constructing such a series does not exist. Rack rents cannot systematically be established. Nor can the actual rents paid be determined for all properties. And even if actual gross rents could be known, such a series would lack comparability for measurements based on real wealth, since not all landlords levied full economic rents, and owner-occupiers paid none. Nor were all properties comparably or fully improved.

Despite these deficiencies in the data, it is possible to approximate a satisfactory solution to the problem. Several systematic valuations of real wealth in the North Riding exist for the early nineteenth century, the land tax series being only one of them. We shall therefore turn our attention in the next chapter to constructing fuller and more reliable estimates of the land tax burden by determining, first, which of the available valuation series *maximally* estimates real property in each township of the riding. In chapter 14 these maximal, and therefore more accurate, estimates will be further tested throughout the three ridings of Yorkshire by evaluating the inherent plausibility of the regional patterns they produce. A more comparable series should thus also be achieved. This new rental series will then be employed throughout Yorkshire to compute new rent-to-tax ratios which will more accurately and reliably measure regional inequalities in tax burden. In chapter 15 this new method will be applied to fourteen additional and regionally distributed counties of England and, at an aggregate level, to every county of England and Wales.

CHAPTER THIRTEEN

A Method for Estimating Inequalities in the Regional and National Distribution of the Land Tax: Finding a Maximum Valuation Series

A search for a maximum series of real property values that will measure inter-township and regional differences in the burden of the land tax is governed by two constraints. First, the values must be available for all, or at least a large proportion, of the townships of England and Wales. Documents such as estate records, where accurate accounts of actual rental values may be obtained, are available for only a small and unrepresentative minority of holdings in any region and often do not even include all of the real property of the township within which they lie. They are therefore wholly unsuitable for a regional or national survey of land tax burdens which is based on ratios of total rental value to total tax quota. Only those valuational series which were systematically collected and reported by national or local government can be of any value for such a purpose. The problem lies in determining which of the available governmental series report valuations that most nearly and consistently approximate full rental values. There are four such series available in the North Riding of Yorkshire, where our tests for a maximum series will be made. The ''rent'' valuations reported in the land tax duplicates of 1826–32 comprise one of those series. As we have seen, the land tax valuations are incomplete in the North Riding, being reported on only 41 percent of the duplicates. But that sample, while statistically unrepresentative in any strict sense, is nevertheless large and widely distributed. It is probable that equivalently large and well distributed samples could be drawn from the duplicates of other counties. The land tax valuations will therefore be tested against the other available series of the North Riding for the fullness of their values.

A second constraint in the search for a maximal series of rental values is related to the chronological period in which the valuations were made and reported. Let us say, for example, that we were able to obtain two full series of valuations from two different types of documents, one made and reported in 1790, the second in 1815. It would be impossible to determine which of those two independently compiled series reported rental values more fully. A simple direct comparison would fail because actual rentals between those dates more than doubled on many large estates in the riding, but did not equivalently increase within all townships or on all estates. During the years 1815–30, actual rentals tended to stabilize throughout the North Riding, and indeed throughout the country. Where declines were erratic and regional, they were not to a degree which would unduly disturb comparisons in the magnitudes of valuations. If Gilling East wapentake is characteristic, during those years valuation totals tended to stabilize along with actual rentals (appendix E). It can therefore be argued that any valuational series reported between 1815 and 1830 can usefully be directly compared in their magnitudes, allowing for acceptable margins of error. If we accept only large differences as significant (remembering that declines in actual rentals nationally during those years are believed to have been generally on an order of 10 to 15 percent), then that series which reports the highest levels of values may be accepted as reporting values which are genuinely more full and therefore which more closely approach rack rent.[1] One of the four available valuation series, the one derivable from the 1803 poor law report, must be excluded from the comparison, since it lies within a period of steeply increasing actual rentals.

There are three North Riding series which report valuations systematically for all or nearly all townships and which fall within the 1815 to 1830 period of relatively stable rents. The first is the series reported in the land tax duplicates themselves from 1826–32. The deficiencies of this series, consisting principally in its wide range of departures from a constant standard such as rack rent, have already been noted. But we shall compare the land tax series against the remaining two, in order to determine which series tends more consistently to report the highest values. Underlying this approach is the assumption that a series with higher values inherently allows less latitude for large departures from true values, or rack rent. Estimation error is thereby reduced and some degree of standardization is achieved, making comparisons more meaningful.

A second series of valuations we shall employ are those reported for schedule A of the property tax. Normally these are only available in our period at the township level for 1815; but in 1824, when undertaking revaluations for the county rate, the North Riding magistrates obtained the schedule A valuations for the property tax as returned to the Board of Taxes for the year 1814. These 1814 returns will be used in the analysis that follows (even though the 1815 returns are available and will be employed in other administrative counties) for three reasons: the 1814 returns are more detailed, giving shillings and pence; they only rarely depart more than marginally from the 1815 values (table 13.1); and they are the property tax series used by the magistrates in settling the valuations of 1824 and are therefore more appropriate for other internal comparisons within the riding. Schedule A of the property tax is, with two exceptions, precisely equivalent to the land tax in the wealth included in its valuations: The schedule includes all gross income accruing to owners of land, houses, tithes, mines of all types, quarries, water works, iron works and inland navigations. The early nineteenth century land tax returns irregularly included two additional categories of taxable wealth: stock-in-trade and the salaries of certain government officials such as excisemen and customs officers. The calculations which follow will exclude the latter two categories from land tax valuations, where they occur, in order to ensure comparability with the other two series.

Unlike the land tax or the local rates, the property tax was actively and closely administered by a centralized bureaucracy. After 1808 travelling inspectors oversaw the process of valuation in the countryside, and all modern authorities agree that by the time the tax was repealed, in 1816, its administration and collection had reached a high degree of efficiency. Schedule A has been thought to be particularly reliable because of the visibility of the wealth being valued and the way in which it was defined in the statutes. But in one respect the schedule may be misleading. Statute required that its real property valuations be based on gross rack rent, exempting only cottages with an annual rent of £2 or less. But rack rents could not always be determined. In practice rental contracts and sales concluded within the previous seven years, being attuned to market conditions, were taken to be equivalent to rack rent. But not all farmland and houses had been recently sold or leased, or were even leased at all. Current rental and sale values would therefore seem to have been mixed in the valuations with rents and sales figures which were longer established and unrevised. Certainly visual comparisons with other local properties were often undertaken, especially for owner-occupied lands and houses, and in some cases special valuations were authorized by statute. But for our purposes no more than a rough consistency need be expected from the property tax series. With this caution in mind, however, there is every reason to believe it was as internally consistent as any series contemporaries were capable of constructing.[2]

A third and final series we shall employ in our search for maximum valuations is that which was reported to Quarter Sessions by the overseers of the poor for each township of the North Riding, after a general revaluation was ordered for the county rate in 1824. In the early nineteenth century the county rate was undergoing substantial transformation, in the North Riding and throughout England. A full understanding of the nature and reliability of the 1824 North Riding valuations requires an understanding of the process and pressures that produced them. The legislative history and nature of the county rate has recently been well recounted by John

Table 13.1
The 1814 property tax as a percentage of the 1815 property tax, all townships, North Riding

Numbered columns: 1 = Allertonshire wapentake; 2 = Birdforth wapentake; 3 = Bulmer wapentake; 4 = Gilling East wapentake; 5 = Gilling West wapentake; 6 = Hallikeld wapentake; 7 = Hang East wapentake; 8 = Hang West wapentake; 9 = Langbaurgh wapentake; 10 = Pickering Lythe wapentake; 11 = Ryedale wapentake; 12 = Whitby Strand wapentake

%	1	2	3	4	5	6	7	8	9	10	11	12	All cases N	All cases %
0.0–4.9														
5.0–9.9														
10.0–14.9														
15.0–19.9														
20.0–24.9														
25.0–29.9														
30.0–34.9														
35.0–39.9														
40.0–44.9		1											1	0.2
45.0–49.9														
50.0–54.9														
55.0–59.9														
60.0–64.9														
65.0–69.9														
70.0–74.9	1	1	1										3	0.6
75.0–79.9			1										1	0.2
80.0–84.9														
85.0–89.9	1							1	1				3	0.6
90.0–94.9								2	3	1			6	1.2
95.0–99.9	3	5						7	20	2		3	40	8.3

Table 13.1 continued

%	1	2	3	4	5	6	7	8	9	10	11	12	All cases N	All cases %
100.0–104.9	25	37	57	29	41	26	30	28	48	27	44	9	401	83.0
105.0–109.9									3				3	0.6
110.0–114.9	1								1				2	0.4
115.0–119.9														
120.0–124.9														
125.0–129.9														
130.0–134.9														
135.0–139.9														
140.0–144.9														
145.0–149.9									1				1	0.2
≥150.0		2									1		3	0.6
def.						1			3	6	3		13	2.7
NR		1	1		1					2	1		6	1.2
N	31	47	60	29	42	27	30	38	80	38	49	12	483	100.0
Mean	98.8	99.9	98.9	100.0	100.0	100.0	100.0	99.1	99.7	99.4	102.2	100.0	99.8	
Minimum	72.4	43.2	73.7	100.0	100.0	100.0	100.0	89.4	88.1	93.0	100.0	99.6	43.2	
Maximum	113.3	198.2	100.2	100.1	100.5	100.1	100.1	100.4	148.4	100.1	371.4	100.8	371.4	

Note: def. = defective. NR = no return.
Source: Appendix M.

Beckett.[3] Suffice it to say that during the eighteenth century a great hodgepodge of statutory responsibilities had been assigned to this rate, whose proceeds went into the county treasury. By 1785, Burn's *Justice of the Peace* was able to list twenty-five separate types of charges for which this one rate was responsible, ranging from the maintenance of militia men's families to the construction and repair of county roads, bridges, and gaols and the prosecution, conveying, and maintenance of prisoners.[4] By the late eighteenth century by far the most onerous burden on the tax in most counties related to the expenses associated with criminal justice, although in upland divisions such as the North Riding the expenses of bridge repair and construction could also be quite significant.

The basis for the county rate was once again quite similar to that of the land tax and property tax, provided stock-in-trade and salary entries are deducted from the former. There is one further incompatibility in the county rate which could be significant in some regions of the country, however. The valuational basis of the county rate was identical to that of the poor rate, and indeed, after 1739, statute provided that the county rate simply be collected as an addition or appendage to the poor rate and paid into the county treasury as a surplus from poor rate funds. As a result the county rate, like the poor rate, was assessed only on coal mines, rather than on all mines, and only on saleable underwoods, rather than on all woodlands. Entries in these categories cannot be deleted from the property tax aggregates and are not always clearly or consistently identified in the land tax. In the North Riding the only troubling case that can be identified arises from the Swaledale lead mines of Gilling West, most notably in the townships of Muker and Melbecks.[5] The incompatibility thus does not appear to impose significant impediments to the establishment of a maximal valuation series in the North Riding.

Before 1815 the county rate was perhaps the classic example of a tax being collected on the basis of parish or township quotas which were truly ancient in their origins.[6] A few counties revised their allocations shortly after the passage in 1739 of 12 Geo. II c. 29. But the courts quickly came to interpret that statute as prohibiting general quota revisions within counties. By the end of the century, clerks of the peace in most counties could not identify the provenance or origins of the quota systems they were administering. Before the later eighteenth century the pressures to revise were perhaps not very great, since the burden of the tax had always been relatively light. But, towards the end of the century, the county rate shared in the general explosion of local administrative expenses and began to rise alarmingly. Between 1792 and 1832, collections for the county rate rose nationally by 148 percent, not so sharp a rise perhaps as the 251 percent experienced after 1784 by the poor rate, but quite enough to propel many local communities desperately into action. Between 1797 and 1814, six counties revalued for the county rate by introducing private bills in the House. Finally, in 1815, Parliament broke the prohibitions of 1739 by passing general enabling legislation (55 Geo. III c. 51). By the early 1830s almost 65 percent of the counties and administrative divisions of England and Wales had valuations for the county rate which had been freshly revised at least once since 1800 (table 13.2 and appendix N). After 1830 the incidence and frequency of revaluation, in the county rate as in all others, increased rapidly. Indeed it is not too much to say that the early decades of the nineteenth century, and especially the 1830s, witnessed a fiscal revolution in the countryside that, under the compelling impetus of soaring administrative expenses, permanently and fundamentally altered the nature of local government. Especially in those communities experiencing rapid economic and demographic growth, this revolution contributed materially and irreversibly to changes in the very fabric and texture of English society.

The impetus for revising the county rate, not only in Yorkshire but throughout England, did not arise from any sense of internal inequalities in the distribution of the tax within individual parishes or townships. The complaints were more regional in nature. They were directed against the outdated quota systems which assigned the burdens of the rate disproportionately to the agricultural districts of a county. Oddly enough, all contemporary evidence indicates that the commercial and industrializing districts, which had grown enormously in population and wealth during the preceding one hundred years, did not seriously object to the prospect of revaluations which would shift significantly heavier burdens of the tax onto their districts; and after the revaluations occurred and new quotas were assigned, these non-agricultural districts, in counties such as Lancashire and the West Riding, did not appeal the results. It may be that they had feared an even worse result; indeed there is evidence that they felt the justice of the redistribution. George Broadrick, a leading West Riding magistrate, whose seat at Hampole Stubbs lay in an agricultural district seven miles northwest of the commercial centre of Doncaster, testified to the unrest of the agricultural gentry of such districts before a committee of the House of Commons in 1834:

> When I first undertook to examine the accounts [in 1831], it was evident that the old rate [stemming from a property-tax-based fresh valuation and reassignment of quotas in 1817] bore very unequally on the agricultural and commercial interests, and that such towns as Sheffield, which had increased in importance and value, and from whence crime emanates in the proportion of 28 cases out of 32, should be called upon to contribute in a larger proportion.

Table 13.2
Bases of valuations for the county rate in sixty administrative counties, England and Wales, c. 1815

Basis	No.	%
Property tax alone	20	33.9
Property tax plus another basis	2	3.4
Rack rent	1	1.7
Other (such as overseer returns)	15	25.4
Old valuation (a. 1800)	11	18.6
Unknown or not reported	10	17.0
TOTAL	59	100.0

Source: Appendix N.

By 1831, only fourteen years after an initial revaluation for quotas, even the commercial districts of the West Riding were complaining loudly. In that year, again under pressures from the agricultural districts and on a motion of Broadrick, the West Riding sessions formed its first standing finance committee, under Broadrick's chairmanship, a measure which led to greatly reduced expenditures. By 1834 a general revaluation of the riding was under way; this time, under the close supervision of the magistrates, it employed standardizing techniques that had been pioneered in 1829 in Lancashire and widely employed in other counties thereafter.

Similar pressures for tax redistributions had long been felt within Yorkshire as a whole. But these were not aimed at the internal inter-township distributions within the East or North Ridings so much as at the proportionate burdens assigned to each of the ridings in meeting the common fiscal obligations of the historical county.[7] By the early 1820s the two predominantly agricultural ridings were complaining, like Broadrick and the West Riding gentry, that the frighteningly soaring burdens on the county rate were arising principally from criminal prosecutions originating in the industrial West Riding. And, to make matters worse, extensive and expensive alterations to the county prison at York Castle were proposed by a committee of magistrates at the 1823 assizes and begun three years later. For some years the West Riding magistrates, contrary to the wishes of the East and North Riding sessions, had been sending convicted felons to the prison, thus swelling its population and increasing the cost and complexity of its per-capita administration. Despite the cessation of this practice in 1824, and an initial drop in the number of prisoners, the prison population rose from 89 in 1824 to 162 in 1833. The new prison wing built to hold these prisoners was completed in 1835, at a total cost to the county of a staggering £203,000. It is little wonder that the East and North Ridings, seeing such costs as stemming from conditions in the industrial West Riding, reacted sharply to these developments.[8]

The East Riding made the first move. In 1823 the North Riding summer sessions received a letter from Richard Bethell of Rise, chairman of the East Riding sessions,

respecting the Proportions in which the several Ridings have contributed to the general Expenses of the County for the last seventy four years [i.e. since the revisions following the act of 1739], the great change which has since taken place in the comparative value of the rateable Property in the different Ridings and the propriety of making a more equal Rate previous to the great Expense likely to be incurred by the proposed alterations of the Castle of York.

The North Riding magistrates agreed to take the matter into consideration at their Michaelmas sessions the following October. In that second meeting the bench warmly concurred with the proposal and undertook to join both the East Riding and West Riding in negotiations which would lead to an "equalization" of the rate between the three ridings. By the summer of 1825 the North Riding sessions was ready to delegate one of its members to lay a proposal to that effect before the general sessions of the county during the next Lent assize week. It was in preparation for such negotiations that the riding decided in 1823 to get its own house in order. In October a revaluation of quotas for the county rate within the North Riding in accordance with 55 Geo. III c. 51 was proposed. At Christmas sessions the proposal was accepted, and directions were given to the clerk of the peace to immediately distribute notices for carrying the same into effect.

The justices seem hardly to have realized the complexity of the undertaking they had set in motion. The general process and its associated problems faced by the North Riding justices were well expressed in the programme distributed by the clerk of the peace of the West Riding on the eve of that riding's revaluation in 1833:

To obtain the relative value of one township to another, the most obvious method is to ascertain the real *bona fide* annual value of each township; in other words, the rack rent, or actual rent, for which every description of property either is or might be let. It is well known to be frequently the case, indeed generally it is so, that townships are valued at one-half, one-third, two-thirds, and various other proportions of the *bona fide* annual value, and in the same township different kinds of property are rated in different proportions. Now, the equality of the county rate would be the same if the whole Riding were rated at one-half, or one-third, or two-thirds, or any other proportion of the actual value; but as that is not the case, the most simple mode of arriving at an equalization of this rate is by endeavouring to ascertain the *bona fide* annual value. It is therefore suggested to the magistrates

> that they should impress upon the overseers, and other parochial officers within their divisions, that it will not be sufficient to return that annual value of their townships upon which the parochial rates are assessed, unless that value be the actual *bona fide* value, or rack rent, which may be the case in some instances. In many cases, and indeed in most cases, the proportion is well known which the rated value bears to the actual value, and in such cases the actual value is easily obtained by calculation.

Broadrick, in his testimony before the House of Commons, also noted that the West Riding magistrates possessed a detailed local knowledge of property values in their divisions and were able to apply that knowledge in revising the overseers' returns: "generally speaking, they could give the fair average value of each township." If this was true of the West Riding magistrates, one would suppose that the more bucolic bench of the North Riding would be even more intimately informed and better positioned to effect revisions. Well, then, surely the process of inter-township revaluation, whatever its difficulties, proceeded with some smoothness in the North Riding.

It did not. The North Riding may have been more bucolic than the West Riding, but it was also clearly more stiffly conservative and entrenched in tradition. In these rural counties the ancient traditions of the local community were still very much alive and well. The entire process of original revaluation broke down completely in Yorkshire, even in the West Riding on its first attempt in 1817. We shall follow the story of this failed attempt in some detail in the North Riding, where the evidence is unusually rich. Much can be learned from this story about the general process and problems of revaluation for all forms of rating, especially at the inter-township level.

The instructions from the North Riding bench in December 1823 had set the riding into motion, but not to anyone's satisfaction. Judging from the simplicity and vagueness of their initial instructions, the magistrates who had assembled in December seem to have anticipated a straightforward procedure. If so, they were naive. By April 1824, when the magistrates assembled at Easter sessions, they were clearly exasperated, perhaps even angry, and arguing both among themselves and with the overseers as to the proper mode and basis for revaluation. Many of the returns received from townships were obviously deficient. Often they merely conveyed a valuation which departed from full values in a locally traditional manner. Numerous other townships had as yet made no return at all, and it is clear that some justices were refusing to enforce the instructions of sessions in their own divisions. The court reacted sharply and with energy, and over the next twelve months did everything in its power to effect a full and fair revaluation of the riding. It began by issuing the following detailed instructions at the 1824 Easter sessions.

It appearing to this Court as well from the great deficiency of Returns for the purposes of the County Rate directed at the last Sessions to be made of the rateable Property in the several Parishes Townships &c. throughout the North Riding as also by the statements made by many of the Justices now assembled that great difference of opinion has prevailed and considerable doubts have arisen respecting the Principles upon which the Court wished them to proceed in receiving the said Returns. – The Court without either intending to control such discretionary powers as the Law has vested in the Justices in their respective Divisions or doubting their readiness and anxiety to carry its orders into effect are nevertheless of opinion that some general expression of the view they take of the subject will materially tend to remove the present unsettled state of practice and facilitate the objects contemplated by their order. –

It must be obvious to the Magistrates that unless one uniform standard and scale of assessing the rateable Property throughout the Riding be adopted the result will be a Rate deficient in its primary ingredient, Equality – Independently also of Equality another principle of the County Rate is that it is an ad valorum Rate or in other words a full and fair assessment of the actual value of such Property as is by Law rateable; – and in order to establish this – the Court suggest the following Rules as applicable to all cases where any difficulties may arise. –

First – That the Returns do contain a true account of the full and fair value of all such Property in the respective Townships &c. – as is by Law rateable to the Poors' Rate. –

Secondly, – When the same is Let to Tennants without fraud collusion or favor and the actual Rent can be ascertained such Rent [is] to be taken as the Value; but in cases where it shall appear to the said Justices that the actual value exceeds the Rent such value alone without reference to the Rent shall be taken as the fair annual value for the purposes of the said Returns. –

Thirdly – In cases of Persons occupying their own Property the value of such Property [is] to be estimated with reference to the rent or value (taken as aforesaid) of other Property of the same nature quality and situation in the same Township. –

Fourthly – With respect to the valuation of Houses and Land occupied by small Freeholders maintaining themselves chiefly by farming the Court suggest that such Houses should be valued separately in such cases only where House Duty is paid. –

Fifthly – In estimating the value of Rateable Property particularly small parcels of Land in the vicinity of large and populous Towns and Villages which obtain an enhanced value and are Let at Rents probably exceeding the actual Produce of such Land in consequence of their contiguity to the said Towns and Villages: – The Court upon mature deliberation are of opinion that such enhanced Value to what causes soever it is owing is the value at which the same ought to be charged to the County Rate. –

The Court are desirous if possible of obviating the necessity of a general valuation of the Riding and hope that by the strenuous and united attention of the

Justices in their respective Divisions acting upon one uniform system, Returns satisfactory to the Court and beneficial to the whole Riding may be obtained – With this view the Court hope that the above expression of their opinion and the principles which will best conduct the Justices to a safe conclusion operating equally in every part and on all the Rateable Property in the Riding will meet with a corresponding attention by the said Justices in their Divisions, and the Court in furtherance of this object respites the time for receiving the remainder of the said Returns until the next Midsummer Sessions. –

By Midsummer sessions, the following July, the court found that several townships had still failed to make returns and that numerous returns received by the clerk of the peace remained deficient. The magistrates therefore decided on a more direct line of action.

It appearing to the Court that notwithstanding its Orders at the last Quarter Sessions several of the Returns directed to be made for the purpose of equalizing the County Rate have not yet been delivered to the Clerk of the Peace: – Ordered that the Clerk of the Peace do write to the Churchwardens and Overseers of the Poor of such Townships as have made default; and to the Clerks of the Magistrates in the respective Divisions within which the same are situate requiring such Returns to be made without delay, and that the same be transmitted to his Office on or before the 27.th day of August next – And that such said Returns be made in strict conformity with the Rules laid down in the Orders of the Easter Sessions. – And as considerable doubts have been expressed whether the Returns already made by the respective Divisions are made upon one uniform principle of Valuation Ordered that the following Gentlemen be appointed a Committee for the purpose of comparing and equalizing the same (namely) –

Allertonshire	Richard W.C. Peirse Esqre
Birdforth	The Revd William Dent
Bulmer	The Revd William Dealtry
Gilling East	The Earl of Tyrconnel
Gilling West	The Revd William Wharton
Hang East	The Hon. Thomas Monson
Hang West	Foster L. Coore Esqre
Hallikeld	John C. Ramsden Esqre
Langbarugh East	John Wharton Esqre
Langbarugh West	Bartholomew Rudd Esqre
Pickering Lythe East	Thomas Mitchelson Esqre
Pickering Lythe West	Sir George Cayley Bar.^{t}
Rydale	Charles Duncombe Esqre
Whitby Strand	James Wilson Esqre

And that five of the said Committee be a Quorum, and that the Committee be open to all other Justices of the Riding who can make it convenient to attend. – And that the first Meeting of the said Committee be holden at the Sessions House in Northallerton on Friday the 27.th Day of August next at Eleven o'Clock in the forenoon. – And the Court delegates to the said Committee all the powers and provisions which the Statute 55th Geo. 3rd Chap. 51 has enacted for assessing the County Rate. – And Orders that all the Returns from the respective Divisions be laid before them; – that they be empowered to Summon and examine Witnesses, – to call such professional Assistance as they think proper, – and to direct Valuations of any particular Townships to be made in order to inform themselves of the actual value of the several Rateable Properties rated in the said Returns; – and to ascertain how far the several Divisions are rated in a fair and equal Proportion with each other; – and to take all such further measures as they think best calculated to obtain an equal Rate throughout the Riding and to report thereon to the next Sessions.

There is abundant evidence on the returns themselves that the committee was active in pursuing its mandate. A sizeable number of returns contain the committee's annotated revisions, which increased the values of some or all individual entries as well as the township total. There is every indication that a detailed scrutiny took place. It should be noted, however, that the members of the committee seem for the most part to have acted in pairs when actually undertaking revision, and that they were acting in those divisions or wapentakes where they themselves were major landed proprietors. One could argue that their efforts were biased by their own vested interests and by the need to maintain friendly relations with their neighbours and tenantry.

The evidence presented in table 13.3 could be regarded as supporting such an argument. Few landowners could have been more dominant within their divisions than was Charles Duncombe in Ryedale. Several townships in which he held large properties were significantly undervalued by their overseers. Does this mean that Duncombe, though a member of the committee, was willfully lightening the load on his own turf? It is difficult to draw that conclusion if one looks at the entire pattern. Five of his twelve townships reported at 90 percent or better of the property tax, and only three fell below the wapentake mean. One exceeded the property tax by almost one-third. Some other individual returns within the same wapentake give us further insights into the process which occurred. The magistrates noted on the return for Kirby Moorside that the valuation had been reduced by 20 percent due to economic depression. The small agricultural township of North Holme, whose lands were entirely in the hands of one non-resident proprietor and his single tenant, reported 93.2 percent

Table 13.3
Ryedale townships in which Charles Duncombe of Duncombe Park held substantial property

Township	1824 county rate as % of 1814 property tax
Bilsdale Kirkham and Midcable	84.3
Farndale East and West Side and Bransdale East Side	86.8
Gillamoor and Fadmoor	92.6
Harome	79.6
Helmsley Blackmoor	71.2
Kirby Moorside	92.4
Nawton and Beadlam	131.2
Pockley	80.6
Rievaulx	82.1
Skiplam and Bransdale West Side	96.2
Sproxton	78.7
Wombleton	101.9
WAPENTAKE MEAN	83.4

Sources: Appendix M; land tax duplicates, NYCRO.

of the property tax. That single tenant, who made the return as overseer and must himself have been a man of some substance and standing, could easily have made a lesser valuation – if anyone could do so – but he did not. Perhaps there is something to be said for an argument that pure self-interest and favouritism were at work in the countryside, but the evidence of the returns suggests the contrary. More convincing arguments would focus on the role of a tradition of self-governance, the inherent complexity of any process of revaluation, and the fears which must have arisen for other modes of assessment when anciently established procedures were disturbed. Those committee members appointed by the bench, such as Duncombe, were among the most active of the North Riding magistracy, and they seem to have engaged their task with characteristic energy and every appearance of integrity. Even so, they failed.

When the court reassembled on 18 October at Michaelmas sessions, it remained deeply suspicious and dissatisfied. It directed the clerk of the peace to apply to the Board of Taxes for the gross amounts returned for each township of the riding under schedule A of the property tax for 1814. A new committee was appointed whose task was to compare the property tax valuations for each township against those returned by the overseers of the poor for the county rate.[9] The committee was to "report to the next Sessions whether any and what alterations and amendments they would recommend to be made in the said Returns." The committee met, examined the accounts, and did not like what it found.

What it found is summarized in table 13.4, which presents the 1824 valuations, as a percentage of the 1814 property tax valuations, in the form of a frequency distribution. The riding mean of 85.5 percent shows that the general pattern within the 483 townships of the riding was to undervalue for the county rate – provided one assumes land values remained generally unchanged between 1814 and 1824 – and that is bad enough. But the truly disturbing statistics are the extraordinary spread of the departures from the valuations of the property tax. The departures ranged through the riding as a whole from 36.7 to 181 percent of the property tax. Within individual wapentakes the spread of percentages was also large. Even if one were to make a case that property values between 1814 and 1824 had in fact fallen 15 percent on average, thus making the riding mean percentage more acceptable (a dubious conclusion), it is by no means probable that alterations in the *relative* values of real property would have caused the erratic departures from that mean within the riding as a whole and within each of its wapentakes. Moreover, in some wapentakes, the patterns of dispersal, along with the means and ranges, differ sharply from the general pattern. In Bulmer the 1824 valuations range uniformly at or below the property tax, while in the adjacent wapentake of Birdforth the majority of the 1824 valuations considerably exceed the property tax. It is clear that the revising committee of magistrates appointed by the court had been utterly unable, despite all their conferred powers and local influence, to effect an "equalization" of the rate, either individually within their respective divisions or collectively within the riding as a whole.

The County Rate Committee made its report at Christmas sessions in January 1825. In effect, the magistracy threw up its hands and abandoned all effort at effecting a new and fresh valuation of the riding. Instead the sessions accepted the recommendation of the committee that the county rate quota for each division, or wapentake, be simply levied in accordance with the valuation returned for schedule A of the 1814 property tax, but reduced, characteristically, by one-third. The magistrates for each division were then empowered to impose on each of their townships whatever portion of the quota seemed "fair and equal." In the end the county rate valuation of every township in the riding was set at two-thirds of the 1814 property tax (appendix M).

How is it that the magistracy, the traditional rulers of the countryside, failed so utterly, where the royal bureaucracy administering the property tax had succeeded? For there is no mistaking the matter: The property tax inspectors do appear to have done a better job of it than the ancient machinery of local government. The magistrates themselves clearly thought so, and who should know better than they? And, as we have begun to see, the statistical evidence leads to the same conclusion. Judging from the numerous comments and annotations attached to the returns, the fault

Table 13.4
Frequency distribution, 1824 overseers' valuations for the county rate as a percentage of the 1814 property tax valuations (schedule A), all townships, North Riding

Numbered columns: 1 = Allertonshire wapentake; 2 = Birdforth wapentake; 3 = Bulmer wapentake; 4 = Gilling East wapentake; 5 = Gilling West wapentake; 6 = Hallikeld wapentake; 7 = Hang East wapentake; 8 = Hang West wapentake; 9 = Langbaurgh wapentake; 10 = Pickering Lythe wapentake; 11 = Ryedale wapentake; 12 = Whitby Strand wapentake

%	1	2	3	4	5	6	7	8	9	10	11	12	All cases N	All cases %	Summary Range	Summary % of cases[a]
0.0–4.9																
5.0–9.9															0.0–19.9	
10.0–14.9																
15.0–19.9																
20.0–24.9																
25.0–29.9															20.0–39.9	0.2
30.0–34.9																
35.0–39.9					1								1	0.2		
40.0–44.9			1					1					2	0.4		
45.0–49.9			1		1								2	0.4	40.0–59.9	6.0
50.0–54.9			3		1			3	1		2	1	11	2.3		
55.0–59.9		1	2	1				2	5	1	1		13	2.7		
60.0–64.9	1		7			2		1	5	1			17	3.5		
65.0–69.9			10		2	2		4	12		1	1	32	6.6	60.0–79.9	31.3
70.0–74.9			18	2	2	3		9	4	4	5	1	47	9.7		
75.0–79.9	1	4	9		7		1	5	9	9	4	2	51	10.6		
80.0–84.9	7	1	3	5	4	7	4	1	13	5	8	2	60	12.4		
85.0–89.9	1	1	2		2	1	6	1	15		8		37	7.7	80.0–99.9	37.1
90.0–94.9	3	4	2	8	8	2	2	4	5	5	6	1	50	10.4		

Table 13.4 continued

%	1	2	3	4	5	6	7	8	9	10	11	12	All cases N	All cases %	Summary Range	Summary % of cases[a]
95.0–99.9	2	2	1	2	3	3	6	2	2	3	1		27	5.6		
100.0–104.9	2	6	1	4	3	1	4	3	5	1	3		33	6.8		
105.0–109.9	2	7		3	1	1	4		3		3	1	25	5.2	100.0–124.9	21.3
110.0–114.9		4		2	2			1	1		1		11	2.3		
115.0–119.9	3	4			3	2	2					2	16	3.3		
120.0–124.9	3	3		2	1	2	1	1		1		1	15	3.1		
125.0–129.9	3	4									1		8	1.7		
130.0–134.9		1									1		2	0.4	≥125.0	4.0
135.0–139.9	3												3	0.6		
140.0–144.9		1											1	0.2		
145.0–149.9		1						1					2	0.4		
150.0–154.9																
155.0–159.9		1											1	0.2		
160.0–164.9		1											1	0.2		
≥165.0		1											1	0.2	90.0–109.9	28.5
def.						1				6	3		10	2.1		
NR					1					2	1		4	0.8		
N	31	47	60	29	42	27	30	38	80	38	49	12	483	100.0		
Mean	104.3	108.8	68.9	93.8	82.4	87.0	96.2	80.4	79.8	82.5	83.4	96.3	85.5			
Minimum	61.1	59.2	40.4	56.3	36.7	60.5	77.4	44.6	53.2	58.1	53.2	51.0	36.7			
Maximum	136.7	181.0	100.6	122.6	122.3	123.0	124.4	149.0	112.2	123.8	131.2	122.8	181.0			

Note: [a]Defective (def.) and no return (NR) cases are excluded from the denominator.
Source: Appendix M.

seems to lie with the overseers themselves, with the vestries to which they were responsible and which frequently directed their activities and determined their response, and with the various occupiers – often men of middling to small substance – whose willingness to cooperate restricted the capacity of the overseers to comply with their directives.

Some townships were cooperative. Several reported valuations which had recently been undertaken by professional land surveyors. Several others reported acreages for each real property other than houses and then converted those acres to monetary values. A larger number of returns reported houses and other forms of property separately from land. Some returns included properties, identified as such, which for some reason – often poverty or their small value – were normally excluded from the poor rate. The magistrates in their turn sometimes noted their rejections of traditional percentage adjustments. In the joint township of Bowes and Boldron, in Gilling West division, the magistrates noted at the bottom of the return: "20 per cent having been deducted from the Rental, ordered that it be replaced." Bowes and Boldron thus reported at 90.9 percent of the property tax in a division where the mean percentage was 82.4. The revising magistrates were not always even-handed, however. The return for Startforth township in the same division bears the following annotation: "20 per cent having been deducted from the Land on a Valuation in 1819–This is thought too much and 10 per cent allowed." While one could observe that the Startforth rental was based on a valuation completed within the previous seven years, and therefore by growing administrative convention it was tantamount to rack rent, the resulting valuation nevertheless achieved only 80.4 percent of the property tax. There may have been some favouritism shown towards Startforth, but such instances are rarely documented. In both Hang East and Pickering Lythe divisions, the magistrates corrected long-standing anomalies in reassigning small portions of farms and estates to the neighbouring townships in which they actually lay. Evidence of this type strongly suggests that, within their own divisions, the magistrates, and especially the committee of revising magistrates, in general earnestly sought to enforce a valuational process which was both meticulous and fair, and in many instances they received a large measure of cooperation.

There is reason to believe that the effort often failed – despite this spirit of diligence and cooperation – due to procedures which were inconsistent. One township which reported its land in acres, for example, converted those acres to rental values by a constant factor. The joint townships of Bedale and Firby in Hang East division, after separately reporting all of their non-landed properties, then appended two summary entries listing separately the total summary values of land for Bedale and for Firby. The lands of Bedale and Firby had been converted at £1 10s. and £1 3s. per acre, respectively, and the township as a whole reported at 96.5 percent of the 1814 property tax. But, within the riding, no other townships reporting acres had employed a standard conversion factor. Catterick, lying within the same division, reported with widely varying acreage values, and most of its values were at £2 per acre or greater. It returned a county rate valuation that was 84.4 percent of the property tax. There is no way of knowing whether acreages were equivalently employed in the valuation procedure in those townships which failed to report them as such; nor, if they were employed, can one know whether comparable conversion factors were used.

Similarly, it is comforting that some returns listed and valued houses separately from landed property. For one thing, it is good to know for a certainty that houses and buildings, when lying on agricultural land, were being valued at all. Not all estate valuations appear to have taken much separate account of houses, unless the buildings were either inadequate or exceptionally good. Separate reporting is also important because houses are generally more valuable than the land on which they specifically lie. But the separate listing of houses in some townships can suggest that they were not being separately and accurately valued in the majority of others, where they were not separately listed. In its instructions at Easter sessions the court had directed that farm houses should be separately valued only "where House Duty is paid." But we do not know how uniformly that payment was made among the townships. We simply cannot be certain what procedures were being followed, and what seems reassuring may also be worrying. Indeed, if some townships were good enough to include properties which were normally excluded from the poor rate, for whatever reasons, may we not then infer that other townships, in adhering to their instructions that the basis for the county rate was to be that for the poor rate, continued to exclude those properties from the returns of their overseers? In many instances the magistrates themselves, even with their extensive local knowledge and investigative powers, must often have been ignorant of what was omitted or included or of whether unwarranted reductions were made. Certainly it would have been difficult for magistrates to alter specific local procedures which had long been observed, however inconsistent they might have been among the townships, without at the same time threatening the entire consensual basis of local taxation. Better to allow inconsistencies to remain. Fundamental alterations in the local bases of government finance were not part of their mandate. Quotas were. And yet an equitable system of quotas could not be obtained so long as the process of valuation was radically decentralized and subject to local tradition.

If there were any real culprits in the failure to effect a fair valuation, they were the townships themselves. Two townships in Hallikeld wapentake simply refused to the end to provide full values. The magistrates for that division added the following annotation to the return of the joint township of Swainby and Allerthorpe, where the land was entirely in the hands of three large tenants: "Full rental required by tenth of July." Nothing further was received by July, and the total on the undervalued return was entered by the County Rate Committee as the final amount returned by the overseer. That amount only comprised 74.9 percent of the property tax. The more urban and commercial township of Kirby Hill, lying on the Great North Road and within the same division, similarly refused to revise its return. The combined final valuations of Kirby Hill and neighbouring Langthorpe comprised only 60.5 percent of the property tax.

Some returning officers seriously disagreed with the entire basis of the valuation procedure which the court had outlined in its instructions. Edward Strangeways, a farmer who acted as special valuer for Aiskew township in Hang East wapentake, expressed his reservations at some length on his return. He may have found himself in the same position as many overseers and other returning officers when he candidly admitted that he knew no other actual rental "but my own." He was therefore, as a matter of necessity, forwarding details of an actual survey completed (in a year unspecified) by a Mr Calvert, giving acreages and values of all land, non-agricultural houses, and tithes. The total amount of that valuation is what in the end the magistrates accepted. But Strangeways took this opportunity to protest that "land cannot be valued but by the Quantity, Quality, and Value of its produce." He then gave the average prices of crops within the township over the last three years, and added: "I declare that the land within the Township of Aysecough [is] worth no such money to farm for a living profit as is contained in this Valuation but several hundred pounds pr Ann less – and that a number of acres in it will not pay assessments and the expense of cultivating." Strangeways may not have been correct. Aiskew returned 103.5 percent of the valuation for the property tax, but we do not know when Calvert made his survey. Strangeways was surely not merely eccentric, however. What he suggested was not unreasonable; and disagreement with the procedures outlined by quarter sessions was widespread and heated throughout the riding that spring. Such disagreements may well have fostered inconsistencies in procedure and, whether intended or not, substantial evasion.

In some townships the valuers seem to have been diligent to a fault, but in return they were harassed by one or more of their neighbours. Most of the initial returns from Gilling East wapentake are dated at the Scorton petty sessions held on 9 April 1824. On 10 June, before the appointment of the revising committee, an adjourned petty sessions again gathered to scrutinize the returns made by the overseers of the division, with the Earl of Tyrconnel, George Hartley, and James Robson acting as magistrates. At the end of those proceedings the following note was added by the magistrates to the return for Ainderby Steeple:

> We hereby certify that we have examined the above named Parties [*i.e.*, every occupier of the township, the returning officer not having signed] on oath or have otherwise ascertained the above to be a true and correct account of the total amount of the full and fair annual value of the several Estates and rateable Property within the Township of Ainderby Steeple charged or liable to be charged to the County Rate, with the Exception of Jos. Todd, who alone has refused to give in his Rent and whose return is on valuation only.

Joseph Todd, a tenant of William Chapman, reported a rent of £138 18s., which was the fifth largest holding on the return and comprised 6.4 percent of the total. Todd ultimately succeeded in defying the sessions. On 2 February 1825, Tyrconnel and Robson added the following to the return: "Upon due Examination we are satisfied with the foregoing Returns." Their satisfaction undoubtedly stemmed from the results of the scrutiny by the County Rate Committee, which by that time would have discovered that the valuation for Ainderby Steeple already exceeded the property tax at 113.8 percent in a wapentake where the mean percentage was 93.8. Their mandate to "equalize" quotas had been fulfilled.

The returning officers of Great Ayton in Langbaurgh wapentake seem to have met widespread recalcitrance through their own stubborn efficiency, and at some cost to themselves and to their reputations. They reported a valuation which comprised 100.2 percent of the property tax, when the wapentake as a whole achieved only 79.8 percent. The returning officers (two overseers, two constables, and two churchwardens) wryly added the following note to the magistrates at the bottom of their return:

> Gentlemen you will have the goodness to alow [sic] us our Bill which we do herein charge

£	s.	
6	6	for loss of time
1	1	for Spite hatred and malice that we may expect from the inhabitants of this Parish
7	7	

In the Swaledale townships, spite and hatred would seem to have been directed against the magistracy itself, and indeed against what these upland yeomen and small tenants in a mixed economy saw as a policy of exploitation and neglect directed against themselves by the wealthier mixed-husbandry townships of the vales. These huge sprawling townships were often ill-defined and heavily characterized by copyhold. They were thus difficult to value. They were not producing the crime that was placing an increasingly heavy burden on the county rate, and their numerous stone bridges, which serviced an important artery into Lancashire and Cumbria, were frequently maintained by the townships themselves and not by the county. They clung steadfastly to their traditional valuations in 1824 and bitterly resented the pressures placed upon them by lowland magistrates. They were suspicious, too, that the lowland townships, where the magistrates resided and held their principal properties, were not themselves reporting full values. Muker was alone among the larger Swaledale townships in reporting relatively high values. As it happens, Muker had been professionally valued by a land surveyor in the autumn of 1818. The constable then reported this valuation, which amounted to 90.6 percent of the 1814 property tax. But, when Muker made its return on 17 March 1824, eight members of its vestry appended the following note to quarter sessions:

> We whose Names are subscribed have in a full Vestry assembled perused the preceding account, and on making a comparison between the Benefits received on Payment of a very large Proportion, and others who pay very inadequate sums. In the Constablery of Muker there are Eight Stone Bridges on the Publick Highways, not one of which is on the County. We humbly hope that we are not trespassing on the Equity of the said regulations, in earnestly requesting your particular attention in order to our relief the first opportunity.

The neighbouring township of Reeth was more severe and defiantly uncooperative in its reaction. On 3 April 1824 the township submitted a detailed valuation to the magistrates, who rejected it and called for a revision. Their concerns were certainly justified: The April return amounted to only 36.7 percent of the 1814 property tax. On 19 June, Reeth submitted a new return on which it did no more than repeat the same unrevised totals for each of its three hamlets and for the township as a whole. For details Reeth referred sessions to its return of April, and appended the following note:

> At a Vestry holden at Reeth on Saturday the 12th day of June 1824 it was resolved that, the Constable be directed to present to the Magistrates a Return prepared by the overseers for the purposes of the County Rate & to represent to them the utter impracticability of obtaining the Rack Rents of all the Property in the Township – and at the same time to state that this Township will cheerfully contribute its full proportion towards the Expense of a general survey of the Riding as the only likely means of obtaining a fair & equitable Valuation for the County Rate –

The vestry at Reeth was in fact entirely correct. The only way the magistracy was going to be able to ensure a fair and equitable fresh valuation of the riding was to authorize precisely what the court at its Easter sessions admitted it was seeking to avoid: a general survey of every township by a single team of professional valuers. Why did the magistrates not wish to do so? Other counties reached the conclusion during those years that a general valuation was unavoidable. What they found was that such revaluations by professional land surveyors were prohibitively expensive. In 1834 a committee of the House of Commons, while investigating the basis for the county rate, estimated that general professional revaluations would cost a county from £15,000 to as much as £50,000. It was only after 1829, when Lancashire pioneered a method for effecting a centralized general county revaluation for less than £1,000, that it became feasible for counties to break with the peculiarities inherent and seemingly ineradicable in local returns and to undertake standardized and more truly equitable procedures.

Meanwhile the 1824 revaluation of the North Riding was doomed to failure. The failure was not so much due to deficiencies in the House of Commons. There was little the House could do politically, or even administratively, even if it had found the political will, to improve the traditional methods of tax collection which were so deeply embedded in the townships and parishes of England. Nor could the treasury intervene in a matter of local taxation. To all appearances the magistrates exerted themselves to the fullest, employing traditional means to meet the demands of a county financial crisis which, there is reason to believe, was genuinely felt in the countryside. But different townships experienced the crisis in different ways. In the North Riding the crisis accentuated old grievances between the upland and lowland communities and prompted the riding to rally against what it viewed as unfair impositions arising principally from problems in the industrial districts of the West. Suspicion and resentment thus played their role in further impeding a deeply traditional and, because it was so radically decentralized, inherently inconsistent process of county revaluation. The results displayed in table 13.4 could hardly have been otherwise.

Turning once again to more purely statistical evidence, we shall see that only the property tax, with its centralized organization of inspectors, was able to produce a relatively consistent maximum series of valuations. Table 13.4 shows that, with the exception of Allertonshire and Birdforth wapentakes, the property tax valuations were generally superior throughout the riding to those produced for the county rate. The superiority of the property tax is even more clearly brought out in table 13.5, where the property tax is compared for the level of its valuation against both of the

Table 13.5
Townships (by wapentake) in which the 1814 or 1815 property tax, the 1824 overseers' returns for the county rate, or the land tax c. 1830 reports the highest valuation, North Riding

Wapentake	No. of Townships	Property tax No.	Property tax % of N	County rate No.	County rate % of N	Land tax No.	Land tax % of reported cases
Allertonshire	31	16	51.6	15	48.4	0 (12)	0.0
Birdforth	47	15	31.9	31	66.0	1 (9)	11.1
Bulmer	60	57	95.0	1	1.7	2 (39)	5.1
Gilling East	29	17	58.6	11	37.9	1 (24)	4.2
Gilling West	42	30.5	72.6	9.5	22.6	2 (17)	11.8
Hallikeld	27	21	77.8	6	22.2	0 (8)	0.0
Hang East	30	20	66.7	10	33.3	0 (7)	0.0
Hang West	38	33	86.8	4	10.5	1 (5)	20.0
Langbaurgh	80	73	91.2	7	8.8	0 (31)	0.0
Pickering Lythe	38	34	89.5	0	0.0	4 (15)	26.7
Ryedale	49	38	77.6	10	20.4	0 (6)	0.0
Whitby Strand	12	8	66.7	4	33.3	0 (0)	0.0
TOTAL	483	362.5	75.0	108.5	22.5	11 (173)	6.7

Note: The number of non–defective townships reporting rents in the land tax is indicated in parentheses. The highest total valuation for the wapentake is underscored. No valuation has been found for Hildenley in Ryedale. Tied ranks are assigned decimal values.
Source: Appendix M.

other candidates for a maximum valuation, the county rate valuations of 1824 and the land tax valuations of c. 1830. Even in Allertonshire, where the county rate produced the highest total valuation for the wapentake as a whole, a slightly larger number of townships produced higher valuations for the property tax. In Hallikeld the county rate again produced the highest total for the wapentake, but twenty-one out of twenty-seven of its townships reported their highest valuations for the property tax. We must not be misled by aggregates, which are driven by outliers. The method we are here seeking must be useful at the township and parish level. Table 13.5 also shows that the land tax valuations of c. 1830 are, by any standard of measurement, an exceedingly inadequate measure of maximal rental values. In only 11 of 173 cases does the land tax produce the highest valuation among the three series, and in no wapentake does it reveal any general tendency to do so.

Information gathered from the other counties of England and Wales shows that our analysis of the differences between the county rate and the property tax in the North Riding do not overestimate the problem. Table 13.6 displays the range of mean percentage differences between the county rate and the property tax in thirty-nine of the fifty-five administrative counties. The North Riding mean of 85.5 percent is in fact slightly above the mean for the English counties, and it approximates the median.

But while, in our search for a maximum series of rental estimates, we may easily dismiss the land tax valuations as a candidate, it is that tax which forms the subject matter of this book. It is therefore worth pausing to compare the land tax valuations more systematically against those for the other rates and to determine, if possible, what underlies their apparent deficiencies. The land tax valuations are compared against the 1815 property tax and the 1824 overseers' returns for the county rate in appendices O.1–2. Appendix O.3 compares them against the amount settled on each township for the county rate in 1825, that is, against two-thirds of the 1814 valuation for the property tax. In appendix O.4 the land tax is compared against whichever of the above constitutes the highest valuation.[10] Table 13.7 summarizes the results.

The first thing to notice is that the dispersal of frequencies on every table is exceedingly great. But such dispersals are not peculiar to comparisons from the land tax. Similar dispersals were encountered on table 13.4, when comparing the valuations for the county rate against those for the property tax. It may be that, if reliable data were available, a comparison between valuational totals for the poor rate and those produced in 1824 for the county rate would reveal a close correspondence. They were supposed to have had the same basis, and the county rate was most often paid out of the funds produced by an enlarged collection for the poor rate. But in no other case does there appear to be a close correlation

Table 13.6
Frequency distribution, county rate valuation as a percentage of property tax valuation, all counties, England and Wales, c. 1830

%	English counties	Welsh counties
0.0–9.9		
10.0-19.9		1
20.0-29.9		1
30.0-39.9		
40.0-49.9	2	
50.0-59.9	1	
60.0-69.9	3	
70.0-79.9	7	
80.0-89.9	4	
90.0-99.9	11	1
100.0-109.9	5	
110.0-119.9	1	
120.0-129.9		
130.0–139.9		1
140.0-149.9		
150.0–159.9		1
County rate unknown	8	6
County rate not reported	1	1
N	43	12
Mean	81.9	94.9

Note: The total number of administrative counties and divisions differs from the total on table 13.2 due to aggregation of divisions on this table.
Source: Appendix N.

between valuations for taxation, whether the taxation being compared was local or national. All statistical evidence indicates that in general there was no single valuation – or, more correctly, no single valuational total – which each township as a whole employed when its real property was assessed. Each type of assessment, with the possible (but as yet untested) exception of the parish rates themselves, proceeded in most townships on the basis of its own uniquely devised valuation. A second observation which might be made from these tables is that the land tax valuations are generally lower, and often considerably so, than those for either the property tax or the county rate. And yet the land tax valuations were recorded and employed well after the other two had been undertaken and given wide publicity. Certainly each village knew its own valuation for the property tax and county rate, even if it did not know its neighbours'; and every township had felt the pressure from quarter sessions for revised valuations only five or six years previously. It is therefore remarkable that the land tax, while undergoing an almost continuous process of internal revaluation which in many cases allowed valuational totals to rise,[11] nevertheless remained strikingly independent and seemingly oblivious to alternative procedures associated with other forms of taxation. The land tax continued to be administered in a manner which was far more traditional than that governing either the property tax or the county rate. The reason for the conservatism of its administration is probably simply that, unlike the other two taxes, the pressures for its collection, following the decline of its burden and the spread of redemption, were diminishing at a time when the pressures on virtually all other taxes were increasing. The land tax could afford the luxury of the good old ways.

When both the dispersal of the percentages and the low mean of those percentages are taken into account, it is apparent that the deviations of the land tax valuations from those of the other series are not merely the result of declining values for real property following the peace with France. Even allowing for an average 10 to 15 percent decline in real property values, the land tax valuations are still generally too low and, even more tellingly, they are far too erratic in their departures from such a pattern. No more than 20 to 25 percent of the townships report land tax valuations which fall within plus or minus 10 percent of those for other taxes. Just over three-quarters of the townships report valuations c. 1830 that were less than 85 percent of the totals estimated for the property tax in 1815. Precisely half of the land tax valuations fell short of the valuations for the county rate by at least that proportion. In only eleven of the cases was the land tax valuation the highest of any of the series. It would seem, then, that in only a relatively small proportion of cases could one hope to argue that land tax valuations, in their total values reported, represent anything like the rack rents, or even the actual rentals, of their respective townships. It is necessary to return again and again to the same conclusion: The valuational rents recorded on land tax duplicates, like the tax values themselves, are not comparable between townships, however reliable they might be in representing proportionate distributions of wealth within their own boundaries. Certainly they can be seriously misleading to those attempting to measure relative burdens of the tax within larger regions.

How are these differences in the valuational bases of the various national and local taxes explained? Must we conclude that each township actually maintained several wholly independent and different valuations for each property within its community? I think not. Such a conclusion would surely have seemed as absurd and bothersome to the villagers of the day as it might to modern historians, and it is unnecessary. The tables we have been examining show only that the valuational totals per township varied with each form of taxation; they do not show that the proportional relations between each property failed to be equivalent for each tax. The proportional burdens of each tax could have varied internally in a comparable manner. Differences in valuational totals do not rule out the possibility of

Table 13.7
The land tax valuations c. 1830 as a percentage of (1) the 1815 property tax, (2) the 1824 overseers' valuations for the county rate, (3) the amounts settled for the county rate in 1825 and (4) the maximum valuation reported, North Riding

	(1)		(2)		(3)		(4)	
%	N	%	N	%	N	%	N	%
0.0–4.9	1	0.6	1	0.6	1	0.6	1	0.6
5.0–9.9								
10.0–14.9	1	0.6					1	0.6
15.0–19.9								
20.0–24.9	1	0.6			1	0.6	1	0.6
25.0–29.9	2	1.2	3	1.7			2	1.2
30.0–34.9	3	1.7	4	2.3	1	0.6	6	3.5
35.0–39.9	8	4.6					7	4.1
40.0–44.9	4	2.3	4	2.3	2	1.2	5	2.9
45.0–49.9	9	5.2	12	7.0	2	1.2	14	8.1
50.0–54.9	9	5.2	5	2.9	1	0.6	9	5.2
55.0–59.9	9	5.2	6	3.5	6	3.5	11	6.4
60.0–64.9	20	11.6	8	4.6	4	2.3	17	9.9
65.0–69.9	17	9.9	14	8.1	4	2.3	17	9.9
70.0–74.9	13	7.6	10	5.8	9	5.2	16	9.3
75.0–79.9	16	9.3	11	6.4	7	4.1	17	9.9
80.0–84.9	14	8.1	8	4.6	5	2.9	11	6.4
85.0–89.9	2	1.2	18	10.5	8	4.6	5	2.9
90.0–94.9	10	5.8	9	5.2	15	8.7	7	4.1
95.0–99.9	13	7.6	19	11.0	10	5.8	14	8.1
100.0–104.9	7	4.1	11	6.4	8	4.6	11	6.4
105.0–109.9	3	1.7	4	2.3	9	5.2		
110.0–114.9	2	1.2	8	4.6	11	6.4		
115.0–119.9			2	1.2	11	6.4		
120.0–124.9	1	0.6	2	1.2	8	4.6		
125.0–129.9			3	1.7	8	4.6		
130.0–134.9			2	1.2	2	1.2		
135.0–139.9					5	2.9		
140.0–144.9	1	0.6	2	1.2	7	4.1		
145.0–149.9			2	1.2	9	5.2		
150.0–154.9					6	3.5		
155.0–159.9					4	2.3		
160.0–164.9	1	0.6	1	0.6	1	0.6		
≥165.0			3	1.7	4	2.3		
def.	3	1.7			3	1.7		
NR	2	1.2						
N	172	100.0	172	100.0	172	100.0	172	100.0
Mean	69.4		80.0		103.9		66.7	
Minimum	3.2		3.6		4.8		3.2	
Maximum	163.9		252.5		245.7		100.0	

Table 13.7 continued

SUMMARY

Percentage of cases[a]

Range (%)	(1)	(2)	(3)	(4)
0.0–19.9	1.2	0.6	0.6	1.2
20.0–39.9	8.4	4.1	1.2	9.3
40.0–59.9	18.6	15.7	6.5	22.7
60.0–79.9	39.5	25.0	14.2	39.0
80.0–99.9	23.4	31.4	22.5	21.5
100.0–124.9	7.8	15.7	27.8	6.4
≥125.0	1.2	7.6	27.2	
90.0–109.9	19.8	25.0	24.8	18.6

Note: [a]Defective (def.) and no return (NR) cases are excluded from the denominator.
Sources: Appendices O.1–4.

a single valuational process, or even a common list of valuations for each property.

Based on the evidence presented in earlier chapters, it is possible to infer that the differences in valuational totals stem principally from three causes. First, as this and chapter 11 have shown, discounting from a derived valuation was a commonplace throughout England and Wales when undertaking tax assessments. Each township, according to the requirements of the tax in question and in keeping with its own unique local traditions, would assess at a rate – for example 25 or 33 or 50 percent – below full valuation. Taxes based on quotas seem to have been peculiarly susceptible to this practice. It was especially common in assessing to the land tax, and we have seen evidence of its widespread use in revaluing for the county rate. The inspectors for the property tax would have been peculiarly alert to preventing any such discounting within their districts. If discounting was widespread, then, and if we accept the probability that different discount rates might have been applied for different tax purposes, much regarding the differences between valuational totals would be explained. And, as a matter of course, we would expect that land tax valuations would in general be the lowest, and those for the property tax the highest, of the three series being examined.

A second contributing factor to the differences in valuational totals undoubtedly derives from differences in taxable population. As revealed in chapter 3, not all properties that were assessed to the county rate, and presumably to the poor rate, were included in the land tax. Since principally small properties seem to have been omitted, the total valuation of the omitted properties may not have been great, and such differences in policies of omission cannot have seriously affected the extraordinary dispersions found when comparing the three valuation series. But neither would the impact of such omissions be insignificant. Since it is also evident that the policy of omission was employed differently in each township, the effect of the policy would be to enhance differential departures from rack rent, and that is the pattern observed.

Simple ignorance could also contribute to explaining the differences in valuational totals. There is no reason to assume, for example, that each township was equivalently knowledgeable about the value of its properties. Townships with high population densities and extensive non-agricultural acres must have found it relatively difficult to establish full valuations. Similarly, many of the huge sprawling upland townships must have shared the reaction of the vestry of Reeth when in 1824 it protested to the magistrates "the utter impracticability of obtaining Rack Rents of all the Property in the Township." Most townships, through decades or even centuries of experience in local taxation and the adjudication of its disputes, may well have come to an understanding of the *relative* values of their properties. William Marshall's "provincial valuers," men with local knowledge, may also have been able to speculate with some accuracy on what current saleable values might be in the land market of the district. But full values at rack rent could still be beyond their grasp.[12] The inspector for the property tax, coming into this township in his capacity as professional valuer, might be expected to have broader perspectives and different views.

When all of these considerations are taken into account, it should not be surprising that the valuational totals among the townships and parishes of England should differ for each local and national tax or that the differences should be as striking as those found in the tables. The situation could hardly be otherwise. Such differences do not necessarily impugn the proportionality of each tax in its internal distribution within each township. Nor do they negate the possibility that each township employed a single valuational basis for all of its taxes. But the differences displayed in the tables underscore once again that none of these taxes, with the possible exception of the property tax, are suitable for inter-township comparisons of absolute tax values. The tax values are not comparable for such purposes, partly for the reasons suggested in this chapter, and partly because of differential changes in land values. Comparisons between townships do seem on comparatively safe grounds when the valuational totals from schedule A of the 1815 property tax are employed. But even here safety is not absolute. Nevertheless, the property tax is clearly the optimal choice for a maximum valuation series with which to test the relative burdens of the land tax, and we shall now employ it in that fashion in each of the three ridings of Yorkshire.

CHAPTER FOURTEEN

Testing the Maximum Series for Comparability: Spatial Distribution Patterns in the North, East, and West Ridings of Yorkshire

Maximum estimates of tax burden will now be derived by dividing the land tax quota of each township into the total value of its real property as reported on schedule A of the 1815 property tax.[1] The resulting statistic is a ratio of valuation, or "rent," to tax, low ratios indicating a relatively heavy burden of tax. It is fortunate that the property tax turns out to be the most reliable rental series, because one could scarcely have asked for a better year than 1815 in which to undertake such an analysis, coming as it does precisely at the end of the great wartime rise in rents and before the period of slow secular decline and economic dislocation has had an opportunity to begin. The 1815 valuations enjoy the considerable additional advantage of being available at the parish or township level for every county of England and Wales. They make possible extensive comparisons which could not be achieved with any other valuational series which can be tested.

Before beginning this examination of the ratios, let us consider for a moment what we might expect to find. All of the literature on the land tax has taught us to expect to find large regional differences at the national or county level in the way the burden of the tax was distributed. But disputes have arisen regarding the equality of distributions within counties. Few have doubted that such inequalities existed; but their degree, and whether they were regionally patterned within counties, is a subject about which we know almost nothing. For more than a century every writer on the land tax has assumed that some inequalities occurred over short distances, largely due to differing rates of agricultural improvement. It is therefore possible that we shall find the tax burdens, as reflected in the ratios, to be patterned regionally within counties in accordance with patterns of improvement. If improvement causes disproportionate rises in land values within a county, then those townships or regions which were most subject to improvement will have experienced relatively sharp rises in the values of their real property. These values will in turn have departed more significantly from their ossified land tax quotas than would those in less improved townships. Improved regions should thus produce relatively high ratios.

Agricultural improvement is not the only factor which might cause disproportionate rises in land values and thus produce these patterns. Expanding urbanization or the development of commercial and transport infrastructures might also cause ratios to rise, for example, and at different rates than does agricultural improvement. There are in fact a myriad of factors which might be expected to have affected differential rises in urban and rural land values; and each of these factors, or combinations of them, might have produced meaningful patterns of tax burden in the countryside. If such patterns emerge, and if they prove to be consistent within different administrative counties, then they will prove invaluable as a basis for further economic analysis and generalization. Equally important, perhaps, a patterned distribution of the ratios would enable us to predict in a general way the tax burden of a group of townships from their more readily known economic characteristics.

But it may be that patterns in the geographical distribution of the land tax burden will not appear. The tests we shall apply to the ratios will be ones whose conditions should be easily met. Rather than attempt complex estimates of the impact of enclosure, or to track the great estates, we shall look quite simply for global differences between the mixed husbandry districts in the lowlands and the sheep runs of the high dales and moorlands. And we shall look at urban centres and industrial regions. If no global differences between such regions emerge with reasonable consistency, then we may conclude that ratios cannot be predicted from known economic characteristics and that the relationships between those factors which caused rises in land values and the ratios themselves are very complex indeed. It is possible, for example, that the quotas themselves were originally distributed in a way which so ill-conformed to current land values that meaningful patterns in subsequent tax burdens cannot emerge. The tax quotas, as well as the 1815 property tax valuations, will be tested individually for their patterns of spatial distribution. If these two variables forming the basis of the ratios are themselves regionally patterned, then we may conclude that any lack of pattern among the ratios is not due to the unreliability of their constituent variables. We shall also test the comparability of the ratios, and of the two variables employed to compute them, by the consistency of our observations in the three ridings of Yorkshire, each of which will be examined in turn. In general, then, we shall ask two questions of the ratios: Are they regionally distributed in ways which conform to known economic characteristics? And how serious are the dispersions in tax burden which they measure?

The ratios for the North Riding of Yorkshire are displayed on map 7 and are presented as frequency distributions in table 14.1. The first thing that strikes the eye is that the real burden of the land tax in the North Riding bears no relationship to the statutory rate of four shillings in the pound, which would produce a ratio of 5:1. No township in the riding has a ratio that low, although one township approaches it, at 7.7. The preponderance of townships, 76 percent of them, produce ratios ranging from 20.0 to 59.9, the mean for the riding as a whole being 44.8. Moreover, the distribution is skewed in the direction of even lighter tax burdens. Only 3 percent of the townships have ratios lower than 20, but in almost 21 percent of the townships the ratios exceed 60, reflecting very light tax burdens indeed. Variation within the riding as a whole extends from a ratio of 7.7 in East and West Ness to a ratio of 188 in Reeth. Ness must thus be interpreted as bearing a real tax burden which is more than 24 times greater than that experienced in Reeth; or, to put it another way, the value of each individual tax entry in Ness must be multiplied by a factor of 24.4 before it can be assumed to represent real wealth in a manner which is approximately equivalent to entries in Reeth.[2] Even setting aside those townships which produce ratios well in excess of one standard deviation from the mean, we still find a tightly patterned group (76 percent of the cases) ranging in ratio from 20 to the upper 50s. That range is a large one. A township with a ratio of 20 carries a burden of tax that is 3 times more severe than a township with a ratio of 60. Error of this magnitude can be fatal to sophisticated statistical calculations and can significantly distort less rigorous applications.

The dispersions of tax burdens are similarly large within each wapentake division. The most heavily assessed township in Whitby Strand bears a tax burden 2.5 times greater than the town of Whitby, which is the most lightly taxed within the wapentake. Elsewhere the differences in burden are more extreme. In most wapentakes the differences range from a factor of 3 to a factor of 8, but in Gilling West the most heavily taxed township bears a burden more than 15 times that of its most lightly taxed neighbour, while in Ryedale the difference is by a factor of 20. Such extraordinary differences are all the more noteworthy since these wapentakes were coterminous with land tax divisions[3] and the townships of each division were governed by the same body of commissioners. In any case there are assuredly no grounds for assuming, as some scholars have done,[4] that significant inequalities in tax burden, to the extent that they existed, were confined to the level of the administrative county. On the contrary, such inequalities were large at all levels, extending down to the level of the land tax division, or hundred, and even, among the townships of northern England, down to the parish or township itself.

Table 14.1
Frequency distribution, net* ratio of 1815 property tax valuations (schedule A) to land tax quotas, all townships, North Riding

Numbered columns: 1 = Allertonshire wapentake; 2 = Birdforth wapentake; 3 = Bulmer wapentake; 4 = Gilling East wapentake; 5 = Gilling West wapentake; 6 = Hallikeld wapentake; 7 = Hang East wapentake; 8 = Hang West wapentake; 9 = Langbaurgh wapentake; 10 = Pickering Lythe wapentake; 11 = Ryedale wapentake; 12 = Whitby Strand wapentake

Ratio	1	2	3	4	5	6	7	8	9	10	11	12	All cases N	All cases %	Summary Range	Summary % of cases[a]
0.0–4.9																
5.0–9.9											1		1	0.2	0.0–19.9	3.0
10.0–14.9	2		1		1				1				5	1.0		
15.0–19.9	1	3		2	1	1							8	1.7		
20.0–24.9	4	4	3	2	4	1	2		2	1	2		25	5.2		
25.0–29.9	9	7	6	3	4		5		7	1	3		45	9.3	20.0–39.9	37.8
30.0–34.9	4	7	6	7	3	2	3		8	3	5		48	9.9		
35.0–39.9	5	8	10	3	5	5	3	4	8	3	4	3	61	12.5		
40.0–44.9	2	5	10	1	5	5	5	2	10	4	6		55	11.4		
45.0–49.9	1	6	9	3	3	3	5	2	12	4	4	3	55	11.4	40.0–59.9	38.3
50.0–54.9	1	5	4	5	3	3	5	7	7	5	5	2	52	10.8		
55.0–59.9	1		3		2	1	1	2	6	2	1		19	3.9		
60.0–64.9	1		5		3			3	4	2	6		24	5.0		
65.0–69.9			1	2	1	1	1	2	1	2	3	1	15	3.1	60.0–79.9	13.3
70.0–74.9					1	1		2	2	2	3		11	2.3		
75.0–79.9					1	2		3	2	3	1	1	13	2.7		
80.0–84.9			1		2			1	3	1	1		9	1.9		
85.0–89.9					1	1		3		1		1	7	1.4	80.0–99.9	4.4
90.0–94.9				1		1		1				1	4	0.8		
95.0–99.9									1				1	0.2		

Table 14.1 continued

Ratio	1	2	3	4	5	6	7	8	9	10	11	12	All cases N	All cases %	Summary Range	Summary % of cases[a]
100.0–104.9								1	2		1		4	0.8		
105.0–109.9									1				1	0.2		
110.0–114.9								3		1			4	0.8		
115.0–119.9								1					1	0.2		
120.0–124.9															100.0–149.9	2.8
125.0–129.9		1								1			2	0.4		
130.0–134.9								1					1	0.2		
135.0–139.9																
140.0–144.9																
145.0–149.9																
150.0–154.9											1		1	0.2		
155.0–159.9																
160.0–164.9																
165.0–169.9															≥150.0	0.4
170.0–174.9																
175.0–179.9																
180.0–184.9																
185.0–189.9					1								1	0.2		
190.0–194.9																
195.0–199.9																
≥200.0																
def.					1				3				4	0.8		
NR		1	1							2	2		6	1.2		
N	31	47	60	29	42	27	30	38	80	38	49	12	483	100.0		
Mean	32.8	37.6	39.7	38.4	44.4	48.3	40.0	65.9	46.6	52.2	54.3	60.9	44.8			
Minimum	12.9	17.4	13.1	19.1	12.1	19.2	21.0	36.6	12.3	20.8	7.7	36.8	7.7			

Table 14.1 continued

Ratio	1	2	3	4	5	6	7	8	9	10	11	12	All cases		Summary	
													N	%	Range	% of cases[a]
Maximum	55.2	128.2	82.2	90.6	188.0	90.3	65.2	134.6	105.9	128.7	154.8	91.0	188.0			
Maximum as % of minimum	428	737	627	474	1,554	470	310	368	861	619	2,010	247	2,442			

Notes: *Salaries and stock-in-trade have been deducted from the quotas.
[a]Defective (def.) and no return (NR) cases are excluded from the denominator.
Source: Appendix M.

The North Riding affords numerous examples of extraordinary disparities in tax burdens among the townships of a single parish, as well as among contiguous townships in different parishes. The wholly urban township of New Malton bears a ratio of 154.8 while the neighbouring parish of Old Malton, which also holds a small urban centre but further includes extensive agricultural acreage, produces a ratio of 104.1. The ratio of the large agricultural township that contains the market town of Easingwold is 40.7. The wholly agricultural township of Raskelf, lying within the same parish, bears a tax burden which is 3 times greater, with a ratio of 13.1. But, one might object, urban townships may be expected to produce such differences, since urban land values had generally risen steeply over the preceding century as internal markets developed. However, the same sharp differences are observed in the more purely agricultural townships. The township of East and West Ness, which produces the lowest ratio in the riding, at 7.7, shares a parish with the townships of Newton (33.1) and Stonegrave (63.7). Two contiguous townships outside its parish have ratios of 28 and 38, but the five remaining townships surrounding Ness all produce ratios in the 60s and 70s. The Swaledale township of Reeth, which is the most lightly burdened township in the riding (188), shares the same parish and is contiguous with Melbecks (37.6). Indeed these two townships often acted jointly and were frequently reported jointly in the documentation of the day. The adjacent parish of Arkengarthdale, immediately to the north and similarly including mining properties, produces a ratio of 76.3. In the lowland mixed husbandry regions, comparable differences in tax burdens are equally easy to find. South Cowton township, lying in Gilling East wapentake, is heavily taxed at 19.1, while the second township within the parish, North Cowton, is much more lightly taxed at 34.4. Their neighbouring joint township to the west, Scorton and Uckerby, lying in a separate Gilling East parish, is strikingly more lightly taxed, at 90.6. Yafforth (19.9), also in Gilling East, shares its parish with Danby Wiske (29.2) and is surrounded by townships whose ratios range from 25 to 55. No matter where one looks within this largely rural stretch of the English countryside, there are wide disparities in the real burden of the land tax. And these disparities occur within very short distances.

What is equally notable is that virtually no regional differences emerge in the distribution of the real burden of the land tax. There is perhaps a slight tendency for lighter burdens to occur in the upland and more pastoral portions of the riding. The mean ratios in Hang West and Whitby Strand are well above the riding mean. But the high mean ratio in Whitby Strand is driven by the light tax burdens in Whitby itself and is therefore more an urban than an upland phenomenon. The equally upland but non-urbanized wapentake of Gilling West stands almost precisely at the riding mean, as do many of its most upland and remote townships. Indeed, even within the upland wapentakes there is no *general* tendency for their more upland townships to have a lighter tax burden. There is some tendency to that effect on the North Yorkshire Moors, but in Wensleydale precisely the opposite occurs. It is the dale townships in this wapentake (Hang West) which produce the higher ratios, and indeed this region displays the only rational distribution of tax burdens to be found in the riding. If higher ratios and lighter tax burdens are to be found, one would expect to find them on the better soils, where improvements were most likely to have occurred. This pattern is found in the dales and moorlands of Hang West, where the lower dairy pastures are more lightly taxed than the moorland sheep runs. With the exception of this one wapentake, however, one searches in vain for differences in tax burden which can reasonably be associated with variations in elevation, in soil regions, or in agricultural regime.

Before completing this examination of ratios in the North Riding it may be well to make a first attempt to dispell any remaining doubts that the dispersions in tax burden we have been examining are real ones and not simply a function of our having selected the property tax for this equation. Table 14.2 presents a frequency distribution of ratios constructed by employing the highest valuation recorded for each township, selected from among the land tax valuations of c. 1830, the county rate valuations returned by the overseers in 1824, the amounts settled for the county rate in 1825, and the property tax valuations of 1815. The riding and wapentake means all rise on this table, but only marginally. The dispersions in the riding as a whole fall, but only from a factor of 24 to a factor of just under 22. They increase sharply in Hang East and diminish in Ryedale, but remain virtually constant elsewhere. The proportion of ratios lying between 20 and 59 falls from 76.1 to 75.3 percent. If it is reasonable to assume that townships are unlikely on any of these occasions to have reported total valuations which exceeded the true rack rental values of their real properties, then this procedure, by removing downward outliers among the ratios, should tend to eliminate significant underassessments and improve the maximal estimates of tax burden. No significant differences emerge in doing so, apart from individual instances. It would appear that, allowing for error and anomalies among individual townships, the property tax does provide a regionally reliable method for analyzing the relative burdens of the land tax.

Ratios employing the 1815 property tax for the East Riding are displayed on map 10 and are presented as a frequency distribution in table 14.3. The patterns are much like those found in the North Riding. The East Riding mean is slightly higher[5] at 50, and the dispersions are slightly larger, with only just over 70 percent of the cases falling between 20 and

59. The distribution is more strongly skewed upwards, with only 1.2 percent of the ratios falling below 20 and over 28 percent exceeding 59. One township, Kilnsea, actually bears a tax burden in excess of the statutory rate (with a ratio of 4). Such a ratio is not wholly implausible in Kilnsea, which was located on Spurn Head at the mouth of the Humber and where a considerable number of acres had been lost into the sea.[6] Similarly, the unusually high ratio of 101 found in Ottringham and Sunk Island, also in South Holderness, is clearly due to the alluvial formation of the latter during the eighteenth and early nineteenth centuries. Alluvial deposit along the rich siltlands may also explain the high ratio in neighbouring Paull, although the influence of Hull may also be a factor since the ratios northward and eastward along the Humber are generally high. Certainly the effects of suburban development and concomitant rises in land values are evident in the immediate vicinity of Hull and, to some extent, of Beverley and Bridlington.

In the riding as a whole, however, the dispersions are great, as they were in the North Riding. The tax burden at Kilnsea is 70 times greater than it is at Sculcoates (280) on the outskirts of Hull. The dispersions within wapentake divisions are also proportionately great, the heavier burdens being generally 3 to 10 times greater than the lighter. In the Hunsley Beacon division of Harthill, near Hull, the dispersion is at a factor of more than 15. In South Holderness the factor rises to 25. In some divisions the more extreme dispersions are caused by a small minority of outliers, but such is not universally the case. In Buckrose and Dickering wapentakes, where the high wolds fall away to lowlands, the ratios are fairly evenly distributed from the low 40s to the low 130s. In every part of the riding, differences in burden of 100 percent or more are found among contiguous parishes and townships. It is impossible in the East Riding, as it was in the North Riding, to find an administrative level which in general would encompass townships with roughly equivalent burdens of land tax.

But unlike in the North Riding, there is some correlation in the East Riding between high ratios and elevation. There is a pattern of markedly lighter tax burdens on the high wolds, and the pattern almost precisely follows the contours of the natural topography of the area. The escarpment to the west is clearly discernible on map 10, and tax burdens do indeed gradually increase as the wolds taper off onto the coastal lowlands in the east. It is worrisome that the pattern stops abruptly on the south at the wapentake lines, however. The wolds are highest in elevation in the two northern wapentakes, and it may be that the extensive enclosures which occurred on the wolds after 1750 were more dramatically felt at these higher elevations. But the fact remains that enclosures were equally extensive during those years on the more southerly wolds.[7] If we accept

Table 14.2
Frequency distribution, ratio of highest valuation to land tax quota, all townships, North Riding

Numbered columns: 1 = Allertonshire wapentake; 2 = Birdforth wapentake; 3 = Bulmer wapentake; 4 = Gilling East wapentake; 5 = Gilling West wapentake; 6 = Hallikeld wapentake; 7 = Hang East wapentake; 8 = Hang West wapentake; 9 = Langbaurgh wapentake; 10 = Pickering Lythe wapentake; 11 = Ryedale wapentake; 12 = Whitby Strand wapentake

												All cases		Summary	
Ratio	1	2	3	4	5	6	7	8	9	10	11	12	N	%	Range	% of cases[a]
0.0–4.9																
5.0–9.9															0.0–19.9	2.1
10.0–14.9	1		1		1								3	0.6		
15.0–19.9	1	2		1	1	1			1				7	1.4		
20.0–24.9	2	1	3	2	2	1	2		3	1	2		19	3.9		
25.0–29.9	9	8	7	3	3		4		6		3		43	8.9	20.0–39.9	34.4
30.0–34.9	3	5	5	6	4	1	4		8	4	5		45	9.3		
35.0–39.9	6	6	10	4	5	4	2	3	8	3	5	2	58	12.0		
40.0–44.9	3	7	10	2	6	5	4	2	10	3	6	1	59	12.2		
45.0–49.9	2	4	9	2	3	4	4	2	14	5	3	3	55	11.4	40.0–59.9	40.9
50.0–54.9	2	9	5	5	4	4	6	6	8	5	5	2	61	12.6		
55.0–59.9			3	1	2	1	2	3	5	2	2		21	4.4		
60.0–64.9	1	2	4		3			3	4	2	6		25	5.2		
65.0–69.9	1	1	2	2	1	1		2	2	2	3	1	18	3.7	60.0–79.9	14.0
70.0–74.9					1	1	1	2	2	2	2		11	2.3		
75.0–79.9					1	2		4	2	3	1		13	2.7		
80.0–84.9		1	1		2	1		1	3	1	1		11	2.3		
85.0–89.9					1			3		1		1	6	1.2	80.0–99.9	5.0
90.0–94.9				1		1		1			2	1	6	1.2		
95.0–99.9									1				1	0.2		

Table 14.2 continued

Ratio	1	2	3	4	5	6	7	8	9	10	11	12	All cases N	All cases %	Summary Range	Summary % of cases[a]
100.0–104.9								1			1		2	0.4		
105.0–109.9									3			1	4	0.8		
110.0–114.9								3		1			4	0.8		
115.0–119.9								1					1	0.2		
120.0–124.9																
125.0–129.9										1			1	0.2	100.0–149.9	2.9
130.0–134.9								1					1	0.2		
135.0–139.9																
140.0–144.9		1											1	0.2		
145.0–149.9																
150.0–154.9																
155.0–159.9											1		1	0.2		
160.0–164.9																
165.0–169.9																
170.0–174.9															≥150.0	0.6
175.0–179.9																
180.0–184.9																
185.0–189.9					1								1	0.2		
190.0–194.9																
195.0–199.9																
≥200.0							1						1	0.2		
def.					1								1	0.2		
NR										2	1		3	0.6		
N	31	47	60	29	42	27	30	38	80	38	49	12	483	100.0		
Mean	36.1	43.0	40.0	39.4	45.4	49.6	41.3	67.4	47.1	52.4	56.1	65.7	46.3			
Minimum	13.6	18.4	13.1	19.1	12.4	19.2	21.0	36.6	18.3	20.8	22.6	37.2	12.4			

Table 14.2 continued

Ratio	1	2	3	4	5	6	7	8	9	10	11	12	All cases N	All cases %	Summary Range	Summary % of cases[a]
Maximum	68.9	144.2	82.2	90.6	188.0	90.3	270.3	134.7	109.1	128.7	155.4	105.5	270.3			
Maximum as % of minimum	507	784	627	474	1,516	470	1,287	368	596	631	688	284	2,180			

Note: [a]Defective (def.) and no return (NR) cases are excluded from the denominator.
Source: Appendices J and M.

Table 14.3
Frequency distribution, net* ratio of 1815 property tax valuations (schedule A) to land tax quotas, all townships, East Riding

Numbered columns:
1 = Buckrose wapentake
2 = Dickering wapentake
3 = Harthill wapentake, Bainton Beacon division
4 = Harthill wapentake, Holme Beacon division
5 = Harthill wapentake, Hunsley Beacon division
6 = Harthill wapentake, Wilton Beacon division
7 = Holderness wapentake, Middle division
8 = Holderness wapentake, North division
9 = Holderness wapentake, South division
10 = Howdenshire wapentake
11 = Hullshire, city and county
12 = Ouse and Derwent wapentake
13 = Beverley borough and liberties

Ratio	1	2	3	4	5	6	7	8	9	10	11	12	13	All cases N	All cases %	Summary Range	Summary % of cases[a]
0–4									1					1	0.3		
5–9																0–19	1.2
10–14																	

Table 14.3 continued

Ratio	1	2	3	4	5	6	7	8	9	10	11	12	13	All cases N	%	Summary Range	% of cases[a]
15–19					1	1	1							3	0.9		
20–24	1	1		2	2	2	2					2		12	3.6		
25–29	1	1	1	3	1	8	3		3	2		3		26	7.8	20–39	32.1
30–34	4		3	1	4	3	7	3	3	3		4	2	37	11.1		
35–39			4	1	1	3	3	5	2	4		5		28	8.4		
40–44	5	1	2	7	1	1	6	6	3	4		4	1	41	12.3		
45–49	3	3	4	2	1	2	3	2	2	2		1	1	26	7.8	40–59	38.6
50–54	6	3	2		1	2	2	3	4	3		1		27	8.1		
55–59	4	5	3	4	3	1	2	2		3		2	1	30	9.0		
60–64	2	2		1	2	1		3						11	3.4		
65–69		3	2					3		2				10	3.0	60–79	11.5
70–74	1	1		2	1	1	2		1			1		10	3.0		
75–79		2	1	1	1			1						6	1.8		
80–84	3	4						1		1			1	10	3.0		
85–89	2	2			1			1						6	1.8	80–99	7.5
90–94	1	1												2	0.6		
95–99	1	3					1					1		6	1.8		
100–104	1	3					1		1					6	1.8		
105–109	1	1	1					1						4	1.2		
110–114		1												1	0.3	100–149	7.5
115–119	2	1			1									4	1.2		
120–124	2	1												3	0.9		
125–129	1						1							2	0.6		
130–134	2	2												4	1.2		
135–139																	
140–144																	

Table 14.3 continued

Ratio	1	2	3	4	5	6	7	8	9	10	11	12	13	All cases N	All cases %	Summary Range	Summary % of cases[a]
145–149																	
150–154																	
155–159																	
160–164																	
165–169		1												1	0.3	≥150	1.6
170–174																	
175–179																	
180–184		1												1	0.3		
185–189																	
190–194		1												1	0.3		
195–199																	
≥200	1				1									2	0.6		
def.																	
NR			1		2						8		1	12	3.6		
N	44	44	24	24	24	25	34	31	20	24	8	24	7	333	100.0		
Mean	60	76	49	44	62	36	48	53	39	41	NA	40	36	50			
Minimum	21	23	29	23	18	18	19	30	4	26		22	32	4			
Maximum	208	190	109	77	280	70	126	105	101	80		95	81	280			
Maximum as % of minimum	990	826	376	335	1,556	389	663	350	2,525	308	NA	432	253	7,000			

Notes: *Salaries and stock-in-trade have been deducted from the quotas.
[a]No return (NR) cases are excluded from the denominator.
Source: Appendix P.1.

that substantial enclosure should significantly raise parish land values, as most scholars have found, then the pattern of higher ratios found on the northern wolds must be considered a disrupted pattern which should have extended further southward. As we shall see shortly, the 1815 property tax values on the high wolds are smaller per acre, but these values rise only gradually on lands to the south. The abrupt discontinuity of ratios on the wolds at the southern boundary of Buckrose and Dickering is due to the significantly lighter assessment of these wapentakes in their original quota assignments. Lightened quotas would tend to produce higher ratios. In this case it is the spatial discontinuities in the quotas that cause the discontinuities in the ratios.

It is instructive to observe that some regions of the riding which had experienced dramatic improvement, but before the assignment of the quotas, do not produce high ratios in 1815. The improvements resulting from fen drainage in Howdenshire occurred largely in the seventeenth century, before the quotas were imposed. It should therefore not be surprising to find the tax burdens in Howdenshire fundamentally similar to those in the surrounding vale. On the high wolds the lightness of the original quotas, assigned as they were at the end of the seventeenth century, allow eighteenth and early nineteenth century enclosures to have an unusual local impact on the ratios, corresponding to dramatically lightened tax burdens. But it must also be observed that, for whatever reasons, there is no clear *general* correlation in the East Riding between lighter tax burdens and enclosure and only a very limited one with elevation.

The West Riding, with its industrial regions and its extensive and remote uplands, is an even more diversified world, in its patterns of taxation as well as in its economy (map 13 and table 14.4). Its mean ratio is the highest of the three ridings, at 58.7, and the dispersions are more extreme. Only just over 66 percent of its townships produce ratios between 20 and 59, and again the distribution is heavily skewed towards lighter tax burdens; 1.9 percent of the cases have ratios which fall below 20, but almost 32 percent exceed 59. The township bearing the lowest ratio, Warley in Halifax parish (3.6), is taxed at a rate which is 107 times more severe than that of Bradford (385.2). Both are in the industrial wapentake of Morley. In four out of ten wapentakes the highest ratios are more than 10 times greater than the lowest. In only one is the difference less than a factor of 5. Even more than in the North or East ridings, sharp differences in tax burden may be observed among contiguous townships and within the same parish. The greatest differences among neighbours are associated with the largest West Riding towns, whose rapid growth in the eighteenth century had rendered their land tax quotas grievously out of date by 1815. But significant short-distance differences in tax burden, on a scale

Table 14.4
Frequency distribution, net* ratio of 1815 property tax valuations (schedule A) to land tax quotas, all townships, West Riding

Numbered columns: 1 = Agbrigg wapentake; 2 = Barkston Ash wapentake; 3 = Claro wapentake and the Liberty of Ripon; 4 = Ewecross wapentake; 5 = Morley wapentake; 6 = Osgoldcross wapentake; 7 = Skyrack wapentake; 8 = Staincliffe wapentake; 9 = Staincross wapentake; 10 = Strafforth and Tickhill wapentake

Ratio	1	2	3	4	5	6	7	8	9	10	All cases N	All cases %	Summary Range	Summary % of cases[a]
0.0–4.9					1						1	0.2		
5.0–9.9													0.0–19.9	1.7
10.0–14.9			3								3	0.5		
15.0–19.9	1		5								6	1.0		
20.0–24.9	2	3	9			1	1	2		1	19	3.1		
25.0–29.9	3	6	16		1	5	2		2	4	39	6.3	20.0–39.9	33.6
30.0–34.9	8	12	15		4	8	6		3	10	66	10.6		
35.0–39.9	11	4	20		5	10	2	2	5	10	69	11.1		
40.0–44.9	5	9	10	1	1	7	3	4	5	10	55	8.9		
45.0–49.9	6	2	8		6	8	6	6	4	8	54	8.7	40.0–59.9	32.9
50.0–54.9	6	6	2		7	5	1	3	5	7	42	6.8		
55.0–59.9	1	4	1		1	4	2	11	4	10	38	6.1		
60.0–64.9	3		2	1	7	3	1	9	3	8	37	6.0		
65.0–69.9	3		4	2	1	1	4	9	3	2	29	4.7	60.0–79.9	18.5
70.0–74.9	1		4	3	5	1	1	9	2	3	29	4.7		
75.0–79.9	1		1	1			3	5			11	1.8		
80.0–84.9	3	1			2	1	3	4			14	2.3		
85.0–89.9			1	1	2		2	2	1	1	10	1.6	80.0–99.9	7.3
90.0–94.9			1		2		1	2	1	1	8	1.3		
95.0–99.9	3					1	1	3		2	10	1.6		

Table 14.4 continued

Ratio	1	2	3	4	5	6	7	8	9	10	All cases N	All cases %	Summary Range	Summary % of cases[a]
100.0–104.9			1	1				5		1	8	1.3		
105.0–109.9	1			1						2	4	0.6		
110.0–114.9		1						1		1	3	0.5	100.0–149.9	3.8
115.0–119.9								2		1	3	0.5		
120.0–124.9					1						1	0.2		
125.0–129.9								1			1	0.2		
130.0–134.9														
135.0–139.9														
140.0–144.9										1	1	0.2		
145.0–149.9	1										1	0.2		
150.0–154.9														
155.0–159.9	1		1								2	0.3		
160.0–164.9														
165.0–169.9			1								1	0.2	≥150.0	2.1
170.0–174.9														
175.0–179.9					1						1	0.2		
180.0–184.9										1	1	0.2		
185.0–189.9														
190.0–194.9														
195.0–199.9														
≥200.0	1				1				1	4	7	1.1		
def.	2		3		2	1					8	1.3		
NR	2		10		8	2	7	2		7	38	6.1		
N	65	48	118	11	58	58	46	82	39	95	620	100.0		
Mean	67.3	38.9	40.0	71.5	70.6	43.7	56.1	71.0	56.1	71.6	58.9			
Minimum	15.1	23.1	12.8	42.8	3.6	21.8	20.0	21.9	25.4	20.3	3.6			

Table 14.4 continued

Ratio	1	2	3	4	5	6	7	8	9	10	All cases N	%	Summary Range	% of cases[a]
Maximum	273.6	110.2	167.1	106.2	385.2	96.6	99.9	126.6	212.4	316.4	385.2			
Maximum as % of minimum	1,812	477	1,305	248	10,700	443	500	578	836	1,559	10,700			

Notes: *Salaries and stock-in-trade have been deducted from the quotas.
[a]Defective (def.) and no return (NR) cases are excluded from the denominator.
Source: Appendix P.2.

comparable to those found in the North and East, are evident throughout the more agricultural portions of the riding.

Once again, as in the North and East ridings, there are no consistent regional differences in the distribution of the tax burden. The lighter burdens on the Thorne and Hatfield levels, extending from Fockerby on the north to the vicinity of Doncaster and Blyth on the south, are interspersed with ratios, such as those in Hatfield parish, which fail to conform with an explanation based on drainage and improvement. Most of the ratios in the fenland parishes of Adlingfleet and Whitgift are in fact very low, some of them reflecting tax burdens which are among the heaviest in the riding. Moreover, in the case of the East Riding, the tax burdens on the drained fenlands of Howdenshire, across the Ouse and immediately to the east, are not unlike those of the vale which surround them. It would therefore be unwise to suggest, as a general proposition, that fenlands which had been subject to extensive further drainage and warping within the last century (though they had been originally drained in the seventeenth) were, by 1815, experiencing unusually light tax burdens.

An even more perplexing pattern may be observed in the West Riding uplands. The wapentakes of Staincliffe and Ewecross in the northwest generally bear tax burdens that are markedly lighter than those of other major regions of the riding. The mean ratios of those two wapentakes are 71.5 and 71.0 respectively. The equally agricultural but lowland wapentakes of Barkston Ash and Osgoldcross have mean ratios of 38.9 and 42.6, reflecting much heavier burdens of tax. It is also notable that the lowland wapentakes of all three ridings, when relatively uncontaminated by major urban influences, tend uniformly to produce mean ratios in the upper 30 to upper 40 range, placing Barkston Ash and Osgoldcross comfortably into a more general county-wide pattern. We have seen that in the East Riding the two high wold wapentakes of Buckrose and Dickering also bore significantly lighter tax burdens than their lowland neighbours. Does this mean that Staincliffe and Ewecross can now be offered in support of a general proposition that upland pastoral areas were, by 1815, experiencing significantly lighter tax burdens than were lowland mixed-husbandry regions? It does not. We have already noted that such a generalization cannot be supported in the North Riding, an administrative county ideally suited for such a test. The more upland townships of Gilling West, which are among the most elevated and remote in the county, generally bear burdens of taxation which are indistinguishable from those in the upper Vale of York; and throughout the riding generally the uplands fail to provide a pattern which is consistent with other variables, such as soil and farming regime, or internally coherent.

Upland patterns similarly fail in the West Riding. With the exception of Saddleworth and the townships west of Sheffield, whose light burdens could be explained on industrial grounds, the upland Pennine parishes to the south of Staincliffe and bordering on the industrial districts most often bear ratios in the 20s and 30s, very much like the most heavily taxed townships of lowland mixed husbandry districts. Many of these lower Pennine townships themselves have industrial characteristics, however, and such characteristics might distort their upland land values – although it would be odd if they were distorted toward heavier tax burdens.

The townships of Claro wapentake, immediately to the east of Staincliffe, are intrinsically more interesting as a comparison. The western and northern portions of Claro have no industrial or commercial characteristics. The high moors of Ewecross and upper Staincliffe extend in unbroken series across northern Claro and fall off, through moors and narrow dales, southward along the Staincliffe-Claro boundary. The predominantly boulder clays and limestones of Staincliffe and Ewecross give way to the predominantly millstone grits of Claro and the more southern Pennines at that point, as they do at the same point on the southern moorlands of Wensleydale just across the riding boundary to the north. But no significant changes in either topography or agrarian regime occur along those soil and wapentake boundaries. The high moors were uniformly given over to lightly stinted sheep runs. The lower elevations and better soils, especially in the Vale of Craven, were primarily dairying with little or no arable. The pastures tended to be permanent, or nearly so. Regular regimes of convertible husbandry had scarcely penetrated the region by the end of the eighteenth century, and the local landlords were sharply criticized by some agricultural improvers.[8] There seems little basis for concluding that land values should have risen disproportionately in any of the northern upland townships of the West Riding during the eighteenth or early nineteenth centuries due to improvement. And while the lands in the Craven lowlands were undoubtedly more valuable than others to the north or east of them, they had always been so. Certainly there is no reason to believe that different portions of the high moors should be markedly different in value; values on the moors should remain fairly consistent until elevations diminish and the terrain flattens considerably on approaching the Forest of Knaresborough and the Vale of York in the southern and westerly portions of Claro.

Yet the ratios fall startlingly and abruptly moving from the high moors and dairy lands of Staincliffe eastward into the equally upland townships of western Claro. The tax burden of Claro as a whole is more than three-quarters greater than those of Staincliffe or Ewecross. Although the same pattern may also be observed on the neighbouring high moorlands of Wensleydale, variations of such magnitude in tax burden on lands such as these seem economically irrational. Lighter tax burdens only begin to appear in Claro as the highlands fall off, further to the east, clustering around the important commercial and administrative centre of Ripon. Here the tax burdens are once again equivalent to those in Craven, but this is hardly a development which could support an argument for lighter upland burdens. Even within Staincliffe and Ewecross, there are only mild differences between the high Pennine and moorland townships and the relatively rich pastoral lowlands of the Vale of Craven. Attempts to find consistent variations in tax burden between upland and lowland regions in the West Riding fail everywhere one looks, just as they did in the North Riding.

The industrial regions of the West Riding, located especially in the wapentakes of Agbrigg and Morley and in the southwestern portions of Strafforth and Tickhill, present further patterns in tax burden which are also puzzling and seem to defy expectations based on the economic, geological, and topographic characteristics of the region. The great industrial and commercial towns of the riding – Bradford, Sheffield, Barnsley, Wakefield – do tend to produce exceptionally high ratios, characteristically falling in the 200 and 300 range. Such towns had enormously increased their housing and industrial structures – and thus their tax units – during the preceding century. Because the value of their real property was thereby greatly increased, the burden of their land tax was reduced. There are some surprises, however. Halifax, despite its small agricultural acreage, and Huddersfield have ratios (123.0 and 108.5, respectively) which are less than half those of the other major industrial centres. The effects on contiguous townships of such centres is also uneven. The entire subregion around Sheffield represents an extended island of high ratios with a corridor extending to Barnsley on the north, following routes of heavy commercial intercourse. There is further evidence of a corridor from Barnsley to Wakefield and thence to Leeds and Bradford, and perhaps from Leeds to Huddersfield, but these traces are difficult to discern. In other respects the major industrial centres, unlike Sheffield, seem to have exercised little effect on the tax burdens of their nearest neighbours.

The industrial region as a whole fails entirely to produce distinctive patterns of tax burden. The industrial townships of Agbrigg and Morely to the west of Leeds, with the exception of the large towns, are not unlike the agricultural and mildly commercial wapentakes of Barkston Ash and Osgoldcross. The high mean ratios of the industrial wapentakes are essentially driven by the large values of their principal centres. The woollen industries of Agbrigg and Morley and the cutlery industries around Sheffield were both still heavily organized on the domestic system and widely dispersed among small household manufacturers outside urban areas. Since those industries were growing enormously during the half century prior to 1815, one would hardly expect these regions to display tax burdens similar to those of the more agricultural districts of the county. Saddleworth is taxed more as one would expect. This Pennine township on the route to Manchester was dotted with small dispersed manufacturers engaged in subsistence agriculture. The tax burden in Saddleworth (158.7) is lighter than that in either Halifax or Huddersfield. Why such effects were not equally experienced in the other industrial districts of the riding is puzzling, if only ratios are considered. As we shall see shortly, land values per acre on the coal measures were in fact generally high by 1815, dropping off as the Pennine slope rises. But the original quota assignments on the coal measures were also high, being essentially comparable to those on the agriculturally much richer lands to the west. The quota assignments had clearly taken industrial wealth into account to some extent in these regions, and these heavier quotas had a permanently inflating effect on the land tax burdens of the industrial townships outside the major centres.

Our discussion of urban centres, in the West Riding and elsewhere, has thus far emphasized their lighter tax burdens. The literature on the land tax has long recognized that higher land values are generally found in urban parishes and on the agricultural lands immediately surrounding them. Such lands were often rendered more valuable, not only for the opportunities they afforded for the construction of suburban housing and villas but also because of the marketing opportunities in foodstuffs provided by the urban populations. In the urban centres themselves houses were generally taxed at lower rates than were agricultural acres. Thus it has been widely assumed that urban centres in general, and often the agricultural lands immediately surrounding the large centres, were taxed progressively more lightly as those centres grew in the eighteenth and early nineteenth centuries. Because they were taxed more lightly, and because the tax entries in their duplicates so often applied only to houses and buildings which were taxed at different and lighter rates, historians utilizing the land tax have frequently excluded such parishes from their analyses – or have recommended that others do so.

Houses and buildings do appear to have been taxed at different rates than land in urban townships, or at least a large proportion of them. The findings of Sir Frederick Morton Eden, presented in appendix H, offer abundant evidence to that effect, and there is no reason to doubt it. It is not true, however, that urban townships as a whole were generally or necessarily more lightly taxed in their total real properties than were the rural districts. The larger industrial and heavily commercialized towns of the West Riding were certainly lightly taxed on their land and buildings, but even in that riding so important a market and commercial centre as Selby (40.4) appears only at the mean of its agricultural wapentake. Outside the more intensely market-oriented West Riding, the pattern is even more diverse. Table 14.5 presents the ratios for the nineteen principal market towns of the North Riding. It is not true that these towns, most of which were no more than service centres for the surrounding agricultural districts,

Table 14.5
Land tax burdens in North Riding market towns, 1815

Wapentake	Township	Ratio: Property tax/ land tax	Ratio: Property tax/acre	Ratio: Acres/ land tax
Allertonshire		32.8	1.16	28
	Northallerton	55.2	1.92	29
Birdforth		37.6	.87	43
	Coxwold	34.6	1.24	51
	Thirsk	128.2	2.67	48
Bulmer		39.7	1.25	31
	Easingwold	40.7	1.46	28
Gilling West				
	Richmond	def.	def.	def.
Hang East		40.0	1.01	39
	Bedale	32.5	1.97	16
	Masham	49.0	.84	58
Hang West		65.9	.54	121
	Askrigg	71.5	.60	119
	Hawes	64.3	.29	221
	Middleham	113.0	1.88	60
Langbaurgh		46.6	1.02	45
	Guisborough	57.2	1.26	48
	Stokesley	42.5	3.10	14
	Yarm	44.3	3.52	13
Pickering Lythe		52.2	.71	73
	Pickering	128.7	def.	157
	Scarborough	NR	NR	NR
Ryedale		54.3	.85	65
	Helmsley Blackmoor	58.5	.73	80
	Kirby Moorside	67.9	1.39	49
	New Malton (combined parishes)	154.8	218.09	0.7
Whitby Strand		60.9	.92	66
	Whitby	91.0	111.07	0.8

Note: NR = no returns. def. = defective.
Source: Appendix M.

were uniformly more lightly taxed than were neighbouring rural townships – so long at least as we consider the townships as a whole in which those market towns were located. More than half of the townships containing market towns fail to depart significantly in their ratios from the wapentake mean.

But the boundaries of many of these townships were relatively extensive and included large proportions of agricultural acres which might drive down the average tax burden of the township as a whole. The boundaries of New Malton and Whitby enclosed virtually no agricultural lands, and in both of these purely urban townships the tax burdens were considerably under those of their agricultural neighbours. But New Malton and Whitby were two of the most intensely commercialized centres in the riding, and for that reason they may be exceptional in the lightness of their burdens. A better test of urban tax burdens might be made by looking at smaller centres, such as Coxwold, or more moderately important centres, such as Stokesley and Yarm, none of which had major agricultural acreages within their township boundaries. Their ratios scarcely depart from their wapentake means. Middleham had few agricultural acres and departs strongly from the wapentake mean, but its ratio is no lighter than those of several other more purely agricultural townships in lower Wensleydale. Easingwold (40.7) does far better than non-urban Raskelf (13.1), which shared its parish; but Raskelf is an outlier, and Easingwold's ratio is almost precisely at the mean for its region. It may be that the extensive agricultural acres within its township are distorting its ratio downward; but Thirsk, whose agricultural acres were equally extensive, enjoys one of the highest ratios and lightest tax burdens of any lowland township. Pickering, whose township encompasses vast rising dales and uplands which swamp its small urban acreage, similarly produces a surprisingly high ratio. But the town of Pickering is in sharp contrast with Helmsley Blackmoor and Kirby Moorside, two nearby market towns which also stood at the foot of townships with extensive moorland acreages. In short, it is not certain that all towns, and especially rural market towns, enjoyed significantly lighter tax burdens by 1815. Some clearly did, but others apparently did not. In particular, when such towns stood in the midst of townships with extensive non-urban acreages, the tax burden on real property for the township as a whole often did not depart significantly from that of its immediate region.

A more surprising finding which emerges from this analysis is that some of the larger and more ancient cities of England were experiencing relatively severe tax burdens on their real property by 1815. Unlike the great industrial and commercial centres of the West Riding, or even some of the rural market towns in the county, the City of York bore a land tax burden which would have been considered heavy in the lowland agricultural districts of the three ridings. Like New Malton and Whitby, York provides a precise test of urban burdens because its boundaries excluded virtually all adjacent agricultural acreages. The ratios for the City of York and for the Ainsty, a wapentake lying within its administrative jurisdiction, are displayed on map 13 and presented in table 14.6 as a frequency distribution. The mean ratio for the twenty-eight parishes lying within the City of York is 21. None of the market towns of the North Riding bear ratios this low; and, as we have seen, the great centres in the West Riding generally have ratios ranging in the 200s or 300s, ratios in the 100s at

Table 14.6
Frequency distribution, net* ratio of 1815 property tax valuations (schedule A) to land tax quotas, all townships, City of York and the Ainsty

Numbered columns: 1 = Ainsty wapentake 2 = City of York

			All cases		Summary	
Ratio	1	2	N	%	Range	% of cases[a]
0–4						
5–9		1	1	1.6	0–19	27.6
10–14	2	4	6	9.8		
15–19	1	8	9	14.8		
20–24	2	3	5	8.2		
25–29	1	4	5	8.2	20–39	53.4
30–34	7	3	10	16.4		
35–39	10	1	11	18.0		
40–44	5	1	6	9.8		
45–49	1	1	2	3.3	40–59	15.5
50–54						
55–59	1		1	1.6		
60–64						
65–69		1	1	1.6	60–79	3.4
70–74	1		1	1.6		
75–79						
80–84						
85–89					80–99	
90–94						
95–99						
100–104						
105–109						
110–114						
115–119						
120–124					100–149	
125–129						
130–134						
135–139						
140–144						
145–149						
150–154						
155–159						
160–164						
165–169					≥150	
170–174						
175–179						
180–184						
185–189						
190–194						
195–199						
≥200						
def.						
NR	2	1	3	4.9		
N	33	28	61	100.0		

Table 14.6 continued

Ratio	1	2	All cases N	All cases %	Summary Range	Summary % of cases[a]
Mean	32	21	26			
Minimum	10	7	7			
Maximum	74	67	74			
Maximum as % of minimum	740	957	1,057			

Notes: *Salaries and stock-in-trade have been deducted from the quota.
[a]Defective (def.) and no return (NR) cases are excluded from the denominator.
Source: Appendix P.3.

Halifax and Huddersfield being low for their group. Even the ancient centre of Ripon, which like York was a cathedral town and administrative centre, though a less fashionable and important one, produces a ratio of 167.1. Nor can the heavy burdens within the walls of York be explained by the walls themselves. While cities such as Hull and Sheffield are contributing to higher ratios in their suburbs, the townships adjacent to York are, with the possible exception of Gate Fulford in the East Riding and of Murton in the North, essentially similar in their tax burdens to their agricultural neighbours. The fact is that York began with a heavy quota assignment; and its land values, while rising, never sufficiently lightened its burden to bring the city into alignment with other large centres. Once again we find that land tax burdens cannot be predicted on the basis of the economic or social characteristics of their townships or parishes. There seem to be no general patterns to the distribution of land tax burdens by the end of the Napoleonic wars, if ever there had been.

The City of York is also instructive due to the internal distribution of the tax among its twenty-eight parishes. Some recent political studies have treated tax data within such cities as though the tax entries among the various parishes were comparable in their absolute values.[9] Table 14.6 makes it clear that such an assumption, at least with respect to the land tax, is unwarranted. The ratios of the parishes lying within the City of York range from 7 to 67. The burden of the land tax in St Cuthbert and its associated parishes is almost 10 times that in St Giles. Most of the parishes fall within a well-distributed range extending from 12 to 34. The analysis of taxation within ancient cities with multiple parishes must clearly be undertaken with the utmost caution. The distributions of tax burdens among their internal parishes are subject to all the variations normally encountered elsewhere in the English countryside.

Finally, as we have had some occasion to note, whatever patterns we do find in the ratios tend to persist across riding boundaries. The lowland agricultural districts in all three ridings tend to have ratios falling mostly in the 20 to 60 range. The peculiarities along the Staincliffe and Ewecross boundary in the West Riding continue into the North Riding on the southern Wensleydale moors. The higher ratios around Ripon extend across the Ouse into the adjacent townships of the North Riding. The East Riding township across the riding boundary from New Malton has a similarly lighter tax burden than its region. It may not be possible to discern consistent regional differences within any one of the ridings, but patterns at the micro level, few as they might be, persist even across the boundaries of administrative counties. This observation again encourages confidence in the ability of the ratios to measure real differences in land tax burdens and in their suitability for making both local and inter-county comparisons.

Why are the land tax burdens generally distributed across the countryside in so dazzling an array? The patterns of those burdens most often seem almost random in their complexity. It is surely reasonable to expect tax burdens, even when associated with ossified and ancient quotas, to bear some consistent relationship to known land values, or to patterns of agricultural improvement, or at least to differences between moorland and vale or broadly defined agricultural regimes – unless the quotas or the valuation series employed in constructing the ratios are themselves so distorted in their distributions as to prevent the emergence of meaningful patterns of tax burden. We shall therefore examine separately the spatial distributions of the property tax and of the quotas. If each produces rational patterns of distribution, then we may be certain that the more irrational distributions of the ratios are due to the way the two variables interact, that is, that they are the result of differential departures of changing land values from ossified tax quotas. We may then feel even more comfortable with our conclusion that the ratios measure tax burdens with some accuracy in the three ridings of Yorkshire and that they may be applied with some assurance in other counties, as we shall do in chapter 15.

The only way in which the distributions of the property tax valuations and the land tax quotas may be tested is by calculating them on a per acre basis. This is not a wholly satisfactory method. As we have seen in chapter 5, parishes and townships are not homogeneous in their soils or land values. Nor are there tight correlations between elevation and soils. But in general a plotting of property tax per acre, with which we shall begin, should distribute itself in such a way that pastoral upland areas with abundant waste are clearly discernible in having lower per acre values than the mixed husbandry lowlands; and major towns, with their immediate hinterlands, should have values which are significantly higher than those found in the best agricultural districts.

Patterns such as these are in fact discernible with remarkable clarity within the North Riding (map 8). The low values per acre throughout the moorland townships of the western dales stand out sharply, as do the slightly higher values of both Swaledale and Wensleydale. Precisely the same patterns are evident throughout the North Yorkshire Moors. In both regions the values rise gradually upon entering the prime mixed-husbandry districts of the vales. Similarly, the principal towns are notable for their unusually high values. Indeed the acreage values in some towns are far greater than contemporary literature would have led us to believe (table 14.5). New Malton and Whitby again provide good tests, being wholly urban in their acreages. New Malton registers an incredible £218 per acre and Whitby £111. Scarborough stands at over £10 per acre. But most towns with moderate agricultural acreage, such as Richmond or Yarm, produce values in the £3 range. Towns with larger proportions of agricultural acreages sometimes display high values, such as Thirsk (£2.67); many others, such as Northallerton (£1.92) or Easingwold (£1.46), blend into their agricultural surroundings. But so they should in such large townships. It is also comforting that, moving from suburban townships in the area of major cities towards the city, the increase in values is gradual. Land within the City of York is valued at over £22, and is nearly equalled by that of its suburban township of St Olave in Marygate (£20.50). Contiguous townships on all sides of York bear land values that are well above those of their agrarian neighbours.

It is not that the acreage values derived from the property tax are not dispersed around the means of their districts. They are even more dispersed than were the ratios employed to calculate land tax burdens (table 14.7). What distinguishes these dispersions from those of the ratios is that, broadly speaking, they are consistently related to what we know about the economy and topography of the riding. The distributions of the property tax acreage values are those we would normally expect. Those of the ratios are not.

Turning to the East Riding, the land values produced by the property tax are distributed once again precisely as we would expect (map 11). The lowest values are on the high wolds and on the poor clays and sands of the vale. Higher values in the vale tend to occur along the Ouse, Derwent, and Humber rivers, where the fields and siltlands can be well watered or warped, and in the fenlands of Howdenshire. The best agricultural land values of the riding are generally on the lower wolds and in Holderness, as they should be. Land values in Hull are over £76 per acre, and the city is surrounded by a wide arc of suburban townships bearing exceptionally high values, an arc which extends in a corridor to Beverley. The dispersions around the division means of the East Riding (table 14.8) are again greater than those of the ratios; but, as in the North Riding, the land values are distributed in a way that enables one quickly to discern the principal economic and topographical features of the administrative county.

Even the extraordinary economic and topographical diversity of the West Riding is reflected in the land values derived from the property tax (map 14). The low acreage values on the high moors of Ewecross and Staincliffe do not halt abruptly at the Claro boundary, as the ratios had done, but continue eastward in accordance with elevation and general topography. Values in Claro rise slowly only as they approach the Forest of Knaresborough and the vale. The mixed husbandry wapentakes to the east, as well as the dairying lowlands of Craven, are very much like those of the East and North Riding vales. The Pennine townships on the west, like those along the northern moorlands of the riding, are characterized by lowering land values as one ascends the slope, except in Saddleworth and those townships in Morley which are most affected by industrialization. Land values in the industrial wapentakes are generally very high, but primarily as a function of spread effects immediately surrounding the major industrial cities. All of the major cities and towns, including non-industrial centres such as Ripon, are adjoined by neighbouring townships with high values. While the dispersion of the acreage values is great throughout the riding (tables 14.9 and 14.10), they conform remarkably well – except for mixed patterns in the fenlands – to its economic and natural features.

If there are any surprises in the West Riding, they lie in the comparatively low land values per acre of its major urban centres. While land values in Hull stand at £76 per acre, and even New Malton and Whitby produce values of £218 and £111 respectively, the highest West Riding value at Wakefield is merely £95.15, followed by Bradford at £48.13, Halifax at £38.41, and central Leeds at £37.80. Sheffield (£24.84) is not significantly different than York (£22.51), which is only about twice as valuable as Scarborough (£10.38). None of these urban centres are significantly diluted by agricultural acreages.

We may conclude that the economically and topographically irrational distributions of the land tax burden ratios are not due to the property tax valuations. But what about the land tax quotas themselves? Since John Beckett and others have shown that these quotas were, in some counties at least, derived from very ancient valuations, perhaps their distributions, when calculated by acreage, are as irrational as those of the ratios and are at the root of the disturbance. Examining the North Riding on map 9, it is immediately apparent that such is not the case. The same broad regions which appeared on the property tax map are repeated here, and to a degree that is greater than most of us would have expected. The highest acreages, representing the lightest tax burdens per pound of quota, are once again distributed precisely where one would want them in the North Yorkshire Moors and in the western dales. Traces of heavier burdens in the Wensleydale lowlands and in Swaledale are readily apparent. Quota burdens tend to increase progressively as elevations decline. Regions consisting

Table 14.7
Frequency distribution, 1814 property tax valuations (schedule A) per acre, all townships, North Riding

Numbered columns: 1 = Allertonshire wapentake; 2 = Birdforth wapentake; 3 = Bulmer wapentake; 4 = Gilling East wapentake; 5 = Gilling West wapentake; 6 = Hallikeld wapentake; 7 = Hang East wapentake; 8 = Hang West wapentake; 9 = Langbaurgh wapentake; 10 = Pickering Lythe wapentake; 11 = Ryedale wapentake; 12 = Whitby Strand wapentake

£/acre	1	2	3	4	5	6	7	8	9	10	11	12	All cases N	All cases %	Summary Range	Summary % of cases[a]
.00–.09																
.10–.19		1			2			2	2	3			10	2.1	.00–.49	13.8
.20–.29		1			3			5		2	3		14	2.9		
.30–.39		2			7		3	2	1	4	4	1	24	5.0		
.40–.49		3			2			4	4	2	3		18	3.7		
.50–.59	1	2	1		2		2	5	2			3	18	3.7		
.60–.69		4	2				3	4	2	3	4		22	4.6	.50–.99	29.4
.70–.79	1	1	3		3			2	2	3	5	4	24	5.0		
.80–.89	2	2	3	2			4	1	3	5	4	1	27	5.6		
.90–.99	4	8	7	1	5	1	2	4	6	5	6	1	50	10.4		
1.00–1.09	5	5	4	3	2	2	1		14	3	3		42	8.7		
1.10–1.19	4	6	8	4	1	2			4	1	3		33	6.8	1.00–1.49	39.2
1.20–1.29	5	3	5	4	4	4	3	1	12	2	2		45	9.3		
1.30–1.39	4	4	7	2	1	7	4	1	9	2	2		43	8.9		
1.40–1.49		1	3	4	2	2	1	1	8	1	2		25	5.2		
1.50–1.59	3	2	2	5	2	2	3		3		1		23	4.8		
1.60–1.69			5	1	2	1	2	5	3				19	3.9	1.50–1.99	12.7
1.70–1.79	1	1	3	1		2							8	1.7		
1.80–1.89				1	1	2		1					5	1.0		
1.90–1.99	1		1	1			1			1	1		6	1.2		

Table 14.7 continued

£/acre	1	2	3	4	5	6	7	8	9	10	11	12	All cases N	All cases %	Summary Range	Summary % of cases[a]
2.00–2.09			1			1			1		2		5	1.0		
2.10–2.19											1		1	0.2	2.00–2.49	2.1
2.20–2.29							1						1	0.2		
2.30–2.39																
2.40–2.49					1	1					1		3	0.6		
2.50–2.59			1										1	0.2		
2.60–2.69		1	1										2	0.4	2.50–2.99	1.2
2.70–2.79			1		1								2	0.4		
2.80–2.89									1				1	0.2		
2.90–2.99																
≥3.00			2						2	1	1	2	8	1.7	≥3.00	1.7
def.																
NR					1						1		3	0.6		
N	31	47	60	29	42	27	30	38	80	38	49	12	483	100.0		
Mean	1.16	.87	1.25	1.29	.53	1.42	1.01	.54	1.02	.71	.85	.92	.87			
Minimum	.57	.13	.57	.83	.10	.95	.36	.19	.17	.13	.20	.30	.10			
Maximum	1.92	2.67	20.50	1.98	2.79	2.41	2.22	1.88	3.52	10.38	218.09	111.07	218.09			
Maximum as % of minimum	337	2,054	3,596	238	2,790	254	617	989	2,070	7,985	109,045	37,023	218,090			

Notes: Valuations are those of 1814. 1815 valuations are substituted in eight cases where 1814 values are defective or not reported.
[a]Defective (def.) and no return (NR) cases are excluded from the denominator.
Source: Appendix M.

Table 14.8

Frequency distribution, 1815 property tax valuations (schedule A) per acre, all townships, East Riding

Numbered columns:
1 = Buckrose wapentake
2 = Dickering wapentake
3 = Harthill wapentake, Bainton Beacon division
4 = Harthill wapentake, Holme Beacon division
5 = Harthill wapentake, Hunsley Beacon division
6 = Harthill wapentake, Wilton Beacon division
7 = Holderness wapentake, Middle division
8 = Holderness wapentake, North division
9 = Holderness wapentake, South division
10 = Howdenshire wapentake
11 = Hullshire, city and county
12 = Ouse and Derwent wapentake
13 = Beverley borough and liberties

£/acre	1	2	3	4	5	6	7	8	9	10	11	12	13	All cases N	All cases %	Summary Range	Summary % of cases[a]
.00–.09																	
.10–.19																.00–.49	0.9
.20–.29																	
.30–.39																	
.40–.49		1			1	1								3	0.9		
.50–.59	1	6		1	1	1								10	3.0		
.60–.69	1	3		3		1				1		2		11	3.3	.50–.99	29.7
.70–.79	3	3	2	3	2	6			1			3		23	6.9		
.80–.89	8	2	2	4	1	1	1	2				1		22	6.6		
.90–.99	7	4	1	4	1	7	1	2		2		3		32	9.6		
1.00–1.09	6	3	4	3	2	2	2	4		1		3		30	9.0		
1.10–1.19	4	6	5	1	1	4	3	8		4		4		40	12.0	1.00–1.49	47.3
1.20–1.29	2	2	2	1	2		5	3	1	3		3		24	7.2		
1.30–1.39	5	5		2	2		4	2	6	3		1		30	9.0		
1.40–1.49	3	3	4	1	1		7	3	4	2	1	1	2	32	9.6		
1.50–1.59	1	1	1	1	1	1	3	3	2	2	1	1		18	5.4		
1.60–1.69		2	1		3		1	1	1	2		1		12	3.6	1.50–1.99	12.7
1.70–1.79	1	1								2				4	1.2		

Table 14.8 continued

£/acre	1	2	3	4	5	6	7	8	9	10	11	12	13	All cases N	All cases %	Summary Range	Summary % of cases[a]
1.80–1.89					1		1				2			4	1.2		
1.90–1.99								2	2					4	1.2		
2.00–2.09					1			1						2	0.6		
2.10–2.19					1		1		1	1				4	1.2	2.00–2.49	4.6
2.20–2.29	1	1											1	3	0.9		
2.30–2.39							1		1		1			3	0.9		
2.40–2.49			1		1								1	3	0.9		
2.50–2.59	1					1				1				3	0.9		
2.60–2.69											1		1	2	0.6	2.50–2.99	2.4
2.70–2.79											1			1	0.3		
2.80–2.89													1	1	0.3		
2.90–2.99												1		1	0.3		
≥3.00		1			1		4				1		1	8	2.4	≥3.00	2.4
def.									1					1	0.3		
NR			1		1									2	0.6		
N	44	44	24	24	24	25	34	31	20	24	8	24	7	333	100.0		
Mean	1.06	1.02	1.20	.94	1.92	.90	1.80	1.29	1.60	1.35	8.10	1.14	3.72	1.28			
Minimum	.56	.41	.73	.58	.45	.47	.87	.80	.71	.61	1.43	.66	1.44	.41			
Maximum	2.58	3.27	2.41	1.50	44.24	2.53	11.42	2.00	2.33	2.59	76.68	2.91	7.43	76.68			
Maximum as % of minimum	461	798	330	259	9,831	538	1,313	250	328	424	5,362	441	516	18,702			

Note: [a]Defective (def.) and no return (NR) cases are excluded from the denominator.
Source: Appendix P.1.

Table 14.9

Frequency distribution, 1815 property tax valuations (schedule A) per acre, all townships, West Riding

Numbered columns: 1 = Agbrigg wapentake; 2 = Barkston Ash wapentake; 3 = Claro wapentake and the Liberty of Ripon; 4 = Ewecross wapentake; 5 = Morley wapentake; 6 = Osgoldcross wapentake; 7 = Skyrack wapentake; 8 = Staincliffe wapentake; 9 = Staincross wapentake; 10 = Strafforth and Tickhill wapentake

£/acre	1	2	3	4	5	6	7	8	9	10	All cases N	All cases %	Summary Range	Summary % of cases[a]
.00–.09			1								1	0.2		
.10–.19			2		1			1			4	0.6	.00–.49	7.9
.20–.29	2		3	1				3	1		10	1.6		
.30–.39	4		3	2	2		2	4			17	2.7		
.40–.49		1	2	1		1		7	1	3	16	2.6		
.50–.59	2	1	3	2			3	3		2	16	2.6		
.60–.69		1	8	2		2	3	7	2	1	26	4.2		
.70–.79	1	4	9			5		9	1	3	32	5.2	.50–.99	26.4
.80–.89		2	6	1	5	5	3	7	2	8	39	6.3		
.90–.99	3	7	10	1	1	8	4	7	3	4	48	7.7		
1.00–1.09	2	7	14			7	2	7	2	7	46	7.4		
1.10–1.19	1	6	9		4	6	4	6	3	8	47	7.6		
1.20–1.29	3	7	9		2	5	4	5	2	7	44	7.1	1.00–1.49	33.2
1.30–1.39	2	3	7		2	4		5	3	4	30	4.8		
1.40–1.49	4	2	8		3	3	1	6	3	6	36	5.8		
1.50–1.59	6		7			1	3	3	1	10	31	5.0		
1.60–1.69	6	1	2			2	1	1	3	6	22	3.6		
1.70–1.79	3	1	2		3		2		5	3	19	3.1	1.50–1.99	16.0
1.80–1.89	3				3		3		2	3	14	2.3		
1.90–1.99	1		1		3	1		1	2	3	12	1.9		

Table 14.9 continued

£/acre	1	2	3	4	5	6	7	8	9	10	All cases N	All cases %	Summary Range	Summary % of cases[a]
2.00–2.09	3	2	1	1	1	1	2		1		12	1.9		
2.10–2.19	1		1		1		4	1			8	1.3		
2.20–2.29	2		2		1					2	7	1.1	2.00–2.49	5.7
2.30–2.39	1		1							1	3	0.5		
2.40–2.49	2				1		2				5	0.8		
2.50–2.59	2	1			2	2					7	1.1		
2.60–2.69	1	1			2						4	0.6		
2.70–2.79									1	1	2	0.3	2.50–2.99	3.0
2.80–2.89					3					1	4	0.6		
2.90–2.99					1						1	0.2		
≥3.00	6	1	5		17	3	3	1	1	11	48	7.7	≥3.00	7.9
def.	2					2					4	0.6		
NR	2		2							1	5	0.8		
N	65	48	118	11	58	58	46	82	39	95	620	100.0		
Mean	1.99	1.21	.96	.53	2.48	1.22	2.30	.80	1.32	1.78	1.40			
Minimum	.28	.46	.08	.23	.15	.43	.32	.12	.28	.41	.08			
Maximum	95.15	4.08	9.51	2.03	48.13	4.88	37.80	3.77	6.30	24.84	95.15			
Maximum as % of minimum	33,982	887	11,888	883	32,087	1,135	11,812	3,142	2,250	6,058	118,938			

Note: [a]Defective (def.) and no return (NR) cases are excluded from the denominator.
Source: Appendix P.2.

Table 14.10
Frequency distribution, 1815 property tax valuations (schedule A) per acre, all townships, City of York and the Ainsty

Numbered columns: 1 = Ainsty wapentake 2 = City of York

£/acre	1	2	All cases N	All cases %	Summary Range	Summary % of cases[a]
.00–.09						
.10–.19					.00–.49	
.20–.29						
.30–.39						
.40–.49						
.50–.59						
.60–.69					.50–.99	15.2
.70–.79						
.80–.89	3		3	4.9		
.90–.99	2		2	3.3		
1.00–1.09	1		1	1.6		
1.10–1.19	1		1	1.6	1.00–1.49	54.6
1.20–1.29	10		10	16.4		
1.30–1.39	4		4	6.6		
1.40–1.49	2		2	3.3		
1.50–1.59	2		2	3.3		
1.60–1.69	1		1	1.6	1.50–1.99	18.2
1.70–1.79	1		1	1.6		
1.80–1.89						
1.90–1.99	2		2	3.3		
2.00–2.09	1		1	1.6		
2.10–2.19	1		1	1.6	2.00–2.49	9.1
2.20–2.29	1		1	1.6		
2.30–2.39						
2.40–2.49						
2.50–2.59						
2.60–2.69					2.50–2.99	
2.70–2.79						
2.80–2.89						
2.90–2.99						
≥3.00	1		1	1.6	≥3.00	3.0
def.		28	28	45.9		
NR						
N	33	28	61	100.0		
Mean	1.31	22.51	2.13			
Minimum	.85					
Maximum	3.26					
Maximum as % of minimum	384	NA	def.			

Note: [a]Defective (def.) cases are excluded from the denominator.
Source: Appendix P.3.

primarily of sheep runs carry the lightest quota burdens, followed by dairying regions and then by the mixed husbandry districts of cereal production. Even the Bulmer sands are marked on the map by their lighter burdens (as they were by their lower per-acre values on the property tax map). Market towns (table 14.5) such as New Malton (0.7 acres) and Whitby (0.8), along with St Olave in Marygate (2) on the outskirts of York, have quota burdens which are far more onerous than those of the prime agricultural districts of the surrounding vale, which range mostly from 20 to 40 acres. Smaller market towns such as Stokesley (14) and Yarm (13), when not diluted by agricultural acreages, also produce heavy quota burdens for their immediate regions. Sharp differences in quota assignment among neighbouring townships are not confined to the vicinity of towns, however. They appear throughout the riding and within all of its regions. As with the property tax distributions, the dispersions in quota burden are very great indeed at all administrative levels, and to a far greater degree than those of the ratios (table 14.11). But also like the property tax, the quotas are distributed within the riding in a manner which conforms surprisingly well with its topography and traditional economy.

There are also significant differences between the quota and the property tax maps, however, particularly in the lowland vales. The Vale of Cleveland is far more lightly taxed by its quotas, when compared to the Vale of York, than it was later to be by the property tax. And, throughout the Vale of York itself, the quota burdens are far less differentiated than are the acreage values derived from the property tax. This is a comforting observation. Although larger regional differences, related principally to topography, should have persisted over the years, differing rates of improvement and a myriad of other considerations should have evolved a more highly differentiated pattern of land values throughout the vales by the end of the Napoleonic wars. Any failure by these maps to display increasing differentiation, especially in the mixed husbandry districts, would cause them to be suspect.

The regional parallels which we found on the North Riding property tax and quota maps are again encountered on those for the East Riding, and they are accompanied by even stronger indications of differential rates of agricultural improvement. The high wolds bear the lightest tax quota burdens (map 12). The poorer soils in the Vale of York also have light quotas when compared to other regions; but, unlike the acreage values of the property tax, the vale quotas are generally twice as heavy as those of the wolds. Quotas tend to fall most heavily on the prime lands of the southern wolds and Holderness and most especially in the vicinity of Hull and Beverley. Market towns generally bear heavy quotas within their regions. Dispersions in the per acre burdens imposed by the quotas are great (table 14.12), but they broadly conform to the regional character of the riding.

Table 14.11

Frequency distribution, acres per £1 gross* land tax quota, all townships, North Riding

Numbered columns: 1 = Allertonshire wapentake; 2 = Birdforth wapentake; 3 = Bulmer wapentake; 4 = Gilling East wapentake; 5 = Gilling West wapentake; 6 = Hallikeld wapentake; 7 = Hang East wapentake; 8 = Hang West wapentake; 9 = Langbaurgh wapentake; 10 = Pickering Lythe wapentake; 11 = Ryedale wapentake; 12 = Whitby Strand wapentake

													All cases		Summary	
acres/£	1	2	3	4	5	6	7	8	9	10	11	12	N	%	Range	% of cases[a]
0–4			1								1	1	3	0.6	0–9	0.6
5–9																
10–14	2	1		1	1	1	1		2				9	1.9	10–19	7.5
15–19	2	5	8	3	1	1	2		3	1	1		27	5.6		
20–24	9	3	11	6	4	4	1		6		2	1	47	9.7		
25–29	8	2	7	5	4	4	3		7		3		43	8.9	20–39	41.2
30–34	5	6	5	4	3	5	9		12		6		55	11.4		
35–39	1	8	11	7	2	4	2		10	3	3	1	52	10.8		
40–44	2	4	5	2	3	3	1	2	6	2	3		33	6.8		
45–49		5	6		3	1	2	1	9	3	4	1	35	7.2	40–59	19.9
50–54		3	1		2	2		1	1	1	2		13	2.7		
55–59		2				1	1	1	6	1	2		14	2.9		
60–64		1	3	1	1		1	5	1	2	1	1	17	3.5		
65–69	1	2	1		1		1		2	1	1		10	2.1	60–79	10.0
70–74					1	1	1		1	2	1	2	9	1.9		
75–79	1				1		3	2	1	2	1	1	12	2.5		
80–84			1					4	4		2		11	2.3		
85–89		1			1				2	2	1		7	1.4	80–99	7.3
90–94		1			1		1	2		2	2		9	1.9		
95–99					1			1		3		3	8	1.7		

Table 14.11 continued

acres/£	1	2	3	4	5	6	7	8	9	10	11	12	All cases N	All cases %	Summary Range	Summary % of cases[a]
100–149		2			5		1	8	3	5	9		33	6.8		
150–199		1			3			5	2	3	2	1	17	3.5	≥100	13.4
200–249					1			5		1			7	1.4		
250–299					1			1		1			3	0.6		
≥300					1				1	1	1		4	0.8		
def.					1								1	0.2		
NR									1	2	1		4	0.8		
N	31	47	60	29	42	27	30	38	80	38	49	12	483	100.0		
Mean	28	43	31	30	83	34	39	121	45	73	65	66	51			
Minimum	10	14	2	12	14	13	13	41	13	16	0.7	0.8	0.7			
Maximum	76	152	83	63	590	70	148	275	317	363	322	154	590			
Maximum as % of minimum	760	1,086	4,150	525	4,214	538	1,138	671	2,438	2,269	46,000	19,250	84,286			

Notes: *No deductions have been made for salary or stock-in-trade.
[a]Defective (def.) and no return (NR) cases are excluded from the denominator.
Source: Appendix M.

Table 14.12

Frequency distribution, acres per £1 gross* land tax quota, all townships, East Riding

Numbered columns:
1 = Buckrose wapentake
2 = Dickering wapentake
3 = Harthill wapentake, Bainton Beacon division
4 = Harthill wapentake, Holme Beacon division
5 = Harthill wapentake, Hunsley Beacon division
6 = Harthill wapentake, Wilton Beacon division
7 = Holderness wapentake, Middle division
8 = Holderness wapentake, North division
9 = Holderness wapentake, South division
10 = Howdenshire wapentake
11 = Hullshire, city and county
12 = Ouse and Derwent wapentake
13 = Beverley borough and liberties

														All cases		Summary	
Acres/£	1	2	3	4	5	6	7	8	9	10	11	12	13	N	%	Range	% of cases[a]
0–4													1	1	0.3		
5–9					1		2		1					4	1.2	0–9	1.6
10–14		1					1						1	3	0.9		
15–19	2			1	1	2	2		1	1			2	12	3.6	10–19	4.7
20–24	1	1	2		1	3	9		6	4		1	1	29	8.7		
25–29	4	1	4	3	3	3	7	3	6	6		6		46	13.8	20–39	46.9
30–34	2	2	4		6	3	7	5	2	4		6		41	12.3		
35–39	3	3	2	2	2	3	1	9	2	4		4		35	10.5		
40–44	5	3	3	3	3	4	3	4	1	1		3		33	9.9		
45–49	2	4	2	6	1	1	1	5		1				23	6.9	40–59	26.4
50–54	4	2	2	1	1	2		3				2		17	5.1		
55–59	1	1	1	3			1	1		2		1	1	12	3.6		
60–64	3	2	1	1	1	1						1		10	3.0		
65–69	1				1									2	0.6	60–79	8.1
70–74	1	1	1	1	1	1								6	1.8		
75–79		4	2		1			1						8	2.4		
80–84	1													1	0.3		
85–89		2		2										4	1.2	80–99	3.7

Table 14.12 continued

Acres/£	1	2	3	4	5	6	7	8	9	10	11	12	13	All cases N	All cases %	Summary Range	Summary % of cases[a]
90–94		1		1						1				3	0.9		
95–99		3				1								4	1.2		
100–149	12	6				1								19	5.7		
150–199	2	3												5	1.5		
200–249		4												4	1.2	≥100	8.7
250–299																	
≥300																	
def.									1					1	0.3		
NR					1						8		1	10	3.0		
N	44	44	24	24	24	25	34	31	20	24	8	24	7	333	100.0		
Mean	57	69	40	47	32	40	26	41	24	30	NA	35	9	38			
Minimum	15	13	21	18	6	16	7	25	6	17		22	4	4			
Maximum	181	249	78	92	78	100	56	76	41	93		61	56	249			
Maximum as % of minimum	1,207	1,915	371	511	1,300	625	800	304	683	547	NA	277	1,400	6,225			

Notes: *No deductions have been made for salary or stock-in-trade.
[a]Defective (def.) and no return (NR) cases are excluded from the denominator.
Source: Appendix P.1.

In the West Riding the dispersion of the quota burdens are again very large (tables 14.13 and 14.14), but the regional patterns stand out less distinctly on map 15 than they did on the quota burden maps for the North and East ridings. The distinctions between the industrial townships and the mixed husbandry districts to the east are especially unmarked. The larger industrial towns themselves bear significantly heavier burdens, but they cause relatively few spread effects among their neighbours. Moreover, their burdens are from 3 to 14 times lighter than that of York (0.96) or of such North Riding centres as New Malton (0.7) and Whitby (0.8). A centre such as Blyth (3) on the Great North Road bears the same burden of quota as Halifax (3) and almost 3 times that of Bradford (8). The quota of Boroughbridge (2) is even heavier. Saddleworth (140) is very lightly taxed. The patterns on the fenlands and the lower western Pennines are mixed, and the quotas of the Craven lowlands, unlike the land values derived from the property tax, are considerably lighter than those of the mixed husbandry districts to the east. Such patterns suggest that the quotas, in the West Riding especially, are relatively ancient ones. Quota burdens in the high Pennine and moorland districts of Staincliffe and Ewecross are consistently light, however; and they continue light across the Claro boundary, as they do on the property tax map. In short, regional patterns are perceptible on the West Riding quota map, but they are not always so well marked, nor do they always bear the same inter-regional relations, as those found for the later valuations of the property tax. The disparities between these two West Riding maps are those we might expect to find in an administrative county that had undergone such profound economic change during the two centuries prior to 1815.

This extended discussion of the areal distributions of the property tax valuations and land tax quotas leads in the end to the conclusion that both variables conform reasonably well with the known topographical and economic features of the three ridings. The correlations are not perfect ones; uplands and lowlands are easily distinguished, but some important distinctions in agrarian regime which should produce significant differences in land values – between dairying and mixed husbandry areas, for example – do not always emerge with clarity. Wensleydale stands out separately on both variables; but the Craven lowlands, when examined by the property tax (but not the quotas) look much like the mixed husbandry districts to the east. No one should have expected that per acre conversions of these variables would uniformly yield fine distinctions, however. Influences on real values, such as soils and improvements, vary quickly and widely as one moves across the landscape and do not neatly coincide with township boundaries. The correlations should be imperfect. If larger patterns emerge, as they do in a rough way, that is enough for our purpose, which is a comparative one. The ratios, by contrast, are not distributed in consistent regional patterns, and they do not conform to known topographic and economic characteristics of the ridings. Since the property tax and the quotas do, then the fact that there is no pattern to the ratios cannot be due to inherent deficiencies in the two variables employed to create them. What does cause the failure?

One answer is a simple technical one. The property tax distributes into regional patterns largely for two reasons: It is a relatively reliable valuation of real property values, and real property values – whether on improved or unimproved land – do in general conform reasonably well with soil and elevation; and the valuations were transformed into per acre values, which standardized them by size but also introduced a geographical bias. Similarly, the quotas were transformed into inverted per acre values; and it would seem that their correspondence with the values of real property, while perhaps less perfect (especially in the West Riding), was sufficient to prevent any gross distortions in expected regional variation. The ratios, on the other hand, were not computed employing acreages. They are direct estimates of actual land tax burdens in 1815, computed by dividing tax quotas into total valuation for each township. Unlike for the other two series, there is no logical necessity for such tax burdens to conform to any other variables whatsoever, be it topography or economic characteristics – or at least there is no necessity that these burdens conform to any *single* or any easily specifiable group of variables. Obviously something caused the distribution of the burdens; but it need not be entirely evident to us what the cause or causes might have been, and they need not have produced orderly patterns on the map.

But the narrow technical answer is not a sufficient one. A more sufficient answer to the question is that the ratios fail to pattern themselves into meaningful regional distributions because of the way the two variables used to create the ratios come together. Land values, reflected in the property tax valuations, had by 1815 departed at differential rates from whatever surrogate for land values was embodied in the quotas. If the quotas ever to any degree corresponded to a system of regionally distributed land values, it was to a system current at the end of the seventeenth century, if not many decades earlier. The property tax values conform to the economy of 1815. The ratios, in effect, superimpose the economy of 1815 on that of an earlier century. Much had happened to transform the economy of Yorkshire during the two centuries prior to 1815, and no place more so than in the West Riding. No part of the county was untouched by steeply rising rents and land values. But the value of some lands rose more sharply than others. Improvement was assuredly a key to the more dramatic lightenings of burden. As improvements occurred, rents would tend to rise, and at higher rates than on lands which were less improved or less susceptible to improvement. Arden is a

Table 14.13
Frequency distribution, acres per £1 gross* land tax quota, all townships, West Riding

Numbered columns: 1 = Agbrigg wapentake; 2 = Barkston Ash wapentake; 3 = Claro wapentake and the Liberty of Ripon; 4 = Ewecross wapentake; 5 = Morley wapentake; 6 = Osgoldcross wapentake; 7 = Skyrack wapentake; 8 = Staincliffe wapentake; 9 = Staincross wapentake; 10 = Strafforth and Tickhill wapentake

Acres/£	1	2	3	4	5	6	7	8	9	10	All cases N	All cases %	Summary Range	Summary % of cases[a]
0–4	1		1		1					1	4	0.6	0–9	1.0
5–9					1					1	2	0.3		
10–14	4	2	4		4	3				3	20	3.2	10–19	7.3
15–19	4	1	11		3	1		1	1		22	3.6		
20–24	15	6	13		11	6	1		4	10	66	10.6		
25–29	10	7	16		11	5	5	2	6	12	74	11.9	20–39	45.0
30–34	6	10	11		1	10	4	3	3	13	61	9.8		
35–39	4	5	9		6	3	7	2	8	14	58	9.4		
40–44	5	7	6		1	7	7	4	3	8	48	7.7		
45–49	5	4	7			5	3	3	5	9	41	6.6	40–59	24.5
50–54	1	4	5	1	1	5	4	6	4	3	34	5.5		
55–59	1		6		2	1	1	4	2	1	18	2.9		
60–64	3		2		1	3	3	8		1	21	3.4		
65–69							2	2		4	8	1.3	60–79	9.4
70–74			2		1	1		5	1	1	11	1.8		
75–79			2		1	2	1	6		2	14	2.3		
80–84			2	1	1		1	2	1	2	10	1.6		
85–89			1							1	2	0.3	80–99	4.9
90–94	2				1			7			10	1.6		
95–99								5	1		6	1.0		

Table 14.13 continued

Acres/£	1	2	3	4	5	6	7	8	9	10	All cases N	%	Summary Range	% of cases[a]
100–149	3	2	4	5	1	1		11		3	30	4.8		
150–199	1		2	3				3			9	1.4		
200-249								2			2	0.3	≥100	8.0
250–299				1				2			3	0.5		
≥300								2			2	0.3		
def.			2		2	3					7	1.1		
NR			12		8	2	7	2		6	37	6.0		
N	65	48	118	11	58	58	46	82	39	95	620	100.0		
Mean	32	32	40	134	29	37	45	86	41	42	44			
Minimum	2	13	2	51	3	10	24	18	18	3	2			
Maximum	172	112	154	270	101	118	82	334	98	113	334			
Maximum as % of minimum	8,600	862	7,700	529	3,367	1,180	342	1,856	544	3,767	16,700			

Notes: *No deductions have been made for salaries or stock-in-trade.
[a]Defective (def.) and no return (NR) cases are excluded from the denominator.
Source: Appendix P.2.

Table 14.14
Frequency distribution, acres per £1 gross* land tax quota, all townships, City of York and the Ainsty

Numbered columns: 1 = Ainsty wapentake 2 = City of York

Acres/£	1	2	All cases N	All cases %	Summary Range	Summary % of cases[a]
0–4					0–9	
5–9						
10–14	4		4	6.6	10–19	19.4
15–19	2		2	3.3		
20–24	7		7	11.5		
25–29	8		8	13.1	20–39	74.2
30–34	7		7	11.5		
35–39	1		1	1.6		
40–44	2		2	3.3		
45–49					40–59	6.4
50–54						
55–59						
60–64						
65–69					60–79	
70–74						
75–79						
80–84						
85–89					80–99	
90–94						
95–99						
100–149						
150–199						
200–249					≥100	
250–299						
≥300						
def.		28	28	45.9		
NR	2		2	3.3		
N	33	28	61	100.0		
Mean	24	0.96	12			
Minimum	11					
Maximum	42					
Maximum as % of minimum	382	NA	def.			

Notes: *No deductions have been made for salaries or stock-in-trade.
[a]Defective (def.) and no return (NR) cases are excluded from the denominator.
Source: Appendix P.3.

township in the high moorlands of Birdforth. Its property tax per acre was the lowest in the North Riding. Its quota, when computed in acres, was also one of the lightest. But, by 1815, its tax burden was one of the heaviest.[10] It remained unenclosed high pasture. The large towns of the West Riding, by contrast, had always been encumbered by relatively heavy tax quotas. It was only because their land values had outperformed their neighbours' so strongly that by 1815 they enjoyed the lightest tax burdens in Yorkshire.

Improvement explains much. But it does not explain everything. Location with respect to markets and the regional development of those markets, the introduction of canals and turnpikes or extension of common carrier routes, the persistence of copyhold and the varying prosperity of mines, the development of spas and fashionable centres – a variety of factors other than agricultural improvement, narrowly defined, or urban development may influence land values. But our purpose here is not to explain the differential rises in land values but to note their consequences for the land tax.

There can be no doubt that the burden of the land tax was most unevenly distributed within each of the three ridings of Yorkshire by the end of the Napoleonic wars. As we now prepare to turn to other counties, it will be useful to keep our Yorkshire findings clearly in mind. Burdens throughout Yorkshire were well below the statutory rate, ranging in the agricultural districts mostly between 20 and 60, but with the distribution of ratios skewed towards even lighter burdens. Sharp disparities in burden are everywhere observed over very short distances and among neighbouring townships. These disparities are often more striking than any isolated regional differences which might emerge. Indeed it was found to be impossible to discern any regional differences which might provide a basis for broad general explanations of variations in burden. Tax burdens cannot be consistently associated with variations in elevation, in soil regions, or in agricultural regime. If any one pattern emerges, it is that large industrial towns (though not necessarily their surrounding districts) tend to have very light burdens. But there is no general urban pattern. Smaller market towns have mixed patterns, and an ancient city such as York is shown to bear a burden which is far in excess of large industrial centres and is onerous even by rural standards within its region. In short, the distribution of land tax burdens in the Yorkshire countryside, even in the agricultural districts, is a homogeny of diversity. It remains to see what that distribution was like in other counties of England and Wales.

CHAPTER FIFTEEN

The National Distribution of the Land Tax Burden: New Estimates for 1815

There has never been any serious dissent from the view that the burden of the land tax among the counties of England and Wales was from the outset a most unequal one. It has generally been thought, both among contemporaries and by modern historians, that the county quota burdens were lightest in the West and North and heaviest in the southeastern counties. Some have attributed these inequalities to persistent and vigorous efforts by northern and western Members of Parliament. Others have supplemented this political explanation by noting that the distribution of the tax conforms to regional patterns of support either for Parliament in the 1650s or for the ministries of William III in the 1690s. The southeastern counties were willing to pay more and therefore had more imposed upon them. If John Beckett is correct, however, the regional inequalities may be more ancient than such an explanation allows, in Cumbria dating back to compositions for purveyance during the reign of James I. There are suggestions in the work of James Tait that the quotas are even earlier in their origins. Important work remains to be done on the origins of the quota systems and the regional distibutions of the burden of national taxation before the eighteenth century. This study has little new to offer on that subject and will focus on the distribution of burdens in 1815. But it is worth reminding ourselves, as a basis for comparisons, that contemporary opinion estimated that land tax burdens at the beginning of the eighteenth century in the northwestern counties were perhaps at 9d. in the pound on a statutory rate of 4s., while Professor Habakkuk has assured us that on the estates he has examined in Bedfordshire and Northamptonshire the Queen Anne tax produced the full statutory burden. If these estimates are correct, then the early eighteenth century quotas must have borne on the northwestern counties at a rent to tax ratio of about 27:1 while Habakkuk's midland (and presumably home) counties would have staggered under a burden of 5:1. The burden would thus have been 5 to 6 times greater in the southeastern midlands than it was in such northwestern counties as Cumberland.[1]

We shall begin our national analysis by constructing estimates of 1815 land tax burdens at the county level for each of the historical counties of England and Wales. Those ratios will once again be interpreted by comparing them against the areal distributions of 1815 real property values and of the quotas. We shall then proceed to examine the distribution of ratios in every township or parish of fourteen historical counties of England, in the way we have done for Yorkshire. In the end evidence will have been presented for fifteen historical English counties (nineteen if one counts separately the three ridings of Yorkshire and the three parts of Lincolnshire) distributed regionally throughout the kingdom, and for each of their 5,231 parishes or townships.[2]

Mean ratios of 1815 property tax to land tax have been computed for each of the fifty-two historical counties of England and Wales. Those ratios are presented on table 15.1, where the counties are listed in rank order of their land tax burdens. The historical counties experienced only minor boundary changes during the later nineteenth and early twentieth centuries, so it has also been possible to compute the property tax and the quotas at the county level as acreage series. These two series are also presented on table 15.1. Each series is displayed separately on maps 16, 21, and 22.

We shall reverse our usual procedure and begin with an examination of the acreage distributions of the 1698 county quotas. With the exception of a few counties, the distribution of the land tax quotas (map 16) conforms broadly with a pattern that is very familiar to English economic and social historians. It is the pattern we are accustomed to observing on maps of national taxation from the fourteenth to the sixteenth centuries, particularly when those maps are based on per-acre or square mile computations and are presented at the county level (maps 17–20). Some of the details of the pattern are different. Unlike the pattern shown in those earlier maps, the land tax quotas bore too heavily on Essex, Worcestershire, and the wealden and lowlands counties southwest of London, and they bore too lightly on Lincolnshire and the East Riding, for example. But the heaviest burdens of the land tax fell on East Anglia and the home counties and on that diagonal belt of midlands counties running northeasterly from Dorset towards the Humber, where the two- and three-field systems are supposed to have concentrated. These were the traditional regions of highest land values, and throughout the medieval and early modern centuries the population and the wealth of England had concentrated here. The remainder of map 16 in fact conforms fairly well with traditional perceptions of land values. The quotas became progressively lighter per acre towards Devon and Cornwall and lighter still in the upper midlands.

Table 15.1
(1) Gross ratio of 1815 property tax valuation (schedule A) to land tax quota (in rank order), (2) 1815 property tax valuation (schedule A) per acre, and (3) acres per £1 gross land tax quota; all counties, England and Wales (ranked by tax burden)

Rank by 1815 land tax burden	County	(1) Ratio (P.T.:L.T.)	(2) P.T./acre (£)	(3) Acres/L.T.
1	Bedfordshire	12.0	1.13	11
2	Hertfordshire	13.4	1.41	9
3	Buckinghamshire	13.6	1.34	10
4	Sussex	15.1	.98	15
5	Suffolk	15.3	1.19	13
6	Berkshire	15.9	1.40	11
7	Middlesex (including London)	17.1	25.03	0.7
8	Essex	17.4	1.59	11
9.5	Oxfordshire	18.2	1.49	12
9.5	Norfolk	18.2	1.17	16
11	Northamptonshire	19.6	1.48	13
12	Kent	19.7	1.68	12
13	Cambridgeshire	20.0	1.18	17
14	Hampshire	20.5	1.07	19
15	Huntingdonshire	20.7	1.37	15
16	Dorset	21.1	1.12	19
17	Wiltshire	22.4	1.34	17
18	Devonshire	23.0	1.14	20
19	Surrey	23.7	3.42	7
20	Worcestershire	23.8	1.74	14
21	Rutland	24.2	1.37	18
22	Leicestershire	26.0	1.69	15
23	Gloucestershire (including Bristol)	26.6	1.82	15
24	Nottinghamshire	27.0	1.36	20
25.5	Lincolnshire	28.6	1.21	24
25.5	Cornwall	28.6	1.06	27
27	Somerset (excluding Bristol)	29.2	1.83	16
28	Herefordshire	29.6	1.12	26
29	Monmouthshire	30.1	.84	36
30	Warwickshire	31.0	2.04	15
31	*Mongomeryshire*	35.4	.41	87
32	Shropshire	35.7	1.20	30
33	*Denbighshire*	35.9	.52	63
34	Derbyshire	36.8	1.36	27
35	*Radnorshire*	37.0	.33	112
36	Cheshire	37.9	1.65	23
37	*Glamorgan*	42.3	.64	66
38	Staffordshire	42.4	1.55	27
39	*Merioneth*	45.8	.26	174
40	*Brecon*	48.0	.31	154
41	Yorkshire	51.6	1.22	42
42	*Carnarvonshire*	53.6	.34	157
43	*Anglesey*	56.7	.52	108

Table 15.1 continued

Rank by 1815 land tax burden	County	(1) Ratio (P.T.:L.T.)	(2) P.T./acre (£)	(3) Acres/L.T.
44	*Carmarthenshire*	63.5	.47	135
45	*Flintshire*	66.5	.94	71
46	*Pembrokeshire*	69.2	.56	124
47	Durham	74.7	1.22	61
48	Northumberland	85.3	.96	89
49	Westmorland	97.9	.59	166
50	*Cardiganshire*	103.3	.32	323
51	Lancashire	147.1	2.58	57
52	Cumberland	189.9	.72	262
England		25.5[a]	1.53[b]	17[c]
Wales		49.0	.44	109
England and Wales		26.0	1.39	19

Notes: Welsh counties are italicized.
[a]27.2 excluding Middlesex.
[b]1.36 excluding Middlesex.
[c]20 excluding Middlesex.
Sources: PP 1818 XIX (1815 property tax); Andrew Browning, ed., *English Historical Documents, 1660–1714* (London, 1953), 318–21 (1707 county quotas for the land tax); *Gazetteer of the British Isles*, 9th ed. (Edinburgh: John Bartholomew, 1966) (acres).

The relatively poor soils of Lancashire fell into a pre-industrial pattern with Durham and Northumberland and parts of Wales. The lightest burdens per acre occurred in Cumbria and the more remote parts of Wales. What could be more appropriate or more natural – from a traditional perspective? It is unnecessary to resort to stories about political bias and regional attitudes towards the King's government, as contemporaries were wont to do, in order to explain this pattern of quota distributions. It was in its broad contours an intrinsically traditional and conservative one. If the distribution was flawed, it was in failing to adjust to relative movements in land values which, by the end of the seventeenth century, had made the traditional patterns no longer wholly appropriate. It is in resisting adjustment, rather than in forming the distribution itself, that politics undoubtedly came into play.[3]

By the end of the seventeenth century the traditional patterns of population and wealth distribution were already beginning those shifts which were to be so marked a feature of English growth in the later eighteenth and early nineteenth centuries.[4] Map 21 displays those shifts as they had occurred in real property values by 1815. The traditional patterns of wealth distribution had by then been entirely disrupted. The lower and eastern midlands counties of two- and three-field agriculture no longer bore the highest acreage values. Nor did Norfolk and Suffolk. Dominance had shifted to the west midlands, to Lancashire, to Gloucestershire and Somerset, and to those home counties most affected by the spread of metropolitan London. Industry and commerce had made their impact. If it is remembered that the land tax quotas were imposed on counties at a time when the tax was designed to be levied on personal as well as on real property – and by a pound rate – then we may appreciate that the quotas, in conforming to the most ancient and traditional of patterns, failed even more acutely to reflect actual contemporary distributions of wealth among the counties than the real property values shown on map 21 would indicate.

The actual burdens of the land tax as it was distributed in 1815 are displayed for every county of England and Wales on map 22. The patterns of their distribution are once again essentially those we are accustomed to seeing on late-medieval and early-modern taxation maps. While the rank order of the 1815 burdens tended not (except very roughly) to remain those originally imposed by the 1698 quotas, the ratios and quotas were highly correlated.[5] But there were also important differences between the quotas and the 1815 ratios. It is marginally possible to characterize the 1698 quotas as having fallen more lightly in "the north and west." This was Ward's impression, citing the views of contemporaries. But by 1815 the distribution of lighter burdens had become more strictly northwesterly. The southwestern counties now had burdens that were essentially similar to those of counties in the east midlands. Even the Welsh counties had increased their relative burdens and conformed to a more integrated national pattern.

It is impossible to construct reliable rent-to-tax ratios at the county level for the end of the seventeenth century, and it is therefore difficult to estimate the varying degrees to which the 1815 tax burdens had departed from the patterns imposed in 1698. But, provided we remember that all early estimates are merely approximations, we may reasonably conclude that the range of mean variation among the counties had greatly increased during the intervening years. According to Habakkuk and contemporary opinion, the land tax burden of Cumbria during the Queen Anne wars was 5 to 6 times lighter than that of both Bedfordshire and Northamptonshire, each of which paid the full statutory rate.[6] By 1815 the difference in tax burden between Cumberland, the most lightly taxed county, and Bedfordshire, then the most heavily taxed, had increased to a factor of 16. Inequality within the system had greatly increased. It is not that Bedfordshire had not improved its tax burden, which had dropped from 4s. to 1s. 8d. on a 4s. statutory rate, a decline of 58 percent. But the actual rate in Northamptonshire had dropped even more sharply, to only 1s., a decline in burden of 75 percent. Northamptonshire had begun with a quota per acre which was only 18 percent lighter than that of Bedfordshire. It ended with a real burden which was 40 percent lighter. Even Westmorland had not done quite so well as Northamptonshire, having experienced a decline in burden of 73 percent (assuming a 9d. actual rate in 1698). Neighbouring Cumberland maintained its relative position as the most lightly taxed county in England and Wales (perhaps capturing that title from Cardiganshire) by diminishing its tax burden 86 percent (again assuming a 1698 actual rate of 9d.).[7]

To some extent the pattern of the 1815 county ratios is the result of the overlaying of later economic conditions on real property values which, to some degree, may have been more appropriate at the end of the seventeenth century, or (more likely) at some earlier period. But not all of the changes were due to differential improvements in land values. Some were due to the vagaries of how counties reported their own valuations in 1693. As Ward has shown, some counties, such as Lancashire and Cornwall, reported as much as 14 percent less taxable value in 1693 than they had done for the monthly assessment of 1691. Other counties, and particularly those near London, such as Bedfordshire (33 percent), Buckinghamshire (49 percent), Sussex (37 percent), and Oxfordshire (42 percent), reported taxable property at levels which were well above the mean national increase of 16 percent. Middlesex and London returned 68 percent more taxable value. These increases compounded the relatively heavy burdens that these counties had always historically borne. For whatever reasons, some counties had not been so prudent as others in responding to the financial demands of government. It is probably for this reason, more than any other, that improving counties – those most characterized by industrialization, urbanization, and advanced agriculture – form no distinguishable patterns among the ratios. Counties most subject to the urban sprawl of the metropolis, such as Surrey, Hertfordshire, and Middlesex itself, began with heavy quotas and ended in 1815 with tax burdens that were still unusually heavy. Some of the west midlands counties, such as Worcestershire (which had reported in 1693 at 27 percent above its 1691 assessment), also ended with relatively heavy burdens. Others such as Staffordshire appear to have improved their standing. Lancashire began prudently and ended splendidly, ranking only behind Cumberland as the most lightly taxed county of England and Wales. But apart from the general northwesterly pattern itself, there are no consistent features to the distribution of the ratios. They bear no consistent relationship to known patterns of improvement, wealth, or demography. They are in economic terms quite irrational.[8]

The county level ratios are not good news for those who would directly compare land tax entries in their absolute values across county boundaries. Lee Soltow, who drew a national sample of such entries from all counties in 1798, encountered more error than he seems to have imagined. By 1815 the values on Bedfordshire duplicates represented on average 16 times more wealth in real property than did entries on duplicates for Cumberland. Perhaps the differences were not so great in 1798. In many regions land values had doubled during the intervening years. But since we cannot directly estimate 1798 burdens, and because land values may not have increased at comparable rates in all counties, it would surely be prudent to assume that the differences in 1798 tax burdens were large.[9] Similarly, when Davies classified owners from eight counties according to the amount of land tax they paid, his class intervals were unavoidably spurious. The mean 1815 land tax burdens within his counties varied by more than 100 percent.[10] Indeed it should be noted that differences in burden are not only great at the national level, they are also great among counties within the traditional regions. It is difficult to select a region for study – the home counties, the east or west midlands, the north – without including counties whose mean burdens differed by 100 percent or more. It is fortunate that relatively few studies have undertaken direct inter-county comparisons based on absolute values derived from the land tax.[11]

If the news concerning relative tax burdens at the level of the counties seems bad, the news becomes worse when we look within the counties. It is there that the full panorama of inequalities fully emerges.[12] The extent of the intra-county inequality in burdens is far worse, I think, than any of us have imagined. I have constructed ratios of 1815 property tax valuation to land tax quota for every reporting and non-defective parish or township in fifteen historical counties of England, comprising a total of 5,231 parishes or townships, or about one-third of all places reporting separately on the English census. The variations in land tax burden were large within every county, and within virtually every hundred. Taking these fifteen counties as a whole, and remembering that the statutory ratio was 5:1, the actual ratios ranged nationally from as low as 2 to as high as 1,346.[13]

Table 15.2 summarizes the distribution of the ratios within each of the sampled counties, the counties being grouped by region.[14] Table 15.3 summarizes the dispersion of the ratios within each county by presenting the highest ratio as a percentage of the lowest ratio. The dispersions are presented for each hundred and for each county as a whole. It is immediately apparent that the distributions of ratios at the township level generally rose in the northwesterly counties. The county means displayed in table 15.1 have already taught us to expect a southeasterly to northwesterly distribution. The southeastern counties were not without their high ratios, however; and we shall see whether these conform to any pattern. It is also notable from table 15.3 that only in Surrey among the fifteen sampled counties was the dispersion of ratios in the majority of the hundreds less than 200 percent; that is to say, within most hundreds

Table 15.2
Percentage distribution, net ratios of 1815 property tax valuations (schedule A) to land tax quotas, all townships (5,231) in nineteen sampled administrative counties, by region

	Range of ratios (%)							
County	0–19	20–39	40–59	60–79	80–99	100–149	≥150	Mean[a]
HOME COUNTIES								
Hertfordshire	92.3	6.7	1.0					14
Surrey	58.2	34.2	3.4	1.4		2.0	0.7	25
LOWER EAST MIDLANDS								
Bedfordshire	92.2	7.8						13
Northamptonshire	44.8	53.4	1.8					20
Oxfordshire	47.6	48.7	2.6	0.8	0.4			20
EAST ANGLIA								
Norfolk	51.2	43.5	1.7	1.5	0.5	1.2	0.3	20
UPPER EAST MIDLANDS								
Leicestershire	31.6	51.8	13.8	2.0	0.7			26
Lincolnshire								
Holland	11.1	63.9	19.4	5.6				28
Kesteven	30.0	41.8	17.6	7.1	2.9		0.6	27
Lindsey	17.3	53.6	21.0	4.7	2.2	0.7	0.5	30
SOUTHWEST								
Cornwall	25.9	62.6	4.2	2.4	2.4	1.2	1.2	29
Wiltshire	32.1	57.6	7.2	2.4	0.3	0.3		23
BORDER								
Herefordshire	5.4	54.0	24.8	6.4	1.0	3.0	0.5	33
NORTH								
Cumberland		0.6	4.0	6.2	9.0	21.5	58.8	199
Lancashire	0.5	1.8	8.4	16.0	11.9	34.9	26.6	126
Westmorland			10.6	25.5	20.2	29.8	13.8	102
Yorkshire								
East Riding	1.2	31.8	38.6	11.2	7.8	7.8	1.6	50
North Riding	3.0	37.4	38.3	13.3	4.4	2.8	0.4	45
West Riding	1.9	33.7	32.6	18.5	7.3	3.8	2.1	59
York and Ainsty	27.6	53.4	15.5	3.4				26

Note: [a]The county means presented in this column are those calculated from the reporting non-defective parishes and townships of each county. Missing values cause them to differ marginally from those calculated from county aggregates and reported in table 15.1.
Source: Appendices M, P.1-3, and Q.1-16.

examined the burden of the most heavily taxed township was at least twice (and usually much more than twice) that of its most lightly taxed neighbour. It would seem that significant inequalities in burdens cannot generally be avoided by historians, even by restricting investigations to the hundred level – not even within hundreds which were relatively homogeneous in their soils and rural in their economies, which is the usual restriction currently observed by most land tax studies.

The magnitude of the inequalities in burden grow enormously in most regions when the scope of the investigation is extended to the county level.

Table 15.3

Frequency distribution, highest township ratio (property tax/land tax) as a percentage of lowest township ratio within each hundred division, all sampled administrative counties, by region

County	Percentage spread (number of hundreds)[a]										% spread within county	County mean ratio[b]
	100–199	200–299	300–399	400–499	500–599	600–699	700–799	800–899	900–999	≥1,000		
HOME COUNTIES												
Hertfordshire	4	4					1				700	14
Surrey	13	7		3	1	2	1		1		7,500	25
LOWER EAST MIDLANDS												
Bedfordshire	3	4	1	1	1						800	13
Northamptonshire	2	10	6		1						638	20
Oxfordshire	1	3	5	2					1	2	2,225	20
EAST ANGLIA												
Norfolk	5	6	5	3	4	2	1	1	2	4	8,100	20
UPPER EAST MIDLANDS												
Leicestershire			1		2	1		1		1	4,450	26
Lincolnshire												
Holland		1		2							427	28
Kesteven			2	3	2	3			1	1	6,089	27
Lindsey	1	4	8	2	4	3	2			2	8,486	30
SOUTHWEST												
Cornwall	2	3			1		1			2	2,260	29
Wiltshire	9	11	2	3	3	1				1	3,400	23
BORDER												
Herefordshire		2	7		1		1			1	1,382	33
NORTH												
Cumberland			1	1				1		3	3,959	199
Lancashire	1			1		1		1		4	3,777	126
Westmorland		1	1	1						1	2,649	102

Table 15.3 continued

County	Percentage spread (number of hundreds)[a]										% spread within county	County mean ratio[b]
	100–199	200–299	300–399	400–499	500–599	600–699	700–799	800–899	900–999	≥1,000		
Yorkshire												
East Riding		1	5	1		1		1	1	2	7,000	50
North Riding		1	2	3		2	1	1		2	2,442	45
West Riding		1		1	2		1	1		4	10,700	59
York and Ainsty							1		1		1,057	26

Notes: [a]In some counties incorporated towns have been treated separately as hundreds. The identification of hundreds, and of the parishes and townships lying within them, was based on early nineteenth century county directories. In some counties one or more hundreds are non-reporting or defective and are not tabulated in this table. See appendix Q.

[b]The county means presented in this column are those calculated from the reporting non-defective parishes and townships of each county. They differ from those on table 15.1, which should be considered more reliable for the county as a whole.

Source: Appendices M, P.1-3, and Q.1-16.

Holland in Lincolnshire presents relatively modest problems. Its most heavily taxed township bore a burden only 4.27 times that of its most lightly taxed township. But in the West Riding of Yorkshire the difference in burdens was at a factor of 107, the entire range occurring within one industrial wapentake (Morley). Even in rural Oxfordshire, where land tax studies have focused so much attention, the difference was at a factor of more than 22, while overwhelmingly rural administrative counties like Norfolk and the Parts of Lindsey could produce factors of more than 80. When we remember that the *county* mean ratio of Cumberland was no more than 16 times that of Bedfordshire, it is apparent that the problem of inequalities in burdens was far more serious *within* individual counties than it was among the counties as a whole. To push this point a little further, taking all 5,231 of the townships which I have examined in the fifteen counties, the difference in burden between the most heavily and most lightly taxed townships was at a factor of 673.

With dispersions of these magnitudes running throughout the countryside, it would be useful if one were able to specify types of townships where high or low ratios were most likely to be found. Were there any identifiable economic or topographical conditions which tended to produce consistently high or low burdens or which would enable us to infer them with some probability? Unfortunately a close examination of the ratios among the townships of our additional sample of fourteen counties reveals few consistent regional or economic patterns in the distribution of the burden of the 1815 land tax, confirming the impressions formed in the preceding chapter by our detailed examination of the three ridings of Yorkshire. There is some noticeable tendency in some counties for lighter tax burdens to have occurred on uplands. In Oxfordshire the pattern is strongly evident, with lighter burdens occurring in the Chilterns to the south and, even more strongly, in the Cotswolds to the north. But it would be quite wrong to suggest that in general the uplands were more lightly taxed. The pattern of lighter burdens we have observed on the East Riding wolds was not continued on the wolds of Lincolnshire. The uplands of Cumbria were taxed comparatively heavily by northwestern standards. In Cumberland the lightest burdens fell on the lowland townships and on the coastal ports. In Westmorland they fell on the lowland woollen districts surrounding Kendal. We may recall that in the adjacent dales of the North Riding the most remote upland townships tended to have heavy burdens, while lighter burdens occurred in the lower townships of Wensleydale and on the North Yorkshire Moors. In Herefordshire, too, lighter burdens tended to concentrate along the Welsh border, but among parishes which were comparatively low in elevation. The more mountainous parishes along the Herefordshire boundary with Brecon and Monmouthshire were heavily taxed and are hardly distinguishable on the ratio map from the remainder of the county.

Fenland districts also present inconsistent patterns. A pattern of lighter burdens appears to be developing on the Norfolk map as one descends from the sands onto Freebridge Marshland hundred and south onto the Bedford Levels of Clackclose. But a glance at the patterns of Kesteven and Holland quickly disabuses one of any such tendency. The patterns of Holland do, to some extent, continue the burdens of the Norfolk fens; but Holland was not more lightly taxed than the hill and vale districts of Kesteven. The predominant pattern within Lincolnshire as a whole was for land tax burdens to lighten progressively proceeding northward and westward from Holland along the limestone ridge to the Isle of Axholme. The fenlands of the Isle, unlike those of Holland, had significantly higher ratios than adjacent Lincolnshire districts. But the fenlands of the West Riding, just across the county boundary, were less burdened still. Yet, as we have seen, the light fenland burdens of the West Riding were confined to the Thorne and Hatfield district. The fenland townships slightly to the north along the Humber, and Howdenshire in the East Riding, were heavily taxed. Fenlands in general display no consistent patterns of tax burden.

There are no discernible differences between the tax burdens of farming regimes, even within single counties. Pastoral districts, for example, were generally neither more heavily nor more lightly taxed than corn and sheep districts. The low Weald of Surrey was taxed at about the same actual rates as the cornlands of Bedfordshire or northeast Hertfordshire. Burdens on the prime dairy lands of southern Craven were not unlike those in the corn-producing wapentakes of Barkston Ash or Osgoldcross in the West Riding. Even the proverbial differences between chalk and cheese fail to appear in the Wiltshire map of tax burdens.

In some counties there was a tendency for lighter burdens to occur on the best soils.[15] But the patterns, even where they can be detected, are far from perfect ones. Despite the relative lack of differentiation among the soils of Bedfordshire, the ratios in that county were somewhat higher on the prime sands of its central region and in the market gardens of Sandy parish. But some of the parishes lying on inferior heavy wet clays enjoyed equally light burdens. The peats around Flitton, which were often associated with the Bedfordshire sands by agricultural improvers, were highly mixed in their ratios. In Oxfordshire the lightest burdens tended to concentrate on the red soils along the Warwickshire and Northamptonshire boundary. These were the best soils in the county, highly suitable to both arable and pastoral production. But, in Oxfordshire, it is not clear that the quality of soils as such was causing ratios to rise. High ratios also occurred widely among the inferior soil parishes of the central Cotswolds and along the Chiltern edge. There is considerable evidence in this county, as in others, that light tax burdens were associated with extensive recent enclosure.

In some counties very light burdens may be commonly found on the worst of soils. Although the wood pasture districts of Norfolk were heavily taxed, the poorest soils in the county, the light sands, generally enjoyed burdens which were far lighter than those on either the rich loams of the broads or even the good sands of northwestern Norfolk, the legendary heartland of the agricultural revolution. In Surrey the best soils lay between Croydon and Epsom; and those parishes, under the additional stimulus of the London market, experienced rapidly rising rents and increasingly light tax burdens during the eighteenth and early nineteenth centuries. But still-lighter tax burdens may be found on the Surrey heathlands along the Berkshire and Hampshire boundaries. The burdens on some of the heaths were by 1815 even lighter than those of the suburban metropolitan parishes along the south bank of the Thames. As with Oxfordshire, the extraordinarily light burdens on the Surrey heaths were often associated with extensive recent enclosure.

There is no doubt that throughout many counties those parishes or townships displaying the lightest tax burdens had experienced extensive parliamentary enclosure, sometimes of arable but often only of waste.[16] Since it is well established that enclosure generally caused land values to rise significantly, we would expect that those parishes which underwent extensive enclosure after 1698 would be marked within their regions by valuational rents which had departed disproportionately from their assigned quotas. It is precisely such departures which cause ratios of rent to tax to rise. We would therefore expect to be able to predict high ratios in those parishes which are known to have undergone extensive enclosure. This study has made no attempt to correlate systematically enclosure and tax burdens. But in every county examined it was quite easy to find cases which undermine the expected relationship between enclosure and tax burden. Some cases are merely questionable. High ratios are found in the Surrey heathland parishes of Frimley and Egham, for example, and both parishes had secured extensive enclosure acts early in the nineteenth century. But in neither parish had the actual award been made by 1815. To suggest that unusually light burdens in 1815 were due to enclosure in those parishes is to antedate the effects. Similar enclosures during the same years in Godalming or Send or Chertsey, where the awards had been made, produced no such dramatic effects. Shirburn, Watlington, and Pishill are adjacent parishes along the Chiltern edge in Oxfordshire. Shirburn and Watlington had recently undergone extensive enclosure. The ratio of Watlington was 39, one of the highest in the district. The ratio of Shirburn (5) remained one of the heaviest in the county. Pishill, which had not experienced any parliamentary enclosure, had the highest ratio (89) in the county. The same contradictions may be found in the central Cotswolds. Spelsbury had been extensively enclosed by parliamentary act and enjoyed a high ratio within its district (37). The parish of Enstone, immediately to its north, was not extensively enclosed until 1836; yet, in 1815, its ratio

(38) was almost precisely that of Spelsbury. If examples such as these are so easily found, it would seem prudent – so long as we lack a more systematic statistical demonstration – to resist any firm generalization regarding the relationship between enclosure and tax burdens.

The literature would lead us to expect light burdens in most urban parishes, but the pattern among such parishes is in fact a highly mixed one. Smaller market towns are peculiarly unpredictable. Their ratios are sometimes quite high, as in New Malton (155), but their ratios are equally likely to range between 2 and 12, as they did in the parishes of Guildford. The ancient county towns and ecclesiastical centres were also capable of exceptionally low ratios and onerous burdens. The great medieval centres of Norwich (with a ratio of 11) and York (whose internal parishes had a mean ratio of 21) were heavily taxed. The ratios of the suburban parishes in metropolitan London seem to have been consistently high, but one should proceed here with some caution; those of the inner Southwark parishes ranged upward from as low as 7. Suburbs such as these, which had been early urbanized, seem not to have experienced significant tax relief. The impact of London on tax burdens seems also not to have extended very far into the home counties. That influence is discernible among the parishes of Hertfordshire; but since they are more distant from London, it is much less pronounced than among the Vale of London parishes of Surrey. The lightest burdens within Hertfordshire concentrated strongly in the southwest, along the route of Watling Street and the Middlesex boundary. The heaviest burdens tended to locate along Ermine Street in the eastern district. Again, the patterns are imperfect. Bushey, Chipping Barnett, and Totteridge, and even Watford, all lying along the Middlesex boundary, were quite heavily taxed, while the northeastern parishes bore unusually low ratios even by southeastern county standards. Their burdens were no lighter than those of the remotest Surrey Weald. The renowned and widely scattered suburban villas and country houses of Hertfordshire did not have equally marked effects in all districts of the county.[17]

If consistently high ratios are to be found among our sample counties, it is among the expanding industrial towns and the larger ports of the kingdom. But some cautionary observations are in order here as well. If the chief industrial towns consistently produced high ratios, their surrounding industrial districts did not necessarily do so. We have seen that the industrial districts of the West Riding appear to have begun with high quota assignments which they were not wholly able to overcome. Even in Lancashire, where the industrial districts were relatively more urbanized, the northern and mostly rural hundred of Lonsdale produced a higher mean ratio (133) than the industrial and heavily urbanized hundred of Salford (127 when Manchester is excluded). West Derby hundred, lying west of

Manchester towards Liverpool, had one of the lowest mean ratios and heaviest burdens in the county (84 excluding Liverpool), rivalled only by the upland hundred of Higher Blackburn (82). The highest ratio in the country was produced for one of the smallest (albeit very prosperous) ports, Whitehaven. But Cumberland was that sort of place.

Time after time what one appears to be observing, even within individual counties, is the same general pattern found at the national level. Ratios tend to rise as one proceeds in a northwesterly direction. Such a pattern is observable in Lincolnshire, in Wiltshire, in Norfolk, in Leicestershire, in Herefordshire, and even (given the economic and topographical characteristics of the county) in Lancashire. Perhaps this internal pattern within counties is accidental. It baffles me how it might be explained.

Do the lack of consistent patterns among the ratios suggest that such things as agricultural improvement or the creation of new tax units due to urbanization do not cause lighter tax burdens? I think not. Such a conclusion would defy logic, and it is unnecessary. Improvement and other factors did lead to lighter burdens, but they did so in highly complex ways. Any number of factors might have impeded or distorted their impacts. Some valuations, even for the property tax, might have been based more on actual rents than on rack rents, for example. In fact the entire notion that regional differences should have emerged among the ratios assumes to some degree that the original quota assignments were themselves rationally distributed on a regional basis. As we have seen, the quotas were, to some degree, rationally distributed within the three ridings of Yorkshire; but even there one could find anomalies, such as in the industrial districts. The distribution may have been less perfect in other counties. There is no limit to a list of possible causes for distortion. In the end it is important to bear clearly in mind that one cannot go to the maps of ratios and identify from them which were the parishes or regions which were most subject to improvement between 1698 and 1815. This information does not necessarily appear. Nor are the least improving regions evident. There is no simple bivariate relationship between improvement and tax burden. Or if there is, the data presented in this study is too flawed to reveal it.

PART FIVE

Conclusions

CHAPTER SIXTEEN

A New Look at the Historiography of Land Tax Studies

Professor Mingay suggested more than twenty years ago that the "detailed investigation of land tax assessments is simply not worth while" when tracing the declining fortunes of the small landowner and the impact of enclosure.[1] It is now time to draw together the conclusions of this study and to assess the extent to which Mingay was correct. Such an assessment must go beyond a consideration of enclosure and smallholder studies, which formed the focus for land tax investigation prior to the 1960s. Land tax studies faltered somewhat during the later 1960s, perhaps due to Mingay's criticisms, but since the 1970s there has been a strong resurgence, and presently there are indications that both the diversity of applications and the quantity of output may increase enormously. Within the last few years the land tax duplicates have been employed on a vast scale to investigate wealth inequalities throughout the whole of England. The duplicates have been linked with poll books in large, computerized data bases to investigate the socio-economic characteristics of the late eighteenth century English electorate. Others have employed the duplicates to construct typologies of "open" and "closed" parishes, the typologies reflecting the degree to which property was concentrated into the hands of a few large landowners. While traditionally those who have employed the land tax duplicates have avoided urban and industrial regions, two recent studies have undertaken analyses of urban morphology and the spread of industrialization based largely on data derived from the land tax. In the paragraphs which follow we shall therefore examine each of these topics, beginning with the impact of enclosure and the decline of the small landowner. The investigative methods employed will be summarized and then, in the light of our findings, subjected to criticism. Those interpretations that seem based on reliable procedures will be identified. It will be suggested that the remainder are dubious at best and certainly unproven. Any procedures which seem to offer hope for expanding our knowledge on the subject in future by means of the land tax will be adumbrated.

THE DECLINE OF THE SMALL LANDOWNER AND THE IMPACT OF ENCLOSURE

Central to all land tax studies is the overriding need to create a single type of statistic which makes inter-township comparisons possible. A secondary requirement of that statistic for most studies is that it support the analysis of long secular trends, either within single townships or among sample groups of townships. Studies of the decline of the small landowner and the impact of enclosure have employed several types of statistic which, it has been hoped, have met both requirements. The most recently devised method, using what are called "turnover rates," will be examined shortly, after first reviewing the methods employed in the classic literature. One of the earliest methods employed, and one of the crudest, did no more than classify smallholders by the raw amount of land tax they owed. Smallholders were grouped by class intervals according to tax amount, sometimes within single townships, but most often the class intervals included all sampled smallholders from many townships or even counties. The intervals would then be compared as sheer numbers or as percentages. The comparisons were made to analyse differences between holders of different size, or to establish long secular trends, or to examine regional differences within or between counties at a single point in time.

None of the procedures associated with this first method are capable of producing statistically reliable results, and for several reasons. The first and most fundamental reason, as we have seen in the preceding two chapters, is that raw tax values are not comparable across township boundaries, and any procedure that attempts to group holders from various townships into a single class-interval scheme on the basis of such values is doomed to fail. A £10 entry in one township is simply not equivalent to a £10 entry in another township – not even when they are drawn from neighbouring townships. Class interval analyses employing these values from varying townships are therefore peculiarly inappropriate. The problems are particularly acute when the class intervals are small. It is relatively easy to classify a holder incorrectly when the range of most of the intervals is no more than £1. But even larger intervals can be highly susceptible to error. When an interval is established at, for example, £100 to £499, its upper boundary is still only 5 times greater than its lower. Such intervals may easily be swamped by the enormous magnitudes of error associated with variations in rent-to-tax ratios. The error produced will proceed in both directions, that is, holders will be misclassified both upward and downward along the interval scale, and to a degree which inherently cannot be estimated for any year other than 1815.[2] The error will increase as the areal unit of analysis expands, but no areal unit can in general be expected to produce reliable results. The townships in most hundreds, and especially those outside the home counties, will produce error sufficient to cause widespread misclassifications within such schemes, at least to the extent of one interval. In most hundreds the misclassifications will exceed one interval. When the areal level of analysis is raised from the hundred to the county, misclassifications will become far more severe. Above the county level, the error becomes devastating. Inter-county comparisons can create distortions of truly enormous proportions, particularly when the selection of counties occurs along the southeasterly to northwesterly axis of rising mean ratios.

The land tax is thus incapable of providing a statistic in the form of raw tax values that will make inter-township comparisons possible. But neither can the duplicates meet the secondary requirement for that statistic demanded by smallholder and enclosure studies: Counts of smallholders based on raw tax values – or on any conversions of those values – cannot be made shortly after the passage of the Redemption Act in 1798. As we have seen in chapter 8, redemption in effect creates two quotas in each township, one for redeemed and one for unredeemed entries. The process of redemption therefore creates *within* each township all of the problems of incomparability – albeit less severe ones – associated with inter-township analysis. The use of the land tax for smallholder and enclosure studies, when the studies are based on tax values or their transformations, should therefore terminate at 1798 or very shortly thereafter.

But what of the period before 1780? The years 1780–98 do not offer much scope for the secular analysis of the fortunes of the small owner-occupier, and it is tempting to extend that analysis to an earlier period. Whatever might be said of the suitability of early manorial surveys and enclosure awards, the pre-1780 land tax duplicates do not generally provide documentation for extending the period of analysis. The single-columned land tax duplicates of the earlier period simply do not distinguish proprietors and occupiers and they are therefore wholly unsuitable for counting and tracing owner-occupiers. One does not know what one is counting in these earlier returns. Certainly there is no reason to believe that counts from single-column duplicates would in any way be comparable to those made from the multi-columned duplicates of the later period. It would hardly be surprising if we found more "owner-occupiers" on the Queen Anne duplicates for a township if that early count included non-owning tenants. The conclusion is a sad one, but it must be faced: The land tax duplicates are only fully reliable (to the extent that they are) in their multi-columned format and prior to redemption. The period of their usefulness for most statistical purposes is therefore restricted approximately to the years 1780–98, or shortly thereafter.

One would suppose on the basis of what has been said so far that the land tax duplicates might still perform valuable services in tracing the fortunes of the small landowner and the impact of enclosure. Although the period of effective investigation may be confined to the last two decades of the eighteenth century, those are nevertheless years of widespread enclosure. And while inter-township tabulations of individual smallholders may have to be avoided, discrete counts of owner-occupiers within individual townships just prior to and following enclosure could surely be undertaken. Townships could then be classified by the nature of their enclosure experience and the townships within each type tabulated and related to other factors such as farming regime. Unfortunately our problems cannot be solved so easily, however. Other problems arise to bedevil the researcher.

Historians whose analyses focus on small owner-occupiers cannot be comforted to learn, as we did in chapter 3, that huge proportions of smallholders are commonly and continually missing from land tax duplicates – sometimes as many as 50 to 80 percent of the smallholders of a township. From time to time a small number of these missing smallholders will temporarily appear in the duplicates. Some historians have noted such occasions in association with enclosure and have concluded that enclosure "created" smallholders whose legal rights to land were now formalized. Others have speculated that smallholders whose valuations were under £1 were normally and perhaps inconsistently omitted, in accordance with statute. I have found that, on the contrary, no consistent patterns of valuational cutoff are to be found, even within single townships. Omissions occur both below and well above the £1 level, and quite erratically. Temporary appearances of smallholders in the land tax duplicates are a common feature of all occasions of major revaluation (such as the lifting of double assessments on Roman Catholics or the settlement of enclosure awards) and those appearances that accompany enclosure may in part, as in other cases, be no more than accommodations to pressures on an unalterable township quota.

To make matters worse, an examination of valuational rent-to-tax ratios of each property within townships further shows that very significant inequalities of tax burdens do often appear, as many historians would have expected, but they appear overwhelmingly on the smaller properties – and again the error proceeds in both directions, that is, small properties bear both heavier and lighter burdens than the mean. Largeholder burdens also occasionally depart from the mean but, contrary to what everyone would have expected, they tend to depart in the direction of heavier burdens. It is clear, then, that those who pursue the fortunes of smallholders will unavoidably be confronted by two types of error, both types occurring in very large magnitudes and *within* individual townships: Large proportions of their smallholders will be missing from the land tax duplicates, and the smallholders who are recorded will vary widely in the ratios of their rentals to their assessed tax values. If we were to think of all the uses to which the land tax duplicates might be put, we would have to conclude that the study of smallholders is the one for which they are most peculiarly ill-adapted.

But the pitfalls for those who study the decline of the small landowner and the impact of enclosure through the land tax duplicates do not end here. Those who pursue such studies have given insufficient attention to the problems posed by the duplicates in defining smallness – even assuming all the difficulties I have been enumerating did not exist. Professor Mingay pointed out some years ago that some farmers might be "small" as owners but "large" as tenants, and sometimes very large indeed.[3] This type of problem may be accommodated through aggregation of holdings when the farmer both owns and leases in the same township; but if any of his holdings are located in more than one township, then the proper aggregation cannot be made. Nominal record linkage between townships should never be undertaken, except very cautiously in the case of the greatest landowners. And yet we know – from poll books, for example – that it was a commonplace in the English countryside for working farmers as well as persons with non-farming occupations to have multiple holdings in scattered, and sometimes in widely scattered, townships. Indeed I have been able to verify that even within a single township the land tax entries do not necessarily represent single unified "farms." On a portion of the North Riding estates of the Earl of Ailesbury, precisely half of his newly consolidated farms spilled over into one or more adjacent townships. The tenants on those farms were reported separately in the land tax duplicates of each township in which a portion of their farm was located. They were not nearly so "small" – nor so numerous within the region – as the duplicates would force us to believe. The very structure of the land tax duplicates fragments and distorts the real structural characteristics of landholding society. While most of these difficulties of analysis may be overcome for large landowners, they are impossible to overcome for the holders of smaller properties.

Not all studies have based their analyses on raw land tax values. Most historians who have traced the decline of the small landowner have followed the lead of Johnson and Gray in transforming their raw tax values into acres by means of acreage equivalents. The early studies adopted county level equivalents. More recent studies have rightly insisted on parish-by-parish conversions. Such a procedure has two potential advantages. First, if the procedure were successful it would overcome the problems of the ratios and differing tax burdens by standardizing the statistic on acres – a very considerable advantage indeed, providing acres as such are acceptable as a variable for measuring "size" of holding. The second advantage, and probably the one being sought by most practitioners, lies in making the land tax statistics compatible with those based on earlier or contemporary manorial surveys and enclosure awards. The surveys and awards normally report only acres, and in the surveys sometimes rent. Acres cannot be converted to land tax assessments. Secular analysis therefore demands that land tax values be converted to acres. Comparisons with sixteenth and seventeenth century smallholder conditions, and even most comparisons with pre-1780 conditions in the eighteenth century, are wholly dependent upon such acreage conversions. Without them it is impossible to establish that identical statistical populations are being compared in the various periods under review. It is unfortunate that no systematic test of acreage conversions has ever been undertaken – though there has been much minor testing and discussion – since so much work rests on their reliability.

The results I have presented in chapter 5 suggest that only in Lancashire and Yorkshire, where the six-inch Ordnance Survey was conducted prior to major parish boundary alterations, can accurate, pre-1850, acreage totals be obtained for most parishes and townships. The acres reported in the 1831 or 1841 census, upon which most historians seem to have relied, and most twentieth century acreages, diverge very significantly from the unreformed acres. If acres cannot be reliably established, then acreage conversions cannot be made. The only way out of this dilemma in the southern counties is to select only those townships where it can clearly be established that no boundary changes had occurred since the earliest period under study. But the burden of proof must clearly be on historians to demonstrate that case; if successful, then they may employ modern acreages such as those found in Bartholomew's or on later Ordnance Survey maps. They must also, of course, confine their analysis to the years prior to redemption. Even if reliable acres are obtained for the township as a whole, redeemed tax entries are not subject to revisions and quickly become liable to lose their proportional relationship to the total real wealth (and perhaps acres) of the township.

But even if reliable acres could be obtained for each township under study and the period of redemption avoided, there remain the residual objections to the conversion of individual tax entries on the basis of mean "acreage equivalents" calculated for the township as a whole. In chapter 5 evidence was presented from the Ailesbury estates that acreage values within individual farms – let alone among all the farms of a township – and even among the fields under identical land-use on a single farm, are subject to wide variation in value per acre. Small holdings, which involve few fields or buildings, must therefore be peculiarly subject to variations in mean value per acre. They are thus equivalently inappropriate for acreage conversions – more so than any other size of property. Recent calls for the examination only of those parishes which are relatively homogeneous in their soils and rural in their characteristics are pointless. There are no parishes which are sufficiently homogeneous in their soils; it is doubtful if there are many farms. Even if acreage conversions were suitable for largeholder studies, which is highly dubious, it is surely foolish to employ them when those smaller classes of property, which are most susceptible to large error, comprise the whole focus of the analysis.

The best argument against the employment of acreage equivalents goes beyond these considerations, however. The argument that acreage conversions cannot reliably be made is not a bad argument, but in one sense it is irrelevant. Let us set aside for a moment the desire to link land tax statistics to earlier surveys and enclosure awards. Are acres a suitable measurement of "size" of holding? Surely they are a deplorable measurement of size when we are tracing the decline of the yeoman farmer and the impact of enclosure. What is "small" in acres in a region of breeding and rearing is not equally small in a dairying region, or under conditions of arable agriculture, or for market gardening. Even within one township the same number of acres under corn is not equivalent in value to the same number of acres under grass. Nor are all cornlands and grasslands equally profitable. Surely when discussing the "small" independent yeoman our central concern is his economic independence and social status and his viability in the face of fluctuating market conditions. But these and other such conditions are related to the potential profitability of his holdings, not to the sheer numbers of his acres as such. Acres are not a constant in the profitability equation. A better surrogate for profitability and economic viability – and even for status – is the rental value of his holding. It is precisely on rental values that the tax assessments in the land tax duplicates are purportedly based. What could be a happier result? Why should we expend ingenuity in converting a good statistic into a bad one that is both more error prone and intrinsically less suitable as a measurement of the qualities in which we are centrally interested? If the land tax duplicates reported only acres rather than tax values based purportedly on rent, I would hope that we would all be busily engaged – if we could – in converting those acres into measurements of wealth.

The remaining methods employed in small landowner studies are generally vulnerable to the same objections I have raised to the tabulation and grouping of holders by raw tax value. If we put to one side the classification of holders by size, many land-tax-based studies have attempted to establish the sheer numbers of holders within each township, distinguishing between owner-occupiers, non-occupying owners, and mere occupiers. One or more of these categories are then used to calculate a percentage of total owners or, in some cases, of total occupiers. If we also put to one side the peculiar difficulties posed by the duplicates when we count total occupiers – such as their failure to report any tenants at all or their tendancy to report them summarily as "sundry tenants" on some proportion of the properties – then we may treat the counting of both proprietors and occupiers as comprising essentially the same problem. The total number of proprietors and occupiers cannot reliably be established from the land tax duplicates, and for reasons which are now familiar. Large numbers of smallholders are regularly and inconsistently omitted from the duplicates of a large proportion of townships. The proportion of omissions varies from year to year within single townships; but, even more importantly for comparative purposes, the rate and level of omissions vary widely among different townships. Thus the "total" estimated owners or occupiers would not only be erroneous within individual townships; the degree of error would necessarily also vary widely among the townships being sampled. The denominators employed for calculating the percentages of each landholding category within each township would therefore lack comparability. In short, any statistic that employs either the total number of proprietors or the total number of occupiers in its equation may be expected to have incorporated large and significant margins of error. Such statistics can be very misleading for most individual townships, but they are peculiarly unsuitable as a basis for comparative analysis.

In 1975 Michael Turner developed a new adaptation of this method of studying the effects of enclosure on the structure of landholding. He sought to avoid the problems associated with tax values and acreage conversions by simply not employing those variables. He focused instead on the surnames of proprietors found in the duplicates. All proprietors were examined regardless of size. He selected those parishes within Buckinghamshire which were enclosed during the 1780s and 1790s, and then added a small group, which had been more anciently enclosed as a control. By tabulating the total number of names which had appeared annually within each parish over an approximately ten-year period spanning the year of enclosure, and by further tabulating the annual turnover in names as those in the original base year dropped out of the duplicates, he was able to calculate annual turnover rates that measure the impact of enclosure on landholding.[4] "Turnover studies" have since spread rapidly and are presently thought to hold the most promise for reliable results in studying the impact of enclosure. Those studies that have appeared have generally found that turnover rates during the year or so following enclosure are significantly higher – sometimes by 100 percent – than those found in the same parishes prior to enclosure or in non-enclosing parishes. Some students have tried to enhance these conclusions by observing that "small" holdings seem most affected. J.M. Martin has extended the method for longer secular analysis by linking land tax tabulations with those for mid-eighteenth century enclosure awards.[5]

Several midlands studies have confirmed that turnovers in surnames do occur in the duplicates at higher rates immediately following enclosure, and there is no reason to doubt that future studies in other regions will find similar patterns. After all, the same phenomenon occurs on a smaller scale when double assessments on Roman Catholics are lifted during the 1790s. As I have suggested earlier, every occasion of major reassessment seems to have been followed – for reasons that are not entirely clear – by a period of erratic inclusion and exclusion of names, and especially of the names of smallholders. Turnover studies have not generally described the full characteristics of the townships under study, but it would not be suprising to find, as Martin did,[6] that turnovers were most pronounced in those parishes or townships which normally recorded large numbers of middling to small proprietors. It is precisely in those townships that one tends to find the largest proportions of regularly missing smallholders. In short, the turnover phenomenon may to a considerable degree be no more than a function of revaluation and of the larger problem of widespread and significant smallholder exclusions.[7]

The turnover method is also misleading in that it *appears* to calculate a rate against a constantly *full* population of proprietors. But, again as we have seen, the land tax duplicates in most townships do not report all proprietors. Nor do all townships exclude them in equal proportions. The denominators employed in calculating the rates – and probably also the numerators – therefore lack comparability. Introducing enclosure awards into the analysis, as Martin has done, only further reduces comparability. Even assuming that the awards include every property in the township no matter how small – which is difficult to demonstrate – there is no reason to believe the patterns of inclusion or exclusion in the awards are comparable to those in the duplicates. If one were to leap to any conclusions, it would be that enclosure awards, when purportedly covering the entire township, are more inclusive. Arithmetic differences derived from comparisons of these two sources, such as secular ''declines'' in smallholders, are likely to reflect – at least to some degree – differences in documentation rather than in real alterations in landholding structure. If turnover studies must be undertaken, then, let them be pursued by means of a single type of documentation. If they were pursued through the land tax duplicates and were somehow confined to larger holdings, I have no reason to doubt that the observed turnovers would be real in almost all cases. But those studies which either include or focus upon smaller proprietors (whose sheer numbers often enlarge the denominator and therefore drive the rates)[8] may well be reporting no more than the ephemera of bookkeeping within a system of fixed quotas.

Everyone who has engaged in turnover studies has noted one further difficulty inherent in this method. A simple tabulation of turnovers in surname runs the risk of overcounting real property transfers. Adrian Henstock, who perhaps has the most detailed experience with this type of tabulation, warns that the rates of overcounting may be significantly higher than others have realized.[9] Strictly speaking, changes of surname should not be counted when a widow marries and merely changes her name, or when a son-in-law inherits. On the other hand, undercounting can occur when changes in Christian name mask genuine sales rather than inheritances. Henstock, working through the duplicates year by year in an unusually well-documented and wholly urbanized township with the assistance of an adult education team, has been able to establish whether many apparent turnovers were by inheritance or genuine alienation. But, even in his town of Ashbourne, such a determination could not be made in all cases. In most other towns it seems doubtful the required supplementary sources would be available. In rural environs the problems would be far more acute, except perhaps among the largest of proprietors. Short of massive family reconstitutions from parish registers or a monumental searching of deeds, small proprietors would seem to be generally untraceable. It must be emphasized that land tax duplicates alone cannot, except in a small minority of instances (when annotations occur as they sometimes do), independently solve these linkage problems arising from inheritance. We must therefore conclude that turnover studies measure a mixture of phenomena within a single statistic: genuine alienations of family holdings, and occasions of inheritance.[10] We cannot determine to what extent each is responsible for driving the rates. Nor do we know that their respective contributions to those rates are constant through time. For these reasons alone it would be prudent to conclude that turnover rates as such are subject to error, probably of considerable magnitudes, and in the direction of overestimations.

In the end it is difficult to avoid the conclusion of Professor Mingay that the land tax duplicates cannot ''bear the weight of detailed interpretation which has been placed on them'' in pursuing the fortunes of the small landowner and the impact of enclosure.[11] The tax values themselves lack comparability for this form of comparative analysis. They cannot reliably be transformed into acres, nor should we want them to be. The duplicates do not provide accurate or even consistent counts, either in their tax entries or in the names they record, of the entire spectrum of the landowning population. As a crowning blow, all of these problems are peculiarly associated with smaller holdings. Not all of my conclusions regarding the reliability of the data are equally well established, however. It is unlikely that future research will significantly modify my conclusions regarding the valuational base of the land tax. The sample I employed for that analysis was too large and nationally distributed. But my evidence for missing smallholders, for example, was limited essentially to one rural, non-urbanized and non-enclosing northern wapentake. I have reason to believe those results could easily be replicated in other northern wapentakes. But it is possible that townships in the southeastern midlands, where the burdens of the tax were generally much greater, were more inclined to include the full extent of their landowning population regardless of size. Though a few earlier studies have similarly found that large numbers of smallholders are missing from the land tax duplicates, and even from the local rates, clearly more research is needed. Perhaps it is fair to suggest that a heavy burden of proof is now on the other side, however. Unless the principal deficiencies which I have detected in the land tax can be shown clearly not to exist – in regions and not merely in casually selected townships – then it is very difficult to see how anything useful about the fortunes of the small landowner or the impact of enclosure has been learned or can be learned from a detailed study of the land tax duplicates.

URBAN MORPHOLOGY

The last two decades have seen interesting new applications of the land tax in the study of the evolution of urban morphology. The most promising method is that which has been most fully developed by Adrian Henstock and his Ashbourne group and is called "house repopulation." This method attempts to link personal names of both proprietors and occupiers with each individual urban property within a town over a long series of years. The linkage is accomplished by tracking each property bundle within a town year by year through a long secular series of duplicates. The Ashbourne project linked each property annually from 1780 to 1832 in the land tax duplicates and then to the 1846 tithe map. The value of the resulting data base lies not so much in its independent statistical qualities as in its usefulness in conjunction with other supplementary sources. So long as one avoids statistics derived exclusively and uncritically from the land tax, much can be learned about the changing physical structure of a town, the rates and causes of change, and who was responsible for them.[12]

It cannot be too much emphasized, however, that the Ashbourne study is of a single, almost wholly urbanized township that is blessed with appropriate supplementary sources which a large team appears to be fully utilizing. I have had a good deal of experience linking property bundles. So long as it is done annually, it can be done reliably in almost all cases. But, if "house repopulation" studies are to succeed, several severely limiting conditions must be observed. The township selected should be almost wholly urbanized, as was Ashbourne; otherwise, severe confusions will arise between urban and rural properties, as Henstock notes. The township should also provide some clear evidence that the land tax property bundles are not lumping together multiple "houses" or "cottages," a practice which is frequently seen on the duplicates of the later 1820s and is undoubtedly a silent feature of earlier duplicates. Care must be exercised not to classify the "size" or "wealth" represented by each property on the basis of its tax entry. Small tax entries, which are rampant in most urban settings, are those which are most subject to wild fluctuations in ratios of valuational rent to tax. Redeemed properties, after 1798, are no longer subject to revaluation in their tax amounts and are especially subject to such error. It should be remembered, too, that the most important forms of wealth among urban residents are seldom in real property; other forms of property are not taxed directly by the land tax – or by local rates – except occasionally in token amounts as "stock in trade." The Ashbourne researchers also believe that their earlier land tax duplicates list the properties street by street in topographical order. Perhaps they are correct, but it is doubtful this assumption would be correct in most other towns. If clear and convincing evidence cannot be presented on this point, then great difficulty will be experienced in linking the land tax property bundles to specific buildings. Much change could have occurred between 1832, when the land tax duplicates cease, and the 1840s or later, when the tithe maps provide an inventory of specific properties. Supplementary sources at scattered points in time are clearly of the utmost importance. Finally, if a complete inventory of proprietorship or occupancy in the town is required, then convincing evidence must be provided that small proprietors and tenants in general are not omitted in significant proportions or on a regular basis from the duplicates.

The Ashbourne project appears to meet these restricting conditions admirably. It is not clear how many towns would lend themselves to such studies with equal facility. Certainly it seems unlikely that regional systems of urban centres could be studied in this manner, which is a great pity. If centres are to be treated in geographical isolation as sources permit, then some attempt should be made to select them typologically, thus avoiding mere arguments by illustrative example. As we have seen in chapter 3, studies of urban morphology based on aggregate statistics, such as those recently pursued by Margaret Noble, are too error prone to be judged promising.

INDUSTRIAL DEVELOPMENT

Robert Unwin's recent venture into the industrial history of the West Riding coalfield also makes innovative use of the land tax duplicates, and it seems likely his method will be emulated. Unlike the other applications we have been discussing, however, the use Unwin has made of the duplicates is not a systematic one. The land tax duplicates in the heavily industrialized wapentake of Staincross, where he focuses on the fortunes of coal masters and the development of mining, sometimes record coal mines as such; but they do so only on rare occasions and inconsistently. The duplicates also tend to exclude ascriptions which separately identify other forms of industrial or transport property. The land tax cannot therefore act as systematic documentation in the development of industrial statistics. Unwin's principal sources, and those which make his research possible, are necessarily of a different provenance. It is from them that he must first identify his coal masters and locate their mines. The land tax may then supply supplementary information of considerable value.

Unwin has made effective use of the duplicates, for example, in tracing the holdings of his coal masters as proprietors and occupiers throughout the region. Since he already knows a good deal about them and their interests, his nominal record linkages are plausible even when less than prominent local families are involved. He is also able to follow their financial fortunes in a rough way by tracking the proportions of tax they paid in each of their townships.

But his method has strict limitations, and more than he seems to appreciate. The information he derives from the duplicates necessarily follows the fortunes of the coal masters and not of the coal mines. When he plots the proportional increases or declines in tax paid by his coal masters within their townships, he cannot distinguish between the industrial and agricultural values of those properties. Are we to assume that the agricultural soils that lie above the coal are susceptible to no improvement? Or that coal masters are never also agriculturalists? The answer to both questions is of course no. Based on land tax evidence alone, the problem remains as to what proportion the agricultural and industrial values contributed to the tax owed on these unlabelled property bundles. The failure of the land tax to make such distinctions becomes particularly significant when gentry, or aspiring gentry, families are involved.[13]

THE MEASUREMENT OF WEALTH INEQUALITIES

The most extraordinary use to which the land tax has been put, and the largest in scale, resulted in Lee Soltow's 1981 study of wealth inequalities in England and Wales. Utilizing the complete 1798 series of duplicates housed in the Public Record Office, Soltow drew an enormous sample of 1,073,000 property bundles distributed nationally. He recognized that the original distribution of the quotas among the counties was an unequal one and that the quotas assigned to the townships had never been adjusted to reflect the later increases in real property values associated with improvement. He tested his aggregate distribution for "robustness" by increasing all assessments in half of his counties. This manipulation produced "only slightly more inequality." He was therefore able to convince himself that the quota inequalities were "probably not very serious within counties, and do not make a great difference even at county level." He then proceeded to transform each of his individual tax values into wealth values by assuming "the tax was 20 per cent of rent assessed [i.e., that the valuational rent was taxed at the statutory rate of 4s. in the pound], that rent assessed was one-third or one-fourth of actual market rent, and that market rent was 3 and one-third or 5 per cent of market value." Applying this formula uniformly throughout his data base, he multiplied each tax value by factors of 300 and 600, thereby attempting to establish generous upper and lower boundaries of error. Given his assumptions, this was a plausible and statistically correct procedure and should have produced Gini coefficients of wealth inequality that were reasonably reliable at the national level in 1798, at least in terms of real property, and that were suitable for comparative analysis.[14]

The assumptions Soltow employed were grievously wrong. I rehearsed my principal objections at the time, and I have found no reason to change them.[15] On the contrary, the new evidence I have presented in this book demonstrates that I erred only in having grossly understated the objections I then posed. Even if Soltow were reliably able to transform his tax entries into a system of compatible wealth values, he would still not be measuring inequalities between units of analysis which are of any intrinsic interest for such studies. He believes his units represent "farms." They do not. Nor do they represent all of the wealth in real property of any individual, or of any nuclear family, or of any household. They are no more than what I have termed property bundles. While Soltow might in principle have been able to unify nationally all of the holdings of the largest proprietors, he could not have done so for the vast majority of holders – even in principle. The requirements which have commonly come to be accepted for nominal record linkage prohibit it. Property bundles as such – and that is all his sample comprises, one hopes – cannot, under any conceivable circumstances, be of the slightest interest for analysis at the national level.

But even if Soltow had somehow employed a unit of analysis which had been of interest, his transformation and use of tax values are wholly unacceptable. The first component of his transformation formula assumes that all tax values within all townships represent *in fact* a 4s. in the pound assessment on valuational rent. He applied this and the two remaining components as constants in the transformation of all tax values. That was a grave and fatal error. As we have seen, the relationship of tax to rent – even to valuational rents directly employed for assessing the land tax – varied enormously within the North Riding. When mean ratios of the more reliable property tax valuations were computed for each of the 5,231 townships I examined in fifteen counties, I found that the real burdens of the land tax could vary from as low as 2:1 to as high as 1,346:1. Gini coefficients, which are a statistic based on an analysis of individual cases, cannot sustain error of these magnitudes. Arguments regarding the Pareto or lognormal character of his distributions, which comprise an important element in his riposte, cannot further his case. Even an unreal world might be lognormally distributed. Given the extraordinary effort he put into his project, and the highly interesting objectives he pursued, it is sad to conclude that no other study in the historiography of the land tax has failed so utterly in the methods it has employed.

THE ECONOMIC CLASSIFICATION OF THE UNREFORMED ELECTORATE

Since the Second World War the land tax has come to be applied to political analyses of the eighteenth century electorate in ways which have seemed highly promising. These studies were pioneered, like so much in the field of popular politics in England, by George Rudé in his study of the Middlesex electorate during the Wilkes campaign. Rudé sought to establish the socio-economic characteristics of those who voted for Wilkite and pro-government candidates, and he did so partially by linking names in poll books with "rents" recorded in land tax duplicates and poor rate books. He successfully did so for 1,021 electors, or about one-half the total electors in forty-four sampled parishes in Westminster and Middlesex. Rudé first totalled the raw valuational rents of the voters for each candidate within each of his parishes. He then aggregated those totals across parish boundaries and calculated mean rentals. He further reported, for each candidate, the total number of electors whose rentals individually exceeded either £50 or £100. He then reported these totals at both the individual parish and aggregate levels. His most impressive use of his data was to group his voters into seven class intervals according to valuational rent, the intervals themselves being further grouped into socio-economic strata described as "substantial," "middling," and "lesser." The boundaries of the middling group were at £10 and £49.[16]

Rudé did not work with tax values as such; he restricted himself to the valuational rents reported in the land tax duplicates or rate books. This was probably a fortunate selection and prevented even larger margins of error.[17] But, as we have seen in chapter 14, the valuational rents reported in the land tax are not generally comparable across township boundaries. When land tax valuations were compared against those reported for the property tax and for the county rate, the land tax was almost uniformly reported at the lowest level, and usually by a wide margin. The land tax valuations of each township also failed to conform to any pattern in their departures from rack rent. The departures among townships were erratic and inherently unpredictable. It was not unusual for them to be 25, or 30, or even 50 percent or more below valuations for the property tax. There is evidence too that land tax valuations, as well as tax amounts, are peculiarly unreliable for the smallest properties, and especially when those properties are in urbanized areas. Such erratic valuation is further exacerbated because the land tax rents, even in urban areas, fail to include significant amounts of non-real property. Occasional inclusions of stock-in-trade are clearly too small to have been more than token amounts. Such amounts were surely employed, like the real property valuations themselves, to make some degree of proportional adjustment for actual wealth in an urban context and are not meaningful in their absolute values. Absolute rental values, we must remember, were irrelevant for purposes of tax collection; internal proportionality was not.

Such considerations are fatal to the reliability of those portions of Rudé's analysis which rely on land tax rentals. He should not have aggregated across parish boundaries. By doing so he constructed a rental series that is incompatible. His class intervals are therefore not homogeneous and, undoubtedly, incorporate substantial and significant error. Since much of his analysis focuses on the lesser orders within the electorate, it is important to remember that small holdings are especially subject to valuational error, and it is smallholders whom the land tax duplicates and parish rates tend to omit in large numbers. It is therefore not surprising that Rudé (and John Phillips) have failed to find large proportions of their voters in their tax documents. Small values are also those which are most sensitive arithmetically to the omission of non-real property. But smallholders are not the only classes whose rentals have been underestimated in these studies. The farther up the social scale one proceeds, the more likely it is that the holder owns properties outside the parish being examined and which have not been linked and added to the rent total he has been assigned. Underestimations and incorrect interval assignments therefore abound at all social levels, and no true, or even approximately reliable, estimates of wealth have been made by Rudé. I must emphasize that I am in no way questioning Rudé's larger conclusions, which rest on far more evidence than land tax and poor rate rentals. The larger importance of his work is little affected by my few remarks. But those statistics which are derived from the land tax do not, I am afraid, serve the purpose which he intended.

Rudé completed his research at a time when historians had not in general been introduced to the mysteries of computers and advanced statistics. In 1982 John Phillips transformed our approach to unreformed electoral politics in an enormously important book on the English urban electorate of the late eighteenth century. His analysis was principally grounded in a huge machine-readable data base in which he systematically linked poll book information on all who voted in each contested parliamentary and municipal election in four typologically selected boroughs: Norwich, Northampton, Maidstone, and Lewes. The first two of those boroughs contained multiple parishes within their urban and electoral boundaries. The poll books provided occupational as well as electoral variables for each of his voters. But Phillips went further, by linking each voter, where possible, to either a land tax duplicate or a poor rate book. He was thus able to add a quantifiable socio-economic variable in the form of a valuational rent. These rents, he hoped, would enable him to overcome the notorious difficulties that all historians have encountered when they attempt to undertake the statistical analysis of social strata on the basis of ascribed occupations. Like Rudé before him, Phillips did not use the tax values as such. Instead he undertook both nonparametric and linear analyses (but relying especially on the former) of his voters based on rents, treating them collectively as a single population across parish boundaries within each of his towns. He also characterized each of the four grand wards of Norwich (each ward being composed of several internal parishes) in terms of its mean rental. Mean and median rentals were compared in their absolute values across parish boundaries and between the four towns themselves. The results of his analyses based on rentals were also employed to confirm the reliability of the analyses he had independently conducted using occupations.[18]

The objections which I have raised to the methods employed by Rudé apply equally to those adopted by Phillips. But the procedures adopted by Phillips, and the towns he has selected for study, raise further difficulties which extend the nature and range of possible error. In the first place, variables based on land tax rentals and tax values are wholly unsuitable for linear analysis employing dummy variables if the rent or tax variable is derived from more than one parish. Strong correlations would mean nothing; weak ones, such as Phillips found, would hardly be surprising. The same is probably true of nonparametric routines. If such analyses are to be conducted, they should be completed parish by parish, even among the internal parishes of a single parliamentary borough.

One of my more important findings is that the valuational rents, as well as taxes, reported on the land tax duplicates are not comparable across parish boundaries, even when those boundaries lie within the walls of a single ancient town such as Norwich or Northampton or a metropolitan centre such as Westminster. Boroughs and cities which contain multiple parishes within their electoral boundaries, such as Norwich or Northampton in Phillips' case, or Westminster in Rudé's, present all of the problems of intertownship analysis. Although Rudé and Phillips did not use tax values as such, it is prudent to observe that the City of York – an ancient ecclesiastical centre similar in many respects to Norwich – contained twenty-eight parishes within its parliamentary boundaries and its mean rent to tax ratio in 1815 was 21:1. But the ratios among its various parishes ranged from 7 to 67, a factor difference of almost 10. There was clearly no unified system of assessment among the parishes of York. The same may be said of the five urban parishes of Bedford, where the ratios ranged from 14 to 25, or of St Albans, where the range was from 10 to 18. The parishes of Southwark ranged from 7 to 31, those of Guildford from 2 to 12. Three of the parishes of Carlisle bore ratios of 296, 654, and 1,210. The ratios of the two parishes of Devizes were 20 and 55. Those of Marlborough were 6 and 8. Everywhere I have looked within my fifteen sample counties, the internal parishes of urban centres show every evidence of having been valued and taxed on entirely separate and independent systems, just like the rural parishes which surrounded them. Since land tax valuational rents among the rural parishes generally departed sharply from full rentals, and did so erratically, one must conclude that the parishes lying within the boundaries of urban centres shared equally in those weaknesses. Moreover, the extraordinary differences in rent-to-tax ratios which are found between the inner parishes of Southwark and the more newly settled suburbs of metropolitan Surrey suggest that differences in modes of assessment among urbanized parishes might be very great indeed.

In short, Phillips should not have suggested that the differences in mean rental between his parishes, wards, or towns either measured or necessarily reflected actual differences in real wealth. His finding that the mean wealth of his elite-dominated Lewes electorate was far smaller than the mean wealth of his occupationally lower-status Norwich electorate suggests the extent to which a comparative use of raw rental values can be misleading. His classification of the Norwich great wards into wealthiest and poorest by mean rental was similarly flawed, and it impeded his ecological analysis. He wisely relied principally on occupational analysis, and I am not questioning his general conclusions. But his use of rentals cannot be said to sustain his findings based on occupations. Instead they merely serve to introduce a spurious precision. It must also be emphasized, as with Rudé, that rental values based principally or exclusively on real property are peculiarly deficient in measuring the wealth, and therefore the status, of urban residents – even putting to one side all of the real property that those persons might own outside the parish or township in which they are being tabulated. By any standards, urban wealth is underestimated by the land tax. The substitution of poor rate for land tax values, as both Phillips and Rudé have sometimes done, will not appear to solve any of these problems – or at least it will not do so before the 1830s when the process of local valuation begins to alter radically in the countryside. Even then the poor rates do not assess personal property. Before the 1830s, at least, the poor rates also have missing smallholders, though not so many, and the poor rate and the land tax seem to have shared a common valuational base in a large proportion of townships throughout England. The use of poor rate values through nominal record linkage with all voters holds no more promise for electoral analysis than does the employment of land tax duplicates, and for the same reasons. Both uses should probably be discouraged.[19]

This review of the literature has thus far been one of virtually uninterrupted gloom and destruction. The land tax appears to be useful for house repopulation studies, but only in carefully selected towns. The duplicates can also provide valuable supplementary information on individual properties and persons. But the reputation of the land tax has always rested on its qualities as a systematic documentation, covering virtually every township in the kingdom and (in a large proportion of cases) for a period of more than fifty years when industrialization, enclosure, and agricultural improvement were at their height. There is one further application of the land tax duplicates to which I will now turn, an application that will permit the reputation of the duplicates as systematic documentation to remain largely undiminished – at least in the geographical scale of their coverage. I refer to those methods which have been devised for classifying townships typologically by their landholding characteristics. Those methods, or modifications of them, will permit historians to utilize the land tax duplicates on a national scale and in a systematic and fully comparable manner, albeit during a limited span of years. This is the only application of the land tax – or the only one yet devised – which will do so.

THE TYPOLOGICAL CLASSIFICATION OF TOWNSHIPS BY LANDHOLDING STRUCTURE

A typological use of the land tax duplicates is one which classifies each township according to the degree to which the proprietorship of its lands is either concentrated into the hands of one or a few largeholders, or is much divided among many middling to small holders. Those "types" of townships where the land is concentrated into the hands of a few are commonly called "close" or "closed." Much divided townships are called "open." These typological classifications have become increasingly employed among historians who have sought to understand the fortunes of the small landowner, the incidence and effects of enclosure, the operation of the poor laws, the distribution of the rural labour force, the structure of communities, and, especially more recently, the nature of landlord paternalism and of political deference.

All schemes with which I am familiar – except my own – have employed four classification types within the "open" to "closed" spectrum. The method appears to have been first employed by H.L. Gray in his pioneering study of enclosure and the small landowner. Gray classified every township of Oxfordshire into one of four landowning types. In the first type, one proprietor pays three-quarters of the tax of the township; in the second, two to three proprietors pay three-quarters of the tax; in the third, two to three proprietors pay one-half of the tax; and in the fourth, the property is much subdivided (a residual category). Gray also stipulated how many of the townships within his first type were entirely owned by one man, though he failed to distribute that figure or to establish it as a separate type. He then tabulated the number of townships within each of his four types and associated those types with the incidence of owner-occupancy within the county.

This ingenious use of the duplicates rested on a number of assumptions which Gray did not thoroughly test. He assumed that the percentages he was deriving were measuring the amount of real property "owned" by a man in terms of "acres." Perhaps even more critically, he assumed the land tax was equitably distributed within each township among its proprietors. The first two assumptions, as we have seen, were not well founded. Not all proprietors held property in freehold, or even by copyhold of inheritance. Nor did Gray's percentages measure proportions of acres. They did measure proportions of real wealth held in effective proprietorship, however; and that measurement satisfied his central objective. Since the mode of classification was exclusively dependent on the tax values of the largest holders, it also evaded one of the two most catastrophic deficiencies of the land tax duplicates, namely, the incidence of missing smallholders and the unreliability of their tax and rental values. The great majority of largeholders, as we have seen in chapter 9, appear to have been taxed at the mode of the township burden. When large holdings depart from the mode, they tend to do so in the direction of heavier burdens. Those cases will therefore produce overestimations of holding size when Gray's method is applied. But such cases are relatively few in any sample population, and the estimation errors are thus comparatively slight. Such holders appear unavoidably as very large within their townships and are unlikely to affect typological classification seriously. Gray's method was therefore essentially reliable *for his purposes* in its measurement of holding size. Gray's method also avoided the second of the catastrophic deficiencies of the land tax. Since a typological classification is entirely derived by a discrete analysis of tax values within each township, it evades the error inherent in all statistics computed from inter-township bodies of data. The uses to which he put these classifications may have been questionable and his interpretations flawed, but Gray's method was fundamentally sound and promising.[20]

Apart from a brief and confused sortie by Davies,[21] Gray's landholding classification scheme was inexplicably neglected for decades, despite the interesting relationships suggested by his table between patterns of landholding and the incidence and impact of enclosure. Later historians made numerous references to regional differences within the counties they studied, implying differences in landholding, but the classification scheme itself was not generally applied. It was only after the Second World War, when Dennis Mills began to apply a similar scheme to the townships of Kesteven and Leicestershire, that the method began to play a more central role in economic and social analysis. David Grigg's important work on Kesteven and Holland apparently owed much to Mills. James Obelkevich also borrowed substantially from it for his innovative study of popular religion in south Lindsey. This typological use of the duplicates, which appears to be proliferating, should be strongly encouraged.

Although everyone who has made a major published use of landholding classifications has employed four types, it is unfortunate that they have adopted units of measurement for each of their types which are unique to their own projects. It has therefore become impossible to compare their results in a direct and precise manner. The more influential of the models, constructed by Mills, specifies two types of "closed" townships: one in which a single proprietor pays 50 percent or more of the tax, and a second in which two or three *absentee* proprietors (the emphasis is Mills') pay two-thirds or more of the tax (no one proprietor paying as much as 50 percent). Two further classifications are superimposed on the two "closed" types and appear to overlap them (Mills is confusing on this as on other points): "estate villages" are those in which a largeholder is "resident" or (which is not the same thing) has a "seat" (Mills seems to mean more than "in occupation" of the holding); and "absentee landlord townships" in which there is no resident largeholder, a category which could apply to either of the two "closed" types. His "open" types are composed of those townships in which the two or three largest proprietors pay less than two-thirds of the tax and the largest pays less than half. These townships are broken down into two discrete types. The lowest type category, termed a "peasant village," includes all townships reported in the duplicates as having twenty or more proprietors *and* where the mean acres per owner is forty or less. In addition, peasant villages include all townships in which the duplicates report fifty or more proprietors, regardless of mean acres per proprietor (or what Mills terms "density of owners"). His third category, "divided townships," is a residual type and includes all remaining examples.[22]

Mills' scheme is, in some respects, a curious one. Estate villages may occur in any of the four type categories, although they obviously do not tend to occur in the fourth and are most likely in the first. These would be useful subdivisions if the term "residence" were clarified and assigned a precise meaning. If only occupancy was meant, then the requirement could be satisfied from the land tax duplicates themselves in a uniform manner – unless one shares my doubts regarding the interpretation of occupancy in the duplicates. But if genuine residence was meant, or if Mills intended to go further, as he seems to have done, and require that the residence be a genuine ''seat'' of the family in residence (one which is untenanted by others and is peculiarly associated with the family), then the requirement can only be satisfied by research in other supplementary sources. I am not suggesting that such a search is impossible or would be unimportant – the presence of a family in its seat is of the utmost significance and can often be established – however, it must be clearly understood by those who wish to employ this method that the land tax cannot systematically (though it may occasionally) provide information on that fact.

Mills' types are also constructed in a manner which some historians may find unsatisfying. The requirements for his second type are especially unfortunate and too restrictive, being confined to townships with only absentee largeholders whose combined holdings constitute at least two-thirds of the tax. Many townships would be, and surely ought not to be, excluded from this category under the terms of this definition. For example, a township whose top two proprietors paid 90 percent of the tax, one of whom paid 45 percent and was in residence, would either be unclassifiable or, one supposes, would be classed within the third type as ''divided.'' Neither result seems within the meaning or analytical intent of the scheme. More critically, his two lowest or ''open'' types are unworkable since they depend on the calculation of mean acres per proprietor. Mills has generally taken his acres from the 1841 census, supplementing them in some instances by directories and later census reports of the nineteenth and early twentieth centuries. Even if those acreage estimates were reliable within the counties in which he was working, the mean acreages would be subject to large error because the denominator for his calculation is composed of total proprietors. The calculation of mean acreages is most unreliable when it is to be principally applied in those townships where smallholders were numerically predominant, as it was in Mills' scheme. The statistic is highly vulnerable to smallholder omission. One of the principal advantages of the typological mode of analysis – its avoidance of a dependence on smallholders and their tax values – thereby vanishes.

Obelkevich used a scheme which was closely patterned on that of Mills, but Obelkevich incorporated important modifications. He employed two ''closed'' and two ''open'' types. His highest type (type A) was what he termed a ''squire's parish'' and comprised all townships in which one proprietor paid more than 50 percent of the tax. The second type (type B) was vaguely defined as those townships in which ''a few'' (how many not being specified) paid ''most'' (how much not being specified) of the tax with no one proprietor paying as much as 50 percent. This type he termed ''oligarchic parishes.'' The lowest of his ''open'' types (unfortunately sequenced as type C) were his "freeholders' parishes," which he defined as those "owned by smallholders averaging less than 40 acres each." This was the equivalent of Mills' "peasant parish" and was dependent on the calculation of Mills' "density of owners" (or mean acres per total number of proprietors recorded in the duplicate). Type D was a residual category for Obelkevich, as it had been for Mills, and was also termed "divided." As he and Mills both noted, type D, or "divided" townships, often included "several large landlords with small or medium holdings." Also like Mills, he overlayered his typology with a second classification scheme in which he distinguished "primary parishes," where there were "resident" squires, and "secondary parishes," where his largeholders in occupation were only occasionally resident, or were resident with smaller holdings, or were resident in other adjacent parishes. Both of his classification schemes are subject to all of the objections and restrictions I have specified for those of Mills.[23]

Grigg adopted a scheme which was significantly different. His highest "closed" type was composed of those townships in which one proprietor "owned" all of the real property (that is, paid all of the tax). A second type was one in which at least half of the township was owned by one proprietor. A third type of township comprised those in which one or two proprietors (unlike Gray or Mills's three) owned at least two-thirds of the real property. The fourth type residually included all remaining townships and was treated analytically as "open" or divided. The second and third types were not arranged analytically along a "closed-open" spectrum. Nor were all three of the closed types fully employed in the analysis. Only the third appeared on Grigg's map of landholding, the fourth type appearing residually by implication (although the map and text are ambiguous on this point). It is not clear, as well, how on reflection Grigg would wish to treat a township in which one proprietor paid, let us say, 45 percent, and a second paid 15 percent, of the tax. His scheme would force him to classify the township into his lowest type, even if the larger holder were in residence. Many historians would therefore consider his lowest category to be too undiscriminating. But all of his categories maintain the advantage of having been calculated exclusively from the tax values of the largest holders. Whether those values should have been restricted to those of the two largest holders, rather than the three largest, as Gray and Mills suggested, is a matter which historians might endlessly debate.[24]

All of these typological schemes hold considerable promise for the classification of townships by pattern of landholding. But, if such work is to be fruitful, it must maintain its reliability and suitability for comparative analysis. There are a number of requirements if these conditions are to be met. First, the types must rely exclusively on the tax values of the largest proprietors. Any attempt to treat townships by the numbers or tax values of their smallholders is certain to fail. The numbers of such holders will be seriously undercounted to an extent which cannot be estimated in an unpredictable number of cases and their tax values will be unreliable. Second, the data to be used for the construction of types must be collected and published in a manner which maximally facilitates recalculation within the requirements of varying schemes. It is unlikely that all historians will agree on a single number or definition of types. Such agreement is unnecessary, provided recalculation can be simply accomplished and published results include such recalculations. It would also be helpful if data were publicly deposited or in some other way made available to others.[25] Third, computations based in part on acres are hazardous and wholly unnecessary. "Size" should be thought of as percentage of tax paid, and that percentage should be considered to represent the proportion of *wealth* in real property within the township. Fourth, proprietorship should not be misrepresented categorically as "ownership." Differing forms of tenure may be accommodated if proprietorship is understood to be in many cases no more than effective proprietary control in the formulation of those leases which actually govern the current use of the land and the revenues derivable therefrom. Fifth, if the tax values are to represent proportions of real wealth, then those entries in the duplicates which represent salaries (such as those for excise officers) and "stock in trade" must be excluded from all proprietor totals and from the total tax owed by the township. Some would wish to exclude tithe entries in the same way. But unless tithes can be uniformly identified as such – and in most regions I firmly believe they cannot – they should uniformly be included (but, where identifiable, flagged for separate evaluation). Unlike salaries and stock-in-trade, they are a form of wealth derived directly from real property. If their inclusion is a compromise, it is not a wholly inappropriate one. Sixth, the "total tax" of each township should be the actual sum of each included individual property bundle. Such a total will be more precise. It will also accommodate those duplicates which lump other local rates into their land tax values. The "totals" at the bottom of the duplicate are more likely to be the land tax quota; they are therefore unsuitable as a denominator in these townships. Finally, typologies based on data which can be gleaned systematically from the land tax should doubtless be supplemented by information regarding seats and genuine residence. Such information cannot be obtained systematically from the duplicates. Some preliminary evidence regarding occupation (negative evidence is probably reliable) can be so derived, however, and should form part of the typology data base.

Further guidelines should be observed regarding the format and date of the duplicates. If post-1798 land tax duplicates are to be used, then tax values cannot be employed. There is a simple and compelling reason for this restriction: Redeemed tax entries (unlike redeemed valuational rents) were not subject to revision and were therefore unaffected by internal revaluation within the township. Proportionality among redeemed tax values thus quickly deteriorates following passage of the Redemption Act of 1798. The later duplicates could be used through their valuational rent values, however; but such a procedure only becomes acceptable when the typology depends exclusively on the proportional estimation of the largest holdings. It is small holdings that are especially susceptible to internal inequalities in their rentals. Unfortunately, it will be found that in most regions and counties only a minority of townships completely reported their valuational rents, even after they become widely reported during the later 1820s and early 1830s. If only one year is to be selected for analysis, it should therefore fall between 1780 and 1798, or shortly thereafter. Since duplicates for 1798 are uniformly available in the Public Record Office, and widely extant in county search rooms, comparability for comparative analysis would be greatly enhanced if all studies were to adopt 1798, or an adjacent year, as a baseline. Comparisons with later years could then be made for those townships where valuational rents are available.[26]

As a baseline for comparative analysis, the year 1798 also enjoys two advantages over earlier years. Since the discrete identification of proprietors is required, only those multi-columned duplicates which explicitly distinguish between proprietors and occupiers may be employed. A sizeable proportion of townships continue to employ the single-column format into the 1780s and early 1790s. By 1798 they are rare. In addition, the double assessment of Roman Catholics can create huge amounts of error in typological classifications. Double assessment was commonly, but not invariably, ascribed on the duplicates, as we have seen. It is unlikely that its effects can be systematically eliminated. By the mid-1790s double assessment seems to have disappeared on virtually all duplicates except those where the Catholic proprietor held almost all of the real property. When almost all of the real property was double assessed, typological classification is not significantly affected. There is every reason, then, to confine the period of initial analysis to the later 1790s, after double assessment has effectively ceased, when multi-columned formats are generally available, and redemption has not yet begun.[27]

If these guidelines are observed, the townships of England and Wales may reliably be classified by their landholding characteristics in a manner which is sufficiently error free to permit both quantitative and qualitative comparative analyses. Provided some attention is given to the possible underassessment of emparked mansions (whose valuational rents impressionistically often seem small, even when the estate as a whole appears fully assessed), then there is reason to believe that an adaptation of these guidelines would also permit a parallel analysis of tenancy, an endeavour which has not to my knowledge been attempted.[28] In fact, historians undertaking analyses based on landholding typologies can meet many of the objectives which have traditionally been pursued by other historians employing less successful methods. Typological configurations of landholding may be associated with the incidence of enclosure – though not with the incidence of smallholders. Generalizations about the association of landholding types with upland and lowland regions and different farming regimes could be made with more precision. Landholding typologies may also be correlated with demographic variables such as population growth and decline, household size, marriage patterns and fertility, geographical mobility and the distribution of occupations, or the distribution of farm and domestic servants. The land tax may not allow electoral analyses to classify individual voters by their wealth, but the behaviour of voting communities could be evaluated within the conditions of their specific landholding environment. Precise operational meaning could then be assigned to those juggernauts of analytical clarity: deference and influence. Far from being a source unsuited to detailed analysis, the land tax is able to provide systematic documentation for an enormous range of questions at a crucial period in the socio-economic and political development of England and Wales. Its misuse should be brought to an end, but its full potential has never been tapped.

GENERAL OBSERVATIONS

Data critique and the evaluation of empirical method makes dry reading at best. Work of this type can only be justified by its impact on the field. It is hoped that the importance of this book will also be reflected in a number of more positive interpretive contributions. The study of the mechanisms and nature of national and local taxation, for example, has added considerable emphasis and definition to a phenomenon which in some sense has always been understood: The local community essentially governed itself and was, in most matters that touched the daily lives of ordinary people, largely independent of royal and parliamentary direction. In some instances the literal meaning of the law itself was successfully and habitually – and irremediably – evaded. What we have not appreciated, I think, is the extent to which the local community was able to exercise this independence. We have also not understood that governance in the countryside was, in many instances, in defiance of the magistracy and the landed elite who, as in the revision of the county rates for the North Riding, found themselves utterly unable to force the yeomanry and tenantry within the immediate vicinity of their own large holdings to comply with their commands. We have found reason to believe, too, that attitudes towards governance and economic vested interests sometimes differed sharply between upland and lowland regions, giving rise to inter-regional jealousies and political conflict. In some instances this book provides no more than clues to such phenomena. They are clues which should be pursued.

There is also evidence, sometimes only briefly alluded to in this volume, that the independence of the local community in its patterns of governance, and its attitudes towards the fiscal support of governmental functions, were beginning a revolutionary change by the second and third decades of the nineteenth century. The pressures of monumentally rising local rates, along with national taxation and the crucial administrative precedent set by the first property tax, affected, with astonishing speed, a local acceptance of modern forms of full rating valuations. By the 1830s regular professional township valuations for local rates had probably become commonplace in the countryside. During the eighteenth century, when revaluation as such was universal and incessant, professional general valuations were a rarity and were almost never settled at full values. The sea changes which occurred in the administration of the countryside during the early decades of the nineteenth century were of the utmost psychological importance and probably did as much, if not more, than any development at the national level to usher in more modern forms of social and economic governance. These developments deserve to be better understood.

We have always known, too, that the national burden of the land tax was most unequally distributed throughout the period of its administration, and especially so during the eighteenth and nineteenth centuries when land values rose differentially. But no one ever guessed the truly staggering extent and magnitude of those inequalities. The analysis presented in this book of the inequalities in 1815 provides a sound basis for estimating systematically and with some precision the full impact and regional distributions of national and local tax burdens on British farming at the end of the Napoleonic wars. It also underscores the unusually light burdens that were then being experienced by the leading northwestern manufacturing and commercial centres. We should remember that most forms of urban and industrial wealth, especially after the repeal of Pitt's property tax, were only indirectly or lightly taxed during these years. By comparison with the landed interest, the commercial and industrial enterprises of Britain were increasingly (in the case of the land tax) being afforded surplus capital for investment precisely during those years when capital formation was most crucial to industrial takeoff.

The landed classes increasingly bore the significant burdens of the land tax. Those burdens were still sufficiently severe in the southeastern counties and in numerous northern townships in 1815, at the end of more than a century of steeply rising rents. Why did the landed interest tolerate such a state of affairs when it seems to have been so dramatically contrary to its own economic well-being? Certainly the ministers of the Crown, at least as early as Walpole, were privately and sometimes publicly (to their cost) more than anxious to end this most inequitable and inefficient of taxation systems. What defeated those intentions was not economics. It was politics. Nothing – nothing at all – so aroused the English countryside against ministers in the eighteenth century as a cry of "general excise."[29] The landed interest clung to the land tax partly in fear of even heavier burdens if it were wholly replaced – and certainly some regions were enormously advantaged by the lightness of its real burdens – and partly, and I think more importantly, because the mode of taxation employed by the land tax was a profoundly traditional one. Excise, as a form of taxation, was unacceptable precisely because it was administered through a centrally appointed body of men of no particular estate or local standing whose business it was to poke their noses into the private affairs of their new neighbours. This sort of practice was what Englishmen understood to be the very essence of French despotism. God save the ancient liberties of England! They had been secured by Magna Carta and by every successful baronial uprising of the medieval period. The local community had always essentially, or to some degree, governed itself. The Glorious Revolution, to the extent that it secured the liberties and freedoms of English local institutions, ensured that it would always be so. Or so it seemed to the landed interest in the eighteenth century. The land tax ensured a suitable distance between the country and the Crown. It enabled men of landed property to rule in the manner of a true aristocracy and in accordance with their natural political rights. With the land went political power – or at least it should do so theoretically in a well-ordered and traditional society. Men might accede to a limited excise, whenever the requirements of government clearly demanded it. They might even consent to the full valuations and the centralized bureaucracy of the property tax under the extraordinary pressures of the Napoleonic wars. But under any other circumstances an attack on the land tax was viewed by the landed interest as an attack on property itself. As such it was politically intolerable. As for the commercial and industrial interests, who were most often, in the northwest at least, scarcely bothered by the tax, what could have been more pleasant? Their economic interests were well-defined with respect to the tax. Who could blame them if they preferred it? Why was this extraordinary form of taxation so long retained? Why, it was retained because there were few beyond the ministers of the Crown themselves who failed to perceive its immemorial and immediate virtues.

PART SIX

Maps

MAP 1 Wapentakes, East Riding

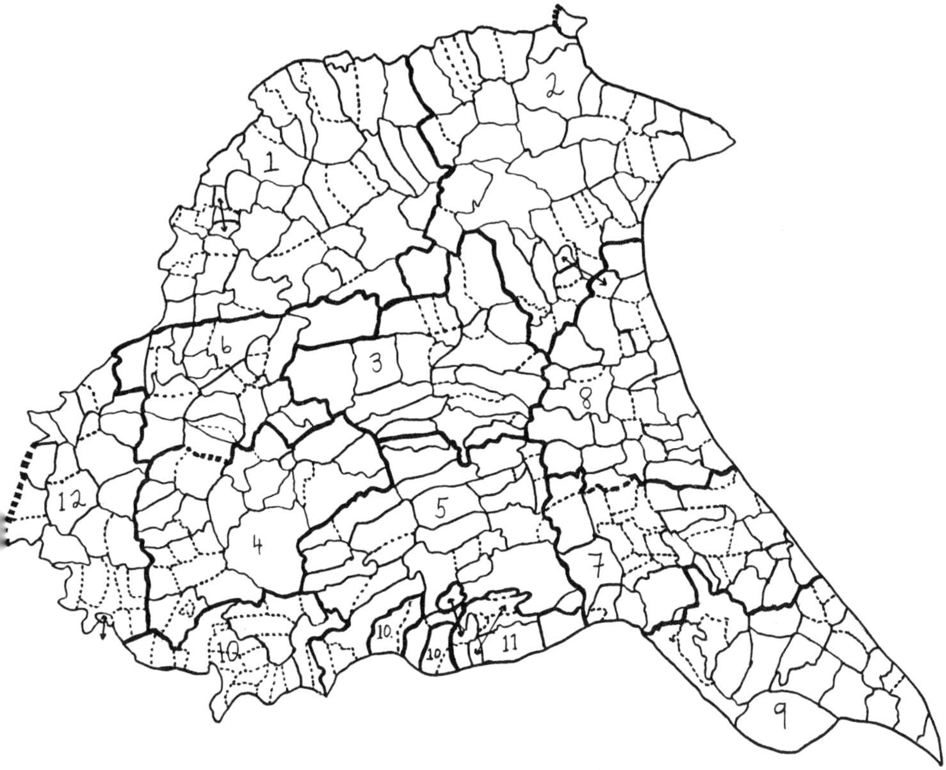

Wapentake
Parish boundary
Township boundary
Detached area

Wapentakes

1 = Buckrose
2 = Dickering
3 = Harthill, Bainton Beacon
4 = Harthill, Holme Beacon
5 = Harthill, Hunsley Beacon
6 = Harthill, Wilton Beacon
7 = Holderness, Middle division
8 = Holderness, North division
9 = Holderness, South division
10 = Howdenshire
11 = Hullshire
12 = Ouse and Derwent

Sources: Humphery-Smith, *The Phillimore Atlas and Index of Parish Registers*; 6-inch Ordnance Survey maps (OS), East Riding.

MAP 2 Wapentakes, North Riding

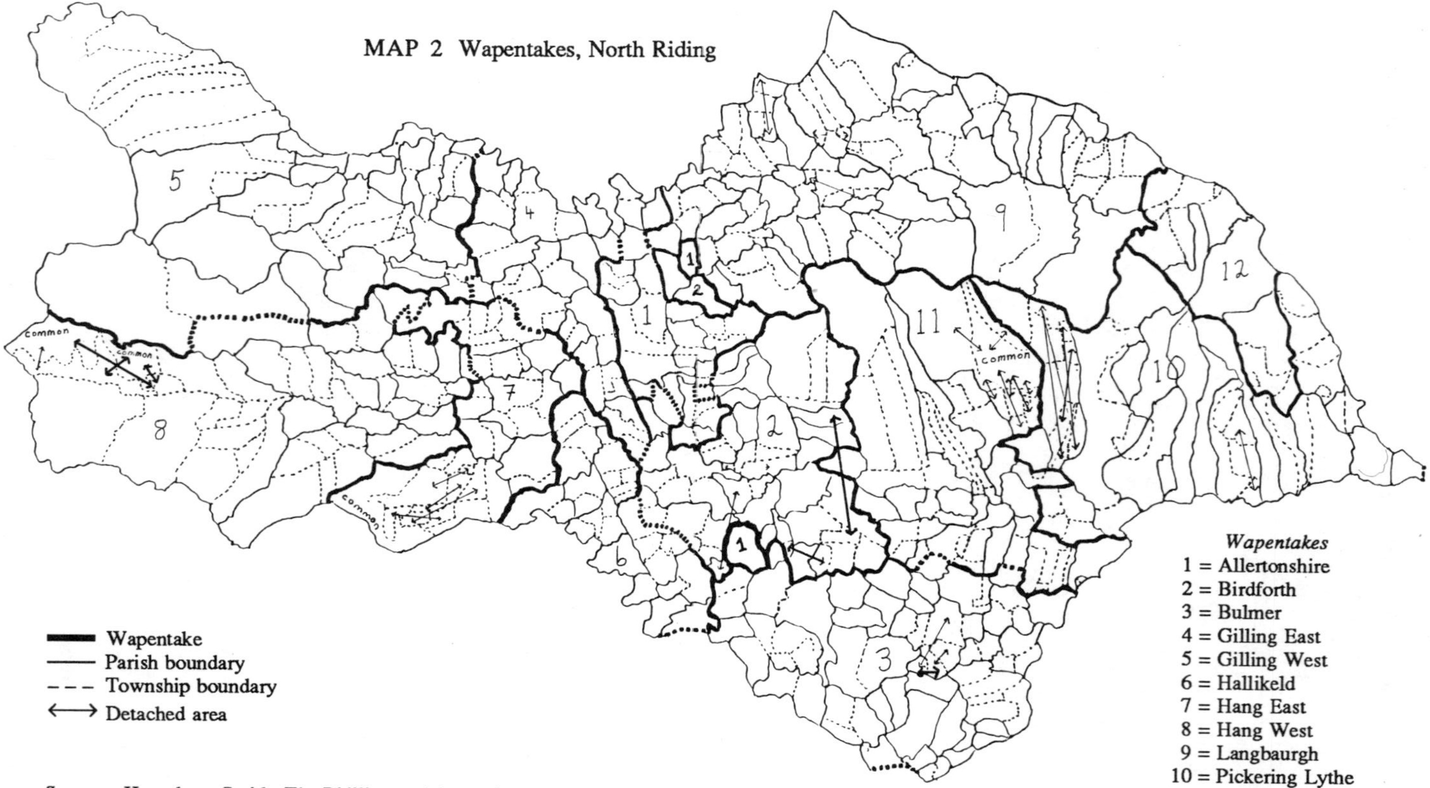

- Wapentake
- Parish boundary
- Township boundary
- ⟷ Detached area

Wapentakes
1 = Allertonshire
2 = Birdforth
3 = Bulmer
4 = Gilling East
5 = Gilling West
6 = Hallikeld
7 = Hang East
8 = Hang West
9 = Langbaurgh
10 = Pickering Lythe
11 = Ryedale
12 = Whitby Strand

Sources: Humphery-Smith, *The Phillimore Atlas and Index of Parish Registers*; 6-inch Ordnance Survey maps (OS), North Riding.

MAP 3 Wapentakes; West Riding, the Ainsty and the City of York

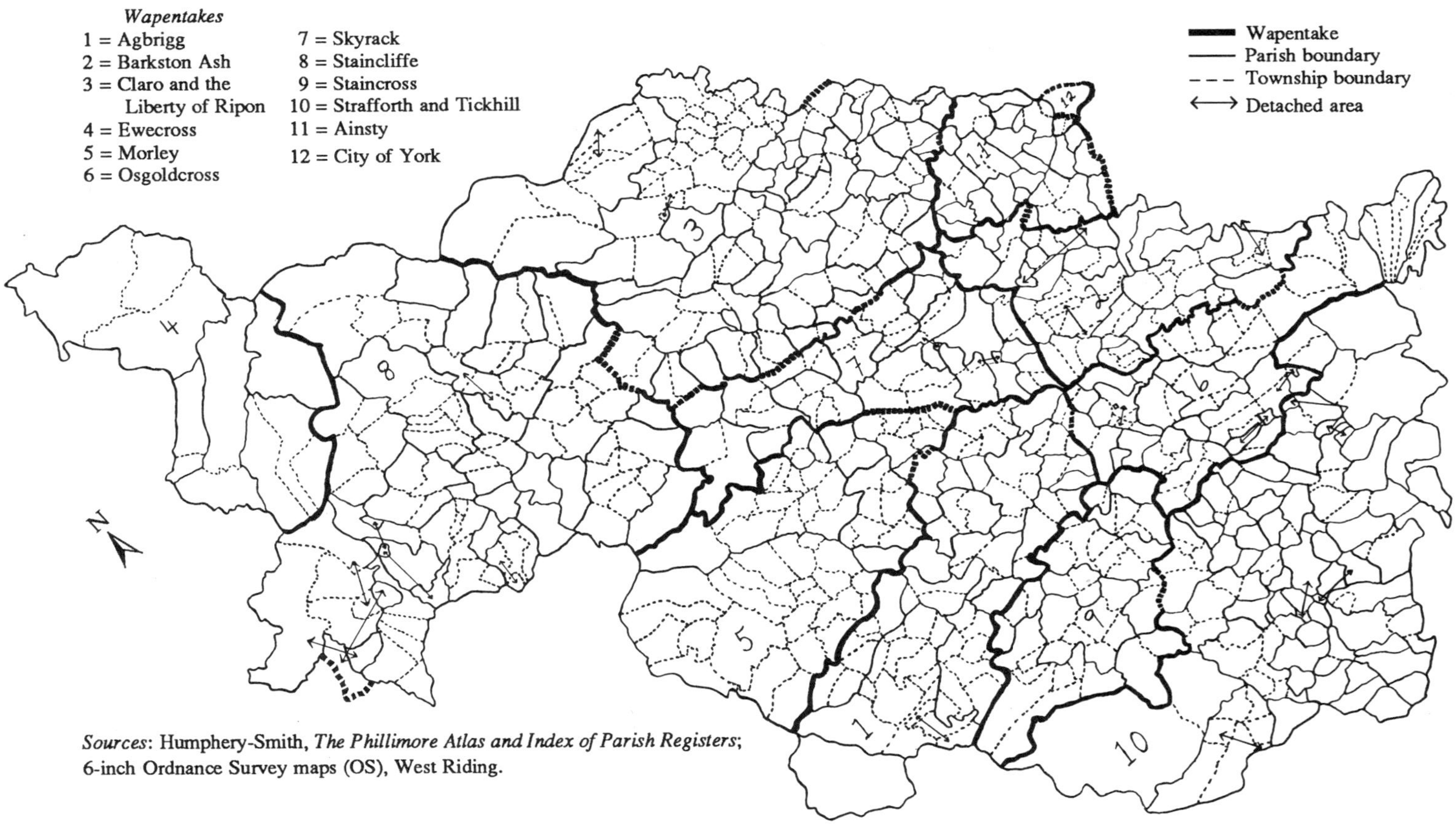

Sources: Humphery-Smith, *The Phillimore Atlas and Index of Parish Registers*; 6-inch Ordnance Survey maps (OS), West Riding.

MAP 4 1831 Census acres as a percentage of six-inch Ordnance acres, North Riding, township level

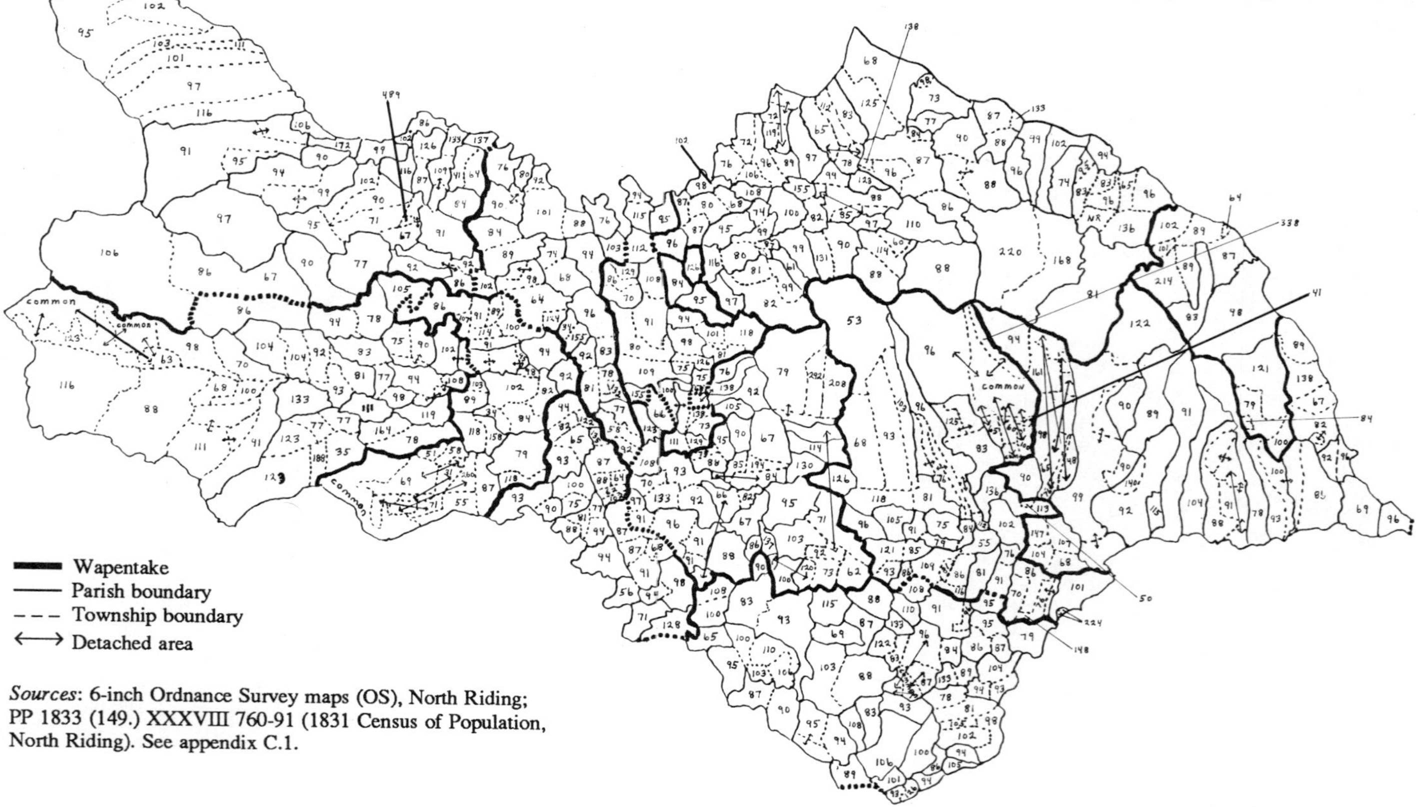

Sources: 6-inch Ordnance Survey maps (OS), North Riding; PP 1833 (149.) XXXVIII 760-91 (1831 Census of Population, North Riding). See appendix C.1.

MAP 5 1831 Census acres as a percentage of six-inch Ordnance acres, North Riding, parish level

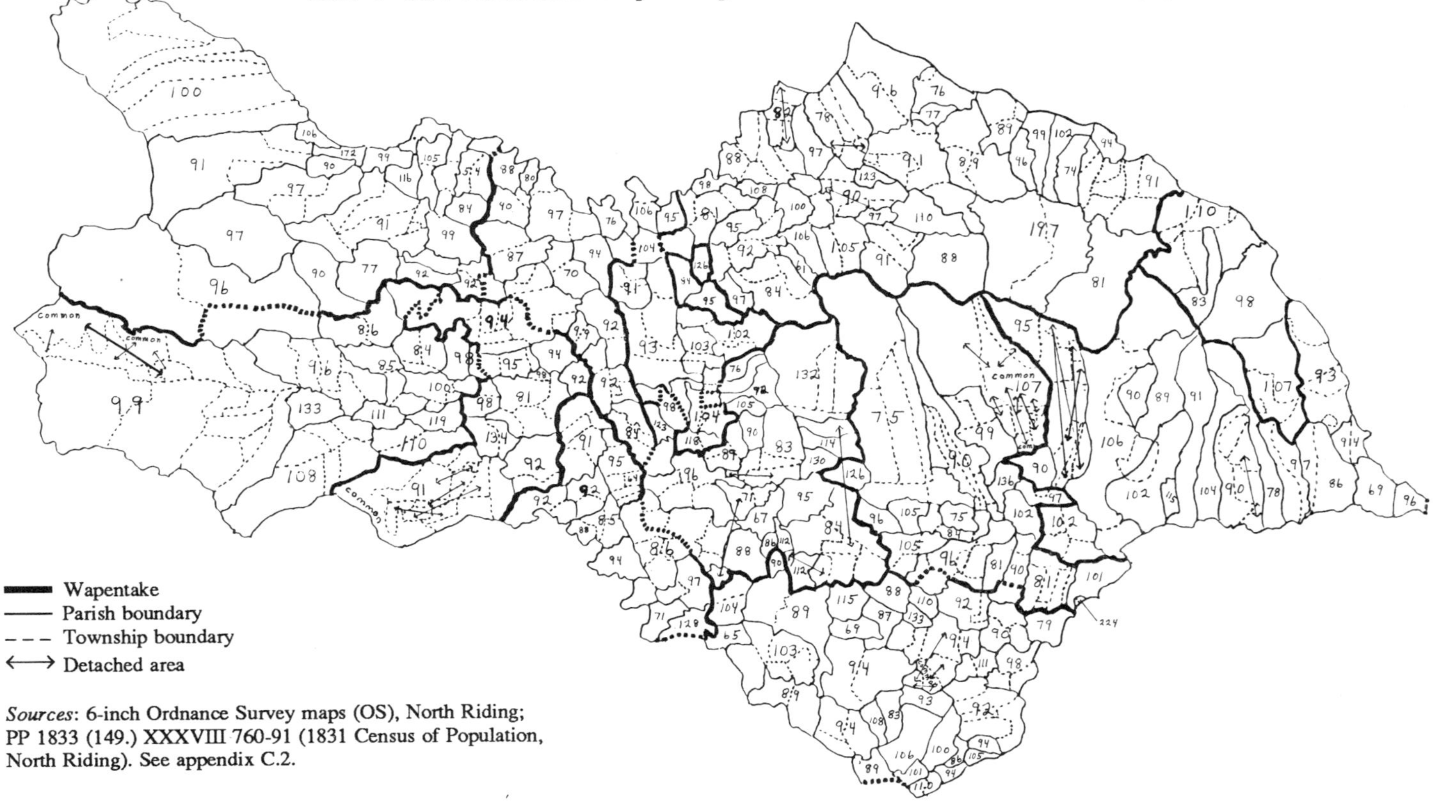

Sources: 6-inch Ordnance Survey maps (OS), North Riding; PP 1833 (149.) XXXVIII 760-91 (1831 Census of Population, North Riding). See appendix C.2.

MAP 6 Ratios of reported land tax valuations to land tax quotas, North Riding sample (all townships reporting "rent"), c. 1830

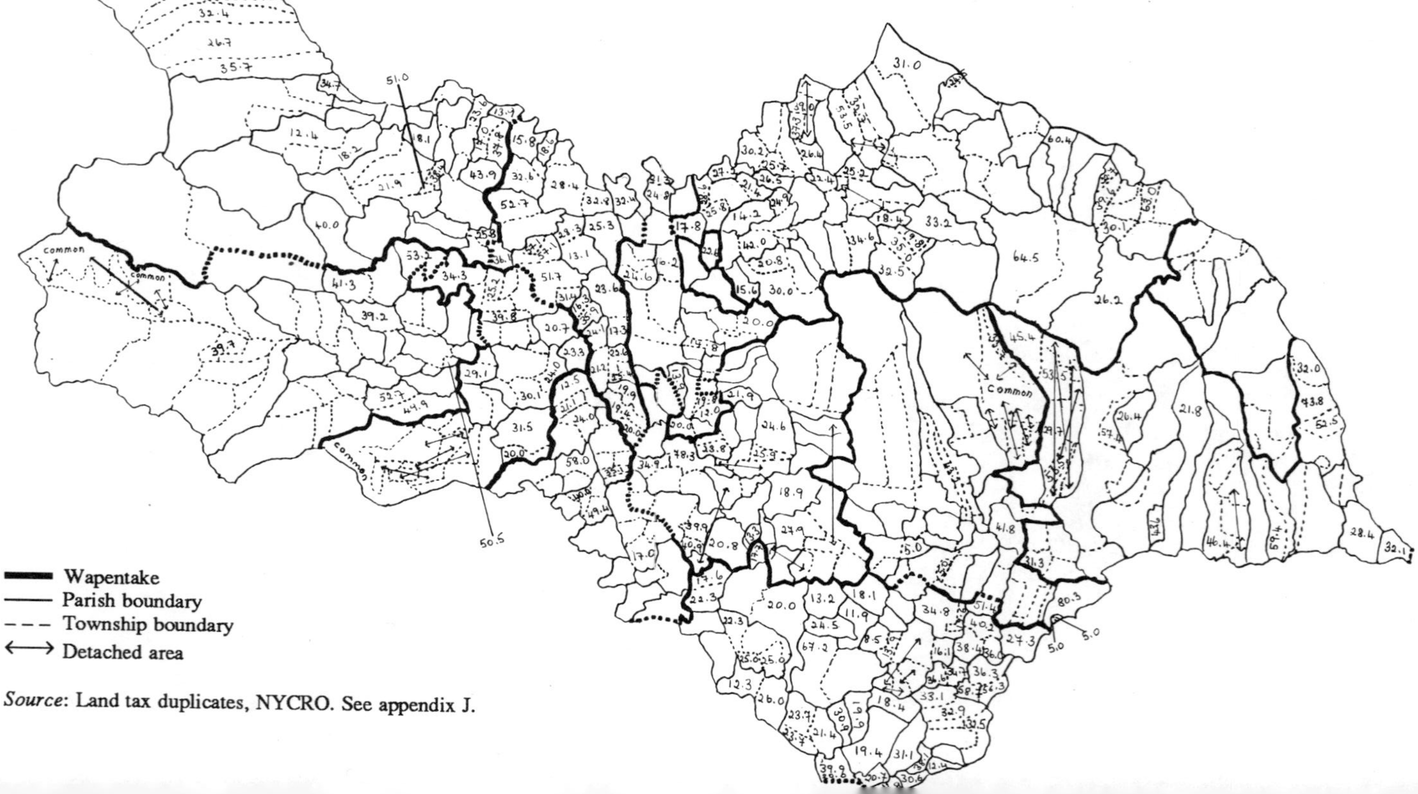

Source: Land tax duplicates, NYCRO. See appendix J.

MAP 7 Net ratios of 1815 property tax valuations (schedule A) to land tax quotas, all townships, North Riding

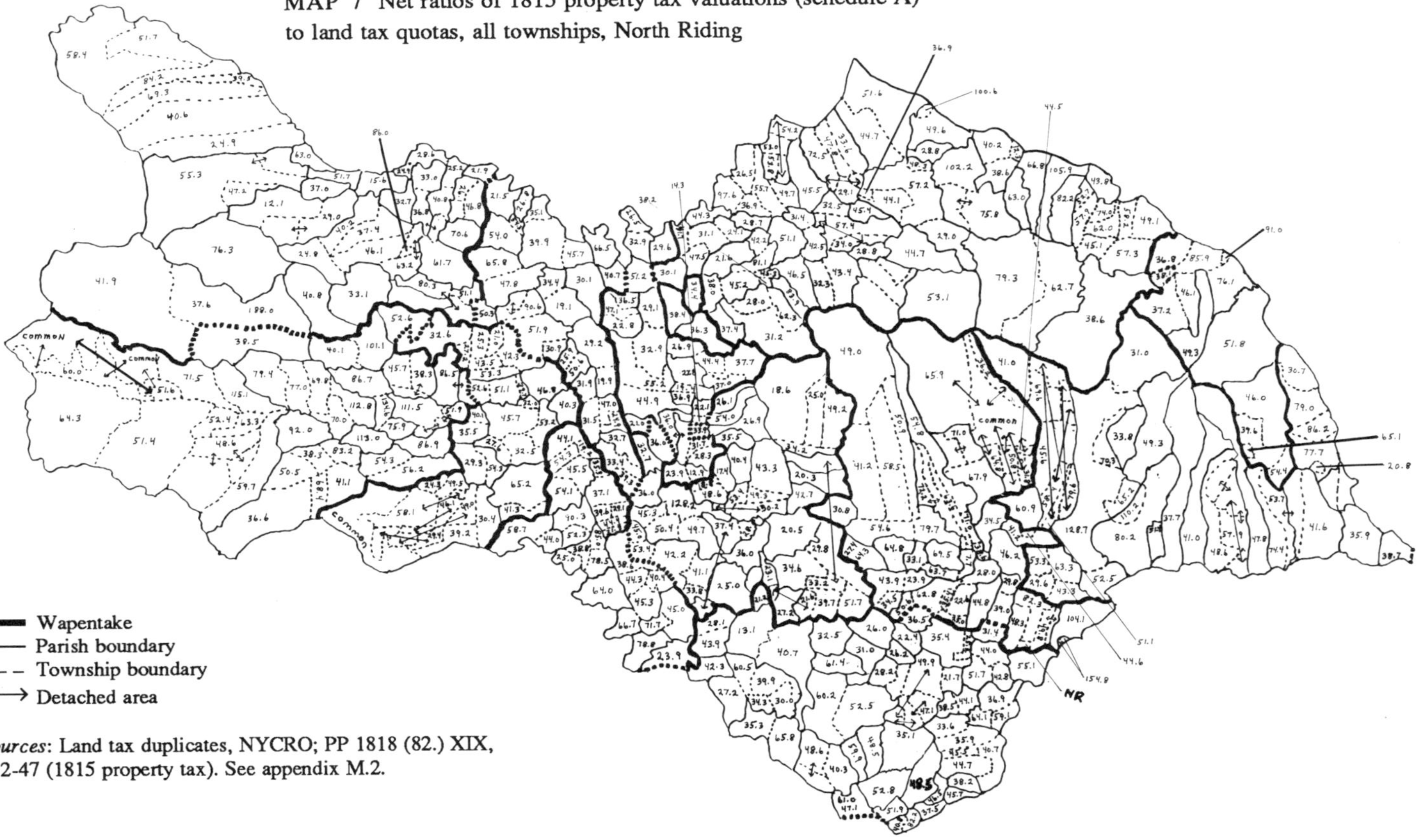

▬ Wapentake
— Parish boundary
- - - Township boundary
⟷ Detached area

Sources: Land tax duplicates, NYCRO; PP 1818 (82.) XIX, 532-47 (1815 property tax). See appendix M.2.

MAP 8 1815 property tax valuations (schedule A) per acre (£), all townships, North Riding

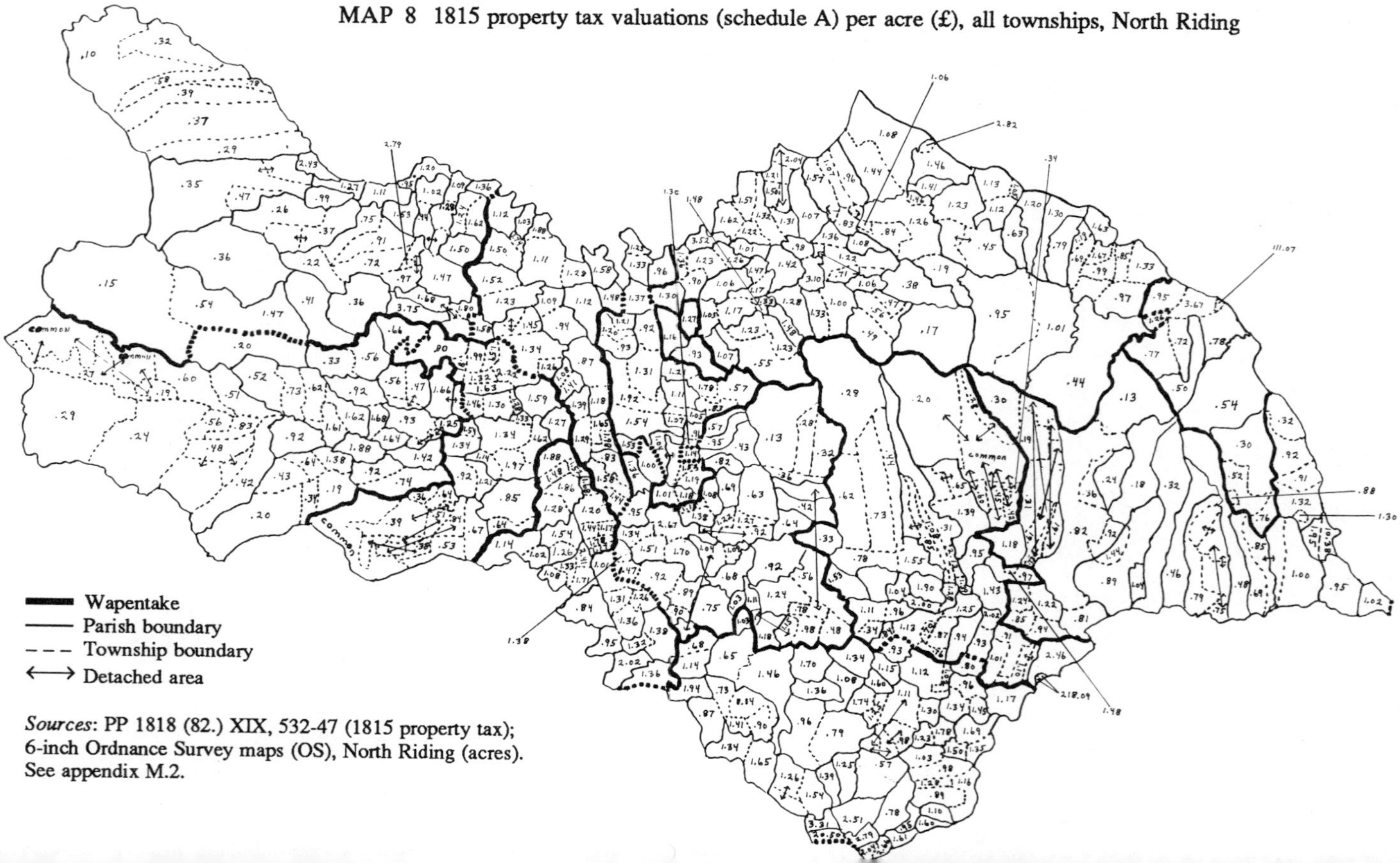

Wapentake
Parish boundary
Township boundary
Detached area

Sources: PP 1818 (82.) XIX, 532-47 (1815 property tax); 6-inch Ordnance Survey maps (OS), North Riding (acres). See appendix M.2.

MAP 9 Acres per £ of land tax quota, all townships, North Riding

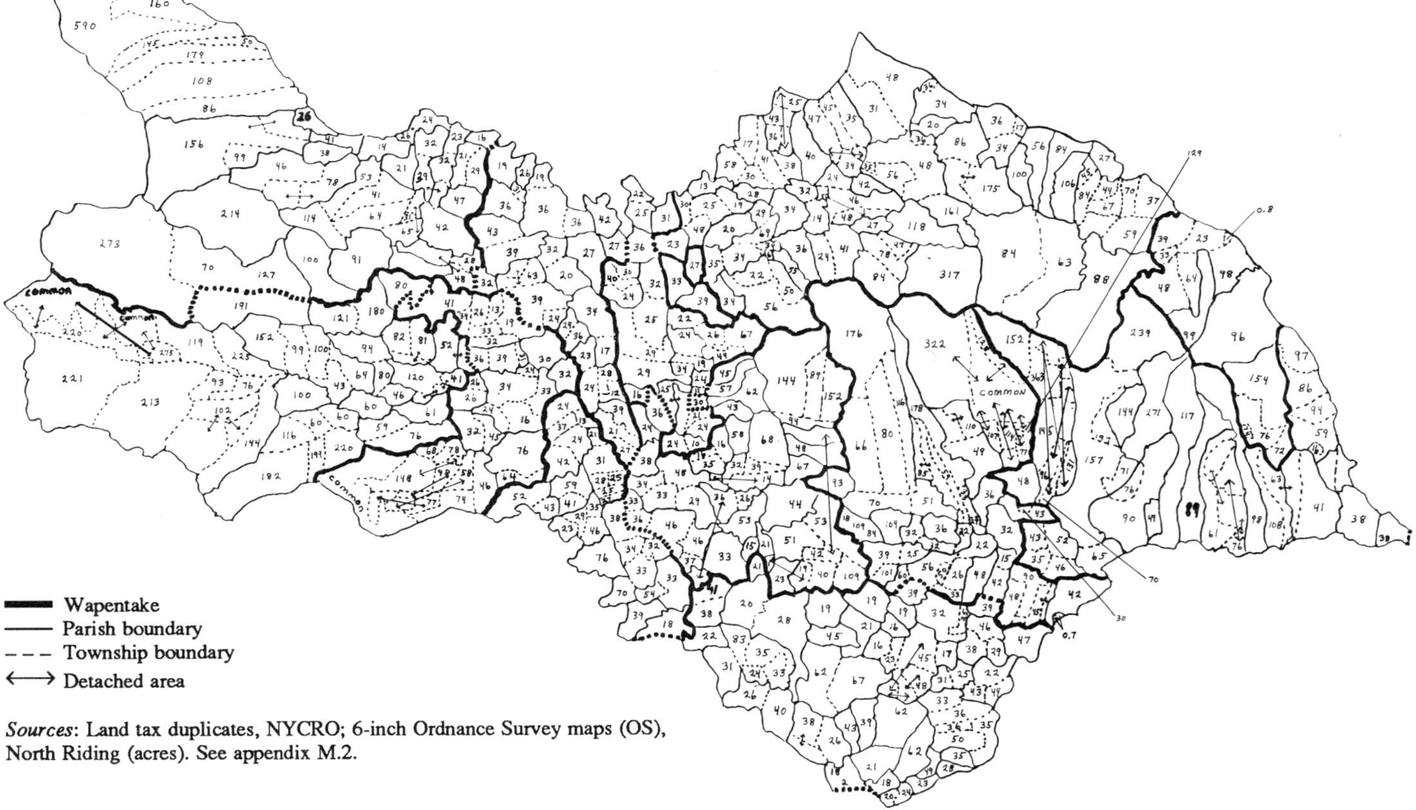

Wapentake
Parish boundary
Township boundary
Detached area

Sources: Land tax duplicates, NYCRO; 6-inch Ordnance Survey maps (OS), North Riding (acres). See appendix M.2.

MAP 10 Net ratios of 1815 property tax valuations (schedule A) to land tax quotas, all townships, East Riding

▬ Wapentake
—— Parish boundary
- - - Township boundary
⟷ Detached area

Sources: Land tax duplicates, Humberside County Record Office; PP 1818 (82.) XIX, 516-26 (1815 property tax). See appendix P.1.

MAP 11 1815 property tax valuations (schedule A) per acre (£), all townships, East Riding

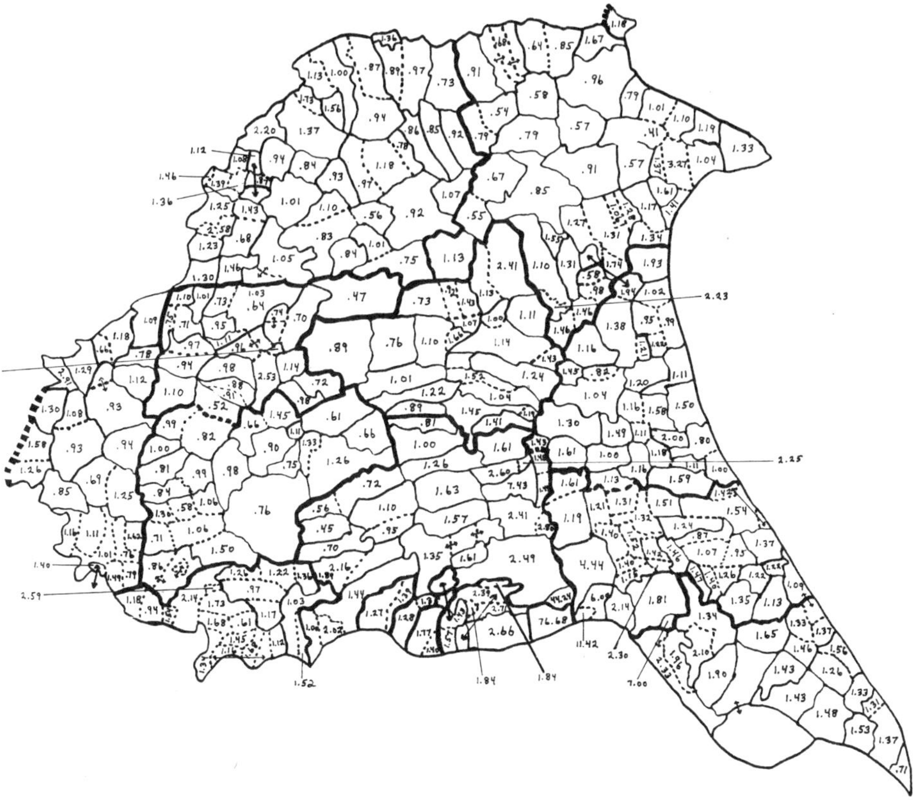

▬ Wapentake
—— Parish boundary
- - - Township boundary
⟷ Detached area

Sources: PP 1818 (82.) XIX, 516-26 (1815 property tax); 6-inch Ordnance Survey maps (OS), East Riding (acres). See appendix P.1.

MAP 12 Acres per £ of land tax quota, all townships, East Riding

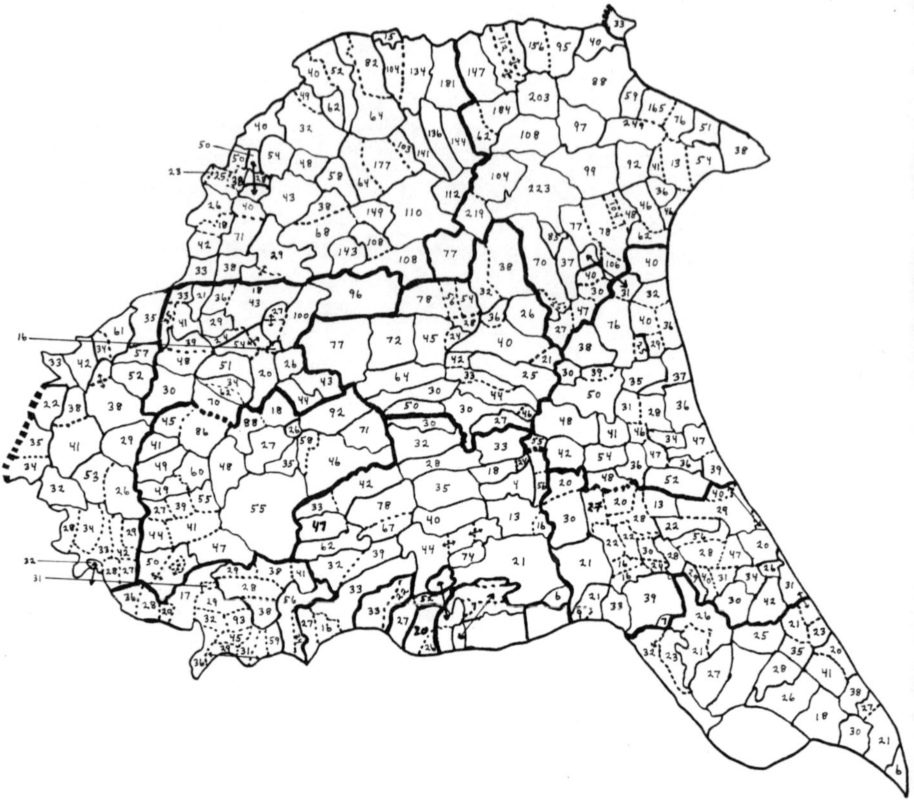

▬ Wapentake
—— Parish boundary
- - - Township boundary
⟷ Detached area

Sources: Land tax duplicates, Humberside County Record Office; 6-inch Ordnance Survey maps (OS), East Riding (acres). See appendix P.1.

MAP 13 Net ratios of 1815 property tax valuations (schedule A) to land tax quotas, all townships; West Riding, the Ainsty and the City of York

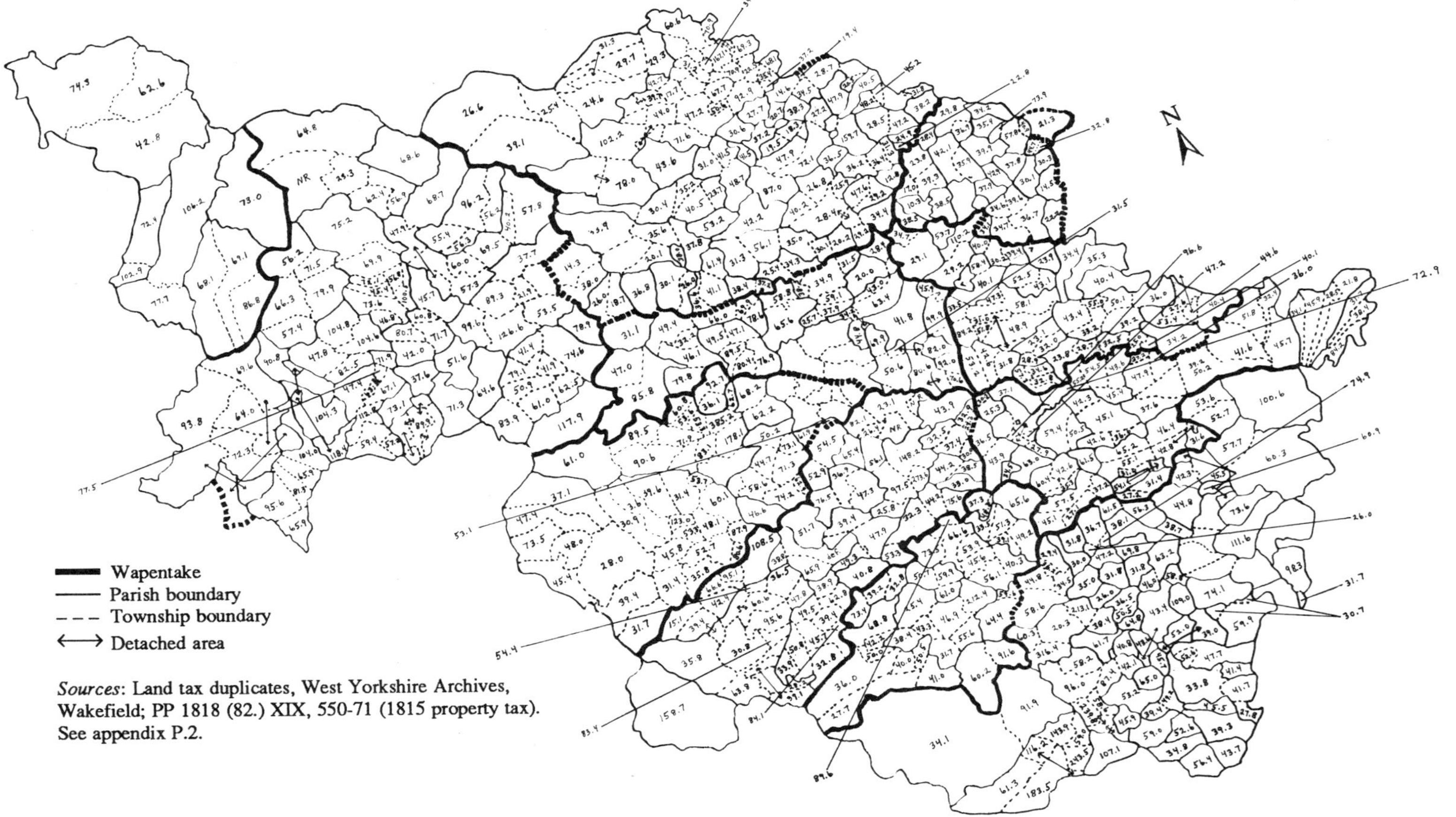

- Wapentake
- Parish boundary
- Township boundary
- ⟷ Detached area

Sources: Land tax duplicates, West Yorkshire Archives, Wakefield; PP 1818 (82.) XIX, 550-71 (1815 property tax). See appendix P.2.

MAP 14 1815 property tax valuations (schedule A) per acre (£), all townships; West Riding, the Ainsty and the City of York

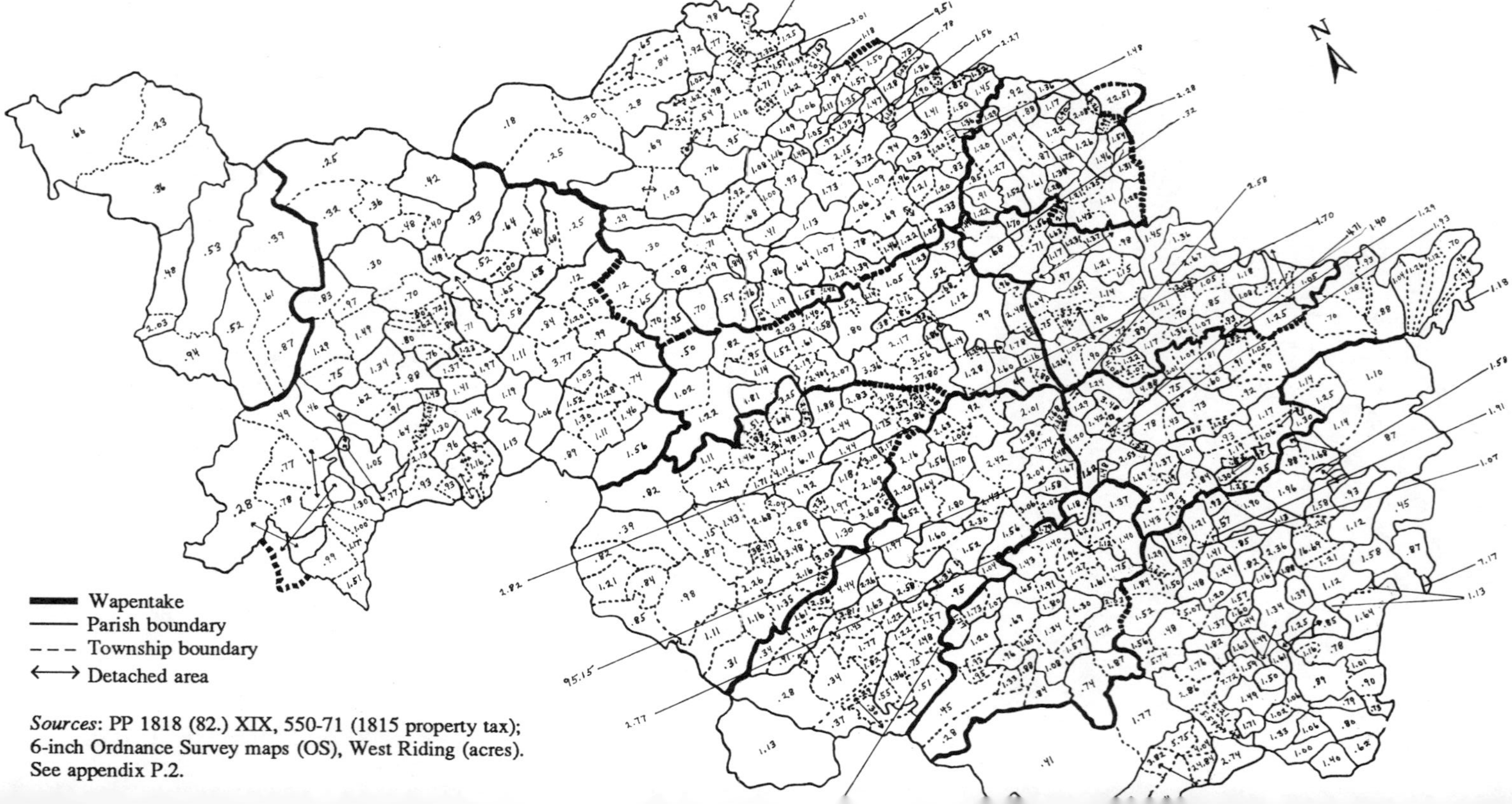

Sources: PP 1818 (82.) XIX, 550-71 (1815 property tax); 6-inch Ordnance Survey maps (OS), West Riding (acres). See appendix P.2.

MAP 15 Acres per £ of land tax quota, all townships; West Riding, the Ainsty and the City of York

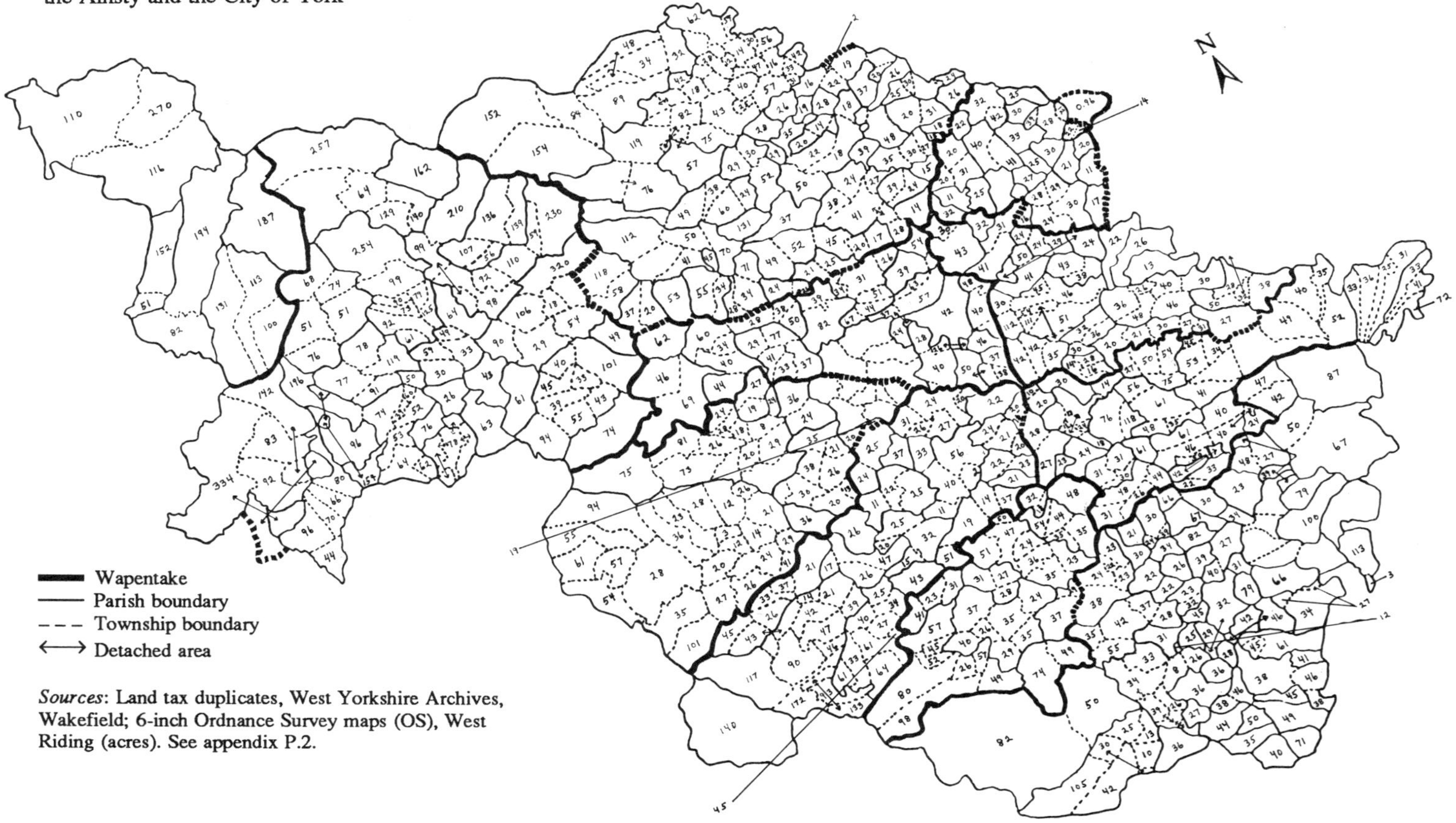

Sources: Land tax duplicates, West Yorkshire Archives, Wakefield; 6-inch Ordnance Survey maps (OS), West Riding (acres). See appendix P.2.

MAP 16 Acres per £ of gross land tax quota, all counties,

Sources: Browning, *English Historical Documents, 1660–1714*, 318–21 (1707 county quotas for the land tax); *Gazetteer of the British Isles*, 9th ed., (acres). See table 15.1.

MAP 17 Assessment per square mile (s.) in 1225, English counties

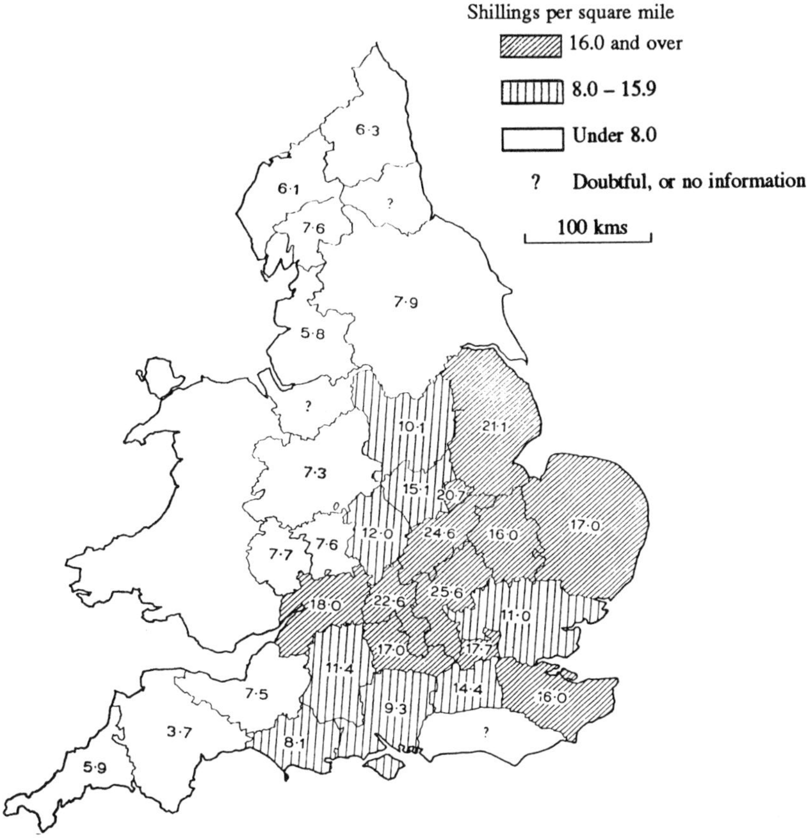

Source: Darby, *A New Historical Geography of England.* Published by permission of Cambridge University Press.

MAP 18 Assessment per square mile (s.) in 1334, English counties

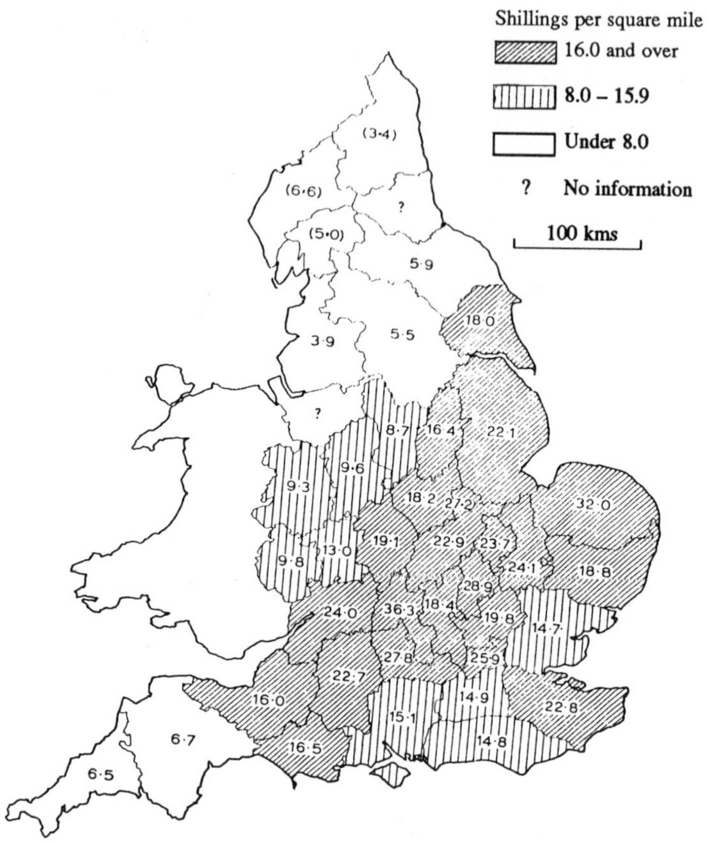

Source: Darby, *A New Historical Geography of England.* Published by permission of Cambridge University Press.

MAP 19 Poll tax population per square mile (s.) in 1377, English counties

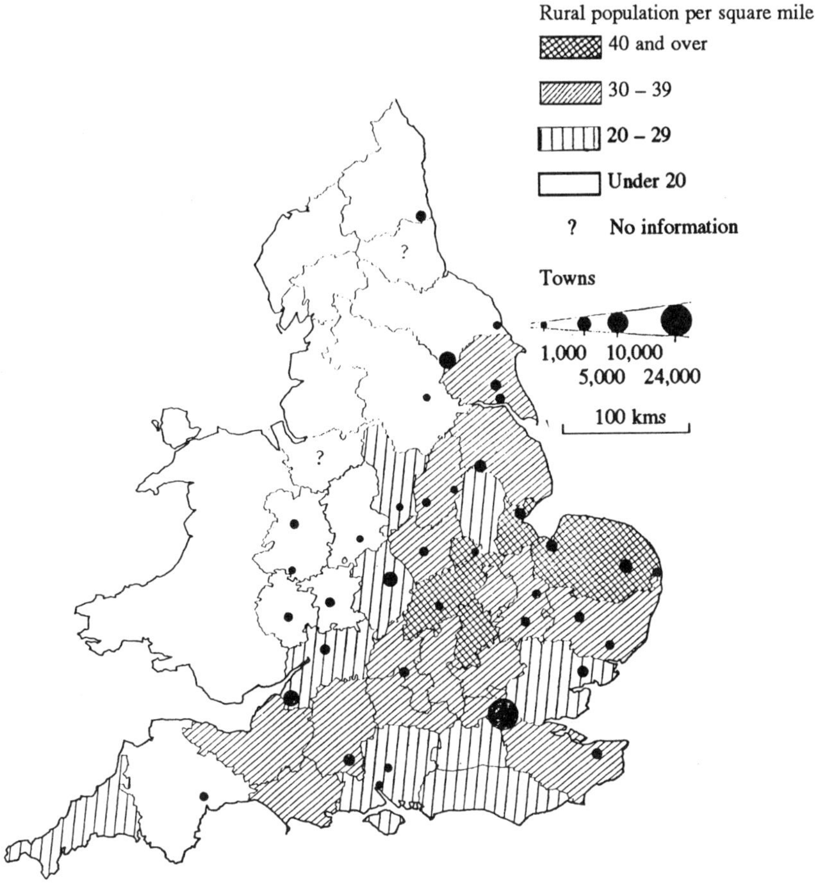

Source: Darby, *A New Historical Geography of England.* Published by permission of Cambridge University Press.

MAP 20 Assessment per square mile in 1524/5, parish level

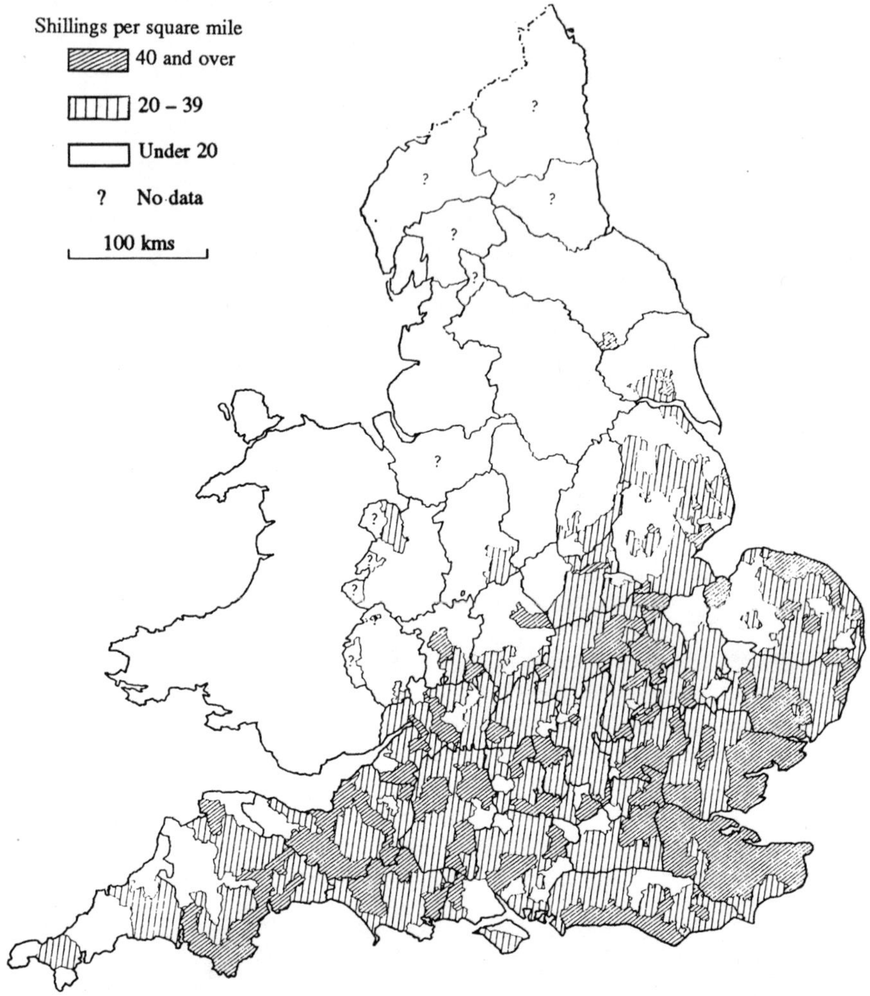

Source: Darby, *A New Historical Geography of England.* Published by permission of Cambridge University Press.

MAP 21 1815 property tax valuations (schedule A) per acre (£), all counties, England and Wales

Sources: PP 1818 (82.) XIX (1815 property tax); *Gazetteer of the British Isles*, 9th ed. (acres). See table 15.1.

MAP 22 Mean gross ratios of 1815 property tax valuations (schedule A) to land tax quotas, all counties, England and Wales

Sources: PP 1818 (82.) XIX (1815 property tax); Browning, *English Historical Documents, 1660–1714*, 318–21 (1707 county quotas for the land tax). See table 15.1.

MAP 23 Net ratios of 1815 property tax valuations (schedule A) to land tax quotas, all parishes, Bedfordshire

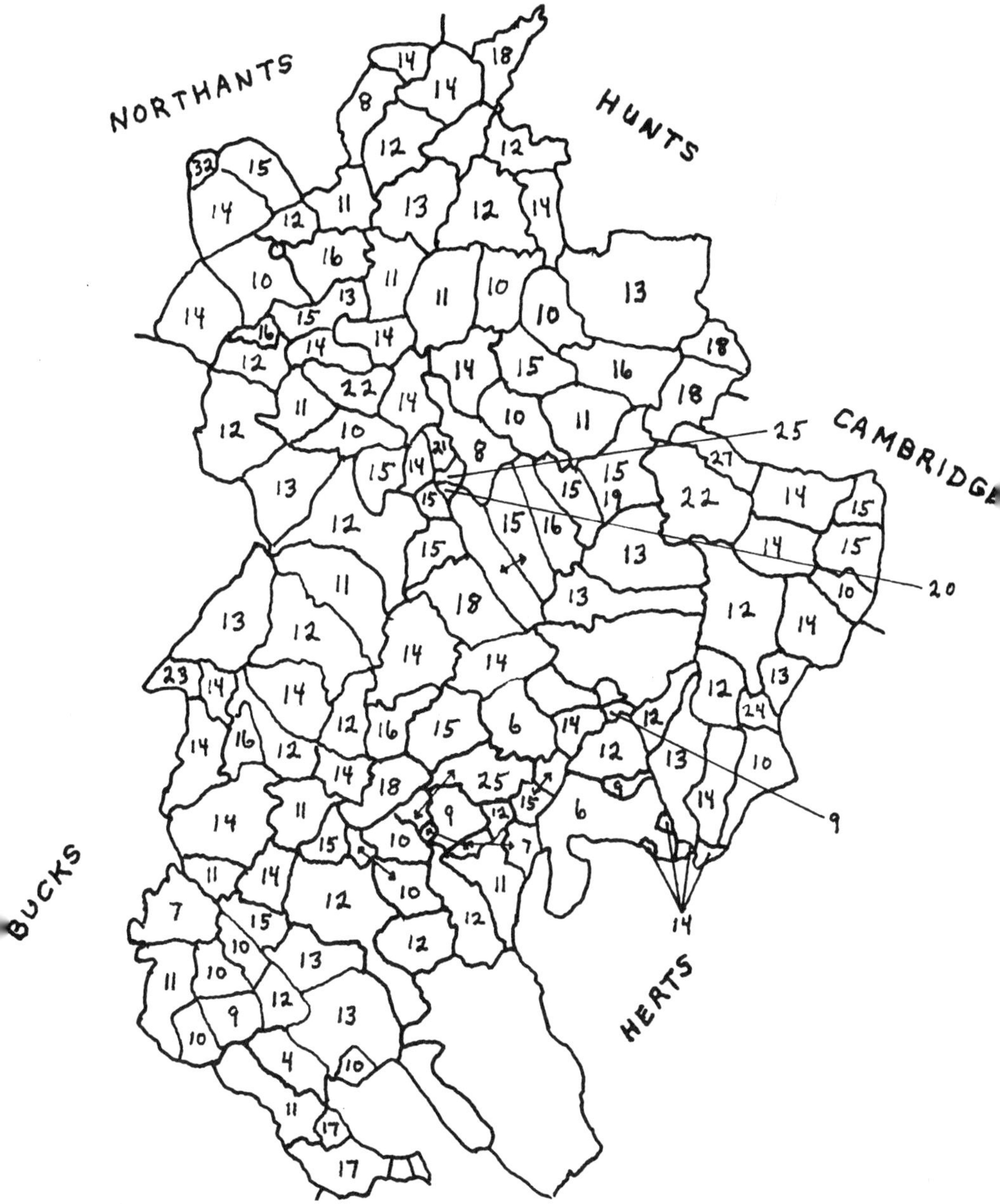

Sources: Land tax duplicates, Bedfordshire Record Office; PP 1818 (82.) XIX (1815 property tax); Humphery-Smith, *The Phillimore Atlas and Index of Parish Registers* (parish boundaries).

MAP 24 Net ratios of 1815 property tax valuations (schedule A) to land tax quotas, all parishes, Cornwall

Sources: Land tax duplicates, Cornwall Record Office; PP 1818 (82.) XIX (1815 property tax); Humphery-Smith, *The Phillimore Atlas and Index of Parish Registers* (parish boundaries).

MAP 25 Net ratios of 1815 property tax valuations (schedule A) to land tax quotas, all townships, Cumberland

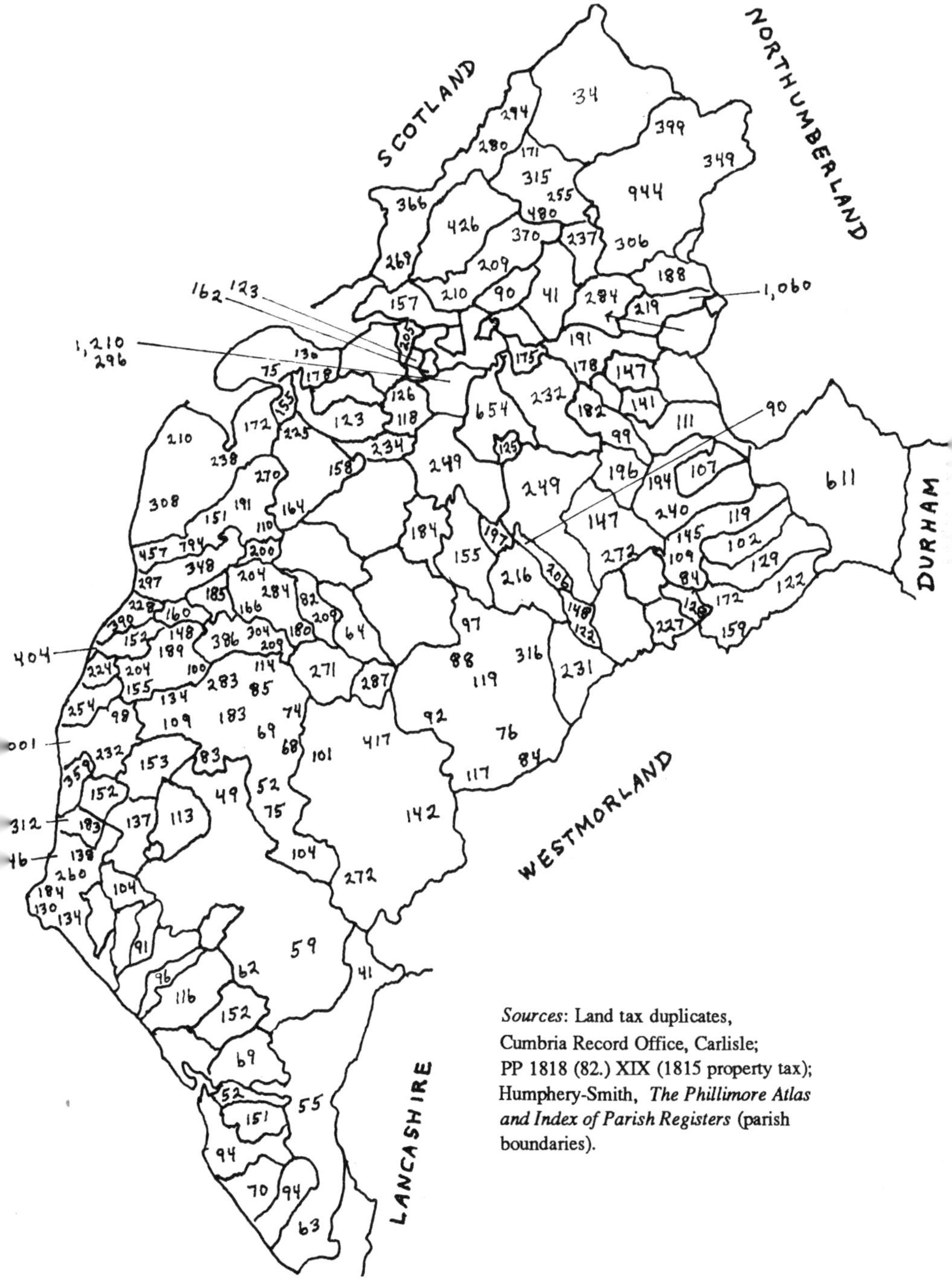

Sources: Land tax duplicates,
Cumbria Record Office, Carlisle;
PP 1818 (82.) XIX (1815 property tax);
Humphery-Smith, *The Phillimore Atlas and Index of Parish Registers* (parish boundaries).

MAP 26 Net ratios of 1815 property tax valuations (schedule A) to land tax quotas, all townships, Herefordshire

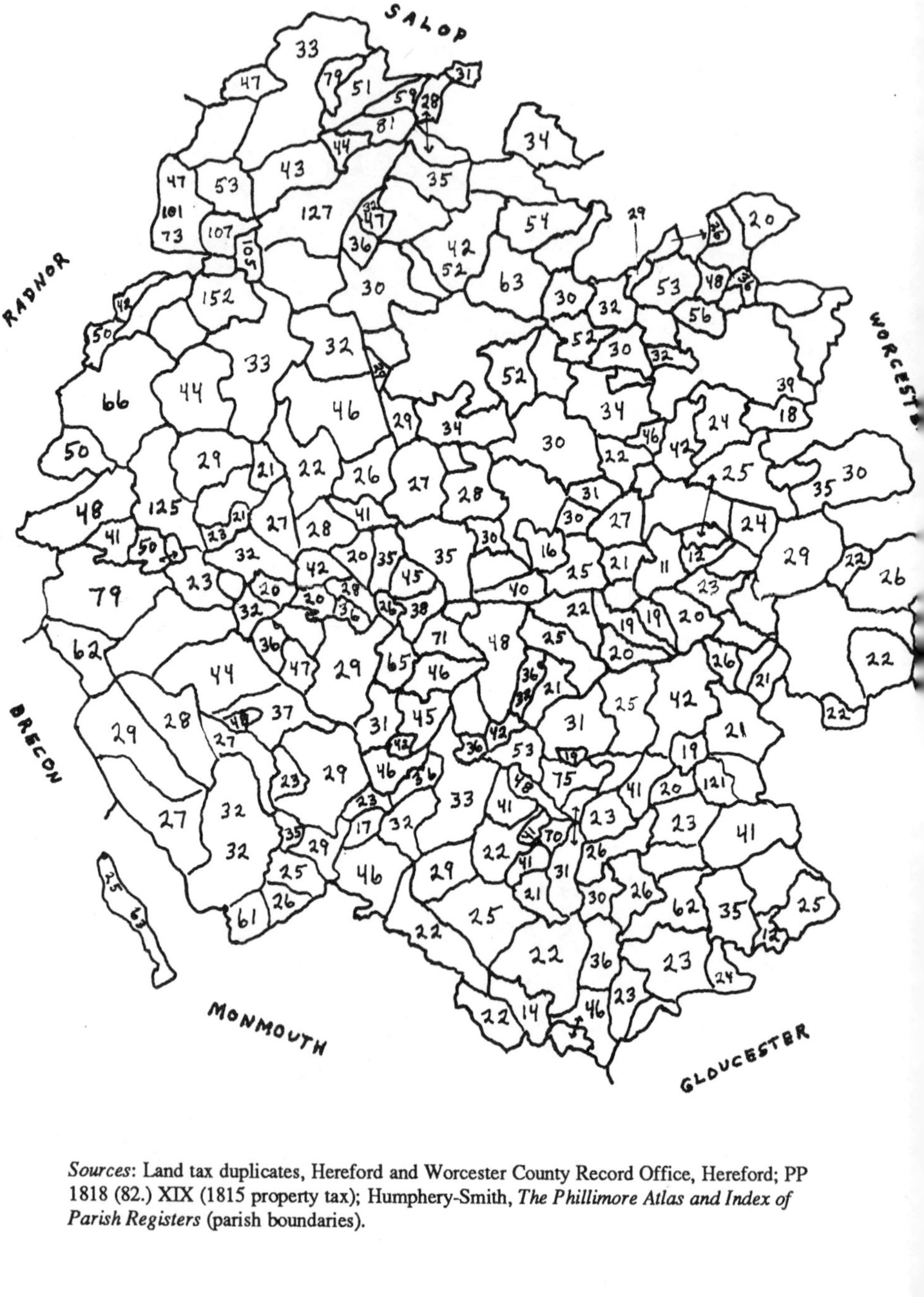

Sources: Land tax duplicates, Hereford and Worcester County Record Office, Hereford; PP 1818 (82.) XIX (1815 property tax); Humphery-Smith, *The Phillimore Atlas and Index of Parish Registers* (parish boundaries).

MAP 27 Net ratios of 1815 property tax valuations (schedule A) to land tax quotas, all parishes, Hertfordshire

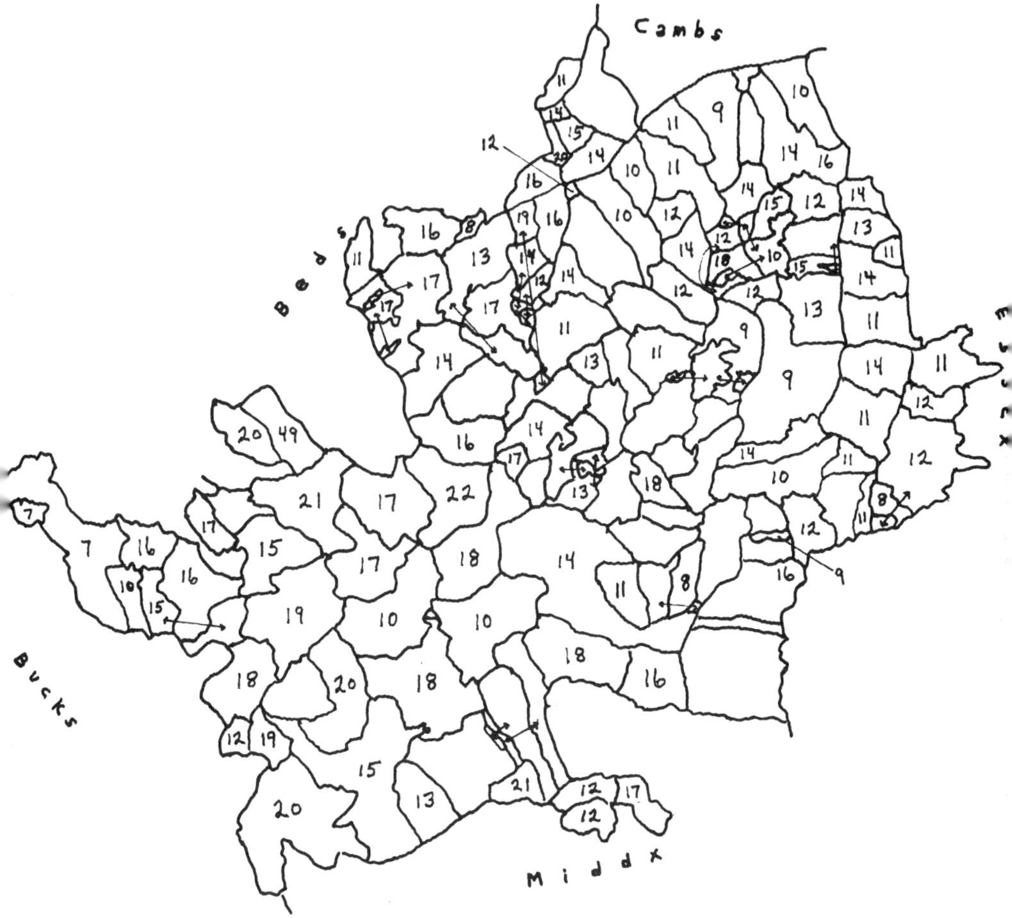

Sources: Land tax duplicates, Hertfordshire Record Office; PP 1818 (82.) XIX (1815 property tax); Humphery-Smith, *The Phillimore Atlas and Index of Parish Registers* (parish boundaries).

MAP 28 Net ratios of 1815 property tax valuations (schedule A) to land tax quotas, all townships, north Lancashire

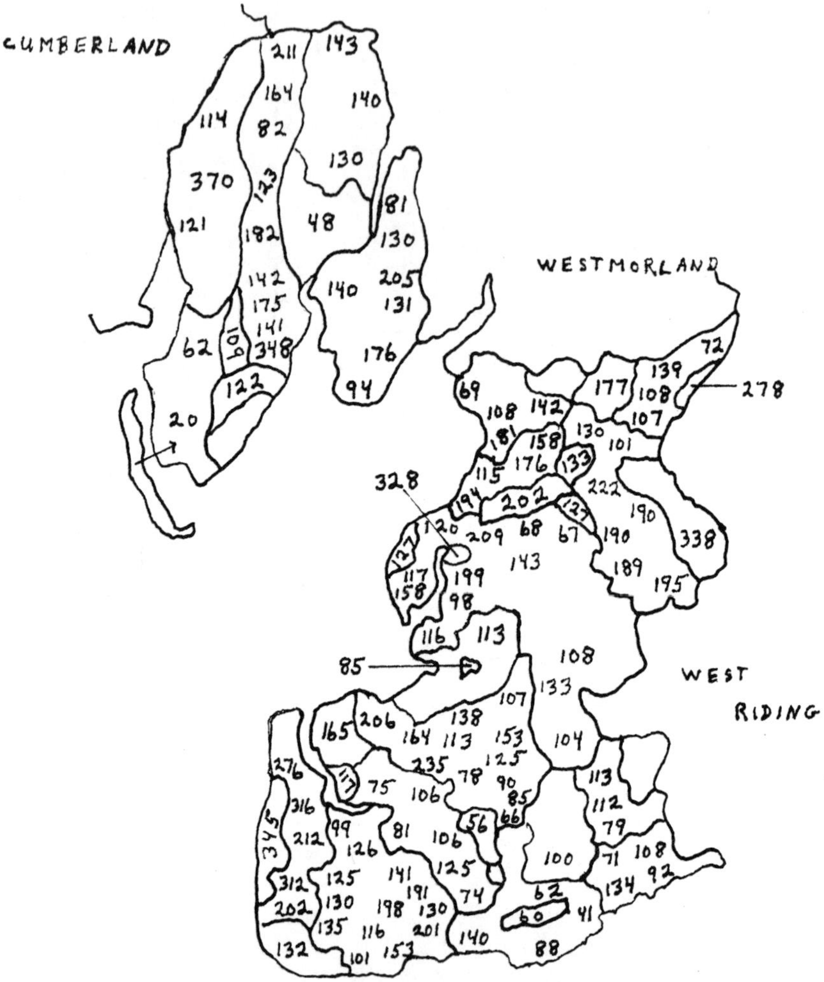

Sources: Land tax duplicates, Lancashire Record Office; PP 1818 (82.) XIX (1815 property tax); Humphery-Smith, *The Phillimore Atlas and Index of Parish Registers* (parish boundaries).

MAP 29 Net ratios of 1815 property tax valuations (schedule A) to land tax quotas, all townships, southeast Lancashire

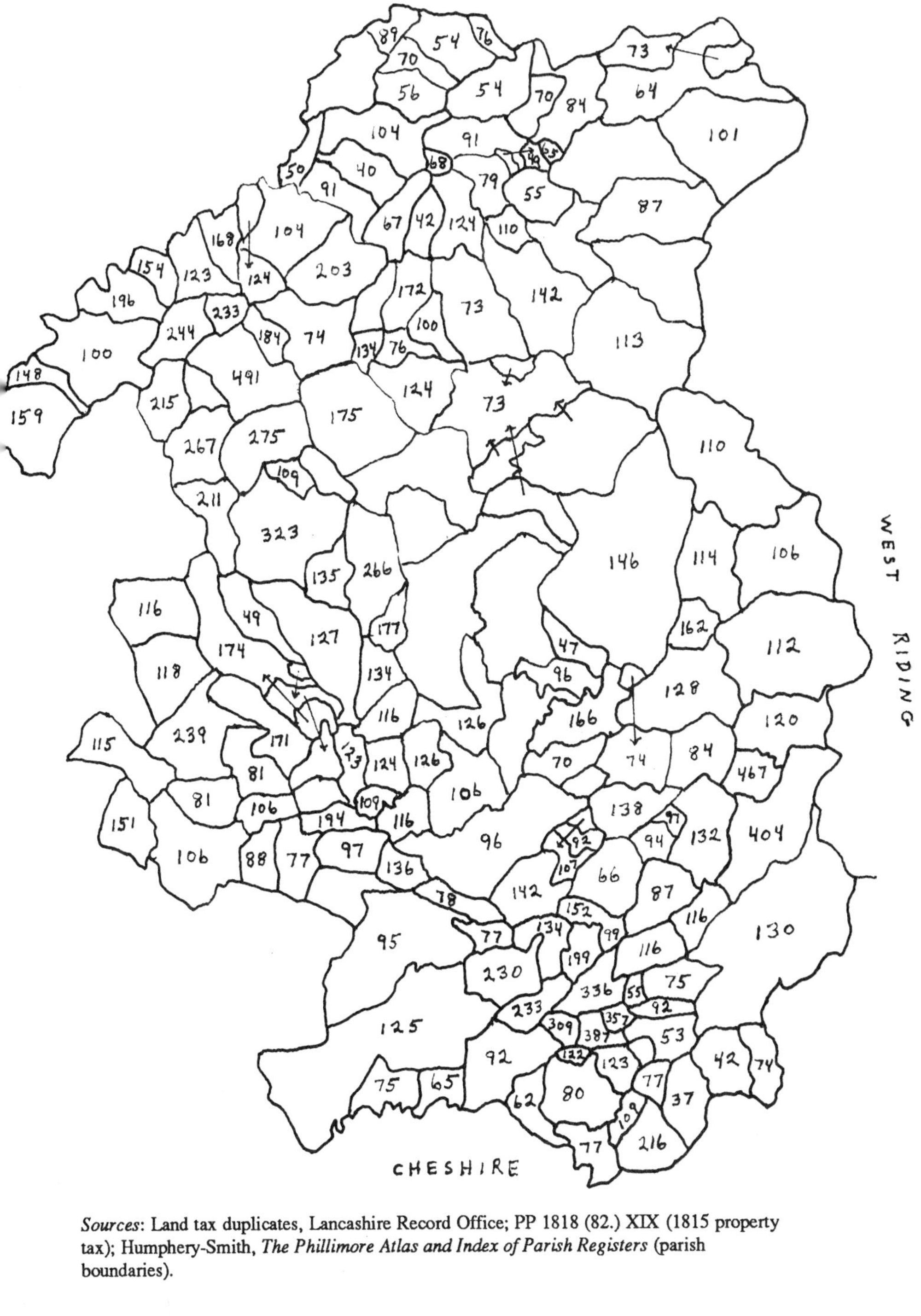

Sources: Land tax duplicates, Lancashire Record Office; PP 1818 (82.) XIX (1815 property tax); Humphery-Smith, *The Phillimore Atlas and Index of Parish Registers* (parish boundaries).

MAP 30 Net ratios of 1815 property tax valuations (schedule A) to land tax quotas, all townships, southwest Lancashire

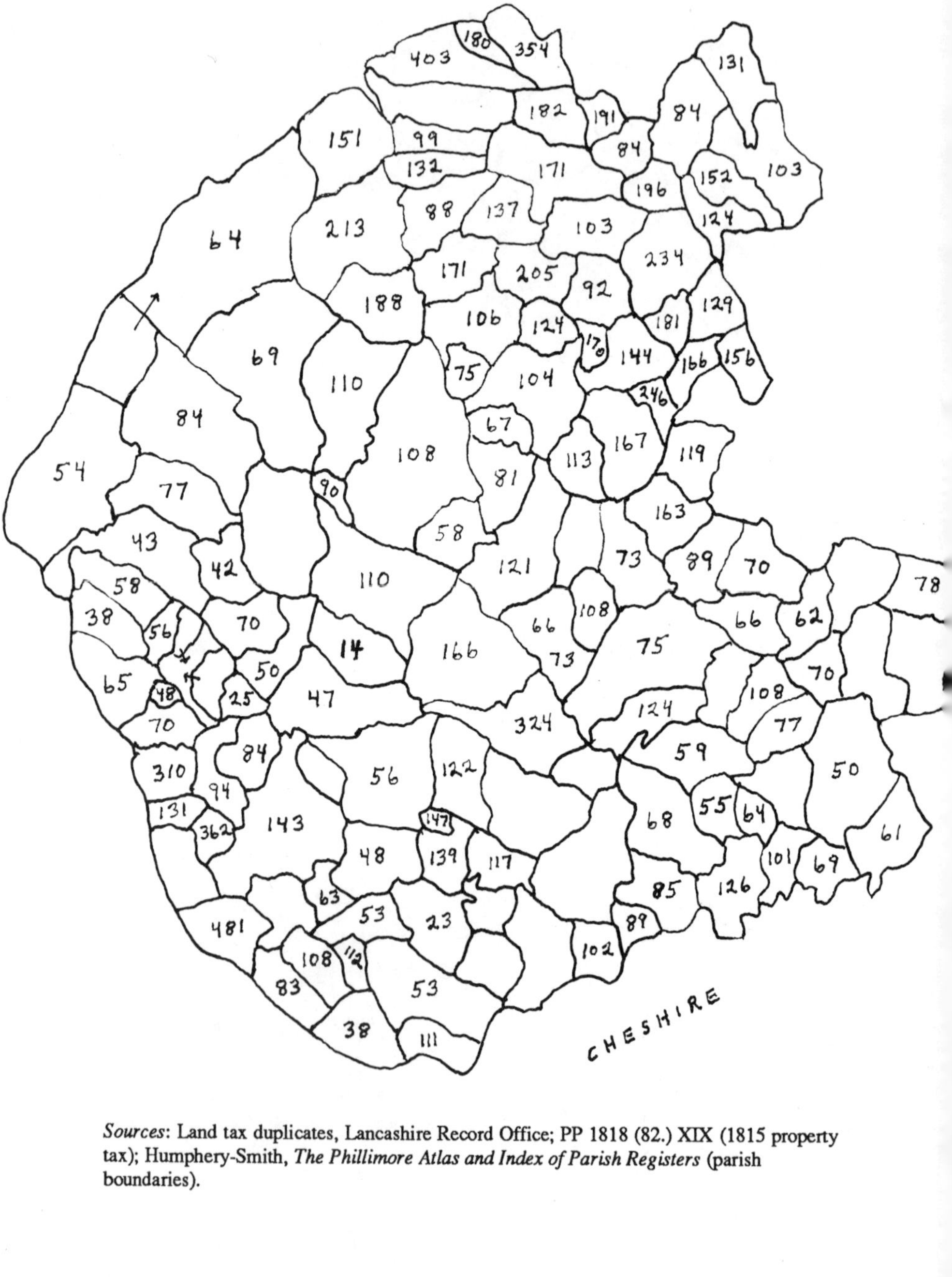

Sources: Land tax duplicates, Lancashire Record Office; PP 1818 (82.) XIX (1815 property tax); Humphery-Smith, *The Phillimore Atlas and Index of Parish Registers* (parish boundaries).

MAP 31 Net ratios of 1815 property tax valuations (schedule A) to land tax quotas, all townships, Leicestershire

Sources: Land tax duplicates, Leicestershire Record Office; PP 1818 (82.) XIX (1815 property tax); Humphery-Smith, *The Phillimore Atlas and Index of Parish Registers* (parish boundaries).

MAP 32 Net ratios of 1815 property tax valuations (schedule A) to land tax quotas, all townships, Parts of Kesteven and Holland, Lincolnshire

Sources: Land tax duplicates, Lincolnshire Archives Office; PP 1818 (82.) XIX (1815 property tax); Humphery-Smith, *The Phillimore Atlas and Index of Parish Registers* (parish boundaries).

MAP 33 Net ratios of 1815 property tax valuations (schedule A) to land tax quotas, all townships, Parts of Lindsey, Lincolnshire

Sources: Land tax duplicates, Lincolnshire Archives Office; PP 1818 (82.) XIX (1815 property tax); Humphery-Smith, *The Phillimore Atlas and Index of Parish Registers* (parish boundaries).

MAP 34 Net ratios of 1815 property tax valuations (schedule A) to land tax quotas, all parishes, Norfolk

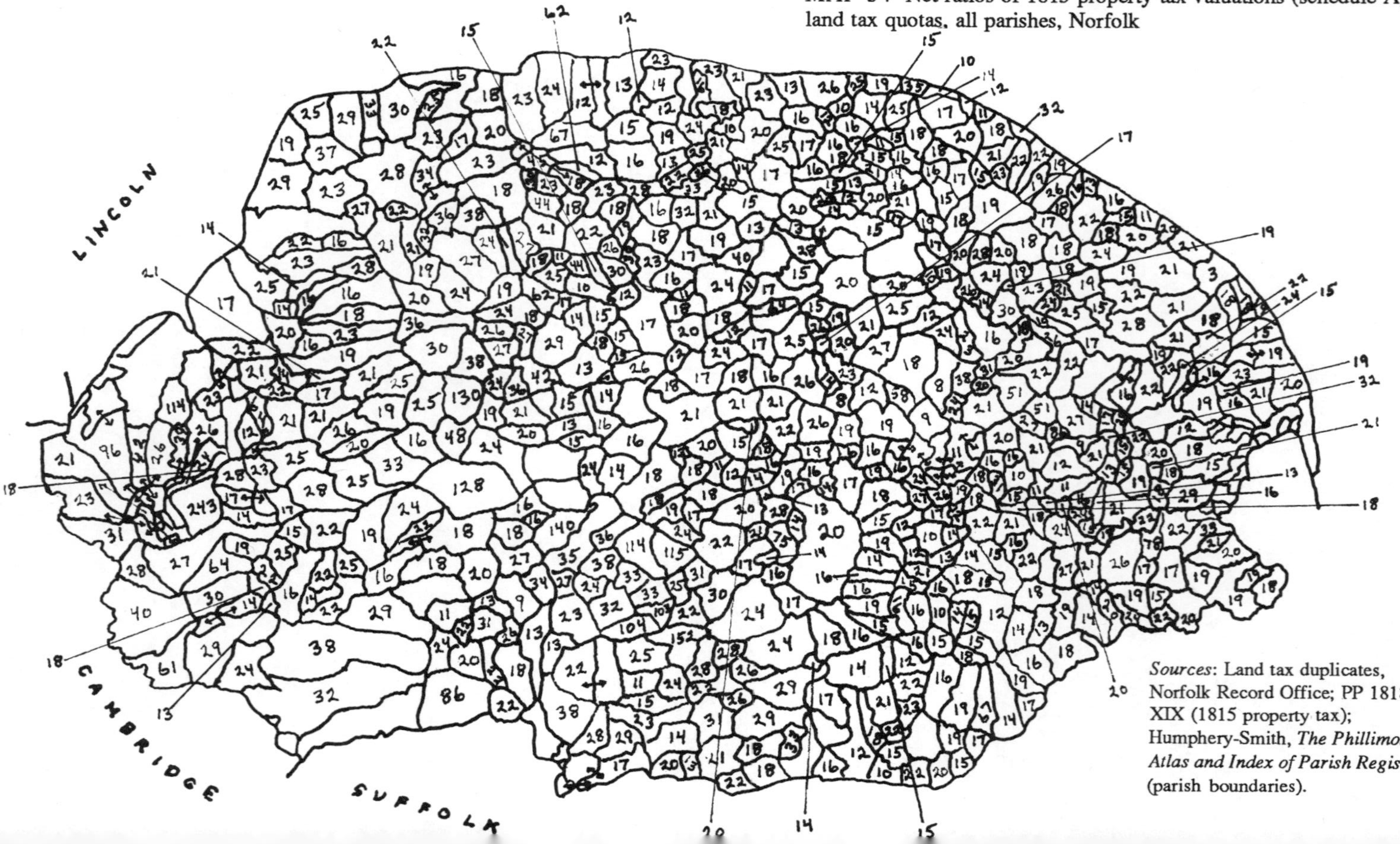

Sources: Land tax duplicates, Norfolk Record Office; PP 1818 (82.) XIX (1815 property tax); Humphery-Smith, *The Phillimore Atlas and Index of Parish Registers* (parish boundaries).

MAP 35 Net ratios of 1815 property tax valuations (schedule A) to land tax quotas, all parishes, Northamptonshire

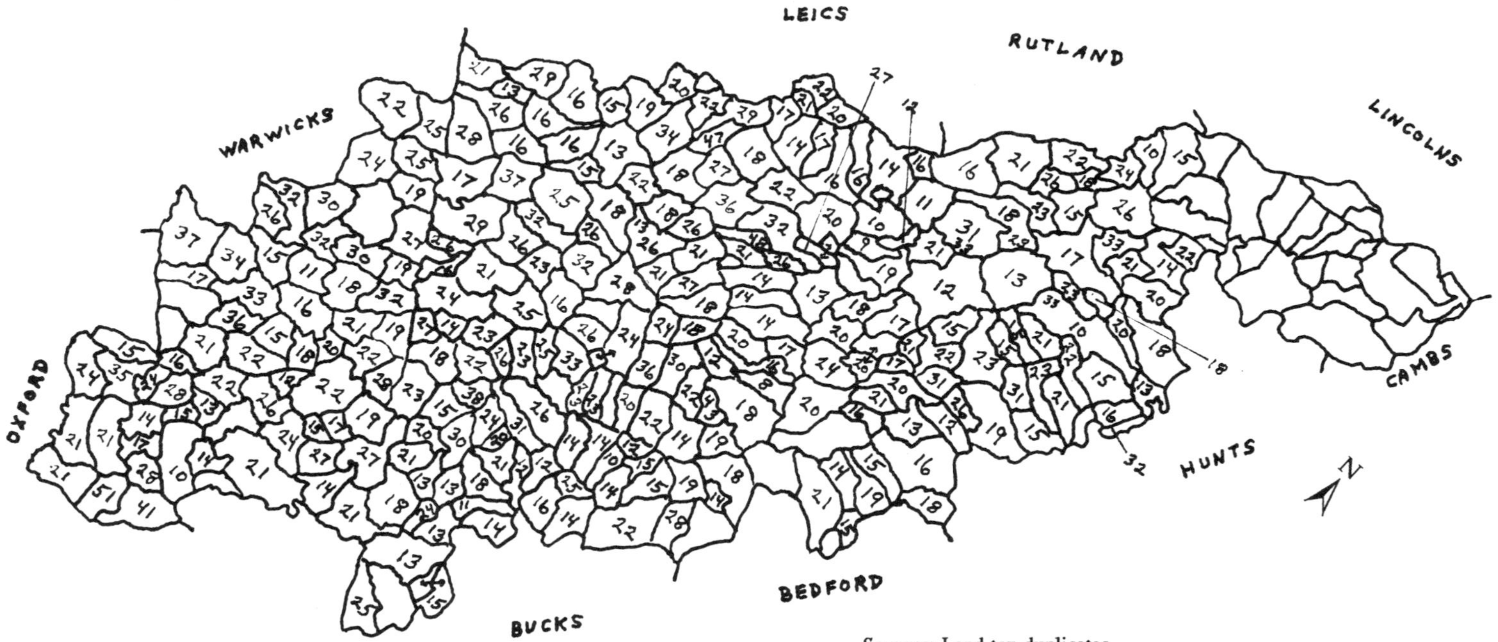

Sources: Land tax duplicates, Northamptonshire Record Office; PP 1818 (82.) XIX (1815 property tax); Humphery-Smith, *The Phillimore Atlas and Index of Parish Registers* (parish boundaries).

MAP 36 Net ratios of 1815 property tax valuations (schedule A) to land tax quotas, all parishes, Oxfordshire

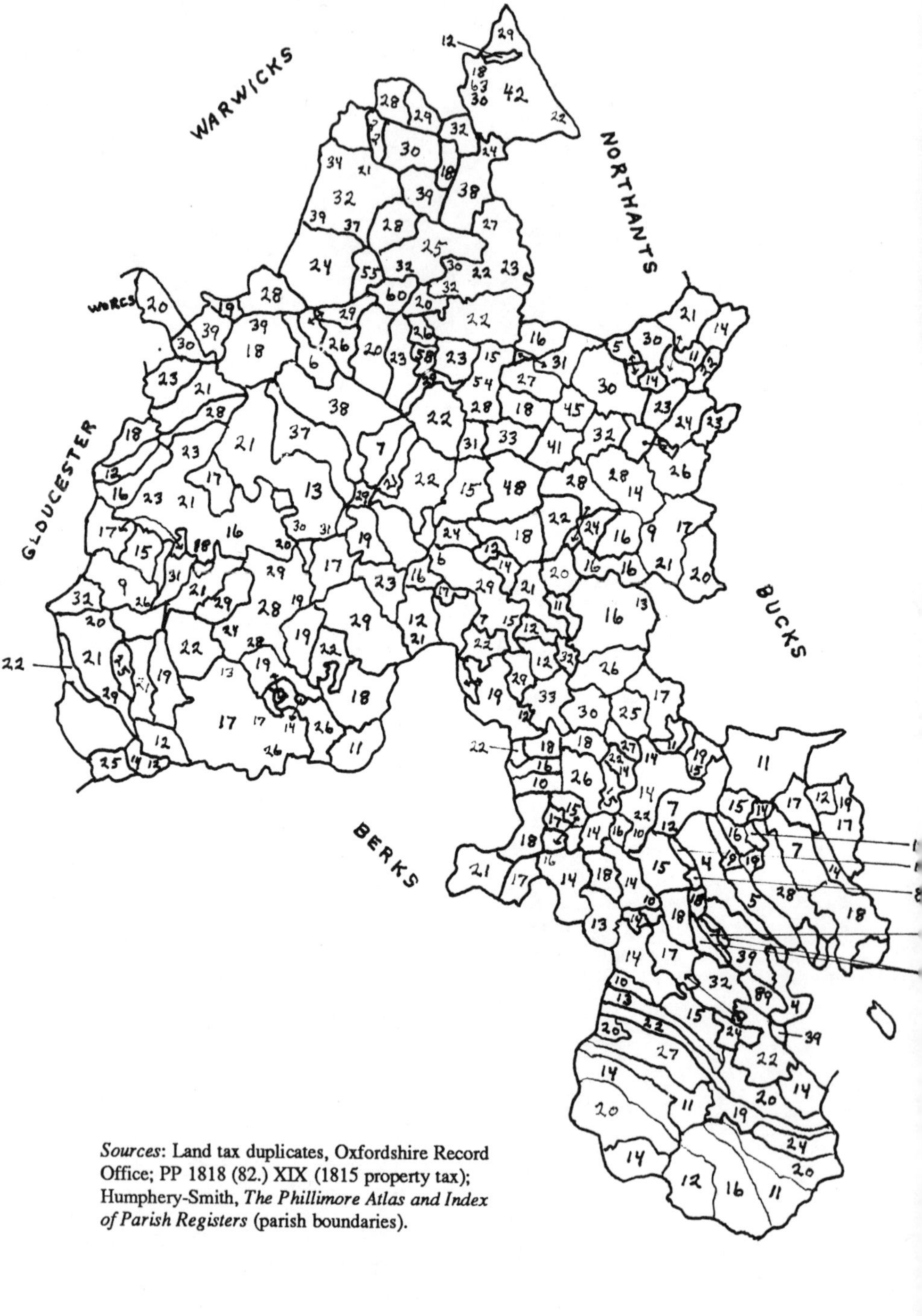

Sources: Land tax duplicates, Oxfordshire Record Office; PP 1818 (82.) XIX (1815 property tax); Humphery-Smith, *The Phillimore Atlas and Index of Parish Registers* (parish boundaries).

MAP 37 Net ratios of 1815 property tax valuations (schedule A) to land tax quotas, all townships, Surrey

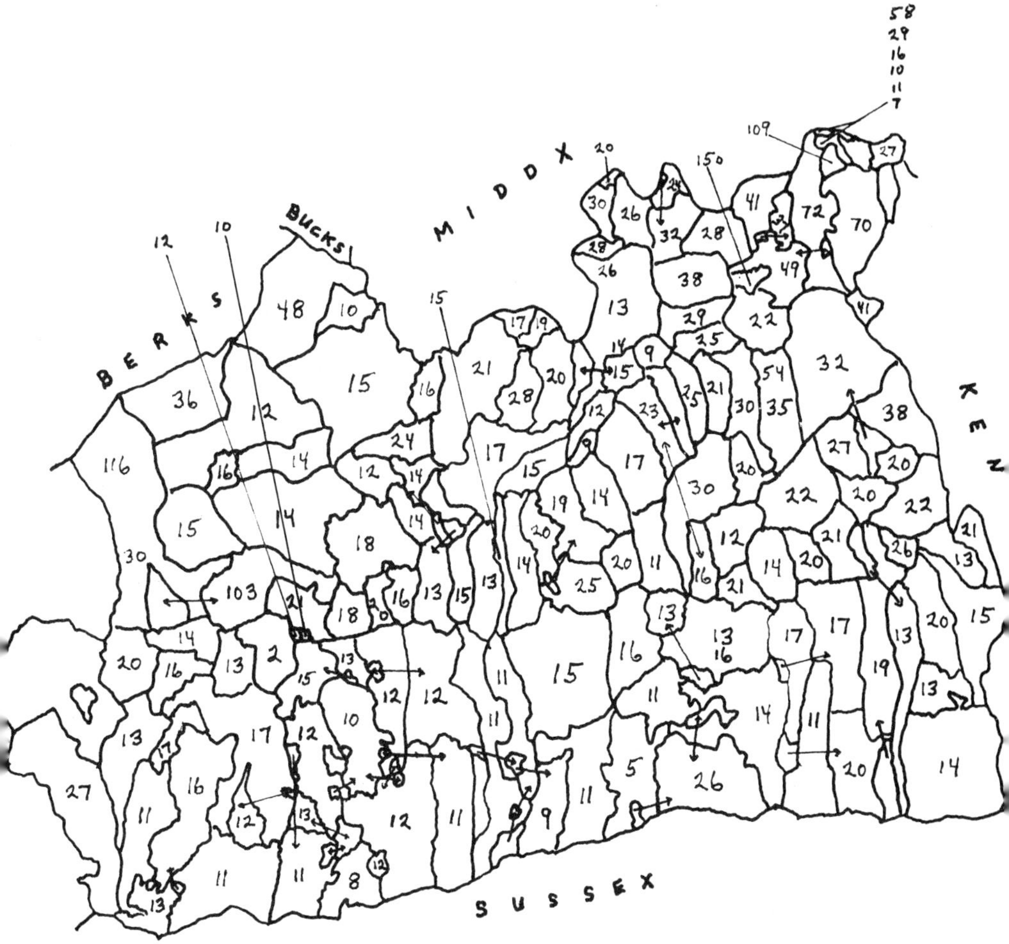

Sources: Land tax duplicates, Surrey Record Office; PP 1818 (82.) XIX (1815 property tax); Humphery-Smith, *The Phillimore Atlas and Index of Parish Registers* (parish boundaries).

MAP 38 Net ratios of 1815 property tax valuations (schedule A) to land tax quotas, all townships, Westmorland

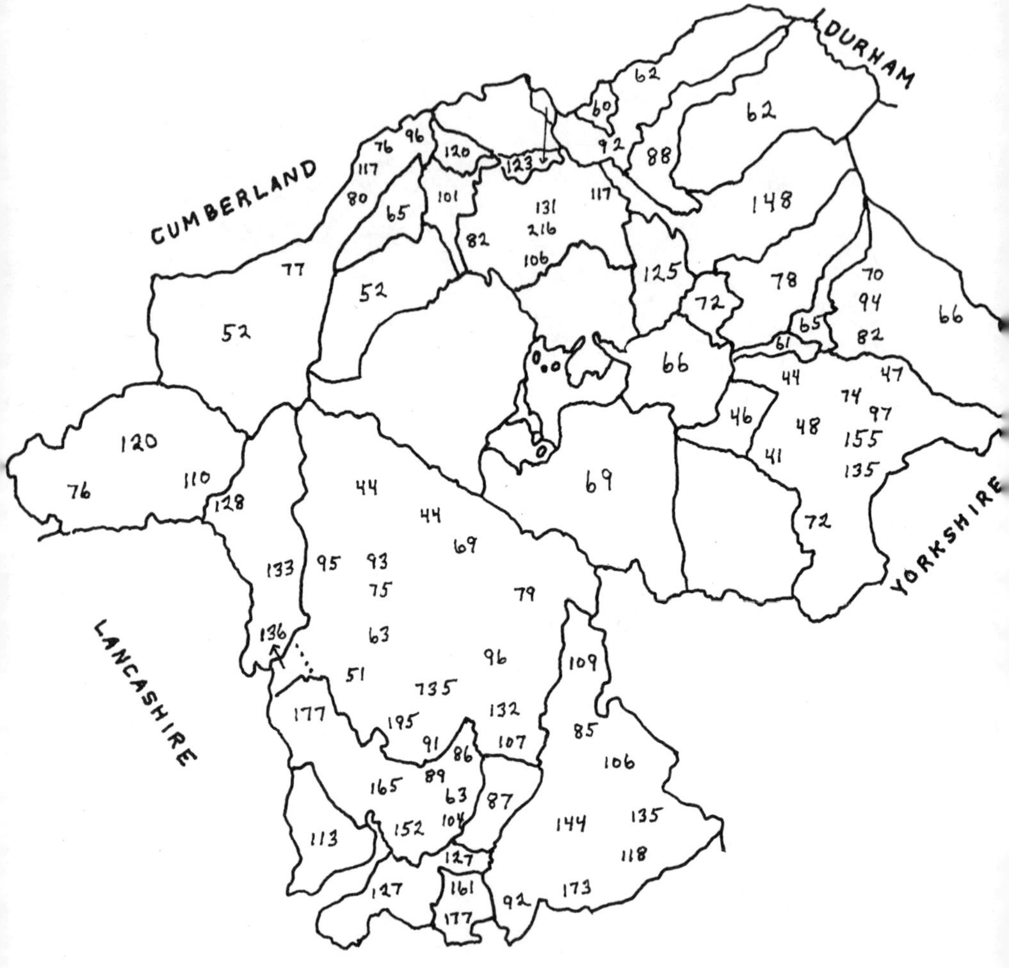

Sources: Land tax duplicates, Cumbria Record Office, Kendal; PP 1818 (82.) XIX (1815 property tax); Humphery-Smith, *The Phillimore Atlas and Index of Parish Registers* (parish boundaries).

MAP 39 Net ratios of 1815 property tax valuations (schedule A) to land tax quotas, all tithings, Wiltshire

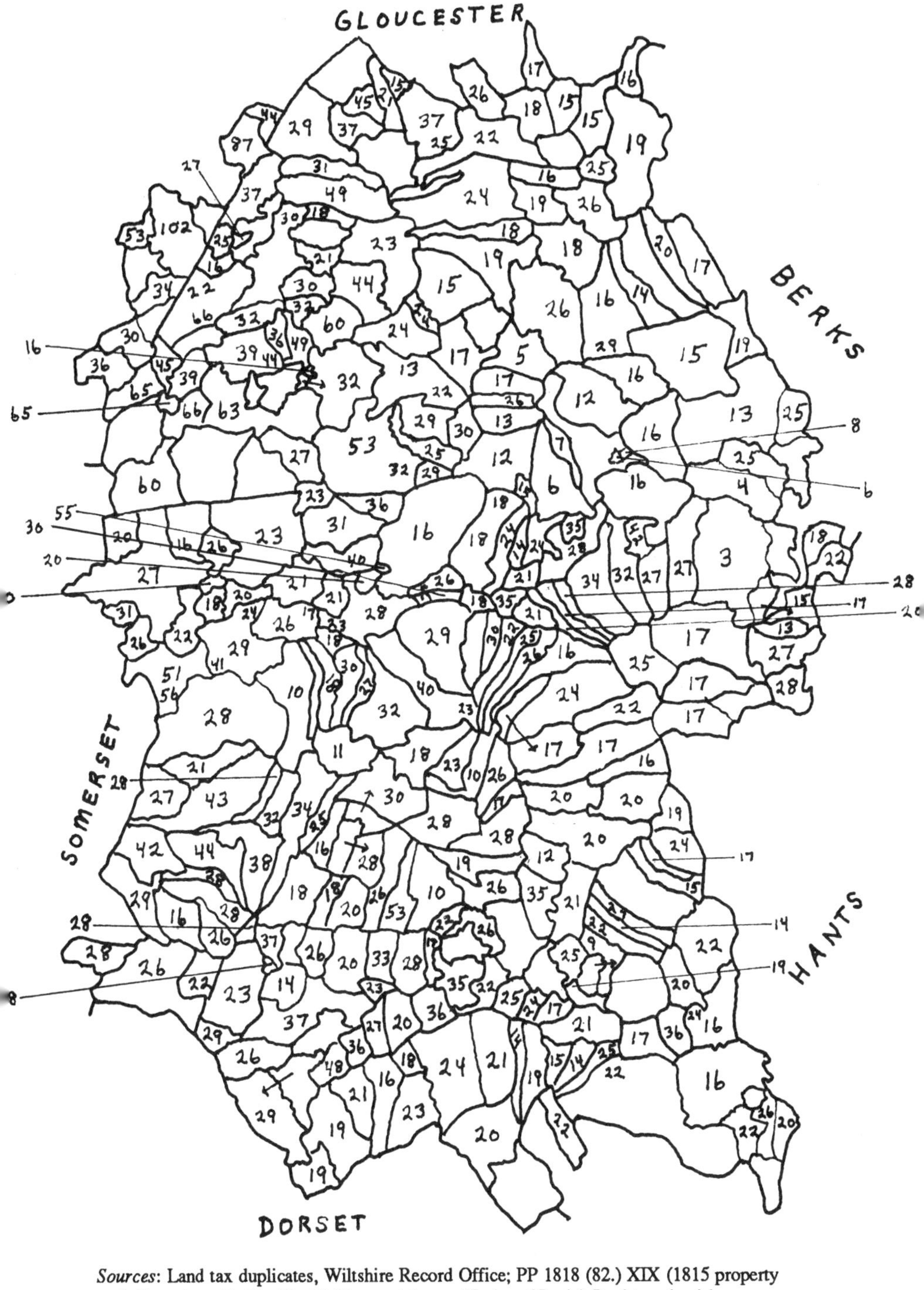

Sources: Land tax duplicates, Wiltshire Record Office; PP 1818 (82.) XIX (1815 property tax); Humphery-Smith, *The Phillimore Atlas and Index of Parish Registers* (parish boundaries).

PART SEVEN

Appendices

APPENDIX A

Consolidated farms on the North Riding estate of the Earl of Ailesbury in Thornton Steward and Rookwith townships, 1804

Tenant	Township	Old acres a. r. p.	New acres a. r. p.	Value	Total old rent	Total new rent	Land tax[b]	% increase in rent
Wm & John Fryer	Thornton Steward		115. 0.39.	123. 5. 8.			1. 6. 5.	
	East Witton		35. 0. 4.	27.16. 0			0.11. 3.	
	FARM TOTAL	118. 2.13.	150. 1. 3.	151. 1. 8.	50. 0. 0.	150. 0. 0.		200.0
Geo. Winn, now Wm Wilson	Thornton Steward	0. 3.15.	6. 1. 7.	9. 1. 3.	1.15. 0.	9. 0. 0.	0. 2. 0.[c]	414.3
John Haw	Thornton Steward	0. 3.23.	7. 3.13.	12. 1. 6	1.15. 0.	12. 0. 0.	0. 0. 8.	585.7
John Dent	Thornton Steward		40. 3.20.	37. 6. 6.			0.14. 0½	
	Rookwith		46. 2. 8.	45.10.10.			1.12. 5.	
	Newton le Willows		10. 3.39.	8. 4. 4.			0. 4. 0.	
	FARM TOTAL	89. 2.33	98. 1.27.	98.10. 5.[a]	60. 6. 0.	98. 0. 0.		62.5
Wm Mitchell	Rookwith		151. 1. 5.	120.15. 6.			4.17. 3.	
	Thornton Steward		63. 0.36.	50. 1. 3.			0.15. 4½	
	Newton le Willows		45. 3. 9.	41. 2. 0.			1. 3. 4.	
	FARM TOTAL	260. 1.10.	260. 1.10.	242.19. 9.[a]	138. 0. 0.	240. 0. 0.		73.9
Wm Beckwith	Rookwith	320. 0.17	233. 2.15.	234. 9. 0.[a]	178. 5. 0.	234. 0. 0.	7.15. 9.	31.3
	Thornton Steward		11. 2.32	23. 5. 0.		16. 0. 0.	0. 4. 6.	
	FARM TOTAL		245. 1. 7.	257.14. 0.		250. 0. 0.		
Adam Russell	Rookwith	7. 3.37	7. 3.37	12. 8.11.[a]	5. 2. 0.	6. 0. 0.	0. 4. 3.	17.6
Overseers of Rookwith		0. 0.23.	0. 0.23.		0.10. 0.	1. 0. 0.	no entry	100.0
Wm Fryer	Thornton Steward		174. 3. 5.	166. 7. 7.[f]			no entry	
	Rookwith		26. 0.26.	34.17. 6.			0.14. 1.[d]	
	FARM TOTAL	242. 2. 8.	200. 3.31.	221. 5. 1.[a]	146.10. 0.	200. 0. 0.		36.5

APPENDIX A (continued) page 338

Tenant	Township	Old acres a. r. p.	New acres a. r. p.	Value	Total old rent	Total new rent	Land tax[b]	% increase in rent
Edw. Wilson	Rookwith	93. 2. 6.	174. 0.15.	201. 7. 7.[a]	52.10. 0.	190. 0. 0.	6.13.11.	261.9
Gabriel Burton	Rookwith		7. 1. 7.	14. 5. 0.[a]		14. 0. 0.	0. 9.10.	
Christopher Firbank	Rookwith	310. 1.38.	112. 1.20.	113. 8. 2.[a]	162. 0. 0.	112. 0. 0.	3.18.11.	-30.9
Mark Barrowby and Geo. Tetlow	Rookwith		146. 0.27.	130.14. 1.[a]		130. 0. 0.	4.11. 7.	
Francis Scott	Rookwith	47. 2. 1.	47. 2. 1.	58. 6.10.[a]	27. 0. 0.	44. 0. 0.		63.0
	Thirn		29. 3. 9.	31. 0. 2.[a]		30. 0. 0.		
	FARM TOTAL	47. 2. 1.	77. 1.10.	89. 7. 0.		74. 0. 0.	1.15. 3.	
John Ward	Rookwith & Thirn	28. 3. 4.	28. 3. 4.	36. 2. 4.[a]	18. 0. 0.	18. 0. 0.	0.11. 3. 0. 4. 6.	0.0
Richard Simpson	Thirn	91. 1.20.	112. 3. 7.	106. 1. 5.	60. 0. 0.	105. 0. 0.	2.16.10.	75.0
William Burton	?	16. 1.10.			7.10. 0.		no entry	
Christopher Todd	Rookwith	0. 0. 7.	0. 0. 7.		0. 0. 4.	0. 5. 0.	no entry	1400.0
Plantations in hand	Thornton Steward	25. 3.10.	25. 3.10.				0. 0. 9.[f]	
TOTAL	Thornton Steward			255. 1. 2.			3. 3. 0.	
TOTAL	Rookwith & Thirn			1,139. 7. 4.			36. 5.10.	
TOTAL	Combined	1622. 0.35.	1622. 0.35.		908. 3. 4.	1549. 5. 0.		70.6

Tenant	Township	Ratio: value/ land tax	Ratio: old rent/ land tax	Ratio: new rent/ land tax	No. of fields	Range of values (s.)/acre/field: arable	pasture	meadow	fallow	value(s.)/ acre/ farm[e]
Wm and John Fryer	Thornton Steward	93			19	16-20	15-35	25-30		
	East Witton	49			6	16	15		18	
	FARM TOTAL									20
Geo. Winn, now Wm Wilson	Thornton Steward	91		90	2			25		25
John Haw	Thornton Steward	362	52	360	2			25		25
John Dent	Thornton Steward	53			10	15-20	18-21		20	
	Rookwith	28			9	14-15	16-18	21	18-20	
	Newton le Willows	41			3	16-18				
	FARM TOTAL									17
Wm Mitchell	Rookwith	25			25	14-16	12-20	16-25	14-16	
	Thornton Steward	65			9	16	14	20	16	
	Newton le Willows	35			7	18				
	FARM TOTAL									16
Wm Beckwith	Rookwith	30	23	30	39	14-25	15-25	15-25	18-25	
	Thornton Steward	103			1		40			
	FARM TOTAL									21
Adam Russell	Rookwith	58	24	28	4		25	25		25
Overseers of Rookwith										
Wm Fryer	Thornton Steward				28	14-20	14-25	21-25	14-20	
	Rookwith	50			3	20-25	30			
	FARM TOTAL									20
Edw. Wilson	Rookwith	30	8	28	36	15-25	15-25	20-30		20
Gabriel Burton	Rookwith	29		28	2			30-35		33

APPENDIX A (continued) page 340

Tenant	Township	Ratio: value/ land tax	Ratio: old rent/ land tax	Ratio: new rent/ land tax	No. of fields	Range of values (s.)/acre/field				value (s.)/ acre/ farm[e]
						arable	pasture	meadow	fallow	
Christopher Firbank	Rookwith	29	41	28	19	8–18	15–20	20–21	18	16
Mark Barrowby and Geo. Tetlow	Rookwith	28		28	25	12–20	12–20	25	15–16	14
Francis Scott	Rookwith				12	18–21	16–21	21–30		
	Thirn				9	14–18	20	25–35	18	
	FARM TOTAL	51		42						20
John Ward	Rookwith and Thirn	46	23	23	9	20–25	20	25	25	22
Richard Simpson	Thirn	37	21	37	21	16–21	12–25	25	18	19
William Burton	?									
Christopher Todd	Rookwith									
Plantations in hand	Thornton Steward									
TOTAL	Thornton Steward	81								
TOTAL	Rookwith and Thirn	31								
TOTAL	Combined									

Notes: [a]Includes tithe.
[b]All tenants of the Earl of Ailesbury in Thornton Steward and Rookwith/Thirn are accounted for on the land tax except the Rookwith overseer, Christopher Todd, the second Thornton Steward property of William Fryer, and William Burton. All land tax entries for which Ailesbury is the proprietor are in the field book.
[c]Entered in the land tax for Isabella Wilson, who does not appear in the field book.
[d]Entered in the land tax for George Fryer, who does not appear in the field book.
[e]Tithes and non-agricultural fields (farmhouse, etc.) have been deducted from acreage and rents.
[f]Not included in township total.
Source: 1804 survey and valuation of the estates of the Earl of Ailesbury in the North Riding, vol. 2, Western Division, ZJX 4/31/2, NYCRO.

APPENDIX B.1

The rate of exclusion of occupiers and properties from the land tax duplicates, aggregate tabulations, Hallikeld wapentake, North Riding.

Numbered columns:
1 = Total occupiers in 1824 land tax (holdings aggregated for each individual).
2 = Total occupiers in 1824 valuation for the county rate.
3 = Column 1 as a percentage of column 2.
4 = Total separate line entries in 1824 valuation for the county rate indicating one house or building (with or without land). Total number without land is indicated in parentheses.
5 = Total separate line entries in 1824 valuation for the county rate indicating multiple houses or buildings (with or without land).
6 = Total houses reported in 1821 census.
7 = Total houses reported in 1831 census.
8 = Total separate line entries in 1831 land tax indicating one house or building (with or without land).
9 = Total separate line entries in 1831 land tax indicating multiple houses or buildings (with or without land).
10 = Total occupiers with aggregated county rate valuation (as occupiers) less than £1 (number omitted in land tax are indicated in parentheses).
11 = Total occupiers with aggregated county rate valuation £1 but less than £2 (number omitted in land tax are indicated in parentheses).
12 = Total occupiers with aggregated county rate valuations £2 but less than £5 (number omitted in land tax are indicated in parentheses).
13 = Total occupiers with aggregated county rate valuation £5 or more (number omitted in land tax are indicated in parentheses).
14 = 1824 valuer for the county rate is also an assessor for the 1824 land tax.

Township	1	2	3	4	5	6	7	8	9	10	11	12	13	14
Ainderby Quernhow	7	12	58	def.	def.	19	24	0	8	0	1 (1)	4 (4)	7	yes
Asenby	36	39	92	26 (0)	4 (1)	51	49	24	4	0	0	4 (2)	35 (2)	no
Baldersby	15	19	79	4[d] (2)	1 (1)	48	56	def.	def.	2 (2)	1 (1)	0	16 (1)	no
Burneston	30	31	97	3 (0)	0	64	68	def.	def.	0	3 (1)	4	24	yes
Carthorpe	38	54	70	22[e] (2)	0	79	83	18[i]	0	0	4 (4)	6 (3)	44 (9)	yes
Cundall, Leckby, and Thornton Bridge	27	26	104	def.	def.	47	48	26	0	0	0	7	19	yes
Dishforth	33	52	63	19 (11)	5 (3)	62	80	def.	def.	0	1 (1)	11 (9)	40 (9)	def.
East Tanfield	7	7	100	def.[f]	def.	3	3	def.	def.	0	0	0	7	yes
Exelby, Leeming, and Scab Newton	110	132	83	114 (33)	7 (1)	138	162	131	4	10 (5)	33 (9)	28 (4)	61 (4)	no
Gatenby	8	7	114[a]	0	0	15	14	def.	def.	0	0	0	7	yes

APPENDIX B.1 (continued) page 342

Township	1	2	3	4	5	6	7	8	9	10	11	12	13	14
Howe	4	4	100	def.[f]	def.	7	8	def.	def.	0	0	0	4	yes
Humburton and Milby	11	11	100[b]	0	0	30	33	0	0	0	0	3	8 (1)	yes
Kirby Hill and Langthorpe	def.	def.	def.	def.	def.	63	83	11	0	def.	def.	def.	def.	def.
Kirklington and Upsland	30	50	60	44 (21)	0	64	64	def.	def.	0	0	11 (10)	39 (10)	no
Langthorne	17	21	81	3[g] (1)	2 (2)	29	32	def.	def.	0	5 (2)	4 (1)	12 (1)	yes
Marton le Moor	14	17	82	14 (0)	2 (1)	43	45	def.	def.	0	0	1 (1)	16 (3)	yes
Melmerby	35	46	76	43 (21)	0	39	71	27	0	17 (11)	4 (2)	7 (1)	18	yes
Middleton Quernhow	8	12	67	8 (4)	0	19	23	8	0	0	0	4 (4)	8	no
Norton le Clay	10	9	111	10 (0)	0	29	30	def.	def.	0	1	0	8	no
Pickhill and Roxby	22	80	28	61 (52)	0	75	89	def.	def.	0	31 (31)	24 (23)	25 (5)	no
Rainton and Newby	def.	37	def.	32 (6)	3 (2)	79	84	def.	def.	1	0	5	31	no
Sinderby	14	14	100[c]	def.	def.	19	20	def.	def.	0	1 (1)	1	12 (1)	def.
Sutton	14	14	100	10 (0)	0	19	26	12	0	0	0	2	12	yes
Swainby and Allerthorpe	3	3	100	3 (0)	0	5	5	0	3	0	0	0	3	yes
Theakston	19	19	100[b]	2 (0)	0	18	16	0	0	0	0	1	18 (1)	def.
Wath	31	33	94	def.	def.	46	47	33	0	0	4 (1)	2 (1)	27 (2)	yes
West Tanfield	83	81	102	51[h] (9)	4 (3)	153	161	131[j]	2	0	6 (1)	16	59	no

Notes: [a]The tithes were separately distributed to each occupier on the county rate valuation; they were aggregated and reported under the vicar on the land tax. Thus the land tax has one additional ''occupier.''

[b]But one occupier is missing from each column.

[c]But two occupiers are missing from each column.

[d]Thirteen additional entries were described as ''Farm.'' Land was not separately distinguished in other entries.

[e]Eleven additinal entries reported as ''Farm.'' These ''farms'' may have included a house. ''Land'' was separately distinguished in other entries.

[f]All principal entries were described only as ''Farm.'' There was no clear attempt to distinguish buildings.

[g]Six additional entries reported ''Farm.'' These may have included a house. ''Land'' was separately distinguished.

[h]Twenty-one additional entries reported as ''A Farm.'' These may have included a house. ''Land'' was separately distinguished.

[i]Thirteen additional entries reported as ''Farm.'' These may have included a house. ''Land'' was separately distinguished.

[j]Includes seventeen entries described as ''House and Farm.''

Sources: 1824 land tax duplicates, NYCRO; 1824 valuations for the county rate, QFR 1/1-18, NYCRO; 1821 and 1831 census, North Riding.

APPENDIX B.2

Individual properties excluded from the 1824 land tax duplicates, Hallikeld wapentake, North Riding

Numbered columns:
1 = Description of property.
2 = Value of property, as reported in the valuations for the county rate, June 1824 (£. s. d.).
3 = Land tax assessed on property, approved by the commissioners May 1824 (£. s. d.).
4 = Ratio of total 1824 county rate valuation of township to total land tax (as reported at the bottom of the 1824 duplicate).
5 = The 1824 total valuation for the county rate as a percentage of the 1814 total valuation for the property tax (see appendix M).
6 = Total number of properties listed in the 1824 county rate valuation.
7 = Number of county rate properties omitted in the 1824 land tax.
8 = Percentage of county rate properties omitted in the 1824 land tax.

Township	1	2	3	4	5	6	7	8
Ainderby Quernhow	Public House	4.16. 0.						
	House and Shop	2. 8. 0.						
	Shop[a]	16. 0.						
	House[b]	1.12. 0.						
	Shop[b]	16. 0.						
	ND[c]	1. 4. 0.						
	House[a]	1.16. 0.						
	TOTAL OMITTED	13. 8. 0.					7	
	TOTAL VALUE	768.14. 0.	21. 6. 8 1/2	36	81.0	16		
	% OMITTED	1.7	0.0					43.8
Asenby	House and Land	10. 0. 0						
	House and Land	39.10. 0.						
	Land	2.10. 0.						
	Land	4.10. 0.						
	ND[c]		0. 2. 1.[d]					
	TOTAL OMITTED	56.10. 0	0. 2. 1.				4	
	TOTAL VALUE	1,729.19. 0.	36. 3. 4.	48	116.7	41		
	% OMITTED	3.3	0.3					9.8
Baldersby	Cottage and Garden	1.10. 0.						
	Cottage and Garden	10. 0.						

Appendix B.2 (continued) page 344

Township	1	2	3	4	5	6	7	8
Baldersby (continued)	Cottage and Garden	2. 6.						
	Cottage Rents	10. 0. 0.						
	TOTAL OMITTED	12. 2. 6.					4	
	TOTAL VALUE	2,167. 4. 4.	48. 0. 0.	45	116.9	21		
	% OMITTED	0.6	0.0					19.0
Burneston	Lands	1.10. 0.						
	TOTAL OMITTED	1.10. 0.					1	
	TOTAL VALUE	1,704. 0. 0.	50. 0. 0.	34	74.5	32		
	% OMITTED	0.1	0.0					3.1
Carthorpe	Land	17.10. 0.						
	Land	4.10. 0.						
	Land	15. 0. 0.						
	House and Land	6.10. 0.						
	Farm	103. 0. 0.						
	House and Land	1. 1. 0						
	House and Land	8. 0. 0						
	House and Land	1. 0. 0.						
	House and Land	12. 0. 0.						
	House and Land	6. 0. 0.						
	House and Land	2.10. 0.						
	Land	4.10. 0.						
	House and Land	12.10. 0.						
	House	1. 0. 0.						
	House	1. 0. 0.						
	Land	21. 0. 0.						
	ND[c]		0. 1. 4.					
	TOTAL OMITTED	217. 1. 0.	0. 1. 4.				16	
	TOTAL VALUE	2,208.10. 0.	50. 0. 0.	44	81.7	57		
	% OMITTED	9.8	0.1					28.1

Cundall, Leckby, and Thornton Bridge	ND[c]		0.17. 2.[d]					
	TOTAL OMITTED		0.17. 2.				0	
	TOTAL VALUE	4,166. 0. 0.	100. 9. 6.	41	96.1	27		
	% OMITTED	0.0	0.8					0.0
Dishforth	Land	4. 0. 0.						
	Land	4.10. 0.						
	House and Land	14.12. 0.						
	Garden	1. 0. 0.						
	Tithes of Corn and Hay	269. 0. 0.[e]						
	Cottage and Land	8. 0. 0.						
	Cottage and Garden	4. 0. 0.						
	Cottage	2. 0. 0.						
	Cottages	2. 0. 0.						
	Cottage and Garden	4.10. 0.						
	Land[a]	184.17. 0.						
	Chapel[a]	2. 0. 0.						
	Cottage	2. 0. 0.						
	Poor Houses belonging to township	11. 0. 0.						
	Cottages etc.	8. 0. 0.						
	Cottage and Garden	4. 0. 0.						
	Cottages	3. 0. 0.						
	House and Land	21. 0. 0.						
	Vicarial Tithes	76.10. 0.[e]						
	Cottage and Garth	6. 8. 0.						
	TOTAL OMITTED	632. 7. 0.					20	
	TOTAL VALUE	2,915. 2. 0.	def.	def.	121.2	56		
	% OMITTED	21.7	0.0					35.7
East Tanfield	TOTAL OMITTED						0	
	TOTAL VALUE	1,180. 0. 0.	30. 2. 3.	39	89.1	7		
	% OMITTED	0.0	0.0					0.0
Exelby, Leeming, and Scab Newton	Cottage and Garden	1. 5. 0.						
	Cottage	10. 0.						

Township	1	2	3	4	5	6	7	8
Exelby, Leeming, and Scab Newton (continued)	Farm House and Land	34. 8. 0.						
	Cottage and Land	7. 2. 0.						
	House and Land	15.17. 6.						
	Cottage and Croft	4. 0. 0.						
	Cottage	1. 0. 0.						
	Willow Garth	10. 0.						
	Cottage	10. 0.						
	Shop	1. 0. 0.						
	Land	5. 5. 0.						
	Cottage, Shop and Garden	3. 0. 0.						
	Cottage	1. 0. 0.						
	Cottage and Land	3.10. 0.						
	Cottage and Garden	1.15. 0.						
	Cottage	3. 0. 0.						
	Garden	7. 6.						
	Cottage and Garden	1. 5. 0.						
	Cottage	10. 0.						
	Cottage and Garden	1. 0. 0.						
	Cottage	1.10. 0.						
	Cottage	1. 0. 0.						
	ND[c]		6.10.					
	ND[c]		10. 3.					
	ND[c]		18. 9 1/2.					
	ND[c]		10 1/4.					
	TOTAL OMITTED	89. 5. 0.	1.16. 8 3/4.				22	
	TOTAL VALUE	3,873.16. 0.	103.11. 7 1/2.[f]	37	84.7	133		
	% OMITTED	2.3	1.8					16.5
Gatenby	TOTAL OMITTED						0	
	TOTAL VALUE	1,292.14. 5.	69. 5. 0.	19	97.2	7		
	% OMITTED	0.0	0.0					0.0

Howe	TOTAL OMITTED						0	
	TOTAL VALUE	577. 0. 0.	15. 0. 0.	38	123.0	5		
	% OMITTED	0.0	0.0					0.0
Humburton and Milby	Land	18. 0. 0.						
	ND[c]		4. 2.					
	TOTAL OMITTED	18. 0. 0.	4. 2.				1	
	TOTAL VALUE	1,333. 0. 0.	35.12. 0.	37	def.	13		
	% OMITTED	1.4	0.6					7.7
Kirklington and Upsland	Land	6. 0. 0.						
	Land	12. 0. 0.						
	House	8. 0. 0.						
	House	4. 0. 0.						
	House	3. 0. 0.						
	House	10. 0. 0.						
	House	4. 0. 0.						
	House	3. 0. 0.						
	House	10. 0. 0.						
	House	4. 0. 0.						
	House	8. 0. 0.						
	House	3. 0. 0.						
	House	10. 0. 0.						
	House	8. 0. 0.						
	House	4. 0. 0.						
	House	6. 0. 0.						
	House	3. 0. 0.						
	House	3. 0. 0.						
	House	5. 0. 0.						
	House	3. 0. 0.						
	TOTAL OMITTED	117. 0. 0.					20	
	TOTAL VALUE	2,461.15. 0.	33.16.10.	73	80.5	51		
	% OMITTED	4.8	0.0					39.2
Langthorne	Fox Covers	20. 0. 0.						
	Lands	2.13. 4.						
	Lands	1. 6. 8.						
	Lands	1.10. 0.						

APPENDIX B.2 (continued) page 348

Township	1	2	3	4	5	6	7	8
Langthorne continued	TOTAL OMITTED	25.10. 0.					4	
	TOTAL VALUE	765. 9. 0.	35. 1. 6 1/4.	22	68.9	22		
	% OMITTED	3.3	0.0					18.2
Marton le Moor	Paupers Houses and Wasteland[h]	5. 0. 0.						
	Labourers' Cottages[h]	2.10. 0.						
	Vicarage Tithes[g,h]	40. 0. 0.						
	Plantation[h]	25. 0. 0.						
	ND[c] (clerical proprietor)		1. 9. 0.					
	TOTAL OMITTED	72.10. 0.	1. 9. 0.				4	
	TOTAL VALUE	1,473.10. 0.	23.18. 4.	62	92.3	18		
	% OMITTED	4.9	6.1					22.2
Melmerby	House	10. 0.						
	House	10. 0.						
	House	10. 0.						
	House	10. 0.						
	House	10. 0.						
	House	10. 0.						
	House	2. 0. 0.						
	House	1. 0. 0.						
	House	1. 0. 0.						
	House	10. 0.						
	House	10. 0.						
	House	10. 0.						
	House	10. 0.						
	House	10. 0.						
	ND[c,i]		0.2.					
	ND[c]		0.2.					
	ND[c,i]		0.2.					
	TOTAL OMITTED	9.10. 0.	0.6.				14	
	TOTAL VALUE	1,249. 0. 0.	22.14.10.	55	64.2	46		
	% OMITTED	0.8	0.1					30.4

Middleton Quernhow	House	2. 0. 0.						
	House	2. 0. 0.						
	House	2. 0. 0.						
	House	2. 0. 0.						
	TOTAL OMITTED	8. 0. 0.					4	
	TOTAL VALUE	1,238. 0. 0.	22. 1. 4.	56	67.3	13		
	% OMITTED	0.6	0.0					30.8
Norton le Clay	ND[c]		1.11. 9.					
	TOTAL OMITTED		1.11. 9.				0	
	TOTAL VALUE	1,205.18. 6.	20. 1.11.	60	83.6	10		
	% OMITTED	0.0	8.0					0.0
Pickhill and Roxby	Cottage	1. 0. 0.						
	Cottage	1. 0. 0.						
	Cottage	1. 0. 0.						
	Cottage	2. 0. 0.						
	Cottage	2. 0. 0.						
	Cottage	2. 0. 0.						
	Cottage	3. 0. 0.						
	Cottage	2. 0. 0.						
	Cottage	1. 0. 0.						
	Cottage	2. 0. 0.						
	Cottage	1. 0. 0.						
	Cottage	3. 0. 0.						
	Cottage	2. 0. 0.						
	Cottage	1. 0. 0.						
	Cottage	1. 0. 0.						
	Cottage	1. 0. 0.						
	Cottage and Garden	6. 0. 0.						
	Cottage	1. 0. 0.						
	Cottage	1. 0. 0.						
	Land	9. 0. 0.						
	Inn	3. 0. 0.						
	Cottage	1. 0. 0.						
	Cottage	1. 0. 0.						
	Cottage	1. 0. 0.						
	Cottage	1. 0. 0.						
	Cottage and Garth	6. 0. 0.						
	Cottage and Land	4. 7. 0.						
	Cottage	3. 0. 0.						

APPENDIX B.2 (continued) page 350

Township	1	2	3	4	5	6	7	8
Pickhill and Roxby	Cottage	1. 0. 0.						
	Cottage	3. 0. 0.						
	Cottage	2. 0. 0.						
	Cottage	1. 0. 0.						
	Cottage	2. 0. 0.						
	Cottage	1. 0. 0.						
	Cottage and Garden	3. 0. 0.						
	Cottage	3. 0. 0.						
	Cottage	2. 0. 0.						
	Chapel	2. 0. 0.						
	Inn	5. 0. 0.						
	Inn	6. 0. 0.						
	Cottage	1. 0. 0.						
	Cottage	2. 0. 0.						
	Cottage and Garden	2. 0. 0.						
	Cottage	2. 0. 0.						
	Cottage	1. 0. 0.						
	Cottage	1. 0. 0.						
	Cottage	1. 0. 0.						
	Cottage and Garden	2. 0. 0.						
	Cottage	1. 0. 0.						
	Cottage	1. 0. 0.						
	Cottage	2. 0. 0.						
	Cottage	1. 0. 0.						
	Cottage	1. 0. 0.						
	Cottage	1. 0. 0.						
	Cottage	1. 0. 0.						
	Cottage	1. 0. 0.						
	Cottage	1. 0. 0.						
	Cottage	1. 0. 0.						
	Cottage	1. 0. 0.						
	ND[c]		7. 2.					
	TOTAL OMITTED	118. 7. 0.	7. 2.				59	
	TOTAL VALUE	2,800.12. 0.	70. 7. 0.	40	107.1	82		
	% OMITTED	4.2	0.5					72.0

Rainton and Newby		def.[j]	def.					
	TOTAL OMITTED	def.	def.				def.	
	TOTAL VALUE	1,995. 5. 2.	46.13. 4.	43	96.6	37		
	% OMITTED	def.	def.					def.
Sinderby	A Farm	6. 0. 0.						
	A Farm	1. 0. 0.						
	ND[c]		1.17.10.[k]					
	ND[c]		0. 8 1/4.[k]					
	TOTAL OMITTED	7. 0. 0.	1.18. 6 1/4.				2	
	TOTAL VALUE	579. 7. 6.	20. 4.10.	29	72.2	14		
	% OMITTED	1.2	9.5					14.3
Sutton	TOTAL OMITTED						0	
	TOTAL VALUE	699. 0. 0.	14. 6. 1.	49	93.1	14		
	% OMITTED	0.0	0.0					0.0
Swainby and Allerthorpe	TOTAL OMITTED						0	
	TOTAL VALUE	1,112. 0. 0.	42. 0. 0.	26	74.9	3		
	% OMITTED	0.0	0.0					0.0
Theakston	House and Land	125. 0. 0.						
	ND[e]		3. 0.					
	TOTAL OMITTED	125. 0. 0.	3. 0.				1	
	TOTAL VALUE	1,211.10. 0.	26. 6. 7 1/2	46	84.6	19		
	% OMITTED	10.3	0.6					5.3
Wath	Rent and Tithe	5. 0. 0.						
	Rent and Tithe	5. 0. 0.						
	Rent and Tithe	1.10. 0.						
	Rent and Tithe	2. 0. 0.						
	ND[e]		1. 9. 8.[i]					
	ND[e]		0. 4.					
	TOTAL OMITTED	13.10. 0.	1.10. 0.				4	
	TOTAL VALUE	1,054. 0. 0.	24.17.2.	42	103.7	36		
	% OMITTED	1.3	6.0					11.1
West Tanfield	Cottage	1. 5. 0.						
	ND[e]		0. 6 1/4.					

APPENDIX B.2 (continued) page 352

Township	1	2	3	4	5	6	7	8
	ND[c]		8.11.					
	ND[c]		1. 7.					
	TOTAL OMITTED	1. 5. 0.	10. 0 1/4.				1	
	TOTAL VALUE	3,063.15. 0.	63.13. 4.	48	82.0	84		
	% OMITTED	0.0	0.8					1.2

Notes: [a]Occupied by same person.
[b]Occupied by same person.
[c]The property is not described.
[d]Occupancy changed between 1824 and 1825.
[e]Tithes of Wool and Lamb are included in the 1824 land tax and identified as such.
[f]Four additional entries are taxed at less than 1s. and listed as ''unoccupied.''
[g]Tithes of Wool and Lamb are reported on the land tax. They are valued at £18 and pay 3s. 6d. tax.
[h]Annotated in the county rate valuation as ''Not Charged to Assessments by the Township.''
[i]Occupier described as deceased.
[j]Ten out of eighteen proprietors are listed as self ''and Tenants'' in the occupier column.
[k]The 1825 land tax duplicate reports the £1. 17s. 10d. property as having been purchased by the 8 1/4d. owner-occupier.
Sources: 1824 land tax duplicates, NYCRO; 1824 valuations for the county rate (includes 1814 property tax), QFR 1/1-18, NYCRO.

APPENDIX C.1

A comparison of total acres per township recorded on the six-inch Ordnance Survey maps and in the 1831 Census, all townships, North Riding

Wapentake	Township	(a) 6-inch Ordnance acres	(b) 1831 Census acres	(b) as % of (a)
Allertonshire	Birkby	1,203	1,030	86
	Borrowby	924	1,280	138
	Brompton	3,842	3,490	91
	Deighton	2,036	2,210	108
	Dinsdale, Over	858	810	94
	Ellerbeck	870	880	101
	Girsby	1,227	1,410	115
	Harlsey, West	1,505	1,410	94
	Holme	550	350	64
	Hornby	1,828	2,050	112
	Hutton Bonville	1,546	1,080	70
	Hutton Conyers	3,212	3,010	94
	Kilvington, North	935	1,210	129
	Knayton and Brawith	1,906	1,390	73
	Landmoth, Catto, and Cotcliffe	872	600	69
	Leake	309	210	68
	Northallerton	4,478	3,600	80
	Norton Conyers	1,041	920	88
	Osmotherley	3,196	3,780	118
	Otterington, North	819	1,270	155
	Romanby	2,060	2,250	109
	Rounton, West	1,456	1,840	126
	Sessay and Hutton Sessay	3,772	3,340	88
	Sigston	1,242	1,560	126
	Smeaton, Little	1,001	1,290	129
	Sowerby under Cotcliffe	812	610	75
	Thimbleby	2,052	1,670	81
	Thornton le Beans and Crosby	2,524	2,520	100
	Thornton le Street	1,389	1,540	111
	Winton, Stank, and Hallikeld	1,366	1,340	98
	Worsall, High	1,625	1,550	95
	SUBTOTAL	52,456	51,500	98
Birdforth	Arden and Dale Town	6,297	9,090	144
	Bagby and Fawdington	2,534	1,680	66
	Balk	946	780	82
	Bilsdale Westside and Snilesworth	8,071	6,090	75
	Birdforth	628	540	86
	Boltby	4,712	3,140	67
	Byland Membris, Oldstead, Wass, and Thorpe le Willows	4,419	3,130	71
	Byland, Old	2,737	3,120	114
	Carlton Husthwaite	819	1,120	137
	Carlton Miniott	1,552	2,070	133
	Catton	842	770	91
	Cold Kirby	1,617	2,100	130
	Cowsby	1,165	2,220	105
	Coxwold, Angram Grange, and Wildon Grange	2,518	2,590	103

APPENDIX C.1 (continued) page 354

Wapentake	Township	(a) 6-inch Ordnance acres	(b) 1831 Census acres	(b) as % of (a)
Birdforth continued				
	Dalton	1,263	1,150	91
	Elmire and Crakehill	986	900	91
	Felixkirk	1,190	1,010	85
	Harlsey, East	3,057	2,910	95
	Hawnby	2,421	7,070	292
	Husthwaite	1,677	1,680	100
	Kepwick	2,742	2,520	92
	Kilburn, Low; Osgoodby; and Hood Grange	3,120	3,670	118
	Kilvington, South	1,067	940	88
	Kirby Knowle	1,580	1,420	90
	Newburgh and Murton	4,074	3,770	92
	Newsham and Breckenbrough	1,914	2,060	108
	Otterington, South	1,450	1,780	123
	Oulston	1,513	1,100	73
	Sand Hutton	1,349	940	70
	Silton, Nether; and Gueldable	1,886	2,610	138
	Silton, Over	1,235	940	76
	Skipton upon Swale	844	820	97
	Sowerby	2,614	2,420	92
	Sutton under Whitestonecliffe	1,908	1,610	84
	Thirkleby	2,690	1,800	67
	Thirlby	634	1,230	194
	Thirsk	3,250	3,030	93
	Thornborough	561	440	78
	Thornton and Baxby	1,448	1,740	120
	Thornton le Moor	1,527	1,010	66
	Topcliffe	4,202	4,030	96
	Upsall	1,292	1,230	95
	Welbury	2,401	2,020	84
	Yearsley	2,792	1,720	62
	SUBTOTAL	97,544	97,010	99
Bulmer	Aldwark	2,336	2,220	95
	Alne	2,263	2,490	110
	Barton le Willows	1,046	980	94
	Brafferton	1,847	1,990	108
	Brandsby and Stearsby	3,077	2,700	88
	Bulmer	1,666	1,430	86
	Buttercrambe and Bossall	2,692	2,640	98
	Claxton	838	880	105
	Clifton, Rawcliffe, and St Olave in Marygate	2,370	2,120	89
	Coneysthorpe	1,205	1,150	95
	Cornbrough	1,104	920	83
	Crambe	1,169	1,090	93
	Crayke	2,874	3,300	115
	Easingwold	6,999	6,520	93
	Farlington	1,224	1,490	122
	Flaxton on the Moor	1,865	1,460	78
	Foston	922	820	89
	Ganthorpe	730	700	96

Wapentake	Township	(a) 6-inch Ordnance acres	(b) 1831 Census acres	(b) as % of (a)
Bulmer continued	Harton	2,002	1,620	81
	Haxby	2,208	1,840	83
	Helmsley, Gate	496	520	105
	Helmsley, Upper	832	780	94
	Helperby	1,894	1,900	100
	Henderskelf	1,706	1,620	95
	Heworth	1,312	1,330	101
	Holtby	901	850	94
	Huby	4,658	4,790	103
	Huntington	2,606	2,760	106
	Huttons Ambo	2,896	2,300	79
	Lillings Ambo	1,763	1,530	87
	Linton upon Ouse	2,321	2,030	87
	Marton in the Forest and Moxby	2,715	2,370	87
	Murton	844	1,060	126
	Myton upon Swale and Ellingthorpe	2,283	1,480	65
	Newton upon Ouse and Beningbrough	2,826	2,560	90
	Osbaldwick	730	680	93
	Raskelf	4,281	3,550	83
	Sand Hutton	2,242	2,280	102
	Scackleton	1,357	1,460	108
	Sheriff Hutton	4,486	4,310	96
	Shipton and Overton	3,341	3,170	95
	Skelton	2,473	2,320	94
	Skewsby and Dalby	1,347	1,480	110
	Stillington	2,158	1,490	69
	Stittenham	1,599	1,340	84
	Stockton on the Forest and Sandburn	3,267	3,270	100
	Strensall, Earswick, and Towthorpe	5,146	4,780	93
	Sutton on the Forest	5,996	5,280	88
	Terrington, Menthorpe, and Wiganthorpe	3,223	2,930	91
	Tholthorpe and Flawith	2,380	2,370	100
	Thormanby	1,002	900	90
	Thornton le Clay	954	1,270	133
	Tollerton	2,199	2,340	106
	Warthill	1,003	860	86
	Welburn	865	750	87
	Whenby	1,042	1,390	133
	Whitwell	1,574	1,640	104
	Wigginton	1,880	2,040	108
	Youlton	803	830	103
	SUBTOTAL	125,838	118,970	94
Gilling East	Ainderby Steeple	1,158	910	78
	Barton and Newton Morrell	3,084	2,790	90
	Brompton on Swale	1,670	1,710	102
	Cleasby	1,205	970	80
	Cowton, East	3,369	3,150	94
	Cowton, North	1,396	1,030	74
	Cowton, South	2,239	1,530	68

Wapentake	Township	(a) 6-inch Ordnance acres	(b) 1831 Census acres	(b) as % of (a)
Gilling East continued				
	Croft	4,632	4,700	101
	Dalton upon Tees	1,635	1,440	88
	Danby Wiske	3,364	3,230	96
	Ellerton upon Swale, Bolton on Swale, and Whitwell	3,601	2,300	64
	Eryholme	2,345	1,790	76
	Kiplin	1,011	1,250	124
	Kirby Wiske	1,108	1,020	92
	Langton, Great	872	300	34
	Langton, Little	1,006	1,560	155
	Manfield	2,918	2,230	76
	Maunby	1,546	890	58
	Middleton Tyas	3,202	2,700	84
	Morton on Swale and Fareholm	1,540	1,250	81
	Moulton	3,041	2,720	89
	Newby Wiske	1,430	1,100	77
	Scorton and Uckerby	3,512	3,460	98
	Smeaton, Great	1,648	1,700	103
	Stapleton	998	920	92
	Thrintoft	1,228	1,130	92
	Warlaby and Low Sober	767	1,010	132
	Yafforth	1,350	1,120	83
	SUBTOTAL	56,875	49,910	88
Gilling West	Aldbrough	1,807	1,150	64
	Arkengarthdale	14,566	14,180	97
	Barforth	2,025	1,750	86
	Barningham and Hope	6,130	6,050	99
	Bowes and Boldron	19,150	17,430	91
	Brignall	2,116	1,910	90
	Caldwell	1,588	2,000	126
	Cliffe	707	970	137
	Cotherstone	8,364	8,120	97
	Dalton	2,706	2,450	90
	Easby and Aske	3,046	2,610	86
	Eppleby	1,118	1,490	133
	Forcett and Carkin	2,270	2,480	109
	Gailes	2,575	1,840	71
	Gilling	4,876	4,440	91
	Gilmonby	2,472	2,350	95
	Holwick	5,788	5,910	102
	Hunderthwaite	6,336	6,390	101
	Hutton Longvillers	1,304	1,510	116
	Kirkby Ravensworth	227	1,110	489
	Lartington	5,436	6,300	116
	Layton, East and West	1,818	1,580	87
	Lunedale	22,770	21,680	95
	Marrick	6,206	5,560	90
	Marske	6,759	5,220	77
	Melbecks	7,974	6,820	86
	Melsonby	2,742	2,310	84
	Mickleton	4,749	4,890	103
	Muker	30,201	32,170	106

Wapentake	Township	(a) 6-inch Ordnance acres	(b) 1831 Census acres	(b) as % of (a)
Gilling West continued				
	New Forest	3,002	2,850	95
	Newsham	3,407	3,490	102
	Ovington	520	530	102
	Ravensworth and Whashton	3,473	2,330	67
	Reeth	5,698	3,820	67
	Richmond	2,520	2,310	92
	Rokeby and Egglestone Abbey	1,808	1,990	110
	Romaldkirk	1,324	1,470	111
	Scargill	5,170	4,880	94
	Skeeby	834	770	92
	Stanwick, St John	1,398	570	41
	Startforth	1,010	1,070	106
	Thorpe and Wycliffe	2,229	2,200	99
	SUBTOTAL	210,219	200,950	96
Hallikeld	Ainderby Quernhow	532	330	62
	Asenby	1,178	800	68
	Baldersby	1,830	1,600	87
	Burneston	1,228	800	65
	Carthorpe	2,111	1,960	93
	Cundall, Leckby, and Thornton Bridge	3,140	3,090	98
	Dishforth	1,765	1,600	91
	Exelby, Leeming, and Newton	2,439	2,300	94
	Gatenby	876	1,070	122
	Howe	400	410	102
	Humburton and Milby	1,819	2,320	128
	Kirby Hill and Langthorpe	2,239	1,590	71
	Kirklington and Upsland	1,986	1,980	100
	Langthorne	833	820	98
	Marton le Moor	1,678	940	56
	Melmerby	1,138	1,070	94
	Middleton Quernhow	764	590	77
	Norton le Clay	1,092	1,030	94
	Pickhill and Roxby	2,184	1,910	87
	Rainton and Newby	1,576	1,370	87
	Sinderby	559	490	88
	Sutton and Howgrave	883	660	75
	Swainby and Allerthorpe	882	1,190	135
	Tanfield, East	1,295	1,160	90
	Tanfield, West	3,286	3,070	93
	Theakston	969	790	82
	Wath	766	620	81
	SUBTOTAL	39,448	35,560	90
Hang East	Ainderby Myers, High Holtby, Hackforth, and Hornby	3,881	3,690	95
	Aiskew	2,035	1,660	82
	Appleton, East and West	1,631	1,480	91

Wapentake	Township	(a) 6-inch Ordnance acres	(b) 1831 Census acres	(b) as % of (a)
Hang East continued				
	Bedale, Firby, and Rand Grange	2,724	2,300	84
	Brough	1,176	1,050	89
	Burrill and Cowling	1,071	370	34
	Burton upon Ure	3,358	2,920	87
	Catterick and Killerby	2,460	2,460	100
	Colburn	1,357	1,240	91
	Crakehall	1,885	1,920	102
	Ellingstring	1,498	760	51
	Ellingtons	2,860	1,670	58
	Fearby	1,960	600	31
	Healey and Sutton	6,062	4,180	69
	Hipswell and St Martins Abbey	2,917	2,290	78
	Ilton and Pott	3,379	2,400	71
	Kirkby Fleetham	3,154	2,950	94
	Masham	3,416	8,890	260
	Newton le Willows and Ruswick	1,858	1,660	89
	Patrick Brompton	1,238	1,280	103
	Rookwith, Thirn, and Clifton upon Ure	2,227	2,510	113
	Scotton	1,406	1,500	107
	Scruton	2,114	1,940	92
	Snape	4,610	3,520	76
	Swinton and Warthermarske	2,776	1,520	55
	Thornton Watlass	1,482	2,340	158
	Tunstall	1,284	1,470	114
	Well	2,079	2,360	114
	SUBTOTAL	67,898	62,930	93
Hang West	Abbotside, High	11,170	13,740	123
	Abbotside, Low	6,887	4,360	63
	Askrigg	4,907	4,790	98
	Aysgarth	1,214	1,220	100
	Bainbridge	16,200	14,210	88
	Barden	1,779	1,330	75
	Bellerby	3,063	2,540	83
	Burton and Walden	7,606	6,950	91
	Burton, Constable	2,650	2,480	94
	Caldbergh and East Scrafton	3,449	1,200	35
	Carlton	2,742	3,380	123
	Carlton Highdale	10,133	12,480	123
	Carperby	4,914	3,460	70
	Castle Bolton	4,956	5,160	104
	Coverham and Agglethorpe	1,410	1,090	77
	Downholme and Walburn	3,166	2,470	78
	Ellerton and Stainton	3,542	3,330	94
	Finghall, Akeber, and Hutton Hang	1,930	1,980	102
	Grinton	8,182	7,000	86
	Harnby	1,111	860	77
	Hauxwell, East and West; and Garriston	2,811	2,520	90
	Hawes	16,821	19,500	116

Wapentake	Township	(a) 6-inch Ordnance acres	(b) 1831 Census acres	(b) as % of (a)
Hang West continued				
	Hudswell	3,028	3,180	105
	Hunton and Arrathorne	2,581	2,620	102
	Leyburn	2,515	2,040	81
	Melmerby	1,212	930	77
	Middleham	2,154	2,400	111
	Preston under Scar	2,577	2,380	92
	Redmire	2,318	2,420	104
	Scrafton, West	1,615	3,040	188
	Spennithorne	1,303	1,280	98
	Thoralby, Newbiggin, and Bishopdale	9,346	10,420	111
	Thornton Rust	1,939	1,330	68
	Thornton Steward	2,158	2,570	119
	Wensley	2,079	1,930	93
	Witton, East (within)	2,610	4,280	164
	Witton, East (without)	4,444	3,450	78
	Witton, West	3,874	5,140	133
	SUBTOTAL	166,396	165,460	99
Langbaurgh	Acklam, West	976	1,160	119
	Aislaby	1,072	1,080	101
	Appleton Wiske	1,865	1,800	96
	Arncliffe, Ingleby	1,893	1,840	97
	Ayton, Great	3,589	3,160	88
	Ayton, Little	1,378	1,170	85
	Barnby, East	2,140	1,400	65
	Battersby	1,230	740	60
	Borrowby	682	650	95
	Brotton	2,076	1,800	87
	Broughton, Great	3,091	2,780	90
	Busby, Great	2,109	2,090	99
	Carlton in Cleveland	1,358	830	61
	Castle Leavington	1,071	730	68
	Commondale	3,057	2,630	86
	Crathorne	2,598	2,460	95
	Danby	6,289	13,860	220
	Easby	1,210	1,170	97
	Easington	3,766	3,850	102
	Egton	15,657	13,570	87
	Ellerby	759	630	83
	Eston	2,252	1,870	83
	Faceby	1,382	1,370	99
	Glaisdale	4,967	8,370	168
	Greenhow	3,484	3,050	88
	Guisborough	7,013	6,120	87
	Hemlington	1,118	1,000	89
	Hilton	1,392	1,510	108
	Hinderwell	1,655	1,550	94
	Hutton Lowcross	1,569	1,510	96
	Hutton Mulgrave	1,086	1,480	136
	Hutton Rudby	2,371	1,890	80
	Ingleby Barwick	1,556	1,190	76
	Ingleby Greenhow	2,288	2,610	114
	Kildale	5,192	5,730	110
	Kilton	1,724	1,510	88

Wapentake	Township	(a) 6-inch Ordnance acres	(b) 1831 Census acres	(b) as % of (a)
Langbaurgh continued				
	Kirby in Cleveland	1,708	2,240	131
	Kirkleatham	4,330	2,960	68
	Kirk Leavington	2,202	1,770	80
	Linthorpe and Middlesbrough	3,215	2,300	72
	Liverton	2,454	2,360	96
	Lofthouse	3,737	3,700	99
	Lythe	3,770	3,620	96
	Maltby	1,116	1,180	106
	Marske	3,970	2,910	73
	Marton in Cleveland	3,519	3,430	97
	Mickleby	1,398	1,340	96
	Middleton upon Leven	1,144	850	74
	Moorsholm, Great; and Stanghow	7,472	6,610	88
	Morton	1,006	780	78
	Newby	1,254	1,940	155
	Newton	1,172	1,440	123
	Newton Mulgrave	2,345	1,950	83
	Normanby	1,462	1,640	112
	Nunthorpe	1,427	1,410	99
	Ormesby and Upsall	3,396	3,210	94
	Picton	1,004	870	87
	Pinchingthorpe	858	1,180	138
	Potto	1,532	1,240	81
	Redcar	604	590	98
	Rounton, East	1,622	1,890	116
	Rousby	3,250	2,410	74
	Rudby in Cleveland	888	880	99
	Seamer	2,650	2,650	100
	Sexhow	528	540	102
	Skelton	4,263	3,830	90
	Skinningrove	188	250	133
	Skutterskelfe	1,008	880	87
	Stainton	2,306	2,220	96
	Stokesley	1,817	1,490	82
	Thornaby	1,695	1,230	72
	Tocketts	668	560	84
	Ugthorpe	NR	2,180	NR
	Upleatham	1,426	1,100	77
	Westerdale	9,881	8,750	88
	Whorlton	6,812	5,590	82
	Wilton	4,050	5,070	125
	Worsall, Low	1,362	1,190	87
	Yarm	1,198	1,180	98
	SUBTOTAL	198,622	193,390	97
Pickering Lythe	Aislaby	1,468	1,110	76
	Allerston	10,043	9,110	91
	Ayton, East and West	4,756	4,770	100
	Barugh, Great and Little	1,461	2,150	147
	Brompton, Sawdon, and Troutsdale	6,520	5,930	91
	Burniston	2,099	1,400	67
	Cayton, Deepdale, Killerby, and Osgodby	3,504	2,430	69
	Cloughton	2,538	3,510	138

Wapentake	Township	(a) 6-inch Ordnance acres	(b) 1831 Census acres	(b) as % of (a)
Pickering Lythe continued				
	Cropton and Cawthorn	5,470	5,350	98
	Ebberston	6,094	6,350	104
	Falsgrave	1,103	1,020	92
	Farmanby	1,813	2,530	140
	Goathland	9,032	11,030	122
	Habton, Great and Little	1,423	1,480	104
	Hartoft Dale	2,940	4,740	161
	Hutton Bushel	3,787	3,510	93
	Kingthorpe	1,208	1,090	90
	Kirby Misperton	1,791	1,910	107
	Lebberston and Gristhorpe	2,479	2,390	96
	Levisham	2,974	2,670	90
	Lockton	7,423	6,610	89
	Middleton	2,699	1,310	48
	Pickering, Marishes, and Newton	20,768	20,640	99
	Rosedale East Side	5,394	5,100	94
	Ryton	2,324	1,590	68
	Scalby, Newby, and Throxenby	4,119	3,370	82
	Scarborough	1,190	1,140	96
	Seamer and Irton	5,951	5,150	86
	Sinnington and Marton	2,892	2,600	90
	Snainton	4,836	4,250	88
	Staintondale	3,114	2,780	89
	Thornton Dale	6,461	5,940	92
	Wilton	1,784	2,060	115
	Wrelton	1,888	1,230	65
	Wykeham	8,248	6,480	78
	SUBTOTAL	151,594	144,730	95
Ryedale	Airyholme, Baxter Howe, and Howthorpe	595	690	116
	Amotherby	1,830	1,580	86
	Ampleforth Oswaldkirk, St Peter, and Birdforth	2,370	2,270	96
	Appleton le Moors	2,583	2,570	100
	Appleton le Street	1,633	1,140	70
	Barton le Street	1,675	1,530	91
	Bilsdale Kirkham, Midcable, and Laskill Pasture	15,878	8,380	53
	Butterwick and Newsam	660	500	76
	Cawton	1,056	900	85
	Coulton	1,086	930	86
	Edstone, Great and Little	1,458	1,980	136
	Farndale East Side and West Side and Bransdale East Side	18,010	17,360	96
	Fryton	1,134	970	86
	Gillamoor and Fadmoor	2,944	3,680	125
	Gilling	2,071	2,500	121
	Grimston	997	930	93

Wapentake	Township	(a) 6-inch Ordnance acres	(b) 1831 Census acres	(b) as % of (a)
Ryedale continued	Harome	2,359	1,920	81
	Helmsley Blackmoor	8,812	8,200	93
	Hildenley	304	450	148
	Hovingham	2,853	3,110	109
	Hutton le Hole	2,345	1,520	65
	Kirby Moorside	4,506	3,730	83
	Lastingham	1,678	690	41
	Malton, New, St Leonard and St Michael	49	110	224
	Malton, Old	3,968	4,020	101
	Nawton, Beadlam, and Wombleton	3,853	2,920	76
	Ness, East and West; and Muscoates	2,388	2,000	84
	Newton and Laysthorp	940	860	91
	Normanby	1,784	2,020	113
	North Holme	546	610	112
	Nunnington	2,122	1,600	75
	Oswaldkirk	2,195	2,310	105
	Pockley	3,440	3,560	103
	Rievaulx	5,311	3,590	68
	Rosedale West Side	2,340	7,900	338
	Salton and Brawby	2,761	2,810	102
	Scawton	2,876	3,610	126
	Skiplam, Bransdale West Side, and Welburn	6,299	6,080	96
	Slingsby	2,570	2,090	81
	South Holme	904	500	55
	Spaunton	2,544	1,540	60
	Sproxton	2,868	3,370	118
	Stonegrave	914	720	79
	Swinton and Broughton	2,120	1,610	76
	Thornton Riseborough	620	310	50
	Wath	371	300	81
	SUBTOTAL	132,620	121,970	92
Whitby Strand	Broxa	533	450	84
	Eskdaleside	1,940	4,150	214
	Fylingdales	9,826	13,010	132
	Hackness	2,457	1,940	79
	Harwood Dale and Silpho	6,984	8,430	121
	Hawsker and Stainsacre	7,314	3,330	46
	Newholm and Dunsley	2,196	2,250	102
	Ruswarp	1,740	1,550	89
	Sneaton	4,850	4,040	83
	Suffield and Everley	1,911	1,910	100
	Ugglebarnby	2,470	2,210	89
	Whitby	78	50	64
	SUBTOTAL	42,299	43,320	102
RIDING	TOTAL	1,341,809	1,285,700	96

Note: The census acres for Ugthorpe in Langbaurgh wapentake are excluded from the totals.
Sources: 6-inch Ordnance Survey maps (OS), North Riding; PP 1833 (149.) XXXVIII 760-91 (1831 Census of Population, North Riding). See map 4.

APPENDIX C.2

A comparison of total acres recorded on the six-inch Ordnance Survey maps and in the 1831 Census, aggregated at the parish level (detached townships being separately reported), all parishes, North Riding

Wapentake	Parish	(a) 6-inch Ordnance acres	(b) 1831 Census acres	(b) as % of (a)
Allertonshire	Birkby	3,750	3,400	91
	Holme	550	350	64
	Hutton Conyers	3,212	3,010	94
	Leake	5,897	6,090	103
	Northallerton	12,416	11,550	93
	Norton Conyers	1,041	920	88
	Osmotherley	7,623	7,740	102
	Otterington, North	4,870	4,800	98
	Rounton, West	1,456	1,840	126
	Sessay and Hutton Sessay	3,772	3,340	88
	Sigston	3,420	3,510	103
	Smeaton, Great	5,341	5,550	104
	Sockburn	2,085	2,220	106
	Thornton le Street	2,324	2,750	118
	Worsall, High	1,625	1,550	95
	SUBTOTAL	59,382	58,620	99
Birdforth	Bagby and Balk	3,480	2,460	71
	Birdforth	628	540	86
	Byland, Old	2,737	3,120	114
	Cold Kirby	1,617	2,100	130
	Cowsby	1,165	1,220	105
	Coxwold	16,764	14,050	84
	Felixkirk	8,444	6,990	83
	Harlsey, East	3,057	2,910	95
	Hawnby	16,789	22,250	132
	Husthwaite	2,496	2,800	112
	Kepwick	2,742	2,520	92
	Kilburn	3,120	3,670	118
	Kilvington, South	2,920	2,610	89
	Kirby Knowle	1,580	1,420	90
	Otterington, South	1,450	1,780	123
	Silton, Over	1,235	940	76
	Thirkleby	2,690	1,800	67
	Thirsk	8,765	8,460	96
	Topcliffe	16,164	13,980	86
	Welbury	2,401	2,020	84
	SUBTOTAL	100,244	97,640	97
Bulmer	Alne	9,981	10,250	103
	Bossall	9,639	8,880	92
	Brafferton	3,741	3,890	104
	Brandsby	3,077	2,700	88
	Bulmer	4,237	3,800	90
	Clifton, Rawcliffe, and St Olave in Marygate	2,370	2,120	89
	Crambe	3,789	3,710	98
	Crayke	2,874	3,300	115
	Dalby	1,347	1,480	110
	Easingwold	11,280	10,070	89
	Foston	1,876	2,090	111
	Haxby	2,208	1,840	83
	Helmsley, Gate	496	520	105

APPENDIX C.2 (continued) page 364

Wapentake	Parish	(a) 6-inch Ordnance acres	(b) 1831 Census acres	(b) as % of (a)
Bulmer continued	Helmsley, Upper	832	780	94
	Heworth	1,312	1,330	101
	Holtby	901	850	94
	Huntington	2,606	2,760	106
	Huttons Ambo	2,896	2,300	79
	Marton in the Forest	2,715	2,370	87
	Myton upon Swale	2,283	1,480	65
	Newton upon Ouse	5,147	4,590	89
	Osbaldwick	1,574	1,740	110
	Overton	5,814	5,490	94
	Sheriff Hutton	10,176	9,590	94
	Stillington	2,158	1,490	69
	Stockton on the Forest	3,267	3,270	100
	Strensall	5,146	4,780	93
	Sutton on the Forest	10,654	10,070	94
	Terrington	3,953	3,630	92
	Thormanby	1,002	900	90
	Warthill	1,003	860	86
	Whenby	1,042	1,390	133
	Wigginton	1,880	2,040	108
	SUBTOTAL	123,276	116,360	94
Gilling East	Ainderby Steeple	4,693	4,300	92
	Barton and Newton Morrell	3,084	2,790	90
	Cleasby	1,205	970	80
	Cowton, East	3,369	3,150	94
	Cowton, North and South	3,635	2,560	70
	Croft	7,265	7,060	97
	Danby Wiske	4,714	4,350	92
	Eryholme	2,345	1,790	76
	Kirby Wiske	5,998	5,070	84
	Langton, Great and Little	1,878	1,860	99
	Manfield	3,625	3,200	88
	Middleton Tyas	6,243	5,420	87
	SUBTOTAL	48,054	42,520	88
Gilling West	Arkengarthdale	14,566	14,180	97
	Barningham	11,300	10,930	97
	Bowes	21,622	19,780	91
	Brignall	2,116	1,910	90
	Caldwell and Layton East and West	3,406	3,580	105
	Easby	5,550	5,090	92
	Gilling	10,809	10,690	99
	Grinton	52,055	49,810	96
	Hutton Longvillers	1,304	1,510	116
	Kirkby Ravensworth	15,390	14,070	91
	Marrick	6,206	5,560	90
	Marske	6,759	5,220	77
	Melsonby	2,742	2,310	84
	Richmond	2,520	2,310	92
	Rokeby	1,808	1,990	110
	Romaldkirk	54,767	54,760	100
	Stanwick, St. John; and Aldbrough	3,205	1,720	54

Wapentake	Parish	(a) 6-inch Ordnance acres	(b) 1831 Census acres	(b) as % of (a)
Gilling West continued				
	Startforth	1,010	1,070	106
	Wycliffe	2,229	2,200	99
	SUBTOTAL	219,364	208,690	95
Hallikeld	Burneston	7,621	6,920	91
	Cundall	4,232	4,120	97
	Humburton and Milby	1,819	2,320	128
	Kirby Hill and Langthorpe	2,239	1,590	71
	Kirklington	2,869	2,640	92
	Langthorne	833	820	98
	Pickhill	4,557	4,330	95
	Tanfield, East and West	4,581	4,230	92
	Wath	2,668	2,280	85
	SUBTOTAL	31,419	29,250	93
Hang East	Bedale	7,715	6,250	81
	Catterick	23,383	21,680	93
	Hornby	3,881	3,690	95
	Kirkby Fleetham	3,154	2,950	94
	Masham	25,309	22,940	91
	Patrick Brompton	5,677	5,560	98
	Scruton	2,114	1,940	92
	Thornton Watlass	3,709	4,850	131
	Well	6,689	5,880	88
	SUBTOTAL	81,631	75,740	93
Hang West	Aysgarth	81,004	79,980	99
	Coverham	20,561	22,120	108
	Downholme	6,708	5,800	86
	Finghall	4,580	4,460	97
	Hauxwell	4,590	3,850	84
	Middleham	2,154	2,400	111
	Spennithorne	5,477	4,680	85
	Thornton Steward	2,158	2,570	119
	Wensley	14,445	13,930	96
	Witton, East	7,054	7,730	110
	Witton, West	3,874	5,140	133
	SUBTOTAL	152,605	152,660	100
Langbaurgh	Acklam	4,227	3,460	82
	Ayton, Great	6,374	5,740	90
	Brotton	3,988	3,560	89
	Carlton	1,358	830	61
	Crathorne	2,598	2,460	95
	Danby	11,256	22,230	197
	Easby	1,210	1,170	97
	Easington	3,766	3,850	102
	Egton	15,657	13,570	87
	Guisborough	13,165	12,000	91
	Hilton	1,392	1,510	108
	Hinderwell	1,655	1,550	94
	Ingleby Arncliffe	1,893	1,840	97
	Ingleby Greenhow	7,002	6,400	91

APPENDIX C.2 (continued) page 366

Wapentake	Parish	(a) 6-inch Ordnance acres	(b) 1831 Census acres	(b) as % of (a)
Langbaurgh continued				
	Kildale	5,192	5,730	110
	Kirby in Cleveland	4,799	5,020	105
	Kirkleatham	8,380	8,030	96
	Kirk Leavington	5,639	4,560	81
	Liverton	2,454	2,360	96
	Lofthouse	3,737	3,700	99
	Lythe (excluding Ugthorpe)	12,180	11,070	91
	Marske	4,574	3,500	76
	Marton in Cleveland	3,519	3,430	97
	Newton	1,172	1,440	123
	Ormesby	8,116	7,500	92
	Rousby	3,250	2,410	74
	Rudby in Cleveland	7,561	6,930	92
	Seamer	2,650	2,650	100
	Skelton	11,735	10,440	89
	Stainton	7,791	6,820	88
	Stokesley	5,180	5,520	106
	Upleatham	1,426	1,100	77
	Westerdale	9,881	8,750	88
	Whorlton	9,726	8,200	84
	Yarm	1,198	1,180	98
	SUBTOTAL	195,701	190,510	97
Pickering Lythe	Allerston	10,043	9,110	91
	Brompton	11,356	10,180	90
	Cayton	3,504	2,430	69
	Ebberston	6,094	6,350	104
	Hutton Bushel	8,543	8,280	97
	Kirby Misperton	6,999	7,130	102
	Lebberston	2,479	2,390	96
	Levisham	2,974	2,670	90
	Lockton	7,423	6,610	89
	Middleton	19,859	18,840	95
	Pickering	31,008	32,760	106
	Scalby	11,870	11,060	93
	Scarborough	2,293	2,160	94
	Seamer	5,951	5,150	86
	Sinnington	2,892	2,600	90
	Thornton Dale	8,274	8,470	102
	Wilton	1,784	2,060	115
	Wykeham	8,248	6,480	78
	SUBTOTAL	151,594	144,730	95
Ryedale	Ampleforth	2,370	2,270	96
	Appleton le Street	5,887	4,780	81
	Barton le Street	3,540	3,180	90
	Gilling	4,124	4,330	105
	Great Edstone	1,458	1,980	136
	Helmsley	38,668	29,020	75
	Hovingham	8,300	7,960	96
	Kirby Moorside	7,450	7,410	99
	Kirkdale	10,698	9,610	90
	Lastingham	29,500	31,580	107
	Malton, New	49	110	224
	Malton, Old	3,968	4,020	101

Wapentake	Parish	(a) 6-inch Ordnance acres	(b) 1831 Census acres	(b) as % of (a)
Ryedale continued	Normanby	2,404	2,330	97
	Nunnington	2,122	1,600	75
	Oswaldkirk	2,195	2,310	105
	Salton	2,761	2,810	102
	Scawton	2,876	3,610	126
	Slingsby	2,570	2,090	81
	Stonegrave	4,242	3,580	84
	SUBTOTAL	135,182	124,580	92
Whitby Strand	Fylingdales	9,826	13,010	132
	Hackness	11,885	12,730	107
	Sneaton	4,850	4,040	83
	Whitby	16,810	14,620	87
	SUBTOTAL	43,371	44,400	102
RIDING	TOTAL	1,341,809	1,285,700	96

Sources: 6-inch Ordnance Survey maps (OS), North Riding; PP 1833 (149.) XXXVIII 760-91 (1831 census of population, North Riding). See map 5.

APPENDIX D.1

Fluctuations in township quotas (£. s. d.), Birdforth wapentake, North Riding, 1693–95, 1699, 1712–18, 1798

Township	1693	1694	1695	1699	1712	1713
Ampleforth Birdforth	31.12. 4.	31.12. 0.	31.12. 4.	36. 1.11.	31. 2. 3.	31. 2. 3.
Arden	32. 0. 0.	32. 0. 0.	32. 0. 0.	32. 9. 8.	31. 8. 61/4.	31. 8. 61/2.
Bagby and Fawdington	71.10. 0.	76.11. 0.[a]	76. 5. 0.	73. 6.11.[b]	76. 2. 01/4.[c]	76. 2. 01/2.
Balk	36. 6. 2.	36. 9. 1.	36. 6. 4.	36.18. 4.	35.14. 6.	35.14. 6.
Bilsdale Westside and Snilesworth	54. 5. 0.	54. 5. 0.	54. 5. 0.	55. 5.10.	53. 1. 111/2.	53. 2. 0.
Birdforth	39.19. 6.	39.19. 6.	39.19. 6.	40. 9. 5.	40.18. 81/2.	40.18. 9.
Boltby	70.17. 0.	70.17. 0.	70.17. 0.	71.18. 2.	69.14. 11/2.	69.14. 11/2.
Byland Membris	80. 0. 0.	77.16. 0.	77.16. 0.	81. 4. 2.	82.13. 31/2.	82.13. 31/2.
Byland, Old	33.18. 0.	33.18. 0.	33.18. 0.	33.17.11.[d]	NR	56. 7.11.[d]
Carlton Husthwaite	40. 0. 0.	40. 0. 0.	40. 0. 0.	40.18. 0.	39. 7.10.	39. 7.10.
Carlton Miniott	47. 2. 0.	47. 2. 0.	47. 2. 0.	47.15. 4.	46. 6.10.	46. 6.101/2.
Catton	23.12. 0.	23.12. 0.	23.12. 0.	23.19. 7.	23. 3. 81/2.	23. 3. 81/2.
Cold Kirby	24. 9. 4.	24. 9. 4.	24. 9. 4.	24.16. 0.	24. 2. 3.	24. 2. 3.
Cowsby	27. 8. 0.	25. 8. 0.	25. 8. 0.	27.16. 4.	26.19. 1.	26.19. 1.
Coxwold etc.	35.14. 0.	35.14. 0.	35.14. 0.	37.16. 1.[d]	NR	57.13. 0.[d]
Dale Town	19. 1. 0.	19. 1. 0.	19. 1. 0.	19. 6. 8.[d]	NR	18.14. 6.[d]
Dalton	27. 4. 0.	27. 2. 0	27. 2. 0.	27. 8. 8.	27. 5. 4.	27. 5. 4.
East Harlsey	107.11. 71/2.	107.11. 6.	107.11. 6.	83. 9.10.[i]	78.13. 9.	78.13. 9.
Elmire and Crakehill	25.14. 4.	25. 1. 0.	25.14. 4.	26. 1.10	NR	25. 6. 2.
Felixkirk	37.10. 0.	37.10. 0.	41. 2. 0.	37. 0. 7.	36.17. 4.	36.18. 8.
Gueldable and Borrowby (Allertonshire)	17.15. 8.[k]	13. 2. 0.[k]	13. 2. 0.[k]	11. 3. 3.[k]	10.16. 0.[k]	10.16. 0.[k]
Hawnby	27.16. 0.	27.16. 0.	27.16. 0.	28. 3. 9.	27. 0. 8.	27. 0. 8.
Husthwaite	73.13. 8.	73. 2. 0.	72.12. 0.	74.14.11.	72.10. 8.	72.10. 8.
Kepwick	32. 0. 0.	32. 2. 0.	32. 2. 0.	33. 4. 0.[d]	NR	38.14. 3.[d]
Kilburn, Low, etc.	71.18. 8.	71.18. 8.	71.18. 8.	69. 0. 4.	70.15. 0.	70.15. 0.
Kirby Knowle	27.10. 0.	27.10. 0.	27.10. 0.	29. 5. 0.	27. 1. 0.	27. 1. 0.
Nether Silton	37. 5.101/2.	40. 7. 0.	40. 7. 0.	37. 9. 83/4.	34. 4.11.	27. 2. 1.[l]
Newburgh and Murton	68. 0. 0.	68. 0. 0.	68. 0. 0.	70. 2. 3.[d]	NR	95.17. 2.[d]
Newsham and Breckenbrough	77.10. 0.	77.10. 0.	77.10. 0.	52.10. 7.[m]	50.14. 8.	50.14. 8.
Oulston	36.12. 0.	36.12. 0.	36.12. 0.	37. 3. 5.[e]	NR	35.19. 9.[e]
Over Silton	19.10. 0.	19.10. 0.	19.10. 0	14.16. 3.[e]	NR	27. 3. 61/2.[e]

Sand Hutton	40. 4. 0.	40. 4. 0.	40. 4. 0	40.14. 7.	39.12. 8.	39.12. 8.
Skipton	25.16. 0.	25.16. 0.	25.16. 0.	26. 4. 01/2.	NR	25. 7. 3.
South Kilvington	33.15. 0.	33.15. 6.	33.15. 0.	34. 5. 5.	33. 3. 7.	33. 3. 7.
South Otterington	60.18. 0.	60.18. 0.	60.18. 0.	61.14. 1.	60. 1. 0.	60. 1. 0.
Sowerby[n]	109. 7. 4.	112. 6. 4.	112. 6. 4.	138.14. 0.	88.12. 8.	88.12. 8.
Sutton under Whitestonecliffe	132. 8. 2.	138. 8. 2.[q]	138. 8. 2.	136. 8. 3.	136. 3. 4.	136. 3. 4.
Thirkleby	52.10. 2.	50.18. 6.	50.18. 6.	53.11. 7.	51. 2. 0.	51. 2. 0.
Thirlby	13.14. 0.	13.14. 0.	13.14. 0.	14. 0. 8.	16. 2. 2.	16. 2. 2.
Thirsk	NR	110. 6.10.	104.16.10.	103.13. 8.	102. 2. 7.	102. 2. 7.
Thornborough	34.17. 4.	23.17. 4.[o]	34.17. 4.	35. 4. 7.	34. 9. 9.	34. 9. 9.
Thornton and Baxby	57.18. 0.	58. 1. 0.	57.11. 8.	58.16. 1.	76.16. 3.[f]	76.18. 5.
Thornton le Moor	40. 2. 0.	40. 2. 0.	38.19. 4.	40.14. 3.	39. 9. 2.	39.19. 2.
Topcliffe	104. 9. 4.	93. 5. 4.[p]	71. 3.101/2.	NR	91.18.11.	91.18.11.
Upsall	82. 4. 0.	82. 4. 0.	88.18. 0.	82.17. 3.	81.11. 8.	81.11. 8.
Welbury	73.11. 41/2	73.11. 4.	73.11. 4.	74. 8. 0.	72.12.10.	72.12.10.
Yearsley	26. 2. 0.	26. 2. 0.	26. 2. 0.	26.10. 0.[d]	NR	25.13. 0.[d]
TOTAL (excluding Thirsk and Topcliffe)	2,138.13. 61/2.		2,152.14. 8.	2,139.17. 61/4.		2,146.18.101/2.

Township	1714	1715	1716	1717	1718	1798
Ampleforth Birdforth	31. 2. 21/2.	31. 2. 3.	31. 2. 3.	31. 2. 3.	31. 2. 3.	31. 2. 3.
Arden	31. 8. 71/2.	31. 8. 71/2.	31. 8. 61/2.	31. 8. 7.	31. 8. 7.	31. 8. 8.
Bagby and Fawdington	76. 2. 2.	76. 2. 2.	76. 2. 01/2.	70.17. 1.	70.17. 1.	70.17. 1.
Balk	35.14. 6.	35.14. 6.	35.14. 6	35.14. 6.	35.14. 6.	35.14. 6.
Bilsdale Westside and Snilesworth	53. 1.111/2.	53. 1.111/2.	53. 1.111/2.	53. 1.111/2.	53. 2. 0.	53. 2. 0.
Birdforth	40.18. 81/2.	40.16. 9.	40.18. 81/2.	40.18. 81/2.	40.18. 81/2.	40.18. 9.
Boltby	69.14. 11/2.	69.14. 11/2.	69.14. 11/4.	69.14. 11/4.	69.14. 11/4.	69.14. 3.
Byland Membris	82.13. 31/2.	82.13. 31/2.	82.13. 31/2.	83. 6. 8.	82.13. 4.	82.13. 4.
Byland, Old	56. 7.11.	56. 7.11.	56. 7.11.	56. 7.11.	56. 7.11.	56. 7.11.
Carlton Husthwaite	39. 7.10.	39. 7.10.	39. 7.10.	39. 7. 8.	39. 7. 8.	39. 7.10.
Carlton Miniott	46. 6.101/2.	46. 6.101/2.	46. 6.101/2.	46. 6.101/2.	46. 6.101/2.	46. 6.11.
Catton	23. 3. 81/2.	23. 3. 81/2.	23. 3. 81/2.	23. 3. 81/2.	23. 3. 81/2.	23. 3. 9.
Cold Kirby	24. 2. 3.	24. 2. 2.	24. 2. 3.	24. 2. 3.	24. 2. 4.	24. 2. 4.
Cowsby	26.19. 1.	26.19. 1.	26.19. 1.	26.19. 1.	26.19. 1.	26.19. 1.

APPENDIX D.1 (continued) page 370

Township	1714	1715	1716	1717	1718	1798
Coxwold etc.	57.13. 0.	57.13. 0.	57.13. 0.	57.13. 0.	57.13. 0.	57.13. 0.
Dale Town	18.14. 61/2.	18.14. 61/2.	18.14. 7.	23.19. 7.[g]	23.19. 7.[g]	18.14. 7.
Dalton	27. 5. 4.	27. 5. 4.	27. 5. 4.	27. 5. 4.	27. 5. 4.	27. 5. 4.
East Harlsey	78.13. 9.	NR	78.13. 9.	78.13. 9.	78.13. 9.	78.13. 9.
Elmire and Crakehill	25. 6. 2.	25. 6. 2.	25. 6. 2.	25. 6. 2.	25. 6. 2.	25. 6. 2.
Felixkirk	36.19. 4.	18. 8. 8.[j]	36.18. 8.	NR	36.18. 8.	36.18. 8.
Gueldable and Borrowby (Allertonshire)	10.16. 0.[k]	10.16. 0.[k]	10.16. 0.[k]	10.16. 0.[k]	10.16. 0.[k]	54. 3. 2.
Hawnby	27. 0. 8	27. 0. 8.	27. 0. 8.	27. 0. 8.	27. 0. 8.	27. 0. 8.
Husthwaite	72.10. 8.	72.10. 8.	72.10. 8.	72.10. 4.	72.10. 4.	72.10. 8.
Kepwick	38.14. 3.	38.14. 3.	38.14. 3.	38.14. 3.	38.14. 3.	43.19. 3.
Kilburn, Low, etc.	70.15. 0.	70.15. 0.	70.15. 0.	70.15. 0.	70.15. 0.	70.15. 0
Kirby Knowle	27. 1. 0.	27. 1. 0.	27. 1. 0.	27. 1. 0.	27. 1. 0.	27. 1. 0.
Nether Silton	27. 2. 1.	27. 2. 1.	27. 2. 1.	27. 2. 1.	27. 2. 1.	27. 2. 1.
Newburgh and Murton	95.17. 2.	95.17. 2.	95.17. 2.	95.17. 2.	95.17. 2.	95.17. 2.
Newsham and Breckenbrough	50.14. 8.	50.14. 8	50.14. 8.	50.14. 8.	50.14. 8.	50.14. 8.
Oulston	37. 5. 9.[h]	37. 5. 9.	37. 5. 9.	37. 5. 9.	37. 5. 9.	37. 5. 9.
Over Silton	27. 3. 7.	27. 3. 7.	27. 3. 7	27. 3. 7.	27. 3. 7.	27. 3. 7.
Sand Hutton	39.12. 8.	39.12. 8.	39.12. 8.	39.12. 8.	39.12. 8.	39.12. 8.
Skipton	25. 7. 3.	NR	25. 7. 3.	25. 7. 3.	25. 7. 3.	25. 7. 3.
South Kilvington	33. 3. 7.	33. 3. 7.	33. 3. 7.	33. 3. 7.	33. 3. 7.	33. 3. 7.
South Otterington	60. 1. 0.	60. 1. 0.	60. 1. 0.	60. 1. 0.	60. 1. 0.	60. 1. 0.
Sowerby[n]	88.12. 8.	88.12. 8.	88.12. 8.	88.12. 8.	88.12. 8.	88.12. 8.
Sutton under Whitestonecliffe	134.17. 4.[h]	134.17. 4.	134.17. 4.	134.17. 5.	134.17. 4.	134.17. 4.
Thirkleby	51. 2. 0.	51. 2. 0.	51. 2. 0.	51. 2. 0.	51. 2. 0.	51. 2. 0.
Thirlby	16. 2. 2.	16. 2. 2.	16. 2. 2.	16. 2. 2.	16. 2. 2.	16. 4. 6.
Thirsk	102. 2. 7.	102. 2. 7.	102. 2. 7.	102. 2. 7.	102. 2. 7.	102. 2. 7.
Thornborough	34. 9. 9.	34. 9. 9.	34. 9. 9.	34. 9. 9.	34. 9. 9.	34. 9. 9.
Thornton and Baxby	76.18. 5.	76.18. 5.	76.18. 5.	76.18. 5.	76.18. 5.	76.18. 5.
Thornton le Moor	39.19. 2.	39.19. 2.	39.19. 2.	39.19. 2.	39.19. 2.	39.19. 2.
Topcliffe	91.18.11.	91.18.11.	91.18.11.	91.18.11.	91.18.11.	91.18.11.
Upsall	81.11. 8.	81.11. 8.	81.11. 8.	81.11. 8.	81.11. 8.	81.11. 8.
Welbury	72.12.10.	72.12.10.	72.12.10.	72.12.10.	72.12.10.	72.12.10.

Yearsley	25.13. 0.	25.13. 0.	25.13. 0.	25.13. 0.	25.13. 0.	25.13. 0.
TOTAL (excluding Thirsk and Topcliffe)						2,190. 9. 0.

Notes: All dates are New Style. The totals are given at a statutory rate of 4s. in the pound. 1699, 1717, and 1718 have been converted from a 3s. rate. 1713-15 have been converted from a 2s. rate. The total for the year in which the 1798 quota was first achieved (within 12d.) is underscored.

[a]The increase is due to the new imposition of a double assessment.

[b]The decrease is due to a reduction in some proportion of the double assessed lands.

[c]The increase is due to an increased imposition on some proportion of double assessed lands.

[d]Wholly owned by the Third Viscount Fauconberg (ob. Nov. 1718), a Catholic recusant.

[e]Almost wholly owned by Viscount Fauconberg.

[f]The increase occurs entirely on the Thornton property, which is wholly owned by Viscount Fauconberg.

[g]The addition is annotated as ''laid on by the Commissioners.''

[h]The register records a small portion (about 13s.) having been reassigned by the commissioners from Sutton under Whitestonecliffe to Oulston.

[i]The decrease is due to an apparent ending of double assessment on the property of George Lawson.

[j]The drop is doubtless due to the recording of only a half year's total, although the register fails to annotate it as such.

[k]Borrowby is adjacent to Gueldable (which is in Birdforth) but is in Allertonshire wapentake. By the late eighteenth century Borrowby is always separately assessed in Allertonshire and is not associated with Gueldable for tax purposes. The return recorded in this register is thus probably geographically incommensurate with the two 1798 townships, whose combined quotas are reported in this table. The 1693 entry suggests that the payments recorded were quarterly, but that possibility is dispelled by the 1717 entry, which specifies the total to be for the whole year. Double assessment is recorded on one large property bundle (£13. 12s. 0d.) in 1693. That property was sold and split up, however, and cannot be clearly traced. Some degree of double assessment appears to continue in the township.

[l]The decrease is due to the sale of double assessed properties of a Catholic recusant, John Pinkney, to two non-Catholic gentry.

[m]The decrease occurs wholly on the Breckenbrough property, which is entirely owned by a Catholic recusant, Sir Hugh Smithson (ob. 1729), who apparently conformed at some point in his life. His assessment is halved between 1695 and 1699. Edgar E. Estcourt and John Orlebar Payne, eds., *The English Catholic Nonjurors of 1715* (London, 1885), 325.

[n]Variations in the Sowerby quota appear to be due principally to variations in the proportions assessed to the six largest estates and especially to the assessment of Sowerby Parks. Boundary changes may have been involved. There is no indication of double assessment. One of the larger properties (Meynell) is Roman Catholic, but its assessments vary relatively little.

[o]The 1694 register for Thornborough is clearly defective. A comparison with 1693 and 1695 shows that one major property (out of a total of only three entries) was omitted in 1694 and that the proprietor was incorrectly assigned to another entry (where the correct proprietor was omitted).

[p]The decline in quota is due to an assessment of £11. 3s. 4d., which was imposed in 1693 on an excise officer, having been dropped in 1694.

[q]A £6 assessment on the personal property of Sir William Ashworth is added in 1694 and 1695, but disappears thereafter.

Source: Land tax register, Birdforth wapentake, 1693-1718; land tax duplicates, Birdforth wapentake, 1798, NYCRO.

APPENDIX D.2

Tax assessments (£. s. d.) on all Roman Catholic properties labelled as double assessed, North Riding, 1790–95, 1798

Wapentake	Township	Proprietor	1790	1791	1792	1793
Allertonshire	High Worsall		53. 6. 5.	53. 6. 5.	53. 6. 5.	53. 6. 5.
		Edw. Meynell, Esq.	(5.11. 8.)	(5.11. 8.)	(5.11. 8.)	(5.11. 8.)
	Thornton le Street		58.10. 6.	58.10. 6.	58.10. 6.	58.10. 6.
		Edw. Meynell, Esq.	(20.11.10.)	(20.11.10.)	(20.11.10.)	(19.15.11 1/2.)
Birdforth	Welbury		72.12.10.	72.12.10.	72.12.10.	72.12.10.
		Joseph Tate	(3.16. 3.)	(3.17. 6.)	(3.17. 6.)	(4. 0. 0.)
		John Meynell	(3. 6. 1.)	(3. 7. 2.)	(3. 7. 1.)	(3. 9. 4.)
Gilling East	Cowton, East		125. 0. 0.	125. 0. 0.	125. 0. 0.	125. 0. 0.
		Sir John Webb, Bt.	(51.13. 1.)	(51.13. 1 1/2.)	(51.13. 1 1/2.)	(50.14. 4 1/2.)
	Cowton, North		43. 6. 8.	43. 6. 8.	43. 6. 8.	43. 6. 8.
		Sir John Webb, Bt.[i]	(1.15. 0.)	(1.17. 7.)	(3. 6. 8.)	(3. 5. 0.)
	Cowton, South		110. 0. 0.	110. 0. 0.	110. 0. 0.	110. 0. 0.
		Sir John Webb, Bt.	(70.16.10 3/4.)	(71. 8. 9 1/2.)	(71. 8. 7 3/4.)	(74. 5. 3 1/2.)
	Danby Wiske		107. 0. 0.	107. 0. 0.	107. 0. 0.	107. 0. 0.
		Sir John Webb, Bt.	(8.17. 9.)	(8. 2. 0.)	(8. 2. 0.)	(8. 2. 0.)
	Ellerton, Bolton and Whitwell		92. 0. 0.	92. 0. 0.	92. 0. 0.	92. 0. 0.
		Sir John Webb, Bt.	(24.13. 5.)	(24.13. 5.)	(23.18. 7 3/4.)	(22.14. 8 1/2.)
	Manfield		152.14. 0.	NT	152. 0. 0.	152. 0. 0.
		William Witham, Esq.	(94.19. 0.)	(92.10. 2.)	(92.10. 2.)	(94. 6. 0.)
	Thrintoft		53. 6. 8.	53. 6. 8.	53. 6. 8.	53. 6. 8.
		Edw. Meynell, Esq.	(31. 1. 9.)	(31. 4.10.)	(31. 4.10.)	(30. 5. 7.)
Gilling West	Aldbrough		70.18. 8.	70.18. 8.	70.18. 8.	70.18. 8.
		James Brown	(1. 0. 0.)	(0.16.11.)	(0.15. 5.)	(0. 7.11.)
		William Witham, Esq.	(6. 0. 0.)	(5.17. 0.)	(5.11. 0.)	(5.14. 0.)
		William Westwood	(0. 6. 8.)	(0. 6. 7 1/2.)	(0. 6. 2.)	(0. 3. 2.)
	Cliffe		43.14.10	43.14.10.	43.14.10.	43.14.10.
		William Witham, Esq. (seat)	(0.10. 1 1/2.)[a]	(0.10. 1 1/2.)	(0.10. 1 1/2.)	(0.10. 1 1/2.)

Gilling West	Dalton		65.12.10.	65.12.10.	65.12.10.	65.12.10.
		Simon Scroop, Esq.	(48. 9. 9.)	(49.16. 3.)	(49.12.11.)	(49.14. 2.)
		Anthony Langstaff	(0.10. 2.)	(0.10. 5.)	(0.10. 6.)	(0.10. 8.)
		Eliz. & Ann Berwick	(0. 6. 8.)	(0. 7. 6.)	(0. 7. 8.)	(0. 7. 8.)
	Eppleby		48.15. 3.	48.15. 3.	48.13.11.	48.13.10.
		Mathew Gibbon	(8.16. 3.)	(8.16. 3.)	(8.17. 9 1/2.)	(8. 8. 8.)
	Hutton Longvillers		60. 0. 4.	60. 0. 4.	60. 0. 4.	60. 0. 4.
		Marm. Tunstall, Esq.	(58.17. 0.)	(58.17. 0.)[r]	(58.17. 0.)[s]	(58.17. 0.)[t]
	Kirkby Ravensworth		7.16. 4.	7.16. 4.	7.16. 4.	7.16. 4.
		Anthony Langstaff	(0. 6. 0.)	(0. 6. 6.)	(0. 3. 4.)	(0. 6. 6.)
		Eliz. & Ann Berwick	(0. 1. 6.)	(0. 1. 7.)	(0. 0.10.)	(0. 1. 8.)
	Lartington		64.12. 8.	64.12. 8.	64.12. 8.	64.12. 8.
		Henry Maire, Esq. (seat)	(53. 3. 8.)	(54. 2. 4.)	(54. 2. 2.)	(54.10. 5.)
		William Hogget	(0.18. 6.)[b]	(0. 6. 9.)	(0. 6. 9.)	--
	Newsham		63.14. 8.	63.14. 8.	63.14. 8.	INC.
		James Shaw	(0.15. 9.)	(0.15. 9.)	(0.15. 9.)	(0. 7.10 1/2.)
		Catherine Bays	(0. 3. 4 1/2.)	--	(0. 3. 4 1/2.)	(0. 3. 4 1/2.)
		George Cash	(0. 3. 0 1/2.)	(0. 8. 1.)	(0. 4. 8 1/2.)	(0. 4. 8 1/2.)
		John Boldron	(0. 3. 1.)	(0. 3. 1.)	(0. 3. 1.)	INC.
		Jonathan Rutter	(0. 3. 1.)	(0. 3. 1.)	(0. 3. 1.)	(0. 3. 1.)
		Robert Robinson	(3.19. 9 1/2.)	(3.19. 9 3/4.)	(3.19. 9 3/4.)	(3.19. 9 3/4.)
		Marm. Tunstall, Esq.[c]	(1. 5. 8 3/4.)	(1. 5. 8 3/4)	(1. 5. 8 3/4.)	(1. 5. 8 3/4)[s]
	Ovington		19.18. 0.	19.18. 0.	19.18. 0.	19.18. 0.
		Marm. Tunstall, Esq.	(8. 6. 6.)	(8. 2.11.)[r]	(7.15.10.)[t]	(7.10. 6.)[t]
		Peter Pearson	(0.18. 2.)	(1. 2. 6 1/2.)[h]	(1.11. 2.)	(1. 1. 5.1/4)[v]
	Thorpe		159. 2. 2.	159. 2. 2.	159. 2. 2.	159. 2. 2.
		Marm. Tunstall, Esq. (seat)	(108. 6. 5.)	(106.15. 0.)[x]	(103. 0. 1.)[j,u]	(111.14.11.)[j,u]
Hallikeld	Gatenby		69. 5. 0.	69. 5. 0.	69. 5. 0.	69. 5. 0.
		Lord Langdale (heirs)	(62. 9. 9.)	(62. 9. 9.)	(62. 9. 9.)	(61. 7. 4.)
	Pickhill and Roxby		70. 7. 0.	70. 7. 0.	70. 7. 0.	70. 7. 0.
		Edw. Meynell, Esq.	(26.13. 4 1/2.)	(27. 4. 8 1/2.)	(27. 4. 8 1/2.)	(27. 4. 8 1/2.)
		Ralph Waiting	(0. 2.10.)	(0. 2.10.)	(0. 2.10.)	(0. 2.10.)
	Sinderby		20. 4.10.	20. 4.10.	20. 4.10.	20. 4.10.
		Edw. Meynell, Esq.	(1.18.10 1/4.)	(1.18.10 1/4.)	(2. 0. 6.)	(2. 0. 6.)

APPENDIX D.2 (continued) page 374

Wapentake	Township	Proprietor	1790	1791	1792	1793
Hang East	Aiskew		75.15. 8.	75.15. 8.	75.15. 8.	75.15. 8.
		Mr Foss	(2. 3. 11/2.)[d]	(2. 3. 11/2.)[d]	(1.15. 91/4.)	(1.15. 91/4.)
		Thos Stapleton, Esq.	(21. 9. 73/4)	(21.19.101/4)	(18. 2. 13/4)[k]	(17. 3. 13/4.)[k]
		Mr Swailes	(0.17.111/4.)	(0.17.111/4)	(0.14.101/2.)	(0.14.101/2.)
	Bedale & Firby		156. 8. 3.	156. 8. 3.	156. 8. 3.	156. 8. 3.
		Thos Stapleton, Esq.	def.	def.	(80. 9. 71/4.)	(80.12. 71/4)
	Catterick & Killerby		129. 6.11.	129. 6.11.	129. 6.11.	129. 6.11.
		Strickland, Esq. (heirs)	(53.15. 0.)	(53.15. 0.)	(53.15. 0.)[y]	(53.15. 0.)[y]
		Sir John Lawson, Bt.	(26.13. 8.)	(26. 13. 8.)	(26.13. 0.)	(26.13. 0.)
		Wm Charlton, Esq.	(23. 7. 4.)	(23. 7. 4.)	(23. 7. 4.)	(23. 7. 4.)
	Colburn		52.11.101/2.	52.11.10.	52.11.10.	52.11.10.
		Philip Saltmarshe, Esq.	(28. 8. 41/2.)	(28. 8. 41/2.)	(28. 8. 41/2.)	(27.15. 61/2.)
	Tunstall		38.19. 9.	38.19. 9.	38.19. 9.	38.19. 9.
		Sir John Lawson, Bt.	(8. 0. 4.)	(8. 0. 4.)	(7. 7. 4.)	(7. 7. 4.)
Hang West	Leyburn[f]		48.10. 8.	48.10. 8.	48.10. 8.	48.10. 8.
		Ralph Riddle, Esq.	(12.16. 5.)	(12.16. 11/2.)	(12.11. 8.)	(12.16. 21/2.)
		John Blenkinsop Sr.	(0. 0. 51/2.)	(0. 0. 51/4)	(0. 0. 5.)	(0. 0. 5.)
		Wm Allen Sr.	(3. 0.10)	(3. 6.10.)	(3. 6.10.)	(3. 6.10.)
		Mrs Mary Allen	(0. 4. 5.)	(0. 4. 5.)	(0. 4. 5.)	(0. 4. 5.)
		Mr Sampson	(0. 4. 8.)	(0. 2. 4.)[aa]	(0. 2. 4.)[aa]	(0. 2. 4.)[aa]
	Thornton Steward		36.11. 1.	36.11. 1.	36.11. 1.	36.11. 1.
		Simon Thos Scroop, Esq.	(16.18. 8.)	(16.18. 8.)	(16.18. 8.)	(16.18. 8.)
		Geo. Kirkley	(0. 3. 4.)[e]	(0. 3. 4.)	(0. 3. 4.)	(0. 3. 4.)

Wapentake	Township	Proprietor	1794	1795	1798
Allertonshire	High Worsall		53. 6. 5.	NR	53. 6. 5.
		Edw. Meynell, Esq.	(2.18.11.)		(2.18.11.)

Allertonshire	Thornton le Street		58.10. 6.	NR	58.10. 6.
		Edw. Meynell, Esq.	(11.19. 5.)[l]		(11.12. 0.)
Birdforth	Welbury		72.12.10.	72.12.10.	72.12.10.
		Joseph Tate	(1.18. 9.)[m]	(2.10. 8.)	(3. 1. 3.)
		John Meynell	(3. 7. 2.)	(1.14. 8.)	(1. 6. 3.)
Gilling East	Cowton, East		125. 0. 0.	125. 0. 0.	125. 0. 0.
		Sir John Webb, Bt.	(29. 7. 0 1/4.)[l]	(26.16. 7 1/2.)	(28.12. 5.)[q]
	Cowton, North		43. 6. 8.	43. 6. 8.	43. 6. 8.
		Sir John Webb, Bt.[i]	(1.13. 9.)	(1.14. 2.)	(1.13.10.)
	Cowton, South		110. 0. 0.	110. 0. 0.	110. 0. 0.
		Sir John Webb, Bt.	(53.13. 9.)[l]	(53.13. 9.)	(53.14. 0 1/2.)
	Danby Wiske		107. 0. 0.	107. 0. 0.	107. 0. 0.
		Sir John Webb, Bt.	(8. 2. 0.)	(4. 1. 0.)	(3.19. 1 3/4.)
	Ellerton, Bolton, and Whitwell		92. 0. 0.	92. 0. 0.	92. 0. 0.
		Sir John Webb, Bt.	(13. 5. 2 1/2.)[l]	(13. 1. 5.)	(11.16.10.)
	Manfield		152. 0. 0.	152. 0. 0.	152. 0. 0.
		William Witham	(64.15.11.)[l]	(70.15.11.)	(66.15. 4.)
Gilling East	Thrintoft		53. 6. 8.	53. 6. 8.	53. 6. 8.
		Edw. Meynell, Esq.	(21. 3. 8.)[l]	(21. 3. 7.)	(21.15. 7.)
Gilling West	Aldbrough		70.18. 8.	70.18. 8.	70.18. 8.
		James Brown	(0. 7.11.)	(0. 7.11.)	(0. 6. 5 1/2.)
		William Witham, Esq.	(2.17. 0.)	(2.17. 0.)	(2. 1. 4.)
		William Westwood	(0. 6. 4.)	(0. 6. 4.)	(0. 2. 7.)
	Cliffe		43.14.10.	43.14.10	43.14.10
		William Witham, Esq. (seat)	(0.10. 1.)	(0.10. 1)	(0. 8.10)
	Dalton		65.12.10.	65.12.10.	65.12.10.
		Simon Scroop, Esq.	(40. 1. 5.)[l]	(40. 1. 5.)	(40. 1. 5.)
		Anthony Langstaff	(0. 8. 7 1/4.)	(0. 8. 7 1/4.)	(0. 6. 7 1/4.)
		Eliz. & Ann Berwick	(0. 8. 7 1/4.)	(0.10. 7 1/4.)	(0. 8. 7 1/4.)
	Eppleby		NR	48.13. 4.	48.13. 4.
		Mathew Gibbon		(4.16. 2 3/4.)[q]	(4.16. 1.)[q]
	Hutton Longvillers		60. 0. 4.	60. 0. 4.	60. 0. 4.

APPENDIX D.2 (continued) page 376

Wapentake	Township	Proprietor	1794	1795	1798
Gilling West		Marm. Tunstall, Esq.	no prop.	no prop.	no prop.
	Kirkby Ravensworth		7.16. 4.	7.16. 4.	7.16. 4.
		Anthony Langstaff	(0. 6. 6.)	(0. 3. 21/2.)	(0. 4. 2.)[q]
		Eliz. & Ann Berwick	(0. 1. 8.)	(0. 0. 91/2.)	(0. 0.10.)
	Lartington		64.12. 8.	64.12. 8.	64.12. 8.
		Henry Maire, Esq. (seat)	(53. 0.10.)	(53.13. 81/4.)[g]	(52.19. 8.)
		William Hogget	--	--	--
	Newsham		65. 8. 6.	63.14. 8.	63.14. 8.
		James Shaw	(0. 8. 7.)	(0. 8. 7.)	--
		Catherine Bays	(0. 1.10.)	(0. 1.10.)	--
		George Cash	(0. 2. 7.)	(0. 2. 7.)	(0. 3. 91/2.)
		John Boldron	(0. 1. 81/4.)	(0. 1. 81/4.)	(0. 1. 9.)
		Jonathan Rutter	(0. 1. 81/4.)	(0. 1. 81/4.)	(0. 1. 81/2.)
		Robert Robinson	(2. 4. 8.)	(2. 3. 8.)	(2. 5. 6.)
		Marm. Tunstall, Esq.[c]	(0.14. 03/4.)[s]	(0.14. 03/4.)[s]	(0.14. 6.)[s]
	Ovington		19.18. 0.	19.18. 0.	19.18. 0.
		Marm. Tunstall, Esq.	(4.15.10.)[t]	(4.15.10.)[t]	(4.15.10.)[u]
		Peter Pearson	(1. 0. 41/2.)[v]	(1. 0. 41/2.)[v]	(1. 4. 91/2.)[w]
	Thorpe		159. 2. 2.	159. 2. 2.	159. 2. 2.
		Marm. Tunstall, Esq. (seat)	(89.11. 6.)[1,u]	(87. 7. 7.)[u]	(85.14. 3.)[u]
Hallikeld	Gatenby		69. 5. 0.	69. 5. 0.	69. 5. 0.
		Lord Langdale (heirs)	(55. 1. 81/4.)[1]	(55. 1. 81/4.)	(55. 1. 81/2.)
	Pickhill & Roxby		70. 7. 0.	70. 7. 0.	70. 7. 0.
		Edw. Meynell, Esq.	(27. 4. 81/2.)	(17.18. 9.)	(17.18. 9.)
		Ralph Waiting	(0. 2.10.)	(0. 1. 9.)	(0. 1. 9.)
	Sinderby		20. 4.10.	20. 4.10.	20. 4.10.
		Edw. Meynell, Esq.	(1. 4. 41/2.)	(1. 2. 41/2.)	(1. 2. 41/2.)
Hang East	Aiskew		75.15. 8.	75.15. 8.	75.15. 8.[o]
		Mr Foss	(0.13. 4.)	(0.13. 4.)	(0.11. 6.)
		Thos Stapleton, Esq.	(10.12.11.)[k]	(10.12.11.)	(9.18. 7.)

Hang East		Mr Swailes	(0. 8. 9.)	--	--
	Bedale & Firby		156. 8. 3.	156. 8. 3.	156. 8. 3.
		Thos Stapleton, Esq.	(62.13. 4.)[l]	(58. 9. 11/4.)	(54.19. 7.)
	Catterick & Killerby		129. 6.11.	NT	129. 6.11.
		Strickland, Esq. (heirs)	(60.15. 0)	(61. 5. 0.)[y]	
		Sir John Lawson, Bt.	(26.12. 8.)	(26.12. 8.)	(69.10. 91/2.)[z]
		Wm Charlton, Esq.	(16. 7. 4.)[n]	(15.17. 4.)	(12.13. 51/2.)[q]
	Colburn		52.11.10.	52.11.10.	52.11.10.
		Philip Saltmarsh, Esq.	(19.18. 31/2.)[l]	(19. 6.111/4.)	(19. 7. 61/4.)
	Tunstall		38.19. 9.	38.19. 9.	38.19. 9.
		Sir John Lawson, Bt.	(3.17.101/4.)[l]	(3.17.101/4.)	(3.11. 61/2.)
Hang West	Leyburn[f]		48.10. 8.	48.10. 8.	48.10. 8.
		Ralph Riddle, Esq.	(8. 1. 01/2.)[l]	(5. 2. 71/2.)	(7. 7. 51/2.)
		John Blenkinsop Sr.	(0. 0. 31/2.)	(0. 0. 31/2.)	(0. 0. 3.)
		Wm Allen Sr.	(2. 5.10.)	(2. 5.10.)	(1.18. 5.)
		Mrs Mary Allen	(0. 2. 6.)	(0. 2. 6.)	(0. 2. 4.)
		Mr Sampson	(0. 8. 4.)[aa]	(0. 8. 4.)[aa]	(0.10. 5.)[aa]
	Thornton Steward		NR	36.11. 1.	36.11. 1.
		Simon Thos Scroop, Esq.		(13. 9.10)	(13.12. 8.1/4)
		Geo. Kirkley		(0. 3. 1.)	(0. 3. 1.)

Notes: Entries designated ''double assessed'' in the duplicate are underscored. NT means no total is entered at the bottom of the duplicate. NR means no duplicate has survived. A dash indicates the property is no longer listed. INC means the duplicate is incomplete. ''No prop.'' means no proprietor is listed.

[a]William Witham is proprietor for the entire township of Cliffe, which was his seat. Only the small tax entry assigned in the occupier column to ''himself'' is double assessed. All of his tenants appear to have normal assessments.

[b]William Hogget is proprietor of two properties in 1790. One is taxed at 18s. 6d. and is labelled as double assessed. A second small property (taxed at 6s. 9d.) purchased by Hogget within the year is not labelled as double assessed in 1790. In 1791 Hogget's 18s. 6d. property appears to have been absorbed into Maire's holdings. A double assessment label appears on Hogget's remaining 6s. 9d. property for the first time in 1792.

[c]His tenant is Anthony Langstaff (see Dalton and Kirkby Ravensworth). The Tunstall property was marked as double assessed in 1789, as were all other cases not underscored in 1790 (see Gatenby; Catterick and Killerby; Thornton Steward; Hutton Longvillers).

[d]A second property owned by Foss (taxed in 1790 at 15s. 91/2d. and included in this table) is not labelled as double assessed until 1792.

APPENDIX D.2 (continued) page 378

[e]George Kirkley is a co-proprietor with the Duke of Bolton. Bolton was not Roman Catholic, and his other properties in this and other townships were not double assessed. Joint ownership with Kirkley was in this case sufficient reason for him to incur the penalty. Kirkley's co-proprietorship is indicated on the 1790 duplicate, but on duplicates for subsequent years he appears as Bolton's tenant.

[f]Thomas Stapleton, Esq. (see Hang East) holds £1. 10s. 6d. in this township but is not entered as double assessed.

[g]Valuational rents are reported this year, along with tax assessed. The ratio of reported ''rent'' to tax on Maire's entry (17:1) is the same as that for all other non-Catholic properties. Therefore the ''rent'' must also be doubled.
No entries are labelled as doubled, however.

[h]In 1791 Pearson acquired a second property which now, for the first time, becomes double assessed. In 1793 both properties (one of which is tithe) are jointly owned by Pearson and Edward Constable, Esq., the latter having come into the Tunstall properties.

[i]This tax is on tithes. The glebe, in the hands of the vicar, is designated in an adjacent entry as ''single assessed'' in 1792.

[j]The entries for all other proprietors are explicitly designated as ''single assessed.''

[k]No alteration has occurred in the number of property bundles assigned to Stapleton in 1792. Only one less bundle (taxed in 1792 at 17s.) is assigned in 1793. One is added (taxed at 11s. 8d.) in 1794. The tax on non-Catholic properties generally rose in 1794.

[l]The tax on non-Catholic properties in this township tended to rise proportionately this year as double assessment ended on the Catholic property.

[m]Joseph Tate continues as occupier in 1794, but a different proprietor is now listed,and double assessment ends on this property bundle.

[n]The entire £7 reduction on Charlton's assessment in 1794 was added to the old Strickland double assessment. No other tax entries change this year.

[o]The 1798 duplicate is missing. A 1799 duplicate has been substituted.

[p]The 1798 duplicate is missing. A 1799 duplicate has been substituted. ''Rents'' are reported for all properties and indicate that double assessment has ended - provided one assumes the rents themselves are not doubled.

[q]Proprietor has deceased (indicated by executors, the ''late,'' etc.).

[r]The proprietor is now listed as William Constable, Esq.

[s]The proprietor is now listed as Edward Sheldon, Esq.

[t]The proprietor is now listed as Edward Constable, Esq.

[u]The proprietor is now listed as Francis Sheldon, Esq.

[v]Now joint proprietor with Edward Constable, Esq.

[w]Now joint proprietor with Francis Sheldon, Esq.

[x]No proprietor listed.

[y]The proprietor is now listed as Sir John Lawson.

[z]The Strickland and Lawson properties are now aggregated into a single entry under Lawson as proprietor.

[aa]The proprietor is now listed as Thomas Stapleton, Esq.

Source: Land tax duplicates, NYCRO.

APPENDIX E

Percentage increase in total rent at approximately five-year intervals, all townships, Gilling East wapentake, North Riding, 1785–1830

Township	1785 Total rent	c. 1790 Total rent	% Diff.	1795 Total rent	% Diff.	1801 Total rent	% Diff.	c. 1806 Total rent	% Diff.
Ainderby Steeple						955. 0. 0.		977. 0. 0.	2.3
Barton						2,186. 0. 0.		2,387.10. 0.	9.2
Brompton on Swale		1,622. 0. 0.		1,635. 0. 0.	0.8	1,903. 0. 0.	16.4	1,903. 0. 0.	0.0
Cleasby		796. 0. 0.		827. 0. 0.	3.9	839. 0. 0.	1.4	841. 0. 0.	0.2
Cowton, East		2,086. 0. 0.				2,426. 0. 0.	16.3	3,088. 0. 0.	27.3
Cowton, North		1,004. 0. 0.		1,030.10. 0.	2.6	1,049.10. 0.	1.8	1,158. 0. 0.	10.3
Cowton, South		1,251.10. 0.				1,253. 0. 0.	0.1	1,559. 0. 0.	24.4
Croft	2,474. 0. 0.					2,410. 0. 0.	-2.6	3,242. 0. 0.	34.5
Dalton upon Tees				976. 0. 0.		1,057. 0. 0.	8.3	1,554. 0. 0.	47.0
Danby Wiske						2,170.10. 0.		2,427. 0. 0.	11.8
Ellerton upon Swale, Bolton on Swale, and Whitwell		2,424. 7. 0.		2,876. 4. 0.	18.6	3,120. 8. 0.	8.5	3,603. 2. 0.	15.5
Eryholme						1,740. 0. 0.		1,928. 0. 0.	10.8
Kiplin		638.10. 0.		761.10. 0.	19.3	796.10. 0.	4.6	806.10. 0.	1.2
Kirby Wiske	868. 0. 0.	917. 0. 0.	5.6	922. 0. 0.	0.5	920. 0. 0.	-0.2	920. 0. 0.	0.0
Langton, Great						552. 0. 0.[b]		543. 0. 0.	-1.6
Langton, Little		674. 0. 0.		670. 0. 0.	-0.6	760. 0. 0.	13.4	760. 0. 0.	0.0
Manfield		1,992. 1. 6.				1,732.18. 0.	-13.0	2,232. 0. 0.	28.8
Maunby	1,105. 0. 0.	1,191. 0. 0.	7.8	1,210. 0. 0.	1.6	1,411.10. 0.	16.6	1,412.10. 0.	0.1
Middleton Tyas						3,317.10. 0.		3,667. 7. 3.	10.5
Morton on Swale						1,435. 0. 0.		1,435. 0. 0.	0.0
Moulton						1,904. 0. 0.		1,944. 0. 0.	2.1
Newby Wiske	578. 0. 0.	613. 0. 0.	6.0	623. 0. 0.	1.6	651.10. 0.	4.6	651.10. 0.	0.0
Newton Morrell						463. 0. 0.		681. 0. 0.	47.1
Scorton and Uckerby						2,628. 0. 0.		2,646. 0. 0.	0.7
Smeaton, Great	1,329. 0. 0.			1,397. 0. 0.	5.1	1,492. 0. 0.	6.8	1,525. 0. 0.	2.2
Stapleton						966.10. 0.		981.10. 0.	1.6
Thrintoft						1,053.10. 0.		1,179.10. 0.	12.0
Warlaby						1,005. 0. 0.		1,011. 0. 0.	0.6

APPENDIX E (continued) page 380

Township	1785 Total rent	c. 1790 Total rent	% Diff.	1795 Total rent	% Diff.	1801 Total rent	% Diff.	c. 1806 Total rent	% Diff.
Yafforth		1,051. 5. 0.		1,342. 0. 0.	27.6	1,382. 0. 0.	3.0	1,381. 0. 0.	-0.1
TOTAL[c]	6,354. 0. 0.	16,260.13. 6.	6.7	14,270. 4. 0.	8.8	43,580. 6. 0.	7.8	48,444. 9. 3.	11.2

Township	1810 Total rent	% Diff.	1815 Total rent	% Diff.	1820 Total rent	% Diff.	1826 Total rent	% Diff.	1830 Total rent	% Diff.	1801–1830 % Diff.
Ainderby Steeple	983. 0. 0.	0.6	972.10. 0.	-1.1			916. 0. 0.	-5.8	916.10. 0.	0.0	-4.0
Barton	2,683.10. 0.	12.4	2,884. 0. 0.	7.5			2,487.10. 0.	-13.7	2,214.18. 4.	-11.0	1.3
Brompton on Swale	1,883. 0. 0.	-1.0	1,898. 0. 0.	0.8	1,898. 0. 0.	0.0	1,809.10. 0.	-4.7	1,899.10. 0.	5.0	-0.2
Cleasby	841. 0. 0.	0.0	842. 0. 0.	0.1			862. 0. 0.	2.4	862. 0. 0.	0.0	2.7
Cowton, East	3,328. 0. 0.	7.8	3,752. 0. 0.	12.7			3,517. 0. 0.	-6.3	3,168. 0. 0.	-9.9	30.6
Cowton, North	1,191. 0. 0.	2.8	1,185.10. 0.	-0.5			1,248. 7. 0.	5.3	1,251.17. 0.	0.3	19.3
Cowton, South	1,559. 0. 0.	0.0	1,554. 0. 0.	-0.3			1,445.10. 0.	-7.0	1,446. 0. 0.	0.0	15.4
Croft	3,242. 0. 0.	0.0	3,234. 0. 0.	-0.2	3,164. 0. 0.	-2.2	3,658. 0. 0.	15.6	3,646. 0. 0.	-0.3	51.3
Dalton upon Tees	1,898. 0. 0.	22.1	1,892. 0. 0.	-0.3	1,679. 0. 0.	-11.2	1,497. 0. 0.	-10.8	1,507.11. 0.	0.7	42.6
Danby Wiske	2,427. 0. 0.	0.0	2,431. 0. 0.	0.2							
Ellerton upon Swale, Bolton on Swale, and Whitwell	3,949. 5. 0.	9.6	4,572. 3. 0.	15.8	4,641. 0. 0.	1.5	4,742.19. 0.	2.2	4,812. 6. 0.	1.5	54.2
Eryholme	1,927. 0. 0.	0.0	1,927. 0. 0.	0.0	1,927. 0. 0.	0.0	1,828. 0. 0.	-5.1	1,805. 0. 0.	-1.2	3.7
Kiplin	1,055.10. 0.	30.9	1,179.10. 0.	11.7	1,309.10. 0.	11.0	1,268.10. 0.	-3.1	1,298.10. 0.	2.4	63.0
Kirby Wiske	920. 0. 0.	0.0	920. 0. 0.	0.0			919.18. 0.[a]	0.0	920. 0. 0.[a]	0.0	0.0
Langton, Great	543. 0. 0.	0.0	537. 0. 0.	-1.1			675. 0. 0.[b]	25.7	648. 0. 0.[b]	-4.0	17.4
Langton, Little	760. 0. 0.	0.0	760. 0. 0.	0.0			1,005.10. 0.	32.3	1,005.10. 0.	0.0	32.3
Manfield	2,270. 0. 0.	1.7	2,279. 0. 0.	0.4			2,380.10. 0.	4.4	2,406.10. 0.	1.1	38.9
Maunby	1,412.10. 0.	0.0	1,412.10. 0.	0.0	1,412.10. 0.	0.0	1,412.10. 0.	0.0	1,412.10. 0.	0.0	0.1
Middleton Tyas	3,945. 5. 0.	7.6	3,914.15. 0.	-0.8			3,903. 0. 0.	-0.4	3,901. 5. 0.	0.0	17.6
Morton on Swale	1,422.10. 0.	-0.9	1,391.10. 0.	-2.2	1,392. 0. 0.	0.0	1,356. 0. 0.	-2.6	1,340. 0. 0.	-1.2	-6.6
Moulton	1,944. 0. 0.	0.0	2,057. 0. 0.	5.8							

Newby Wiske	719.10. 0.	10.4	719.10. 0.	0.0	725. 0. 0.	0.8	725. 0. 0.	0.0	726. 5. 0.	0.2	11.5
Newton Morrell	681. 0. 0.	0.0	1,080. 0. 0.	58.6							
Scorton and Uckerby	3,249.10. 0.	22.8	3,218.10. 0.	-1.0	3,223.10. 0.	0.2	3,214.10. 0.	-0.3	3,203. 0. 0.	-0.4	21.9
Smeaton, Great	1,525. 0. 0.	0.0	1,501. 0. 0.	-1.6							
Stapleton	981.10. 0.	0.0	981.10. 0.	0.0							
Thrintoft	1,179.10. 0.	0.0	1,179.10. 0.	0.0			1,288.10. 0.	9.2	1,288.10. 0.	0.0	22.3
Warlaby	1,011. 0. 0.	0.0	1,010. 0. 0.	-0.1			1,593.10. 0.	57.8	1,547.10. 0.	-2.9	54.0
Yafforth	1,381. 0. 0.	0.0	1,383. 0. 0.	0.1			1,376. 0. 0.	-0.5	1,382. 0. 0.	0.4	0.0
TOTAL[c]	50,912.10. 0.	5.1	52,668. 8. 0.[d]	3.4	21,371.10. 0.	-0.3	45,130. 4. 0.	0.6[e]	44,609. 2. 4.	-1.2	21.9

Notes: Properties whose rent was omitted in appendix K, because the matching tax entry was not present in the return, are here included in township and wapentake totals.

[a]16 entries for tithe failed to report rent this year. In 1815 these tithes amounted to £107. 2s. 0d. This amount has been added to the reported total rent in this table.

[b]One entry for tithe failed to report rent this year. In 1806, 1810, and 1815 these tithes amounted to £56. 0s. 0d. This amount has been added to the reported total rent in this table.

[c]The % difference in the total row includes only those townships reporting rent in both years defining a five-year interval. In township rows the % difference includes the value from the latest year previously reporting rent.

[d]The % difference for 1801-15 is 20.8.

[e]The % difference for all townships reporting in both 1815 and 1826 is 1.1.

Source: Land tax duplicates, Gilling East wapentake, NYCRO.

APPENDIX F

Changes in numbers of property bundles and percentage changes in total valuational rent at approximately five-year intervals for redeemed and unredeemed properties, all townships, Gilling East wapentake, North Riding, 1801–30

Township	1801–1806						1806–1810					
	Redeemed property bundles			Unredeemed property bundles			Redeemed property bundles			Unredeemed property bundles		
	1801 No.	1806 No.	Rent % change	1801 No.	1806 No.	Rent % change	1806 No.	1810 No.	Rent % change	1806 No.	1810 No.	Rent % change
Ainderby Steeple	10	14	24.2	21	22	-7.2	14	15	13.4	22	21	-6.8
Barton	8	8	15.2	35	40	6.9	8	15	10.0	40	45	13.4
Brompton on Swale	32	31	11.3	47	44	-11.0	31	32	-6.5	44	44	-7.2
Cleasby	2	2	0.0	14	15	0.2	2	2	0.0	15	15	0.0
Cowton, East	0	0	NA	32	44	27.3	0	0	NA	44	46	7.8
Cowton, North	24	24	1.5	22	22	15.1	24	22	9.4	22	19	-0.2
Cowton, South	4	4	25.2	13	14	24.1	4	4	0.0	14	14	0.0
Croft	0	0	NA	32	33	34.5	0	0	NA	33	34	0.0
Dalton upon Tees	2	2	28.0	11	10	50.0	2	2	0.5	10	19	25.0
Danby Wiske	9	9	15.4	32	33	10.8	9	9	0.0	33	36	0.0
Ellerton, etc.	0	1	NA	38	44	14.8	1	1	0.0	44	43	9.7
Eryholme	3	3	4.5	6	6	11.1	3	3	0.0	6	6	0.0
Kiplin	0	0	NA	8	8	1.2	0	0	NA	8	8	30.9
Kirby Wiske	6	9	115.2	32	28	-32.9	9	9	0.0	28	28	0.0
Langton, Great	4	4	0.0	8	9	-2.7	4	4	0.0	9	9	0.0
Langton, Little	2	2	0.0	5	5	0.0	2	2	0.0	5	5	0.0
Manfield	2	2	33.6	26	21	28.4	2	2	0.3	21	24	1.9
Maunby	7	15	511.4	40	28	-46.8	15	15	24.8	28	22	-26.2
Middleton Tyas	46	42	0.4	22	60	33.1	42	46	9.3	60	35	2.4
Morton on Swale	12	15	15.1	18	18	-24.5	15	18	0.0	18	26	-3.0
Moulton	3	4	68.8	15	15	-10.6	4	6	35.0	15	13	-12.6
Newby Wiske	2	2	0.0	25	26	0.0	2	9	892.8	26	19	-50.4
Newton Morrell	0	0	NA	2	2	47.1	0	0	NA	2	2	0.0
Scorton-Uckerby	22	22	2.8	32	33	-1.1	22	20	0.0	33	33	43.6
Smeaton, Great	7	9	56.6	17	15	-24.1	9	8	0.0	15	14	0.0
Stapleton	2	3	20.4	9	9	-7.9	3	3	0.0	9	9	0.0
Thrintoft	13	16	26.2	14	14	0.5	16	16	0.0	14	14	0.0
Warlaby	5	6	4.7	5	4	-0.6	6	6	0.0	4	4	0.0

Yafforth	5	6	6.2	19	24	-1.1	6	6	0.0	24	26	0.0
TOTAL	232		23.5			8.0			8.0			3.7

	1810-1815						1815-1820					
	Redeemed property bundles			Unredeemed property bundles			Redeemed property bundles			Unredeemed property bundles		
	1810	1815	Rent	1810	1815	Rent	1815	1820	Rent	1815	1820	Rent
Township	No.	No.	% change	No.	No.	% change	No.	No.	% change	No.	No.	% change
Ainderby Steeple	15	16	-2.8	21	23	0.2						
Barton	15	16	-3.9	45	39	10.9						
Brompton on Swale	32	33	-13.1	44	44	0.9	33	32	16.1	44	43	0.0
Cleasby	2	2	0.0	15	18	0.1						
Cowton, East	0	0	NA	46	46	12.7						
Cowton, North	22	21	0.5	19	17	-1.0						
Cowton, South	4	4	0.0	14	14	-0.4						
Croft	0	0	NA	34	38	-0.2	0	0	NA	38	41	-2.2
Dalton upon Tees	2	2	0.0	19	15	-0.4	2	2	1.1	15	10	-12.6
Danby Wiske	9	8	0.0	36	39	0.2						
Ellerton, etc.	1	2	950.2	43	43	10.5	2	2	-15.2	43	44	2.4
Eryholme	3	3	0.0	6	6	0.0	3	3	0.0	6	6	0.0
Kiplin	0	0	NA	8	8	11.7	0	0	NA	8	7	11.0
Kirby Wiske	9	9	8.4	28	28	0.0						
Langton, Great	4	4	31.0	9	6	-22.8						
Langton, Little	2	2	0.0	5	5	0.0						
Manfield	2	1	0.0	24	27	0.4						
Maunby	15	15	0.0	22	21	0.0	15	15	0.0	21	30	0.0
Middleton Tyas	46	45	-1.7	35	34	1.5						
Morton on Swale	18	18	0.0	26	24	-7.7	18	17	0.0	24	26	0.1
Moulton	6	9	8.3	13	13	4.4						
Newby Wiske	9	7	0.0	19	18	0.0	7	7	-0.1	18	20	2.0
Newton Morrell	0	0	NA	2	2	58.6						
Scorton-Uckerby	20	23	-0.1	33	32	-1.5	23	26	0.4	32	31	0.0
Smeaton, Great	8	7	0.0	14	14	-2.9						
Stapleton	3	3	0.0	9	10	0.0						
Thrintoft	16	15	0.0	14	16	0.0						
Warlaby	6	7	32.4	4	3	-10.6						

APPENDIX F (continued) page 384

Township	1810-1815 Redeemed property bundles 1810 No.	1815 No.	Rent % change	1810-1815 Unredeemed property bundles 1810 No.	1815 No.	Rent % change	1815-1820 Redeemed property bundles 1815 No.	1820 No.	Rent % change	1815-1820 Unredeemed property bundles 1815 No.	1820 No.	Rent % change
Yafforth	6	4	2.9	26	27	-0.3						
TOTAL			1.6			3.8			2.2			-0.3

Township	1815- or 1820-1826 Redeemed property bundles 1815 or 1820 No.	1826 No.	Rent % change	1815- or 1820-1826 Unredeemed property bundles 1815 or 1820 No.	1826 No.	Rent % change	1826-1830 Redeemed property bundles 1826 No.	1830 No.	Rent % change	1826-1830 Unredeemed property bundles 1826 No.	1830 No.	Rent % change
Ainderby Steeple	16	15	6.3	23	23	-14.1	15	15	0.0	23	25	0.1
Barton	16	13	-5.6	39	42	-25.4	13	19	1.3	42	44	-13.9
Brompton on Swale	32	32	-3.0	43	43	6.2	32	33	3.2	43	45	-5.7
Cleasby	2	2	0.0	18	14	2.4	2	2	0.0	14	15	0.0
Cowton, East	0	0	NA	46	53	-6.3	0	0	NA	53	56	-9.9
Cowton, North	21	23	11.7	17	19	1.9	23	23	0.8	19	25	0.0
Cowton, South	4	4	-17.3	14	17	-3.2	4	4	0.0	17	17	0.0
Croft	0	0	NA	41	46	15.6	0	0	NA	46	44	-0.3
Dalton upon Tees	2	4	-15.6	10	12	-10.2	4	3	-1.3	12	11	0.9
Danby Wiske	8	9	NA	39	43	-5.0	9	9	NA	43	46	-0.1
Ellerton, etc.	2	2	-8.2	44	46	2.6	2	3	8.9	46	48	1.2
Eryholme	3	3	-13.0	6	6	-4.7	3	3	0.0	6	7	-1.3
Kiplin	0	0	NA	7	7	-3.1	0	0	NA	7	7	2.4
Kirby Wiske	9	9	-14.3	28	30	-1.4	9	9	0.0	30	30	0.0
Langton, Great	4	9	113.9	6	3	-98.0	9	9	-4.9	3	3	60.0
Langton, Little	2	2	34.4	5	5	26.9	2	2	0.0	5	5	0.0
Manfield	1	1	-13.8	27	26	5.8	1	1	21.4	26	24	-0.2
Maunby	15	15	0.0	30	29	0.0	15	15	0.0	29	28	0.0

Middleton Tyas	45	69	-0.4	34	48	-1.0	69	74	0.1	48	47	-0.2
Morton on Swale	17	17	0.0	26	27	-9.7	17	17	0.0	27	30	-4.8
Moulton												
Newby Wiske	7	7	0.0	20	20	0.0	7	7	0.1	20	20	0.2
Newton Morrell												
Scorton-Uckerby	26	27	0.0	31	38	-8.6	27	27	0.0	38	38	-0.6
Smeaton, Great												
Stapleton												
Thrintoft	15	15	18.7	16	15	-0.2	15	15	0.0	15	15	0.0
Warlaby	7	7	84.2	3	2	45.1	7	6	-7.8	2	2	0.1
Yafforth	4	4	-28.9	27	15	-20.0	4	7	8.7	15	12	-0.4
TOTAL			-1.7[a]			1.1[b]			0.2			-1.8

Notes: This appendix is not fully comparable with appendices J and K. ''Splits'' reported in appendices J and K cannot normally be included in the % change computations for this table, though very large amounts have been assigned when sufficiently clear. Some distortion is unavoidable, however. The rents of ''omissions'' entries have been included. The number of entries is based on the number of ''rent'' entries where the latter is different from the number of tax entries. But such counts are subject to interpretation, and some distortion is thus again unavoidable. Error should not be sufficient to affect larger conclusions.

[a]The % change for 1815-26 is 5.9.

[b]The % change for 1815-26 is -2.8.

Source: Land tax duplicates, Gilling East wapentake, NYCRO.

APPENDIX G.1

Frequency distributions, ratios of valuational rent (as reported in the land tax) to tax for each property bundle, Gilling East townships reporting "rent", North Riding, 1795, c.1806, c. 1830

I. 1795

Township	Redeemed Ratio	Redeemed Total cases	Redeemed Rent ≤£10	Redeemed Rent ≥£100	Unredeemed Ratio	Unredeemed Total cases	Unredeemed Rent ≤£10	Unredeemed Rent ≥£100
Brompton on Swale					31.0	61	32	3
Cleasby					17.8	18	9	3
Dalton upon Tees					21.3	12	3	5
Ellerton etc.					31.0	4	3	
					31.1	3	3	
					31.2	18	1	12
					31.3	4	2	
					31.5	2		
					31.8	1		
					32.0	3	3	
					32.5	2	2	
					33.0	1	1	
Kiplin					18.4	6		4 (1)
					18.5	2	1	
Kirby Wiske					20.0	25	8	3 (1)
Maunby					16.5	3		1
					16.6	37	22	3
					16.8	2		
Newby Wiske					16.2	1		
					17.1	14	9	1
Scorton (excluding Uckerby)					49.6	1	1	
					50.3	2		
					50.5	43	14	6 (3)
					50.6	1		
Smeaton, Great					23.2	5	4	
					23.3	14		8 (1)
					23.4	4	4	
Yafforth					16.8	13	1	3
					16.9	1	1	
					17.1	2	2	

II. c. 1806

Township	Ratio	Redeemed Total cases	Redeemed Rent ≤£10	Redeemed Rent ≥£100	Ratio	Unredeemed Total cases	Unredeemed Rent ≤£10	Unredeemed Rent ≥£100
Ainderby Steeple	23.4	2			16.2	1		
	23.5	1	1		22.2	1		
	23.6	1	1		23.7	1		
	23.7	1			23.9	4		
	24.0	3	2		24.0	11	6	
	24.5	1			24.2	2		
	26.1	1	1		24.5	1	1	
	31.0	1			28.0	1	1	
Barton	32.0	1	1		34.3	40	24	4
	33.4	1		1				
	34.7	1						
	38.6	1						
	45.2	1						
	46.3	1		1				
	49.1	1						
	57.6	1						
Brompton on Swale	34.3	1			36.9	42	24	1
	35.5	2	1	1 (1)	37.0	2		
	35.6	13	4	1				
	35.8	1	1					
	36.0	1						
	36.8	1						
	36.9	11	2					
	42.2	1	1					
Cleasby	18.1	2	2		18.1	15	6	3
Cowton, East	NA				24.6	44	21	12 (1)
Cowton, North	22.8	1	1		30.0	22	8	1 (1)
	23.1	1	1					
	23.7	8	4					
	23.8	10	9					
	23.9	1	1					

APPENDIX G.1 (continued) page 388

	II. c. 1806							
		Redeemed				Unredeemed		
Township	Ratio	Total cases	Rent ≤£10	Rent ≥£100	Ratio	Total cases	Rent ≤£10	Rent ≥£100
Cowton, North continued								
	26.9	1						
	29.3	1	1					
	38.5	1	1					
Cowton, South	13.5	1			13.9	1		
	13.7	1		1	14.1	1	1	
	14.0	1		1	14.2	7		1
	14.5	1			14.3	5	1	3
Croft	NA				25.3	31	5	15 (1)
					25.4	1		1
					25.5	1		1
Dalton upon Tees	23.2	1		1	34.3	10	3	5 (1)
	30.1	1	1					
Danby Wiske	17.6	1	1		22.3	27	8	8
	19.6	1	1		22.4	6	6	
	20.3	1		1				
	20.6	1						
	22.6	1						
	23.5	1						
	25.4	1						
	25.7	1						
	28.0	1						
Ellerton, etc.	35.9	1			37.9	1		
					38.8	1		1
					38.9	1		
					39.1	16		11
					39.2	1		1
					39.5	1	1	
					39.9	2		
					40.0	20	17	
					40.1	1	1	

Eryholme	31.2	2			30.7	1		1
	46.8	1			31.2	1		1
					34.8	1		1
					39.0	2		2
					56.8	1		
Kiplin	NA				19.3	1	1	
					19.5	7		4 (1)
Kirby Wiske	20.0	8	1		20.0	24	14	1 (1)
					20.3	1	1	
					20.7	1	1	
					21.0	1	1	
Langton, Great	13.4	4			13.3	1	1	
					13.4	7	2	1
					14.9	1	1	
Langton, Little	27.1	1		1 (1)	24.0	1	1	
	27.2	1			27.2	2		1
					27.4	1	1	
					28.0	1		
Manfield	15.2	2	1	1	10.2	1	1	
					11.0	1		1
					15.1	1		1
					15.2	13	3	3
					15.3	1	1	
					15.4	1	1	
					15.8	1		1
					17.0	1		
					17.3	1		1
Maunby	17.3	1	1		19.6	12	4	2
	17.4	1						
	17.5	1						
	19.2	1						
	19.3	1		1 (1)				
	19.6	2		1				
Middleton Tyas	21.1	1		1	27.2	1		
	23.8	1			50.5	1	1	
	39.4	1		1	54.7	1		
	40.0	3	3		56.0	2	2	
	40.7	1	1		56.5	3	2	1
	40.8	2	2		56.6	1	1	

II. c. 1806

Township	Ratio	Redeemed Total cases	Redeemed Rent ≤£10	Redeemed Rent ≥£100	Ratio	Unredeemed Total cases	Unredeemed Rent ≤£10	Unredeemed Rent ≥£100
Middleton Tyas cont.	40.9	1			56.8	1	1	
	41.0	6	2		56.9	2		
	42.4	1	1		57.1	6	2	1
	42.7	2			57.2	2		1
	43.5	1		1	57.3	6	1	
	44.6	1			57.4	1		
	45.2	1		1 (1)	57.5	1		
	45.3	2			57.6	5	2	
	45.7	1		1	57.9	1		
	46.7	1		1	60.0	20	19	
	46.8	1			62.5	1	1	
	47.2	1		1	67.2	1	1	
	47.5	1			72.0	1	1	
	47.8	1			84.0	2	2	
	48.0	1		1	96.0	1	1	
	48.8	1						
	51.1	1	1					
	51.3	1		1				
	54.4	1		1				
	58.5	1		1 (1)				
	60.0	1	1					
	63.1	1		1 (1)				
	100.0	1		1				
	174.5	1						
Morton on Swale	21.1	1	1		22.1	1	1	
	22.7	3		3	22.5	3	3	
	22.8	10	4	2	22.6	2	2	
	26.2	1	1		22.7	2		
					22.8	8	5	2 (1)
					23.1	1	1	
					23.2	1	1	

Moulton	23.3	1		1 (1)	25.1	12		5 (1)
	24.5	2		1 (1)	25.2	3		
	24.9	1		1				
Newby Wiske	17.8	2			17.8	25	16	1
					18.4	1		
Newton Morrell	NA				33.5	2		2
Scorton and Uckerby	35.3	2		1	35.3	1		1
	52.6	2	2		52.6	7	6	
	52.9	3		1	52.9	3		
	53.0	13	6	3 (3)	53.0	12	2	4
	53.1	1			53.1	1		
	53.3	1	1		53.3	9	8	
Smeaton, Great	23.2	1		1	25.0	2	2	
	25.0	1	1		25.1	3		2 (1)
	25.1	3	1	1	25.2	4		
	25.2	2		1	25.3	4	4	
	27.6	1		1	25.9	1		
	30.7	1			26.3	1		1
Stapleton	17.0	1			18.5	3	3	
	18.1	1		1	18.6	4		2 (1)
	18.6	1			18.9	1		
					19.2	1	1	
Thrintoft	19.4	2	2		24.0	14	9	1
	19.6	1	1					
	19.7	2	1	1				
	19.8	5						
	20.0	5	5					
	24.0	1		1				
Warlaby	16.6	5			16.6	4		3 (1)
	16.7	1	1					
Yafforth	17.1	1			17.1	18	15	
	17.9	3	1	1 (1)	17.2	6		2

APPENDIX G.1 (continued) page 392

III. c. 1830

Township	Redeemed Ratio	Redeemed Total cases	Redeemed Rent ≤£10	Redeemed Rent ≥£100	Unredeemed Ratio	Unredeemed Total cases	Unredeemed Rent ≤£10	Unredeemed Rent ≥£100
Ainderby Steeple	23.4	1			21.3	22	11	
	23.9	2			21.4	1		
	24.0	10	7		24.0	1		
	24.2	1						
	24.7	1						
Barton	12.0	1	1		30.4	1	1	
	25.7	1	1		30.5	1	1	
	33.2	1			30.7	1	1	
	34.3	1	1		30.8	1	1	
	36.0	3	2		31.0	13	8	2
	36.9	1			31.1	4		1
	38.1	1			31.2	3		
	38.6	1		1	31.3	2	2	
	40.9	1			31.4	1	1	
	47.4	1			31.5	1	1	
	48.0	1	1		31.8	1	1	
	55.7	1			32.0	2	2	
	62.9	1	1		33.9	1	1	
	106.7	1	1		34.3	3	3	
					35.0	1	1	
					35.1	1	1	
					35.3	2	2	
					40.1	1	1	
					49.4	1	1	
Brompton on Swale	33.4	1			36.6	1	1	
	34.3	1			36.9	43	26	
	35.6	10	4		39.4	1		1
	35.8	2	1	1				
	36.0	1						
	36.6	1		1 (1)				
	36.9	12	5					

Brompton on Swale continued	37.9	1						
	40.0	2	2					
	42.2	1	1					
Cleasby	18.1	2	2		18.1	14	8	2 (1)
					19.4	1		1
Cowton, East	NA				24.8	3	3	
					25.1	4	4	
					25.2	1		
					25.3	46	28	12 (1)
					25.4	1		
					25.5	1	1	
Cowton, North	26.7	1	1		27.0	1	1	
	27.8	2	1		28.2	21	10	
	28.0	1	1		28.3	1		
	28.1	4	4		28.4	1		
	28.2	6	3		28.5	1	1	
	28.3	1	1					
	28.4	3						
	28.5	2	1					
	29.0	2	1	1 (1)				
	29.6	1	1					
Cowton, South	10.3	1		1	4.2	1	1	
	11.7	1			12.5	1		1 (1)
	12.0	1			13.7	10		3
	12.8	1		1	13.8	2	2	
					13.9	2	2	
					14.6	1		1
Croft	NA				28.2	41	7	14 (1)
					28.6	1		
					28.9	1		
					32.6	1		1
Dalton upon Tees	def.				34.3	10	2	5 (2)
					34.4	1		1
Danby Wiske	def.				21.4	1	1	
					21.5	1		
					21.6	27	6	5
					21.7	8	7	
					21.8	9	9	

APPENDIX G.1 (continued) page 394

Township	Ratio	Redeemed Total cases	Redeemed Rent ≤£10	Redeemed Rent ≥£100	Ratio	Unredeemed Total cases	Unredeemed Rent ≤£10	Unredeemed Rent ≥£100
				III. c. 1830				
Ellerton, etc.	53.3	1		1	48.0	2	2	
	88.5	1			49.4	1	1	
					49.6	1	1	
					50.0	1	1	
					50.3	1		
					50.4	10	9	
					50.5	7	1	4 (1)
					50.6	3		
					50.8	3		2
					50.9	3		3
					51.0	5		5 (1)
					51.4	3	3	
					52.1	4	4	
					52.2	2	2	
					53.3	1	1	
					59.1	1		1 (1)
Eryholme	27.3	2			30.9	1		1
	39.0	1	1		31.2	2		2
					34.8	1		1
					35.9	1		1
					38.9	1	1	
					42.9	1		
Kiplin	NA				31.0	1		
					31.3	2		2
					31.4	1		1 (1)
					31.5	2		2
					32.3	1	1	
Kirby Wiske	20.0	7	1		19.8	1	1	
					20.0	11	4	1 (1)
Langton, Great	10.8	1	1		13.4	2	2	
	11.8	1						

Langton, Great cont.	13.3	1	1	
	13.4	1		
	15.8	1		1
	16.0	1		
	17.4	1		
	18.2	1		1
	19.3	1		1 (1)
Langton, Little	27.2	1		
	36.8	1		1
Manfield	16.2	1		1
Maunby	17.3	1	1	
	17.4	1		
	17.5	1		
	19.2	1		
	19.3	1		1 (1)
	19.6	3		2 (1)
Middleton Tyas	30.5	1	1	
	30.8	1	1	
	33.6	2		
	34.3	1	1	
	36.4	1		1
	37.6	1	1	
	38.0	1		
	38.2	1		
	38.4	3	1	
	38.5	1		
	38.7	1	1	
	40.0	3	1	
	41.0	1	1	
	42.7	1		
	42.9	1		1
	44.6	1		1
	45.3	1		
	45.7	1	1	
	46.0	1	1	
	46.8	1		

24.0	1	1	
26.1	1		1
27.4	1	1	
28.0	1		
46.5	1		1 (1)
15.7	24	6	7 (2)
18.5	1	1	
19.0	1		
19.1	1		
19.6	23	16	1
20.0	1	1	
20.1	1		
59.2	2		
59.3	1		
59.4	2		1
59.5	3		1
59.6	1		
59.8	1		
60.0	24	21	

APPENDIX G.1 (continued) page 396

	III. c. 1830							
		Redeemed				Unredeemed		
Township	Ratio	Total cases	Rent ≤£10	Rent ≥£100	Ratio	Total cases	Rent ≤£10	Rent ≥£100
Middleton Tyas cont.	47.0	1	1					
	47.4	1		1				
	48.0	1	1					
	50.0	1		1				
	52.0	2		2				
	52.6	1		1				
	54.1	1		1				
	55.6	1	1					
	60.0	2	1					
	60.6	2		1 (1)				
	61.2	1		1				
	67.1	1		1				
	75.3	2	2					
	81.8	1						
	85.7	1	1					
	90.0	1						
	140.0	1	1					
	200.0	1	1					
Morton on Swale	21.2	2	2		17.4	22	16	1
	22.5	1	1		17.5	2	2	
	22.7	2		2	17.6	6	6	
	22.8	11	6	4				
	23.3	1	1					
Newby Wiske	14.0	1		1	19.2	1		
	17.8	3			22.0	1	1	
	18.3	1			23.3	5	4	
	18.5	1	1		23.4	11	7	
	24.5	1			24.0	1	1	
					26.9	1	1	
Scorton and Uckerby	35.3	2		1	35.3	1		1
	35.4	1	1		71.6	1		

Scorton and Uckerby continued								
	51.2	1	1		75.6	1		1
	51.9	1	1		78.3	1		
	52.6	1	1		79.9	1		1
	52.9	2		1 (1)	80.0	32	20	3
	53.0	7	1	2 (1)				
	53.1	4						
	53.3	6	6					
	53.9	1		1				
Thrintoft	22.8	2	2		24.0	15	10	2
	23.3	1	1					
	23.7	1	1					
	23.8	1						
	24.0	5	1	1				
	24.1	1						
	24.3	2	2					
	24.8	1		1				
	25.0	1	1					
Warlaby	26.8	2		1	24.0	2		2 (2)
	27.3	1		1 (1)				
	29.0	1						
	30.1	1		1				
	40.0	1						
Yafforth	17.1	4	3		17.0	1		
	17.9	1	1		17.1	7	3	1
	18.6	1		1 (1)	17.2	2		1
					17.4	1		1

Note: Figures in parentheses in the columns for properties with rents ≥£100 indicate the number of owner-occupiers included in the tabulation.
Source: Land tax duplicates, Gilling East wapentake, North Riding, NYCRO.

APPENDIX G.2

Size of holding and rent-to-tax ratios of each assessor to the land tax, all North Riding townships reporting valuational rent c. 1830

			Assessor as Proprietor			Assessor as tenant			
Wapentake	Township	Cases	Rent	%	Ratio	Rent	%	Ratio	% of his Proprietor
Allertonshire	Borrowby	a				5. 0. 0.	0.6	20.0	0.6
	Deighton	a				140. 0. 0.	13.6	16.2	90.9
		b				120. 0. 0.	11.6	12.3	90.9
	Dinsdale, Over	a				400. 0. 0.	47.4	21.3	47.4
		b				147. 0. 0.	17.4	21.6	35.0*
	Girsby	a				380. 0. 0.	31.2	25.0	31.2
	Hutton Bonville	a				150. 0. 0.	9.6	23.0	100.0
		b				68. 0. 0.	4.4	23.0	100.0
	Knayton & Brawith	a				66.13. 4.	6.9	12.0	34.6
								12.0	
		b	51. 0. 0.[a]	5.3	12.0				
					12.0				
	Osmotherley	a				17. 0. 0.	1.8	20.0	0.5
									1.6
		b				13. 0. 0.	1.5	20.0	1.5*
	Sessay and Hutton Sessay	a				55. 0. 0.	2.3	21.0	92.3
		b				44. 0. 0.	1.9	21.4	92.3
	Sigston	a				94.10. 0.	9.9	15.2	46.0
		b	67. 3. 8.	7.0	15.2	174. 7. 6.	18.2	15.2	46.0
					14.4				
	Thornton le Beans	a				51. 0. 0.	3.6	13.5	6.4
		b				80. 0. 0.	5.7	15.6	35.4*
	Thornton le Street	a				120. 0. 0.	10.2	20.0	61.5
		b				132. 0. 0.	11.3	20.0	19.8*
	West Rounton	a	39. 0. 0.	3.2	22.2	101. 0. 0.	8.4	22.8	20.3
					22.3			26.5	2.2
					21.8			22.3	2.2
		b				32. 0. 0.	2.7	23.9	20.8*
								21.0	

Wapentake	Township	Cases	Mean ratio of township: Redeemed	Mean ratio of township: Unredeemed	% difference from mean ratio: Proprietor	% difference from mean ratio: Tenant	Total % of control: Proprietors	Total % of control: Tenants
Allertonshire	Borrowby	a	19.7	20.0		0.0	0.6	0.6
	Deighton	a				5.2		
		b	15.4	35.7		-20.1	90.9	25.2
	Dinsdale, Over	a				-0.5		
		b	18.7	21.4		0.9	82.4	64.8
	Girsby	a	24.3	25.3		2.9	31.2	31.2
	Hutton Bonville	a				-6.5		
		b	NA	24.6		-6.5	100.0	14.0
	Knayton & Brawith	a				0.0		
						0.0		
		b			0.0			
			12.0	12.0	0.0		39.9	12.2
	Osmotherley	a				0.0		
		b	20.0	20.0		0.0	3.6	3.3
	Sessay and Hutton Sessay	a				-0.5		
		b	13.4	21.1		1.4	92.3	4.2
	Sigston	a				0.0		
		b			12.6	0.0		
			13.5	15.2	-5.3		53.0	35.1
	Thornton le Beans	a				0.0		
		b	13.5	14.1		10.6	41.8	9.3
	Thornton le Street	a				0.0		
		b	20.0	20.0		0.0	81.3	21.5
	West Rounton	a			0.0	2.7		
					0.4	14.2		
					-6.0	0.4		
		b				3.0		
			23.2	22.2		-5.4	48.7	14.3

APPENDIX G.2 (continued) page 400

			Assessor as Proprietor			Assessor as tenant			
Wapentake	Township	Cases	Rent	%	Ratio	Rent	%	Ratio	% of his Proprietor
Birdforth	Birdforth	a				100. 0. 0.	18.2	13.3	64.2
		b				112. 0. 0.	20.4	13.3	20.4*
	Boltby	a				61.19. 6.	3.7	24.6	def.
		b				40. 0. 0.	2.4	24.6	def.
	Cowsby	a				72. 0. 0.	12.2	22.6	90.0
		b				42. 0. 0.	7.1	22.6	90.0
	Coxwold	a				12. 0. 0.	0.9	26.7	100.0
		b				14.10. 0.	1.1	26.7	100.0
	Dalton	a	7. 3. 0.[a]	0.6	39.9	33. 0. 0.	3.0	40.0	13.4
								40.0	0.1
		b				81.10. 0.	7.5	40.0	49.0*
	Elmire & Crakehill	a				135. 0. 0.	12.5	44.7	90.0
		b				130. 0. 0.	12.0	43.9	90.0
	Kilburn, Low	a	18. 0. 0.[a]	1.3	18.0				
		b	23. 0. 0.[a]	1.7	18.2	5. 0. 0.	0.4	19.0	0.4
	Kilvington, South	a				def.			
		b				def.			
	Sand Hutton	a				NL			
		b				NL			
	Thirlby	a				5. 0. 0.	1.2	25.9	85.8
		b				30.10. 0.	7.2	26.0	85.8
	Thirsk	a	16.13. 4	0.3	80.0				
		b				6.13. 4.	0.1	80.0	0.2
Bulmer	Barton le Willows	a				39. 0. 0.	2.7	54.6	83.4
		b	16. 0. 0.	1.1	30.2	103. 0. 0.	7.2	56.4	83.4
								50.0	2.8*
	Brafferton	a				170. 0. 0.	21.6	17.2	70.2
		b				17. 0. 0.	2.2	17.2	70.2
	Brandsby & Stearsby	a				494. 0. 0.	17.1	20.8	91.0
		b				338. 0. 0.	11.7	20.8	91.0

Wapentake	Township	Cases	Mean ratio of township: Redeemed	Mean ratio of township: Unredeemed	% difference from mean ratio: Proprietor	% difference from mean ratio: Tenant	Total % of control: Proprietors	Total % of control: Tenants
Birdforth	Birdforth	a				0.0		
		b	13.3	13.3		0.0	84.6	38.6
	Boltby	a				0.0		
		b	NA	24.6		0.0		6.1
	Cowsby	a				3.2		
		b	NA	21.9		3.2	90.0	19.3
	Coxwold	a				-4.3		
		b	NA	27.9		-4.3	100.0	2.0
	Dalton	a			1.3	0.2		
						1.5		
		b	39.4	39.9		0.2	63.1	11.1
	Elmire & Crakehill	a				9.3		
		b	NA	40.9		7.3	90.0	24.5
	Kilburn, Low	a			-3.7			
		b	20.8	18.7	-2.7	1.6	3.4	3.4
	Kilvington, South	a						
		b	NA	23.8				
	Sand Hutton	a						
		b	43.4	33.4				
	Thirlby	a				0.0		
		b	NA	25.9		0.4	85.8	8.4
	Thirsk	a			3.0			
		b	79.6	77.7		3.0	0.5	0.4
Bulmer	Barton le Willows	a				-7.4		
		b			-48.8	-4.4		
			50.0	59.0		0.0	87.3	11.0
	Brafferton	a				0.0		
		b	17.2	18.8		0.0	70.2	23.8
	Brandsby & Stearsby	a				14.9		
		b	NA	18.1		14.9	91.0	28.8

APPENDIX G.2 (continued) page 402

			Assessor as Proprietor			Assessor as tenant			
Wapentake	Township	Cases	Rent	%	Ratio	Rent	%	Ratio	% of his Proprietor
Bulmer	Bulmer	a				118. 0. 0.	7.1	29.1	48.5
		b				145. 0. 0.	8.7	29.1	48.5
		.						75.0	0.9*
	Buttercrambe & Bossall	a				315. 0. 0.	12.6	35.8	56.2
		b				NL			
	Clifton	a	8. 0. 0.[a]	0.2	40.0				
		b				NL			
	Coneysthorpe	a				96. 0. 0.	6.1	53.3	58.3
		b				68. 0. 0.	4.3	53.3	58.3
	Cornbrough	a				NL			
		b	48. 0. 0.[a]	7.3	14.5				
	Crayke	a				def.			
		b				def.			
	Crambe	a				NL			
		b				168. 0. 0.	11.2	56.5	100.0
	Easingwold	a				def.			
						def.			
	Farlington	a				86. 0. 0.	13.4	8.6	60.4
		b				48. 0. 0.	7.5	8.6	60.4
	Flaxton on the Moor	a				55. 0. 0.	2.9	28.5	2.9
		b				70. 0. 0.	3.7	236.6	11.5*
	Foston	a				55. 5. 0.	4.3	32.0	57.8
		b				82. 0. 0.	6.4	31.8	23.2*
	Ganthorpe	a				205. 0. 0.	35.4	19.6	91.9
		b				112. 0. 0.	19.3	19.6	91.9
	Gate Helmsley	a	20.10. 0.[a]	9.6	11.6	8. 0. 0.	3.7	11.6	3.7
					24.6				
		b				2. 0. 0.	0.5	17.4	2.1*
	Harton	a				100. 0. 0.	5.6	32.8	100.0
		b				67. 0. 0.	3.7	32.8	100.0

Wapentake	Township	Cases	Mean ratio of township: Redeemed	Unredeemed	% difference from mean ratio: Proprietor	Tenant	Total % of control: Proprietors	Tenants
Bulmer	Bulmer	a				-14.9		
		b				-14.9		
			58.5	34.2		119.3	49.4	15.8
	Buttercrambe & Bossall	a				3.8		
		b	26.7	34.5				
	Clifton	a			0.5			
		b	39.8	39.9				
	Coneysthorpe	a				3.7		
		b	NA	51.4		3.7	58.3	10.4
	Cornbrough	a						
		b	12.9	14.3	1.4			
	Crayke	a						
		b	NA	13.2				
	Crambe	a						
		b	NA	56.3		0.4		
	Easingwold	a						
		b	NA	20.0				
	Farlington	a				0.0		
		b	8.2	8.6		0.0	60.4	20.9
	Flaxton on the Moor	a				-27.8		
		b	25.4	39.5		831.5	14.4	6.6
	Foston	a						
		b	def.	def.			81.0	10.7
	Ganthorpe	a				0.0		
		b	NA	19.6		0.0	91.9	54.7
	Gate Helmsley	a			-4.9 89.2	-10.8		
		b	12.2	13.0		42.6	15.4	13.8
	Harton	a				-0.3		
		b	NA	32.9		-0.3	100.0	9.3

APPENDIX G.2 (continued) page 404

			Assessor as Proprietor			Assessor as tenant			
Wapentake	Township	Cases	Rent	%	Ratio	Rent	%	Ratio	% of his Proprietor
Bulmer	Haxby	a				41.15. 0.	3.7	20.0	0.5
								20.2	3.4
								21.8	0.1
								20.0	1.4
		b				24.15. 0.	2.2	20.4	0.8*
								20.0	1.3*
								20.2	0.2*
								20.9	
	Helperby	a	def.[a]						
		b	def.[a]						
	Henderskelf	a				NL			
		b				NL			
	Heworth	a				200. 0. 0.	13.7	21.2	13.7
		b	80. 0. 0.[a]	5.5	20.8	31. 0. 0.	2.1	20.9	1.1*
								23.8	1.0*
	Holtby	a				56. 0. 0.	4.7	83.6	3.9
								28.9	0.8
		b	10. 0. 0.	0.8	def.	84. 0. 0.	7.1	def.	13.0*
	Huby	a				15. 0. 0.	0.3	109.1	0.3
		b				63. 0. 0.	1.2	def.	1.2*
	Huntington	a				34. 0. 0.	1.4	19.9	1.4
		b				NL			
	Huttons Ambo	a				50. 0. 0.	3.0	49.2	44.3
		b				62.11. 0	3.7	35.9	44.3
	Linton upon Ouse	a				126. 0. 0.	11.6	12.3	100.0
		b				122. 0. 0.	11.3	12.3	100.0
	Marton in the Forest	a				62. 0. 0.	def.	12.0	def.
		b	63. 0. 0.[a]	def.	12.0				

Wapentake	Township	Cases	Mean ratio of township: Redeemed	Mean ratio of township: Unredeemed	% difference from mean ratio: Proprietor	% difference from mean ratio: Tenant	Total % of control: Proprietors	Total % of control: Tenants
Bulmer	Haxby	a				22.7		
						23.9		
						8.4		
						0.5		
		b				25.2		
						22.7		
						0.5		
			16.3	20.1		4.0	7.7	5.9
	Helperby	a						
		b	NA	22.3				
	Henderskelf	a						
		b	NA	40.2				
	Heworth	a				-32.2		
		b			-1.4	-0.9		
			20.2	21.1		12.8	21.3	21.3
	Holtby	a						
		b	def.	def.			18.5	12.6
	Huby	a				61.2		
		b	67.0	67.7			1.5	1.5
	Huntington	a				9.3		
		b	18.2	20.3				
	Huttons Ambo	a				92.9		
		b	35.9	25.5		40.8	44.3	6.7
	Linton upon Ouse	a				0.0		
		b	NA	12.3		0.0	100.0	22.9
	Marton in the Forest	a				0.8		
		b	NA	11.9	0.8			

APPENDIX G.2 (continued) page 406

			Assessor as Proprietor			Assessor as tenant			
Wapentake	Township	Cases	Rent	%	Ratio	Rent	%	Ratio	% of his Proprietor
Bulmer	Murton	a				126. 0. 0.	12.3	def.	32.7
		b	15.10. 0.[a]	1.5	def.	67. 0. 0.	6.5	28.6	1.9*
								28.6	1.6*
								21.0	3.8*
	Newton upon Ouse	a	30. 7. 9.[a]	1.6	26.0	11. 6. 9.	0.6	25.9	87.4
		b				125.10. 0	6.8	25.9	87.4
	Osbaldwick	a				151.10. 0.	15.3	27.8	1.3
								27.8	9.2
								25.1	4.8
		b	11. 0. 0.[a]	1.1	27.8				
			6. 0. 0.	0.6	27.4				
					51.4				
	St. Olave in Marygate	a				NL			
		b	3. 0. 0.[a]	def.	20.0	2.10. 0.	def.	20.0	def.
	Shipton & Overton	a				102. 0. 0.	5.0	23.4	86.9
		b				179. 0. 0.	8.7	23.3	86.9
	Skelton	a				110. 0. 0.	def.	21.3	def.
		b				NL			
	Stillington	a	12.10. 0[a]	def.	25.3				
		b	1. 0. 0.	def.	25.3	4.10. 0.	def.	26.3	def.
	Stittenham	a				256.17. 6.	16.6	15.9	100.0
		b				93.15. 0.	6.1	18.8	100.0
	Stockton on the Forest	a				NL			
	Strensall	a				22. 10. 0.	1.5	20.0	2.7
									0.9
		b				17.10. 0.	1.1	20.0	3.5*
	Terrington	a				77. 0. 0.	2.2	39.0	41.7
		b				30. 0. 0.	0.8	40.9	0.8*
	Tholthorpe and Flawith	a				59. 0. 0.	9.2	22.6	9.2
		b				42. 0. 0.	6.6	37.8	6.6*

Wapentake	Township	Cases	Mean ratio of township Redeemed	Unredeemed	% difference from mean ratio Proprietor	Tenant	Total % of control Proprietors	Tenants
Bulmer	Murton	a						
		b				-8.9		
						4.0		
			27.5	31.4		-23.6	41.5	20.3
	Newton upon Ouse	a			0.4	0.0		
		b	def.	25.9		0.0	89.0	9.0
	Osbaldwick	a				0.7		
						0.7		
						-9.0		
		b			4.1			
					2.6			
			27.6	26.7	92.5		17.0	17.0
	St. Olave in Marygate	a						
		b	NA	20.0	0.0	0.0		
	Shipton & Overton	a				0.0		
		b	26.4	23.4		-0.4	86.9	13.7
	Skelton	a				-0.5		
		b	NA	21.4				
	Stillington	a				3.3		
		b	NA	24.5	3.3	7.3		
	Stittenham	a				-1.2		
		b	NA	16.1		16.8	100.0	22.7
	Stockton on the Forest	a	26.5	31.7				
	Strensall	a				2.0		
						2.0		
		b	17.5	19.6		2.0	7.1	2.6
	Terrington	a				2.9		
		b	29.8	37.9		37.2	42.5	3.0
	Tholthorpe and Flawith	a				-5.4		
		b	21.7	23.9		74.2	15.8	15.8

APPENDIX G.2 (continued) page 408

			Assessor as Proprietor			Assessor as tenant			
Wapentake	Township	Cases	Rent	%	Ratio	Rent	%	Ratio	% of his Proprietor
Bulmer	Thormanby	a				119.10. 0.	13.9	17.8	68.6
		b				28. 0. 0.	3.2	17.8	68.6
	Thornton le Clay	a	1.10. 0.[a]	0.1	60.0	68.11. 0.	6.2	30.3	24.8
		b	6. 0. 0.[a]	0.5	68.6	131.11. 0.	11.8	30.1	24.8
	Tollerton	a				def.			
		b				def.			
	Warthill	a	89. 0. 0.[a]	11.4	29.9	22. 0. 0.	2.8	16.6	2.8
		b				70. 0. 0.	9.0	50.0	9.0*
	Welburn	a	15. 0. 0.[a]	1.4	66.7				
		b				def.	def.	32.2	80.4
	Whitwell	a				128. 0. 0.	4.9	37.1	100.0
		b				162.10. 0.	6.2	36.9	100.0
	Wigginton	a				5. 0. 0.	0.4	35.3	0.7
		b	8. 0. 0.[a]	0.6	32.0	34. 0. 0.	2.5	30.8	16.0*
								40.0	
	Youlton	a				216. 0. 0.	26.2	24.9	26.4
		b				NL			
Gilling East	Ainderby Steeple	a				NL			
	Barton	a				58.10. 0.	2.6	def.	14.7
		b				NL			
	Brompton on Swale	a				50. 0. 0.	2.6	35.6	2.6
	Cleasby	a				253. 0. 0.	29.4	18.1	66.4
		b				NL			
	Cowton, East	a				218. 0. 0.	6.9	25.3	17.3
		b				175.10. 0.	5.6	25.3	26.8*
	Cowton, North	a				138.10. 0.	11.1	28.2	5.4
								28.3	12.5
	Cowton, South	a				110.10. 0.	7.6	10.3	14.8
	Croft	a				250. 0. 0.	6.8	28.2	48.8

Wapentake	Township	Cases	Mean ratio of township Redeemed	Mean ratio of township Unredeemed	% difference from mean ratio Proprietor	% difference from mean ratio Tenant	Total % of control Proprietors	Total % of control Tenants
Bulmer	Thormanby	a				0.0		
		b	16.7	17.8		0.0	68.6	17.1
	Thornton le Clay	a						
		b	NA	NA			24.8	18.0
	Tollerton	a						
		b	NA	25.0				
	Warthill	a			-14.8	-52.7		
		b	35.1	42.9		42.4	23.2	23.2
	Welburn	a			85.8			
		b	51.1	35.9		-10.3	81.8	
	Whitwell	a				2.2		
		b	NA	36.3		1.6	100.0	11.1
	Wigginton	a				13.5		
		b			2.9	-1.0		
			30.5	31.1		28.6	17.3	3.5
	Youlton	a				-9.8		
		b	22.5	27.6				
Gilling East	Ainderby Steeple	a	24.0	21.5				
	Barton	a						
		b	38.8	27.7				
	Brompton on Swale	a	36.6	35.6		-2.7	2.6	2.6
	Cleasby	a				-2.7		
		b	18.1	18.6				
	Cowton, East	a				0.0		
		b	NA	25.3		0.0	44.1	12.5
	Cowton, North	a				0.0		
			28.4	28.2		0.4	17.9	11.1
	Cowton, South	a	11.5	13.6		-10.4	14.8	7.6
	Croft	a	NA	28.4		-0.7	48.8	6.8

APPENDIX G.2 (continued) page 410

Wapentake	Township	Cases	Assessor as Proprietor: Rent	Assessor as Proprietor: %	Assessor as Proprietor: Ratio	Assessor as tenant: Rent	Assessor as tenant: %	Assessor as tenant: Ratio	Assessor as tenant: % of his Proprietor
Gilling East	Dalton upon Tees	a	7. 0. 0.[a]	0.5	34.3	14. 0. 0.	0.9	25.4	9.7
		b				132. 0. 0.	8.8	34.3	28.1*
	Danby Wiske	a	17.10. 0.[a]	def.	21.5	87.10. 0.	def.	21.6	def.
		b				198. 5. 0.	def.	21.6	def.*
	Ellerton etc.	a				393. 0. 0.	8.2	51.0	77.3
		b				580. 0. 0.	12.0	50.5	77.3
	Eryholme	a				522. 0. 0.	28.9	30.9	62.9
	Kiplin	a				335. 0. 0.	25.8	31.5	96.1
		b				360. 0. 0.	27.7	31.5	96.1
	Kirby Wiske	a				def.			
	Langton, Great	a				52. 0. 0.	8.8	17.4	8.8
	Langton, Little	a				NL			
		b				NL			
	Manfield	a				170. 0. 0.	7.1	16.2	7.1
	Maunby	a				247. 0. 0.	17.5	19.6	31.8
								19.6	7.4
	Middleton Tyas	a	2. 0. 0.[a]	0.0	def.	370. 0. 0.	9.5	54.1	68.3
								40.0	13.1
								61.2	
								59.5	
								88.7	
	Morton on Swale	a				155.10. 0.	11.6	22.8	65.0
	Newby Wiske	a				306. 0. 0.	42.1	24.5	62.6
								23.4	10.2
								19.2	17.0
	Scorton and Uckerby	a	2. 0. 0.[a]	0.1	80.0				
			5. 0. 0.	0.2	80.0				
		b	20. 0. 0.	0.6	53.0	327. 0. 0.	10.2	35.3	10.2
	Thrintoft	a				206.10. 0.	16.1	24.0	39.2
	Warlaby	a				126. 0. 0.	8.1	26.8	8.1
	Yafforth	a				465. 0. 0.	33.6	17.1	33.6

Wapentake	Township	Cases	Mean ratio of township Redeemed	Mean ratio of township Unredeemed	% difference from mean ratio Proprietor	% difference from mean ratio Tenant	Total % of control Proprietors	Total % of control Tenants
Gilling East	Dalton upon Tees	a			0.9	0.0		
		b	25.4	34.0		0.9	37.8	9.7
	Danby Wiske	a			-8.9	-8.5		
		b	NA	23.6		-8.5		
	Ellerton etc.	a				0.2		
		b	80.4	50.9		-0.8	77.3	20.2
	Eryholme	a	28.4	32.6		-5.2	62.9	28.9
	Kiplin	a				0.3		
		b	NA	31.4		0.3	96.1	53.5
	Kirby Wiske	a	20.0	20.0				
	Langton, Great	a	16.4	13.4		6.1	8.8	8.8
	Langton, Little	a						
		b	36.5	34.5				
	Manfield	a	16.2	15.7		0.0	7.1	7.1
	Maunby	a				1.6		
			19.3	19.5		0.5	39.2	17.5
	Middleton Tyas	a				7.3		
						-20.6		
						21.4		
						-0.2		
			50.4	59.6		48.8	81.4	9.5
	Morton on Swale	a	22.8	17.4		0.0	65.0	11.6
	Newby Wiske	a				36.9		
						0.0		
			17.9	23.4		-17.9	89.8	42.1
	Scorton and Uckerby	a				16.3		
						16.3		
		b	46.4	68.8	14.2	-23.9	11.1	11.1
	Thrintoft	a	24.2	24.0		0.0	39.2	16.1
	Warlaby	a	28.1	24.0		-4.6	8.1	8.1
	Yafforth	a	18.4	17.2		-0.6	33.6	33.6

APPENDIX G.2 (continued) page 412

Wapentake	Township	Cases	Assessor as Proprietor: Rent	%	Ratio	Assessor as tenant: Rent	%	Ratio	% of his Proprietor
Gilling West	Aldbrough	a				244. 0. 0.	10.3	36.9	79.7
		b				480. 0. 0.	20.3	def.	79.7
	Barningham	a				101. 0. 0.	7.1	17.8	49.6
		b				5.10. 0.	0.4	17.8	49.6
									0.1*
	Cliffe	a				NL			
	Cotherstone	a				NL			
		b	30. 0. 0.[a]	1.4	27.4				
	Eppleby	a				184. 0. 0.	16.0	23.9	37.4
		b				NL			
	Gailes	a				NL			
	Hunderthwaite	a				29. 0. 0.	2.5	28.2	0.3
								31.9	2.2
		b	20.10. 0.	1.8	30.8				
	Hutton Longvillers	a				111. 0. 0.	10.1	18.1	98.1
	Kirkby Ravensworth	a	2. 0. 0.[a]	0.5	53.3				
	Lartington	a				66. 0. 0.	2.9	18.8	93.0
		b				56. 0. 0.	2.5	18.8	93.0
								18.8	0.4*
	Lunedale	a	108.10. 0.[a]	6.4	43.4				
					62.5				
					33.2				
	Marrick	a				14. 0. 0.	def.	40.0	def.
									def.
		b				6. 0. 0.	def.	40.0	def.
	Melsonby	a				def.			
	Ravensworth and Whashton	a	6. 0. 0.[a]	0.3	36.9	4. 0. 0.	0.2	16.0	0.2
		b				100. 0. 0.	4.9	45.1	def.*
	Scargill	a				153.10. 0.	11.2	12.3	100.0
	Skeeby	a				226. 0. 0.	29.7	26.7	61.0
								23.1	7.1
		b				133. 0. 0.	17.5	28.0	17.5*

Wapentake	Township	Cases	Mean ratio of township: Redeemed	Mean ratio of township: Unredeemed	% difference from mean ratio: Proprietor	% difference from mean ratio: Tenant	Total % of control: Proprietors	Total % of control: Tenants
Gilling West	Aldbrough	a						
		b	def.	def.			79.7	30.6
	Barningham	a				4.1		
		b				4.1		
			23.9	17.1			49.7	7.5
	Cliffe	a	NA	13.9				
	Cotherstone	a						
		b	26.7	26.6	2.6			
	Eppleby	a				2.6		
		b	23.3	24.3				
	Gailes	a	22.8	24.0				
	Hunderthwaite	a				-1.4		
						-8.8		
		b	35.0	28.6	-12.0		4.3	4.3
	Hutton Longvillers	a	NA	18.1		0.0	98.1	10.1
	Kirkby Ravensworth	a	51.8	51.0	4.5		0.5	0.5
	Lartington	a				-48.4		
		b				-48.4		
			36.4	18.8		0.0	93.4	5.4
	Lunedale	a			-1.4			
					42.0			
			44.0	44.5	-25.4		6.4	6.4
	Marrick	a				0.0		
		b	NA	40.0		0.0		
	Melsonby	a	36.3	45.9				
	Ravensworth and Whashton	a			-6.1	-59.3		
		b	39.3	36.2		14.8		5.4
	Scargill	a	NA	12.4		-0.8	100.0	11.2
	Skeeby	a				6.0		
						-8.3		
		b	28.0	25.2		0.0	85.6	47.2

			Assessor as Proprietor			Assessor as tenant			
Wapentake	Township	Cases	Rent	%	Ratio	Rent	%	Ratio	% of his Proprietor
Gilling West	Stanwick, St. John	a				227. 0. 0.	20.0	16.6	53.2
		b				NL			
	Startforth	a	3. 0. 0.[a]	0.2	55.4				
		b	2. 0. 0.	0.1	29.5	40. 0. 0.	3.0	40.0	22.4
Hallikeld	Ainderby Quernhow	a	181.10. 0.[a]	24.2	39.3				
		b	227.10. 0.[a]	30.4	35.9				
	Burneston	a				NL			
		b	96.10. 0.[a]	8.0	24.0	306. 0. 0.	25.4	24.0	29.4
					24.0				
	Dishforth	a				NL			
		b				6. 0. 0.	0.7	17.1	0.7
	Exelby etc.	a	4.18.10.[a]	0.4	12.8	19.10.10.	1.5	12.6	1.2
								12.7	0.5
		b				71. 0. 8.	5.5	10.1	45.2*
								11.5	
								12.6	
	Kirklington	a				195. 0. 0.	9.9	60.0	69.7
									10.1
		b				192. 0. 0.	9.8	60.0	69.7
	Melmerby	a	132. 0. 0.[a]	10.8	48.0	193. 0. 0.	15.8	57.1	12.5
								48.0	11.6
		b	193. 0. 0.[a]	15.8	48.0	28. 0. 0.	2.3	48.0	11.6
			1. 0. 0.	0.1	48.0				
	Theakston	a				423. 5. 0.	83.8	21.1	89.0
		b				NL			
	Wath	a				14. 0. 0.	1.3	40.0	78.2
		b				107. 0. 0.	10.2	40.0	78.2
									21.8*

			Mean ratio of township		% difference from mean ratio		Total % of control	
Wapentake	Township	Cases	Redeemed	Unredeemed	Proprietor	Tenant	Proprietors	Tenants
Gilling West	Stanwick, St. John	a				-2.4		
		b	NA	17.0				
	Startforth	a			36.4			
		b	27.3	40.6	-27.3	-1.5	22.7	3.3
Hallikeld	Ainderby Quernhow	a			0.2			
		b	39.2	33.8	6.2		54.6	54.6
	Burneston	a						
		b			0.0	0.0		
			24.0	24.0	0.0		37.4	33.4
	Dishforth	a						
		b	17.0	17.1		0.6		
	Exelby etc.	a			0.8	-0.8		
			11.9	12.7		0.0		
		b				-15.1		
						-3.4		
			11.9	12.7		-0.8	47.3	7.4
	Kirklington	a				4.0		
		b	60.5	57.7		4.0	79.8	19.7
	Melmerby	a			0.0	0.2		
						0.0		
		b			0.0	0.0		
			57.0	48.0	0.0		50.8	44.8
	Theakston	a				-0.9		
		b	19.5	21.3				
	Wath	a				0.0		
		b				0.0		
			NA	40.0			100.0	11.5

APPENDIX G.2 (continued) page 416

Wapentake	Township	Cases	Assessor as Proprietor: Rent	%	Ratio	Assessor as tenant: Rent	%	Ratio	% of his Proprietor
Hang East	Aiskew	a				9. 0. 0.	def.	24.0	def.
									def.
		b	2. 0. 0.[a]	def.	24.0				
			1. 0. 0.	def.	24.0				
	Appleton, East and West	a				88. 0. 0.	4.4	33.8	68.3
	Bedale	a				109. 0. 0.	def.	30.0	def.
		b				17. 0. 0.	def.	30.0	def.*
	Colburn	a				136. 0. 0.	10.2	25.3	59.4
		b				12. 0. 0.	0.9	25.3	59.4
	Hipswell	a				229. 0. 0.	def.	34.3	def.
		b				40. 0. 0.	def.	34.3	def.*
	Kirkby Fleetham	a				NL			
		b	22.10. 0.[a]	5.9	54.2	14. 0. 0.	3.6	54.2	3.6
	Newton le Willows	a	9.10. 0.[a]	0.5	30.0	31.13. 0.	1.5	30.0	0.4
								20.9	0.2
								23.7	0.5
								30.1	0.4
		b				76.10. 0.	3.7	30.0	54.3*
	Scruton	a				22. 0. 0.	def.	def.	def.
		b				43.10. 0.	def.	def.	def.*
	Snape	a				67. 0. 0.	3.5	31.2	98.3
		b				87. 0. 0.	4.6	30.7	98.3
	Well	a				7. 0. 0.	1.1	20.0	78.0
		b				111. 0. 0.	17.2	20.0	78.0
Hang West	Bellerby	a	5. 0. 0.[a]	0.4	40.0				
		b				42. 0. 0.	3.3	39.4	30.3
	Ellerton and Stainton	a				40.10. 0.	3.3	37.1	59.8
		b				115. 0. 0.	9.5	31.1	40.2*
	Finghall	a				270. 0. 0.	11.5	50.5	89.0

Wapentake	Township	Cases	Mean ratio of township: Redeemed	Mean ratio of township: Unredeemed	% difference from mean ratio: Proprietor	% difference from mean ratio: Tenant	Total % of control: Proprietors	Total % of control: Tenants
Hang East	Aiskew	a				0.0		
		b			0.0			
			NA	24.0	0.0			
	Appleton, East and West	a	39.0	50.4		-13.3	68.3	4.4
	Bedale	a				-0.3		
		b	NA	30.1		-0.3		
	Colburn	a				0.4		
		b	NA	25.2		0.4	59.4	11.1
	Hipswell	a				0.0		
		b	NA	34.3		0.0		
	Kirkby Fleetham	a						
		b	NA	20.7	161.8	161.8	9.5	9.5
	Newton le Willows	a			0.0	0.0		
						-13.3		
						-1.6		
						0.3		
		b	24.1	30.0		0.0	56.3	5.7
	Scruton	a						
		b	def.	23.4				
	Snape	a				4.3		
		b	42.0	29.9		2.7	98.3	8.1
	Well	a				0.0		
		b	20.0	20.0		0.0	78.0	18.3
Hang West	Bellerby	a			2.8			
		b	39.7	38.9		1.3	30.7	3.7
	Ellerton and Stainton	a				-10.2		
		b	NA	41.3		-24.7	100.0	12.8
	Finghall	a	NA	50.5		0.0	89.0	11.5

APPENDIX G.2 (continued) page 418

Wapentake	Township	Cases	Assessor as Proprietor: Rent	%	Ratio	Assessor as tenant: Rent	%	Ratio	% of his Proprietor
Hang West	Hudswell	a	def.						
		b				183.12. 5.	def.	55.2	def.
								53.4	def.
	Thornton Rust	a				40. 0. 0.	4.8	40.0	1.0
									22.2
		b	24. 0. 0.[a]	2.9	def.				
	Witton, East (within)	a				def.			
	Witton, East (without)	a				213. 0. 0.	def.	49.0	def.
		b				260. 0. 0.	def.	52.0	def.
Langbaurgh	Acklam, West	a				90. 0. 0.	10.4	32.6	98.4
		b				79. 0. 0.	9.2	32.5	98.4
	Appleton Wiske	a				62. 0. 0.	4.3	18.2	4.3
		b				58. 0. 0.	4.0	18.5	8.8*
	Arncliffe, Ingleby	a				NL			
		b				14. 5. 0.	1.6	7.1	41.9
	Barnby, East	a				NL			
		b				20.16. 0.	1.1	<u>51.5</u>	1.1
	Battersby	a				164. 0. 0.	31.4	<u>19.4</u>	97.8
		b				81. 0. 0.	15.5	<u>20.0</u>	97.8
	Borrowby	a				50. 0. 0.	14.4	<u>15.2</u>	14.4
		b				46. 0. 0.	13.3	<u>56.3</u>	26.3*
	Broughton, Great	a	3. 0. 0.[a]	0.1	24.0				
		b	146. 0. 0.[a]	5.6	<u>39.2</u>				
	Castle Leavington	a				180. 0. 0.	15.0	22.1	42.1
		b				180. 0. 0.	15.0	<u>22.1</u>	15.0*
	Crathorne	a				164. 0. 0.	8.8	def.	93.5
	Danby	a				36. 0. 0.	0.7	<u>40.8</u>	1.3
		b				76. 0. 0.	1.6	<u>112.8</u>	2.5*
	Easby	a				93. 0. 0.	11.4	24.9	13.9

Wapentake	Township	Cases	Mean ratio of township Redeemed	Mean ratio of township Unredeemed	% difference from mean ratio Proprietor	% difference from mean ratio Tenant	Total % of control Proprietors	Total % of control Tenants
Hang West	Hudswell	a						
		b				3.8		
			NA	53.2		0.4		
	Thornton Rust	a				-3.4		
		b	40.2	41.4			26.1	7.7
	Witton, East (within)	a	NA	52.7				
	Witton, East (without)	a				-1.8		
		b	NA	49.9		4.2		
Langbaurgh	Acklam, West	a				-12.6		
		b	NA	37.3		-12.9	98.4	19.6
	Appleton Wiske	a				4.6		
		b	18.0	17.4		6.3	8.3	13.1
	Arncliffe, Ingleby	a						
		b	15.1	17.7		-59.9		
	Barnby, East	a						
		b	52.6	67.0		-2.1		
	Battersby	a				-1.5		
		b	19.7	21.4		1.5	97.8	46.9
	Borrowby	a				-38.2		
		b	24.6	20.0		128.9	40.7	27.7
	Broughton, Great	a			-43.7			
		b	31.6	42.6	24.0		5.7	5.7
	Castle Leavington	a				3.8		
		b	22.1	21.3		0.0	57.1	30.0
	Crathorne	a	NA	14.2			93.5	8.8
	Danby	a				-37.9		
		b	65.7	61.8		71.7	3.8	2.3
	Easby	a	17.9	20.4		22.0	13.9	11.4

APPENDIX G.2 (continued) page 420

			Assessor as Proprietor			Assessor as tenant			
Wapentake	Township	Cases	Rent	%	Ratio	Rent	%	Ratio	% of his Proprietor
Langbaurgh	Egton	a				def.	def.	def.	51.7
						60. 0. 0.	1.3	24.9	1.3*
	Greenhow	a				82. 0. 0.	6.1	25.9	98.8
		b				77. 0. 0.	5.7	41.8	98.8
	Hemlington	a				80. 0. 0.	10.2	31.3	10.2
		b				NL			
	Hilton	a				244. 0. 0.	18.8	26.2	100.0
		b				235. 0. 0.	18.1	29.6	100.0
	Hutton	a				5.10. 0.	0.2	41.9	0.2
		b				NL			
	Ingleby Barwick	a				NL			
		b				112. 0. 0.	13.8	25.8	13.8
	Ingleby Greenhow	a				96. 0. 0.	9.4	49.2	91.1
		b				239. 0. 0.	23.3	28.9	91.1
								39.6	
	Kildale	a				256. 0. 0.	17.5	33.1	
		b				NL			
	Kirkleatham	a				NL			
		b				97. 0. 0.	3.5	32.2	95.0
	Linthorpe	a				318. 0. 0.	16.5	44.5	19.3
		b				245. 0. 0.	12.6	45.1	65.0*
	Lofthouse	a				NL			
		b	8. 0. 0.	0.2	256.0				
	Maltby	a	65. 0. 0.	6.7	29.0				
		b				130. 0. 0.	13.4	21.6	13.8
	Middleton upon Leven	a				126. 0. 0.	def.	19.8	def.
								24.4	def.
		b				40. 0. 0.	def.	24.2	def.*
	Newby	a				124. 0. 0.	14.2	22.8	41.5
	Newton Mulgrave	a				40. 0. 0.	3.6	64.0	3.6
		b				NL			

Wapentake	Township	Cases	Mean ratio of township: Redeemed	Mean ratio of township: Unredeemed	% difference from mean ratio: Proprietor	% difference from mean ratio: Tenant	Total % of control: Proprietors	Total % of control: Tenants
Langbaurgh	Egton	a						
			26.5	20.2		-6.0	53.0	
	Greenhow	a				-20.3		
		b	32.5	NA		28.6	98.8	11.8
	Hemlington	a				-6.8		
		b	33.6	21.3				
	Hilton	a				-1.1		
		b	NA	26.5		11.7	100.0	36.9
	Hutton	a				-0.5		
		b	41.9	42.1				
	Ingleby Barwick	a						
		b	27.0	35.8		-27.9		
	Ingleby Greenhow	a				40.6		
		b				-17.4		
			35.0	29.5		13.1	91.1	32.7
	Kildale	a				-0.3		
		b	NA	33.2				
	Kirkleatham	a						
		b	37.6	30.9		4.2		
	Linthorpe	a				9.3		
		b	21.8	40.7		10.8	84.3	29.1
	Lofthouse	a						
		b	63.6	23.0	302.5			
	Maltby	a			12.0			
		b	25.3	25.9		-16.6	20.5	20.1
	Middleton upon Leven	a						
						0.0		
		b	NA	24.4				
	Newby	a	24.0	21.3		-5.0	41.5	14.2
	Newton Mulgrave	a				65.4		
		b	38.7	46.5				

APPENDIX G.2 (continued) page 422

			Assessor as Proprietor			Assessor as tenant			
Wapentake	Township	Cases	Rent	%	Ratio	Rent	%	Ratio	% of his Proprietor
Langbaurgh	Normanby	a				200. 0. 0.	def.	32.7	def.
		b				194. 0. 0.	def.	32.7	def.
	Nunthorpe	a				123. 0. 0.	def.	25.3	def.
		b	def.[a]			117. 0. 0.	def.	25.3	def.
	Ormesby	a				NL			
		b				417. 0. 0.	def.	53.5	def.
	Picton	a				120. 0. 0.	22.4	25.8	22.4
		b				70. 0. 0.	13.1	25.5	13.1*
	Potto	a				155. 0. 0.	10.5	19.1	6.2
								21.5	5.2
									49.0
		b	3. 0. 0.[a]	0.2	19.1	240. 0. 0.	16.3	21.5	4.1*
									49.0
	Recar	a	2. 0. 0.	def.	21.3				
			4. 0. 0.[a]	def.	53.3				
		b				NL			
	Ugthorpe	a				60. 0. 0.	4.8	26.6	4.8
		b				def.		47.3	6.8*
								def.	def.*
	Whorlton	a				68. 0. 0.	1.9	30.0	76.2
		b				110. 0. 0.	3.0	30.0	76.2
	Worsall, Low	a				135. 0. 0.	10.3	30.2	10.3
		b				NL			
	Yarm	a				0.10. 0.	0.0	21.8	23.5
		b				8. 0. 0.	0.3	43.6	0.3*
Pickering Lythe	Allerston	a				90. 0. 0.	def.	21.8	def.
		b	def.[a]						
	Burniston	a				52. 0. 0.	4.4	70.5	4.4
		b				NL			

Wapentake	Township	Cases	Mean ratio of township: Redeemed	Mean ratio of township: Unredeemed	% difference from mean ratio: Proprietor	% difference from mean ratio: Tenant	Total % of control: Proprietors	Total % of control: Tenants
Langbaurgh	Normanby	a				0.0		
		b	32.7	NA		0.0		
	Nunthorpe	a				0.4		
		b	NA	25.2		0.4		
	Ormesby	a						
		b	NA	53.5		0.0		
	Picton	a				0.0		
		b	25.8	25.8		-1.2	35.5	35.5
	Potto	a				0.0		
						0.0		
		b			0.0	0.0		
			19.1	21.5			64.7	27.0
	Recar	a			-13.1			
					117.6			
		b	NA	24.5				
	Ugthorpe	a				-12.5		
		b				55.6		
			30.4	28.0				
	Whorlton	a				-0.3		
		b	27.8	30.1		-0.3	76.2	4.9
	Worsall, Low	a				28.5		
		b	23.5	31.0				
	Yarm	a				-19.0		
		b	28.0	26.9		62.1	23.8	0.3
Pickering Lythe	Allerston	a				0.0		
		b	NA	21.8				
	Burniston	a				39.3		
		b	50.6	def.				

APPENDIX G.2 (continued) page 424

			Assessor as Proprietor			Assessor as tenant			
Wapentake	Township	Cases	Rent	%	Ratio	Rent	%	Ratio	% of his Proprietor
Pickering									
Lythe	Cayton, etc.	a				120. 0. 0.	4.5	22.5	5.0
		b	5. 0. 0.[a]	0.2	33.3	96. 0. 0.	3.6	28.9	6.4*
	Cloughton	a	59. 0. 0.[a]	2.7	80.9				
					71.4				
					99.3				
		b				142. 0. 0.	6.5	def.	6.5
	Cropton	a				NL			
		b				20. 0. 0.	1.8	50.0	2.8
	Habton, Great								
	and Little	a				52. 0. 0.	4.0	175.8	6.9
		b				115. 0. 0.	8.9	27.8	23.3*
	Hartoft Dale	a				31. 0. 0.	7.2	65.3	7.2
		b				24. 0. 0.	5.6	46.3	5.6*
	Hutton Bushel	a				112. 2. 6.	5.4	56.3	5.4
								60.0.	
		b				34. 7. 6.	1.6	60.0	66.3*
	Lebberston and								
	Gristhorpe	a				54. 0. 0.	def.	def.	def.
								21.5	def.
		b				48. 0. 0.	def.	30.3	def.*
	Levisham	a				def.			31.0
		b				79. 0. 0.	14.5	def.	22.4*
	Newton	a	12.10. 0.	2.4	48.8				
			def.[a]						
			0.10. 0.[a]	0.1	34.3				
		b	3. 0. 0.	0.6	55.4	14. 0. 0.	2.7	66.2	2.7
								27.4	
	Rosedale East Side	a				115. 0. 0.	7.2	83.2	100.0
								41.2	
		b				77.10. 0.	4.8	46.9	100.0

Wapentake	Township	Cases	Mean ratio of township Redeemed	Unredeemed	% difference from mean ratio Proprietor	Tenant	Total % of control Proprietors	Tenants
Pickering Lythe	Cayton, etc.	a				-8.2		
		b	31.8	24.5	4.7	-9.1	11.6	8.3
	Cloughton	a			-4.5 -15.7 17.2			
		b	84.7	def.			9.2	9.2
	Cropton	a						
		b	25.8	41.7		19.9		
	Habton, Great and Little	a				251.6		
		b	50.0	30.6		-9.2	30.2	12.9
	Hartoft Dale	a				19.6		
		b	52.8	54.6		-15.2	12.8	12.8
	Hutton Bushel	a				-6.6 -0.5		
		b	60.3	59.2		-0.5	71.7	7.0
	Lebberston and Gristhorpe	a						
		b	def.	31.1		-30.9 -2.6		
	Levisham	a						
		b	27.1	def.			53.4	23.5
	Newton	a				-7.6 -42.8		
		b	52.8	60.0	-7.7	25.4 -54.3	5.8	5.8
	Rosedale East Side	a				82.4 -9.6		
		b	def.	45.6		2.8	100.0	12.0

APPENDIX G.2 (continued) page 426

Wapentake	Township	Cases	Assessor as Proprietor: Rent	%	Ratio	Assessor as tenant: Rent	%	Ratio	% of his Proprietor
Pickering Lythe	Snainton	a				NL			
		b	5. 0. 0.[a]	0.1	48.0				
	Staintondale	a	16. 0. 0.[a]	1.6	45.7	100. 0. 0.	9.7	39.4	def.
		b	112. 0. 0.[a]	10.9	55.6				
			def.[a]						
			112. 0. 0.	10.9	23.0				
					39.4				
	Wilton	a				NL			
		b				120. 0. 0.	6.3	21.9	96.6
	Wrelton	a				NL			
		b				4. 0. 0.	0.4	83.4	0.4
Ryedale	Brawby	a				def.			
	Cawton	a				NL			
	Malton, New (St. Leonard's)	a				def.			
	Malton, New (St. Michael's)	a				def.			
	Malton, Old	a	21. 0. 0.[a]	0.3	90.0	90. 0. 0.	1.2	def.	79.6
		b	5. 0. 0.[a]	0.1	66.7	70. 0. 0.	0.9	80.0	79.6
	Rosedale West Side	a	18. 0. 0.[a]	2.9	30.0	18. 0. 0.	2.9	30.0	2.9
		b	28. 0. 0.[a]	4.6	35.0				
	Wath	a				def.			100.0
	Wombleton	a				47. 0. 0.	5.4	38.5	5.4

No. of townships = 198

No. of assessors = 357

No. of NL = 45

No. of def. for rent = 26

Wapentake	Township	Cases	Mean ratio of township: Redeemed	Mean ratio of township: Unredeemed	% difference from mean ratio: Proprietor	% difference from mean ratio: Tenant	Total % of control: Proprietors	Total % of control: Tenants
Pickering Lythe	Snainton	a						
		b	48.6	35.2	-1.2			
	Staintondale	a			45.5	0.0		
		b			77.1			
					-26.8			
			31.4	39.4	0.0			
	Wilton	a						
		b	43.8	41.5		-50.0		
	Wrelton	a						
		b	58.1	52.4		59.2		
Ryedale	Brawby	a	41.7	39.6				
	Cawton	a	5.0	5.0				
	Malton, New (St. Leonard's)	a	4.8	5.1				
	Malton, New (St. Michael's)	a	5.0	5.0				
	Malton, Old	a						
		b	def.	def.			80.0	2.5
	Rosedale West Side	a			-2.9	-13.5		
		b	34.7	30.9	0.9		10.4	10.4
	Wath	a	NA	5.0			100.0	
	Wombleton	a	34.6	46.8		11.3	5.4	5.4

Notes: A superscript ''a'' for rent designates an owner-occupier. Underscored ratios are for redeemed values. The cases column indicates the row in which values begin for each separate assessor (some townships having more than one assessor). ''% of his proprietor'' entries are asterisked when the proprietor of the second assessor is not the same person as the proprietor of the first assessor. ''Rent'' has been aggregated for each assessor, but when an assessor holds more than one property bundle within the township, each unique ratio which occurs on his holdings is reported.

NA = not applicable.

NL = name of assessor is not listed among assessed entries (although other persons with that surname may in some cases be listed).

def. = defective.

Source: Land tax duplicates c. 1830, North Riding, NYCRO.

APPENDIX H

Average actual rents and local poundage rates for the land tax and poor rate, Eden survey of 1795–96, England and Wales

County / Parish	Average rent: Type of land[a]	Average rent: Rent of land	Average rent: Rent of houses	Land tax: Poundage rate	Land tax: Rent to tax ratio[b]	Poor rate: Poundage rate c. 1795[c]	Bases[d]
Bedfordshire							
Dunstable	pasture	£3		3s.	6.7	4s.	on three-quarters of the the real rental (P.R.)
Houghton Regis	arable	14s.		2s. 8d.	7.5	2s. 6d.	as nearly on the full rental as possible (P.R.)
Humbershoe		15s.		2s. 3½d.	8.7	9s. 6d.	on the net rental (L.T.); on the full rental (P.R.)
Leighton Buzzard	open	10s.					
	enclosed						
	meadow	30s.			7.6*	4s.	
Berkshire							
Pangbourne						3s. 6d.	
Reading, St Mary		30–40s.		2s.	10.0	houses 3s.6d. land 5s.2d.	
Streatley						3s.	
Wallingford, St Mary				1s.10½d.	7.0	7s.	
Wallingford, St Leonard				1s.10½d.	7.0	5s.	
Windsor, New					11.1*	2s. 6d.	a low valued rental (P.R.)
Buckinghamshire							
Buckingham				2s. 6d.	8.0	7s.	on the real rental (L.T.); nominal rental = £3,996.12s.6d.; real rental = c. £5,000.
Maids Moreton	arable	18–20s.		2s.	10.0	3s.9d.	on the net rental (P.R.)
Stony Stratford				3s. 7d.	5.6	6s. 6d.	on the net rental (P.R.)
Winslow	enclosed grassland	£1. 1s. to £2.15s.		7s. 6d.	2.7	6s.	houses on two-thirds of real rent and lands on full value (P.R.)

Cheshire						
Chester (various wards)	near city	£1.10s. to £4; ave. £1.18s.	varies by ward 8d. to 2s. 6d.	30.0 to 8.0	2s. ave.	
High Walton	dairy	20-35s.	1s. 2d.	17.1	2s. 6d.	an old and low valuation (P.R)
Mickle Trafford	dairy	25s.			1s. 6d.	on ''about two-thirds and a little more, of the real rental'' (P.R.)
Cornwall						
Kenwyn					12s. 6d.	on new mining (P.R.)
Cumberland						
Ainstable		18s.			10¾d.	on the full rental (P.R.)
Alston					2s.10d.*	
Bromfield parish	cultivated	£1.			6s. 9d. ''per poll''	which is ''probably about nine pence in the pound'' except Blencogo where ''it seems not to exceed six-pence'' (P.R.)
Caldbeck parish		15s.	3½d.	68.6		on the full rental (L.T.)
Carlisle, St Mary's Quarter			1½d.	160.0	1s. 2d.	on the full rental (L.T., P.R.)
Carlisle, Caldewgate Quarter		£1-£5				
Carlisle, Cumersdale Quarter		15s.	1½d.	160.0	9¾d.	
Carlisle, Rickergate Quarter		£1-£5	0¾d.	320.0	2s. 3d.	
Castle Carrock		18s.	5d.	48.0	10¼d.*	on full and fair rental (L.T., P.R.)
Croglin	open	9s. 6d.				
	enclosed	15-16s.	4½d.	53.3	3¾d.*	on the fair rental (L.T., P.R.)
Cumrew parish		14s.			4d.*	on the full rental (P.R.)
Cumwhitton parish		18s.	3½d.	68.6	4d.*	''by the old purvey'' (L.T., P.R.)

County Parish	Average rent: Type of land[a]	Rent of land	Rent of houses	Land tax: Poundage rate	Rent to tax ratio[b]	Poor rate: Poundage rate c. 1795[c]	Bases[d]
Cumberland							
Gilcrux		6-21s.; ave. 14s.		3¾d.	64.0	9¾d.*	on the full rental (P.R.)
Harrington		5-25s.; ave.13-14s.		2½d.	96.0	1s. 4d.*	on the full rental (L.T., P.R.)
Hesket parish	dairy grass	30-40s.		2½d.	96.0	6½d.*	on the full rental (L.T., P.R.)
Kirkoswald				2¼d.	106.7	9¾d.*	on the full rental (L.T., P.R.)
Sebergham parish		14s.		2¼d.	106.7		
Staffield				2¾d.	87.3	4d.*	on the full rental (L.T., P.R.)
Warwick parish		19-20s.		3d.	80.0		on full and fair rental (L.T.)
Wetheral parish		5-50s.; ave. 14s.		2d.	120.0	6½d.*	on the full rental (L.T.); on the full and fair rental (P.R.)
Workington parish						6d.*	on the fair rental (P.R.)
Derbyshire							
Chesterfield	not built on	£3-£4.10s.				2s.	on the net rental (P.R.)
Derby, St Alkmund		£2.10s.-£4.10s.; ave. £3.				land 2s.3d.; houses 1s.6d.	on the net rental (P.R.)
Derby, All Saints		£2.10s.-£4.10s. ave. £3.				2s.1d.	
Derby, St Michael		£2.10s.-£4.10s.; ave. £3				2s.6d.	on the net rental (P.R.)
Derby, St Peter's		£2.10s.-£4.10s.; ave. £3.				land 3s.; houses 1s.6d.	on the net rental (P.R.)
Derby, St Werburgh		£2.10s.-£4.10s.; ave. £3.				3s.6d.	on the nominal rental (P.R.)

Devonshire						
Wirksworth	mostly grass	£1.1s.-£3.; ave. £2.			land 3s.7d. houses 2s.3d	on the net rental (P.R.)
Clyst St George		40s. incl. all rates, taxes, repairs	2s.	10.0		on the net rental (L.T.)
Dorset						
Blandford parish	arable	£1.10s.	1s. 4d.	15.0	land 4s.5d. houses 3s.4d.	nearly at full rental (P.R.)
Durweston		10s.	2s.	10.0	5s.10d.	
Wimborne Minster					3s.	
Durham						
Durham, St Margaret		10-40s.				
Gateshead					3s.	on the full rental (P.R.)
Holy Island parish	on coast	£1.10s.		coast 4.4* island 35.1*		
Monkwearmouth parish		10s.-£4.				
South Shields Chapelry					11s.	on only one-quarter of the rental (P.R.)
Stanhope parish		15-45s.			1s. 4d.	
Sunderland parish				155.8*	5s.	on the net rental (P.R.); shipping contributes by tonnage (P.R.)
Tanfield		10-50s.			2s.	on the assessed rental (P.R.)
Essex						
Colchester, All Saints	not built on	£1. 2s.	4s. 2d.	4.8	5s.	on the net rental (L.T.); on the nominal rental (P.R.)
Colchester, St James		£2.10s.	4s. 2d.	4.8	9s. 6d.	on the nominal rental (P.R.)
Colchester, St Mary Magdalen		£1.	5s. 6d. or 6s.	3.6 or 3.3	16s.	on nearly the net rental (L.T.); on the nominal rental (P.R.)

APPENDIX H (continued) page 432

County Parish	Average rent: Type of land[a]	Average rent: Rent of land	Average rent: Rent of houses	Land tax: Poundage rate	Land tax: Rent to tax ratio[b]	Poor rate: Poundage rate c. 1795[c]	Bases[d]
Gloucestershire							
Bristol, out-parishes only		£3.-£5.		6d.	40.0	3s. 3d.	on the rack rental (P.R.)
Rodmarton				1s. 4d.	15.0		
Stapleton	pasture 2 mi. from Bristol	£2-£3.		2s.	10.0		
Hampshire							
Gosport						land 4s.6d. houses 3s.	
Hawkley		8-20s.; ave. 12s.		3s.	6.7		on the net rental (L.T.)
Isle of Wight (3 unnamed parishes)						2s. 1s. 3d. 3s. 3d.	on the rack rental (P.R.) on two-thirds of the rent (P.R.)
Newton Valence		5-20s.; ave. 9s.		2s. 6d.	8.0	7s.	on the net rental (L.T.); on the rack rental (P.R.)
Petersfield		£1-£3.		3s. 4d.	6.0	6s.	on the rack rental (P.R.)
Portsea		£1-£3.10s.					
Portsmouth						3s. 6d.	seldom at full rental
Southampton					49.2*	4s.	on three-quarters of the net rental (P.R.)
Herefordshire							
Hereford (all 6 parishes)		£2-£4.		6d.-2s.; ave. 1s.	40.0-10.0 ave. 20.0		
Hereford, All Saints						4s.	on nearly the full rental (P.R.)
Hereford, St Nicholas						2s.	on nearly the full rental (P.R.)

Hertfordshire							
Chipping Barnet				3s. 4d.	6.0	2s.-2s.6d.*	
Redbourn	meadow	£3.		9½d.	25.3	2s. 6d.	as near the net rent as can be ascertained
	arable	15s.					
	ave.	£1.					
St Albans (all 3 parishes)		50s.		3s. 8d.	5.4		on the net rental (L.T.)
St Albans (1 parish)						5s.	at nine-tenths of their real rent, except rebuilt houses which are under-assessed (P.R.)
St Albans (2 parishes)						2s.6d. or 3s.	
Kent							
Ashford				5s. 8d.	3.5	3s.	on the half rental (L.T.)
Chalk		10-15s.		2s. 3d.	8.9	2s.	on the net rental (L.T.)
Chart, Great	arable	8-10s.				3s. 6d.	on the full rental (P.R.)
	pasture	16s.-£1.					
Chart, Little						6s.	on the nominal rental (P.R.)
Cobham	corn land	5s.-£1. 1s.		2s. 9d.	7.3	4s.	on the net rental (L.T.)
Hothfield		16s.			8.4*	2s. 6d.	
Meopham		5-30s.		3s. 6d.	5.7	3s.	
Westwell						4s.*	
20 Weald parishes						ave. 4s.6d.	on the nominal rental (P.R.)
Lancashire							
Bury		15-90s.; ave. 32s.		1¼d.	192.0	3s.	on the net rental (L.T.); said to be at half rental (P.R.)
Lancaster	grass	£2-£6.		1½d.	160.0	3s. 4d.	on the net rental (L.T.); at half rental on land and two-thirds on houses (P.R.)
Liverpool		£4-£6.		6d.	40.0	2s.	on the net rental (L.T.)
Manchester		£4.	2 small rooms £4-£6.	1½d.	160.0	3s.	on the net rental (L.T.); plus personalty (P.R.)

APPENDIX H (continued) page 434

County / Parish	Average rent: Type of land[a]	Average rent: Rent of land	Average rent: Rent of houses	Land tax: Poundage rate	Land tax: Rent to tax ratio[b]	Poor rate: Poundage rate c. 1795[c]	Bases[d]
Lancashire							
Preston	grass	£2-£4.		2 3/4d.	87.3	5s.	on the nominal rental, which is half the real rent on houses and two-thirds the real rent on land (P.R.)
Leicestershire							
Ashby-de-la-Zouch		20-30s.		1s. 6d.	13.3	2s. 9d.	8 years ago fixed at three-quarters the net rental, but today probably one-half the net rental [due to increasing land values] (P.R.)
Carlton Curlieu	grass	£1. 1s.				1s. 4 1/2d.	
Kibworth Beauchamp	grass	25s.			11.6*	4s.	set at full rent on 1780 enclosure, but c. four-fifths now at net rent (P.R.)
Kibworth Harcourt					19.4*	2s. 6d.	
Leicester, St Martin				10d.	24.0	5s. 5d.	houses are usually assessed at about two-thirds of the net rental (P.R.)
Smeeton Westerby					10.1*	6s.	
Lincolnshire							
Alford		15-30s.; ave. 20s.			9.7*	2s. 4d.	
Cockerington (North or South?)		5-25s.; ave. 16s.		1s. 6d.	13.3	1s. 8d.	on the full rental (P.R.)

Lincoln (all parishes)			9d.-2s.	26.7-10.0	2s.-4s.6d.	on the net rental (P.R.)
Louth		10s.-£3.	1s. 3d.	16.0	1s. 9d.	
Spilsby		24s.			2s. 8d.	
Swineshead	fens	20-21s.			1s. 3d.	on the rack or net rental (P.R.)
Tattershall				6.4*	3s.10d.	on the net rental (P.R.)
Willoughby	sheep pasture	9-10s.			2s.	
Middlesex						
Ealing		£2-£4.; ave. £3.			4s.	
Hampton					2s.	
St Martin's in the Fields					3s.	
Monmouthshire						
Abergavenny		10s.-£3.10s.			6s.	''it is probable that on an average, land is not assessed at more than one third of its real value'' (P.R.)
Monmouth	near town	£3-£4.10s.	1s. 2d.	17.1	5s.	
	at a distance	£1				
Norfolk						
Downham					2s. 6d.	
Gressenhall and 50 incorporated parishes of 2 hundreds			2d.-6s.; ave. 1s.	120.0-3.3; ave. 20.0	6d.-3s.; ave. 1s.8d.	
Hilgay					6s.	
Norwich	near town	sometimes £5.		5.4*	18s. 6d.	on half the rack rental and on stock (P.R.)
	farmland	£1.				
Yarmouth			3s. 8d.	5.4		
Northamptonshire						
Brixworth		27s.	1s. 1d.	18.5	2s.	on the net rental (L.T.); on the nominal rental (P.R.)
Kettering					10s. 8d.	on the net rental (P.R.)

APPENDIX H (continued) page 436

County Parish	Average rent: Type of land[a]	Average rent: Rent of land	Average rent: Rent of houses	Land tax: Poundage rate	Land tax: Rent to tax ratio[b]	Poor rate: Poundage rate c. 1795[c]	Bases[d]
Northamptonshire							
Northampton, ward A				1s. 6d.	13.3		on a very old valuation, now averaging about three-quarters of net rental (L.T.)
Northampton, ward B				2s.10½d.	7.0		on a very old valuation, now averaging about three-quarters of net rental (L.T.)
Northampton, ward C				1s.10d.	10.9		on a very old valuation, now averaging about three-quarters of net rental (L.T.)
Northampton, ward D				1s.	20.0		on a very old valuation, now averaging about three-quarters of net rental (L.T.)
Northampton, All Saints ward				2s. 2½d.	9.0	7s. 6d.	
Northampton, St Giles ward		40s.				6s. 2d.	said to be on three-quarters of the rack rental, but probably on only two-thirds of the net rental (P.R.)
Roade		ave. 10s.6d.-12s.; Duke of Grafton 8s.		1s.11d.	10.4	3s. 6d.	on the full rental (P.R.)
Yardley Gobion		18-20s.		2s. 5½d.	8.1	4s.	at nearly full rental (P.R.)
Northumberland							
Carrycoats						9s.	

Newcastle (all 4 parishes)	15s.-£3.	''very low''			
Newcastle, All Saints				6s.	on about four-fifths of the net rental (P.R.)
Newcastle, St Andrew				3s. 6d.	
Newcastle, St John				3s. 3d.	not levied on the full rental (P.R.)
Newcastle, St Nicholas				4s. 4d.	on four-fifths of the net rental (P.R.)
North Shields	£2-£3.			6s.	on two-thirds of the net rental (P.R.)
Tynemouth				3s.	
[name forgotton by reporter]				1s.	
Nottinghamshire					
Hoveringham	15-40s.; ave. 25s.		21.6*	9 1/4d.	on the net rental (P.R.)
Newark	15s.-£6.; ave. £2. 2s.			land 2s.6d. houses 1s.6d.	on the net rental (P.R.)
Nottingham, St Mary	£3.			land 12s. houses 4s.4d.	the houses at half and the land at about seven-eighths the net rental (P.R.)
[farming parishes between Newark and Overingham]				6d.-9d.	
Oxfordshire					
Banbury		1s. 1d.	18.5	19s.	on the nominal rental, which is one-third the rack rental (P.R.)
Deddington				open fields 6s. 6d.	nearly on the full rental (P.R.)
[parishes between Deddington & Oxford]				enclosed 1s.3d.-3s.6d.	
Oxford [11 incorporated parishes]		5s.-6s.	4.0-3.3		
Oxford, St Clement		2s. 5d.	8.3	4s. 8d.	

County Parish	Average rent: Type of land[a]	Average rent: Rent of land	Average rent: Rent of houses	Land tax: Poundage rate	Land tax: Rent to tax ratio[b]	Poor rate: Poundage rate c. 1795[c]	Bases[d]
Rutland							
Empingham		12s.				5s.	
North Luffenham						1s.11d.	
Shropshire							
Bishop's Castle, borough and out hamlet		12s.-£4; ave. 26s.					
Bishop's Castle, borough				1s.	20.0	1s. 2d.	on the net rental (L.T.); as nearly on the full rental as can be ascertained (P.R.)
Bishop's Castle, out hamlet				11d.	21.8	1s. 2d.	on the net rental (L.T.); at full rental (P.R.)
Ellesmere (and 3 neighbouring incorporated parishes)		£1.10s.				4s. 6d.	on one-third of the rack rental (P.R.)
Shrewsbury (6 parishes)	10 miles distance	£1-£2.; ave. £1.5s. or £1.8s. on large farms				2s.	on the rack rental (P.R.)
Somerset							
Frome	grass near town	£3.				land 5s. houses 2s.6d.	on the present rent (P.R.)
	grass at a distance	£1-£2.					
	arable	14-18s.					
Minehead		£1-£3.		1s.10d.	10.9	3d.	on the net rental (P.R.)
Walcot parish		50-60s.		under 1d.	over 240.0	2s.	on the net rental (P.R.)
Staffordshire							
Clifton Campville						1s. 3d.	

Lichfield (all 3 parishes)	distant	ave. 30s.				
	near city	£3-£4.				
Lichfield, St Chad						on the nominal rental, which is half the rack rental (P.R.)
Lichfield, St Mary					4s. 8d.	on the nominal rental (P.R.)
Lichfield, St Michael					1s. 8d.	on the nominal rental, which is half the rack rental (P.R.)
Wolverhampton		£3.			1s. 8d.	on the net rental (P.R.)
Suffolk						
Blything hundred (46 incorporated parishes)		16s.			10d.-3s.	
Loes and Wilford hundreds		16s.			1-2s.	on the net rental (P.R.)
Oulton					1s. 4d.	on the rack rental (P.R.)
Surrey						
Epsom	farm	£1.	2s. 1d.	9.6	2s. 6d.	on the net rental (L.T.)
	non-farm	£2.2s.-£4.4s.				
Esher		15s.-£3.; ave. £1.5s.	1s. 3d.	16.0	3s.	on the net rental (L.T.); on the full rental (P.R.)
Farnham		15s.	2s.	10.0	3s.	on the net rental (P.R.)
Reigate Borough			2s.11d.	6.8	6-7s.	on the rack rental, or 5s. on the nominal (P.R.)
Reigate Foreign			2s. 5d.	8.3	3s. to 3s.6d.	on the rack rental (P.R.)
Walton on Thames	meadow	£2	1s. 3½d.	15.5		on the net rental (L.T.)
	enclosed arable	£1.10s.				
	common arable	£1.				
Sussex						
Burwash					6s. 3d.	
Chailey	breeding & dairy	10s.	2s. 8d.	7.5	12s. 6d.	on two-thirds of the full rental (P.R.)
Peasmarsh					4s.	
Winchelsea	marsh	£1.10s.			5s. 6d.	
	upland	£1.				

APPENDIX H (continued) page 440

County Parish	Type of land[a]	Average rent: Rent of land	Average rent: Rent of houses	Land tax: Poundage rate	Land tax: Rent to tax ratio[b]	Poor rate: Poundage rate c. 1795[c]	Bases[d]
Warwickshire							
Alcester						4s. 6d.	
Birmingham					46.9*	10s.	on the net rental (P.R.)
Coventry	mostly pasture	30-35s.		1s. 6d.	13.3	10s.	on the nominal rental, which is about five-eighths the real rental (P.R.)
Mollington (Oxon.)	all common fields	18s.		1s. 2d.	17.1	2s.	
Southam		£1.		1s. 6d.	13.3	2s. 8d.	on the nominal rental, which at present is about two-thirds the real rental (P.R.)
Sutton Coldfield		23s.		1s. 3d.	16.0	3s.	on the net rental (L.T.); probably about 2s. on the net rental (P.R.)
Westmorland							
Kendal					295.6*	3s. 8d.	on stock in trade, houses and land (P.R.)
Kentmere						1s. 8d.	on the full rental (P.R.)
Kirkby Lonsdale				8d.	30.0	2s. 3d.	on the fair rental (L.T.); houses one-half and land three-fourths of full value on a new valuation (P.R.)
Orton		2s.10d.-£1.10s.			64.2*	9d.	on the full rental (L.T., P.R.)
Underbarrow		10s.-£2.; ave. 16s.		7 1/4d.	33.1	1s. 3 3/4d.	on the full rental (P.R.)

Wiltshire							
Bradford on Avon (borough and 6 hamlets)	near town	£2-£3.			land	2s.9d.	on the rack rental (P.R.)
	hamlets	18s.-£2.			houses	1s.4 1/2d.	
Seend	arable	£1. 5s.				9d.*	on the net rental (P.R.)
	dairy pasture	£2-£3.					
Trowbridge	grazing	40-50s.					
Worcestershire							
Evesham, All Saints					land	4 1/2d.	
					houses	3d.	
Inkberrow	Vale of Evesham						
	garden	£2-£4.					
	other	15s.-25s.					
Yorkshire							
Bradford					land	3s.	on the net rental (P.R.)
					houses	1s.6d.	
Burton in Lonsdale		6s.-£3.; ave. 13s.	4 1/2d.	53.3		1s.10 1/2d.	on the net rental (P.R.)
Ecclesfield	Duke of Norfolk (much under-let)	15s.-16s.	3 3/4d.	64.0		1s. 3d.	on the net rental (L.T., P.R.)
	other	10s.-£2.; ave. £1.1s.					
Great Driffield	2/3 arable	10-12s.					
Halifax		£3-£5.		35.4*		3s.	on the rack or net rental (P.R.)
Kingston upon Hull	contiguous	£4-£5.		22.7*-25.9*			
	4-5 mi. away	ave. £3.					
Hullshire (other townships)				70.4*			
Leeds	in skirts of town	frequently £300.			land	3s.7 1/2d.	on the fair rental (P.R.)
	building land	sometimes £1,000.			houses	2s.	
	other	£2-£5.					
Pocklington	1/2 arable, 1/2 grass	£1-£1.10s.		6.7*		4s. 8d.	on the net rental (L.T.)

APPENDIX H (continued) page 442

County Parish	Average rent: Type of land[a]	Average rent: Rent of land	Average rent: Rent of houses	Land tax: Poundage rate	Land tax: Rent to tax ratio[b]	Poor rate: Poundage rate c. 1795[c]	Bases[d]
Yorkshire							
Settle	mostly feeding	5s.-£3.; ave. 18s.		4½d.	53.3		
Sheffield		£2-£4.		2d.	120.0	2s. 6d.	on the net rental (L.T., P.R.)
Skipton	near town distant	£3. 18s.		8d.	30.0	2s.	on the net rental (L.T., P.R.)
Southowram		10s.-£1.; ave. 15s.6d.		1s. 2d.	17.1	3s. 6d.	on the net rental (P.R.)
Stokesley		ave. £1.10s.; more near town				land 6d. houses 3d.	
Thornton in Lonsdale	cultivated	16-17s.			56.3*	10d.	
Denbighshire							
Llanferres		18-25s.				3s. 4d.	
Wrexham		10s.-£3.; ave. 25s.		1s. or less	20.0 or more	4s.	on the nominal rent, a very old assessment (P.R.)
Pembrokeshire							
Narberth		5s.		6d.	40.0	2s.	on the net rental (L.T.); on the present value of the land (P.R.)
Radnorshire							
Knighton		5s.-£4.; ave. £1.1s.		1s. or 1s.1d.	20.0 or 18.5	2s.	on the net rental (L.T.); houses at two-thirds and land at three-fourths real rent, but actually lower (P.R.)

Presteigne	10s.-£3.; ave. 21s.	8d.	30.0	5s.	on the net rental (L.T.); on the nominal rental, which is scarcely half the real rental (P.R.)

Notes: [a]Eden does not always report rents for every major type of land in a parish.

[b]Ratios are computed from local poundage rates, when these are given by Eden. Asterisked ratios are derived by the following equations (Eden having supplied the data in these cases):

(total poor tax receipts/rate) = total valuational rent

(total valuational rent/land tax quota) = ratio

Note that the ratio series is not wholly reliable, since it is based on a valuation rent series that inconsistently departs from full rental values.

[c]Asterisked rates are averaged over a period of years.

[d]L.T. = land tax. P.R. = parish rate. The bases for the land tax and parish rate, as reported in Eden, are normally intended to convey the real *burden* of each tax. They should not necessarily be understood as also *describing* the valuational base locally employed in actually computing tax entries, though they may do so in some instances. Note that rack rent is seldom employed in characterizing the basis of taxation. The variations in mode of reporting the base suggest widespread variations in modes of calculating tax entries. The variations also make it clear that reported local poundage rates, such as those which appear in the 1803 poor law report, are not comparable for inter-parish analyses and do not usually represent a straight-forward or consistent proportion of either rack or actual rents within the parish. Note that houses are generally assessed at *lower* rates than land. Most students of the land tax have assumed that distortions in acreage conversions and in tax burdens among smallholders are due to houses, which are more valuable than land and comprise a large proportion of such holdings. The evidence in Eden does not support that inference. Adjustments in valuation were commonly made which may well have been sufficiently compensatory.

Source: Sir Frederick Morton Eden, *The State of the Poor* (London, 1797), vols. 2, 3.

APPENDIX I

A comparison of computed valuational rents for the land tax and the poor rate, Eden survey of 1795–96

County Parish	Land tax rent (£)	Basis	Poor rate rent (£)	Basis	Poor rate rent as % of land tax rent
Bedfordshire					
Dunstable	1,652.67		1,493.14	three-fourths of the real rental	90.3
Houghton Regis	3,258.38		2,987.50	as nearly the full rental as possible	91.7
Humbershoe	270.98	net rental	235.17	full rental	86.8
Berkshire					
Wallingford (2 parishes)	3,161.51		1,551.48		49.1
Buckinghamshire					
Buckingham	5,000.00	real rental	3,996.63	nominal rental	79.9
Stony Stratford	686.79		710.04	net rental	103.4
Winslow	623.60		2,652.38	houses two-thirds of real rent and lands full value	425.03
Cheshire					
High Walton	408.00		399.00	an old and low valuation	83.1
Cumberland					
Gilcrux	655.60		773.31*	full rental	118.0
Harrington	1,281.00	full rental	1,512.64*	full rental	118.1
Dorset					
Durweston	545.67		500.00		91.6
Essex					
Colchester, All Saints	782.40	net rental	562.50	nominal rental	71.9
Colchester, St James	1,106.40		925.58	nominal rental	83.6

Essex					
Colchester, St Mary Magdalen	106.00-115.64	nearly the net rental	76.12	nominal rental	65.8-71.8
Gloucestershire					
Bristol, out-parishes	22,720.00		15,384.62	rack rental	67.7
Hampshire					
Petersfield	1,282.02		1,281.67	rack rental	100.0
Hertfordshire					
Chipping Barnet	3,374.25		3,000.00-3,200.00		88.9-94.8
Redbourn	9,581.89		4,340.97	as near the net rent as can be ascertained	45.3
Lancashire					
Bury	11,836.80	net rental	12,921.83	full rental	109.2
Manchester	140,320.00	net rental	145,747.17		103.9
Preston	17,629.09		8,978.67	the nominal rental, which is half the real rent on houses and two-thirds the real rent on land	50.9
Lincolnshire					
Cockerington	1,240.00		1,143.60	full rental	92.2
Monmouthshire					
Monmouth	6,077.14		1,527.62		25.1
Norfolk					
Yarmouth	15,382.66		14,736.84		95.8
Northamptonshire					
Brixworth	4,156.00	net rental	3,128.00	nominal rental	75.3
Roade	735.87		707.78	full rental	96.2
Yardley Gobion	1,113.76		1,080.00	nearly full rental	97.0
Oxfordshire					
Banbury	3,692.31		3,636.63	rack rental	98.5

APPENDIX I (continued) page 446

County Parish	Land tax rent (£)	Basis	Poor rate rent (£)	Basis	Poor rate rent as % of land tax rent
Surrey					
Epsom	6,713.00	net rental	6,462.00		96.3
Esher	3,339.63	net rental	2,965.25	full rental	88.8
Reigate Borough	1,658.58		1,634.50	nominal rental	98.5
Reigate Foreign	5,158.59		4,908.50	nominal rental	95.2
Warwickshire					
Coventry	18,326.50	fair rental	9,509.90	the nominal rental, which is about five-eighths the real rental	51.9
Southam	3,443.78		2,435.88	the nominal rental, which at present is about two-thirds the real rental	70.7
Sutton Coldfield	7,372.27	net rental	6,180.00	the nominal rental, which is about two-thirds of the net rental	83.8
Westmorland					
Underbarrow	2,168.28		2,214.86	full rental	102.1
Yorkshire					
Burton in Lonsdale	1,731.76		1,946.06	net rental	112.4
Ecclesfield	14,310.40	net rental	15,126.53	net rental	105.7
Skipton	4,392.00	net rental	4,471.67	net rental	101.8

Note: Asterisked rents are averaged over a period of years.
Source: Sir Frederick Morton Eden, *The State of the Poor* (London, 1797), vols. 2, 3.

APPENDIX J

Total valuational rent and tax, with rent-to-tax ratios, for all North Riding townships reporting rent (North Riding sample), c. 1830

Numbered columns:
- 1 = Wapentake.
- 2 = Township.
- 3 = Year of tax duplicate, if other than 1830.
- 4 = Number of ''split'' entries, i.e., entries where both a redeemed and an unredeemed tax value have been assigned to a single rent entry. Such ''split'' rent and tax values are omitted from columns 6-7 and 9-10, but are included in columns 8 and 11.
- 5 = Number of ''omission'' entries, i.e., entries where the tax is entered but the rent is missing (in only one case is the rent entered and the tax missing). Such ''omission'' entries are not included in any of the columns.
- 6 = Total redeemed rent.
- 7 = Total unredeemed rent.
- 8 = Total redeemed plus unredeemed rent.
- 9 = Total redeemed tax.
- 10 = Total unredeemed tax.
- 11 = Total redeemed plus unredeemed tax. All rent and tax totals are derived by adding the values reported for each individual property bundle.
- 12 = The ratio of redeemed rent to redeemed tax. All ratios are to the value 1.
- 13 = The ratio of unredeemed rent to unredeemed tax.
- 14 = The ratio of total rent (redeemed plus unredeemed) to total tax.
- 15 = The percent difference between the redeemed ratio and the unredeemed ratio, i.e., ((unred. ratio-red. ratio)/red. ratio) x 100.

1	2	3	4	5	6	7	8	9	10	11	12	13	14	15
Allertonshire														
	Borrowby				517.10. 0	361.10. 0	879. 0. 0	26. 4. 6	18. 1. 6	44. 6. 0	19.7	20.0	19.8	1.5
	Deighton				935.10. 0	94. 0. 0	1,029.10. 0	60.18. 8 1/2	2.12. 7 3/4	63.11. 4 1/4	15.4	35.7	16.2	131.8
	Dinsdale, Over				40. 0. 0	804. 0. 0	844. 0. 0	2. 2.10	37.10. 7	39.13. 5	18.7	21.4	21.3	14.4
	Girsby				605. 0. 0	613. 0. 0	1,218. 0. 0	24.18. 7	24. 3.11	49. 2. 6	24.3	25.3	24.8	4.1
	Hutton Bonville	1831			none	1,559. 6. 0	1,559. 6. 0	none	63. 6.10	63. 6.10	NA	24.6	24.6	NA
	Knayton and Brawith				206. 0. 0	756.10. 0	962.10. 0	17. 3. 4	63. 0.10	80. 4. 2	12.0	12.0	12.0	0.0
	Osmotherley				415. 8. 4	541. 0. 0	956. 8. 4	20.14.11	27. 1. 0	47.15.11	20.0	20.0	20.0	0.0
	Sessay and Hutton Sessay				70. 0. 0	2,289. 0. 0	2,359. 0. 0	5. 4. 7	108. 5. 8	113.10. 3	13.4	21.1	20.8	57.5
	Sigston				219.11. 2	736.16. 4	956. 7. 6	16. 4. 9	48. 8. 7	64.13. 4	13.5	15.2	14.8	12.6
	Thornton le Beans and Crosby		3		413. 0. 0	812. 0. 0	1,399. 0. 0	30.12. 0 1/2	57.12. 5	100.12. 2	13.5	14.1	13.9	4.4

APPENDIX J (continued) page 448

1	2	3	4	5	6	7	8	9	10	11	12	13	14	15
	Thornton le Street				41. 0. 0	1,129.10. 0	1,170.10. 0	2. 1. 0	56. 9. 6	58.10. 6	20.0	20.0	20.0	0.0
	West Rounton		1		390. 0. 0	748. 0. 0	1,203. 0. 0	16.15. 5 1/2	33.14. 2 1/2	53. 5. 9 1/2	23.2	22.2	22.6	-4.3
SUBTOTAL					3,852.19. 6	10,444.12. 4	14,536.11.10	223. 0. 8 1/2	540. 7. 8 1/4	778.12. 2 3/4	17.3	19.3	18.7	11.6
Birdforth														
	Birdforth				134. 5. 0	414. 0. 0	548. 5. 0	10. 1. 6	31. 1. 0	41. 2. 6	13.3	13.3	13.3	0.0
	Boltby				NR	1,653.10. 6 3/4	NA	(2. 6. 7 1/2)	67. 5. 8 3/4	(69.12. 4 1/4)	NA	24.6	NA	NA
	Cowsby	1829			none	589.10. 0	589.10. 0	none	26.19. 1	26.19. 1	NA	21.9	21.9	NA
	Coxwold, Angram Grange and Wildon Grange	1829			none	1,367.13. 0	1,367.13. 0	none	49. 0.11	49. 0.11	NA	27.9	27.9	NA
	Dalton		8		117.14. 0	672.15. 0	1,087. 6. 0	2.19. 9 1/4	16.17. 4	27. 5. 4	39.4	39.9	39.9	1.3
	Elmire and Crakehill				none	1,079.10. 0	1,079.10. 0	none	26. 7. 4	26. 7. 4	NA	40.9	40.9	NA
	Kilburn, Low; Osgoodby; and Hood Grange				164. 0. 0	1,178. 0. 0	1,342. 0. 0	7.17. 6	63. 0. 4	70.17.10	20.8	18.7	18.9	1.1
	Sand Hutton	1829	1	1	159. 0. 0	1,191. 2. 0	1,366.12. 0	3.13. 3 3/4	35.12. 0 3/4	39.14. 8 1/2	43.4	33.4	34.4	-23.0
	South Kilvington	1829		2	NR	430. 9. 0	NA	(12. 3.11)	18. 1. 0 1/2	(30. 4.11 1/2)	NA	23.8	NA	NA
	Thirlby	1829			none	422. 5. 0	422. 5. 0	none	16. 5. 9 1/2	16. 5. 9 1/2	NA	25.9	25.9	NA
	Thirsk			1	1,662. 9. 4	3,650. 0. 7 1/4	5,312. 9.11 1/4	20.17. 8 1/4	46.19. 5	67.17. 1 1/4	79.6	77.7	78.3	-2.4
	SUBTOTAL				2,237. 8. 4	12,648.15. 2	13,115.10.11 1/4	45. 9. 9 1/4	97.10. 0 1/2	365.10. 7 1/4	49.2	31.8	35.9	-35.4
Bulmer														
	Barton le Willows				40. 0. 0	1,395. 0. 0	1,435. 0. 0	0.16. 0	23.12. 8 1/2	24. 8. 8 1/2	50.0	59.0	58.7	18.0
	Brafferton				553. 0. 0	235. 0. 0	788. 0. 0	32. 3. 4	12.10. 0	44.13. 4	17.2	18.8	17.6	9.3
	Brandsby and Stearsby				none	2,886. 0. 0	2,886. 0. 0	none	159. 3. 4	159. 3. 4	NA	18.1	18.1	NA
	Bulmer				438. 0. 0	1,226. 0. 0	1,664. 0. 0	7. 9. 8	35.16. 8	43. 6. 4	58.5	34.2	38.4	-41.5
	Buttercrambe and Bossall				525. 0. 0	1,968. 0. 0	2,493. 0. 0	19.13. 4	57. 0.10	76.14. 2	26.7	34.5	32.5	29.2
	Clifton				2,837. 0. 0	583. 0. 0	3,420. 0. 0	71. 3. 8	14.12. 0	85.15. 8	39.8	39.9	39.9	0.2
	Coneysthorpe	1829			none	1,576.15. 0	1,576.15. 0	none	30.13. 4	30.13. 4	NA	51.4	51.4	NA

Cornbrough				205. 0. 0	454. 0. 0	659. 0. 0	15.17. 0	31.13. 6	47.10. 6	12.9	14.3	13.9	10.8
Crayke				NR	797.19. 9	NA	(89.11. 3 1/4)	60.11. 2 3/4	(150. 2. 6)	NA	13.2	NA	NA
Crambe				none	1,502.12. 0	1,502.12. 0	none	26.13. 4 1/4	26.13. 4 1/4	NA	56.3	56.3	NA
Easingwold				NR	2,101. 6. 4	NA	(146. 5. 7 1/4)	105. 1.11	(251. 7. 6 1/4)	NA	20.0	NA	NA
Farlington				115.10. 0	525.10. 0	641. 0. 0	14. 1.10	61. 7. 0	75. 8.10	8.2	8.6	8.5	4.9
Flaxton on the Moor			6	656. 0. 0	1,232. 0. 0	1,888. 0. 0	25.16. 0 1/4	31. 3.11 1/4	56.19.11 1/2	25.4	39.5	33.1	55.5
Foston				def.	def.	1,288.19. 0	(16.15. 8)	(20. 7. 8)	37. 3. 4	def.	def.	34.7	def.
Ganthorpe				none	579. 2. 0	579. 2. 0	none	29.10. 0	29.10. 0	NA	19.6	19.6	NA
Gate Helmsley				154. 0. 0	60.10. 0	214.10. 0	12.13. 4 1/2	4.13. 3 1/2	17. 6. 8	12.2	13.0	12.4	6.6
Harton				none	1,801. 7. 0	1,801. 7. 0	none	54.15. 6	54.15. 6	NA	32.9	32.9	NA
Haxby				458. 5. 0	673.13. 0	1,131.18. 0	23. 5. 7 1/2	33.11. 4 1/2	56.17. 0	16.3	20.1	19.9	23.3
Helperby				NR	485. 6. 0	NA	(27.13. 7)	21.15. 4 1/2	(49. 8.11 1/2)	NA	22.3	NA	NA
Henderskelf				none	c.1,500. 0. 0	c.1,500. 0. 0	none	37. 6. 8	37. 6. 8	NA	40.2	40.2	NA
Heworth			7	641. 0. 0	818. 0. 0	1,459. 0. 0	31.15.10 1/2	38.15. 9 1/2	70.11. 8	20.2	21.1	20.7	4.4
Holtby			2	def.	def.	1,184.10. 0	(16. 2. 4 3/4)	(22.10. 4)	38.12. 8 3/4	def.	def.	30.6	def.
Huby		4		1,420. 0. 0	3,333. 0. 0	5,012. 0. 0	21. 3.11 3/4	49. 4. 1 1/4	74.12. 2 1/2	67.0	67.7	67.2	1.0
Huntington	1829			963. 0. 0	1,443. 0. 0	2,406. 0. 0	52.16. 9	71. 3. 9	124. 0. 6	18.2	20.3	19.4	11.5
Huttons Ambo				380. 5. 0	1,296. 4. 0	1,676. 9. 0	10.11.11	50.15. 1	61. 7. 0	35.9	25.5	27.3	-29.0
Linton upon Ouse				none	1,081.10. 0	1,081.10. 0	none	87.13. 8	87.13. 8	NA	12.3	12.3	NA
Marton in the Forest and Moxby				NR	1,443.15. 0	NA	(6.17. 9)	120.19. 5 1/2	(127.17. 2 1/2)	NA	11.9	NA	NA
Murton		6		526.10. 0	264. 0. 0	1,026. 0. 0	19. 2. 3 1/4	8. 8. 1	35.11. 9 1/2	27.5	31.4	28.8	14.2
Newton upon Ouse and Beningbrough			6	def.	1,822. 0. 0	1,836. 0. 0	(4.19. 4 3/4)	70. 4. 4 3/4	70.13. 8 1/4	def.	25.9	26.0	def.
Osbaldwick			1	374.10. 0	614. 0. 0	988.10. 0	13.10.10 1/2	22.19. 2	36.10. 0 1/2	27.6	26.7	27.1	-3.3
St Olave in Marygate				NR	192.15. 0	NA	(12. 2. 6)	9.12. 9	(21.15. 3)	NA	20.0	NA	NA
Shipton and Overton				200.10. 0	1,857. 5. 0	2,057.15. 0	7.12. 2	79. 6.10 1/4	86.19. 0 1/4	26.4	23.4	23.7	-11.4
Skelton and Rawcliffe				NR	1,258. 0. 0	NA	(63.17. 9)	58.13. 9	(122.11. 6)	NA	21.4	NA	NA
Stillington			1	NR	889. 0. 0	NA	(11.14. 6 3/4)	36. 5. 6 1/2	(48. 0. 1 1/4)	NA	24.5	NA	NA
Stittenham			1	none	1,543. 2. 6	1,543. 2. 6	none	95.18. 8	95.18. 8	NA	16.1	16.1	NA
Stockton on the Forest and Sandburn				160.10. 0	1,480. 0. 0	1,640.10. 0	6. 1. 1	46.13. 4	52.14. 5	26.5	31.7	31.1	19.6

APPENDIX J (continued) page 450

1	2	3	4	5	6	7	8	9	10	11	12	13	14	15
Bulmer														
	Strensall, Earswick, and Towthorpe		4		465. 0. 0	1,002. 0. 0	1,533. 0. 0	26.10. 9	51. 2. 6	83. 5. 7	17.5	19.6	18.4	12.0
	Terrington, Menthorpe, and Wiganthorpe			2	1,174. 0. 0	2,362. 0. 0	3,536. 0. 0	39. 8. 3 3/4	62. 4.10	101.13. 1 3/4	29.8	37.9	34.8	27.2
	Tholthorpe and Flawith				456. 0. 0	183. 0. 0	639. 0. 0	20.19.11 3/4	7.13. 3 3/4	28.13. 3 1/2	21.7	23.9	22.3	10.1
	Thormanby				45. 0. 0	816. 0. 0	861. 0. 0	2.13.10 3/4	45.16. 8	48.10. 6 3/4	16.7	17.8	17.7	6.6
	Thornton le Clay		4		def.	def.	1,114. 5. 8	(11. 5.10 1/2)	(19. 2. 5 1/2)	30. 8. 4	NA	NA	36.6	NA
	Tollerton			1	NR	887. 0. 0	NA	(30. 3.11)	35. 9. 4	(65.13. 3)	NA	25.0	NA	NA
	Warthill				448. 0. 0	331. 0. 0	779. 0. 0	12.15. 0	7.14. 4	20. 9. 4	35.1	42.9	38.1	22.2
	Welburn				10. 0. 0	1,047.10. 0	1,057.10. 0	0. 3.11	29. 3. 1	29. 7. 0	51.1	35.9	36.0	-29.7
	Whitwell				none	2,615.17. 6	2,615.17. 6	none	72. 0. 0	72. 0. 0	NA	36.3	36.3	NA
	Wigginton				479. 0. 0	868. 0. 0	1,347. 0. 0	15.13. 7 1/2	27.18. 8	43.12. 3 1/2	30.5	31.1	30.9	2.0
	Youlton				377. 0. 0	448. 0. 0	825. 0. 0	16.15. 0	16. 5. 0	33. 0. 0	22.5	27.6	25.0	22.7
	SUBTOTAL				7,480. 0. 0	51,479. 0. 1	61,687.12. 8	520.15. 3	2,033.14. 1 3/4	2,230.11. 7 1/2	14.4	25.3	27.6	75.7
Gilling East														
	Ainderby Steeple				419.10. 0	497. 0. 0	916.10. 0	17. 9. 0	23. 1. 8 3/4	40.10. 8 3/4	24.0	21.5	22.6	-10.4
	Barton		2		704. 0. 0	1,365. 8. 4	2,214.18. 4	18. 2.10	49. 6.11 1/2	67.16. 9 1/2	38.8	27.7	32.6	-28.6
	Brompton on Swale		1		981.10. 0	808. 0. 0	1,899.10. 0	26.16. 3 1/2	22.13. 8	52.10.11 1/2	36.6	35.6	36.1	-2.7
	Cleasby				16. 0. 0	846. 0. 0	862. 0. 0	0.17. 8	45.10.11 1/4	46. 8. 7 1/4	18.1	18.6	18.6	2.8
	Cowton, East				none	3,168. 0. 0	3,168. 0. 0	none	125. 4. 4 1/4	125. 4. 4 1/4	NA	25.3	25.3	NA
	Cowton, North				461. 7. 0	790.10. 0	1,251.17. 0	16. 4. 3	27.19.11	44. 4. 2	28.4	28.2	28.3	-0.7
	Cowton, South				343.10. 0	1,102.10. 0	1,446. 0. 0	29.15. 3	80.14. 8 3/4	110. 9.11 3/4	11.5	13.6	13.1	18.3
	Croft				none	3,646. 0. 0	3,646. 0. 0	none	128.11. 5	128.11. 5	NA	28.4	28.4	NA
	Dalton upon Tees				155. 0. 0	1,352.11. 0	1,507.11. 0	6. 2. 2 1/4	39.16. 3	45.18. 5 1/4	25.4	34.0	32.8	33.8
	Danby Wiske				NR	1,797. 0. 0	NA	(23.16. 8 3/4)	76. 3. 4 1/2	(100. 0. 1 1/4)	NA	23.6	NA	NA
	Ellerton upon Swale, Bolton on Swale, and Whitwell				196. 0. 0	4,616. 6. 0	4,812. 6. 0	2. 8. 9	90.12. 2 1/2	93. 0.11 1/2	80.4	50.9	51.7	-36.7
	Eryholme				80. 0. 0	1,725. 0. 0	1,805. 0. 0	2.16. 4 1/2	52.18. 2 1/2	55.14. 7	28.4	32.6	32.4	14.8

Kiplin				none	1,298.10. 0	1,298.10. 0	none	41. 6. 8	41. 6. 8	NA	31.4	31.4	NA
Kirby Wiske		2	16	364. 4. 0	381. 1. 6	812.18. 0	18. 4. 2 1/4	19. 1. 0 3/4	40.12.10 1/2	20.0	20.0	20.0	0.0
Langton, Great			1	584. 0. 0	8. 0. 0	592. 0. 0	35.14. 0 1/4	0.11.11	36. 5.11 1/4	16.4	13.4	16.3	-18.3
Langton, Little				739. 0. 0	266.10. 0	1,005.10. 0	20. 5. 4	7.14. 8	28. 0. 0	36.5	34.5	35.9	-5.5
Manfield				170. 0. 0	2,236.10. 0	2,406.10. 0	10.10. 0	142. 2. 2	152.12. 2	16.2	15.7	15.8	-3.1
Maunby				904.10. 0	508. 0. 0	1,412.10. 0	46.14.10 3/4	26. 0. 8 3/4	72.15. 7 1/2	19.3	19.5	19.4	1.0
Middleton Tyas		13	1	2,830. 0. 0	932.15. 0	3,901. 5. 0	56. 2. 3	15.13. 2	73.19.11	50.4	59.6	52.7	18.2
Morton on Swale and Fareholm				1,021.10. 0	318.10. 0	1,340. 0. 0	44.17. 9	18. 5. 2 1/2	63. 2.11 1/2	22.8	17.4	21.2	-23.7
Newby Wiske				417. 0. 0	309. 5. 0	726. 5. 0	23. 6. 2	13. 3.10 3/4	36.10. 0 3/4	17.9	23.4	19.9	30.7
Scorton and Uckerby		1		1,265. 0. 0	1,778. 0. 0	3,203. 0. 0	27. 4. 8	25.16. 5	56. 1. 1	46.4	68.8	57.1	48.3
Thrintoft				702.10. 0	586. 0. 0	1,288.10. 0	28.19. 5	24. 8. 4	53. 7. 9	24.2	24.0	24.1	-0.8
Warlaby and Low Sober				555.10. 0	992. 0. 0	1,547.10. 0	19.14. 9	41. 5. 3	61. 0. 0	28.1	24.0	25.4	-14.6
Yafforth		1		163. 0. 0	933. 0. 0	1,382. 0. 0	8.17. 4	54. 8. 0	80. 0. 0	18.4	17.2	17.3	-6.5
SUBTOTAL				13,073. 1. 0	32,262. 6.10	44,446. 0. 4	461. 3. 4 1/2	1,192.11. 2 3/4	1,606. 6. 0 1/4	28.3	27.0	27.7	-4.6
Gilling West													
Aldbrough		3		def.	def.	2,359. 0. 0	(4.13. 1)	(57.13.10 1/2)	62. 6.11 1/2	def.	def.	37.8	def.
Barningham and Hope			5	294.10. 0	1,127.15. 0	1,422. 5. 0	12. 6. 5 1/4	65.18. 7	78. 5. 0 1/4	23.9	17.1	18.2	-28.4
Cliffe	1831			none	610. 0. 0	610. 0. 0	none	43.14.10	43.14.10	NA	13.9	13.9	NA
Cotherstone				1,316. 5. 0	742.17. 0	2,059. 2. 0	49. 4. 1 1/2	27.17. 4	77. 1. 5 1/2	26.7	26.6	26.7	-0.4
Eppleby				843.10. 0	303. 0. 0	1,146.10. 0	36. 3.10	12. 9. 7	48.13. 5	23.3	24.3	23.6	4.3
Gailes		2	2	182. 5. 0	700.15. 0	883. 0. 0	8. 0. 1	29. 4. 3	40. 4.11	22.8	24.0	21.9	5.3
Hunderthwaite			6	740.10. 0	406. 5. 0	1,146.15. 0	21. 3. 2	14. 3. 7	35. 6. 9	35.0	28.6	32.4	-18.3
Hutton Longvillers				none	1,103. 0. 0	1,103. 0. 0	none	60.17. 5	60.17. 5	NA	18.1	18.1	NA
Kirkby Ravensworth		1	1	206. 0. 0	168. 0. 0	374. 0. 0	3.19. 6 1/2	3. 5.10 1/2	7. 6. 7	51.8	51.0	51.0	-1.5
Lartington				2,217.10. 0	48. 0. 0	2,265.10. 0	60.18. 3 1/2	2.11. 0.	63. 9. 3 1/2	36.4	18.8	35.7	-48.4
Lunedale				1,443. 5. 0	256. 5. 0	1,699.10. 0	32.16. 9	5.15. 3	38.12. 0	44.0	44.5	44.0	1.1
Marrick				NR	2,117. 0. 0	NA	(8.18.10 3/4)	52.18. 6	(61.17. 4 3/4)	NA	40.0	NA	NA
Melsonby		7		672. 3. 0	1,616. 0. 0	2,560. 0. 0	18.10. 0 3/4	35. 3. 5	58. 6.10 1/4	36.3	45.9	43.9	26.4
Ravensworth and Whashton			4	1,514. 0. 0	541. 0. 0	2,055. 0. 0	38.10. 8	14.18. 6 1/2	53. 9. 2 1/2	39.3	36.2	38.4	-7.9
Scargill				none	1,375.12. 0	1,375.12. 0	none	111. 6. 5	111. 6. 5	NA	12.4	12.4	NA
Skeeby				198. 0. 0	562.10. 0	760.10. 0	7. 1. 5 3/4	22. 7. 3 1/2	29. 8. 9 1/4	28.0	25.2	25.8	-10.0
Stanwick, St John				none	1,133. 0. 0	1,133. 0. 0	none	66.14. 0	66.14. 0	NA	17.0	17.0	NA

APPENDIX J (continued) page 452

1	2	3	4	5	6	7	8	9	10	11	12	13	14	15
Gilling West														
	Startforth			7	472. 0. 0	880. 0. 0	1,352. 0. 0	17. 5. 4 1/2	21.13. 6 3/4	38.18.11 1/4	27.3	40.6	34.7	48.7
	SUBTOTAL				10,099.18. 0	13,690.19. 0	24,304.14. 0	305.19. 9 3/4	590.19. 5 1/4	914. 3. 2 3/4	33.0	23.2	26.6	-29.7
Hallikeld														
	Ainderby Quernhow	1831			204.10. 0	544. 0. 0	748.10. 0	5. 4. 5 1/2	16. 2. 3	21. 6. 8 1/2	39.2	33.8	35.1	-13.8
	Burneston	1831			483. 0. 0	720. 6. 8	1,203. 6. 8	20. 3. 4	30. 0. 3	50. 3. 7	24.0	24.0	24.0	0.0
	Dishforth	1831	1		749.10. 0	144. 0. 0	904.10. 0	44. 0. 6	8. 8. 6	53. 1.10	17.0	17.1	17.0	0.6
	Exelby, Leeming, and Newton	1831			265. 3. 7	1,033.18. 6	1,299. 2. 1	22. 5. 0	81. 7. 9 1/2	103.12. 9 1/2	11.9	12.7	12.5	6.7
	Kirklington and Upsland	1831		1	230. 0. 0	1,735.10. 0	1,965.10. 0	3.16. 0	30. 1. 4	33.17. 4	60.5	57.7	58.0	-4.6
	Melmerby	1831		2	229. 0. 0	996. 0. 0	1,225. 0. 0	4. 0. 5	20.15. 0	24.15. 5	57.0	48.0	49.4	-15.8
	Theakston	1831			51. 5. 0	504.15. 0	556. 0. 0	2.12. 7 1/2	23.14. 0	26. 6. 7 1/2	19.5	21.3	21.1	9.2
	Wath	1831			none	1,045. 0. 0	1,045. 0. 0	none	26. 2. 6	26. 2. 6	NA	40.0	40.0	NA
	SUBTOTAL				2,212. 8. 7	6,724. 9. 2	8,946.18. 9	102. 2. 4	236.11. 7 1/2	339. 6. 9 1/2	21.7	28.4	26.4	30.9
Hang East														
	Aiskew				NR	1,208. 0. 0	NA	(11.10. 0)	50. 6. 8	(61.16. 8)	NA	24.0	NA	NA
	Appleton, East and West				1,817. 8. 6	175.10. 0	1,992.18. 6	46.11.10	3. 9. 7	50. 1. 5	39.0	50.4	39.8	29.2
	Bedale and Firby				NR	3,654. 0. 0	NA	(22. 6. 4)	121. 5. 9	(143.12. 1)	NA	30.1	NA	NA
	Colburn				none	1,334. 0. 0	1,334. 0. 0	none	52.19. 3	52.19. 3	NA	25.2	25.2	NA
	Hipswell and St Martin's Abbey	1831			NR	1,902.13. 0	NA	(15.14. 4)	55. 9. 7 3/4	(71. 3.11 3/4)	NA	34.3	NA	NA
	Kirkby Fleetham				NR	383.10. 0	NA	NR	18.10. 6	NA	NA	20.7	NA	NA
	Newton le Willows and Ruswick				260. 0. 0	1,783.18. 0	2,043.18. 0	10.15. 9 1/2	59. 6.11	70. 2. 8 1/2	24.1	30.0	29.1	24.5
	Scruton		11		def.	946.17. 0	1,552.19. 0	(17.19. 8 1/2)	40. 7. 7 3/4	66.11. 9 1/2	def.	23.4	23.3	def.
	Snape				341.15. 0	1,555.19. 6	1,897.14. 6	8. 2.11	52. 1. 1	60. 4. 0	42.0	29.9	31.5	-28.8
	Well				117. 5. 0	529.10. 0	646.15. 0	5.17. 4	26. 9. 6	32. 6.10	20.0	20.0	20.0	0.0
	SUBTOTAL				2,536. 8. 6	13,473.17. 6	9,469. 4. 0	71. 7.10 1/2	480. 6. 6 1/2	332. 6. 0	35.5	28.0	28.5	-21.1

Hang West											
Bellerby		575. 0. 0	698. 0. 0	1,273. 0. 0	14. 9.10	17.19. 0 1/2	32. 8.10 1/2	39.7	38.9	39.2	-2.0
East Witton (within)		none	2,342. 1. 6	2,342. 1. 6	none	44. 8. 8 1/2	44. 8. 8 1/2	NA	52.7	52.7	NA
East Witton (without)		NR	2,743.17. 6	NA	(3. 7. 7)	54.19. 2	(58. 6. 9)	NA	49.9	NA	NA
Ellerton and Stainton	1	none	1,210. 0. 0	1,210. 0. 0	none	29. 6. 0 1/2	29. 6. 0 1/2	NA	41.3	41.3	NA
Finghall, Akebar, and Hutton Hang		none	2,355. 0. 0	2,355. 0. 0	none	46.13. 1	46.13. 1	NA	50.5	50.5	NA
Hudswell		NR	1,675.13. 5	NA	(7. 7. 1 1/2)	31. 9. 7	(38.16. 8 1/2)	NA	53.2	NA	NA
Thornton Rust	10	259.15. 0	177. 5. 0	826. 5. 0	6. 9. 3	4. 5. 6 1/2	20.16. 4 1/2	40.2	41.4	39.7	3.0
SUBTOTAL		834.15. 0	11,202.16. 5	8,006. 6. 6	20.19. 1	229. 1. 2	173.13. 1	39.8	48.9	46.1	22.9
Langbaurgh											
Acklam, West		none	862.10. 0	862.10. 0	none	27. 6. 5 3/4	27. 6. 5 3/4	NA	37.3	37.3	NA
Appleton Wiske		961.10. 0	473. 0. 0	1,434.10. 0	53. 9. 9 1/2	27. 2. 9 1/4	80.12. 6 3/4	18.0	17.4	17.8	-3.3
Arncliffe, Ingleby		667. 0. 0	198.10. 0	865.10. 0	44. 4. 5	11. 4. 5 1/2	55. 8.10 1/2	15.1	17.7	15.6	17.2
Barnby, East		445.12. 0	1,471.16. 0	1,917. 8. 0	8. 9. 6	21.19. 0 1/4	30. 8. 6 1/4	52.6	67.0	63.0	27.4
Battersby		504. 0. 0	18. 0. 0	522. 0. 0	25.10. 6	0.16.10	26. 7. 4	19.7	21.4	19.8	8.6
Borrowby		217. 0. 0	129. 0. 0	346. 0. 0	8.16. 0	6. 8.10	15. 4.10	24.6	20.0	22.7	-18.7
Broughton, Great	1	1,731. 0. 0	864. 0. 0	2,595. 0. 0	54.15. 4 3/4	20. 5. 9	75. 1. 1 3/4	31.6	42.6	34.6	34.8
Castle Leavington		180. 0. 0	1,020. 0. 0	1,200. 0. 0	8. 2. 9	47.17. 8	56. 0. 5	22.1	21.3	21.4	-3.6
Crathorne	1832	none	1,855. 0. 0	1,855. 0. 0	none	130.11. 4	130.11. 4	NA	14.2	14.2	NA
Danby		3,353.15. 0	1,483.10. 0	4,837. 5. 0	51. 1. 0 1/2	23.19. 9 1/4	75. 0. 9 3/4	65.7	61.8	64.5	-5.9
Easby		639. 0. 0	175. 0. 0	814. 0. 0	35.14. 5	8.11. 3	44. 5. 8	17.9	20.4	18.4	14.0
Egton		4,481. 0. 0	164. 0. 0	4,645. 0. 0	169. 3. 8	8. 2. 2	177. 5.10	26.5	20.2	26.2	-23.8
Greenhow		1,348. 0. 0	none	1,348. 0. 0	41.10. 4	none	41.10. 4	32.5	NA	32.5	NA
Hemlington	2	410. 0. 0	370. 0. 0	780. 0. 0	12. 4. 3 1/2	17. 6.11	29.11. 2 1/2	33.6	21.3	26.4	-36.6
Hilton		none	1,295. 0. 0	1,295. 0. 0	none	48.17. 0	48.17. 0	NA	26.5	26.5	NA
Hutton Rudby	9	1,636.15. 0	1,179. 1. 0	2,924.11. 0	39. 1. 2 1/2	27.19.10 1/4	69.12.10 1/2	41.9	42.1	42.0	0.5
Ingleby Barwick	1	240. 0. 0	481. 0. 0	813. 0. 0	8.17. 4 3/4	13. 8. 6 1/4	26.19. 3	27.0	35.8	30.2	32.6
Ingleby Greenhow		1,017.10. 0	8. 0. 0	1,025.10. 0	29. 0. 7 1/2	0. 5. 5	29. 6. 0 1/2	35.0	29.5	35.0	-15.7
Kildale		none	1,459.15. 0	1,459.15. 0	none	43.19. 0 1/2	43.19. 0 1/2	NA	33.2	33.2	NA
Kirkleatham		34.10. 0	2,756. 0. 0	2,790.10. 0	0.18. 4	89. 3. 9	90. 2. 1	37.6	30.9	31.0	-17.8
Linthorpe		100. 0. 0	1,843.10. 0	1,943.10. 0	4.11.10 1/2	45. 6. 0 1/2	49.17.11	21.8	40.7	39.0	86.7
Lofthouse		3,925.18. 0	123. 7. 0	4,049. 5. 0	61.14. 7 1/2	5. 7. 2	67. 1. 9 1/2	63.6	23.0	60.4	-63.8
Low Worsall		345. 0. 0	969. 0. 0	1,314. 0. 0	14.13.11 3/4	31. 6. 0 1/4	46. 0. 0	23.5	31.0	28.6	31.9

APPENDIX J (continued) page 454

1	2	3	4	5	6	7	8	9	10	11	12	13	14	15
	Langbaurgh													
	Maltby				325.10. 0	643. 0. 0	968.10. 0	12.17. 7	24.17. 0	37.14. 7	25.3	25.9	25.7	2.4
	Middleton upon Leven				def.	639. 0. 0	NA	(13.13. 0 1/4)	26. 3. 4	(39.16. 4 1/4)	NA	24.4	NA	NA
	Newby	1831			353. 0. 0.	519. 0. 0	872. 0. 0	14.13. 6	24. 6. 9	39. 0. 3	24.0	21.3	22.4	-11.2
	Newton Mulgrave				965. 0. 0	145. 0. 0	1,110. 0. 0	24.18. 5	3. 2. 4	28. 0. 9	38.7	46.5	39.6	20.2
	Normanby				956. 0. 0	NR	NA	29. 5. 2	(3. 7. 1)	(32.12. 3)	32.7	NA	NA	NA
	Nunthorpe				NR	1,238. 0. 0	NA	(10.16.11 1/4)	49. 0. 8	(59.17. 7 1/4)	NA	25.2	NA	NA
	Ormesby				NR	1,911. 0. 0	NA	(36.11. 0 1/4)	35.14.10 1/4	(72. 5.10 1/2)	NA	53.5	NA	NA
	Picton		1		210. 0. 0	275. 0. 0	535. 0. 0	8. 3. 0 3/4	10.13. 3	20.15. 0	25.8	25.8	25.8	0.0
	Potto				360.10. 0	1,114. 0. 0	1,474.10. 0	18.18. 1 1/2	51.17. 1	70.15. 2 1/2	19.1	21.5	20.8	12.6
	Redcar			1	NR	132.15. 0	NA	(11.10. 6 1/4)	5. 8. 6 1/2	(16.19. 0 3/4)	NA	24.5	NA	NA
	Ugthorpe			5	1,124.15. 0	121.10. 0	1,246. 5. 0	37. 1. 0 3/4	4. 6. 9	41. 7. 9 3/4	30.4	28.0	30.1	-7.9
	Whorlton				112. 0. 0	3,509.10. 0	3,621.10. 0	4. 0. 8	116.11. 8	120.12. 4	27.8	30.1	30.0	8.3
	Yarm				766. 0. 0	1,821. 0. 0	2,587. 0. 0	27. 7.11	67.11. 5	94.19. 4	28.0	26.9	27.2	-3.9
	SUBTOTAL				27,410. 5. 0	31,267.14. 0	54,051.19. 0	849. 5. 7 3/4	1,076.19. 8 1/2	1,789.11. 3 1/2	32.3	29.0	30.2	-10.2
	Pickering Lythe													
	Allerston				NR	1,433. 3. 0	NA	(20. 4. 0)	65.13.10 1/2	(85.17.10 1/2)	NA	21.8	NA	NA
	Burniston		13	6	909. 0. 0	def.	1,169. 0. 0	17.19. 6	(2. 0. 8)	22. 5. 1	50.6	def.	52.5	def.
	Cayton, Deepdale, Killerby, and Osgodby		6	1	1,483. 0. 0	891.10. 0	2,646. 0. 0	46.13.10	36. 7. 4	93. 0. 8	31.8	24.5	28.4	-23.0
	Cloughton		9		1,764. 0. 0	def.	2,170. 0. 0	20.16. 6	(4. 5. 7)	29. 7. 8	84.7	def.	73.8	def.
	Cropton and Cawthorn				737. 0. 0	380. 0. 0	1,117. 0. 0	28.10. 4 3/4	9. 2. 4 1/4	37.12. 9	25.8	41.7	29.7	61.6
	Habton, Great and Little				84. 0. 0	1,201. 0. 0	1,285. 0. 0	1.13. 7 1/4	39. 6. 3	40.19.10 1/4	50.0	30.6	31.3	-38.8
	Hartoft Dale				304. 0. 0	127. 0. 0	431. 0. 0	5.15. 2 1/4	2. 6. 6	8. 1. 8 1/4	52.8	54.6	53.3	3.4
	Hutton Bushel				500.13. 8	1,591. 8. 9	2,092. 2. 5	8. 6. 1 3/4	26.17. 8	35. 3. 9 3/4	60.3	59.2	59.4	-1.8
	Levisham		5		245. 0. 0.	def.	545. 0. 0	9. 0. 7	(6. 6. 0 1/2)	20.12. 8 1/4	27.1	def.	26.4	def.
	Lebberston and Gristhorpe		6	18	def.	745. 0. 0	1,597. 0. 0	def.	23.19. 4 1/2	49.13. 8	def.	31.1	32.1	def.
	Newton		5	8	187. 0. 0	233. 5. 0	509.15. 0	3.10.10 1/2	3.17. 9 3/4	8.17. 9	52.8	60.0	57.4	13.6

Rosedale East Side		1		def.	1,531.10. 9	1,605. 0. 9	(0. 5. 2)	33.11. 7¼	35. 7. 8	def.	45.6	45.4	def.
Snainton				3,203. 0. 0	451. 5. 0	3,654. 5. 0	65.17.11	12.16. 0	78.13.11	48.6	35.2	46.4	-27.6
Staintondale			1	927. 0. 0	100. 0. 0	1,027. 0. 0	29.10. 8	2.10. 9	32. 1. 5	31.4	39.4	32.0	25.5
Wilton			1	1,782. 0. 0	125. 0. 0	1,907. 0. 0	40.14. 6	3. 0. 3	43.14. 9	43.8	41.5	43.6	-5.2
Wrelton				820. 0. 0	294. 0. 0	1,114. 0. 0	14. 2. 1¼	5.12. 1¾	19.14. 3	58.1	52.4	56.5	-9.8
SUBTOTAL				12,945.13. 8	9,104. 2. 6	22,869. 3. 2	292.11. 9¾	265. 1.11	555. 7. 7½	44.2	34.3	41.2	-22.4
Ryedale													
Cawton				205. 9. 2	6. 8. 4	211.17. 6	41. 1.10	1. 5. 8	42. 7. 6	5.0	5.0	5.0	0.0
New Malton, St Leonards				68. 6. 0	75.11. 0	143.17. 0	14. 3. 0	14.17. 0	29. 0. 0	4.8	5.1	5.0	6.2
New Malton, St Michaels				134. 0. 0	64.15. 0	198.15. 0 (271. 0. 0) Stock in trade	26.16. 0	12.19. 0	39.15. 0 (13.11. 0) Stock in trade	5.0	5.0	5.0 (20.0)	0.0
Old Malton	1829	55		def.	def.	7,536. 0. 0	(54. 1.11)	(39.15. 2)	93.17. 1	def.	def.	80.3	def.
Rosedale West Side				476. 0. 0	138. 0. 0	614. 0. 0	13.14. 8	4. 9. 4	18. 4. 0	34.7	30.9	33.7	-11.0
Salton and Brawby (Brawby only)		2		339. 0. 0	620. 0. 0	1,175. 0. 0	8. 2. 8½	15.13. 4½	28. 1. 5½	41.7	39.6	41.8	-5.0
Wath				none	36.18. 6	36.18. 6	none	7. 6. 8	7. 6. 8	NA	5.0	5.0	NA
Wombleton		4		396. 0. 0	202. 0. 0	868. 0. 0	11. 8. 9	4. 6. 4¾	20. 2. 2¾	34.6	46.8	43.2	35.3
SUBTOTAL				1,618.15. 2	1,143.12.10	10,784. 8. 0	115. 6.11½	60.17. 5¼	278.13.11¼	14.0	18.8	38.7	34.3
Whitby Strand													
SUBTOTAL				No rents reported									
1	2			6	7	8	9	10	11	12	13	14	15
RIDING				84,301.12. 9	193,442. 5.10	272,218. 9. 2¼	3,008. 2. 7¼	7,104. 0.11¼	9,364. 2. 5¼	28.0	27.2	29.1	-2.8

Notes: Values in parentheses are excluded from wapentake and riding totals. NA = not applicable. NR = not reported. Def. = defective. Townships omitted from this appendix failed to report rents c. 1830, or reported less than half the rentals.
Source: Land tax duplicates, NYCRO. See map 6.

APPENDIX K

Total valuational rent and tax, with rent-to-tax ratios, for all townships of Gilling East wapentake reporting rent, c. five-year intervals 1785–1826

Numbered columns:

1 = Wapentake.
2 = Township.
3 = Year of tax duplicate, if other than that of section.
4 = Number of ''split'' entries (see explanation, Appendix J).
5 = Number of ''omission'' entries (see explanation, Appendix J).
6 = Total redeemed rent.
7 = Total unredeemed rent.
8 = Total redeemed plus unredeemed rent (or simply total rent before 1801 section).
9 = Total redeemed tax.
10 = Total unredeemed tax.
11 = Total redeemed plus unredeemed tax (or simply total tax before 1801 section). All rent and tax totals are derived by adding the values reported for each individual property bundle.
12 = The ratio of redeemed rent to redeemed tax. All ratios are to the value 1.
13 = The ratio of unredeemed rent to unredeemed tax.
14 = The ratio of total rent (redeemed plus unredeemed 1801-26) to total tax.
15 = The percentage difference between the redeemed ratio and the unredeemed ratio, i.e., ((unred. ratio - red. ratio)/red. ratio) x 100.

I. 1785

1	2	3	4	5	6	7	8	9	10	11	12	13	14	15
Gilling East														
	Croft	1784					2,474. 0. 0			127.19.11 3/4			19.3	
	Kirby Wiske	1784					868. 0. 0			46. 8. 4			18.7	
	Maunby						1,105. 0. 0			73.13. 4			15.0	
	Newby Wiske						578. 0. 0			36.10. 0			15.8	
	Smeaton, Great	1783					1,329. 0. 0			60. 0. 0			22.2	
	TOTAL						6,354. 0. 0			344.11. 7 3/4			18.4	

II. 1790

1	2	3	4	5	6	7	8	9	10	11	12	13	14	15
Gilling East														
	Brompton on Swale						1,622. 0. 0			52.12. 8			30.8	
	Cleasby	1791					796. 0. 0			46. 8. 8			17.1	
	Cowton, East	1789					2,086. 0. 0			125.15. 7 1/2			16.6	
	Cowton, North						1,004. 0. 0			43.18. 7 1/2			22.8	
	Cowton, South	1792					1,251.10. 0			110. 0. 4 3/4			11.4	
	Ellerton upon Swale etc.						2,424. 7. 0			92. 1. 4			26.3	
	Kiplin	1791		1			638.10. 0			40.16. 8			15.6	
	Kirby Wiske						917. 0. 0			44.16. 1 1/4			20.5	
	Langton, Little	1791					674. 0. 0			28. 0. 0			24.1	
	Manfield	1789					1,992. 1. 6			152. 7. 6 3/4			13.1	
	Maunby						1,191. 0. 0			73. 4. 0 1/2			16.3	
	Newby Wiske						613. 0. 0			36.11. 0			16.8	
	Yafforth						1,051. 5. 0			80. 0. 0			13.1	
	TOTAL						16,260.13. 6			926.12. 8 1/4			17.5	

III. 1795

1	2	3	4	5	6	7	8	9	10	11	12	13	14	15
Gilling East														
	Brompton on Swale						1,635. 0. 0			52.15.10 3/4			31.0	
	Cleasby						827. 0. 0			46.10. 4 1/2			17.8	
	Cowton, North	1794					1,030.10. 0			43. 9. 3 1/4			23.7	
	Dalton upon Tees						976. 0. 0			45.15. 0 1/4			21.3	
	Ellerton upon Swale						2,876. 4. 0			91.18.10 1/2			31.3	
	Kiplin						761.10. 0			41. 6.11			18.4	
	Kirby Wiske						922. 0. 0			46. 2. 0			20.0	
	Langton, Little	1794					670. 0. 0			28. 0. 0			23.9	
	Maunby						1,210. 0. 0			73. 1.11			16.6	
	Newby Wiske						623. 0. 0			36.13. 0			17.0	
	Smeaton, Great						1,397. 0. 0			60. 0. 0			23.3	
	Yafforth						1,342. 0. 0			80. 0. 0			16.8	
	TOTAL						14,270. 4. 0			645.13. 3 1/4			22.1	

APPENDIX K (continued) page 458

IV. 1801 1 2	3	4	5	6	7	8	9	10	11	12	13	14	15
Gilling East													
Ainderby Steeple				288. 0. 0	667. 0. 0	955. 0. 0	12.11. 5	28. 0. 0	40.11. 5	22.9	23.8	23.5	3.9
Barton		1		254. 0. 0	1,582. 0. 0	2,186. 0. 0	7.13. 9	49. 8. 9	67.18. 1 1/2	33.0	32.0	32.2	-3.0
Brompton on Swale				935.10. 0	967.10. 0	1,903. 0. 0	26. 3. 9 1/4	26. 4. 0 3/4	52. 7.10	35.7	36.9	36.3	3.4
Cleasby				16. 0. 0	823. 0. 0	839. 0. 0	0.17. 7 3/4	45. 8. 8 3/4	46. 6. 4 1/2	18.1	18.1	18.1	0.0
Cowton, East				none	2,426. 0. 0	2,426. 0. 0	none	125. 2. 7	125. 2. 7	NA	19.4	19.4	NA
Cowton, North				367.10. 0	682. 0. 0	1,049.10. 0	15. 9. 8 3/4	28.17. 2	44. 6.10 3/4	23.7	23.6	23.7	-0.4
Cowton, South				331.10. 0	921.10. 0	1,253. 0. 0	29.15. 3	80. 6. 1 1/2	110. 1. 4 1/2	11.1	11.5	11.4	3.6
Croft				none	2,410. 0. 0	2,410. 0. 0	none	128. 3. 0	128. 3. 0	NA	18.8	18.8	NA
Dalton upon Tees				143. 0. 0	914. 0. 0	1,057. 0. 0	6. 2. 2 1/4	39. 7.10	45.10. 0 1/4	23.4	23.2	23.2	-0.8
Danby Wiske	1802			466. 0. 0	1,704.10. 0	2,170.10. 0	23.16. 8 3/4	83. 8.10 3/4	107. 5. 7 1/2	19.5	20.4	20.2	4.6
Ellerton upon Swale, etc.				none	3,120. 8. 0	3,120. 8. 0	none	89.11. 7 1/2	89.11. 7 1/2	NA	34.8	34.8	NA
Eryholme				88. 0. 0	1,652. 0. 0	1,740. 0. 0	2.16. 4 1/2	52.18. 3 1/2	55.14. 8	31.2	31.2	31.2	0.0
Kiplin				none	796.10. 0	796.10. 0	none	41. 9. 8 1/4	41. 9. 8 1/4	NA	19.2	19.2	NA
Kirby Wiske				182. 3. 0	737.17. 0	920. 0. 0	9. 2. 1 3/4	36.17. 9	45.19.10 3/4	20.0	20.0	20.0	0.0
Langton, Great			1	219. 0. 0	277. 0. 0	496. 0. 0	16. 6. 6	19.19. 6 1/2	36. 6. 0 1/2	13.4	13.9	13.7	3.7
Langton, Little	1802			550. 0. 0	210. 0. 0	760. 0. 0	20. 5. 4	7.14. 8	28. 0. 0	27.1	27.2	27.1	0.4
Manfield				122. 0. 0	1,610.18. 0	1,732.18. 0	10.14.10	141.19. 4	152.14. 2	11.4	11.3	11.3	-0.9
Maunby			1	118.10. 0	1,293. 0. 0	1,411.10. 0	6.10. 2 1/2	57. 6. 1 1/4	63.16. 3 3/4	18.2	22.6	22.1	24.2
Middleton Tyas		1		2,635. 0. 0	682.10. 0	3,317.10. 0	56. 4. 6	15.15. 2	74. 0. 0	46.9	43.3	44.8	-7.7
Morton on Swale and Fareholm				887.10. 0	547.10. 0	1,435. 0. 0	39. 0. 1	24. 0.10	63. 0.11	22.8	22.8	22.8	0.0
Moulton				305. 0. 0	1,599. 0. 0	1,904. 0. 0	12.14. 4	65. 5. 8	78. 0. 0	24.0	24.5	24.4	2.1
Newby Wiske				42. 0. 0	609.10. 0	651.10. 0	2. 7. 3	34. 2. 9	36.10. 0	17.8	17.8	17.8	0.0
Newton Morrell				none	463. 0. 0	463. 0. 0	none	20. 7. 0	20. 7. 0	NA	22.8	22.8	NA
Scorton and Uckerby				1,227. 0. 0	1,401. 0. 0	2,628. 0. 0	26.11. 8	28. 8. 6	55. 0. 2	46.2	49.3	47.8	6.7
Smeaton, Great			1	440. 0. 0	1,052. 0. 0	1,492. 0. 0	16.15. 8	42. 5. 6 1/2	59. 1. 2 1/2	26.2	24.9	25.3	-5.0
Stapleton				323.10. 0	643. 0. 0	966.10. 0	17.19. 2	35. 7. 6	53. 6. 8	18.0	18.2	18.1	1.1
Thrintoft				469. 0. 0	584.10. 0	1,053.10. 0	23.15. 0	29.11. 9	53. 6. 9	19.7	19.8	19.8	0.5
Warlaby and Low Sober				236. 0. 0	769. 0. 0	1,005. 0. 0	14.12. 2	46. 8. 1	61. 0. 3	16.2	16.6	16.5	2.5
Yafforth	1800			193. 0. 0	1,189. 0. 0	1,382. 0. 0	10.15. 7	69. 4. 5	80. 0. 0	17.9	17.2	17.3	-3.9
TOTAL				10,839. 3. 0	32,335. 3. 0	43,524. 6. 0	409. 1. 3 1/2	1,493. 1. 4 1/4	1,914.18. 7 1/4	26.5	21.6	22.7	-18.5

V. 1806 1 2	3	4	5	6	7	8	9	10	11	12	13	14	15
Gilling East													
Ainderby Steeple	1807			358. 0. 0	619. 0. 0	977. 0. 0	14.11.11	26. 0. 0	40.11.11	24.5	23.8	24.1	-2.8
Barton	1807			696. 0. 0	1,691.10. 0	2,387.10. 0	18. 3. 1 1/2	49. 6. 8 1/2	67. 9.10	38.3	34.3	35.4	-10.4
Brompton on Swale				1,041.10. 0	861.10. 0	1,903. 0. 0	29. 1. 6 1/4	23. 6. 7 1/4	52. 8. 1 1/2	35.8	36.9	36.3	3.1
Cleasby				16. 0. 0	825. 0. 0	841. 0. 0	0.17. 7 3/4	45.10.11 1/4	46. 8. 7	18.1	18.1	18.1	0.0
Cowton, East				none	3,088. 0. 0	3,088. 0. 0	none	125. 9. 0	125. 9. 0	NA	24.6	24.6	NA
Cowton, North			1	373. 0. 0	785. 0. 0	1,158. 0. 0	15. 9. 9 1/4	26. 3. 4	41.13. 1 1/4	24.1	30.0	27.8	24.5
Cowton, South				415. 0. 0	1,144. 0. 0	1,559. 0. 0	29.15. 3	80. 4. 9	110. 0. 0	13.9	14.2	14.2	2.2
Croft				none	3,242. 0. 0	3,242. 0. 0	none	128. 6. 7	128. 6. 7	NA	25.3	25.3	NA
Dalton upon Tees				183. 0. 0	1,371. 0. 0	1,554. 0. 0	6. 2. 2 1/4	39.19. 9	46. 1.11 1/4	30.0	34.3	33.7	14.3
Danby Wiske				538. 0. 0	1,889. 0. 0	2,427. 0. 0	23.16. 9	84.12. 2	108. 8.11	22.6	22.3	22.4	-1.3
Ellerton upon Swale, etc.	1805			22. 0. 0	3,581. 2. 0	3,603. 2. 0	0.12. 3	91.10. 4 1/4	92. 2. 7 1/4	35.9	39.1	39.1	8.9
Eryholme				92. 0. 0	1,836. 0. 0	1,928. 0. 0	2.16. 4 1/2	52.18. 3 1/2	55.14. 8	32.6	34.7	34.6	6.4
Kiplin				none	806.10. 0	806.10. 0	none	41. 7. 6 1/2	41. 7. 6 1/2	NA	19.5	19.5	NA
Kirby Wiske		1		391.19. 0	495. 1. 0	920. 0. 0	19.11.11 1/4	24.14.11	45.19.10 1/4	20.0	20.0	20.0	0.0
Langton, Great				219. 0. 0	324. 0. 0	543. 0. 0	16. 6. 5 3/4	24. 2. 3 1/2	40. 8. 9 1/4	13.4	13.4	13.4	0.0
Langton, Little				550. 0. 0	210. 0. 0	760. 0. 0	20. 5. 4	7.14. 8	28. 0. 0	27.1	27.2	27.1	0.4
Manfield				163. 0. 0	2,069. 0. 0	2,232. 0. 0	10.13.11 1/4	140. 7. 0 1/4	151. 0.11 1/2	15.2	14.7	14.7	-3.3
Maunby			1	724.10. 0	688. 0. 0	1,412.10. 0	37.11. 1 1/2	35. 2. 5 3/4	72.13. 7 1/4	19.3	19.6	19.4	1.6
Middleton Tyas	1805	1		2,644.15. 0	908.12. 3	3,667. 7. 3	56. 0.11	16. 9. 8	74.10.10 1/2	47.2	55.1	49.2	16.7
Morton on Swale and Fareholm	1807			1,021.10. 0	413.10. 0	1,435. 0. 0	44.17. 9	18. 3. 3	63. 1. 0	22.8	22.8	22.8	0.0
Moulton				515. 0. 0	1,429. 0. 0	1,944. 0. 0	21. 2.11	56.17. 1	78. 0. 0	24.4	25.1	24.9	2.9
Newby Wiske				42. 0. 0	609.10. 0	651.10. 0	2. 7. 3	34. 2. 9	36.10. 0	17.8	17.8	17.8	0.0
Newton Morrell				none	681. 0. 0	681. 0. 0	none	20. 7. 0	20. 7. 0	NA	33.5	33.5	NA
Scorton and Uckerby				1,261. 0. 0	1,385. 0. 0	2,646. 0. 0	27. 4. 4	28. 2. 5 1/2	55. 6. 9 1/2	46.3	49.2	47.8	6.3
Smeaton, Great				689. 0. 0	836. 0. 0	1,525. 0. 0	27. 1. 7	32.18. 5	60. 0. 0	25.4	25.4	25.4	0.0
Stapleton				389.10. 0	592. 0. 0	981.10. 0	21.10. 1	31.16. 7	53. 6. 8	18.1	18.6	18.4	2.8
Thrintoft	1807			592. 0. 0	587.10. 0	1,179.10. 0	28.18. 0	24. 9. 7	53. 7. 7	20.5	24.0	22.1	17.1
Warlaby and Low Sober	1807			247. 0. 0	764. 0. 0	1,011. 0. 0	14.18. 2	46. 2. 1	61. 0. 3	16.6	16.6	16.6	0.0
Yafforth	1807			205. 0. 0	1,176. 0. 0	1,381. 0. 0	11. 9. 7	68.10. 5	80. 0. 0	17.8	17.2	17.3	-3.4
TOTAL				13,389.14. 0	34,907.15. 3	48,444. 9. 3	501. 6. 2 1/4	1,424.16. 8 1/4	1,929.16. 2	26.7	24.5	25.1	-8.2

APPENDIX K (continued) page 460

VI. 1810

1	2	3	4	5	6	7	8	9	10	11	12	13	14	15
Gilling East														
	Ainderby Steeple				406. 0. 0	577. 0. 0	983. 0. 0	16.12. 1	24. 0. 4	40.12. 5	24.4	24.0	24.2	1.6
	Barton				766. 0. 0	1,917.10. 0	2,683.10. 0	18. 3. 1 1/2	51.18. 7 3/4	70. 1. 9 1/4	42.2	36.9	38.3	-12.6
	Brompton on Swale		1		973.10. 0	799.10. 0	1,883. 0. 0	27. 3. 3	20.13. 0 1/2	50.17. 3 1/2	35.8	38.7	37.0	8.1
	Cleasby				16. 0. 0	825. 0. 0	841. 0. 0	0.17. 7 3/4	45.10.11 1/4	46. 8. 7	18.1	18.1	18.1	0.0
	Cowton, East				none	3,328. 0. 0	3,328. 0. 0	none	125. 4.10 1/4	125. 4.10 1/4	NA	26.6	26.6	NA
	Cowton, North				408. 0. 0	783. 0. 0	1,191. 0. 0	15.15. 9 3/4	26. 5. 4	42. 1. 1 3/4	25.8	29.8	28.3	15.5
	Cowton, South				415. 0. 0	1,144. 0. 0	1,559. 0. 0	29.15. 3	80. 4. 9	110. 0. 0	13.9	14.2	14.2	2.2
	Croft				none	3,242. 0. 0	3,242. 0. 0	none	129. 6. 6 1/2	129. 6. 6 1/2	NA	25.1	25.1	NA
	Dalton upon Tees				184. 0. 0	1,714. 0. 0	1,898. 0. 0	6. 2. 2 1/2	42.18. 6	49. 0. 8 1/2	30.1	39.9	38.7	32.6
	Danby Wiske				538. 0. 0	1,889. 0. 0	2,427. 0. 0	23.16. 8 3/4	84.12. 2	108. 8.10 3/4	22.6	22.3	22.4	-1.3
	Ellerton upon Swale, etc.				22. 0. 0	3,927. 5. 0	3,949. 5. 0	0.12. 3	94. 1. 6	94.13. 9	35.9	41.7	41.7	16.2
	Eryholme				92. 0. 0	1,835. 0. 0	1,927. 0. 0	2.16. 4 1/2	52.18. 3 1/2	55.14. 8	32.6	34.7	34.6	6.4
	Kiplin				none	1,055.10. 0	1,055.10. 0	none	41.10.10	41.10.10	NA	25.4	25.4	NA
	Kirby Wiske		1		391.19. 0	495. 1. 0	920. 0. 0	19.11.11 1/4	24.14.11 1/2	45.19.10 3/4	20.0	20.0	20.0	0.0
	Langton, Great				219. 0. 0	324. 0. 0	543. 0. 0	16. 6. 5 3/4	24. 2.10	40. 9. 3 3/4	13.4	13.4	13.4	0.0
	Langton, Little				550. 0. 0	210. 0. 0	760. 0. 0	20. 5. 3 3/4	7.14. 9	28. 0. 0 3/4	27.1	27.1	27.1	0.0
	Manfield				162.10. 0	2,107.10. 0	2,270. 0. 0	10.15. 8 1/2	139. 4. 8	150. 0. 4 1/2	15.1	15.1	15.1	0.0
	Maunby				904.10. 0	508. 0. 0	1,412.10. 0	46.14.10 3/4	25.17.11 1/4	72.12.10	19.3	19.6	19.4	1.6
	Middleton Tyas		2	2	2,889.15. 0	930.10. 0	3,945. 5. 0	55.17. 7	15.19. 0	74. 0. 0	51.7	58.3	53.3	12.8
	Morton on Swale and Fareholm				1,021.10. 0	401. 0. 0	1,422.10. 0	44.17. 9	18. 2. 2	62.19.11	22.8	22.1	22.6	-3.1
	Moulton				695. 0. 0	1,249. 0. 0	1,944. 0. 0	28. 6. 2	49.13.10	78. 0. 0	24.6	25.1	24.9	2.0
	Newby Wiske				417. 0. 0	302.10. 0	719.10. 0	23. 6. 2 1/4	13. 3. 9 3/4	36.10. 0	17.9	22.9	19.7	27.9
	Newton Morrell				none	681. 0. 0	681. 0. 0	none	20. 7. 0	20. 7. 0	NA	33.5	33.5	NA
	Scorton and Uckerby				1,261. 0. 0	1,988.10. 0	3,249.10. 0	27. 4. 4	28. 3. 6 1/2	55. 7.10 1/2	46.3	70.6	58.7	52.5
	Smeaton, Great				689. 0. 0	836. 0. 0	1,525. 0. 0	27. 1. 7	32.18. 5	60. 0. 0	25.4	25.4	25.4	0.0
	Stapleton				389.10. 0	592. 0. 0	981.10. 0	21.10. 1	31.16. 7	53. 6. 8	18.1	18.6	18.4	2.8
	Thrintoft				592. 0. 0	587.10. 0	1,179.10. 0	28.18. 0	24. 9. 7	53. 7. 7	20.5	24.0	22.1	17.1
	Warlaby and Low Sober				247. 0. 0	764. 0. 0	1,011. 0. 0	14.18. 2	45.12. 1	60.10. 3	16.6	16.8	16.7	1.2
	Yafforth				205. 0. 0	1,176. 0. 0	1,381. 0. 0	11. 9. 7	68.10. 4	79.19.11	17.8	17.2	17.3	-3.4
	TOTAL				14,455. 4. 0	36,189. 6. 0	50,912.10. 0	538.18. 6	1,389.17. 2 3/4	1,935.13. 1 3/4	26.8	26.0	26.3	-3.0

VII. 1815

1	2	3	4	5	6	7	8	9	10	11	12	13	14	15
Gilling East														
	Ainderby Steeple				394.10. 0	578. 0. 0	972.10. 0	16.16. 0	24. 7. 1	41. 3. 1	23.5	23.7	23.6	0.8
	Barton			1	736. 0. 0	2,126. 0. 0	2,862. 0. 0	18. 3. 1 1/2	53. 3. 0	71. 6. 1 1/2	40.5	40.0	40.1	-1.2
	Brompton on Swale		2		845.10. 0	806.10. 0	1,898. 0. 0	23.11. 1	21.10.10 1/2	51.17. 2	35.9	37.4	36.6	4.2
	Cleasby				16. 0. 0	826. 0. 0	842. 0. 0	0.17. 7 3/4	45.12. 0 1/2	46. 9. 8 1/4	18.1	18.1	18.1	0.0
	Cowton, East				none	3,752. 0. 0	3,752. 0. 0	none	125. 1. 4	125. 1. 4	NA	30.0	30.0	NA
	Cowton, North				410. 0. 0	775.10. 0	1,185.10. 0	15.15. 1 3/4	27. 9. 3 3/4	43. 4. 5 1/2	26.0	28.2	27.4	8.5
	Cowton, South				415. 0. 0	1,139. 0. 0	1,554. 0. 0	29.15. 3	78.19. 7 1/2	108.14.10 1/2	13.9	14.4	14.3	3.6
	Croft				none	3,234. 0. 0	3,234. 0. 0	none	130. 2.11	130. 2.11	NA	24.8	24.8	NA
	Dalton upon Tees				184. 0. 0	1,708. 0. 0	1,892. 0. 0	6. 2. 2 1/2	38.13. 8	44.15.10 1/2	30.1	44.2	42.2	40.2
	Danby Wiske				538. 0. 0	1,893. 0. 0	2,431. 0. 0	23.16. 8 3/4	83. 3. 4 1/2	107. 0. 1 1/4	22.6	22.8	22.7	0.9
	Ellerton upon Swale, etc.				231. 1. 0	4,341. 2. 0	4,572. 3. 0	2. 8. 9	89.10. 6 1/2	91.19. 3 1/2	94.8	48.5	49.7	-48.8
	Eryholme				92. 0. 0	1,835. 0. 0	1,927. 0. 0	2.16. 4 1/2	52.18. 3 1/2	55.14. 8	32.6	34.7	34.6	6.4
	Kiplin			1	none	1,179.10. 0	1,179.10. 0	none	41. 7. 6	41. 7. 6	NA	28.5	28.5	NA
	Kirby Wiske				424.19. 0	495. 1. 0	920. 0. 0	20. 2.11 1/4	25.16.11 1/2	45.19.10 3/4	21.1	19.2	20.0	-9.0
	Langton, Great				287. 0. 0	250. 0. 0	537. 0. 0	21. 7. 9 1/4	19. 1. 6 1/4	40. 9. 4	13.4	13.1	13.3	-2.2
	Langton, Little				550. 0. 0	210. 0. 0	760. 0. 0	20. 5. 3 3/4	7.14. 9	28. 0. 0 3/4	27.1	27.1	27.1	0.0
	Manfield				162.10. 0	2,116.10. 0	2,279. 0. 0	10.15. 8 1/2	140.11. 8	151. 7. 4 1/2	15.1	15.0	15.0	-0.7
	Maunby				904.10. 0	508. 0. 0	1,412.10. 0	46.14.10 3/4	25.18. 8	72.13. 6 3/4	19.3	19.6	19.4	1.6
	Middleton Tyas		3	2	2,839. 5. 0	944.10. 0	3,911.15. 0	55.17. 1	15.18. 4	74. 0. 0	50.8	59.3	52.9	16.7
	Morton on Swale and Fareholm				1,021.10. 0	370. 0. 0	1,391.10. 0	44.17. 9	18. 2. 2 1/2	62.19.11 1/2	22.8	20.4	22.1	-10.5
	Moulton				752.10. 0	1,304.10. 0	2,057. 0. 0	28. 6. 2	49.13.10	78. 0. 0	26.6	26.2	26.4	-1.5
	Newby Wiske				417. 0. 0	302.10. 0	719.10. 0	23.14. 2 1/4	13. 3. 8 3/4	36.17.11	17.6	22.9	19.5	30.1
	Newton Morrell				none	1,080. 0. 0	1,080. 0. 0	none	20. 7. 0	20. 7. 0	NA	53.1	53.1	NA
	Scorton and Uckerby				1,260. 0. 0	1,958.10. 0	3,218.10. 0	27. 4. 0	27.16. 0	55. 0. 0	46.3	70.4	58.5	52.0
	Smeaton, Great				689. 0. 0	812. 0. 0	1,501. 0. 0	27. 1. 7	32.18. 5	60. 0. 0	25.4	24.7	25.0	-2.8
	Stapleton				389.10. 0	592. 0. 0	981.10. 0	21.10. 1	31.16. 7	53. 6. 8	18.1	18.6	18.4	2.8
	Thrintoft				592. 0. 0	587.10. 0	1,179.10. 0	29.18. 2	24. 9. 7	54. 7. 9	19.8	24.0	21.7	21.2
	Warlaby and Low Sober				327. 0. 0	683. 0. 0	1,010. 0. 0	19.14. 9	41. 5. 6	61. 0. 3	16.6	16.5	16.6	-0.6
	Yafforth				211. 0. 0	1,172. 0. 0	1,383. 0. 0	11. 9. 7	68.10. 6	80. 0. 1	18.4	17.1	17.3	-7.1
	TOTAL				14,689.15. 0	37,579.13. 0	52,643. 8. 0	549. 2. 3 1/2	1,375. 4. 9 3/4	1,933. 6.11 1/4	26.8	27.3	27.2	1.9

APPENDIX K (continued) page 462

VIII. 1820

1 2	3	4	5	6	7	8	9	10	11	12	13	14	15
Gilling East													
Brompton on Swale		1		981.10. 0	806.10. 0	1,898. 0. 0	27. 5. 3 1/2	21.10.10	51.17. 1 1/2	36.0	37.4	36.6	3.9
Croft				none	3,164. 0. 0	3,164. 0. 0	none	128.18.11	128.18.11	NA	24.5	24.5	NA
Dalton upon Tees				186. 0. 0	1,493. 0. 0	1,679. 0. 0	6. 2. 2 1/2	39. 9. 5 3/4	45.11. 8 1/4	30.4	37.8	36.8	24.3
Ellerton upon Swale, etc.				196. 0. 0	4,445. 0. 0	4,641. 0. 0	2. 8. 9	89.15. 1 1/2	92. 3.10 1/2	80.4	49.5	50.3	-38.4
Eryholme				92. 0. 0	1,835. 0. 0	1,927. 0. 0	2.16. 4 1/2	52.18. 6 1/2	55. 4.11	32.6	34.7	34.9	6.4
Kiplin				none	1,309.10. 0	1,309.10. 0	none	41. 6. 9	41. 6. 9	NA	31.7	31.7	NA
Maunby				904.10. 0	508. 0. 0	1,412.10. 0	46.14.10 3/4	26. 1. 0 1/4	72.15.11	19.3	19.5	19.4	1.0
Morton on Swale and Fareholm				1,021.10. 0	370.10. 0	1,392. 0. 0	44.17. 9	18. 2. 3 1/2	63. 0. 0 1/2	22.8	20.4	22.1	-10.5
Newby Wiske				416.10. 0	308.10. 0	725. 0. 0	23.14. 7 1/4	13. 3. 9 3/4	36.18. 5	17.6	23.4	19.6	33.0
Scorton and Uckerby				1,265. 0. 0	1,958.10. 0	3,223.10. 0	27. 4. 8 1/2	27.16. 0	55. 0. 8 1/2	46.4	70.4	58.6	51.7
TOTAL				5,062.10. 0	16,198.10. 0	21,371.10. 0	181. 4. 7	459. 2. 9 1/4	642.18.11 1/4	27.9	35.3	33.2	26.5

IX. 1826 1 2	3	4	5	6	7	8	9	10	11	12	13	14	15
Gilling East													
Ainderby Steeple				419.10. 0	496.10. 0	916. 0. 0	17. 9. 0	23. 1. 3¼	40.10. 3¼	24.0	21.5	22.6	-10.4
Barton		2		695. 0. 0	1,586.10. 0	2,487.10. 0	16.15. 7	45. 3. 5	67.17. 1	41.4	35.1	36.6	-15.2
Brompton on Swale		1	2	951.10. 0	856.10. 0	1,808. 0. 0	26. 9. 0½	19.18. 4¼	49. 8. 4¾	36.0	43.0	36.6	19.4
Cleasby				16. 0. 0	846. 0. 0	862. 0. 0	0.17. 8	45.10.11	46. 8. 7	18.1	18.6	18.6	2.8
Cowton, East				none	3,517. 0. 0	3,517. 0. 0	none	131. 0. 6	131. 0. 6	NA	26.8	26.8	NA
Cowton, North				457.17. 0	790.10. 0	1,248. 7. 0	16. 4. 3¾	27.19.11¼	44. 4. 3	28.2	28.2	28.2	0.0
Cowton, South				343. 0. 0	1,102.10. 0	1,445.10. 0	29.15. 3	80. 4. 8¼	109.19.11¼	11.5	13.7	13.1	19.1
Croft				none	3,658. 0. 0	3,658. 0. 0	none	129.10.11½	129.10.11½	NA	28.2	28.2	NA
Dalton upon Tees				157. 0. 0	1,340. 0. 0	1,497. 0. 0	6. 2. 2¼	39. 7. 9¾	45.10. 0	25.7	34.0	32.9	32.3
Danby Wiske				NR	1,799. 5. 0	NA	(23.16. 8¾)	83. 3. 8½	(107. 0. 5¼)	NA	21.6	NA	NA
Ellerton upon Swale, etc.				180. 0. 0	4,562.19. 0	4,742.19. 0	2. 8. 9	89.10. 3	91.19. 0	73.8	51.0	51.6	-30.9
Eryholme				80. 0. 0	1,748. 0. 0	1,828. 0. 0	2.16. 4½	52.18. 3½	55.14. 8	28.4	33.0	32.8	16.2
Kiplin				none	1,268.10. 0	1,268.10. 0	none	41. 6. 8	41. 6. 8	NA	30.7	30.7	NA
Kirby Wiske		2	16	364. 3. 6	381. 0. 0	812.16. 0	18. 4. 2¼	19. 1. 0¾	40.12.10½	20.0	20.0	20.0	0.0
Langton, Great			1	614. 0. 0	5. 0. 0	619. 0. 0	35.14. 0½	0.11.11	36. 5.11½	17.2	8.4	17.0	-51.2
Langton, Little				739. 0. 0	266.10. 0	1,005.10. 0	20. 5. 4	7.14. 8	28. 0. 0	36.5	34.5	35.9	-5.5
Manfield				140. 0. 0	2,240.10. 0	2,380.10. 0	10.10. 0	142. 6. 4¾	152.16. 4¾	13.3	15.7	15.6	18.0
Maunby				904.10. 0	508. 0. 0	1,412.10. 0	46.14.10¾	26. 0. 8¾	72.15. 7½	19.3	19.5	19.4	1.0
Middleton Tyas		13	1	2,828. 0. 0	934.10. 0	3,901. 0. 0	56. 1. 7	15.13. 9	73.19.10	50.4	59.6	52.7	18.2
Morton on Swale and Fareholm				1,021.10. 0	334.10. 0	1,356. 0. 0	44.17. 9	18. 2. 3½	63. 0. 0½	22.8	18.5	21.5	-18.8
Newby Wiske				416.10. 0	308.10. 0	725. 0. 0	23. 6. 0¾	13. 3.11¼	36.10. 0	17.9	23.4	19.9	30.7
Scorton and Uckerby		1		1,265. 0. 0	1,789.10. 0	3,214.10. 0	25. 4. 2	25.17. 5¾	54. 1. 7¾	50.2	69.2	59.4	37.8
Thrintoft				702.10. 0	586. 0. 0	1,288.10. 0	28.19. 5	24. 8. 4	53. 7. 9	24.2	24.0	24.1	-0.8
Warlaby and Low Sober				602.10. 0	991. 0. 0	1,593.10. 0	19.14. 9	41. 5. 3	61. 0. 0	30.5	24.0	26.1	-21.3
Yafforth		5		150. 0. 0	937. 0. 0	1,376. 0. 0	8. 2. 6	54.12. 7	79.19.11	18.5	17.2	17.2	-7.0
TOTAL				13,047.10. 6		44,963.12. 0		1,197.15. 2		28.6		28.0	
					32,854. 4. 0		456.12.10¼		1,606. 0. 4¼		27.4		-4.2

Note: Values in parentheses are excluded from wapentake totals. NA = not applicable. NR = not reported. Def. = defective. Townships omitted from this appendix failed to report rents circa the date of their section.
Source: Land tax duplicates, NYCRO.

APPENDIX L

The usual valuational basis of the poor rate according to the clerks of the peace and the 1803 Poor Law Report, all counties, England and Wales

County	Usual basis of valuation[a]	No. of parishes or townships in 1803 report	Parishes reporting at rack rent in 1803 report No.	%
Bedfordshire	Rack rent	140	0	
Berkshire	NS	191	1	0.5
Buckinghamshire	Houses two-thirds and lands three-quarters of rack rent; ''quality price'' following enclosure or ''fresh'' valuation	223	1	0.4
Cambridgeshire	NS	175	1	0.6
Cheshire	NS	491	9	1.8
Cornwall	''somewhat, and probably not very considerably, below One Half of the Rented Value''	215	5	2.3
Cumberland	Towns at rack rent less one-eighth; land at rack rent less one-quarter or more	215	2	0.9
Derbyshire	NS	317	0	
Devonshire	NA	474	3	0.6
Dorset	c. two-thirds of rack rent (averaged for county)	286	2	0.7
Durham	Rack rent less one-quarter (averaged for county)	289	5	1.7
Essex	Four-fifths or more of rack rent (''as near the Rack as may be, at least in all Towns and other considerable Places'')	415	8	1.9
Gloucestershire	c. three-quarters of rack rent (averaged for county)	399	4	1.0
Hampshire	c. two-thirds of rack rent (averaged for county)	331	9	2.7
Herefordshire	NS	259	0	
Hertfordshire	[Defective response from Clerk of the Peace]	142	8	5.6
Huntingdonshire	''The Magistrates desired me to say, much of this County has been lately enclosed, and more of it has been valued by Surveyor, for the Purpose of equalizing the Rates, so that, except a small Part, the County stands in the Rates at nearly a Rack-Rent.''	104	0	
Kent	NS	409	7	1.7
Lancashire	NS	452	4	0.9

Leicestershire	c. half of rack rent	323	1	0.3
Lincolnshire				
Holland	NA	41	0	
Kesteven	c. two-thirds of rack rent (averaged for Kesteven)	198	2	1.0
Lindsey	NS	463	7	1.5
Middlesex (including London)	Over three-quarters of parishes at rack rent; 1 at two-thirds rack; 1 at two-fifths rack; 7 at three-quarters rack; 8 at four-fifths rack; 1 at seven-eighths rack; 1 at three-tenths rack. ''Thirty-five Parishes in the City of London have answered ... by stating the Rate to be 'Discretionary.' The Overseers explain this to be a Mode of imposing the Rate with regard to the Ability of the Occupier to pay the Assessment, as well as to the Premises occupied; so that a wealthy Man is rated higher in the Pound than one less able to pay a heavy Assessment; consequently no precise Rate in the Pound could in such Cases be stated.''	208	14	6.7
Monmouth	NS	149	0	
Norfolk	NS	691	149[b]	21.6
Northamptonshire	Rack rent	333	1	0.3
Northumberland	Rack rent less c. one-ninth (averaged for county)	513	2	0.4
Nottinghamshire	NS	269	0	
Oxfordshire	Rack rent	284	5	1.8
Rutland	Rack rent	53	1	1.9
Shropshire	Two-thirds of rack rent	247	8	3.2
Somerset	NS ''but thinks the Rated Rental is somewhat more than Half'' the rack rent	489	7	1.4
Staffordshire	NS	246	2	0.8
Suffolk	NS	510	4	0.8
Surrey	''before the Property Tax took place, the general professed Proportion in most parts of this County was Two-thirds, and at such it continues in the Hundreds of Woking, Blackheath, Godalming, and the Town of Guildford; but, in most other Parts of this County, and particularly in the Hundreds of Kingston, Elmbridge, Reigate, Tandridge, and Wallington, the Parishes since the passing of that Act have been assessed at the Rack Rental.''	151	11	7.3
Sussex	NS	308	7	2.3
Warwickshire	NS	254	2	0.8

APPENDIX L (continued) page 466

County	Usual basis of valuation[a]	No. of parishes or townships in 1803 report	Parishes reporting at rack rent in 1803 report No.	%
Westmorland	NC	108	6	5.6
Wiltshire	Rack rent ''in some places;'' three-quarters of rack rent in ''the greater proportion of parishes;'' ''in others much less.''	336	3	0.9
Worcestershire	NS	225	1	0.4
Yorkshire East	c. three-quarters of rack rent (averaged for riding), but ''irregular.''	422	31	7.4
North	NS	532	8	1.5
West	c. one-third of rack rent (averaged for riding)	644	33	5.1
SUBTOTAL ENGLAND		13,524[c]	374	2.8
Anglesey	NS	74	0	
Breconshire	NS, ''as the same differs very much in every parish''	113	0	
Cardiganshire	c. two-thirds of rack rent	98	0	
Carmarthenshire	NS	126	0	
Carnarvonshire	NA	73	0	
Denbighshire	c. one-half of rack rent (averaged for county)	82	0	
Flint	Two-thirds of rack rent	44	0	
Glamorgan	NS	169	0	
Merioneth	c. one-third of rack rent, ''but it is impossible to be correct in this, as it varies much in different Parts of the County, and also in Dwelling Houses and Gardens, &c. occupied in towns within the County.''	34	0	
Montgomeryshire	Half of rack rent ''in many Parts of the County;'' one-third in ''other Parts;'' rack rent in ''some Parishes.''	69	1	1.4
Pembrokeshire	''there are various Modes of making Rates in the County of Pembroke, viz. by the Plough Land, Ox Land, Land Tax, Value, Old Surveys, New Surveys; and that in the same Parish the Rate frequently varies in the Proportion of twenty to one.''	151	1	0.7

Radnorshire	''varies much;'' one-third of rack rent ''in some parts;'' half ''in others;'' two-thirds ''in others;'' c. three-quarters ''in some.''	63	8	12.7
SUBTOTAL WALES		1,096[d]	10	0.9
TOTAL ENGLAND AND WALES		14,620	384	2.6

Notes: [a]NA = no answer received from the clerk of the peace. NC = no comment in the 1803 report. NS = the clerk of the peace was ''not able to state any thing satisfactory.''
[b]The summary observation in the Report has a total of 152. I count 149.
[c]The summary observation in the Report has a total of 13,517. I count 13,524.
[d]The summary observation in the Report has a total of 1,094. I count 1,096.
Source: PP 1803-04 (175.) XIII.

APPENDIX M.1

A comparison of total valuational rent for all North Riding townships reporting rent in the land tax c. 1830; the 1814 property tax (schedule A); the 1815 property tax (schedule A); the 1824 overseers' valuations for the county rate; and the total valuation settled upon each township by the justices in 1825; all townships, North Riding

Numbered columns:

1 = Total valuational rent (£. s. d.) as reported in the land tax duplicates c. 1830.
2 = Total valuation (£. s. d.) as reported in the 1814 property tax (schedule A).
3 = 1830 land tax rent (column 1) as a percentage of the 1814 property tax valuation (column 2).
4 = Total valuation (£. s. d.) as reported in the 1815 property tax (schedule A).
5 = 1814 property tax valuation (column 2) as a percentage of the 1815 property tax valuation (column 4).
6 = 1830 land tax rent (column 1) as a percentage of the 1815 property tax valuation (column 4).
7 = Total valuation (£. s. d.) reported to justices by overseers in 1824 as a basis for the reassessment of the county rate.
8 = The 1824 overseer's valuation (column 7) as a percentage of the 1814 property tax valuation (column 2).
9 = 1830 land tax rent (column 1) as a percentage of the 1824 overseer's valuation (column 7).
10 = The amount (£. s. d.) settled by justices on each township in 1825 as a basis for the county rate.
11 = The amount settled in 1825 (column 10) as a percentage of the 1824 overseer's valuation (column 7).
12 = The amount settled in 1825 (column 10) as a percentage of the 1814 property tax valuation (column 2).
13 = The 1830 land tax rent (column 1) as a percentage of the amount settled in 1825 (column 10).

Wapentake Township	1	2	3	4	5	6
Allertonshire						
Birkby		1,442. 0. 0.		1,414. 0. 0.	102.0	
Borrowby	879. 0. 0.	1,405. 0. 0.	62.6	1,405. 0. 0.	100.0	62.6
Brompton		5,049.10. 0.		4,993. 0. 0.	101.1	
Deighton	1,029.10. 0.	1,866. 0. 0.	55.2	1,851. 0. 0.	100.8	55.6
Dinsdale, Over	844. 0. 0.	1,072. 0. 0.	78.7	1,051. 0. 0.	102.0	80.3
Ellerbeck		1,547.10. 0.		1,507. 0. 0.	102.7	
Girsby	1,218. 0. 0.	1,634.11. 0.	74.5	1,617. 0. 0.	101.1	75.3
Harlsey, West		1,828. 0. 0.		1,828. 0. 0.	100.0	
Holme and Howgrave		980. 0. 0.		960. 0. 0.	102.1	
Hornby		2,507.10. 0.		2,577. 0. 0.	97.3	
Hutton Bonville	1,559. 6. 0.	1,445. 0. 0.	107.9	1,442. 0. 0.	100.2	108.1
Hutton Conyers		2,705.10. 0.		2,705. 0. 0.	100.0	
Kilvington, North		1,107. 0. 0.		1,246. 0. 0.	88.8	
Knayton and Brawith	962.10. 0.	2,272.10. 0.	42.4	2,272. 0. 0.	100.0	42.4

Landmoth, Catto, and Cotcliffe		797. 0. 0.		797. 0. 0.	100.0	
Leake		403. 0. 0.		403. 0. 0.	100.0	
Northallerton		8,619. 0. 0.		8,552. 0. 0.	100.8	
Norton Conyers		1,130. 0. 0.		1,130. 0. 0.	100.0	
Osmotherley	956. 8. 4.	1,823. 0. 0.	52.5	1,803. 0. 0.	101.1	53.0
Otterington, North		1,254. 0. 0.		1,107. 0. 0.	113.3	
Romanby		3,175. 6. 0.		3,180. 0. 0.	99.8	
Rounton, West	1,203. 0. 0.	1,845.15. 0.	65.2	1,832. 0. 0.	100.8	65.7
Sessay and Hutton Sessay	2,359. 0. 0.	2,835. 0. 0.	83.2	2,834. 0. 0.	100.0	83.2
Sigston	956. 7. 6.	1,309.13. 0.	73.0	1,254. 0. 0.	104.4	76.3
Smeaton, Little		1,213. 0. 0.		1,213. 0. 0.	100.0	
Sowerby under Cotcliffe		867. 5. 0.		867. 0. 0.	100.0	
Thimbleby		1,702.15. 0.		1,702. 0. 0.	100.0	
Thornton le Beans and Crosby	1,399. 0. 0.	2,621. 0. 0.	53.4	3,621. 0. 0.	72.4	38.6
Thornton le Street	1,170.10. 0.	1,398. 0. 0.	83.7	1,398. 0. 0.	100.0	83.7
Winton, Stank, and Hallikeld		1,522.10. 0.		1,547. 0. 0.	98.4	
Worsall, High		1,562.18. 0.		1,563. 0. 0.	100.0	
TOTAL (all townships)		60,941. 3. 0.		61,671. 0. 0.	98.8	
TOTAL (land tax townships only)	14,536.11.10.	21,527. 9. 0.	67.5	22,380. 0. 0.	96.2	65.0

Total of highest valuations (all townships) = £67,997. 3. 1.
Total of highest valuations (land tax townships only) = £25,048. 2. 7.
Land tax rent as % of highest valuations = 58.0.

APPENDIX M.1 (continued) page 470

Wapentake Township	7	8	9	10	11	12	13
Allertonshire							
Birkby	1,141.10. 0.	79.2		961. 6. 8.	84.2	66.7	
Borrowby	1,920.10. 0.	136.7	45.8	936.13. 4.	48.8	66.7	93.8
Brompton	6,499. 0. 0.	128.7		3,366. 6. 8.	51.8	66.7	
Deighton	1,538. 0. 0.	82.4	66.9	1,244. 0. 0.	80.9	66.7	82.8
Dinsdale, Over	874. 0. 0.	81.5	96.6	714.13. 4.	81.8	66.7	118.1
Ellerbeck	1,303. 3. 0.	84.2		1,031.13. 4.	79.2	66.7	
Girsby	1,312. 0. 0.	80.3	92.8	1,089.14. 0.	83.0	66.7	111.8
Harlsey, West	1,505. 0. 0.	82.3		1,218.13. 4.	81.0	66.7	
Holme and Howgrave	1,231.15. 0.	125.7		653. 6. 8.	53.0	66.7	
Hornby	1,531.10. 0.	61.1		1,671.13. 4.	109.2	66.7	
Hutton Bonville	1,823. 3. 0.	126.2	85.5	963. 6. 8.	52.8	66.7	161.9
Hutton Conyers	2,460. 7. 0.	90.9		1,803.13. 4.	73.3	66.7	
Kilvington, North	1,310. 0. 0.	118.3		738. 0. 0.	56.3	66.7	
Knayton and Brawith	3,098. 8. 0.	136.3	31.1	1,515. 0. 0.	48.9	66.7	63.5
Landmoth, Catto, and Cotcliffe	960.19. 6.	120.6		531. 6. 8.	55.3	66.7	
Leake	546.18. 0.	135.7		268.13. 4.	49.1	66.7	
Northallerton	8,910. 0. 0.	103.4		5,746. 0. 0.	64.5	66.7	
Norton Conyers	1,166. 0. 0.	103.2		753. 6. 8.	64.6	66.7	
Osmotherley	1,548. 0. 0.	84.9	61.8	1,215. 6. 8.	78.5	66.7	78.7
Otterington, North	1,197. 0. 0.	95.4		836. 0. 0.	69.8	66.7	
Romanby	3,835. 3. 6.	120.8		2,116.17. 4.	55.2	66.7	
Rounton, West	1,730.10. 0.	93.8	69.5	1,230.10. 0.	71.1	66.7	97.8
Sessay and Hutton Sessay	3,378. 2. 7.	119.2	69.8	1,890. 0. 0.	55.9	66.7	124.8
Sigston	1,125.10. 0.	85.9	85.0	873. 2. 0.	77.6	66.7	109.5
Smeaton, Little	1,295.19. 6.	106.8		808.13. 4.	62.4	66.7	
Sowerby under Cotcliffe	831. 0. 0.	95.8		578. 3. 4.	69.6	66.7	
Thimbleby	1,862. 0. 0.	109.4		1,135. 3. 4.	61.0	66.7	
Thornton le Beans and Crosby	3,233. 0. 0.	123.3	43.3	1,747. 6. 8.	54.0	66.7	80.1

Thornton le Street	1,656. 0. 0.	118.4	70.7	932. 0. 0.	56.3	66.7	125.6
Winton, Stank, and Hallikeld	1,437.15. 6.	94.4		1,015. 0. 0.	70.6	66.7	
Worsall, High	1,308. 0. 0.	83.7		1,041.18. 8.	79.6	66.7	
TOTAL (all townships)	63,570. 4. 7.	104.3		40,627. 8. 8.	63.9	66.7	
TOTAL (land tax townships only)	23,237. 3. 7.	107.9	62.6	14,351.12. 8.	61.8	66.7	101.3

APPENDIX M.1 (continued) page 472

Wapentake Township	1	2	3	4	5	6
Birdforth						
Ampleforth Birdforth		855. 5. 2.		855. 0. 0.	100.0	
Arden		586. 0. 0.		586. 0. 0.	100.0	
Bagby & Fawdington		2,643.13. 1.		2,643. 0. 0.	100.0	
Balk		1,034.17. 6.		1,034. 0. 0.	100.1	
Bilsdale Westside and Snilesworth		2,610.15. 5.		2,610. 0. 0.	100.0	
Birdforth	(548. 5. 0.)	(646.13. 0.)	84.8	NR		
Boltby	def.	2,973.10. 0.		3,013. 0. 0.	98.7	
Byland Membris, Oldstead, Wass, and Thorpe le Willows		2,461.12. 0.		2,461, 0. 0.	100.0	
Byland, Old		1,147. 5.10.		1,147. 0. 0.	100.0	
Carlton Husthwaite		911.18. 0.		911. 0. 0.	100.1	
Carlton Miniott		2,338.16. 6.		2,338. 0. 0.	100.0	
Catton		1,236.17. 6.		1,236. 0. 0.	100.1	
Cold Kirby		1,030.14. 0.		1,030. 0. 0.	100.1	
Cowsby	589.10. 0.	956.14. 6.	61.6	956. 0. 0.	100.1	61.7
Coxwold, Angram Grange, and Wildon Grange	1,367.13. 0.	3,111. 1. 0.	44.0	1,699. 0. 0.	183.1	80.5
Dale Town		641. 2. 0.		641. 0. 0.	100.0	
Dalton	1,087. 6. 0.	1,119. 9. 6.	97.1	1,119. 0. 0.	100.0	97.2
Elmire & Crakehill	1,079.10. 0.	891. 1.10.	121.1	891. 0. 0.	100.0	121.2
Felixkirk		1,454.19. 6.		1,974. 0. 0.	73.7	
Gueldable		395.12. 0.		395. 0. 0.	100.2	
Harlsey, East		2,855. 0. 0.		2,855. 0. 0.	100.0	
Hawnby		680.15. 8.		680. 0. 0.	100.1	
Husthwaite		1,971.17. 6.		1,971. 0. 0.	100.0	
Kepwick		1,186.12. 6.		1,186. 0. 0.	100.0	
Kilburn, Low; Osgoodby, and Hood Grange	1,342. 0. 0.	2,882.13. 4.	46.6	1,454. 0. 0.	198.2	92.3

Kilvington, South	def.	1,473. 8.10.		1,469. 0. 0.	100.3	
Kirby Knowle		1,093. 1. 8.		1,093. 0. 0.	100.0	
Newburgh & Morton		3,187. 8. 0.		3,187. 0. 0.	100.0	
Newsham and Breckenbrough		1,824.14. 8.		1,824. 0. 0.	100.0	
Otterington, South		1,969. 2. 0.		1,994. 0. 0.	98.8	
Oulston		1,480. 1.10.		1,480. 0. 0.	100.0	
Sand Hutton	1,366.12. 0.	1,801. 4. 3.	75.9	1,801. 0. 0.	100.0	75.9
Silton, Nether		1,464.10. 0.		1,464. 0. 0.	100.0	
Silton, Over		709.19. 0.		709. 0. 0.	100.1	
Skipton upon Swale		1,164.11. 6.		1,144. 0. 0.	101.8	
Sowerby		4,441.16. 6.		4,471. 0. 0.	99.3	
Sutton under Whitestonecliffe		1,763.12. 7.		4,080. 0. 0.	43.2	
Thirkleby		1,831. 8. 2.		1,842. 0. 0.	99.4	
Thirlby	422. 5. 0.	803.10. 0.	52.6	803. 0. 0.	100.1	52.6
Thirsk	5,312. 9.11 1/4	8,693. 8. 6.	61.1	8,702. 0. 0.	99.9	61.0
Thornborough		647.12. 3.		647. 0. 0.	100.1	
Thornton and Baxby		1,666. 1. 9.		1,666. 0. 0.	100.0	
Thornton le Moor		1,534.18. 0.		1,534. 0. 0.	100.0	
Topcliffe		3,877. 7. 7.		3,877. 0. 0.	100.0	
Upsall		1,398.16. 0.		1,398. 0. 0.	100.0	
Welbury		2,793.10. 0.		2,793. 0. 0.	100.0	
Yearsley		1,326.19. 3.		1,326. 0. 0.	100.1	
TOTAL (all townships)[a]		84,925. 6. 8.		84,989. 0. 0.	99.9	
TOTAL (non-defective land tax townships only)[a]	12,567. 5.11 1/4	20,259. 2.11.	62.0	17,425. 0. 0.	116.3	72.1

Total of highest valuations (all townships)[a] = £97,276. 6. 5.
Total of highest valuations (non-defective land tax townships only)[a] = £22,852.15. 0.
Land tax rent as % of highest valuations[a] = 55.0.

APPENDIX M.1 (continued) page 474

Wapentake Township	7	8	9	10	11	12	13
Birdforth							
Ampleforth Birdforth	506.13. 0.	59.2		570. 3. 5.	112.5	66.7	
Arden	914.10. 0.	156.0		390.13. 4.	42.7	66.7	
Bagby and Fawdington	2,508. 3. 6.	94.9		1,762. 8. 9.	70.3	66.7	
Balk	1,079.12. 0.	104.3		689.18. 4.	63.9	66.7	
Bilsdale Westside and Snilesworth	2,314. 2. 0.	88.6		1,740.10. 3.	75.2	66.7	
Birdforth	(1,170.13. 0.)	181.0	46.8	(431. 2. 0.)	36.8	66.7	127.2
Boltby	3,595. 6. 6.	120.9		1,982. 6. 8.	55.1	66.7	
Byland Membris, Oldstead, Wass, and Thorpe le Willows	2,624. 8. 0.	106.6		1,641. 1. 4.	62.5	66.7	
Byland, Old	1,873. 2. 0.	163.3		764.17. 3.	40.8	66.7	
Carlton Husthwaite	1,099. 8. 0.	120.6		607.18. 8.	55.3	66.7	
Carlton Miniott	2,402.18. 0.	102.7		1,559. 4. 4.	64.9	66.7	
Catton	1,127.18. 0.	91.2		824.11. 8.	73.1	66.7	
Cold Kirby	979. 4. 0.	95.0		687. 2. 8.	70.2	66.7	
Cowsby	726.11. 6.	75.9	81.1	637.16. 4.	87.8	66.7	92.4
Coxwold, Angram Grange, and Wildon Grange	3,960.19. 2.	127.3	34.5	2,074. 0. 8.	52.4	66.7	65.9
Dale Town	531.10. 8.	82.9		427. 8. 0.	80.4	66.7	
Dalton	1,132.13. 0.	101.2	96.0	746. 6. 4.	65.9	66.7	145.7
Elmire and Crakehill	1,033. 4. 9.	116.0	104.5	594. 1. 3.	57.5	66.7	181.7
Felixkirk	1,505.10. 0.	103.5		969.19. 8.	64.4	66.7	
Gueldable	499. 0. 0.	126.1		263.14. 8.	52.8	66.7	
Harlsey, East	2,971. 0. 0.	104.1		1,903. 6. 8.	64.1	66.7	
Hawnby	515.15. 0.	75.8		453.17. 1.	88.0	66.7	
Husthwaite	1,480.18. 3.	75.1		1,314.11. 8.	88.8	66.7	
Kepwick	1,092. 0. 0.	92.0		791. 1. 4.	72.4	66.7	
Kilburn, Low; Osgoodby, and Hood Grange	2,743. 3. 2.	95.2	48.9	1,921.15. 7.	70.0	66.7	69.8
Kilvington, South	1,924. 9. 0.	130.6		982. 5.11.	51.0	66.7	
Kirby Knowle	1,191. 9. 0.	109.0		728.14. 5.	61.2	66.7	
Newburgh and Morton	3,378. 9. 6.	106.0		2,124.18. 8.	62.9	66.7	

Newsham and Breckenbrough	2,355. 7. 0.	129.1		1,216. 9. 9.	51.6	66.7	
Otterington, South	2,289. 8. 0.	116.3		1,312.14. 8.	57.3	66.7	
Oulston	1,709.19. 4.	115.5		986.14. 7.	57.7	66.7	
Sand Hutton	2,174. 5. 0.	120.7	62.8	1,200.16. 2.	55.2	66.7	113.8
Silton, Nether	1,646. 8. 0.	112.4		976. 6. 8.	59.3	66.7	
Silton, Over	720.15. 0.	101.5		473. 6. 0.	65.7	66.7	
Skipton upon Swale	1,367.10. 0.	117.4		776. 7. 8.	56.8	66.7	
Sowerby	4,675. 4. 0.	105.2		2,961. 4. 4.	63.3	66.7	
Sutton under Whitestonecliffe	2,484.10. 0.	140.9		1,175.15. 1.	47.3	66.7	
Thirkleby	2,071. 5. 0.	113.1		1,220.18. 9.	58.9	66.7	
Thirlby	880. 5. 0.	109.6	48.0	535.13. 4.	60.8	66.7	78.8
Thirsk	9,785.15. 0.	112.6	54.3	5,795.12. 4.	59.2	66.7	91.7
Thornborough	600. 0. 0.	92.6		431.14.10.	72.0	66.7	
Thornton & Baxby	1,830. 7. 1.	109.8		1,110.14. 6.	60.7	66.7	
Thornton le Moor	2,298. 5. 0.	149.7		1,023. 5. 4.	44.5	66.7	
Topcliffe	4,388.10. 0.	113.2		2,584.18. 5.	58.9	66.7	
Upsall	1,473.15. 8.	105.4		932.10. 8.	63.3	66.7	
Welbury	2,230.10. 0.	79.8		1,862. 6. 8.	83.5	66.7	
Yearsley	1,690.10. 3.	127.4		884.12.10.	52.3	66.7	
TOTAL (all townships)[a]	92,384. 7. 4.	108.8		56,616.17. 6.	61.3	66.7	
TOTAL (non-defective land tax townships only)[a]	22,436.16. 7.	110.7	56.0	13,506. 2. 0.	60.2	66.7	93.0

APPENDIX M.1 (continued) page 476

Wapentake Township	1	2	3	4	5	6
Bulmer						
Aldwark		2,031.15. 0.		2,031. 0. 0.	100.0	
Alne		2,580. 7. 0.		2,580. 0. 0.	100.0	
Barton le Willows	1,435. 0. 0.	1,568.10. 0.	91.5	1,568. 0. 0.	100.0	91.5
Brafferton	788. 0. 0.	1,254.19. 0.	62.8	1,254. 0. 0.	100.1	62.8
Brandsby and Stearsby	2,886. 0. 0.	4,131. 0. 0.	69.9	4,131. 0. 0.	100.0	69.9
Bulmer	1,664. 0. 0.	2,239. 3. 4.	74.3	2,239. 0. 0.	100.0	74.3
Buttercrambe and Bossall	2,493. 0. 0.	3,123.17. 6.	79.8	3,123. 0. 0.	100.0	79.8
Claxton		1,068.10. 0.		1,068. 0. 0.	100.0	
Clifton	3,420. 0. 0.	5,238.17. 0.	65.3	5,238. 0. 0.	100.0	65.3
Coneysthorpe	1,576.15. 0.	962.10. 0.	163.8	962. 0. 0.	100.0	163.9
Cornbrough	(659. 0. 0.)	(1,382. 8. 0.)	47.7	NR		
Crayke	def.	4,888.17. 6.		4,880. 0. 0.	100.2	
Crambe	1,502.12. 0.	1,574.10. 6.	95.4	1,574. 0. 0.	100.0	95.5
Easingwold	def.	10,241.10. 6.		10,241. 0. 0.	100.0	
Farlington	641. 0. 0.	2,130. 0. 0.	30.1	2,130. 0. 0.	100.0	30.1
Flaxton on the Moor	1,888. 0. 0.	1,913.16. 0.	98.6	1,913. 0. 0.	100.0	98.7
Foston	1,288.19. 0.	1,638.18. 6.	78.6	1,638. 0. 0.	100.0	78.7
Ganthorpe	579. 2. 0.	742.10. 0.	78.0	742. 0. 0.	100.1	78.0
Harton	1,801. 7. 0.	1,968.17. 0.	91.5	1,968. 0. 0.	100.0	91.5
Haxby	1,131.18. 0.	2,759.18. 0.	41.0	2,759. 0. 0.	100.0	41.0
Helmsley, Gate	214.10. 0.	793. 5. 0.	27.0	793. 0. 0.	100.0	27.0
Helmsley, Upper		918.14. 6.		918. 0. 0.	100.1	
Helperby	def.	2,170. 9. 0.		2,170. 0. 0.	100.0	
Henderskelf	c. 1,500. 0. 0.	1,643. 0. 0.	91.3	1,643. 0. 0.	100.0	91.3
Heworth	1,459. 0. 0.	3,664. 3. 0.	39.8	3,664. 0. 0.	100.0	39.8
Holtby	1,184. 0. 0.	1,448. 0. 6.	81.8	1,448. 0. 0.	100.0	81.8
Huby	5,012. 0. 0.	4,491.15. 0.	111.6	4,491. 0. 0.	100.0	111.6
Huntington	2,406. 0. 0.	6,549. 8. 6.	36.7	6,549. 0. 0.	100.0	36.7
Huttons Ambo	1,676. 9. 0.	3,382.19. 6.	49.6	3,382. 0. 0.	100.0	49.6
Lillings Ambo		1,727.16. 0.		1,727. 0. 0.	100.0	
Linton upon Ouse	1,081.10. 0.	3,100.19. 8.	34.9	3,100. 0. 0.	100.0	34.9
Marton in the Forest and Moxby	def.	2,928. 6. 0.		3,971. 0. 0.	73.7	

Murton	1,026. 0. 0.	2,247. 7. 6.	45.6	2,928. 0. 0.	76.8	35.0
Myton upon Swale and Ellingthorpe		4,430.11. 6.		4,430. 0. 0.	100.0	
Newton upon Ouse and Beningbrough	1,836. 0. 0.	4,652.13. 6.	39.5	4,652. 0. 0.	100.0	39.5
Osbaldwick	988.10. 0.	1,488.15. 0.	66.4	1,488. 0. 0.	100.0	66.4
Raskelf		2,785. 6. 4.		2,785. 0. 0.	100.0	
St Olave in Marygate	def.	1,025. 1. 0.		1,025. 0. 0.	100.0	
Sand Hutton		1,993.15. 0.		1,993. 0. 0.	100.0	
Scackleton		1,267. 7. 0.		1,267. 0. 0.	100.0	
Sheriff Hutton		5,000.10. 0.		5,000. 0. 0.	100.0	
Shipton and Overton	2,057.15. 0.	4,228.11. 6.	48.7	4,228. 0. 0.	100.0	48.7
Skelton and Rawcliffe	def.	4,941. 1. 0.		4,941. 0. 0.	100.0	
Skewsby and Dalby		1,553.12. 0.		1,553. 0. 0.	100.0	
Stillington	def.	2,945. 5.10.		2,945. 0. 0.	100.0	
Stittenham	1,543. 2. 6.	2,082.10. 0.	74.1	2,082. 0. 0.	100.0	74.1
Stockton on the Forest and Sandburn	1,640.10. 0.	2,554.18. 6.	64.2	2,554. 0. 0.	100.0	64.2
Strensall, Earswick, and Towthorpe	1,533. 0. 0.	2,923.13. 5.	52.4	2,923. 0. 0.	100.0	52.4
Sutton on the Forest		4,724.17. 0.		4,724. 0. 0.	100.0	
Terrington, Menthorpe, and Wiganthorpe	3,536. 0. 0.	3,596. 4. 0.	98.3	3,596. 0. 0.	100.0	98.3
Tholthorpe and Flawith	639. 0. 0.	1,733.13. 6.	36.8	1,733. 0. 0.	100.0	36.9
Thormanby	861. 0. 0.	1,032.13. 0.	83.4	1,032. 0. 0.	100.1	83.4
Thornton le Clay	1,114. 5. 8.	1,171. 3. 0.	95.1	1,171. 0. 0.	100.0	95.2
Tollerton	def.	1,971.17. 6.		1,971. 0. 0.	100.0	
Warthill	779. 0. 0.	951.10. 0.	81.9	951. 0. 0.	100.0	81.9
Welburn	1,057.10. 0.	1,257.14. 6.	84.1	1,257. 0. 0.	100.0	84.1
Whenby		1,665. 0. 0.		1,665. 0. 0.	100.0	
Whitwell	2,615.17. 6.	2,656. 5. 0.	98.5	2,656. 0. 0.	100.0	98.5
Wigginton	1,347. 0. 0.	2,612. 3. 8.	51.6	2,612. 0. 0.	100.0	51.6
Youlton	825. 0. 0.	1,133. 1. 0.	72.8	1,133. 0. 0.	100.0	72.8
TOTAL (all townships)[a]		155,504. 4. 9.		157,190. 0. 0.	98.9	
TOTAL (non-defective land tax townships only)[a]	61,028.12. 8.	92,643.15. 1.	65.9	93,305. 0. 0.	99.3	65.4

Total of highest valuations (all townships)[a] = £158,383.19. 9.
Total of highest valuations (non-defective land tax townships only)[a] = £94,480.16. 1.
Land tax rent as % of highest valuations[a] = 64.6.

APPENDIX M.1 (continued) page 478

Wapentake Township	7	8	9	10	11	12	13
Bulmer							
Aldwark	1,216.12. 0.	59.9		1,354.10. 0.	111.3	66.7	
Alne	1,909.17. 0.	74.0		1,720. 4. 8.	90.1	66.7	
Barton le Willows	1,080. 1. 0.	68.8	132.9	1,045.13. 4.	96.8	66.7	137.2
Brafferton	938.16. 9.	74.8	83.9	836.12. 8.	89.1	66.7	94.2
Brandsby and Stearsby	2,594. 0. 0.	62.8	111.2	2,754. 0. 0.	106.2	66.7	104.8
Bulmer	1,638.12. 0.	73.2	101.6	1,492.15. 7.	91.1	66.7	111.5
Buttercrambe and Bossall	2,187. 0. 0.	70.0	114.0	2,082.11. 8.	95.2	66.7	119.7
Claxton	718. 0. 0.	67.2		712. 6. 8.	99.2	66.7	
Clifton	3,814. 0. 0.	72.8	89.7	3,492.11. 4.	91.6	66.7	97.9
Coneysthorpe	624.10. 0.	64.9	252.5	641.13. 4.	102.7	66.7	245.7
Cornbrough	(943.19. 0.)	68.3	69.8	(921.12. 0.)	97.6	66.7	71.5
Crayke	2,500. 0. 0.	51.1		3,259. 5. 0.	130.4	66.7	
Crambe	1,125. 6. 0.	71.5	133.5	1,049.13. 8.	93.3	66.7	143.1
Easingwold	5,382.11. 2.	52.6		6,827.13. 8.	126.8	66.7	
Farlington	1,282. 0. 0.	60.2	50.0	1,420. 0. 0.	110.8	66.7	45.1
Flaxton on the Moor	1,472. 0. 0.	76.9	128.3	1,275.17. 4.	86.7	66.7	148.0
Foston	1,129.16. 0.	68.9	114.1	1,092.12. 4.	96.7	66.7	118.0
Ganthorpe	615. 0. 0.	82.8	94.2	495. 0. 0.	80.5	66.7	117.0
Harton	1,526. 9. 0.	77.5	118.0	1,312.11. 4.	86.0	66.7	137.2
Haxby	2,009. 8. 0.	72.8	56.3	1,839.18. 8.	91.6	66.7	61.5
Helmsley, Gate	750. 0. 0.	94.5	28.6	528.16. 8.	70.5	66.7	40.6
Helmsley, Upper	790. 0. 0.	86.0		612. 9. 8.	77.5	66.7	
Helperby	2,086.12. 2.	96.1		1,446.19. 4.	69.3	66.7	
Henderskelf	1,065. 6. 0.	64.8	140.8	1,095. 6. 8.	102.8	66.7	136.9
Heworth	2,674. 2. 0.	73.0	54.6	2,442.15. 4.	91.3	66.7	59.7
Holtby	584.13. 6.	40.4	202.5	965. 7. 0.	165.1	66.7	122.6
Huby	2,957. 0. 7.	65.8	169.5	2,994.10. 0.	101.3	66.7	167.4
Huntington	4,622. 0. 0.	70.6	52.0	4,366. 5. 8.	94.5	66.7	55.1
Huttons Ambo	3,404.18. 0.	100.6	49.2	2,255. 6. 4.	66.2	66.7	74.3

Lillings Ambo	1,228. 9. 0.	71.1		1,151.17. 4.	93.8	66.7	
Linton upon Ouse	2,203.14. 0.	71.1	49.1	2,067. 6. 5.	93.8	66.7	52.3
Marton in the Forest and Moxby	1,912.17. 0.	65.3		1,952. 4. 0.	102.0	66.7	
Murton	1,038. 0. 0.	46.2	98.8	1,498. 5. 0.	144.3	66.7	68.5
Myton upon Swale and Ellingthorpe	3,061.13.10.	69.1		2,953.14. 0.	96.5	66.7	
Newton upon Ouse and Beningbrough	3,281.12. 1.	70.5	55.9	3,101.15. 8.	94.5	66.7	59.2
Osbaldwick	1,080. 0. 0.	72.5	91.5	992.10. 0.	91.9	66.7	99.6
Raskelf	2,339.14. 0.	84.0		1,856.17. 7.	79.4	66.7	
St Olave in Marygate	895. 0. 0.	87.3		683. 7. 4.	76.4	66.7	
Sand Hutton	1,308.13. 0.	65.6		1,329. 3. 4.	101.6	66.7	
Scackleton	976. 0. 0.	77.0		844.18. 0.	86.6	66.7	
Sheriff Hutton	3,570.10. 0.	71.4		3,333.13. 4.	93.4	66.7	
Shipton and Overton	3,042. 7. 6.	71.9	67.6	2,819. 1. 0.	92.6	66.7	73.0
Skelton and Rawcliffe	2,800. 0. 0.	56.7		3,294. 0. 8.	117.6	66.7	
Skewsby and Dalby	1,056. 0. 0.	68.0		1,035.14. 8.	98.1	66.7	
Stillington	1,600. 0. 2.	54.3		1,963.10. 7.	122.7	66.7	
Stittenham	1,575.16. 0.	75.7	97.9	1,388. 6. 8.	88.1	66.7	111.1
Stockton on the Forest and Sandburn	1,593. 0. 0.	62.3	103.0	1,703. 5. 8.	106.9	66.7	96.3
Strensall, Earswick, and Towthorpe	2,194. 9. 6.	75.1	69.8	1,949. 2. 3.	88.8	66.7	78.6
Sutton on the Forest	2,984.12. 6.	63.2		3,149.18. 0.	105.5	66.7	
Terrington, Menthorpe, and Wiganthorpe	2,790. 0. 6.	77.6	126.7	2,397. 9. 4.	85.9	66.7	147.5
Tholthorpe and Flawith	1,421.19. 3.	82.0	44.9	1,155.15. 8.	81.3	66.7	55.3
Thormanby	787. 8. 0.	76.2	109.3	688. 8. 8.	87.4	66.7	125.1
Thornton le Clay	1,076.16. 8.	91.9	103.5	780.15. 4.	72.5	66.7	142.7
Tollerton	1,474. 3. 0.	74.8		1,314.11. 8.	89.2	66.7	
Warthill	718. 0. 0.	75.4	108.5	634. 6. 8.	88.3	66.7	122.8
Welburn	946. 9. 0.	75.2	111.7	838. 9. 8.	88.6	66.7	126.1
Whenby	1,163. 3. 0.	69.8		1,110. 0. 0.	95.4	66.7	

APPENDIX M.1 (continued) page 480

Wapentake Township	7	8	9	10	11	12	13
Bulmer							
Whitwell	1,621.17. 6.	61.0	161.3	1,770.16. 8.	109.2	66.7	147.7
Wigginton	1,834.10. 0	70.2	73.4	1,741. 9. 1.	94.9	66.7	77.3
Youlton	825. 0. 0.	72.8	100.0	755. 7. 4.	91.6	66.7	109.2
TOTAL (all townships)[a]	107,100. 6. 8.	68.9		103,669. 9. 6.	96.8	66.7	
TOTAL (non-defective land tax townships only)[a]	66,125.18.10.	71.4	92.3	61,762.10. 0.	93.4	66.7	98.8

Wapentake Township	1	2	3	4	5	6
Gilling East						
Ainderby Steeple	916.10. 0.	1,908. 4. 9.	48.0	1,908. 0. 0.	100.0	48.0
Barton	2,214.18. 4.	3,667. 1. 0.	60.4	3,667. 0. 0.	100.0	60.4
Brompton on Swale	1,899.10. 0.	2,645. 2. 0.	71.8	2,645. 0. 0.	100.0	71.8
Cleasby	862. 0. 0.	1,246. 0. 0.	69.2	1,246. 0. 0.	100.0	69.2
Cowton, East	3,168. 0. 0.	3,773. 4. 0.	84.0	3,773. 0. 0.	100.0	84.0
Cowton, North	1,251.17. 0.	1,519. 0. 0.	82.4	1,519. 0. 0.	100.0	82.4
Cowton, South	1,446. 0. 0.	2,107. 1. 4.	68.6	2,107. 0. 0.	100.0	68.6
Croft	3,646. 0. 0.	5,135. 4. 0.	71.0	5,135. 0. 0.	100.0	71.0
Dalton upon Tees	1,507.11. 0.	2,096. 0. 0.	71.9	2,096. 0. 0.	100.0	71.9
Danby Wiske	def.	2,923. 1. 8.		2,923. 0. 0.	100.0	
Ellerton upon Swale, Bolton on Swale, and Whitwell	4,812. 6. 0.	4,828. 1. 0.	99.7	4,829. 0. 0.	100.0	99.6

Eryholme	1,805. 0. 0.	3,708. 0. 0.	48.7	3,708. 0. 0.	100.0	48.7
Kiplin	1,298.10. 0.	1,277. 0. 3.	101.7	1,277. 0. 0.	100.0	101.7
Kirby Wiske	812.18. 0.	1,599. 3. 0.	50.8	1,599. 0. 0.	100.0	50.8
Langton, Great	592. 0. 0.	941.19. 0.	62.8	941. 0. 0.	100.1	62.9
Langton, Little	1,005.10. 0.	1,416.10. 0.	71.0	1,416. 0. 0.	100.0	71.0
Manfield	2,406.10. 0.	3,276.11. 0.	73.4	3,276. 0. 0.	100.0	73.4
Maunby	1,412.10. 0.	2,435. 9. 0.	58.0	2,435. 0. 0.	100.0	58.0
Middleton Tyas	3,901. 5. 0.	4,867. 8. 6.	80.2	4,867. 0. 0.	100.0	80.2
Morton on Swale and Fareholm	1,340. 0. 0.	1,988. 0. 0.	67.4	1,988. 0. 0.	100.0	67.4
Moulton		3,730.10. 0.		3,730. 0. 0.	100.0	
Newby Wiske	726. 5. 0.	1,193. 3. 0.	60.9	1,193. 0. 0.	100.0	60.9
Newton Morrell		1,106. 0. 0.		1,106. 0. 0.	100.0	
Scorton and Uckerby	3,203. 0. 0.	5,080.10. 0.	63.0	5,079. 0. 0.	100.0	63.1
Smeaton, Great		2,444.15. 0.		2,444. 0. 0.	100.0	
Stapleton		1,874. 0. 0.		1,874. 0. 0.	100.0	
Thrintoft	1,288.10. 0.	1,704.15. 0.	75.6	1,704. 0. 0.	100.0	75.6
Warlaby and Low Sober	1,547.10. 0.	1,519. 0. 0.	101.9	1,519. 0. 0.	100.0	101.9
Yafforth	1,382. 0. 0.	1,595.10. 0.	86.6	1,595. 0. 0.	100.0	86.6
TOTAL (all townships)		73,606. 3. 6.		73,599. 0. 0.	100.0	
TOTAL (non-defective land tax townships only)	44,446. 0. 4.	61,527.16.10.	72.2	61,522. 0. 0.	100.0	72.2

Total of highest valuations (all townships) = £75,506. 8. 7.
Total of highest valuations (non-defective land tax townships only) = £63,412. 5. 7.
Land tax rent as % of highest valuations = 70.1.

Wapentake Township	7	8	9	10	11	12	13
Gilling East							
Ainderby Steeple	2,171.13. 3.	113.8	42.2	1,272. 3. 2.	58.6	66.7	72.0
Barton	3,359.11. 6.	91.6	65.9	2,444.14. 0.	72.8	66.7	90.6
Brompton on Swale	2,997. 0. 0.	113.3	63.4	1,763. 8. 0.	58.8	66.7	107.7
Cleasby	1,012. 0. 0.	81.2	85.2	830.13. 4.	82.1	66.7	103.8
Cowton, East	3,461. 0. 3.	91.7	91.5	2,515. 9. 4.	72.7	66.7	125.9
Cowton, North	1,120.10. 0.	73.8	111.7	1,012.13. 4.	90.4	66.7	123.6
Cowton, South	1,927. 0. 9.	91.4	75.0	1,404.14. 2.	72.9	66.7	102.9
Croft	4,928.10. 0.	96.0	74.0	3,423. 9. 4.	69.5	66.7	106.5
Dalton upon Tees	1,746.10. 0.	83.3	86.3	1,397. 6. 8.	80.0	66.7	107.9
Danby Wiske	2,938.18. 0.	100.5		1,948.14. 6.	66.3	66.7	
Ellerton upon Swale, Bolton on Swale, and Whitwell	4,487. 8. 0.	92.9	107.2	3,218.14. 0.	71.7	66.7	149.5
Eryholme	2,088.11. 0.	56.3	86.4	2,472. 0. 0.	118.4	66.7	73.0
Kiplin	1,166.11. 0.	91.4	111.3	851. 6.10.	73.0	66.7	152.5
Kirby Wiske	1,722. 9. 0.	107.7	47.2	1,066. 2. 0.	61.9	66.7	76.2
Langton, Great	948.19. 0.	100.7	62.4	627.19. 4.	66.2	66.7	94.3
Langton, Little	1,143. 0. 0.	80.7	88.0	944. 6. 8.	82.6	66.7	106.5
Manfield	3,340. 0. 0.	101.9	72.0	2,184. 7. 4.	65.4	66.7	110.2
Maunby	2,198. 5. 0.	90.3	64.2	1,623.12. 8.	73.9	66.7	87.0
Middleton Tyas	4,950.14. 0.	101.7	78.8	3,244.19. 0.	65.5	66.7	120.2
Morton on Swale and Fareholm	2,394. 6. 0.	120.4	56.0	1,325. 6. 8.	55.4	66.7	101.1
Moulton	3,129. 5. 2.	83.9		2,487. 0. 0.	79.5	66.7	
Newby Wiske	1,288.13. 0.	108.0	56.4	795. 8. 8.	61.7	66.7	91.3
Newton Morrell	818. 0. 0.	74.0		737. 6. 8.	90.1	66.7	
Scorton and Uckerby	4,692.14. 0.	92.4	68.2	3,387. 0. 0.	72.2	66.7	94.6
Smeaton, Great	2,061. 0. 0.	84.3		1,629.16. 8.	79.1	66.7	
Stapleton	1,737.19. 0.	92.7		1,249. 6. 8.	71.9	66.7	
Thrintoft	1,621.10. 0.	95.1	79.5	1,136.10. 0.	70.1	66.7	113.4
Warlaby and Low Sober	1,862. 7. 0.	122.6	83.1	1,012.13. 4.	54.4	66.7	152.8
Yafforth	1,720. 0. 0.	107.8	80.3	1,063.13. 4.	61.8	66.7	129.9

TOTAL (all townships)	69,034.14. 1.	93.8		49,070.15. 8.	71.1	66.7	
TOTAL (non-defective land tax townships only)	58,349.10. 1.	94.8	76.2	41,018.11. 2.	70.3	66.7	108.4

APPENDIX M.1 (continued) page 484

Wapentake Township	1	2	3	4	5	6
Gilling West						
Aldbrough	2,359. 0. 0.	2,919. 0. 0.	80.8	2,919. 0. 0.	100.0	80.8
Arkengarthdale		5,195.15. 0.		5,195. 0. 0.	100.0	
Barforth and Little Hutton		2,438.15. 0.		2,438. 0. 0.	100.0	
Barningham and Hope	1,422. 5. 0.	2,271. 0. 0.	62.6	2,271. 0. 0.	100.0	62.6
Bowes and Boldron		6,774.15. 0.		6,774. 0. 0.	100.0	
Brignall		2,094.10. 0.		2,084. 0. 0.	100.5	
Caldwell		1,627. 0. 0.		1,627. 0. 0.	100.0	
Cliffe	610. 0. 0.	960. 0. 0.	63.5	960. 0. 0.	100.0	63.5
Cotherstone	2,059. 2. 0.	3,129.10. 0.	65.8	3,129. 0. 0.	100.0	65.8
Dalton		2,461. 5. 0.		2,461. 0. 0.	100.0	
Easby and Aske		5,106.10. 0.		5,106. 0. 0.	100.0	
Eppleby	1,146.10. 0.	1,224. 0. 0.	93.7	1,224. 0. 0.	100.0	93.7
Forcett		2,062. 0. 0.		2,062. 0. 0.	100.0	
Gailes	883. 0. 0.	1,856. 5. 0.	47.6	1,856. 0. 0.	100.0	47.6
Gilling		7,165. 5. 0.		7,165. 0. 0.	100.0	
Gilmonby		1,174. 0. 0.		1,174. 0. 0.	100.0	
Holwick		1,865.10. 0.		1,865. 0. 0.	100.0	
Hunderthwaite	1,146.15. 0.	2,449. 0. 0.	46.8	2,449. 0. 0.	100.0	46.8
Hutton Longvillers	1,103. 0. 0.	1,990. 0. 0.	55.4	1,990. 0. 0.	100.0	55.4
Kirkby Ravensworth	374. 0. 0.	632.10. 0.	59.1	632. 0. 0.	100.1	59.2
Lartington	2,265.10. 0.	1,579. 0. 0.	143.5	1,579. 0. 0.	100.0	143.5
Layton, East and West; and Carkin		2,338. 0. 0.		2,338. 0. 0.	100.0	
Lunedale	1,699.10. 0.	2,256.15. 0.	75.3	2,256. 0. 0.	100.0	75.3
Marrick	def.	2,524. 0. 0.		2,524. 0. 0.	100.0	
Marske		2,445.10. 0.		2,445. 0. 0.	100.0	
Melbecks		4,316. 5. 0.		4,316. 0. 0.	100.0	
Melsonby	2,560. 0. 0.	4,122. 5. 0.	62.1	4,122. 0. 0.	100.0	62.1
Mickleton		2,755. 0. 0.		2,755. 0. 0.	100.0	
Muker		4,634.10. 0.		4,634. 0. 0.	100.0	
New Forest		650. 0. 0.		650. 0. 0.	100.0	

Newsham		2,564. 0. 0.		2,564. 0. 0.	100.0	
Ovington		495.15. 0.		495. 0. 0.	100.2	
Ravensworth and Whashton	2,055. 0. 0.	3,377. 5. 0.	60.8	3,377. 0. 0.	100.0	60.8
Reeth		8,402.15. 0.		8,402. 0. 0.	100.0	
Richmond		NR		(9,452. 0. 0.)		
Rokeby and Egglestone Abbey		2,295. 5. 0.		2,295. 0. 0.	100.0	
Romaldkirk		1,034. 0. 0.		1,034. 0. 0.	100.0	
Scargill	1,375.12. 0.	1,352.15. 0.	101.7	1,352. 0. 0.	100.0	101.7
Skeeby	760.10. 0.	1,504.15. 0.	50.5	1,504. 0. 0.	100.0	50.6
Stanwick, St John	1,133. 0. 0.	1,740. 0. 0.	65.1	1,740. 0. 0.	100.0	65.1
Startforth	1,352. 0. 0.	2,453. 0. 0.	55.1	2,453. 0. 0.	100.0	55.1
Thorpe & Wycliffe		2,480. 0. 0.		2,480. 0. 0.	100.0	
TOTAL (all townships)[a]		110,717. 5. 0.		110,696. 0. 0.	100.0	
TOTAL (non-defective land tax townships only)	24,304.14. 0.	35,817. 0. 0.	67.8	35,813. 0. 0.	100.0	67.9

Total of highest valuations (all townships) = £113,332.15. 0.
Total of highest valuations (non-defective land tax townships only) = £37,608.12. 0.
Land tax rent as % of highest valuations = 64.6.

APPENDIX M.1 (continued) page 486

Wapentake Township	7	8	9	10	11	12	13
Gilling West							
Aldbrough	3,166. 0. 0.	108.5	74.5	1,946. 0. 0.	61.5	66.7	121.2
Arkengarthdale	2,473. 9. 0.	47.6		3,463.16. 8.	140.0	66.7	
Barforth and Little Hutton	2,352.10. 0.	96.5		1,625.16. 8.	69.1	66.7	
Barningham and Hope	2,710. 0. 0.	119.3	52.5	1,514. 0. 0.	55.9	66.7	93.9
Bowes and Boldron	6,156.10. 0.	90.9		4,516.10. 0.	73.4	66.7	
Brignall	1,918. 0. 0.	91.6		1,396. 6. 8.	72.8	66.7	
Caldwell	1,834. 6. 0.	112.7		1,084.13. 4.	59.1	66.7	
Cliffe	908. 0. 0.	94.6	67.2	640. 0. 0.	70.5	66.7	95.3
Cotherstone	2,404.10. 0.	76.8	85.6	2,086. 6. 8.	86.8	66.7	98.7
Dalton	1,926. 0. 0.	78.2		1,640.16. 8.	85.2	66.7	
Easby & Aske	3,429. 0. 0.	67.1		3,404. 6. 8.	99.3	66.7	
Eppleby	1,496.10. 0.	122.3	76.6	816. 0. 0.	54.5	66.7	140.5
Forcett	1,624.10. 0.	78.8		1,374.13. 4.	84.6	66.7	
Gailes	1,913.10. 0.	103.1	46.1	1,237.10. 0.	64.7	66.7	71.4
Gilling	6,530. 6. 4.	91.1		4,776.16. 8.	73.1	66.7	
Gilmonby	1,063.10. 0.	90.6		782.13. 4.	73.6	66.7	
Holwick	1,324.12.11.	71.0		1,243.13. 4.	93.9	66.7	
Hunderthwaite	1,763. 5. 0.	72.0	65.0	1,632.13. 4.	92.6	66.7	70.2
Hutton Longvillers	1,566. 8. 0.	78.7	70.4	1,326.13. 4.	84.7	66.7	83.1
Kirkby Ravensworth	428. 0. 0.	67.7	87.4	421.13. 4.	98.5	66.7	88.7
Lartington	1,545.10. 0.	97.9	146.6	1,052.13. 4.	68.1	66.7	215.2
Layton, East and West; and Carkin	2,736.10. 0.	117.0		1,558.13. 4.	57.0	66.7	
Lunedale	1,800.18. 4.	79.8	94.4	1,504.10. 0.	83.5	66.7	113.0
Marrick	2,114. 8. 0.	83.8		1,682.13. 4.	79.6	66.7	
Marske	2,118. 0. 0.	86.6		1,630. 6. 8.	77.0	66.7	
Melbecks	2,316.12. 0.	53.7		2,877.10. 0.	124.2	66.7	
Melsonby	4,188.15. 0.	101.6	61.1	2,748. 3. 4.	65.6	66.7	93.2
Mickleton	2,661. 0. 0.	96.6		1,836.13. 4.	69.0	66.7	
Muker	4,196.18. 7.	90.6		3,089.13. 4.	73.6	66.7	
New Forest	650. 0. 0.	100.0		433. 6. 8.	66.7	66.7	

Newsham	2,428.12. 4.	94.7		1,709. 6. 8.	70.4	66.7	
Ovington	546. 0. 0.	110.1		330.10. 0.	60.5	66.7	
Ravensworth and Whashton	2,808. 0. 0.	83.1	73.2	2,251.10. 0.	80.2	66.7	91.3
Reeth	3,086.17.10.	36.7		5,601.16. 8.	181.5	66.7	
Richmond	NR			NR			
Rokeby and Egglestone Abbey	1,780. 6. 4.	77.6		1,530. 3. 4.	85.9	66.7	
Romaldkirk	1,201.17. 0.	116.2		689. 6. 8.	57.4	66.7	
Scargill	1,176.15. 0.	87.0	116.9	901.16. 8.	76.6	66.7	152.5
Skeeby	1,177.10. 0.	78.2	64.6	1,003. 3. 4.	85.2	66.7	75.8
Stanwick, St John	1,398. 0. 0.	80.3	81.0	1,160. 0. 0.	83.0	66.7	97.7
Startforth	1,971. 0. 0.	80.4	68.6	1,635. 6. 8.	83.0	66.7	82.7
Thorpe and Wycliffe	2,292. 0. 0.	92.4		1,653. 6. 8.	72.1	66.7	
TOTAL (all townships)[a]	91,184. 7. 8.	82.4		73,811.10. 0.	81.0	66.7	
TOTAL (non-defective land tax townships only)	32,422.11. 4.	90.5	75.0	23,878. 0. 0.	73.6	66.7	101.8

APPENDIX M.1 (continued) page 488

Wapentake Township	1	2	3	4	5	6
Hallikeld						
Ainderby Quernhow	748.10. 0.	948. 8. 3.	78.9	948. 0. 0.	100.0	79.0
Asenby		1,481.19. 0.		1,481. 0. 0.	100.0	
Baldersby		1,853.10. 6.		1,853. 0. 0.	100.0	
Burneston	1,203. 6. 8.	2,286. 4. 1.	52.6	2,286. 0. 0.	100.0	52.6
Carthorpe		2,704. 4. 7.		2,704. 0. 0.	100.0	
Cundall, Leckby, and Thornton Bridge		4,335.12. 8.		4,335. 0. 0.	100.0	
Dishforth	904.10. 0.	2,405. 6. 0.	37.6	2,405. 0. 0.	100.0	37.6
Exelby, Leeming, and Newton	1,299. 2. 1.	4,573. 3. 0.	28.4	4,573. 0. 0.	100.0	28.4
Gatenby		1,330. 2. 1.		1,330. 0. 0.	100.0	
Howe		469. 0. 0.		469. 0. 0.	100.0	
Humburton and Milby		def.		(2,474. 0. 0.)		
Kirby Hill and Langthorpe		4,519. 2. 3.		4,519. 0. 0.	100.0	
Kirklington and Upsland	1,965.10. 0.	3,057. 5. 8.	64.3	3,057. 0. 0.	100.0	64.3
Langthorne		1,110. 5. 0.		1,110. 0. 0.	100.0	
Marton le Moor		1,595.15. 0.		1,595. 0. 0.	100.0	
Melmerby	1,225. 0. 0.	1,943.15. 0.	63.0	1,943. 0. 0.	100.0	63.0
Middleton Quernhow		1,840. 5. 0.		1,840. 0. 0.	100.0	
Norton le Clay		1,442.15. 6.		1,442. 0. 0.	100.0	
Pickhill and Roxby		2,613.15. 8.		2,613. 0. 0.	100.0	
Rainton and Newby		2,065.16. 2.		2,065. 0. 0.	100.0	
Sinderby		802.14. 9.		802. 0. 0.	100.1	
Sutton		750. 9. 1.		750. 0. 0.	100.1	
Swainby and Allerthorpe		1,483.18. 0.		1,483. 0. 0.	100.1	
Tanfield, East		1,324. 0. 0.		1,324. 0. 0.	100.0	
Tanfield, West		3,734. 2. 5.		3,734. 0. 0.	100.0	
Theakston	556. 0. 0.	1,432. 9. 3.	38.8	1,432. 0. 0.	100.0	38.8
Wath	1,045. 0. 0.	1,016. 0. 0.	102.8	1,016. 0. 0.	100.0	102.8

TOTAL (all townships)[a]		53,119.18.11.		53,109. 0. 0.	100.0	
TOTAL (land tax townships only)	8,946.18. 9.	17,662.11. 3.	50.6	17,660. 0. 0.	100.0	50.7

Total of highest valuations (all townships)[a] = £54,524. 5. 1.
Total of highest valuations (land tax townships only) = £18,210. 7. 3.
Land tax rent as % of highest valuations = 49.1.

Wapentake Township	7	8	9	10	11	12	13
Hallikeld							
Ainderby Quernhow	768.14. 0.	81.0	97.4	632. 5. 6.	82.3	66.7	118.4
Asenby	1,729.19. 0.	116.7		987.19. 4.	57.1	66.7	
Baldersby	2,167. 4. 4.	116.9		1,235.13. 8.	57.0	66.7	
Burneston	1,704. 0. 0.	74.5	70.6	1,524. 2. 9.	89.4	66.7	79.0
Carthorpe	2,208.10. 0.	81.7		1,802.16. 5.	81.6	66.7	
Cundall, Leckby, and Thornton Bridge	4,166. 0. 0.	96.1		2,890. 8. 5.	69.4	66.7	
Dishforth	2,915. 2. 0.	121.2	31.0	1,603.10. 8.	55.0	66.7	56.4
Exelby, Leeming, and Newton	3,873.16. 3.	84.7	33.5	3,048.15. 4.	78.7	66.7	42.6
Gatenby	1,292.14. 5.	97.2		886.14. 9.	68.6	66.7	
Howe	577. 0. 0.	123.0.		312.13. 4.	54.2	66.7	
Humburton and Milby	def.			def.			
Kirby Hill and Langthorpe	2,733. 9. 3.	60.5		3,012.14.10.	110.2	66.7	
Kirklington and Upsland	2,461.15. 0.	80.5	79.8	2,038. 3. 9.	82.8	66.7	96.4
Langthorne	765. 9. 0.	68.9		740. 3. 4.	96.7	66.7	
Marton le Moor	1,473.10. 0.	92.3		1,063.16. 8.	72.2	66.7	
Melmerby	1,249. 0. 0.	64.2	98.1	1,295.16. 8.	103.8	66.7	94.5
Middleton Quernhow	1,238. 0. 0.	67.3		1,226.16. 8.	99.1	66.7	
Norton le Clay	1,205.18. 6.	83.6		961.17. 0.	79.8	66.7	
Pickhill and Roxby	2,800.12. 0.	107.1		1,742.10. 6.	62.2	66.7	
Rainton and Newby	1,995. 5. 2.	96.6		1,377. 4. 2.	69.0	66.7	

APPENDIX M.1 (continued) page 490

Wapentake Township	7	8	9	10	11	12	13
Sinderby	579. 7. 6.	72.2		535. 3. 2.	92.4	66.7	
Sutton	699. 0. 0.	93.1		500. 6. 0.	71.6	66.7	
Swainby and Allerthorpe	1,112. 0. 0.	74.9		989. 5. 4.	89.0	66.7	
Tanfield, East	1,180. 0. 0.	89.1		882.13. 4.	74.8	66.7	
Tanfield, West	3,063.15. 0.	82.0		2,489. 8. 3.	81.2	66.7	
Theakston	1,211.10. 0.	84.6	45.9	954.19. 6.	78.8	66.7	58.2
Wath	1,054. 0. 0.	103.7	99.1	677. 6. 8.	64.3	66.7	154.3
TOTAL (all townships)[a]	46,225.11. 5.	87.0		35,413. 6. 0.	76.6	66.7	
TOTAL (land tax townships only)	15,237.17. 3.	86.3	58.7	11,775. 0.10.	77.3	66.7	76.0

Wapentake Township	1	2	3	4	5	6
Hang East						
Ainderby Myers and High Holtby		1,222.16. 6.		1,222. 0. 0.	100.1	
Aiskew	def.	3,289.18. 0.		3,289. 0. 0.	100.0	
Appleton, East and West	1,992.18. 6.	2,666. 0. 0.	74.8	2,666. 0. 0.	100.0	74.8
Bedale and Firby	def.	4,666. 8. 0.		4,666. 0. 0.	100.0	
Brough		1,867. 8. 0.		1,867. 0. 0.	100.0	
Burrill and Cowling		1,221.19. 0.		1,221. 0. 0.	100.1	
Burton upon Ure		2,240. 0. 0.		2,240. 0. 0.	100.0	
Catterick and Killerby		5,468.17. 0.		5,468. 0. 0.	100.0	

Colburn	1,334. 0. 0.	1,340.18. 0.	99.5	1,340. 0. 0.	100.1	99.6
Crakehall		3,005.10. 0.		3,005. 0. 0.	100.0	
Ellingstring		538.10. 0.		538. 0. 0.	100.1	
Ellingtons		1,823.11. 0.		1,823. 0. 0.	100.0	
Fearby		998.16. 4.		998. 0. 0.	100.1	
Hackforth		1,735.19. 0.		1,735. 0. 0.	100.0	
Healey and Sutton		2,372.11. 6.		2,372. 0. 0.	100.0	
Hipswell and St Martin's Abbey	def.	2,323. 2. 0.		2,323. 0. 0.	100.0	
Hornby		2,324. 6. 0.		2,324. 0. 0.	100.0	
Ilton and Pott		1,296. 5. 0.		1,296. 0. 0.	100.0	
Kirkby Fleetham	def.	5,006.17. 7.		5,006. 0. 0.	100.0	
Masham		2,886. 1. 0.		2,886. 0. 0.	100.0	
Newton le Willows and Ruswick	2,043.18. 0.	2,493. 8. 0.	82.0	2,493. 0. 0.	100.0	82.0
Patrick Brompton		1,901.12. 0.		1,901. 0. 0.	100.0	
Rookwith, Thirn, and Clifton upon Ure		2,039. 9. 0.		2,039. 0. 0.	100.0	
Scotton		1,134. 0. 0.		1,134. 0. 0.	100.0	
Scruton	1,552.19. 0.	2,685. 9. 0.	57.8	2,685. 0. 0.	100.0	57.8
Snape	1,897.14. 6.	3,923.11. 0.	48.4	3,923. 0. 0.	100.0	48.4
Swinton and Warthermarske		1,461.16. 0.		1,461. 0. 0.	100.0	
Thornton Watlass		1,792. 6. 4.		1,792. 0. 0.	100.0	
Tunstall		1,698. 0. 0.		1,698. 0. 0.	100.0	
Well	646.15. 0.	1,336. 0. 0.	48.4	1,336. 0. 0.	100.0	48.4
TOTAL (all townships)		68,761. 7. 3.		68,747. 0. 0.	100.0	
TOTAL (Non-defective land tax townships only)	9,469. 4. 0.	14,445. 6. 0.	65.6	14,443. 0. 0.	100.0	65.6

Total of highest valuations (all townships) = £71,010. 7. 9.
Total of highest valuations (non-defective land tax townships only) = £15,427. 6. 0.
Land tax rent as % of highest valuations = 61.4.

APPENDIX M.1 (continued) page 492

Wapentake Township	7	8	9	10	11	12	13
Hang East							
Ainderby Myers and High Holtby	1,279.10. 0.	104.6		815. 4. 4.	63.7	66.7	
Aiskew	3,404. 0. 0.	103.5		2,193. 5. 4.	64.4	66.7	
Appleton, East and West	2,300.18. 6.	86.3	86.6	1,777. 6. 8.	77.2	66.7	112.1
Bedale and Firby	4,502. 0. 0.	96.5		3,110.18. 8.	69.1	66.7	
Brough	1,517. 0. 0.	81.2		1,244.18. 8.	82.1	66.7	
Burrill and Cowling	1,208. 0. 0.	98.8		814.12. 8.	67.4	66.7	
Burton upon Ure	1,735. 0. 0.	77.4		1,493. 6. 8.	86.1	66.7	
Catterick and Killerby	4,618. 0. 0.	84.4		3,645.18. 0.	79.0	66.7	
Colburn	1,339. 0. 0.	99.8	99.6	893.18. 8.	66.8	66.7	149.2
Crakehall	3,236.10. 0.	107.7		2,003.13. 4.	61.9	66.7	
Ellingstring	480. 0. 0.	89.1		359. 0. 0.	74.8	66.7	
Ellingtons	1,600. 0. 0.	87.7		1,215.14. 0.	75.9	66.7	
Fearby	950. 0. 0.	95.1		665.17. 6.	70.1	66.7	
Hackforth	1,827. 8. 0.	105.3		1,157. 6. 0.	63.3	66.7	
Healey and Sutton	2,100. 0. 0.	88.5		1,581.14. 4.	75.3	66.7	
Hipswell and St Martin's Abbey	2,438.18. 0.	105.0		1,548.14. 8.	63.5	66.7	
Hornby	2,392.17. 0.	102.9		1,549.10. 8.	64.8	66.7	
Ilton and Pott	1,150. 0. 0.	88.7		864. 3. 4.	75.1	66.7	
Kirkby Fleetham	4,060. 0. 0.	81.1		3,337.18. 5.	82.2	66.7	
Masham	2,400. 0. 0.	83.2		1,924. 0. 8.	80.2	66.7	
Newton le Willows and Ruswick	2,343.17. 7.	94.0	87.2	1,662. 5. 4.	70.9	66.7	123.0
Patrick Brompton	1,791. 5. 0.	94.2		1,267.14. 8.	70.8	66.7	
Rookwith, Thirn, and Clifton upon Ure	2,361. 0. 0.	115.8		1,359.12. 8.	57.6	66.7	
Scotton	1,124. 0. 0.	99.1		756. 0. 0.	67.3	66.7	
Scruton	3,342. 0. 0.	124.4	46.5	1,790. 6. 0.	53.6	66.7	86.7
Snape	4,249. 0. 0.	108.3	44.7	2,615.14. 0.	61.6	66.7	72.6

Swinton and Warthermarske	1,300. 0. 0.	88.9		974.10. 8.	75.0	66.7	
Thornton Watlass	1,792. 0. 0.	100.0		1,194.17. 7.	66.7	66.7	
Tunstall	1,966. 0. 0.	115.8		1,132. 0. 0.	57.6	66.7	
Well	1,319. 0. 0.	98.7	49.0	890.13. 4.	67.5	66.7	72.6
TOTAL (all townships)	66,127. 4. 1.	96.2		45,840.16.10.	69.3	66.7	
TOTAL (non-defective land tax townships only)	14,893.16. 1.	97.4	63.6	9,630. 4. 0.	68.4	66.7	98.3

APPENDIX M.1 (continued) page 494

Wapentake Township	1	2	3	4	5	6
Hang West						
Abbotside, High		3,033. 1. 7.		3,047. 0. 0.	99.5	
Abbotside, Low		1,294.13. 2.		1,294. 0. 0.	100.0	
Askrigg		2,941.17. 6.		2,941. 0. 0.	100.0	
Aysgarth		1,013. 4. 2.		1,013. 0. 0.	100.0	
Bainbridge		3,891. 7. 6.		3,915. 0. 0.	99.4	
Barden		995. 5. 0.		995. 0. 0.	100.0	
Bellerby	1,273. 0. 0.	2,814.19.10.	45.2	2,815. 0. 0.	100.0	45.2
Burton and Walden		3,156.15.11.		3,157. 0. 0.	100.0	
Burton, Constable		2,469. 7. 0.		2,469. 0. 0.	100.0	
Caldbergh and East Scrafton		645. 3. 4.		645. 0. 0.	100.0	
Carlton		1,191.12. 6.		1,192. 0. 0.	100.0	
Carlton Highdale		2,042.11. 8.		2,042. 0. 0.	100.0	
Carperby		2,506.16. 8.		2,515. 0. 0.	99.7	
Castle Bolton		2,585. 1. 8.		2,585. 0. 0.	100.0	
Coverham and Agglethorpe		1,946. 3. 4.		1,946. 0. 0.	100.0	
Downholme and Walburn		1,775.11. 0.		1,775. 0. 0.	100.0	
Ellerton and Stainton	1,210. 0. 0.	1,176. 0. 0.	102.9	1,176. 0. 0.	100.0	102.9
Finghall, Akebar, and Hutton Hang	2,355. 0. 0.	2,421.17. 0.	97.2	2,421. 0. 0.	100.0	97.3
Grinton		1,642. 4. 4.		1,649. 0. 0.	99.6	
Harnby		1,865. 4. 0.		1,865. 0. 0.	100.0	
Hauxwell, East and West; and Garriston		1,320. 6. 0.		1,320. 0. 0.	100.0	
Hawes		4,890. 7. 0.		4,899. 0. 0.	99.8	
Hudswell	def.	2,012.14. 2.		2,043. 0. 0.	98.5	
Hunton and Arrathorne		4,295. 3. 6.		4,295. 0. 0.	100.0	
Leyburn		4,065.17. 6.		4,460. 0. 0.	91.2	
Melmerby		775. 5. 0.		775. 0. 0.	100.0	
Middleham		4,046.14. 6.		4,062. 0. 0.	99.6	
Preston under Scar		1,609. 5. 0.		1,801. 0. 0.	89.4	

Redmire		1,692.19. 0.		1,809. 0. 0.	93.6	
Scrafton, West		554.18. 0.		554. 0. 0.	100.2	
Spennithorne		2,141.15. 6.		2,141. 0. 0.	100.0	
Thoralby, Newbiggin, and Bishopdale		4,465. 8. 6.		4,465. 0. 0.	100.0	
Thornton Rust	826. 5. 0.	1,091. 7. 6.	75.7	1,091. 0. 0.	100.0	75.7
Thornton Steward		3,076. 1. 6.		3,076. 0. 0.	100.0	
Wensley		3,351.18. 0.		3,351. 0. 0.	100.0	
Witton, East (within)	2,342. 1. 6.	2,413. 0. 0.	97.1	2,413. 0. 0.	100.0	97.1
Witton, East (without)	def.	3,294.18. 0.		3,282. 0. 0.	100.4	
Witton, West		3,555.19. 6.		3,555. 0. 0.	100.0	
TOTAL (all townships)		90,062.15. 4.		90,849. 0. 0.	99.1	
TOTAL (non-defective land tax townships only)	8,006. 6. 6.	9,917. 4. 4.	80.7	9,916. 0. 0.	100.0	80.7

Total of highest valuations (all townships) = £92,953.11. 3.
Total of highest valuations (non-defective land tax townships only) = £10,267.12. 6.
Land tax rent as % of highest valuations = 78.0.

APPENDIX M.1 (continued) page 496

Wapentake Township	7	8	9	10	11	12	13
Hang West							
Abbotside, High	1,985.15. 0.	65.5		2,022. 1. 1.	101.8	66.7	
Abbotside, Low	922.10. 0.	71.2		863. 2. 1.	93.6	66.7	
Askrigg	1,950. 8. 6.	66.3		1,961. 5. 0.	100.6	66.7	
Aysgarth	852. 0. 0.	84.1		675. 9. 5.	79.3	66.7	
Bainbridge	3,961.15. 0.	101.8		2,594. 5. 0.	65.5	66.7	
Barden	741.10. 0.	74.5		663.10. 0.	89.5	66.7	
Bellerby	1,964. 0. 0.	69.8	64.8	1,876.13. 3.	95.6	66.7	67.8
Burton and Walden	2,217.15. 0.	70.2		2,104.10. 7.	94.9	66.7	
Burton, Constable	2,271. 0. 0.	92.0		1,646. 4. 8.	72.5	66.7	
Caldbergh and East Scrafton	413. 0. 0.	64.0		430. 2. 3.	104.1	66.7	
Carlton	836.10. 0.	70.2		794. 8. 4.	95.0	66.7	
Carlton Highdale	1,449.10. 0.	71.0		1,361.14. 6.	94.0	66.7	
Carperby	1,750. 3.10.	69.8		1,671. 4. 6.	95.5	66.7	
Castle Bolton	1,344.18. 0.	52.0		1,723. 7. 9.	128.1	66.7	
Coverham and Agglethorpe	1,001. 0. 0.	51.4		1,297. 8.10.	129.6	66.7	
Downholme and Walburn	1,410. 0. 0.	79.4		1,183.14. 0.	84.0	66.7	
Ellerton and Stainton	1,199. 0. 0.	102.0	100.9	784. 0. 0.	65.4	66.7	154.3
Finghall, Akebar, and Hutton Hang	2,415.13. 0.	99.7	97.5	1,614.11. 4.	66.8	66.7	145.9
Grinton	1,269.19. 6.	77.3		1,094.16. 3.	86.2	66.7	
Harnby	1,366. 7. 0.	73.2		1,243. 9. 4.	91.0	66.7	
Hauxwell, East and West; and Garriston	1,967.10. 0.	149.0		880. 4. 0.	44.7	66.7	
Hawes	5,936. 4. 5.	121.4		3,260. 4. 8.	54.9	66.7	
Hudswell	1,888.10. 5.	93.8		1,341.16. 1.	71.0	66.7	
Hunton and Arrathorne	2,434. 7. 0.	56.7		2,863. 9. 0.	117.6	66.7	
Leyburn	3,692.12. 1.	90.8		2,710.11. 8.	73.4	66.7	
Melmerby	400.15. 0.	51.7		516.16. 8.	129.0	66.7	
Middleham	1,804.16. 0.	44.6		2,697.16. 4.	149.5	66.7	
Preston under Scar	1,551. 0. 8.	96.4		1,072.16. 8.	69.2	66.7	

Redmire	1,758. 1. 7.	103.8		1,128.12. 8.	64.2	66.7	
Scrafton, West	430. 0. 0.	77.5		369.18. 8.	86.0	66.7	
Spennithorne	1,265. 5. 0.	59.1		1,427.17. 0.	112.8	66.7	
Thoralby, Newbiggin, and Bishopdale	4,034.10. 0.	90.3		2,976.19. 0.	73.8	66.7	
Thornton Rust	822.12.10.	75.4	100.4	727.11. 8.	88.4	66.7	113.6
Thornton Steward	2,228. 1. 0.	72.4		2,050.14. 4.	92.0	66.7	
Wensley	2,987.10. 6.	89.1		2,234.12. 0.	74.8	66.7	
Witton, East (within)	2,729. 8. 0.	113.1	85.8	1,608.13. 4.	58.9	66.7	145.6
Witton, East (without)	2,344.14. 0.	71.2		2,196.12. 0.	93.7	66.7	
Witton, West	2,790. 2. 3.	78.5		2,370.13. 0.	85.0	66.7	
TOTAL (all townships)	72,388.15. 7.	80.4		60,041.16.11.	82.9	66.7	
TOTAL (non-defective land tax townships only)	9,130.13.10.	92.1	87.7	6,611. 9. 7.	72.4	66.7	121.1

APPENDIX M.1 (continued) page 498

Wapentake Township	1	2	3	4	5	6
Langbaurgh						
Acklam, West	862.10. 0.	1,469.10. 0.	58.7	1,469. 0. 0.	100.0	58.7
Aislaby		1,345.19. 6.		1,251. 0. 0.	107.6	
Appleton Wiske	1,434.10. 0.	2,427.10. 0.	59.1	2,427. 0. 0.	100.0	59.1
Arncliffe, Ingleby	865.10. 0.	2,027. 2. 0.	42.7	2,074. 0. 0.	97.7	41.7
Ayton, Great		4,373. 0. 0.		4,477. 0. 0.	97.7	
Ayton, Little		983.15. 0.		983. 0. 0.	100.1	
Barnby, East	1,917. 8. 0.	1,823. 0. 0.	105.2	1,772. 0. 0.	102.9	108.2
Battersby	(522. 0. 0.)	(581. 0. 0.)	89.8	def.		
Borrowby	346. 0. 0.	810. 3. 0.	42.7	804. 0. 0.	100.8	43.0
Brotton		2,342. 1. 0.		2,341. 0. 0.	100.0	
Broughton, Great	2,595. 0. 0.	3,081.12. 6.	84.2	3,257. 0. 0.	94.6	79.7
Busby, Great		2,696.10. 0.		2,686. 0. 0.	100.4	
Carlton in Cleveland		2,011.15. 0.		2,084. 0. 0.	96.5	
Castle Leavington	1,200. 0. 0.	1,348. 3. 0.	89.0	1,348. 0. 0.	100.0	89.0
Commondale		573. 5. 0.		551. 0. 0.	104.0	
Crathorne	1,855. 0. 0.	2,762. 5. 0.	67.2	2,822. 0. 0.	97.9	65.7
Danby	4,837. 5. 0.	5,950. 4. 6.	81.3	5,949. 0. 0.	100.0	81.3
Easby	814. 0. 0.	1,278. 0. 0.	63.7	1,278. 0. 0.	100.0	63.7
Easington		4,910. 5. 0.		4,767. 0. 0.	103.0	
Egton	4,645. 0. 0.	6,842. 1. 0.	67.9	6,842. 0. 0.	100.0	67.9
Ellerby		1,266. 0. 0.		1,266. 0. 0.	100.0	
Eston		2,152.10. 0.		2,152. 0. 0.	100.0	
Faceby		1,706. 9. 0.		1,731. 0. 0.	98.6	
Glaisdale		5,002. 0. 0.		4,966. 0. 0.	100.7	
Greenhow	(1,348. 0. 0.)	(1,716. 5. 0.)	78.5	def.		
Guisborough		8,811.10. 0.		8,445. 0. 0.	104.3	
Hemlington	780. 0. 0.	1,462. 0. 0.	53.4	1,469. 0. 0.	99.5	53.1
Hilton	1,295. 0. 0.	1,403. 0. 0.	92.3	1,403. 0. 0.	100.0	92.3
Hinderwell		2,691.13. 0.		2,639. 0. 0.	102.0	
Hutton Lowcross		1,320. 0. 0.		1,245. 0. 0.	106.0	
Hutton Mulgrave		1,050.14.11.		1,051. 0. 0.	100.0	
Hutton Rudby	2,924.11. 0.	2,773.16. 0.	105.4	3,149. 0. 0.	88.1	92.9

Ingleby Barwick	813. 0. 0.	2,529.10. 0.	32.1	2,630. 0. 0.	96.2	30.9
Ingleby Greenhow	(1,025.10. 0.)	(1,277.12. 8.)	80.3	def.		
Kildale	1,459.15. 0.	1,974. 0. 0.	73.9	1,966. 0. 0.	100.4	74.2
Kilton		1,922.10. 0.		1,922. 0. 0.	100.0	
Kirby in Cleveland		2,275.11. 0.		2,327. 0. 0.	97.8	
Kirkleatham	2,790.10. 0.	4,669. 0. 0.	59.8	4,652. 0. 0.	100.4	60.0
Kirk Leavington		2,707. 0. 0.		2,707. 0. 0.	100.0	
Linthorpe	1,943.10. 0.	2,594. 0. 0.	74.9	2,644. 0. 0.	98.1	73.5
Liverton		1,543. 2. 0.		1,543. 0. 0.	100.0	
Lofthouse	4,049. 5. 0.	4,493.19. 6.	90.1	4,480. 0. 0.	100.3	90.4
Lythe		5,029.19. 0.		5,010. 0. 0.	100.4	
Maltby	968.10. 0.	1,363.10. 0.	71.0	1,393. 0. 0.	97.9	69.5
Marske		5,808. 7. 0.		5,808. 0. 0.	100.0	
Marton in Cleveland		3,774. 2. 0.		3,971. 0. 0.	95.0	
Mickleby		1,389.18. 0.		1,300. 0. 0.	106.9	
Middlesbrough		2,207. 0. 0.		2,353. 0. 0.	93.8	
Middleton upon Leven	def.	1,679. 0. 0.		1,679. 0. 0.	100.0	
Moorsholm, Great; and Stanghow		3,343.10. 0.		3,239. 0. 0.	103.2	
Morton		837.19. 4.		868. 0. 0.	96.5	
Newby	872. 0. 0.	1,228.19. 0.	71.0	1,226. 0. 0.	100.2	71.1
Newton		1,270.10. 0.		1,270. 0. 0.	100.0	
Newton Mulgrave	1,110. 0. 0.	1,627.10. 0.	68.2	1,624. 0. 0.	100.2	68.3
Normanby	def.	1,560.10. 0.		1,560. 0. 0.	100.0	
Nunthorpe	def.	1,935. 2. 0.		1,945. 0. 0.	99.5	
Ormesby and Upsall	def.	5,338. 5. 0.		5,320. 0. 0.	100.3	
Picton	535. 0. 0.	901. 0. 0.	59.4	986. 0. 0.	91.4	54.2
Pinchingthorpe		914.12. 0.		914. 0. 0.	100.1	
Potto	1,474.10. 0.	1,881. 2. 0.	78.4	1,981. 0. 0.	95.0	74.4
Redcar	def.	1,705. 6. 0.		1,705. 0. 0.	100.0	
Rounton, East		1,699. 0. 0.		1,759. 0. 0.	96.6	
Rousby		2,571. 0. 0.		2,531. 0. 0.	101.6	
Rudby in Cleveland		1,042.10. 0.		1,042. 0. 0.	100.0	
Seamer		3,770. 5. 0.		3,954. 0. 0.	95.4	
Sexhow		783. 0. 0.		783. 0. 0.	100.0	
Skelton		5,254. 9. 0.		5,076. 0. 0.	103.5	
Skinningrove		197. 9. 0.		133. 0. 0.	148.4	
Skutterskelfe		1,337. 0. 0.		1,337. 0. 0.	100.0	
Stainton		3,037.11. 0.		3,110. 0. 0.	97.7	

Wapentake Township	1	2	3	4	5	6
Stokesley		5,625.10. 3.		5,688. 0. 0.	98.9	
Thornaby		2,558. 0. 0.		2,587. 0. 0.	98.9	
Tocketts		975. 0. 0.		884. 0. 0.	110.3	
Ugthorpe	1,246. 5. 0.	1,876.16. 6.	66.4	1,866. 0. 0.	100.6	66.8
Upleatham		2,017.10. 0.		2,007. 0. 0.	100.5	
Westerdale		1,656. 1. 0.		1,653. 0. 0.	100.2	
Whorlton	3,621.10. 0.	3,758. 1. 0.	96.4	3,757. 0. 0.	100.0	96.4
Wilton		5,836.12. 6.		5,836. 0. 0.	100.0	
Worsall, Low	1,314. 0. 0.	1,847. 0. 0.	71.1	1,917. 0. 0.	96.3	68.5
Yarm	2,587. 0. 0.	4,217.19. 0.	61.3	4,207. 0. 0.	100.3	61.5
TOTAL (all townships)[a]		197,261. 2. 6.		197,848. 0. 0.	99.7	
TOTAL (non-defective land tax townships only)[a]	51,156. 9. 0.	70,420.14. 0.	72.6	71,392. 0. 0.	98.6	71.6

Total of highest valuations (all townships)[a] = £200,154. 7. 9.
Total of highest valuations (non-defective land tax townships only)[a] = £71,845. 4. 6.
Land tax rent as % of highest valuations[a] = 71.2.

Wapentake Township	7	8	9	10	11	12	13
Langbaurgh							
Acklam, West	958. 2. 0.	65.2	90.0	979.13. 4.	102.2	66.7	88.0
Aislaby	774.13. 4.	57.6		897. 6. 4.	115.8	66.7	
Appleton Wiske	2,043. 0. 0.	84.2	70.2	1,618. 6. 8.	79.2	66.7	88.6
Arncliffe, Ingleby	1,570. 0. 0.	77.4	55.1	1,351. 8. 0.	86.1	66.7	64.0
Ayton, Great	4,380.13. 0.	100.2		2,915. 6. 8.	66.6	66.7	
Ayton, Little	992. 0. 0.	100.8		655.16. 8.	66.1	66.7	
Barnby, East	1,946. 8. 0.	106.8	98.5	1,215. 6. 8.	62.4	66.7	157.8
Battersby	(534. 0. 0.)	91.9	97.8	(387. 6. 8.)	72.5	66.7	134.8
Borrowby	615. 2. 0.	75.9	56.2	540. 2. 0.	87.8	66.7	64.1
Brotton	2,362. 2. 3.	100.8		1,561. 7. 4.	66.1	66.7	
Broughton, Great	3,459. 0. 0.	112.2	75.0	2,054. 8. 4.	59.4	66.7	126.3
Busby, Great	1,803. 2. 6.	66.9		1,797.13. 4.	99.7	66.7	
Carlton in Cleveland	1,318. 0. 0.	65.5		1,341. 3. 4.	101.8	66.7	
Castle Leavington	1,200. 0. 0.	89.0	100.0	898.15. 4.	74.9	66.7	133.5
Commondale	504.10. 0.	88.0		382. 3. 4.	75.8	66.7	
Crathorne	2,357. 6.10.	85.4	78.7	1,841.10. 0.	78.1	66.7	100.7
Danby	5,236.10. 0.	88.0	92.4	3,966.16. 4.	75.8	66.7	121.9
Easby	915.10. 0.	71.6	88.9	852. 0. 0.	93.1	66.7	95.5
Easington	2,946. 4. 6.	60.0		3,273.10. 0.	111.1	66.7	
Egton	5,191.18. 0.	75.9	89.5	4,561. 7. 4.	87.9	66.7	101.8
Ellerby	926. 1. 0.	73.1		844. 0. 0.	91.1	66.7	
Eston	2,314. 0. 0.	107.5		1,435. 0. 0.	62.0	66.7	
Faceby	1,063. 0. 0.	62.3		1,137.12. 8.	107.0	66.7	
Glaisdale	4,331. 0. 7.	86.6		3,334.13. 4.	77.0	66.7	
Greenhow	(1,376.10. 0.)	80.2	97.9	(1,144. 3. 4.)	83.1	66.7	117.8
Guisborough	6,607. 3. 0.	75.0		5,874. 6. 8.	88.9	66.7	
Hemlington	1,013. 0. 0.	69.3	77.0	974.13. 4.	96.2	66.7	80.0
Hilton	1,236.15. 0.	88.2	104.7	935. 6. 8.	75.6	66.7	138.4
Hinderwell	2,798.11. 0.	104.0		1,794. 8. 8.	64.1	66.7	
Hutton Lowcross	1,093. 0. 0.	82.8		880. 0. 0.	80.5	66.7	
Hutton Mulgrave	851. 4. 0.	81.0		700. 9.11.	82.3	66.7	
Hutton Rudby	2,807. 0. 0.	101.2	104.2	1,849. 4. 0.	65.9	66.7	158.2
Ingleby Barwick	1,675. 0. 0.	66.2	48.5	1,686. 6. 8.	100.7	66.7	48.2
Ingleby Greenhow	(1,040.10. 0.)	81.4	98.6	(851.15. 1.)	81.9	66.7	120.4

APPENDIX M.1 (continued) page 502

Wapentake Township	7	8	9	10	11	12	13
Langbaurgh							
Kildale	1,748.16. 0.	88.6	83.5	1,316. 0. 0.	75.2	66.7	110.9
Kilton	1,366.16. 0.	71.1		1,281.13. 4.	93.8	66.7	
Kirby in Cleveland	1,344. 4. 0.	59.1		1,517. 0. 8.	112.9	66.7	
Kirkleatham	4,169.15. 0.	89.3	66.9	3,112.13. 4.	74.6	66.7	89.6
Kirk Leavington	2,540.10. 0.	93.8		1,804.13. 4.	71.0	66.7	
Linthorpe	1,966.10. 0.	75.8	98.8	1,729. 6. 8.	87.9	66.7	112.4
Liverton	1,036.16. 0.	67.2		1,028.14. 8.	99.2	66.7	
Lofthouse	4,219.13. 4.	93.9	96.0	2,995.19. 8.	71.0	66.7	135.2
Lythe	3,600. 9. 0.	71.6		3,353. 6. 0.	93.1	66.7	
Maltby	1,050. 0. 0.	77.0	92.2	909. 0. 0.	86.6	66.7	106.5
Marske	5,070.10. 0.	87.3		3,872. 4. 8.	76.4	66.7	
Marton in Cleveland	2,637. 0. 0.	69.9		2,516. 1. 4.	95.4	66.7	
Mickleby	1,212.15. 0.	87.2		926.12. 0.	76.4	66.7	
Middlesbrough	1,536. 3. 0.	69.6		1,471. 6. 8.	95.8	66.7	
Middleton upon Leven	1,001. 1. 0.	59.6		1,119. 6. 8.	111.8	66.7	
Moorsholm, Great; and Stanghow	2,769.10. 0.	82.8		2,229. 0. 0.	80.5	66.7	
Morton	749. 0. 0.	89.4		558.12.11.	74.6	66.7	
Newby	1,006. 0. 0.	81.8	86.7	819. 6. 0.	81.4	66.7	106.4
Newton	1,025. 0. 0.	80.7		847. 0. 0.	82.6	66.7	
Newton Mulgrave	910.13. 4.	56.0	121.9	1,085. 0. 0.	119.2	66.7	102.3
Normanby	1,340. 0. 0.	85.9		1,040. 6. 8.	77.6	66.7	
Nunthorpe	1,570. 0. 0.	81.1		1,290. 1. 4.	82.2	66.7	
Ormesby and Upsall	3,566. 0. 0.	66.8		3,558.16. 8.	99.8	66.7	
Picton	820. 0. 0.	91.0	65.2	600.13. 4.	73.2	66.7	89.1
Pinchingthorpe	806. 0. 0.	88.1		609.14. 8.	75.6	66.7	
Potto	1,547.14. 0.	82.3	95.3	1,254. 1. 4.	81.0	66.7	117.6
Redcar	1,834. 6. 0.	107.6		1,136.17. 4.	62.0	66.7	
Rounton, East	1,348. 0. 0.	79.3		1,132.13. 4.	84.0	66.7	
Rousby	1,621.10. 0.	63.1		1,714. 0. 0.	105.7	66.7	
Rudby in Cleveland	991. 9. 0.	95.1		695. 0. 0.	70.1	66.7	
Seamer	2,291. 0. 6.	60.8		2,513.10. 0.	109.7	66.7	

Sexhow	530. 0. 0.	67.7		522. 0. 0.	98.5	66.7	
Skelton	2,795. 0. 0.	53.2		3,502.19. 4.	125.3	66.7	
Skinningrove	156.17. 0.	79.4		131.12. 8.	83.9	66.7	
Skutterskelfe	770. 0. 0.	57.6		891. 6. 8.	115.8	66.7	
Stainton	2,057. 8. 0.	67.7		2,025. 0. 8.	98.4	66.7	
Stokesley	5,575.10. 0.	99.1		3,750. 6.10.	67.3	66.7	
Thornaby	1,539. 0. 0.	60.2		1,705. 6. 8.	110.8	66.7	
Tocketts	907.16. 0.	93.1		650. 0. 0.	71.6	66.7	
Ugthorpe	1,266. 0. 0.	67.4	98.4	1,251. 4. 4.	98.8	66.7	99.6
Upleatham	1,682.19. 0.	83.4		1,345. 0. 0.	79.9	66.7	
Westerdale	1,412.17. 0.	85.3		1,104. 0. 8.	78.1	66.7	
Whorlton	3,286.10. 0.	87.4	110.2	2,505. 7. 4.	76.2	66.7	144.6
Wilton	4,753. 0. 0.	81.4		3,891. 1. 8.	81.9	66.7	
Worsall, Low	1,509.10. 0.	81.7	87.0	1,231. 6. 8.	81.6	66.7	106.7
Yarm	3,182.10. 0.	75.4	81.3	2,811.19. 4.	88.4	66.7	92.0
TOTAL (all townships)[a]	157,412. 5. 2.	79.8		131,507. 8. 4.	83.5	66.7	
TOTAL (non-defective land tax townships only)[a]	58,908. 3. 6.	83.6	86.8	46,947.17. 8.	79.7	66.7	109.0

APPENDIX M.1 (continued) page 504

Wapentake Township	1	2	3	4	5	6
Pickering Lythe						
Aislaby		1,078. 5. 0.		1,078. 0. 0.	100.0	
Allerston	def.	3,240. 7. 4.		3,240. 0. 0.	100.0	
Ayton, East and West		4,030.11. 0.		4,030. 0. 0.	100.0	
Barugh, Great and Little		1,816.18. 0.		1,816. 0. 0.	100.0	
Brompton, Sawdon, and Troutsdale		4,864. 2.10.		4,994. 0. 0.	97.4	
Burniston	1,169. 0. 0.	1,917.15. 0.	61.0	1,917. 0. 0.	100.0	61.0
Cayton, Deepdale, Killerby, and Osgodby	2,646. 0. 0.	3,338. 0. 0.	79.3	3,338. 0. 0.	100.0	79.3
Cloughton	2,170. 0. 0.	2,324.19. 4.	93.3	2,324. 0. 0.	100.0	93.4
Cropton and Cawthorn	(1,117. 0. 0.)	def.		(1,718. 0. 0.)		65.0
Ebberston		2,814.11. 2.		2,814. 0. 0.	100.0	
Falsgrave		NR		(2,150. 0. 0.)		
Farmanby		2,618.12. 0.		2,618. 0. 0.	100.0	
Goathland		def.		(1,172. 0. 0.)		
Habton, Great and Little	1,285. 0. 0.	1,215.17. 9.	105.7	1,215. 0. 0.	100.1	105.8
Hartoft Dale	(431. 0. 0.)	def.		(564. 0. 0.)		76.4
Hutton Bushel	2,092. 2. 5.	2,619.11.10.	79.9	2,620. 0. 0.	100.0	79.8
Kingthorpe		1,115. 0. 0.		1,115. 0. 0.	100.0	
Kirby Misperton		2,191. 8. 6.		2,191. 0. 0.	100.0	
Lebberston and Gristhorpe	1,597. 0. 0.	2,527. 6. 3.	63.2	2,527. 0. 0.	100.0	63.2
Levisham	545. 0. 0.	699.11. 0.	77.9	699. 0. 0.	100.1	78.0
Lockton		1,351. 1. 6.		1,350. 0. 0.	100.1	
Marishes		def.		(1,888. 0. 0.)		
Middleton		1,636.10. 0.		1,636. 0. 0.	100.0	
Newton	509.15. 0.	854. 0. 0.	59.7	854. 0. 0.	100.0	59.7
Pickering		def.		(13,151. 0. 0.)		
Rosedale East Side	(1,605. 0. 9.)	def.		(1,452. 0. 0.)		110.5
Ryton		2,183. 5. 6.		2,183. 0. 0.	100.0	

Scalby and Newby		4,900.17. 6.		4,900. 0. 0.	100.0	
Scarborough		NR		(12,355. 0. 0.)		
Seamer and Irton		5,976. 0. 0.		5,976. 0. 0.	100.0	
Sinnington and Marton		3,416.11. 0.		3,674. 0. 0.	93.0	
Snainton	3,654. 5. 0.	3,821.12. 3.	95.6	3,821. 0. 0.	100.0	95.6
Staintondale	1,027. 0. 0.	984. 6. 0.	104.3	984. 0. 0.	100.0	104.4
Thornton Dale		5,746. 5. 0.		5,746. 0. 0.	100.0	
Throxenby		520.10. 0.		520. 0. 0.	100.1	
Wilton	1,907. 0. 0.	1,858. 0. 0.	102.6	1,858. 0. 0.	100.0	102.6
Wrelton	1,114. 0. 0.	1,150.19. 0.	96.8	1,150. 0. 0.	100.1	96.9
Wykeham		3,920.19. 3.		4,020. 0. 0.	97.5	
TOTAL (all townships)[a]		76,733.14. 0.		77,208. 0. 0.	99.4	
TOTAL (non-defective land tax townships only)[a]	19,716. 2. 5.	23,311.18. 5.	84.6	23,307. 0. 0.	100.0	84.6

Total of highest valuations (all townships)[a] = £77,380. 8. 4.
Total of highest valuations (non-defective land tax townships only)[a] = £23,473. 2.10.
Land tax rent as % of highest valuations[a] = 84.0.

Wapentake Township	7	8	9	10	11	12	13
Pickering Lythe							
Aislaby	867.18. 0.	80.5		718.16. 8.	82.8	66.7	
Allerston	2,982. 9. 41/2.	92.0		2,160. 4.10.	72.4	66.7	
Ayton, East & West	3,082. 4. 6.	76.5		2,687. 0. 8.	87.2	66.7	
Barugh, Great and Little	1,414. 1. 3.	77.8		1,211. 5. 4.	85.7	66.7	
Brompton, Sawdon, and Troutsdale	3,469.13.11.	71.3		3,242.15. 3.	93.5	66.7	
Burniston	1,524.16. 6.	79.5	76.7	1,278.10. 0.	83.8	66.7	91.4
Cayton, Deepdale, Killerby, and Osgodby	3,278. 0. 0.	98.2	80.7	2,225. 6. 8.	67.9	66.7	118.9
Cloughton	2,141. 5. 9.	92.1	101.3	1,549.19. 7.	72.4	66.7	140.0
Cropton and Cawthorn	(1,421. 2. 0.)		78.6	def.			
Ebberston	2,574. 9. 31/2.	91.5		1,876. 7. 6.	72.9	66.7	
Falsgrave	NR			NR			
Farmanby	2,215. 4. 0.	84.6		1,745.14. 8.	78.8	66.7	
Goathland	(932.10. 0.)			def.			
Habton, Great and Little	1,505. 0. 0.	123.8	85.4	810.11.10.	53.9	66.7	158.5
Hartoft Dale	(476. 0. 9.)		90.5	def.			
Hutton Bushel	1,982. 7. 6.	75.7	105.5	1,746. 7.10.	88.1	66.7	119.8
Kingthorpe	648. 0. 0.	58.1		743. 6. 8.	114.7	66.7	
Kirby Misperton	1,717. 0. 0.	78.3		1,460.19. 0.	85.1	66.7	
Lebberston and Gristhorpe	2,078. 3. 6.	82.2	76.8	1,684.17. 6.	81.1	66.7	94.8
Levisham	547.10. 0.	78.3	99.5	466. 7. 4.	85.2	66.7	116.9
Lockton	1,000. 1. 0.	74.0		900.14. 4.	90.1	66.7	
Marishes	(1,570. 0. 0.)			def.			
Middleton	1,517. 4. 0.	92.7		1,091. 0. 0.	71.9	66.7	
Newton	711. 5. 0.	83.3	71.7	569. 6. 8.	80.0	66.7	89.5
Pickering	(9,899.10. 0.)			def.			
Rosedale East Side	(1,309.16. 0.)		122.5	def.			

Ryton	1,695. 0. 0.	77.6		1,455.10. 4.	85.9	66.7	
Scalby and Newby	3,101. 4. 0.	63.3		3,267. 5. 0.	105.4	66.7	
Scarborough	NR			NR			
Seamer and Irton	4,567.19. 0.	76.4		3,984. 0. 0.	87.2	66.7	
Sinnington and Marton	3,421. 0. 3.	100.1		2,277.14. 0.	66.6	66.7	
Snainton	3,814. 4. 2.	99.8	95.8	2,547.14.10.	66.8	66.7	143.4
Staintondale	909.10. 0.	92.4	112.9	656. 4. 0.	72.2	66.7	156.5
Thornton Dale	4,727. 0. 0.	82.3		3,830.16. 8.	81.0	66.7	
Throxenby	518.10. 0.	99.6		347. 0. 0.	66.9	66.7	
Wilton	1,333. 0. 0.	71.7	143.1	1,238.13. 4.	92.9	66.7	154.0
Wrelton	857. 8. 3.	74.5	129.9	767. 6. 0.	89.5	66.7	145.2
Wykeham	3,100.14. 9.	79.1		2,613.19. 6.	84.3	66.7	
TOTAL (all townships)[a]	63,302. 4. 0.	82.5		51,155.16. 0.	80.8	66.7	
TOTAL (non-defective land tax townships only)[a]	20,682.10. 8.	88.7	95.3	15,541. 5. 7.	75.1	66.7	126.9

APPENDIX M.1 (continued) page 508

Wapentake Township	1	2	3	4	5	6
Ryedale						
Amotherby		1,662.12. 0.		1,662. 0. 0.	100.0	
Ampleforth Oswaldkirk		def.		(675. 0. 0.)		
Ampleforth St Peter's		def.		NR		
Appleton le Moors		1,063. 2. 0.		1,063. 0. 0.	100.0	
Appleton le Street		1,643.14. 9.		1,643. 0. 0.	100.0	
Airyholme, Baxter Howe, and Howthorpe		454. 0. 0.		454. 0. 0.	100.0	
Barton le Street		1,558. 0. 0.		1,558. 0. 0.	100.0	
Bilsdale Kirkham and Midcable, and Laskill Pasture		4,412,10. 0.		4,412. 0. 0.	100.0	
Butterwick & Newsam		1,336. 0. 0.		1,336. 0. 0.	100.0	
Cawton	211.17. 6.	1,015.17. 0.	20.8	1,015. 0. 0.	100.1	20.9
Coulton		918. 0. 0.		918. 0. 0.	100.0	
Edstone, Great and Little		1,382. 0. 0.		1,381. 0. 0.	100.1	
Farndale East Side and West Side, and Bransdale East Side		3,689. 1. 0.		3,689. 0. 0.	100.0	
Fryton		985.18. 0.		985. 0. 0.	100.1	
Gillamoor and Fadmoor		1,907.10. 0.		1,906. 0. 0.	100.1	
Gilling		2,308. 0. 0.		2,308. 0. 0.	100.0	
Grimston		340.10. 0.		340. 0. 0.	100.1	
Harome		3,666. 7. 0.		3,666. 0. 0.	100.0	
Helmsley Blackmoor		6,465.10. 0.		6,465. 0. 0.	100.0	
Hildenley		NR		NR		
Hovingham		3,219.10. 0.		3,219. 0. 0.	100.0	
Hutton le Hole		1,419.19. 0.		1,420. 0. 0.	100.0	
Kirby Moorside		6,257. 4. 0.		6,256. 0. 0.	100.0	
Lastingham		579. 3. 0.		579. 0. 0.	100.0	

Malton, New, St Leonard's and St Michael's	342.12. 0.	10,686.11. 0.	3.2	10,646. 0. 0.	100.4	3.2
Malton, Old	7,536. 0. 0.	9,767.10. 0.	77.2	9,767. 0. 0.	100.0	77.2
Nawton and Beadlam		2,268. 8. 0.		2,267. 0. 0.	100.1	
Ness, East and West; and Muscoates		3,056. 5. 0.		823. 0. 0.	371.4	
Newton and Laysthorp		977. 0. 0.		977. 0. 0.	100.0	
Normanby		1,725. 0. 0.		1,725. 0. 0.	100.0	
North Holme		757. 8. 0.		757. 0. 0.	100.0	
Nunnington		4,031. 7. 0.		4,031. 0. 0.	100.0	
Oswaldkirk		def.		(1,360. 0. 0.)		
Pockley		1,508. 0. 0.		1,508. 0. 0.	100.0	
Rievaulx		3,295. 0. 0.		3,295. 0. 0.	100.0	
Rosedale West Side	614. 0. 0.	658. 0. 0.	93.3	658. 0. 0.	100.0	93.3
Salton and Brawby	def.	3,959.18. 0.		3,955. 0. 0.	100.1	
Scawton		951. 0. 0.		951. 0. 0.	100.0	
Skiplam and Bransdale West Side		1,426.13. 0.		1,426. 0. 0.	100.0	
Slingsby		2,417. 1. 0.		2,416. 0. 0.	100.0	
South Holme		1,127. 0. 0.		1,127. 0. 0.	100.0	
Spaunton		1,135.12. 0.		1,135. 0. 0.	100.0	
Sproxton		2,230. 7. 0.		2,230. 0. 0.	100.0	
Stonegrave		1,832. 0. 0.		1,832. 0. 0.	100.0	
Swinton & Broughton		2,339.16. 0.		2,339. 0. 0.	100.0	
Thornton Riseborough		914.10. 0.		914. 0. 0.	100.0	
Wath	36.18. 6.	260. 0. 0.	14.2	260. 0. 0.	100.0	14.2
Welburn		3,585.17. 0.		3,585. 0. 0.	100.0	
Wombleton	868. 0. 0.	1,279.16. 0.	67.8	1,279. 0. 0.	100.1	67.9
TOTAL (all townships)[a]		108,474. 6. 9.		106,178. 0. 0.	102.2	
TOTAL (non-defective land tax townships only)[a]	10,784. 8. 0.	23,667.14. 0.	45.6	23,625. 0. 0.	100.2	45.6

Total of highest valuations (all townships)[a] = £109,798. 2.11.
Total of highest valuations (non-defective land tax townships only)[a] = £23,732.13. 2.
Land tax rent as % of highest valuations[a] = 45.4.

APPENDIX M.1 (continued) page 510

Wapentake Township	7	8	9	10	11	12	13
Ryedale							
Amotherby	1,217. 0. 0.	73.2		1,108. 8. 0.	91.1	66.7	
Ampleforth Oswaldkirk	(600.17. 6)			def.			
Ampleforth St Peter's	(801. 6. 0.)			def.			
Appleton le Moors	1,087.13. 0.	102.3		708.14. 8.	65.2	66.7	
Appleton le Street	1,313. 0. 0.	79.9		1,095.16. 6.	83.5	66.7	
Airyholme, Baxter Howe, and Howthorpe	580. 0. 0.	127.8		302.13. 4.	52.2	66.7	
Barton le Street	1,166.12. 0.	74.9		1,038.13. 4.	89.0	66.7	
Bilsdale Kirkham and Midcable, and Laskill Pasture	3,719. 1. 0.	84.3		2,941.13. 4.	79.1	66.7	
Butterwick & Newsam	1,130. 0. 0.	84.6		890.13. 4.	78.8	66.7	
Cawton	802. 0. 0.	78.9	26.4	677. 4. 8.	84.4	66.7	31.3
Coulton	813. 5. 0.	88.6		612. 0. 0.	75.2	66.7	
Edstone, Great and Little	1,495. 2. 6.	108.2		921. 6. 8.	61.6	66.7	
Farndale East Side and West Side, and Bransdale East Side	3,202. 2. 0.	86.8		2,459. 7. 4.	76.8	66.7	
Fryton	893. 9. 0.	90.6		657. 5. 4.	73.6	66.7	
Gillamoor and Fadmoor	1,766. 4. 0.	92.6		1,271.13. 4.	72.0	66.7	
Gilling	1,515.10. 0.	65.7		1,538.13. 4.	101.5	66.7	
Grimston	274.12. 0.	80.6		227. 0. 0.	82.7	66.7	
Harome	2,917. 3. 0.	79.6		2,444. 4. 8.	83.8	66.7	
Helmsley Blackmoor	4,602.15. 0.	71.2		4,310. 6. 8.	93.6	66.7	
Hildenley	NR			NR			
Hovingham	1,751.15. 0.	54.4		2,146. 6. 8.	122.5	66.7	
Hutton le Hole	1,258. 4. 3.	88.6		946.12. 8.	75.2	66.7	
Kirby Moorside	5,783.15. 2.	92.4		4,171. 9. 4.	72.1	66.7	

Lastingham	427. 5. 0.	73.8		386. 2. 0.	90.4	66.7	
Malton, New, St Leonard's and St Michael's	9,388. 2. 0.	87.8	3.6	7,124. 7. 4.	75.9	66.7	4.8
Malton, Old	5,192.15. 0.	53.2	145.1	6,511.13. 4.	125.4	66.7	115.7
Nawton and Beadlam	2,975.10. 0.	131.2		1,512. 5. 4.	50.8	66.7	
Ness, East and West; and Muscoates	2,704. 0. 0.	88.5		2,037.10. 0.	75.4	66.7	
Newton and Laysthorp	827. 0. 0.	84.6		651. 6. 8.	78.8	66.7	
Normanby	1,849. 0. 0.	107.2		1,150. 0. 0.	62.2	66.7	
North Holme	706. 0. 0.	93.2		504.18. 8.	71.5	66.7	
Nunnington	3,477.15. 0.	86.3		2,687.11. 4.	77.3	66.7	
Oswaldkirk	(1,026. 2. 0.)			def.			
Pockley	1,215. 3. 0.	80.6		1,005. 6. 8.	82.7	66.7	
Rievaulx	2,706. 4. 0.	82.1		2,196.13. 4.	81.2	66.7	
Rosedale West Side	698.16. 0.	106.2	87.9	438.13. 4.	62.8	66.7	140.0
Salton and Brawby	3,608.11. 0.	91.1		2,639.18. 8.	73.2	66.7	
Scawton	843.10. 0.	88.7		634. 0. 0.	75.2	66.7	
Skiplam and Bransdale West Side	1,372. 8. 0.	96.2		951. 2. 0.	69.3	66.7	
Slingsby	2,174. 5. 0.	90.0		1,611. 7. 4.	74.1	66.7	
South Holme	950. 0. 0.	84.3		751. 6. 8.	79.1	66.7	
Spaunton	1,274.13. 0.	112.2		757. 1. 4.	59.4	66.7	
Sproxton	1,754.17. 0.	78.7		1,486.18. 0.	84.7	66.7	
Stonegrave	1,288. 0. 0.	70.3		1,221. 6. 8.	94.8	66.7	
Swinton and Broughton	2,364.15. 6.	101.1		1,559.17. 4.	66.0	66.7	
Thornton Riseborough	734. 0. 0.	80.3		609.13. 4.	83.1	66.7	
Wath	144. 7. 0.	55.5	25.6	173. 6. 8.	120.1	66.7	21.3
Welburn	3,173.11. 0.	88.5		2,390.11. 4.	75.3	66.7	
Wombleton	1,303.19. 2.	101.9	66.6	853. 4. 0.	65.4	66.7	
TOTAL (all townships)[a]	90,443. 9. 7.	83.4		72,316. 4. 6.	80.0	66.7	
TOTAL (non-defective land tax townships only)[a]	17,529.19. 2.	74.1	61.5	15,778. 9. 4.	90.0	66.7	68.3

APPENDIX M.1 (continued) page 512

Wapentake Township	1	2	3	4	5	6
Whitby Strand						
Broxa		469. 0. 0.		469. 0. 0.	100.0	
Eskdaleside		1,487.10. 0.		1,491. 0. 0.	99.8	
Fylingdales		5,283. 9. 0.		5,304. 0. 0.	99.6	
Hackness		1,286. 0. 0.		1,286. 0. 0.	100.0	
Harwood Dale and Silpho		2,087.19. 6.		2,087. 0. 0.	100.0	
Hawsker and Stainsacre		5,703.13. 0.		5,705. 0. 0.	100.0	
Newholm and Dunsley		2,079. 4. 0.		2,062. 0. 0.	100.8	
Ruswarp		6,390.12. 0.		6,390. 0. 0.	100.0	
Sneaton		2,412. 0. 0.		2,412. 0. 0.	100.0	
Suffield and Everley		1,447. 0. 0.		1,447. 0. 0.	100.0	
Ugglebarnby		1,780.17. 6.		1,788. 0. 0.	99.6	
Whitby		8,663. 5. 0.		8,659. 0. 0.	100.0	
TOTAL (all townships)		39,090.10. 0.		39,100. 0. 0.	100.0	

Total of highest valuations = £42,209. 2. 6.

Wapentake Township	7	8	9	10	11	12	13
Whitby Strand							
Broxa	239. 0. 0.	51.0		312.13. 4.	130.8	66.7	
Eskdaleside	1,380. 5. 0.	92.8		991.13. 4.	71.8	66.7	
Fylingdales	5,609. 2. 6.	106.2		3,522. 6. 0.	62.8	66.7	
Hackness	945.12. 0.	73.5		857. 6. 8.	90.7	66.7	
Harwood Dale and Silpho	1,387. 0. 0.	66.4		1,391.19. 8.	100.4	66.7	
Hawsker and Stainsacre	6,687. 5. 6.	117.2		3,802. 8. 8.	56.9	66.7	
Newholm and Dunsley	2,419. 0. 0.	116.3		1,386. 2. 8.	57.3	66.7	
Ruswarp	7,849.10. 0.	122.8		4,260. 8. 0.	54.3	66.7	
Sneaton	2,011. 0. 0.	83.4		1,608. 0. 0.	80.0	66.7	
Suffield and Everley	1,091. 3. 0.	75.4		964.13. 4.	88.4	66.7	
Ugglebarnby	1,434.10. 0.	80.6		1,187. 5. 0.	82.8	66.7	
Whitby	6,602. 1. 6.	76.2		5,775.10. 0.	87.5	66.7	
TOTAL (all townships)	37,655. 9. 6.	96.3		26,060. 6. 8.	69.2	66.7	

APPENDIX M.1 (continued) page 514

Wapentake Township	1	2	3	4	5	6
Riding						
TOTAL (all townships)[a]		1,119,197.17. 8.		1,121,184. 0. 0.	99.8	
TOTAL (non-defective land tax townships only)[a]	271,043. 9. 21/4.	391,200.11.10.	69.3	390,788. 0. 0.	100.1	69.4

Total of highest valuations (all townships)[a] = £1,160,526.18. 5.
Total of highest valuations (non-defective land tax townships only)[a] = £406,358.17. 6.
Land tax rent as % of highest valuations[a] = 66.7.

Wapentake Township	7	8	9	10	11	12	13
Riding							
TOTAL (all townships)[a]	956,828.19. 8.	85.5		746,131.16. 7.	78.0	66.7	
TOTAL (non-defective land tax townships only)[a]	338,955. 0.11.	86.6	80.0	260,801. 2.10.	76.9	66.7	103.9

Notes: The highest valuation is underscored.
[a]Values in parentheses are excluded.
Sources: Land tax duplicates, NYCRO; PP 1818 (82.) XIX, 532-47 (1815 property tax); 1824 valuations for the county rate (includes 1814 property tax), QFR 1/1-18, NYCRO.

APPENDIX M.2
Valuational rent per acre and land tax burdens, all townships, North Riding

Numbered columns:
1 = Acres per township, rounded to the nearest acre. Commons are equally apportioned among all townships enjoying rights.
2 = Rent per acre (£) computed from the 1814 property tax (appendix M.1, column 2). Values are computed after rounding rents to the nearest shilling.
3 = Rent per acre (£) computed from the highest reported valuation (appendix M.1, columns 1, 2, 4, 7, or 10). Values are computed after rounding rents to the nearest shilling.
4 = The total land tax owed for c. 1830 (£. s. d.) as reported at the bottom of the duplicate (except for townships reporting valuational rent, where total tax has been derived by adding each individual tax entry). Some earlier duplicates have been employed. There are no significant deviations from the 1798 quotas. Taxes on salaries and stock-in-trade have been deducted.
5 = The ratio of the 1815 property tax valuation (appendix M.1, column 4) to the total land tax assessed c. 1830 (appendix M.2, column 4). Ratios have been computed after rounding rents and taxes to the nearest shilling.
6 = The ratio of the highest reported valuation (appendix M.1, columns 1, 2, 4, 7, or 10) to the total land tax assessed c. 1830 (appendix M.2, column 4). Ratios have been computed after rounding rents and taxes to the nearest shilling.
7 = Number of acres per £1 of land tax assessed (appendix M.2, column 4).
8 = Tax for salaries or stock-in-trade deducted from the total land tax owed (£. s. d.).
9 = Type of deduction.

Wapentake Township	1	2	3	4	5	6	7	8	9
Allertonshire									
Birkby	1,203	1.20	1.20	30. 0. 2.	47.1	48.1	40		
Borrowby	924	1.52	2.08	44. 6. 0.	31.7	43.4	21		
Brompton	3,842	1.31	1.69	151.14. 0 3/4.	32.9	42.8	25		
Deighton	2,036	.92	.92	63.11. 4 1/4	29.1	29.4	32		
Dinsdale, Over	858	1.25	1.25	39.13. 5.	26.5	27.0	22		
Ellerbeck	870	1.78	1.78	33.17.11.	44.4	45.6	26		
Girsby	1,227	1.33	1.33	49. 2. 6.	32.9	33.2	25		
Harlsey, West	1,505	1.21	1.21	67.17. 1 1/4.	26.9	26.9	22		
Holme and Howgrave	840	1.17	1.47	33. 0. 0.	29.1	37.3	25		
Hornby	1,828	1.37	1.41	50. 6.10.	51.2	51.2	36		
Hutton Bonville	1,546	.93	1.18	63. 6.10.	22.8	28.8	24		
Hutton Conyers	3,212	.84	.84	42. 4. 8.	64.0	64.0	76		
Kilvington, North	935	1.18	1.40	96. 6. 0.	12.9	13.6	10		
Knayton and Brawith	1,906	1.19	1.62	80. 4. 2.	28.3	38.6	24		

APPENDIX M.2 (continued) page 516

Wapentake Township	1	2	3	4	5	6	7	8	9
Landmoth, Catto, and Cotcliffe	872	.91	1.10	35.19. 71/2.	22.1	26.7	24		
Leake	309	1.30	1.77	28. 3. 8.	14.3	19.4	11		
Northallerton	4,478	1.92	1.99	154.17. 2.	55.2	57.5	29		
Norton Conyers	1,041	1.08	1.12	45. 3.10.	25.0	25.8	23		
Osmotherley	3,196	.57	.57	47.15.11.	37.7	38.1	67		
Otterington, North	819	1.53	1.53	52.16. 0.	21.0	23.8	16		
Romanby	2,060	1.54	1.86	70.15. 0.	44.9	54.2	29		
Rounton, West	1,456	1.27	1.27	53. 5. 91/2.	34.4	34.6	27		
Sessay and Hutton Sessay	3,772	.75	.90	113.10. 3.	25.0	29.8	33		
Sigston	1,242	1.05	1.05	64.13. 4.	19.4	20.2	19		
Smeaton, Little	1,001	1.21	1.29	33. 4. 9.	36.5	39.0	30		
Sowerby under Cotcliffe	812	1.07	1.07	23. 9.111/4.	36.9	36.9	34		
Thimbleby	2,052	.83	.91	46. 1. 21/4.	37.0	40.4	44		
Thornton le Beans and Crosby	2,524	1.04	1.43	100.12. 2.	36.0	36.0	25		
Thornton le Street	1,389	1.01	1.19	58.10. 6.	23.9	28.3	24		
Winton, Stank, and Hallikeld	1,366	1.11	1.13	55.12. 81/2.	27.8	27.8	24		
Worsall, High	1,625	.96	.96	52.16. 5.	29.6	29.6	31		
TOTAL (all townships)	52,746	1.16	1.20	1,882.19. 31/4.	32.8	33.8	28		
TOTAL (land tax townships only)	22,076	.98	1.05	778.12. 23/4.	28.7	29.8	28		
Based on highest valuations (all townships)			1.29			36.1			

Total of highest valuations (all townships) = £67,997. 3. 1.

Wapentake Township	1	2	3	4	5	6	7	8	9
Birdforth									
Ampleforth Birdforth	558	1.53	1.53	31. 4. 9.	27.4	27.4	18		
Arden	4,524	.13	.20	31. 8. 8.	18.6	29.1	144		
Bagby and Fawdington	2,534	1.04	1.04	70.13. 4.	37.4	37.4	36		
Balk	946	1.09	1.14	35.16. 9.	28.8	30.1	26		
Bilsdale Westside and Snilesworth	8,071	.32	.32	53. 2. 0.	49.2	49.2	152		
Birdforth	(628)	1.03	1.86	(41. 2. 6.)	NR	28.4	15		
Boltby	4,712	.63	.76	69.12. 4 1/4.	43.3	51.6	68		
Byland Membris, Oldstead, Wass, and Thorpe le Willows	4,419	.56	.59	82.13. 4 1/2.	29.8	31.8	53		
Byland, Old	2,737	.42	.68	56. 7.11.	20.3	33.2	48		
Carlton Husthwaite	819	1.11	1.34	39. 7.10.	23.1	27.9	21		
Carlton Miniott	1,552	1.51	1.55	46. 6. 8 1/2.	50.4	51.8	33		
Catton	842	1.47	1.47	23. 3. 2.	53.4	53.4	36		
Cold Kirby	1,617	.64	.64	24. 2. 4.	42.7	42.8	67		
Cowsby	1,165	.82	.82	26.19. 1.	35.5	35.5	43		
Coxwold, Angram Grange, and Wildon Grange	2,518	1.24	1.57	49. 0.11.	34.6	80.8	51		
Dale Town	1,773	.36	.36	18.14. 7.	34.2	34.2	94		
Dalton	1,263	.89	.90	27. 5. 4.	41.1	41.6	46		
Elmire and Crakehill	986	.90	1.09	26. 7. 4.	33.8	40.9	37		
Felixkirk	1,190	1.22	1.66	36.18. 8.	53.4	53.4	32		
Gueldable	348	1.14	1.43	11.13. 4.	33.9	42.8	30		
Harlsey, East	3,057	.93	.97	78.13. 8.	36.3	37.8	39		
Hawnby	2,421	.28	.28	27. 2.11.	25.0	25.1	89		
Husthwaite	1,677	1.18	1.18	72.10. 8.	27.2	27.2	23		
Kepwick	2,742	.43	.43	44. 0. 7 3/4.	26.9	26.9	62		
Kilburn, Low; Osgoodby, and Hood Grange	3,120	.92	.92	70.17.10.	20.5	40.6	44		
Kilvington, South	1,067	1.38	1.80	30. 4.11 1/2.	48.6	63.6	35		
Kirby Knowle	1,580	.69	.75	27. 1. 0.	40.4	44.0	58		
Newburgh and Morton	4,074	.78	.83	95.17. 2.	33.2	35.2	42		

APPENDIX M.2 (continued) page 518

Wapentake Township	1	2	3	4	5	6	7	8	9
Birdforth									
Newsham and Breckenbrough	1,914	.95	1.23	50.14. 0.	36.0	46.4	38		
Otterington, South	1,450	1.36	1.58	61. 0. 51/2.	32.7	37.5	24		
Oulston	1,513	.98	1.13	37. 5. 9.	39.7	45.8	40		
Sand Hutton	1,349	1.34	1.61	39.14. 81/2.	45.3	54.7	34		
Silton, Nether	1,538	.95	1.07	27. 2. 1.	54.0	60.8	57		
Silton, Over	1,235	.57	.58	27. 3. 7.	26.1	26.5	45		
Skipton upon Swale	844	1.38	1.62	25. 7.11.	45.0	53.8	33		
Sowerby	2,614	1.70	1.79	89.18. 61/4.	49.7	52.0	29		
Sutton under Whitestonecliffe	1,908	.92	2.14	134.16. 6.	30.2	30.2	14		
Thirkleby	2,690	.68	.77	51. 2. 0.	36.0	40.5	53		
Thirlby	634	1.27	1.39	16. 5. 91/2.	49.3	54.0	39		
Thirsk	3,250	2.67	3.01	67.17. 11/4.	128.2	144.2	48		
Thornborough	561	1.15	1.15	34. 9. 9.	18.8	18.8	16		
Thornton and Baxby	1,448	1.15	1.26	76.18. 63/4.	21.6	23.8	19		
Thornton le Moor	1,527	1.00	1.50	42.11. 2.	36.0	54.0	36		
Topcliffe	4,202	.92	1.04	91.18.11.	42.2	47.7	46		
Upsall	1,292	1.08	1.14	80. 1. 8.	17.4	18.4	16		
Welbury	2,401	1.16	1.16	72.15. 53/4.	38.4	38.4	33		
Yearsley	2,792	.48	.60	25.13. 0.	51.7	65.9	109		
TOTAL (all townships)[a]	97,474	.87	.95	2,260. 4. 3.	37.6	40.9	43		
TOTAL (non-defective land tax townships only)[a]	14,285	1.42	1.57	324. 8. 11/4.	53.7	69.2	44		
Based on highest valuations (all townships)[a]			1.00			43.0			

Total of highest valuations (all townships)[a] = £97,276. 6. 5.

Wapentake Township	1	2	3	4	5	6	7	8	9
Bulmer									
Aldwark	2,336	.87	.87	74.13. 4.	27.2	27.2	31		
Alne	2,263	1.14	1.14	64.13. 51/2.	39.9	39.9	35		
Barton le Willows	1,046	1.50	1.50	24. 8. 81/2.	64.1	64.2	43		
Brafferton	1,847	.68	.68	44.13. 4.	28.1	28.1	41		
Brandsby and Stearsby	3,077	1.34	1.34	159. 3. 4.	26.0	26.0	19		
Bulmer	1,666	1.34	1.34	43. 6. 4.	51.7	51.7	38		
Buttercrambe and Bossall	2,692	1.16	1.16	76.14. 2.	40.7	40.7	35		
Claxton	838	1.28	1.28	23. 9. 3.	45.5	45.6	36		
Clifton	1,581	3.31	3.31	85.15. 8.	61.0	61.0	18		
Coneysthorpe	1,205	.80	1.31	30.13. 4.	31.4	51.4	39		
Cornbrough	(1,104)	1.25	1.25	(47.10. 6.)	NR	29.1	23		
Crayke	2,874	1.70	1.70	150. 2. 6.	32.5	32.6	19		
Crambe	1,169	1.35	1.35	26.13. 41/4.	59.1	59.1	44		
Easingwold	6,999	1.46	1.46	251. 7. 61/4.	40.7	40.7	28		
Farlington	1,224	1.74	1.74	75. 8.10.	28.2	28.2	16		
Flaxton on the Moor	1,865	1.03	1.03	56.19.111/2.	33.6	33.6	33		
Foston	922	1.78	1.78	37. 3. 4.	44.1	44.1	25		
Ganthorpe	730	1.02	1.02	29.10. 0.	25.2	25.2	25		
Harton	2,002	.98	.98	54.15. 6.	35.9	35.9	36		
Haxby	2,208	1.25	1.25	56.17. 0.	48.5	48.5	39		
Helmsley, Gate	496	1.60	1.60	17. 6. 8.	45.7	45.7	28		
Helmsley, Upper	832	1.10	1.10	24. 0. 0.	38.2	38.3	35		
Helperby	1,894	1.14	1.14	49. 8.111/2.	43.9	43.9	38		
Henderskelf	1,706	.96	.96	37. 6. 8.	44.0	44.0	46		
Heworth	1,312	2.79	2.79	70.11. 8.	51.9	51.9	18		
Holtby	901	1.61	1.61	38.12. 83/4.	37.5	37.5	23		
Huby	4,658	.96	1.08	74.12. 21/2.	60.2	67.2	62		
Huntington	2,606	2.51	2.51	124. 0. 6.	52.8	52.8	21		
Huttons Ambo	2,896	1.17	1.18	61. 7. 0.	55.1	55.5	47		
Lillings Ambo	1,763	.98	.98	36.13. 53/4.	47.1	47.1	48		
Linton upon Ouse	2,321	1.34	1.34	87.13. 8.	35.3	35.4	26		

APPENDIX M.2 (continued) page 520

Wapentake Township	1	2	3	4	5	6	7	8	9
Bulmer									
Marton in the Forest and Moxby	2,715	1.08	1.46	127.17. 2 1/2.	31.0	31.0	21		
Murton	844	2.66	3.47	35.11. 9 1/2.	82.2	82.2	24		
Myton upon Swale and Ellingthorpe	2,283	1.94	1.94	104.14. 2.	42.3	42.3	22		
Newton upon Ouse and Beningbrough	2,826	1.65	1.65	70.13. 8 1/4.	65.8	65.8	40		
Osbaldwick	730	2.04	2.04	36.10. 0 1/2.	40.8	40.8	20		
Raskelf	4,281	.65	.65	212.13. 4.	13.1	13.1	20		
St Olave in Marygate	50	20.50	20.50	21.15. 3.	47.1	47.1	2		
Sand Hutton	2,242	.89	.89	44.10. 9.	44.7	44.8	50		
Scackleton	1,357	.93	.93	34.14.10.	36.5	36.5	39		
Sheriff Hutton	4,486	1.11	1.11	100. 3. 1.	49.9	49.9	45		
Shipton and Overton	3,341	1.26	1.26	86.19. 0 1/4.	48.6	48.6	38		
Skelton and Rawcliffe	3,212	1.54	1.54	122.11. 6.	40.3	40.3	26		
Skewsby and Dalby	1,347	1.15	1.15	69. 7. 8 1/2.	22.4	22.4	19		
Stillington	2,158	1.36	1.36	48. 0. 1 1/4.	61.4	61.4	45		
Stittenham	1,599	1.30	1.30	95.18. 8.	21.7	21.7	17		
Stockton on the Forest and Sandburn	3,267	.78	.78	52.14. 5.	48.5	48.5	62		
Strensall, Earswick, and Towthorpe	5,146	.57	.57	83. 5. 7.	35.1	35.1	62		
Sutton on the Forest	5,996	.79	.79	90. 0. 0.	52.5	52.5	67		
Terrington, Menthorpe, and Wiganthorpe	3,223	1.12	1.12	101.13. 1 3/4	35.4	35.4	32		
Tholthorpe and Flawith	2,380	.73	.73	28.13. 3 1/2.	60.5	60.5	83		
Thormanby	1,002	1.03	1.03	48.10. 6 3/4.	21.2	21.3	21		

Thornton le Clay	954	1.23	1.23	30. 8. 4.	38.5	38.5	31
Tollerton	2,199	.90	.90	65.13. 3.	30.0	30.0	33
Warthill	1,003	.95	.95	20. 9. 4.	46.5	46.5	49
Welburn	865	1.45	1.45	29. 7. 0.	42.8	42.8	29
Whenby	1,042	1.60	1.60	63.12. 0.	26.2	26.2	16
Whitwell	1,574	1.69	1.69	72. 0. 0.	36.9	36.9	22
Wigginton	1,880	1.39	1.39	43.12. 3 1/2.	59.9	59.9	43
Youlton	803	1.41	1.41	33. 0. 0.	34.3	34.3	24
TOTAL (all townships)[a]	124,734	1.25	1.26	3,963. 2. 9 3/4.	39.7	39.7	31
TOTAL (non-defective land tax townships only)[a]	71,567	1.29	1.30	2,183. 1. 1 1/2.	42.7	42.7	33
Based on highest valuations (all townships)[a]			1.27			40.0	

Total of highest valuations (all townships)[a] = £158,383.19. 9.

APPENDIX M.2 (continued) page 522

Wapentake Township	1	2	3	4	5	6	7	8	9
Gilling East									
Ainderby Steeple	1,158	1.65	1.88	40.10. 8 3/4.	47.0	53.6	28		
Barton	2,450	1.50	1.50	67.16. 9 1/2.	54.0	54.0	36		
Brompton on Swale	1,670	1.58	1.79	52.10.11 1/2.	50.3	57.0	32		
Cleasby	1,205	1.03	1.03	46. 8. 7 1/4.	26.8	26.8	26		
Cowton, East	3,369	1.12	1.12	124. 4. 4 1/4.	30.1	30.1	27		
Cowton, North	1,396	1.09	1.09	44. 4. 2.	34.4	34.4	32		
Cowton, South	2,239	.94	.94	110. 9.11 3/4.	19.1	19.1	20		
Croft	4,632	1.11	1.11	128.11. 5.	39.9	39.9	36		
Dalton upon Tees	1,635	1.28	1.28	45.18. 5 1/4.	45.7	45.7	36		
Danby Wiske	3,364	.87	.87	100. 0. 1 1/4.	29.2	29.4	34		
Ellerton upon Swale, Bolton on Swale, and Whitwell	3,601	1.34	1.34	93. 0.11 1/2.	51.9	51.9	39		
Eryholme	2,345	1.58	1.58	55.14. 7.	66.5	66.5	42		
Kiplin	1,011	1.26	1.28	41. 6. 8.	30.9	31.4	24		
Kirby Wiske	1,108	1.44	1.55	40.12.10 1/2.	39.3	42.4	27		
Langton, Great	872	1.08	1.09	36. 5.11 1/4.	25.9	26.1	24		
Langton, Little	1,006	1.41	1.41	28. 0. 0.	50.6	50.6	36		
Manfield	2,918	1.12	1.14	152.12. 2.	21.5	21.9	19		
Maunby	1,546	1.58	1.58	72.15. 7 1/2.	33.4	33.4	21		
Middleton Tyas	3,202	1.52	1.55	73.19.11.	65.8	66.9	43		
Morton on Swale and Fareholm	1,540	1.29	1.55	63. 2.11 1/2.	31.5	37.9	24		
Moulton	3,041	1.23	1.23	78. 0. 0.	47.8	47.8	39		
Newby Wiske	1,430	.83	.90	36.10. 0 3/4.	32.7	35.3	39		
Newton Morrell	634	1.74	1.74	20. 7. 0.	54.3	54.3	31		
Scorton and Uckerby	3,512	1.45	1.45	56. 1. 1.	90.6	90.6	63		
Smeaton, Great	1,648	1.48	1.48	60. 0. 0.	40.7	40.7	27		
Stapleton	998	1.88	1.88	53. 6. 8.	35.1	35.1	19		
Thrintoft	1,228	1.39	1.39	53. 7. 9.	31.9	31.9	23		

Gilling East							
Warlaby and Low Sober	767	1.98	2.43	61. 0. 0.	24.9	30.5	12
Yafforth	1,350	1.18	1.27	80. 0. 0.	19.9	21.5	17
TOTAL (all townships)	56,875	1.29	1.29	1,917.19. 9 1/2.	38.4	38.4	30
TOTAL (non-defective land tax townships only)	47,190	1.30	1.30	1,606. 6. 0 1/4.	38.3	38.3	29
Based on highest valuations (all townships)			1.33			39.4	

Total of highest valuations (all townships) = £75,506. 8. 7.

APPENDIX M.2 (continued) page 524

Wapentake Township	1	2	3	4	5	6	7	8	9
Gilling West									
Aldbrough	1,807	1.62	1.75	62. 6.11 1/2.	46.8	50.8	29		
Arkengarthdale	14,566	.36	.36	68. 1. 0.	76.3	76.4	214		
Barforth and Little Hutton	2,025	1.20	1.20	85. 3.10.	28.6	28.6	24		
Barningham and Hope	6,130	.37	.44	78. 5. 0 1/4.	29.0	34.6	78		
Bowes and Boldron	19,150	.35	.35	122. 9. 4.	55.3	55.3	156		
Brignall	2,116	.99	.99	56. 8. 0.	37.0	37.1	38		
Caldwell	1,588	1.02	1.16	49. 6. 4.	33.0	37.2	32		
Cliffe	707	1.36	1.36	43.14.10.	21.9	21.9	16		
Cotherstone	8,364	.37	.37	77. 1. 5 1/2.	40.6	40.6	108		
Dalton	2,706	.91	.91	65.15. 1 1/2.	37.4	37.4	41		
Easby & Aske	3,046	1.68	1.68	63.12. 4.	80.3	80.3	48		
Eppleby	1,118	1.09	1.34	48.13. 5.	25.2	30.8	23		
Forcett	1,606	1.28	1.28	50.11. 2.	40.8	40.8	32		
Gailes	2,575	.72	.74	40. 4.11.	46.1	47.5	64		
Gilling	4,876	1.47	1.47	116. 4. 4.	61.7	61.7	42		
Gilmonby	2,472	.47	.47	24.17. 3.	47.2	47.2	99		
Holwick	5,788	.32	.32	36. 0. 6 1/2.	51.7	51.7	160		
Hunderthwaite	6,336	.39	.39	35. 6. 9.	69.3	69.3	179		
Hutton Longvillers	1,304	1.53	1.53	60.17. 5.	32.7	32.7	21		
Kirkby Ravensworth	227	2.79	2.79	7. 6. 7.	86.0	86.0	31		
Lartington	5,436	.29	.42	63. 9. 3 1/2.	24.9	35.7	86		
Layton, East and West; and Carkin	2,482	.94	1.10	63. 9. 0.	36.8	43.1	39		
Lunedale	22,770	.10	.10	38.12. 0.	58.4	58.5	590		
Marrick	6,206	.41	.41	61.17. 4 3/4.	40.8	40.8	100		
Marske	6,759	.36	.36	73.19. 0.	33.1	33.1	91		
Melbecks	7,974	.54	.54	114.13. 0 1/4.	37.6	37.6	70		
Melsonby	2,742	1.50	1.53	58. 6.10.1/4	70.6	71.8	47		
Mickleton	4,749	.58	.58	32.13. 6.	84.2	84.2	145		
Muker	30,201	.15	.15	110.13. 5.	41.9	41.9	273		
New Forest	3,002	.22	.22	26. 4. 5 3/4.	24.8	24.8	114		

Newsham	3,407	.75	.75	63.16.10 1/4.	40.2	40.2	53
Ovington	520	.95	1.05	19.17.11.	24.9	27.4	26
Ravensworth and Whashton	3,473	.97	.97	53. 9. 2 1/2.	63.2	63.2	65
Reeth	5,698	1.47	1.47	44.13. 7 3/4.	188.0	188.0	127
Richmond	(2,520)	NR	3.75	def.	def.	def.	def.
Rokeby and Egglestone Abbey	1,808	1.27	1.27	44. 7. 8.	51.7	51.7	41
Romaldkirk	1,324	.78	.91	26. 4. 0.	39.5	45.9	50
Scargill	5,170	.26	.27	111. 6. 5.	12.1	12.4	46
Skeeby	834	1.80	1.80	29. 8. 9 1/4.	51.1	51.1	28
Stanwick, St John	1,398	1.24	1.24	66.14. 0.	26.1	26.1	21
Startforth	1,010	2.43	2.43	38.18.11 1/4.	63.0	63.0	26
Thorpe & Wycliffe	2,229	1.11	1.11	159. 2. 0.	15.6	15.6	14
TOTAL (all townships)[a]	207,699	.53	.53	2,494. 3.11 3/4.	44.4	44.4	83
TOTAL (non-defective land tax townships only)	71,401	.50	.50	914. 3. 2 3/4.	39.2	39.2	78
Based on highest valuations (all townships)			.54			45.4	

Total of highest valuations (all townships) = £113,332.15. 0.

APPENDIX M.2 (continued) page 526

Wapentake Township	1	2	3	4	5	6	7	8	9
Hallikeld									
Ainderby Quernhow	532	1.78	1.78	21. 6. 81/2.	44.4	44.4	25		
Asenby	1,178	1.26	1.47	36.13. 4.	40.4	47.2	32		
Baldersby	1,830	1.01	1.18	48. 0. 0.	38.6	45.2	38		
Burneston	1,228	1.86	1.86	50. 3. 7.	45.5	45.5	24		
Carthorpe	2,111	1.28	1.28	50. 0. 0.	54.1	54.1	42		
Cundall, Leckby, and Thornton Bridge	3,140	1.38	1.38	96. 5. 4.	45.0	45.0	33		
Dishforth	1,765	1.36	1.65	53. 1.10.	45.3	54.9	33		
Exelby, Leeming, and Newton	2,439	1.88	1.88	103.12. 91/2.	44.1	44.1	24		
Gatenby	876	1.52	1.52	69. 5. 0.	19.2	19.2	13		
Howe	400	1.17	1.44	15. 0. 0.	31.3	38.5	27		
Humburton and Milby	(1,819)	1.36	1.36	(103. 7. 4.)	23.9	23.9	18		
Kirby Hill and Langthorpe	2,239	2.02	2.02	57. 6. 8.	78.8	78.8	39		
Kirklington and Upsland	1,986	1.54	1.54	33.17. 4.	90.3	90.3	59		
Langthorne	833	1.33	1.33	34.13. 4.	32.0	32.0	24		
Marton le Moor	1,678	.95	.95	23.18. 2.	66.7	66.8	70		
Melmerby	1,138	1.71	1.71	24.15. 5.	78.5	78.5	46		
Middleton Quernhow	764	2.41	2.41	21.13. 4.	85.0	85.0	35		
Norton le Clay	1,092	1.32	1.32	20. 2. 0.	71.7	71.8	54		
Pickhill and Roxby	2,184	1.20	1.28	70. 7. 0.	37.1	39.8	31		
Rainton and Newby	1,576	1.31	1.31	46.13. 4.	44.3	44.3	34		
Sinderby	559	1.44	1.44	20. 4.10.	39.6	39.6	28		
Sutton	593	1.26	1.26	14. 6.10.	52.3	52.3	41		
Swainby and Allerthorpe	882	1.68	1.68	42. 0. 0.	35.3	35.3	21		
Tanfield, East	1,295	1.02	1.02	30. 2. 3.	44.0	44.0	43		
Tanfield, West	3,286	1.14	1.14	63.13. 4.	58.7	58.7	52		
Theakston	969	1.48	1.48	26. 6. 71/2.	54.3	54.4	37		
Wath	766	1.33	1.38	26. 2. 6.	38.8	40.3	29		

TOTAL (all townships)[a]	37,339	1.42	1.42	1,099.11. 6 1/2.	48.3	48.3	34
TOTAL (land tax townships only)	10,823	1.63	1.63	339. 6. 9 1/2.	52.0	52.0	32
Based on highest valuations (all townships)[a]			1.46			49.6	

Total of highest valuations (all townships)[a] = £54,524. 5. 1.

APPENDIX M.2 (continued) page 528

Wapentake Township	1	2	3	4	5	6	7	8	9
Hang East									
Ainderby Myers and High Holtby	953	1.28	1.34	30.15.11 1/2.	39.7	41.5	31		
Aiskew	2,035	1.62	1.67	61.16. 8.	53.2	55.0	33		
Appleton, East and West	1,631	1.63	1.63	50. 1. 5.	53.3	53.3	32		
Bedale and Firby	2,367	1.97	1.97	143.12. 1.	32.5	32.5	16		
Brough	1,176	1.59	1.59	88.14. 5.	21.0	21.0	13		
Burrill and Cowling	1,071	1.14	1.14	44. 2. 7.	27.6	27.7	24		
Burton upon Ure	3,358	.67	.67	73.15. 4.	30.4	30.4	46		
Catterick and Killerby	2,460	2.22	2.22	129. 6.11.	42.3	42.3	19		
Colburn	1,357	.99	.99	52.19. 3.	25.3	25.3	26		
Crakehall	2,242	1.34	1.44	65.16. 0.	45.7	49.2	34		
Ellingstring	1,498	.36	.36	22. 1. 9.	24.3	24.4	68		
Ellingtons	2,860	.64	.64	36.16. 7.	49.5	49.5	78		
Fearby	1,960	.51	.51	21.12. 7 3/4.	46.1	46.1	90		
Hackforth	1,338	1.30	1.36	33.19. 4.	51.1	53.8	39		
Healey and Sutton	6,062	.39	.39	40.17. 0.	58.1	58.1	148		
Hipswell and St Martin's Abbey	2,917	.80	.84	71. 3.11 3/4.	32.6	34.2	41		
Hornby	1,590	1.46	1.50	44. 3. 0.	52.6	54.2	36		
Ilton and Pott	3,379	.38	.38	44. 2. 0.	29.4	29.4	77		
Kirkby Fleetham	3,154	1.59	1.59	106.16.11.	46.8	46.8	30		
Masham	3,416	.84	.84	58.17. 8 1/2.	49.0	49.0	58		
Newton le Willows and Ruswick	1,858	1.34	1.34	70. 2. 8 1/2.	35.5	35.5	26		
Patrick Brompton	1,238	1.54	1.54	47. 8. 1 1/2.	40.1	40.1	26		
Rookwith, Thirn, and Clifton upon Ure	2,227	.92	1.06	69.13. 4.	29.3	33.9	32		
Scotton	1,406	.81	.81	41.15. 4.	27.2	27.2	34		
Scruton	2,114	1.27	1.58	66.11. 9 1/2.	40.3	50.2	32		
Snape	4,610	.85	.92	60. 4. 0.	65.2	70.6	76		

Swinton and Warthermarske	2,776	.53	.53	37. 5. 8.	39.2	39.2	74
Thornton Watlass	1,482	1.21	1.21	33. 0. 0.	54.3	54.3	45
Tunstall	1,284	1.32	1.53	38.19. 9.	43.5	50.4	33
Well	2,079	.64	.64	32. 6.10.	41.3	41.3	64
TOTAL (all townships)	67,898	1.01	1.01	1,718.19. 1.	40.0	40.0	39
TOTAL (non-defective land tax townships only)	13,649	1.06	1.06	332. 6. 0.	55.4	55.4	41
Based on highest valuations (all townships)			1.04			41.3	

Total of highest valuations (all townships) = £71,010. 7. 9.

APPENDIX M.2 (continued) page 530

Wapentake Township	1	2	3	4	5	6	7	8	9
Hang West									
Abbotside, High	11,170	.27	.27	50.15. 3 1/2.	60.0	60.0	220		
Abbotside, Low	6,887	.19	.19	25. 1. 1 1/4.	51.6	51.7	275		
Askrigg	4,907	.60	.60	41. 3. 0.	71.5	71.5	119		
Aysgarth	1,214	.83	.83	15.19. 8.	63.3	63.3	76		
Bainbridge	16,200	.24	.24	76. 3. 4.	51.4	52.0	213		
Barden	1,779	.56	.56	21.14. 9 1/2.	45.7	45.8	82		
Bellerby	3,063	.92	.92	32. 8.10 1/2.	86.7	86.7	94		
Burton and Walden	7,606	.42	.42	52.17. 9 1/2.	59.7	59.7	144		
Burton, Constable	2,650	.93	.93	22. 2. 9.	111.5	111.5	120		
Caldbergh and East Scrafton	3,449	.19	.19	15.13.10.	41.1	41.1	220		
Carlton	2,742	.43	.43	23.11.10 1/4.	50.5	50.5	116		
Carlton Highdale	10,133	.20	.20	55.15.10.	36.6	36.6	182		
Carperby	4,914	.51	.51	21.17. 4 1/4.	115.1	115.1	225		
Castle Bolton	4,956	.52	.52	32.11. 4.	79.4	79.4	152		
Coverham and Agglethorpe	1,410	1.38	1.38	23. 7.11 1/2.	83.2	83.2	60		
Downholme and Walburn	3,166	.56	.56	17.11. 5 3/4.	101.1	101.2	180		
Ellerton and Stainton	3,542	.33	.34	29. 6. 0 1/2.	40.1	41.3	121		
Finghall, Akebar, and Hutton Hang	1,930	1.25	1.25	46.13. 1.	51.9	51.9	41		
Grinton	8,182	.20	.20	42.16. 2.	38.5	38.5	191		
Harnby	1,111	1.68	1.68	13.17. 1.	134.6	134.7	80		
Hauxwell, East and West; and Garriston	2,811	.47	.70	34.10. 0 1/2.	38.3	57.0	81		
Hawes	16,821	.29	.35	76. 3. 4.	64.3	78.0	221		
Hudswell	3,028	.66	.67	38.16. 8 1/2.	52.6	52.6	80		
Hunton and Arrathorne	2,581	1.66	1.66	49.12. 8.	86.5	86.5	52		
Leyburn	2,515	1.62	1.77	39.10. 8.	112.8	112.8	64		
Melmerby	1,212	.64	.64	20. 5. 1.	38.3	38.3	60		
Middleham	2,154	1.88	1.88	35.19. 4 1/2.	113.0	113.0	60		
Preston under Scar	2,577	.62	.70	25.15.10.	69.8	69.8	100		

Redmire	2,318	.73	.78	23. 9. 9 1/4.	77.0	77.0	99
Scrafton, West	1,615	.34	.34	8. 2. 1 1/2.	68.4	68.5	199
Spennithorne	1,303	1.64	1.64	28. 4. 0.	75.9	76.0	46
Thoralby, Newbiggin, and Bishopdale	9,346	.48	.48	91.16. 8 3/4.	48.6	48.6	102
Thornton Rust	1,939	.56	.56	20.16. 4 1/2.	52.4	52.5	93
Thornton Steward	2,158	1.42	1.42	35. 8. 4.	86.9	86.9	61
Wensley	2,079	1.61	1.61	47.17. 4.	70.0	70.0	43
Witton, East (within)	2,610	.92	1.04	44. 8. 8 1/2.	54.3	61.4	59
Witton, East (without)	4,444	.74	.74	58. 6. 9.	56.2	56.5	76
Witton, West	3,874	.92	.92	38.13. 4 3/4.	92.0	92.0	100
TOTAL (all townships)	166,396	.54	.55	1,379. 5.10 1/4	65.9	65.9	121
TOTAL (non-defective land tax townships only)	13,084	.76	.76	173.13. 1.	57.1	57.1	75
Based on highest valuations (all townships)			.56			67.4	

Total of highest valuations (all townships) = £92,953.11. 3.

Wapentake Township	1	2	3	4	5	6	7	8	9
Langbaurgh									
Acklam, West	976	1.50	1.50	27. 6. 53/4.	53.8	53.8	36		
Aislaby	1,072	1.26	1.26	32.16. 0.	38.1	41.0	33		
Appleton Wiske	1,865	1.30	1.30	80.12. 63/4.	30.1	30.1	23		
Arncliffe, Ingleby	1,893	1.07	1.10	55. 8.101/2.	37.4	37.4	34		
Ayton, Great	3,589	1.22	1.25	78. 0. 6.	57.4	57.4	46		
Ayton, Little	1,378	.71	.72	28.19. 4.	34.0	34.3	48		
Barnby, East	2,140	.85	.91	30. 8. 61/4.	58.2	63.9	70		
Battersby	(1,230)	.47	.47	(26. 7. 4.)		22.0	47		
Borrowby	682	1.19	1.19	15. 4.10.	52.7	53.1	45		
Brotton	2,076	1.13	1.14	58. 5. 11/2.	40.2	40.6	36		
Broughton, Great	3,091	1.00	1.12	75. 1. 13/4.	43.4	46.1	41		
Busby, Great	2,109	1.28	1.28	57.15.10.	46.5	46.6	36		
Carlton in Cleveland	1,358	1.48	1.53	24.16. 7.	83.9	83.9	55		
Castle Leavington	1,071	1.26	1.26	56. 0. 5.	24.1	24.1	19		
Commondale	3,057	.19	.19	18.19. 8.	29.0	30.2	161		
Crathorne	2,598	1.06	1.09	130.11. 4.	21.6	21.6	20		
Danby	6,289	.95	.95	75. 0. 93/4.	79.3	79.3	84		
Easby	1,210	1.06	1.06	44. 5. 8.	28.8	28.8	27		
Easington	3,766	1.30	1.30	45. 0. 2.	105.9	109.1	84		
Egton	15,657	.44	.44	177. 5.10.	38.6	38.6	88		
Ellerby	759	1.67	1.67	17. 1. 71/2.	74.0	74.0	44		
Eston	2,252	.96	1.03	63.19. 2.	33.6	36.2	35		
Faceby	1,382	1.23	1.25	27.15. 8.	62.3	62.3	50		
Glaisdale	4,967	1.01	1.01	79. 3. 6.	62.7	63.2	63		
Greenhow	(3,484)	.49	.49	(41.10. 4.)	def.	41.4	84		
Guisborough	7,013	1.26	1.26	147. 9. 81/2.	57.2	59.7	48		
Hemlington	1,118	1.31	1.31	29.11. 21/2.	49.7	49.7	38		
Hilton	1,392	1.01	1.01	48.17. 0.	28.7	28.7	28		
Hinderwell	1,655	1.63	1.69	60. 5. 31/2.	43.8	46.4	27		
Hutton Lowcross	1,569	.84	.84	28. 4.10.	44.1	46.7	56		
Hutton Mulgrave	1,086	.97	.97	18. 7. 5.	57.3	57.3	59		
Hutton Rudby	2,371	1.17	1.33	69.12.101/2.	45.2	45.2	34		

Ingleby Barwick	1,556	1.62	1.69	26.19. 3.	97.6	97.6	58
Ingleby Greenhow	(2,288)	.56	.56	(29. 6. 01/2.)	def.	43.6	78
Kildale	5,192	.38	.38	43.19. 01/2.	44.7	44.9	118
Kilton	1,724	1.12	1.12	49.16. 61/2.	38.6	38.6	34
Kirby in Cleveland	1,708	1.33	1.36	72. 0.11.	32.3	32.3	24
Kirkleatham	4,330	1.08	1.08	90. 2. 1.	51.6	51.8	48
Kirk Leavington	2,202	1.23	1.23	87. 1. 0.	31.1	31.1	25
Linthorpe	2,135	1.21	1.24	49.17.11.	53.0	53.0	43
Liverton	2,454	.63	.63	24.10. 2.	63.0	63.0	100
Lofthouse	3,737	1.20	1.20	67. 1. 91/2.	66.8	67.0	56
Lythe	3,770	1.33	1.33	102. 2. 21/2.	49.1	49.3	37
Maltby	1,116	1.22	1.25	37.14. 7.	36.9	36.9	30
Marske	3,970	1.46	1.46	117. 2. 6.	49.6	49.6	34
Marton in Cleveland	3,519	1.07	1.13	87. 6. 0.	45.5	45.5	40
Mickleby	1,398	.99	.99	20.19. 11/2.	62.0	66.3	67
Middlesbrough	1,080	2.04	2.18	43. 8. 4.	54.2	54.2	25
Middleton upon Leven	1,144	1.47	1.47	39.16. 41/4.	42.2	42.2	29
Moorsholm, Great; and Stanghow	7,472	.45	.45	42.14. 33/4.	75.8	78.3	175
Morton	1,006	.83	.86	29.16. 11/2.	29.1	29.1	34
Newby	1,254	.98	.98	39. 0. 3.	31.4	31.5	32
Newton	1,172	1.08	1.08	27.19. 63/4.	45.4	45.4	42
Newton Mulgrave	2,345	.69	.69	28. 0. 9.	57.9	58.0	84
Normanby	1,462	1.07	1.07	32.12. 3.	47.8	47.9	45
Nunthorpe	1,427	1.36	1.36	59.17. 71/4.	32.5	32.5	24
Ormesby and Upsall	3,396	1.57	1.57	72. 5.101/2.	72.5	73.8	47
Picton	1,004	.90	.98	20.15. 0.	47.5	47.5	48
Pinchingthorpe	858	1.06	1.06	24.14. 9.	36.9	37.0	35
Potto	1,532	1.23	1.29	70.15. 21/2.	28.0	28.0	22
Redcar	604	2.82	3.04	16.19. 03/4.	100.6	108.2	36
Rounton, East	1,622	1.05	1.08	46. 5.10.	38.0	38.0	35
Rousby	3,250	.79	.79	30.16. 2.	82.2	83.5	106
Rudby in Cleveland	888	1.17	1.17	12.16. 8.	81.1	81.1	69
Seamer	2,650	1.42	1.49	77. 8. 1.	51.1	51.1	34
Sexhow	528	1.48	1.48	20.10. 0.	38.2	38.2	26
Skelton	4,263	1.23	1.23	49.13. 41/4.	102.2	105.8	86
Skinningrove	188	1.05	1.05	10.16. 4.	12.3	18.3	17
Skutterskelfe	1,008	1.33	1.33	29. 9.11.	45.3	45.3	34
Stainton	2,306	1.32	1.35	55.17. 4.	55.7	55.7	41

APPENDIX M.2 (continued) page 534

Wapentake Township	1	2	3	4	5	6	7	8	9
Langbaurgh									
Stokesley	1,817	3.10	3.13	133.13. 6.	42.5	42.5	14		
Thornaby	1,695	1.51	1.53	97.12. 0.	26.5	26.5	17		
Tocketts	668	1.46	1.46	18. 6. 3.	48.3	53.3	36		
Ugthorpe	NR	NR	NR	41. 7. 9 3/4.	45.1	45.3	NR		
Upleatham	1,426	1.41	1.41	69.14. 4 3/4.	28.8	28.9	20		
Westerdale	9,881	.17	.17	31. 2. 9.	53.1	53.2	317		
Whorlton	6,812	.55	.55	120.12. 4.	31.2	31.2	56		
Wilton	4,050	1.44	1.44	130. 9. 4.	44.7	44.7	31		
Worsall, Low	1,362	1.36	1.41	46. 0. 0.	41.7	41.7	30		
Yarm	1,198	3.52	3.52	94.19. 4.	44.3	44.4	13		
TOTAL (all townships)[a]	191,620	1.02[b]	1.02[b]	4,245. 7.11 1/4.	46.6	46.6	45		
TOTAL (non-defective land tax townships only)[a]	82,928	.83[b]	.84[b]	1,789.11. 3 1/2.	39.9	39.9	46		
Based on highest valuations (all townships)[a]			1.03[b]			47.1			

Total of highest valuations (all townships)[a] = £200,154. 7. 9.

Wapentake Township	1	2	3	4	5	6	7	8	9
Pickering Lythe									
Aislaby	1,468	.73	.73	21. 1.11.	51.1	51.1	70		
Allerston	10,043	.32	.32	85.17.10 1/2.	37.7	37.7	117		
Ayton, East and West	4,756	.85	.85	75. 1. 7.	53.7	53.7	63		
Barugh, Great and Little	1,461	1.24	1.24	34. 0. 7.	53.3	53.4	43		
Brompton, Sawdon, and Troutsdale	6,520	.75	.76	86. 4. 4.	57.9	57.9	76		
Burniston	2,099	.91	.91	22. 5. 1.	86.2	86.2	94		
Cayton, Deepdale, Killerby, and Osgodby	3,504	.95	.95	93. 0. 8.	35.9	35.9	38		
Cloughton	2,538	.92	.92	29. 7. 8	79.0	79.1	86		
Cropton and Cawthorn	(5,470)	def.	.31	(37.12. 9.)	45.6	45.6	145		
Ebberston	6,094	.46	.46	68.11. 0.	41.0	41.0	89		
Falsgrave	(1,103)	NR	1.95	NR	NR	NR	NR		
Farmanby	1,813	1.44	1.44	23.15. 5.	110.2	110.2	76		
Goathland	(9,032)	def.	.13	(37.16. 9.)	31.0	31.0	239		
Habton, Great and Little	1,423	.85	.90	40.19.10 1/4.	29.6	31.3	35		
Hartoft Dale	(2,940)	def.	.19	(8. 1. 8 1/4.)	69.6	69.6	363		
Hutton Bushel	3,787	.69	.69	35. 3. 9 3/4.	74.4	74.4	108		
Kingthorpe	1,208	.92	.92	17. 0. 7.	65.2	65.2	71		
Kirby Misperton	1,791	1.22	1.22	34.12. 4.	63.3	63.3	52		
Lebberston and Gristhorpe	2,479	1.02	1.02	65. 5. 8.	38.7	38.7	38		
Levisham	2,974	.24	.24	20.12. 8 1/4.	33.8	33.9	144		
Lockton	7,423	.18	.18	27. 8. 4.	49.3	49.3	271		
Marishes	(2,335)	def.	.81	(35.18. 9.)	52.5	52.5	65		
Middleton	2,699	.61	.61	20.11. 3.	79.6	79.6	131		
Newton	2,396	.36	.36	12. 3. 4.	70.3	70.3	197		
Pickering	(16,037)	def.	.82	(102. 3. 2.)	128.7	128.7	157		
Rosedale East Side	(5,394)	def.	.30	(35. 7. 8.)	41.0	45.4	152		
Ryton	2,324	.94	.94	50. 7. 8 1/2.	43.3	43.3	46		
Scalby and Newby	3,720	1.32	1.32	63. 0.11 1/2.	77.7	77.7	59		

APPENDIX M.2 (continued) page 536

Wapentake Township	1	2	3	4	5	6	7	8	9
Pickering Lythe									
Scarborough	(1,190)	NR	10.38	NR	NR	NR	NR		
Seamer and Irton	5,951	1.00	1.00	143. 9. 8.	41.6	41.6	41		
Sinnington and Marton	2,892	1.18	1.27	60. 5. 8.	60.9	60.9	48		
Snainton	4,836	.79	.79	78.13.11.	48.6	48.6	61		
Staintondale	3,114	.32	.33	32. 1. 5.	30.7	32.0	97		
Thornton Dale	6,461	.89	.89	71.12. 3.	80.2	80.2	90		
Throxenby	399	1.30	1.30	24.19.11 1/2.	20.8	20.8	16		
Wilton	1,784	1.04	1.07	36. 2. 8.	51.4	52.8	49		
Wrelton	1,888	.61	.61	19.14. 3.	58.4	58.4	96		
Wykeham	8,248	.48	.49	84. 0. 4.	47.8	47.8	98		
TOTAL (all townships)[a]	108,093	.71	.71	1,477.12. 9 1/4.	52.2	52.2	73		
TOTAL (non-defective land tax townships only)[a]	32,822	.71	.71	485.11. 0 1/4.	48.0	48.0	68		
Based on highest valuations (all townships)[a]			.72			52.4			

Total of highest valuations (all townships)[a] = £77,380. 8. 4.

Wapentake Township	1	2	3	4	5	6	7	8	9
Ryedale									
Amotherby	1,830	.91	.91	20. 4. 21/4.	82.3	82.3	90		
Ampleforth Oswaldkirk	(877)	def.	.77	(10.10. 0.)	64.3	64.3	84		
Ampleforth St Peter's	(935)	def.	.86	(8.11. 3.)	NR	93.7	109		
Appleton le Moors	2,583	.41	.42	33. 8. 0.	31.8	32.6	77		
Appleton le Street	1,633	1.01	1.01	34. 0. 0.	48.3	48.3	48		
Airyholme, Baxter Howe, and Howthorpe	595	.76	.97	18. 3. 2.	25.0	32.0	33		
Barton le Street	1,675	.93	.93	40. 0. 0.	39.0	39.0	42		
Bilsdale Kirkham and Midcable, and Laskill Pasture	15,878	.28	.28	89.18. 6.	49.0	49.0	176		
Butterwick and Newsam	660	2.02	2.02	44.16. 0.	29.8	29.8	15		
Cawton	1,056	.96	.96	42. 7. 6.	23.9	24.0	25		
Coulton	1,086	.84	.84	18. 2. 8.	50.6	50.6	60		
Edstone, Great and Little	1,458	.95	1.02	40. 0. 0.	34.5	37.4	36		
Farndale East Side and West Side, and Bransdale East Side	18,010	.20	.20	55.19. 0.	65.9	65.9	322		
Fryton	1,134	.87	.87	43.12. 4.	22.6	22.6	26		
Gillamoor and Fadmoor	2,944	.65	.65	26.16. 63/4.	71.0	71.0	110		
Gilling	2,071	1.11	1.11	52.12. 0.	43.9	43.9	39		
Grimston	997	.34	.34	9.16. 6.	34.5	34.6	101		
Harome	2,359	1.55	1.55	46. 0. 0.	79.7	79.7	51		
Helmsley Blackmoor	8,812	.73	.73	110.10.10.	58.5	58.5	80	5. 0. 0.	Excise
Hildenley	(304)	NR	NR	NR	NR	NR	NR		
Hovingham	2,853	1.13	1.13	51. 4. 8.	62.8	62.8	56		
Hutton le Hole	2,345	.60	.60	21.18. 2.	64.8	64.8	107		
Kirby Moorside	4,506	1.39	1.39	92. 2.103/4.	67.9	67.9	49		
Lastingham	1,678	.34	.34	13. 0. 0.	44.5	44.6	129		

APPENDIX M.2 (continued) page 538

Wapentake Township	1	2	3	4	5	6	7	8	9
Ryedale									
Malton, New, St Leonard's and St Michael's	49	218.09	218.09	68.15. 0.	154.8	155.4	0.7	13.11. 0.	Stock
Malton, Old	3,968	2.46	2.46	93.17. 1.	104.1	104.1	42		
Nawton and Beadlam	2,666	.85	1.17	31. 8. 0 3/4.	72.2	94.8	85		
Ness, East and West; and Muscoates	2,388	1.28	1.28	107. 8. 0.	7.7	28.4	22		
Newton and Laysthorp	940	1.04	1.04	29.10. 8.	33.1	33.1	32		
Normanby	1,784	.97	1.04	41.16. 8.	41.2	44.2	43		
North Holme	546	1.39	1.39	19.12. 0.	38.6	38.6	29		
Nunnington	2,122	1.90	1.90	57.19. 8.	69.5	69.5	36		
Oswaldkirk	(2,195)	def.	.62	(21. 0. 0.)	64.8	64.8	104		
Pockley	3,440	.44	.44	29.12. 0.	50.9	50.9	116		
Rievaulx	5,311	.62	.62	80. 0. 0.	41.2	41.2	66		
Rosedale West Side	2,340	.28	.30	18. 4. 0.	36.2	38.4	128		
Salton and Brawby	2,761	1.43	1.43	85.10. 0.	46.2	46.3	32		
Scawton	2,876	.33	.33	30.16. 6.	30.8	30.8	93		
Skiplam and Bransdale West Side	4,618	.31	.31	26. 0. 4.	54.8	54.9	178		
Slingsby	2,570	.94	.94	53.19. 1.	44.8	44.8	48		
South Holme	904	1.25	1.25	40. 6. 0.	28.0	28.0	22		
Spaunton	2,544	.45	.50	22. 6.10.	50.8	57.0	114		
Sproxton	2,868	.78	.78	40.17. 0 1/2.	54.6	54.6	70		
Stonegrave	914	2.00	2.00	28.15. 0.	63.7	63.7	32		
Swinton and Broughton	2,120	1.10	1.12	47. 0. 0.	49.8	50.3	45		
Thornton Riseborough	620	1.48	1.48	20.10. 0.	44.6	44.6	30		
Wath	371	.70	.70	7. 6. 8.	35.4	35.4	50		
Welburn	1,681	2.13	2.13	50.10. 0.	71.0	71.0	33		
Wombleton	1,187	1.08	1.10	20. 2. 2 3/4.	63.6	64.9	59		

TOTAL (all townships)[a]	127,751	.85	.85	1,956.15. 9 3/4.	54.3	55.4	65
TOTAL (non-defective land tax townships only)[a]	8,971	2.64	2.64	278.13.11 1/4.	84.8	84.9	32
Based on highest valuations (all townships)[a]			.86			56.1	

Total of highest valuations (all townships)[a] = £109,798. 2.11.

APPENDIX M.2 (continued) page 540

Wapentake Township	1	2	3	4	5	6	7	8	9
Whitby Strand									
Broxa	533	.88	.88	7. 4. 0.	65.1	65.1	74		
Eskdaleside	1,940	.77	.77	40. 2. 0.	37.2	37.2	48		
Fylingdales	9,826	.54	.57	102. 6.10.	51.8	54.8	96		
Hackness	2,457	.52	.52	32. 9. 0.	39.6	39.6	76		
Harwood Dale and Silpho	6,984	.30	.30	45. 6. 8.	46.0	46.0	154		
Hawsker and Stainsacre	7,314	.78	.91	75. 0. 31/4.	76.1	89.2	98		
Newholm and Dunsley	2,196	.95	1.10	56. 1. 2.	36.8	43.2	39		
Ruswarp	1,740	3.67	4.51	74. 7. 6.	85.9	105.5	23		
Sneaton	4,850	.50	.50	48.18. 51/2.	49.3	49.3	99		
Suffield and Everley	1,911	.76	.76	26.12. 0.	54.4	54.4	72		
Ugglebarnby	2,470	.72	.72	38.16. 0.	46.1	46.1	64		
Whitby	78	111.07	111.07	95. 4. 23/4.	91.0	91.0	0.8		
TOTAL (all townships)	42,299	.92	.92	642. 8. 11/2.	60.9	60.9	66		
Based on highest valuations (all townships)			1.00			65.7			

Total of highest valuations (all townships) = £42,209. 2. 6.

Wapentake Township	1	2	3	4	5	6	7	8	9
Riding									
TOTAL (all townships)[a]	1,280,924	.87	.88	25,038.11. 23/4.	44.8	44.8	51		
TOTAL (non-defective land tax townships only)[a]	388,796	1.01	1.01	9,205.12.10.	42.4	42.5	42		
Based on highest valuations (all townships)[a]			.91			46.3			

Total of highest valuations (all townships)[a] = £1,160,526.18. 5.

Notes: NR = no return.
Def. = defective.
[a]Values in parentheses are excluded.
[b]Excludes Ugthorpe from the numerator.
Sources: Land tax duplicates, NYCRO; PP 1818 (82.) XIX, 532-47 (1815 property tax); 1824 valuations for the county rate (includes 1814 property tax), QFR 1/1-18, NYCRO; 6-inch Ordnance Survey maps (OS), North Riding (acres). See maps 7, 8, and 9.

APPENDIX N

The valuation for the county rate c. 1815 as a percentage of the 1815 valuation for the property tax, with the reported basis of the county rate valuation, all counties, England and Wales

County	1815 valuation for property tax	Valuation for county rate (£. s. d.)	Year of county rate valuation	County rate as % of property tax
Bedfordshire	343,685	139,584	1739	40.6
Berkshire	643,781	707,827	1822[a]	110.0
Buckinghamshire	643,492	627,245	1814[b]	97.5
Cambridgeshire	645,554	608,374.1. 2.	1827[c]	94.2
Cheshire	1,083,083	857,968	1821	79.2
Cornwall	(916,060)	UNKNOWN	Ancient	
Cumberland	705,446	761,231.17. 0.	1825[d]	107.9
Derbyshire	887,659	795,836.14. 3.	1816[e]	89.7
Devonshire	1,897,515	905,984.12. 41/4.	1816[f]	47.8
Dorset	(698,395)	UNKNOWN	1740	
Durham	791,359	700,219.17. 6.	1823[g]	88.5
Essex	1,556,836	1,138,713. 4. 61/4.	1815[h]	73.1
Gloucestershire	(1,463,259)	UNKNOWN	1825[i]	
Hampshire	1,130,952	631,708	1821[j]	55.9
Herefordshire	604,614	513,893.18. 2.	1819[k]	85.0
Hertfordshire	571,107	350,246.10. 0.	1824[l]	61.3
Huntingdonshire	320,188	262,335	1817	81.9
Kent	1,644,179	1,056,891. 1. 0.	1807[m]	64.3
Lancashire	3,087,774	3,106,009	1815[q]	100.6
Leicestershire	902,217	651,197.14.10.	1805[n]	72.2
Lincolnshire	2,061,830			79.4
Holland		184,690. 3. 0.	1818[o]	
Kesteven		506,676.16. 7.	1818[l]	
Lindsey		897,417. 4. 61/4.	1822[o]	
City of Lincoln		47,833. 9. 9.	1830	
Middlesex	5,595,537	4,044,736	1815[g]	72.3
Monmouthshire	295,097	305,698	1827[a]	103.6
Norfolk	(1,540,952)	UNKNOWN	Ancient	
Northamptonshire	(942,162)	UNKNOWN	1732	
Northumberland	1,240,594	1,117,656.16. 21/2.	1830[g]	90.1

Nottinghamshire	(737,229)	Not reported	1818[p]	
Oxfordshire	713,147	651,164	1813[q]	91.3
Rutland	(133,487)	UNKNOWN	1693[r]	
Shropshire	(1,037,988)	UNKNOWN	1740	
Somerset	1,900,651	1,900,651	1818[s]	100.0
Staffordshire	1,150,285	1,114,994. 7. 8.	1817[t]	96.9
Suffolk	(1,127,404)	UNKNOWN (except 1 division)	Ancient (except 1 division)	
Surrey	1,579,173	1,528,710. 2. 4.	1816[u]	96.8
Sussex	915,348	838,939	1816[v]	91.6
Warwickshire	1,236,727	1,173,080	1816[l]	94.8
Westmorland	298,199	270,859.18. 8.	1816[w]	90.8
Wiltshire	1,155,459	1,184,565.18. 43/4.	1818[x]	102.5
Worcestershire	799,605	750,253. 6. 63/4.	1825[y]	93.8
Yorkshire, East Riding	1,120,434	826,112	1815[l]	73.7
Yorkshire, North Riding	1,166,948	766,742	1824[z]	65.7
Yorkshire, West Riding	2,396,222	1,686,027	1817[aa]	70.4
Yorkshire, York and Ainsty	106,251	105,557. 3. 4.	1824	99.4
ENGLAND SUBTOTAL	41,190,948	33,717,629.17. 93/4.		81.9
Anglesey	92,581	15,138.10. 0.	Not reported	16.4
Breconshire	(146,539)	UNKNOWN	UNKNOWN	
Cardiganshire	(141,889)	UNKNOWN	1748	
Carmarthenshire	(277,455)	UNKNOWN	UNKNOWN	
Carnarvonshire	125,198	188,755. 9. 5.	1829[bb]	150.8
Denbighshire	(221,783)	Not reported	UNKNOWN	
Flint	(153,930)	UNKNOWN	UNKNOWN	
Glamorgan	334,192	323,670	1826[u]	96.8
Merioneth	111,436	25,506.13. 4.	Ancient	22.9
Montgomeryshire	207,286	273,353	1827[u]	131.9
Pembrokeshire	(219,589)	UNKNOWN	Ancient	
Radnor	(99,717)	UNKNOWN	UNKNOWN	
WALES SUBTOTAL	870,693	826,423.12. 9.		94.9
TOTAL	42,061,641	34,544,053.10. 63/4.		82.1

APPENDIX N (continued) page 544

Notes: [a]Valuation was based on the 1815 property tax, schedule A.

[b]Valuation was based on the 1814 property tax, schedule A.

[c]Valuation was based on the ''actual value of property.''

[d]Valuation was based on ''the poor rates, and examination of overseers as to actual value of properties rated.''

[e]Valuation was based on the 1816 property tax, schedule A.

[f]Valuation was based on the ''actual value of county,'' as reported by overseers of the poor.

[g]Valuation was based on ''the full and fair annual value.''

[h]Valuation was based on the 1815 property tax, schedule A, less 25 percent.

[i]The deputy clerk of the peace reports he ''believes'' the valuation was ''taken from the last property tax assessments, but inasmuch as he had not the preparation of that rate, he is unable to set forth that particular.''

[j]Valuation was based on the 1815 property tax, schedule A, less 33 percent.

[k]Valuation was based on the property tax (year and schedule unspecified), less 25 percent.

[l]Valuation (according to the parliamentary reports) was based on the property tax (year and schedule unspecified). The Quarter Sessions Special Order Book for the North Riding, 1836, QFR 6/4/43, NYCRO, indicates the East Riding valuation was at 1d. in the pound on 4/5 of the 1815 property tax valuation. The parliamentary reports are clearly incomplete and sometimes in error.

[m]Valuation was based on rack rent.

[n]Valuation was based on the 1804 property tax, schedule A.

[o]Valuation was based on the ''estimated annual value.''

[p]Valuation was based on the 1816 property tax (schedule unspecified), ''with such alterations as appeared just and proper upon examination of the Churchwardens or Overseers of each parish.''

[q]Valuation was based on the 1813 property tax, schedule A.

[r]Valuation dates from ''when land tax first imposed.''

[s]Valuation was based on the property tax, schedule A, (year unspecified).

[t]Valuation was based on the ''full annual value.''

[u]Valuation was based on the ''annual value.''

[v]Valuation of the western division was based on the property tax (year and schedule unspecified); valuation of the eastern division was based on the ''full and fair annual value of all property assessed to the poor rate, or liable to be so.''

[w]Valuation was based on ''the average of the three preceding years of the Property Tax, under Schedule (A.), deducting one-fourth part.''

[x]Valuation was based on the property tax, schedules A and B (year unspecified).

[y]Valuation was based on the ''full and fair annual value'' as returned by overseers of the poor and ''altered by magistrates where insufficient.''

[z]Valuation was based on the 1814 property tax, schedule A, less 33 percent.

[aa]Valuation was based upon a ''comparison of returns of overseers of the poor, and collector of the property tax, allowing a deduction of one-fourth from the average of these returns.''

[bb]Valuation was based on ''one-fifth part of the annual value.''

Sources: PP 1831-32 (577.) XLIV; PP 1834 (542.) XIV.

APPENDICES O.1–4

Frequency distributions comparing North Riding land tax valuations c. 1830 with other valuations

Numbered columns (appendices O.1-4):

1 = Allertonshire wapentake
2 = Birdforth wapentake
3 = Bulmer wapentake
4 = Gilling East wapentake
5 = Gilling West wapentake
6 = Hallikeld wapentake
7 = Hang East wapentake
8 = Hang West wapentake
9 = Langbaurgh wapentake
10 = Pickering Lythe wapentake
11 = Ryedale wapentake
12 = Whitby Strand wapentake

APPENDIX O.1 page 546

Frequency distribution, the North Riding land tax valuations c. 1830 as a percentage of the 1815 property tax valuations (schedule A)

%	1	2	3	4	5	6	7	8	9	10	11	12	All cases N	All cases %	Summary Range	Summary % of cases[a]
0.0-4.9											1		1	0.6		
5.0-9.9																
10.0-14.9											1		1	0.6	0.0-19.9	1.2
15.0-19.9																
20.0-24.9											1		1	0.6		
25.0-29.9			1			1							2	1.2	20.0-39.9	8.4
30.0-34.9			2						1				3	1.7		
35.0-39.9	1		5			2							8	4.6		
40.0-44.9	1		1						2				4	2.3		
45.0-49.9			2	2	2		2	1					9	5.2	40.0-59.9	18.6
50.0-54.9	1	1	2	1	1	1			2				9	5.2		
55.0-59.9	1			1	3		1		2	1			9	5.2		
60.0-64.9	1	2	2	4	4	2			3	2			20	11.6		
65.0-69.9	1		3	3	2				6	1	1		17	9.9	60.0-79.9	39.5
70.0-74.9			3	5			1		4				13	7.6		
75.0-79.9	2	1	3	1	1	1		1	1	4	1		16	9.3		
80.0-84.9	3	1	4	3	1		1		1				14	8.1		
85.0-89.9				1					1				2	1.2	80.0-99.9	23.4
90.0-94.9		1	3		1				3	1	1		10	5.8		
95.0-99.9		1	5	1			1	2	1	2			13	7.6		
100.0-104.9				2	1	1		1		2			7	4.1		
105.0-109.9	1								1	1			3	1.7	100.0-124.9	7.8
110.0-114.9			1							1			2	1.2		
115.0-119.9																
120.0-124.9		1											1	0.6		
125.0-129.9																
130.0-134.9															≥ 125.0	1.2
135.0-139.9																
140.0-144.9					1								1	0.6		
145.0-149.9																
150.0-154.9																
155.0-159.9																

160.0-164.9			1										1	0.6		
≥ 165.0															90.0-109.9	19.8
def.									3				3	1.7		
NR		1	1										2	1.2		
N	12	9	39	24	17	8	7	5	31	15	6	0	172	100.0		
Mean	65.0	72.1	65.4	72.2	67.9	50.7	65.6	80.7	71.6	84.6	45.6		69.4			
Minimum	38.6	52.6	27.0	48.0	46.8	28.4	48.4	45.2	30.9	59.7	3.2		3.2			
Maximum	108.1	121.2	163.9	101.9	143.5	102.8	99.6	102.9	108.2	110.5	93.3		163.9			

Note: [a]Defective (def.) and no return (NR) cases are excluded from the denominator.
Source: Appendix M.

APPENDIX O.2 page 548

Frequency distribution, the North Riding land tax valuations c. 1830 as a percentage of the 1824 overseers' valuations for the county rate

%	1	2	3	4	5	6	7	8	9	10	11	12	All cases N	All cases %	Summary Range	Summary % of cases
0.0-4.9											1		1	0.6		
5.0-9.9															0.0-19.9	0.6
10.0-14.9																
15.0-19.9																
20.0-24.9																
25.0-29.9			1								2		3	1.7	20.0-39.9	4.1
30.0-34.9	1	1				2							4	2.3		
35.0-39.9																
40.0-44.9	1		1	1			1						4	2.3		
45.0-49.9	1	3	2	1	1	1	2		1				12	7.0	40.0-59.9	15.7
50.0-54.9		1	3		1								5	2.9		
55.0-59.9			2	2					2				6	3.5		
60.0-64.9	1	1		3	2			1					8	4.6		
65.0-69.9	3		3	2	3				2		1		14	8.1	60.0-79.9	25.0
70.0-74.9	1		1	2	3	1			1	1			10	5.8		
75.0-79.9				3	1	1			3	3			11	6.4		
80.0-84.9		1	1	2	1				2	1			8	4.6		
85.0-89.9	2		1	4	2		2	1	4	1	1		18	10.5	80.0-99.9	31.4
90.0-94.9	1		2	1	1				3	1			9	5.2		
95.0-99.9	1	1	2			3	1	1	8	2			19	11.0		
100.0-104.9		1	4					2	3	1			11	6.4		
105.0-109.9			2	1						1			4	2.3		
110.0-114.9			4	2					1	1			8	4.6	100.0-124.9	15.7
115.0-119.9			1		1								2	1.2		
120.0-124.9									1	1			2	1.2		
125.0-129.9			2							1			3	1.7		
130.0-134.9			2										2	1.2		
135.0-139.9															≥ 125.0	7.6
140.0-144.9			1							1			2	1.2		
145.0-149.9					1						1		2	1.2		
150.0-154.9																
155.0-159.9																

160.0-164.9			1										1	0.6		
≥ 165.0			3										3	1.7		
															90.0-109.9	25.0
def.																
NR																
N	12	9	39	24	17	8	7	5	31	15	6	0	172	100.0		
Mean	62.6	56.0	92.3	76.2	75.0	58.7	63.6	87.7	86.8	95.3	61.5		80.0			
Minimum	31.1	34.5	28.6	42.2	46.1	31.0	44.7	64.8	48.5	71.7	3.6		3.6			
Maximum	96.6	104.5	252.5	111.7	146.6	99.1	99.6	100.9	121.9	143.1	145.1		252.5			

Source: Appendix M.

APPENDIX O.3 page 550

Frequency distribution, the North Riding land tax valuations c. 1830 as a percentage of the amounts settled for the county rate in 1825

%	1	2	3	4	5	6	7	8	9	10	11	12	All cases N	All cases %	Summary Range	Summary % of cases[a]
0.0-4.9											1		1	0.6		
5.0-9.9															0.0-19.9	0.6
10.0-14.9																
15.0-19.9																
20.0-24.9											1		1	0.6		
25.0-29.9															20.0-39.9	1.2
30.0-34.9											1		1	0.6		
35.0-39.9																
40.0-44.9			1			1							2	1.2		
45.0-49.9			1						1				2	1.2	40.0-59.9	6.5
50.0-54.9			1										1	0.6		
55.0-59.9			4			2							6	3.5		
60.0-64.9	1		1						2				4	2.3		
65.0-69.9		2	1						1				4	2.3		
70.0-74.9			3	2	2		2						9	5.2	60.0-79.9	14.2
75.0-79.9	1	1	2	1	1	1							7	4.1		
80.0-84.9	2				2				1				5	2.9		
85.0-89.9				1	1		1		4	1			8	4.6	80.0-99.9	22.5
90.0-94.9	1	2	1	4	3	1			1	2			15	8.7		
95.0-99.9	1		3		3	1			2				10	5.8		
100.0-104.9			1	3					3		1		8	4.6		
105.0-109.9	1		1	4					3				9	5.2		
110.0-114.9	1	1	2	2	1		1	1	2				11	6.4	100.0-124.9	27.8
115.0-119.9	1		3			1			2	3	1		11	6.4		
120.0-124.9	1		2	1	1		1		2				8	4.6		
125.0-129.9	1	1	2	3					1				8	4.6		
130.0-134.9									2				2	1.2		
135.0-139.9			3						2				5	2.9	≥ 125.0	27.2
140.0-144.9			2		1				1	2	1		7	4.1		
145.0-149.9		1	3	1			1	2		1			9	5.2		
150.0-154.9				2	1	1		1		1			6	3.5		
155.0-159.9									2	2			4	2.3		

160.0-164.9	1												1	0.6		
≥ 165.0		1		2	1								4	2.3		
															90.0-109.9	24.8
def.										3			3	1.7		
NR																
N	12	9	39	24	17	8	7	5	31	15	6	0	172	100.0		
Mean	101.3	93.0	98.8	108.4	101.8	76.0	98.3	121.1	109.0	126.9	68.3		103.9			
Minimum	63.5	65.9	40.6	72.0	70.2	42.6	72.6	67.8	48.2	89.5	4.8		4.8			
Maximum	161.9	181.7	245.7	152.8	215.2	154.3	149.2	154.3	158.5	158.5	140.0		245.7			

Note: [a]Defective (def.) cases are excluded from the denominator.
Source: Appendix M.

APPENDIX O.4 page 552

Frequency distribution, the North Riding land tax valuations c. 1830 as a percentage of the maximum valuation among the preceding three

%	1	2	3	4	5	6	7	8	9	10	11	12	All cases N	All cases %	Summary Range	Summary % of cases
0.0-4.9											1		1	0.6		
5.0-9.9															0.0-19.9	1.2
10.0-14.9											1		1	0.6		
15.0-19.9																
20.0-24.9											1		1	0.6		
25.0-29.9			1			1							2	1.2	20.0-39.9	9.3
30.0-34.9	1	1	2			1			1				6	3.5		
35.0-39.9	1		5			1							7	4.1		
40.0-44.9			1	1			1		2				5	2.9		
45.0-49.9	1	3	3	2	2		2	1					14	8.1	40.0-59.9	22.7
50.0-54.9	1	1	2		2	1			2				9	5.2		
55.0-59.9	1			3	3				3	1			11	6.4		
60.0-64.9	2	2	4	3	2				2	2			17	9.9		
65.0-69.9	2		3	2	2				6	1	1		17	9.9	60.0-79.9	39.0
70.0-74.9	3		3	4	1		1		4				16	9.3		
75.0-79.9	1		3	2	2	1		1	2	4	1		17	9.9		
80.0-84.9			4	4			1		2				11	6.4		
85.0-89.9	1							1	2		1		5	2.9	80.0-99.9	21.5
90.0-94.9			3						3	1			7	4.1		
95.0-99.9		1	5	1		1	1	1	2	2			14	8.1		
100.0		1	2	1	2			1		4			11	6.4	100.00	6.4
															90.0-100.0	18.6
def.																
NR																
N	12	9	39	24	17	8	7	5	31	15	6	0	172	100.0		
Mean	58.0	55.0	64.6	70.1	64.6	49.1	61.4	78.0	71.2	84.0	45.4		66.7			
Minimum	31.1	34.5	27.0	42.2	46.1	28.4	44.7	45.2	30.9	59.7	3.2		3.2			
Maximum	85.5	100.0	100.0	100.0	100.0	99.1	99.5	100.0	98.5	100.0	87.9		100.0			

Source: Appendix M.

APPENDIX P.1

Ratios of 1815 property tax valuation (schedule A) to land tax quota, property tax valuation per acre, and acres per land tax quota; all townships, East Riding

Wapentake Parish/Township	1815 property tax	Land tax gross quota	Land tax net quota	Gross ratio	Net ratio	Deductions Amount	Deductions Type	Acres	Property tax/ acre	Acres/ gross L.T. quota
Buckrose										
Acklam	1,592	33. 0. 0.		48				2,358	.68	71
Birdsall	4,090	93. 0. 0.		44				4,030	1.01	43
Bugthorpe	2,805	51. 1. 8.		55				1,917	1.46	38
Burythorpe	1,394	25. 0. 0.		56				1,250	1.12	50
Cowlam	2,200	18. 8. 0.		116				2,052	1.07	112
Duggleby	1,661	26.16. 0.		62				1,714	.97	64
Eddlethorpe and Firby	1,687	33. 0. 0.		51				1,243	1.36	38
Fimber	1,940	17.16. 0.		109				1,924	1.01	108
Fridaythorpe	1,619	13. 8. 0.		121				1,919	.84	143
Grimston, North	1,319	32. 6. 0.		41				1,565	.84	48
Helperthorpe	2,214	19. 0. 0.		116				2,593	.85	136
Heslerton, East	3,469	26.16. 0.		129				3,584	.97	134
Heslerton, West	2,618	28. 8. 0.		92				2,954	.89	104
Howsham	2,690	83. 4. 0.		32				2,150	1.25	26
Kennythorpe	470	19. 0. 0.		25				542	.87	28
Kirby Grindalyth	5,319	25.12. 0.		208				4,524	1.18	177
Kirby Underdale and Garrowby	5,386	178.17. 3.		30				5,123	1.05	29
Kirkham	400	12. 0. 0.		33				273	1.46	23
Knapton	2,508	35. 8. 0.		71				2,889	.87	82
Langton	2,139	42. 7. 0.		50				2,284	.94	54
Leavening	1,848	32. 4. 0.		57				1,292	1.43	40
Leppington	3,044	64. 8. 0.		47				1,182	2.58	18
Luttons Ambo	2,262	18.12. 0.		122				1,623	.86	141
Mennythorpe	632	11.12. 0.		54				583	1.08	50
Norton, Sutton and Welham	6,239	71.10. 0.		87				2,838	2.20	40
Rillington	2,448	54. 0. 0.		45				2,170	1.13	40
Scagglethorpe	2,086	24.13. 0.		85				1,206	1.73	49

Wapentake Parish/Township	1815 property tax	Land tax gross quota	Land tax net quota	Gross ratio	Net ratio	Deductions Amount	Deductions Type	Acres	Property tax/ acre	Acres/ gross L.T. quota
Buckrose										
Scampston	2,409	46.16. 0.		51				2,412	1.00	52
Scrayingham	1,925	37. 9. 0.		51				1,560	1.23	42
Settrington	6,814	156.16. 0.		43				4,986	1.37	32
Sherburn	3,461	26. 4. 0.		132				4,739	.73	181
Skirpenbeck	2,135	49. 8. 4.		43				1,644	1.30	33
Sledmere and Croom	6,450	63.19. 0.		101				7,041	.92	110
Thirkleby	1,049	13. 0. 0.		81				1,345	.78	103
Thixendale and Raisthorpe	4,909	87.12. 9.		56				5,923	.83	68
Thorpe Bassett	2,810	29. 6. 0.		96				1,806	1.56	62
Towthorpe	967	11.10. 0.		84				1,710	.56	149
Weaverthorpe	2,750	20.12. 0.		133				2,977	.92	144
Westow	1,653	47.16. 0.		34				1,190	1.39	25
Wetwang	2,573	31.16. 0.		81				3,436	.75	108
Wharram le Street and Grange	1,922	36. 0. 0.		53				2,072	.93	58
Wharram Percy	1,612	38. 8. 0.		42				1,459	1.10	38
Wintringham	5,018	83. 4. 0.		60				5,340	.94	64
Yedingham	792	38. 8. 0.		21				582	1.36	15
SUBTOTAL	115,328	1,909.12. 0.		60				109,004	1.06	57

Dickering										
Bempton and Newsholme	2,343	38.16. 0.		60				1,970	1.19	51
Bessingby	2,045	35. 8. 0.		58				1,270	1.61	36
Boynton	1,479	28. 8. 0.		52				2,613	.57	92
Bridlington and Bridlington Quay	8,248	193. 2. 0.	99. 0. 0.	43	83	47. 0. 0.	Excise	2,519	3.27	13
						47. 2. 0.	Customs			
Brigham	2,016	50.12. 0.		40				1,382	1.46	27
Buckton	2,185	26. 0. 0.		84				1,984	1.10	76
Burton Agnes	3,368	33. 4. 0.		101				2,574	1.31	78
Burton Fleming	2,240	40. 4. 0.		56				3,910	.57	97
Butterwick	1,402	28.12. 0.		49				1,778	.79	62
Carnaby	2,270	42. 0. 0.		54				1,944	1.17	46
Cottam	1,417	11.16. 0.		120				2,586	.55	219
Easton	1,005	17.16. 0.		56				734	1.37	41
Filey	980	25. 4. 0.	9. 4. 0.	39	106	16. 0. 0.	Riding Officer	833	1.18	33
Flamborough	4,113	80. 0. 0.	72. 0. 0.	51	57	8. 0. 0.	Customs	3,084	1.33	38
Flixton	1,629	16. 8. 0.		99				2,561	.64	156
Folkton	2,506	30.16. 0.		81				2,936	.85	95
Foston on the Wolds	1,619	23. 8. 0.		69				1,108	1.46	47
Foxholes and Boythorpe	1,375	13.14. 4.		100				2,526	.54	184
Fraisthorpe and Auburn	2,661	32. 0. 0.		83				1,987	1.34	62
Ganton and Potter Brompton	3,623	27. 0. 0.		134				3,982	.91	147
Garton on the Wolds	4,697	53.16. 0.		87				4,147	1.13	77
Gembling	1,210	41. 4. 0.		29				1,235	.98	30
Gransmoor	2,175	11.16. 0.		184				1,253	1.74	106
Grindale and Argam	1,230	12. 0. 0.		102				2,988	.41	249
Haisthorpe	1,775	29. 0. 0.		61				1,390	1.28	48
Harpham	2,728	27.16. 0.		98				2,144	1.27	77
Hilderthorpe	1,034	16. 0. 0.		65				731	1.41	46
Hunmanby	6,679	79. 0. 0.	69. 0. 0.	84	97	10. 0. 0.	Excise	6,988	.96	88

Wapentake Parish/Township	1815 property tax	Land tax gross quota	Land tax net quota	Gross ratio	Net ratio	Deductions Amount	Deductions Type	Acres	Property tax/ acre	Acres/ gross L.T. quota
Dickering										
Kelk, Great	686	29.12. 0.		23				1,173	.58	40
Kilham	6,961	36.14. 0.		190				8,173	.85	223
Langtoft	2,413	34. 8. 0.		70				3,582	.67	104
Lowthorpe	2,574	52.12. 0.		49				1,969	1.31	37
Muston	3,840	57. 4. 5.		67				2,293	1.67	40
Nafferton	5,401	70. 4. 0.		77				4,899	1.10	70
Newton, Wold; and Fordon	2,013	17. 4. 0.		117				3,493	.58	203
Reighton	1,439	30.17. 4.	28. 7. 4.	47	51	2.10. 0.	Salary	1,818	.79	59
Rudston	5,075	56. 0. 9.		90				5,551	.91	99
Ruston Parva	1,504	11. 8. 0.		132				969	1.55	85
Sewerby and Marton	2,205	39. 4. 0.		56				2,116	1.04	54
Speeton	1,859	11. 4. 0.		166				1,844	1.01	165
Thornholm	1,428	13. 0. 0.		110				1,346	1.06	104
Thwing, Octon, and Octon Grange	3,181	37. 8. 0.		85				4,024	.79	108
Wansford	2,055	42.14. 0.		48				922	2.23	22
Willerby, Binnington, and Staxton	3,098	40.16. 0.		76				4,567	.68	112
SUBTOTAL	115,784	1,645.10.10.	1,514.18.10.	70	76	57. 0. 0.	Excise	113,896	1.02	69
						55. 2. 0.	Customs			
						16. 0. 0.	Riding Officer			
						2.10. 0.	Salary			

Harthill, Bainton Beacon										
Aike	648	11.15. 0.		55				545	1.19	46
Bainton	3,283	66. 9. 0.		49				2,981	1.10	45
Beswick	2,104	46. 5. 2.		45				2,028	1.04	44
Bracken	NR	(16. 0. 0.)		NR				(677)	NR	42
Dalton, North	3,533	64. 9. 0.		55				4,636	.76	72
Driffield, Great and Little	12,557	135. 0. 8.	115. 0. 8.	93	109	20. 0. 0.	Excise	5,202	2.41	38
Eastburn	1,205	15.12. 0.		77				843	1.43	54
Emswell and Kelleythorpe	2,714	74. 6. 8		36				2,398	1.13	32
Holme on the Wolds	1,347	30. 0. 0.		45				1,517	.89	50
Hutton Cranswick	5,473	120. 2. 8.		46				4,814	1.14	40
Kilnwick	2,577	50.15. 0.		51				1,698	1.52	33
Kirkburn	1,270	24.13. 0.		52				1,387	.92	56
Lockington	4,465	104. 0. 0.		43				3,083	1.45	30
Lund	3,742	104. 2. 0.		36				3,078	1.22	30
Middleton on the Wolds	3,714	57. 4. 0.		65				3,664	1.01	64
Neswick	1,640	40. 8. 0.		40				987	1.66	24
Rotsea	1,154	38. 5. 4.		30				805	1.43	21
Scorborough	1,954	50.19. 4.		38				1,384	1.41	27
Skerne	3,065	106. 4. 0.		29				2,757	1.11	26
Southburn	1,177	39. 2. 0.		30				1,103	1.07	28
Sunderlandwick	822	23. 0. 0.		36				822	1.00	36
Tibthorpe	2,112	36.16. 01/4.		57				2,885	.73	78
Warter	6,990	101.18. 8.		68				7,876	.89	77
Watton	5,906	189. 8. 2.		31				4,744	1.24	25
SUBTOTAL	73,452	1,530.15. 81/4.	1,510.15. 81/4.	48	49	20. 0. 0.	Excise	61,237	1.20	40

APPENDIX P.1 (continued) page 558

Wapentake Parish/Township	1815 property tax	Land tax gross quota	Land tax net quota	Gross ratio	Net ratio	Deductions Amount	Deductions Type	Acres	Property tax/ acre	Acres/ gross L.T. quota
Harthill, Holme Beacon										
Aughton	1,648	40. 0. 0.		41				1,952	.84	49
Bielby	1,146	19.16. 0.		58				1,737	.66	88
Breighton and Gunby	1,253	40. 0. 0.		31				1,753	.71	44
Bubwith	2,009	57.10. 8.		35				1,550	1.30	27
Cottingwith, East	1,249	30.14. 6.		41				1,251	1.00	41
Ellerton	2,076	52. 0. 0.		40				2,555	.81	49
Everingham	2,673	110.16. 0.		24				2,980	.90	27
Foggathorpe	1,395	24. 2. 0.		58				1,320	1.06	55
Goodmanham	2,013	42.10. 8.		47				3,026	.66	71
Gribthorpe and Willitoft	1,874	43. 6. 3.		43				1,773	1.06	41
Harlthorpe	438	19. 3. 9.		23				758	.58	39
Harswell	846	32. 0. 0.		26				1,126	.75	35
Hayton	2,756	103.11. 0.		27				1,900	1.45	18
Holme upon Spalding Moor	8,721	208.15. 0.		42				11,514	.76	55
Laytham	1,417	24. 2. 0.		59				1,434	.99	60
Londesborough and Easthorpe	2,592	46. 6. 0.		56				4,256	.61	92
Melbourne	2,595	36. 8. 8.		71				3,148	.82	86
Seaton Ross	3,351	71.19. 4.		46				3,426	.98	48
Shipton	1,962	25. 9. 8.		77				1,474	1.33	58
Spaldington	5,320	76. 0. 0.		70				3,542	1.50	47
Storwood	1,209	27. 6.10 3/4.		44				1,222	.99	45
Thorpe le Street	750	26. 8. 0.		28				676	1.11	26
Weighton, Market; and Arras	7,436	126. 7. 0.	116. 7. 0.	59	64	10. 0. 0.	Excise	5,880	1.26	46

Wressell, Newsholme, Brindleys, and Loftsome	3,592	83. 2. 9.		43				4,156	.86	50
SUBTOTAL	60,321	1,367.16. 13/4.	1,357.16. 13/4.	44	44	10. 0. 0.	Excise	64,409	.94	47
Harthill, Hunsley Beacon										
Bromfleet	2,277	71. 8. 0.		32				1,127	2.02	16
Burton, Bishop	6,935	121. 6. 8.		57				4,259	1.63	35
Burton, Cherry	4,369	123.14.10.		35				3,466	1.26	28
Cave, North	6,532	95. 0. 0.	85. 0. 0.	69	77	10. 0. 0.	Excise	3,027	2.16	32
Cave, South	6,268	130.13.11.	129.17.11.	48	48	0.16. 0.	Stock	4,336	1.44	33
Cliffe, North	728	39.13. 0.		18				1,304	.56	33
Cliffe, South	965	45. 0. 0.		21				2,127	.45	47
Cottingham	24,261	453.10.10.	443.10.10.	53	55	10. 0. 0.	Excise	9,734	2.49	21
Dalton, South	1,500	62. 9. 4.		24				1,844	.81	30
Drewton and Everthorpe	NR	(53.17. 8.)		NR				(2,114)	NR	39
Elloughton and Brough	2,058	60. 0. 0.		34				1,614	1.28	27
Etton	3,739	114.10. 6.		33				3,728	1.00	32
Faxfleet	1,683	62.18. 0.		27				1,681	1.00	27
Hotham	1,952	44.18. 0.		43				2,808	.70	62
Leconfield	5,860	110. 3. 4.		53				3,630	1.61	33
Newbald, North	4,380	51. 6. 8.		85				3,982	1.10	78
Newbald, South	1,894	29.11. 4.		64				1,991	.95	67
New Village	(962)	NR		NR				(510)	1.89	NR
Rowley (Bentley, Risby, and Little Weighton)	8,697	147. 0. 0.		59				6,424	1.35	44
Sancton and Houghton	2,290	75. 0. 0.		30				3,174	.72	42
Sculcoates	32,911	117.14. 0.		280				744	44.24	6
Skidby	2,511	21. 3. 8.		118				1,561	1.61	74

APPENDIX P.1 (continued) page 560

Wapentake Parish/Township	1815 property tax	Land tax gross quota	Land tax net quota	Gross ratio	Net ratio	Deductions Amount	Deductions Type	Acres	Property tax/ acre	Acres/ gross L.T. quota
Harthill, Hunsley Beacon										
Walkington, Provost and Howden Fees	5,859	93.16.4		62				3,725	1.57	40
Wauldby	1,377	19.12. 0.		70				1,021	1.35	52
SUBTOTAL	129,046	2,090.10. 5.	2,069.14. 5.	62	62	20. 0. 0. 0.16. 0.	Excise Stock	67,307	1.92	32
Harthill, Wilton Beacon										
Allerthorpe	1,382	47. 1. 4.		29				1,578	.88	34
Barnby Moor	2,517	50.10. 8.		50				2,578	.98	51
Belthorpe	580	32. 0. 0.		18				561	1.03	18
Bolton	1,042	38. 8. 0.		27				941	1.11	24
Burnby	1,662	38. 4. 0.		44				1,700	.98	44
Catton, High	1,206	41. 0. 0.		29				1,697	.71	41
Catton, Low	1,012	38. 4. 0.		26				1,346	.75	35
Fangfoss and Spittle	1,339	48. 6. 0.		28				1,409	.95	29
Givendale, Great; and Grimthorpe	975	48.12. 0.		20				1,314	.74	27
Huggate	3,310	73. 0. 0.		45				7,004	.47	96
Kilnwick Percy	1,803	60. 0. 0.		30				1,580	1.14	26
Meltonby and Yapham	1,805	34.16. 0.		52				1,888	.96	54
Millington	1,751	25. 0. 0.		70				2,509	.70	100
Newton upon Derwent	1,619	36. 1. 21/2.		45				1,713	.94	48
Nunburnholme	1,332	43. 0. 0.		31				1,857	.72	43
Ousethorpe	516	20. 0. 0.		26				331	1.56	16

Pocklington	6,501	127. 4. 0.	108.11. 8.	51	60	18.12. 4.	Excise	2,570	2.53	20
Stamford Bridge, East	1,229	33.10. 0.		37				1,122	1.10	33
Sutton, Full	889	41.16. 0.		21				881	1.01	21
Sutton on Derwent	4,066	121.18. 8.		33				3,681	1.10	30
Thornton	1,202	33. 0. 0.		36				2,314	.52	70
Waplington	740	13. 4. 0.		56				812	.91	62
Wilberfoss	1,424	38. 1. 4.		37				1,472	.97	39
Wilton, Bishop	2,569	94. 0. 0.		27				4,013	.64	43
Youlthorpe and Gowthorpe	857	33. 2. 0.		26				1,179	.73	36
SUBTOTAL	43,328	1,209.19. 21/2.	1,191. 6.101/2.	36	36	18.12. 4.	Excise	48,050	.90	40
Holderness, Middle										
Aldbrough, Etherdwick, Fosham, and Carlton	5,832	130.19. 7.		44				3,776	1.54	29
Benningholme and Grange	1,775	55. 5. 0.		32				1,470	1.21	27
Bilton	1,390	73. 0. 4.		19				1,204	1.15	16
Burton Pidsea	3,106	77.16. 0.		40				2,303	1.35	30
Coniston	913	27. 4. 0.		34				602	1.52	22
Danthorpe	917	23.12. 0.		39				726	1.26	31
Drypool	2,102	20.16. 0.		101				184	11.42	9
Ellerby	2,964	78.13. 0.		38				2,247	1.32	28
Elsternwick	1,615	28.16. 0.		56				1,155	1.40	40
Fitling	1,449	32. 8. 0.		45				1,529	.95	47
Flinton	1,739	35.18. 5.		48				2,008	.87	56
Ganstead	1,135	51.12. 0.		22				809	1.40	16
Garton in Holderness and Grimston	2,499	91.14. 0.		27				1,822	1.37	20
Hedon	2,239	47.11. 0.	42. 7. 0.	47	53	5. 4. 0.	Excise	320	7.00	7
Hilston	676	20.18. 2.		32				552	1.22	26

APPENDIX P.1 (continued) page 562

Wapentake Parish/Township	1815 property tax	Land tax gross quota	Land tax net quota	Gross ratio	Net ratio	Deductions Amount	Deductions Type	Acres	Property tax/ acre	Acres/ gross L.T. quota
Holderness, Middle										
Humbleton	1,587	53. 0. 0.		30				1,477	1.07	28
Lelley	1,166	27. 8. 0.		42				792	1.47	29
Marfleet	2,752	39. 6. 8.		70				1,285	2.14	33
Marton	1,429	72. 1. 4.		20				946	1.51	13
Meaux	2,345	72. 4. 0.		32				1,457	1.61	20
Newton, East; and Bewick	2,039	36. 4. 8.		56				1,439	1.42	40
Newton, West; Burton Constable, and Tansterne	3,042	109. 4. 0.		28				2,460	1.24	22
Owstwick	1,635	38.15. 2.		42				1,337	1.22	34
Preston	9,062	129. 8. 0.		70				5,012	1.81	39
Roos	2,869	59. 8. 0.		48				2,528	1.13	42
Skirlaugh, South	1,438	54. 4. 0.		26				1,101	1.31	20
Southcoates	7,783	61.12. 0.		126				1,296	6.00	21
Sproatley	2,003	48. 4. 0.		42				1,372	1.46	28
Sutton and Stoneferry	21,124	221. 8. 0.		95				4,760	4.44	21
Swine	3,202	103. 8. 0.		31				2,286	1.40	22
Thirtleby	1,072	25. 0. 0.		43				754	1.42	30
Tunstall and Waxholme	2,061	60. 8. 0.		34				1,888	1.09	31
Waghen	4,740	132. 0. 0.		36				3,983	1.19	30
Wyton	1,820	33.12. 0.		54				792	2.30	24
SUBTOTAL	103,520	2,172.19. 4.	2,167.15. 4	48	48	5. 4. 0.	Excise	57,672	1.80	26

Holderness, North

Atwick and Skirlington	1,961	47.16. 0.		41				1,759	1.11	37
Barmston	4,662	61. 0. 0.	55. 0. 0.	76	85	6. 0. 0.	Riding Officer	2,418	1.93	40
Beeford	5,177	49. 4. 0.		105				3,752	1.38	76
Bonwick	948	26. 8. 0.		36				774	1.22	29
Brandesburton	4,854	93.16. 0.		52				4,672	1.04	50
Catfoss	1,261	35. 0. 0.		36				1,084	1.16	31
Catwick	2,344	38. 8. 0.		61				1,570	1.49	41
Cowdens, Great and Little	1,588	40. 0. 0.		40				1,579	1.00	39
Dringhoe, Upton, and Brough	1,617	42. 0. 1.		38				1,705	.95	40
Dunnington	1,022	33.16. 0.		30				844	1.21	25
Eske	1,575	20. 0. 0.		79				1,098	1.43	55
Frodingham, North	3,660	82. 0. 0.		45				3,147	1.16	38
Goxhill	1,679	24. 9. 8.		68				838	2.00	34
Hatfield, Great	1,659	41. 8. 0.		40				1,489	1.11	36
Hatfield, Little	1,152	20.13. 4.		56				976	1.18	47
Hempholme	1,530	35.12. 0.		43				1,052	1.45	30
Hornsea and Burton	5,012	93. 4. 0.	77. 4. 0.	54	65	8. 0. 0. 8. 0. 0.	Excise Customs	3,332	1.50	36
Leven	4,822	78. 0. 0.		62				3,709	1.30	48
Lissett and Little Kelk	3,639	60.12. 0.		60				1,877	1.94	31
Mappleton and Rowlston	1,562	41. 4. 1.		38				1,954	.80	47
Moor Town	419	13. 0. 0.		32				512	.82	39
Nunkeeling, Arram, and Bewholme	3,418	80.19. 0.		42				2,854	1.20	35
Rise	2,353	56. 0. 0.		42				2,034	1.16	36
Riston, Long	1,843	34. 1. 0.		54				1,834	1.00	54
Routh	3,841	56. 0. 0.		68				2,385	1.61	42
Seaton and Wassand	2,748	61. 0. 4.		45				1,744	1.58	28
Sigglesthorne	1,144	22. 4. 0.		52				1,032	1.11	46

APPENDIX P.1 (continued) page 564

Wapentake Parish/Township	1815 property tax	Land tax gross quota	Land tax net quota	Gross ratio	Net ratio	Deductions Amount	Deductions Type	Acres	Property tax/ acre	Acres/ gross L.T. quota
Holderness, North										
Skipsea	1,575	44.12. 0.		35				1,593	.99	36
Skirlaugh, North; Arnold, and Rowton	2,503	45.12. 0.		55				2,214	1.13	48
Ulrome	1,622	50. 0. 0.		32				1,594	1.02	32
Withernwick	4,478	54.14. 0.		82				2,822	1.59	52
SUBTOTAL	77,668	1,482.13. 6.	1,460.13. 6.	52	53	8. 0. 0.	Excise	60,247	1.29	41
						8. 0. 0.	Customs			
						6. 0. 0.	Riding Officer			
Holderness, South										
Burstwick and Skeckling	5,834	169. 8. 0.		34				4,338	1.34	26
Easington	3,186	109. 0. 0.		29				2,319	1.37	21
Frodingham, South	1,756	34. 8. 0.		51				1,205	1.46	35
Halsham	4,795	115. 0. 0.		42				2,907	1.65	25
Hollym	2,663	52. 0. 0.		51				2,119	1.26	41
Holmpton	2,524	50. 0. 0.		50				1,903	1.33	38
Keyingham	6,762	130.12. 0.		52				3,549	1.90	27
Kilnsea	644	158.12. 0.		4				911	.71	6
Newton, Out	887	24.12. 0.		36				676	1.31	27
Ottringham and Sunk Island	(18,003)	(178.16. 4.)		101				def.	def.	def.
Owthorne	1,439	46. 8. 3.		31				1,052	1.37	23
Patrington	5,356	145.16. 0.	135.16.0	37	39	10.0.0	Excise	3,741	1.43	26
Paull	11,539	157. 0. 0.		73				4,956	2.33	32
Rimswell	1,639	57.18. 0.		28				1,233	1.33	21

Ryhill and Camerton	3,307	74.16. 0.		44				1,571	2.10	21
Skeffling	2,811	61.16. 0.		45				1,834	1.53	30
Thorngumbald	3,239	71.12. 0.		45				1,656	1.96	23
Welwick	5,214	189. 4. 0.		28				3,515	1.48	18
Winestead	3,016	74. 0. 0.		41				2,108	1.43	28
Withernsea	1,163	37.12. 0.		31				746	1.56	20
SUBTOTAL	67,774	1,759.14. 3.	1,749.14.3	38	39	10.0.0	Excise	42,339	1.60	24
Howdenshire										
Asselby	1,091	42. 4. 0.		26				1,163	.94	28
Balkholme	779	13.15. 4.		57				1,281	.61	93
Barmby on the Marsh	2,206	51.15. 6.		42				1,862	1.18	36
Belby	1,255	24.14. 8.		51				724	1.73	29
Bellasize	1,672	62. 6. 4.		27				1,721	.97	28
Blacktoft	2,434	42. 8. 9.		57				2,356	1.03	56
Brantingham and Thorpe Brantingham	1,874	62.11. 4.		30				1,346	1.39	22
Cotness	1,060	20. 0. 0.		53				629	1.68	31
Eastrington	1,964	44. 8. 8.		44				1,678	1.17	38
Ellerker	2,713	64.11. 0.		42				2,143	1.27	33
Gilberdike	1,969	42.16. 0.		46				1,616	1.22	38
Howden	6,390	179. 5. 4.	160. 4. 0.	36	40	19. 1. 4.	Excise	2,981	2.14	17
Kilpin	1,520	27.17. 0.		54				906	1.68	32
Knedlington	1,268	41. 8. 0.		31				824	1.54	20
Laxton	1,918	29. 8. 0.		65				1,326	1.45	45
Melton	1,256	34.16. 0.		36				897	1.40	26
Newport Wallingfen	694	12. 6. 8.		56				510	1.36	41
Portington and Cavil	1,660	44.17. 4.		37				1,316	1.26	29
Saltmarshe and Metham	2,800	82.10. 0.		34				2,402	1.16	29
Scalby	1,760	48.10. 0.		36				1,160	1.52	24

APPENDIX P.1 (continued) page 566

Wapentake Parish/Township	1815 property tax	Land tax gross quota	Land tax net quota	Gross ratio	Net ratio	Deductions Amount	Deductions Type	Acres	Property tax/ acre	Acres/ gross L.T. quota
Howdenshire										
Skelton	2,677	55.16. 8.		48				1,999	1.34	36
Thorpe	803	10. 1. 8.		80				310	2.59	31
Welton	3,149	87.12. 0.		36				1,778	1.77	20
Yokefleet	1,999	30. 4. 0.		66				1,780	1.12	59
SUBTOTAL	46,911	1,156. 4. 3.	1,137. 2.11.	40	41	19. 1. 4.	Excise	34,708	1.35	30
Hullshire										
Anlaby	(3,985)	NR		NR				(1,471)	2.71	NR
Ella, Kirk	(2,780)	NR		NR				(1,162)	2.39	NR
Ella, West	(1,190)	NR		NR				(645)	1.84	NR
Ferriby, North	(1,779)	NR		NR				(1,131)	1.57	NR
Hessle and Garrison Side	(7,373)	NR		NR				(2,775)	2.66	NR
Hull	(77,903)	NR		NR				(1,016)	76.68	NR
Swanland	(4,811)	NR		NR				(3,355)	1.43	NR
Willerby	(1,829)	NR		NR				(996)	1.84	NR
SUBTOTAL	(101,650)	NR		NR				(12,551)	8.10	NR

Wapentake Parish/Township	1815 property tax	Land tax gross quota	Land tax net quota	Gross ratio	Net ratio	Deductions Amount	Deductions Type	Acres	Property tax/ acre	Acres/ gross L.T. quota
Ouse and Derwent										
Barlby	1,718	53. 0. 8.		32				1,482	1.16	28
Brackenholme and Woodhall	1,063	49. 2. 2.		22				1,340	.79	27
Cliffe with Lund	2,760	82. 0. 3.		34				2,740	1.01	33
Deighton	2,167	53. 1. 8.		41				2,002	1.08	38
Duffield, North	4,269	130.16. 0.		33				3,417	1.25	26
Duffield, South	1,274	39.17. 0.		32				1,686	.76	42
Dunnington	2,650	36.17. 0.		72				2,243	1.18	61
Elvington	2,647	45. 4. 6.		58				2,372	1.12	52
Escrick	4,051	105.15. 0.		38				4,346	.93	41
Fulford, Gate and Water	5,841	61. 3. 7.		95				2,007	2.91	33
Grimston	524	23. 1. 0.		23				797	.66	34
Hemingbrough	1,700	41. 2. 9.		41				1,141	1.49	28
Heslington St Lawrence and St Paul	3,425	63. 3. 2.		54				2,645	1.29	42
Kelfield	2,311	53. 6. 8.		43				1,835	1.26	34
Kexby	1,480	33. 4. 3.		44				1,892	.78	57
Menthorpe and Bowthorpe	1,773	37.10. 9.		47				1,095	1.62	29
Naburn	3,414	116.14. 8.		29				2,636	1.30	22
Osgodby	1,736	45. 9. 9.		38				1,558	1.11	34
Riccall	2,278	84.13. 2.		27				2,667	.85	32
Skipwith	1,835	50. 1. 2.		37				2,644	.69	53
Stamford Bridge, West; and Scoreby	2,121	55. 8. 4.		38				1,945	1.09	35
Stillingfleet and Moreby	4,124	73.13. 2.		56				2,605	1.58	35

APPENDIX P.1 (continued) page 568

Wapentake Parish/Township	1815 property tax	Land tax gross quota	Land tax net quota	Gross ratio	Net ratio	Deductions Amount	Deductions Type	Acres	Property tax/ acre	Acres/ gross L.T. quota
Ouse and Derwent										
Thorganby and West Cottingwith	2,771	100. 7. 8.	99.14. 8	28	28	0.13. 0.	Excise	2,938	.94	29
Wheldrake and Langwith	4,957	140.12. 0.		35				5,310	.93	38
SUBTOTAL	62,889	1,575. 6. 4.	1,574.13. 4.	40	40	0.13. 0.	Excise	55,343	1.14	35
Beverley borough and liberties										
Beverley St Martin, Mary, and Nicholas	17,930	559. 7. 3.	529. 7. 3.	32	34	30. 0. 0.	Excise	2,412	7.43	4
Molescroft	3,529	76. 1. 0.		46				1,359	2.60	18
Storkhill and Sandholme	725	13. 5. 4.		55				322	2.25	24
Thearne	1,445	32.19. 4.		44				516	2.80	16
Tickton and Hull Bridge	(1,156)	NR		NR				(779)	1.48	NR
Weel	1,640	20. 4. 0.		81				1,139	1.44	56
Woodmansey and Beverley Parks	7,144	220. 0. 0.		32				2,963	2.41	13
SUBTOTAL	32,413	921.16.11.	891.16.11.	35	36	30. 0. 0.	Excise	8,711	3.72	9

RIDING TOTAL (excluding Hullshire)	928,434	18,822.18.10½.	18,714.16. 6½.	49	50	198.10. 8.	Excise	722,923	1.28	38
						63. 2. 0.	Customs			
						22. 0. 0.	Riding Officer			
						2.10. 0.	Salary			
						0.16. 0.	Stock			

Notes: NR = no record. Def. = defective.
Sources: PP 1818 (82.) XIX, 516-26 (1815 property tax); 6-inch Ordnance Survey maps (acres); land tax duplicates, Humberside County Record Office. See maps 10, 11, and 12.

APPENDIX P.2

Ratios of 1815 property tax valuation (schedule A) to land tax quota, property tax valuation per acre, and acres per land tax quota; all townships, West Riding

Wapentake Township	1815 property tax	Acres	Property tax: £/acre	Net land tax quota	Deductions from land tax quota Amount	Type	Net ratio: property tax/ land tax	Acres/£1 gross land tax
Agbrigg								
Ackton	1,199	968	1.24	52. 2. 3.			23.0	18
Almondbury	4,300	2,636	1.63	117.16. 6	£7. 0. 0	Excise	36.5	21
Altofts	2,539	1,838	1.38	78. 2. 6			32.5	24
Alverthorpe and Thornes	8,129	3,345	2.43	83. 6. 6			97.5	40
Ardsley, East	3,092	1,818	1.70	55. 2. 3			56.1	33
Ardsley, West	3,631	2,326	1.56	55.10. 3	£7. 0. 0.	Excise	65.4	37
Austonley	972	3,316	.29	24.16. 8			39.1	133
Batley	4,488	2,038	2.20	84.15.10			52.9	24
Bretton, West	2,188	2,098	1.04	41. 0.10			53.3	51
Carlton and Lofthouse	NR	1,984	NR	72. 8.11			NR	27
Cartworth	1,252	2,263	.55	36.18. 4			33.9	61
Crigglestone	4,888	3,129	1.56	151. 7. 1	£10. 0. 0.	Excise	32.3	19
Crofton	2,405	1,520	1.58	72.18. 5			33.0	21
Crosland, South; and Linthwaite	4,732	3,263	1.45	78. 2. 6			60.6	42
Cumberworth Half and Skelmanthorpe	2,190	1,185	1.85	26. 1. 0			84.1	45
Dalton	3,031	1,341	2.26	78. 2. 6			38.8	17
Dewsbury	9,580	1,468	6.52	125. 4.10	£7. 0. 0.	Excise	76.5	11
Emley	3,382	3,556	.95	82.18. 5			40.8	43
Farnley Tyas	2,171	1,784	1.22	45. 8.10			47.8	39
Flockton, Nether and Over	3,696	1,108	3.34	74.18. 0			49.3	15
Fulstone	1,689	2,261	.75	36.19. 3 1/2			45.7	61
Golcar	2,255	1,592	1.42	53. 4. 0	£7. 0. 0.	Excise	42.4	26
Hepworth	1,211	2,374	.51	36.18. 4			32.8	64
Holme	524	1,728	.30	18.12. 4			28.2	93

Honley	4,303	2,435	1.77	45. 0. 0	£7. 0. 0. Excise	95.6	47
Horbury	2,948	1,279	2.30	114. 3. 2		25.8	11
Huddersfield, Fartown, and Marsh	17,998	4,056	4.44	165.17. 4	£24. 0. 0. Excise	108.5	21
Kirkburton	2,003	1,286	1.56	51. 9. 0		38.9	25
Kirkheaton and Upper Whitley	def.	3,727	def.	72.18. 5	£7. 0. 0. Excise	def.	47
Lepton, Great and Little	4,803	1,862	2.58	72.18. 4		65.9	26
Lindley and Quarmby	3,819	1,494	2.56	40. 2. 8		95.1	37
Lockwood (North Crosland)	3,274	860	3.81	60. 4. 0		54.4	14
Longwood	2,143	1,334	1.61	32. 2. 8	£8. 0. 0. Excise	66.6	33
Marsden	2,400	8,646	.28	66.18. 6	£7. 0. 0. Excise	35.8	117
Meltham	1,603	4,692	.34	52. 2. 3		30.8	90
Methley	7,023	3,492	2.01	159.17. 6		43.9	22
Middleton	4,774	1,815	2.63	58. 3. 0		82.1	31
Mirfield	7,405	3,765	1.97	143. 4. 2		51.7	26
Morley	5,964	2,766	2.16	109. 7. 4		54.5	25
Normanton and Woodhouse	2,677	1,537	1.74	71.10. 8		37.4	21
Ossett	5,581	3,105	1.80	117.19. 4	£7. 0. 0. Excise	47.3	25
Oulton and Woodlesford	NR	1,360	NR	59. 2. 3	£7. 0. 0. Excise	NR	20
Quick and Saddleworth	21,306	18,796	1.13	134. 4.10		158.7	140
Rothwell, Rothwell Haigh, and Royds Green	3,037	3,300	.92	131. 7.10	£7. 0. 0. Excise	23.1	24
Sandal Magna	4,951	1,617	3.06	112. 0. 7		44.2	14
Scammonden and Deanhead	608	1,806	.34	40. 2. 8		15.1	45
Sharleston	2,007	1,199	1.67	52. 2. 3		38.5	23
Shelley	2,463	1,568	1.57	39. 4. 3	£7. 0. 0. Excise	62.8	34
Shepley	1,840	1,247	1.48	46.14. 2		39.4	27
Shitlington	5,176	3,410	1.52	107.19. 0		47.9	32
Slaithwaite and Lingards	2,880	3,170	.91	73. 3. 0		39.4	43

APPENDIX P.2 (continued) page 572

Wapentake Township	1815 property tax	Acres	Property tax: £/acre	Net land tax quota	Deductions from land tax quota Amount	Type	Net ratio: property tax/ land tax	Acres/£1 gross land tax
Agbrigg								
Snydale	1,563	1,059	1.48	52. 2. 3			30.0	20
Soothill, Nether and Upper	4,042	2,459	1.64	109. 7. 6			36.9	22
Stanley and Wrenthorpe	11,318	4,674	2.42	76. 6. 6	£7. 0. 0.	Excise	148.2	56
Thong, Nether	1,443	795	1.82	17. 6. 2 3/4			83.4	46
Thong, Upper	1,187	3,206	.37	18.12. 4			63.8	172
Thornhill	4,100	2,564	1.60	104. 3. 3			39.4	25
Thorpe on the Hill	546	548	1.00	20.12. 6			26.4	26
Thurstonland	2,579	2,106	1.22	52. 2. 3			49.5	40
Wakefield	72,123	758	95.15	263.12. 4 1/2	£56. 0. 0.	Excise	273.6	2
Walton	3,680	1,824	2.02	48.13. 4			75.6	37
Warmfield and Heath	3,230	1,580	2.04	73. 2. 6			44.2	22
Whitley, Lower	def.	1,038	def.	52. 2. 3			def.	20
Whitwood	1,814	1,082	1.68	55. 2. 3			32.9	20
Wooldale & Scholes	2,932	2,158	1.36	57.14. 3	£7. 0. 0.	Excise	50.8	33
TOTAL	307,087	154,305[a]	1.99					
TOTAL	307,087[b]			4,564. 3. 5 3/4[c]	£189. 0. 0.	Excise	67.3	
TOTAL		161,554[d]		4,823.15. 3 3/4				32

Notes: [a]Excludes acres when property tax value is def. (defective) or NR (no return).
[b]Excludes property tax value when land tax quota is NR.
[c]Excludes land tax quota when property tax value is def. or NR.
[d]Excludes acres when land tax quota is NR.

Wapentake Township	1815 property tax	Acres	Property tax: £/acre	Net land tax quota	Deductions from land tax quota Amount	Type	Net ratio: property tax/ land tax	Acres/£1 gross land tax
Barkston Ash								
Aberford with Lotherton	1,134	1,094	1.04	33.16. 7	£2. 2. 0	Excise	33.5	30
Barkston	1,226	1,164	1.05	25.17. 7			47.3	45
Barlow	2,807	2,371	1.18	77.19. 2			36.0	30
Birkin	2,528	2,160	1.17	105.19. 8			23.8	20
Bramham	2,817	4,170	.68	96.12.11			29.1	43
Brayton	2,040	1,945	1.05	40.14. 5 1/2	£8. 0. 0.	Excise	50.1	40
Brotherton	3,804	933	4.08	66. 6. 6			57.3	14
Burn	2,105	2,482	.85	53.13. 9			39.2	46
Burton Salmon	905	955	.95	31. 7. 4			28.9	30
Byram & Poole	1,008	823	1.22	29. 2. 6			34.6	28
Camblesforth	1,716	1,595	1.08	32. 1. 9			53.4	50
Carlton	5,268	4,217	1.25	154. 3. 0			34.2	27
Cawood	4,194	2,890	1.45	121.19.10	£8. 0. 0.	Excise	34.4	22
Clifford and Micklethwaite Grange	2,616	2,288	1.14	75. 6. 1			34.7	30
Drax	1,940	1,381	1.40	43. 9. 1 1/2			44.6	32
Drax, Long	1,648	1,696	.97	59.13.10 1/2			27.6	28
Fairburn	1,292	1,428	.90	40.13. 0			31.8	35
Fenton, Church	2,390	1,972	1.21	45. 9.10			52.5	43
Fenton, Little; and Biggin	1,727	1,504	1.15	40. 0. 6			43.1	38
Fryston, Monk	1,281	1,771	.72	55. 9. 7			23.1	32
Gateforth	1,440	2,062	.70	43. 7. 9			33.2	48
Grimston	1,457	892	1.63	36. 8. 5			40.0	24
Haddlesey, Chapel	1,245	1,162	1.07	38. 4. 6 1/2			32.5	30
Haddlesey, West	1,617	1,193	1.36	56. 8. 3			28.7	21
Hambleton	2,873	2,380	1.21	66. 3.10			43.4	36
Hillam	1,358	1,527	.89	42. 8.10			32.0	36
Hirst, Courtney	814	630	1.29	20. 5. 6			40.1	31
Hirst, Temple	704	758	.93	28. 3. 4			25.0	27
Huddleston and Lumby	817	1,423	.57	26. 6. 6			31.0	54

APPENDIX P.2 (continued) page 574

Wapentake Township	1815 property tax	Acres	Property tax: £/acre	Net land tax quota	Deductions from land tax quota Amount	Deductions from land tax quota Type	Net ratio: property tax/ land tax	Acres/£1 gross land tax
Barkston Ash								
Kirkby Wharfe and North Milford	1,516	1,230	1.23	50. 3. 4			30.2	24
Ledsham	2,005	1,968	1.02	47. 1. 2			42.6	42
Ledston	2,510	1,986	1.26	47. 4. 4			53.2	42
Micklefield	1,330	1,777	.75	15.16. 0			84.2	112
Milford, South	2,218	2,301	.96	45. 7. 0			48.9	51
Newland	2,419	2,296	1.05	59.15. 8			40.4	38
Newthorpe	347	746	.46	6.14. 0			51.8	111
Newton Kyme and Toulston	2,336	1,371	1.70	43.10. 0			53.7	32
Ryther, Lead, and Ossendyke	3,716	3,779	.98	155. 4. 6			23.9	24
Saxton and Scarthingwell	2,640	2,718	.97	65.18. 0			40.1	41
Selby	9,723	3,643	2.67	240.12. 2	£40. 0. 0.	Excise and Customs	40.4	13
Sherburn	5,546	4,858	1.14	95. 9. 7	£9.12. 0.	Excise	58.1	46
Stutton and Hazlewood	2,110	2,974	.71	72. 3. 4 3/4			29.2	41
Sutton	1,311	632	2.07	40. 0. 0			32.8	16
Tadcaster	5,569	2,172	2.56	50.11. 2	£20. 0. 0.	Excise	110.2	31
Thorpe Willoughby	963	463	2.08	17.10. 2			55.0	26
Towton	1,037	885	1.17	17.14. 9			58.4	50
Ulleskelf	1,819	1,323	1.37	46. 3. 7			39.4	29
Wistow	5,853	4,316	1.36	165.11. 7			35.3	26
TOTAL	111,739	92,304	1.21	2,870. 4. 4 3/4	£47.14. 0. £40. 0. 0.	Excise Excise and Customs	38.9	32

Wapentake Township	1815 property tax	Acres	Property tax: £/acre	Net land tax quota	Deductions from land tax quota Amount	 Type	Net ratio: property tax/ land tax	Acres/£1 gross land tax
Claro								
Aismunderby and Bondgate	2,916	1,701	1.71	43. 0. 8			67.7	40
Aldborough	3,365	2,240	1.50	117. 1. 7			28.7	19
Aldfield	1,251	1,270	.98	70.10. 9			17.7	18
Allerton Mauleverer, Flaxby, and Hopperton	9,931	2,999	3.31	62. 4. 0			159.7	48
Arkendale	2,358	1,603	1.47	86.16. 9			27.2	18
Askwith	1,846	3,392	.54	61. 7. 7			30.1	55
Azerley	3,696	4,018	.92	126. 0. 0			29.3	32
Beamsley	1,409	2,160	.65	37. 1. 8 3/4			38.0	58
Birstwith	1,656	1,801	.92	47. 0. 9			35.2	38
Bishopside, High and Low	4,160	6,004	.69	40.14. 0	£9.16. 0	Excise	102.2	119
Bishopton	1,161	386	3.01	33. 7. 8			34.8	12
Blubberhouses	303	3,736	.08	NR			NR	NR
Boroughbridge	894	94	9.51	46. 4. 0	£9.12. 0	Excise	19.4	2
Brearton	1,647	1,562	1.05	44. 5. 4			37.2	35
Burton Leonard	1,898	1,796	1.06	68. 9. 8			27.7	26
Castley	743	524	1.42	20. 0. 0			37.2	26
Cattal Magna	1,299	1,122	1.16	41.11. 0			31.3	27
Clareton	480	416	1.15	NR			NR	NR
Clifton & Norwood	1,956	3,627	.54	51.14. 4			37.8	70
Clint	2,112	1,945	1.08	68. 0. 0			31.0	29
Clotherholme	525	339	1.55	def.			def.	def.
Coneythorpe	889	392	2.27	NR			NR	NR
Copgrove	955	860	1.11	46. 2. 0			20.7	19
Cowthorpe	1,139	1,370	.83	88.14. 6			12.8	15
Dacre and Bewerley	11,520	11,153	1.03	147.12. 1			78.0	76
Deighton, Kirk	2,729	2,274	1.20	93.11. 0			29.2	24
Deighton, North	1,791	1,475	1.21	37.11. 9			47.6	39
Denton	2,261	3,240	.70	61. 7.10			36.8	53

Wapentake Township	1815 property tax	Acres	Property tax: £/acre	Net land tax quota	Deductions from land tax quota Amount	Type	Net ratio: property tax/ land tax	Acres/£1 gross land tax
Claro								
Dunkeswick	2,043	1,467	1.39	59.11. 0			34.3	25
Dunsforth, High	1,026	1,009	1.02	50. 9. 9			20.3	20
Dunsforth, Low	816	1,048	.78	def.			def.	def.
Eavestone	390	1,142	.34	NR			NR	NR
Farnham	1,360	1,044	1.30	74. 9. 2			18.3	14
Farnley	2,327	1,958	1.19	56.11. 8			41.1	34
Felliscliffe	1,783	2,628	.68	44. 0. 0			40.5	60
Ferrensby	663	425	1.56	NR			NR	NR
Fewston	1,558	2,186	.71	43.13. 8			35.6	50
Follifoot	1,973	1,860	1.06	49. 2. 4			40.2	38
Fountains Earth	2,025	6,744	.30	79.14. 8			25.4	84
Givendale	1,182	848	1.39	52.10. 0			22.5	16
Goldsborough	1,674	1,785	.94	45.17. 8			36.5	39
Grantley and Skelden	1,101	1,762	.62	27.14. 0			39.7	NR
Grewelthorpe	2,950	4,521	.65	94. 4. 8			31.3	48
Hammerton, Green	1,816	1,206	1.50	38.10. 4			47.2	31
Hammerton, Kirk	1,483	1,089	1.36	59. 9. 3			24.9	18
Hampsthwaite	1,133	1,135	1.00	47.16. 9			23.7	24
Harrogate, High; and Bilton	7,142	4,121	1.73	82. 0.10			87.0	50
Hartwith, Warsill, and Winsley	4,098	5,360[a]	.76	93.18. 4			43.6	57
Haverah Park	912	2,245	.41	17. 3. 0			53.2	131
Hazlewood and Storiths	424	3,487	.12	29.13. 0			14.3	118
Hewick, Copt and Bridge	1,961	1,572	1.25	28. 6. 4			69.3	56
Hunsingore	1,390	1,159	1.20	38. 4. 0			36.4	30
Ingerthorpe	1,045	512	2.04	20.12. 8			50.6	25
Kearby and Netherby	2,081	1,422	1.46	69. 1.10			30.1	20
Killinghall	3,262	3,515	.93	67. 0. 0			48.7	52

Kirby Hall	630	426	1.48	13.18. 8		45.2	30
Kirkby Malzeard	2,815	3,363	.84	94.15. 0	£5. 5. 0 Excise	29.7	34
Kirkby Overblow	1,834	2,358	.78	52. 7. 8		35.0	45
Knaresborough	11,194	3,012	3.72	155. 4. 6	£16. 0. 0 Excise	72.1	18
Laverton	1,855	6,697	.28	75. 6. 0		24.6	89
Leathley	2,472	1,565	1.58	64. 8. 0		38.4	24
Lindrick	NR	740	NR	NR		NR	NR
Lindley	1,547	1,789	.86	25. 4. 0		61.4	71
Linton	1,332	1,266	1.05	45.12. 0		29.2	28
Markington and Wallerthwaite	3,492	3,179	1.10	74. 0. 0		47.2	43
Marton and Grafton	2,776	2,165	1.28	57.17.11		47.9	37
Menwith and Darley	1,776	2,858	.62	58.10. 0		30.4	49
Middleton and Stockhill	2,522	2,658	.95	134.14. 4		18.7	20
Minskip	2,227	1,414	1.57	64.12. 4		34.5	22
Monkton, Bishop	3,550	2,186	1.62	38. 4. 0		92.9	57
Monkton, Nun	2,580	1,775	1.45	67. 9. 8		38.2	26
Nesfield and Langbar	1,356	1,924	.70	52. 1. 1		26.0	37
Newall and Clifton	1,965	1,531	1.28	53.14. 1		36.6	28
Newby and Mulwith	851	796	1.07	24. 0. 0		35.4	33
Nidd	1,705	1,203	1.42	41. 0. 8		41.5	29
Nunwick and Howgrave	1,134	938	1.21	16. 0. 0		70.9	59
Ouseburn, Great	2,130	1,568	1.36	52.10. 6	£8. 0. 0 Excise	40.5	26
Ouseburn, Little	1,338	706	1.90	27.15. 0		48.2	25
Pannal and Swindon	5,525	4,898	1.13	131. 0. 0		42.2	37
Plumpton	2,333	2,134	1.09	87. 0. 8		26.8	24
Ribston, Great; and Walshford	1,994	1,933	1.03	55. 0.11		36.2	35
Ribston, Little	823	856	.96	31.15. 0		25.9	27
Rigton	3,343	3,111	1.07	59.12. 0		56.1	52
Ripley	1,905	1,641	1.16	45.17. 8	£8.19. 8 Excise	41.5	30
Ripon	11,430	1,561	7.32	68. 7.11 1/2	£45.10. 6 1/2 Excise	167.1	14
Roecliffe	1,661	1,861	.89	113.13. 1		14.6	16
Sawley	1,759	3,284	.54	40. 0. 2		44.0	82
Scotton	1,096	1,127	.97	56. 3. 8		19.5	20
Scriven and Tentergate	3,930	1,829	2.15	82. 1. 6		47.9	22
Sharow	1,620	722	2.24	24. 1. 8		67.2	30

APPENDIX P.2 (continued) page 578

Wapentake Township	1815 property tax	Acres	Property tax: £/acre	Net land tax quota	Deductions from land tax quota Amount	Type	Net ratio: property tax/ land tax	Acres/£1 gross land tax
Claro								
Sicklinghall	1,822	1,494	1.22	89.19. 8			20.2	17
Skelton	1,508	926	1.63	22. 3. 0			68.1	42
Spofforth and Stockeld	3,792	5,465	.69	133. 7. 8			28.4	41
Stainburn	2,026	3,157	.64	64.14. 0			31.3	49
Stainley, North; and Sleningford	4,146	4,244	.98	68. 6. 71/4			60.6	62
Stainley, South; and Cayton	2,316	2,131	1.09	75.15. 4			30.6	28
Staveley	1,929	1,425	1.35	50. 6. 0			38.3	28
Stonebeck, Down	3,177	12,516	.25	81. 3. 4			39.1	154
Stonebeck, Upper	2,137	12,195	.18	80. 6. 0			26.6	152
Studley Roger	1,104	986	1.12	35. 6. 9			31.2	28
Studley Royal	NR	696	NR	NR			NR	NR
Sutton Grange	790	1,022	.77	def.			def.	def.
Thornthwaite and Padside	1,007	3,480	.29	NR			NR	NR
Thornton, Bishop	2,986	3,135	.95	41.14. 0			71.6	75
Thornville	395	266	1.48	17. 6. 8			22.8	15
Thorpe Underwood	2,133	2,463	.87	NR			NR	NR
Thruscross	1,984	6,529	.30	58.10. 0			33.9	112
Timble, Great	768	1,566	.49	38. 2. 8			20.1	41
Timble, Little	424	504	.84	11. 2. 6			38.0	45
Walkingham and Occaney	331	427	.78	NR			NR	NR
Weeton	1,680	1,376	1.22	66. 0. 8			25.4	21
Weston	1,153	1,510	.76	44. 6. 0			26.0	34
Westwick	500	422	1.18	13. 9. 2			37.2	31
Wetherby	3,727	1,601	2.33	108. 6. 0	£8. 0. 0	Excise	34.4	14
Whitcliffe and Littlethorpe	1,904	1,262	1.51	26.16. 8			70.9	47

Whixley	3,358	2,374	1.41	117.17. 4		28.5	20
Widdington	924	701	1.32	29. 2. 0		31.8	24
Winksley	741	729	1.02	17. 7. 4		42.7	42
TOTAL	255,770	264,989[b]	.96				
TOTAL	247,443[c]			6,185.12.11 3/4	£103. 3. 2 1/2 Excise	40.0	
TOTAL		249,403[d]		6,185.12.11 3/4			40

Notes: [a]Warsill, a separate township, is reported as included in Hartwith for the property tax. Warsill is not mentioned in the Hartwith land tax duplicates, nor is it returned separately. The property tax return may be in error. The 1,029 acres of Warsill are thus not included in the acres assigned here to Hartwith.
[b]Excludes acres when property tax value is NR (no return).
[c]Excludes property tax value when land tax quota is def. (defective) or NR.
[d]Excludes acres when land tax quota is def. or NR.

Ewcross

Austwick	4,567	7,450	.61	66. 1. 0		69.1	113
Bentham	7,286	7,718	.94	93.15.10		77.7	82
Burton in Lonsdale	3,154	1,555	2.03	30.13. 4		102.9	51
Clapham and Newby	6,286	12,080	.52	92. 4. 8		68.1	131
Dent	7,610	20,890	.36	177.17.10	£2.14. 0 Excise	42.8	116
Garsdale	2,827	12,172	.23	45. 2.11 1/2		62.6	270
Horton in Ribblesdale	6,745	17,258	.39	92. 8. 0		73.0	187
Ingleton	9,289	17,508	.53	87.10. 4	£2.11. 0 Excise	106.2	194
Lawkland	4,303	4,949	.87	49.11. 0		86.8	100
Sedbergh	12,967	19,603	.66	174.10. 4	£3.12. 0 Excise	74.3	110
Thornton in Lonsdale	3,571	7,484	.48	49. 6. 8		72.4	152
TOTAL	68,605	128,667	.53	959. 1.11 1/2	£8.17. 0 Excise	71.5	134

APPENDIX P.2 (continued) page 580

Wapentake Township	1815 property tax	Acres	Property tax: £/acre	Net land tax quota	Deductions from land tax quota Amount	Type	Net ratio: property tax/ land tax	Acres/£1 gross land tax
Morley								
Allerton	2,707	1,849	1.46	37.13. 2			71.9	26
Armley	2,982	961	3.10	NR			NR	NR
Barkisland	2,819	2,420	1.16	89.14. 2			31.4	27
Beeston	6,046	1,568	3.86	NR			NR	NR
Bierley, North	6,428	3,342	1.92	NR			NR	NR
Bolton	1,344	712	1.89	37. 4.11			36.1	19
Bowling	9,548	1,562	6.11	53.12. 3			178.1	29
Bradford	76,773	1,595	48.13	199. 6. 31/4			385.2	8
Bramley	7,096	2,505	2.83	NR			NR	NR
Calverley and Farsley	5,997	3,180	1.88	87.17. 5			68.2	36
Churwell	1,378	488	2.82	25.18. 9			53.1	19
Clayton	2,985	1,744	1.71	def.			def.	def.
Cleckheaton	3,455	1,755	1.97	59. 0. 0			58.6	30
Drighlington	3,525	1,136	3.10	48. 4. 2	£5. 0. 0	Excise	73.1	21
Eccleshill	3,115	1,220	2.55	49.14. 5			62.7	24
Elland and Greetland	7,461	3,448	2.16	141.11. 0	£5. 0. 0	Excise	52.7	24
Erringden	2,532	3,012	.84	52.13. 8			48.0	57
Farnley	3,657	2,084	1.75	NR			NR	NR
Fixby	1,834	934	1.96	22.15. 5			80.6	41
Gildersome	3,147	993	3.17	50.16. 1			61.9	20
Gomersal, Great and Little	8,766	3,254	2.69	122.19. 6			71.3	26
Halifax	38,337	998	38.41	311.16. 1			123.0	3
Hartshead and Clifton	3,987	3,070	1.30	85.11. 9			46.6	36
Haworth	6,616	8,114	.82	108. 9. 9			61.0	75
Heaton	2,487	1,323	1.88	46. 6. 8			53.6	28
Heckmondwike	3,268	697	4.69	51.18. 9			62.9	13
Heptonstall	4,439	5,394	.82	93.12. 4	£5. 0. 0	Excise	47.4	55
Hipperholme and Brighouse	7,482	2,598	2.88	124.10. 6			60.1	21

Holbeck	7,829	612	12.79	NR		NR	NR
Horton	8,348	2,033	4.11	100.10. 5		83.1	20
Hunslet	8,507	1,152	7.38	NR		NR	NR
Hunsworth	1,634	1,380	1.18	36.10. 8		44.7	38
Idle	8,006	2,462	3.25	86. 8. 0	£5. 0. 0 Salary	92.7	27
Langfield	2,361	2,784	.85	51.19. 5		45.4	54
Liversedge	7,841	2,130	3.68	105.13. 8		74.2	20
Manningham	3,942	1,318	2.99	74. 0. 3		53.3	18
Midgley	2,287	2,628	.87	73.18.10		30.9	36
Norland	2,883	1,273	2.26	62.19.10		45.8	20
Ovenden	7,674	5,350	1.43	193.15. 3		39.6	28
Owram, North	9,427	3,520	2.68	300. 4. 3		31.4	12
Owram, South	8,853	2,546	3.48	184. 3. 5		48.1	14
Pudsey	6,210	2,546	2.44	99.15. 2	£4. 0. 0 Salary	62.2	24
Rastrick	4,151	1,371	3.03	47. 3. 6		87.9	29
Rishworth	2,058	6,548	.31	64.18. 0		31.7	101
Shelf	2,654	1,302	2.04	49. 7. 8		53.7	26
Shipley	3,527	1,406	2.51	58. 0.10		60.8	24
Skircoat	5,661	1,330	4.26	106. 2.10		53.3	12
Sowerby	6,763	6,894	.98	241.10.10		28.0	28
Soyland	4,757	4,270	1.11	120.15. 5		39.4	35
Stainland	3,155	2,335	1.35	88. 1. 1		35.8	26
Stansfield	7,639	6,330	1.21	103.19. 0		73.5	61
Thornton	5,950	4,785	1.24	65.14. 5		90.6	73
Tong	3,836	2,657	1.44	76. 9. 0		50.2	35
Wadsworth	4,425	11,224	.39	119. 5.11		37.1	94
Warley	622	4,025	.15	174. 2. 4½	£7. 4. 9½ Excise	3.6	23
Wike	1,675	967	1.73	def.		def.	def.
Wilsden	2,927	2,638	1.11	32.14. 4		89.5	81
Wortley, Lower and Upper	3,784	1,054	3.59	NR		NR	NR
TOTAL	379,597	152,826	2.48				
TOTAL	328,608[a]			4,652. 5. 8½	£22. 4. 9½ Excise £9. 0. 0 Salary	70.6	
TOTAL		136,837[b]		4,652. 5. 8½			29

Notes: [a]Excludes property tax value when land tax quota is def. (defective) or NR (no return).
[b]Excludes acres when land tax quota is def. or NR.

APPENDIX P.2 (continued) page 582

Wapentake Township	1815 property tax	Acres	Property tax: £/acre	Net land tax quota	Deductions from land tax quota Amount	Type	Net ratio: property tax/ land tax	Acres/£1 gross land tax
Osgoldcross								
Ackworth	6,686	2,642	2.53	106. 4. 0	£5. 0. 0	Excise	63.0	24
Adlingfleet	1,773	1,848	.96	55.18. 0			31.7	33
Airmyn	4,742	3,707	1.28	91.12. 2			51.8	40
Badsworth	2,616	1,546	1.69	43. 5.11	£6. 0. 0	Excise	60.4	31
Balne	2,638	2,866	.92	70. 2. 8			37.6	41
Beaghall	3,775	1,877	2.01	68. 7. 9			55.2	27
Bramwith, Kirk	1,738	1,334	1.30	55. 0. 0			31.6	24
Burghwallis	2,490	1,920	1.30	46. 0. 0			54.1	42
Campsall	2,120	1,776	1.19	38.10. 0			55.1	46
Carleton	1,133	588	1.93	24. 0. 0			47.2	24
Castleford	1,457	564	2.58	48. 1. 0	£6. 0. 0	Excise	30.3	10
Cowick	3,431	def.	def.	87.10. 31/2			39.2	def.
Cridling Stubbs	1,013	1,355	.75	24. 2. 31/2			42.3	56
Darrington	2,436	3,110	.78	41. 0. 0			59.4	76
Egbrough	1,625	2,010	.81	37. 5. 9			43.6	54
Elmsall, North	2,530	2,118	1.19	44. 0. 0			57.5	48
Elmsall, South	1,463	1,424	1.03	54. 0. 0			27.1	26
Featherstone	1,789	1,380	1.30	49. 0. 0			36.5	28
Fenwick	2,781	2,371	1.17	60. 0. 0			46.4	40
Fockerby	853	910	.94	22. 4. 2			38.4	41
Fryston, Ferry	3,952	3,186	1.24	106.11. 3			37.1	30
Goole	4,280	4,838	.88	93.12. 9			45.7	52
Gowdall	1,276	1,210	1.05	35. 9. 2			36.0	34
Haldenby and Eastoft	3,360	2,858	1.18	39.17. 7			84.2	72
Hardwick, East	810	528	1.53	29. 0. 0			27.9	18
Heck, Great	1,520	1,676	.91	31.14. 4			47.9	53
Hensall	966	1,177	.82	25.18. 7			37.2	45
Hessle	958	645	1.48	27.16. 0			34.5	23
Hook	1,857	2,001	.93	57. 5. 0			32.4	35
Houghton, Glass	1,394	1,079	1.29	55. 0. 0			25.3	20
Kellington	1,928	1,761	1.09	35. 7.11			54.5	50
Kirkby, South	3,385	2,360	1.43	75. 0. 0			45.1	31

Knottingley	5,760	1,180	4.88	79. 0. 0	£5. 0. 0 Excise	72.9	14
Moss	2,569	2,414	1.06	60. 0. 0		42.8	40
Norton	2,150	2,320	.93	33. 0. 0	£5. 0. 0 Excise	65.2	61
Ousefleet	2,025	2,885	.70	92.15. 3		21.8	31
Owston	1,725	1,815	.95	55. 0. 0		31.4	33
Pollington	1,719	1,920	.90	def.		def.	def.
Pontefract and Monk Hill	9,452	2,712	3.48	NR		NR	NR
Pontefract Park	1,975	1,394	1.42	NR		NR	NR
Purston Jaglin, Hill Top, West Hardwick, Huntwick, Foulby, Nostell, and Wragby	4,700	2,892	1.62	107. 0. 0		43.9	27
Rawcliffe	3,258	4,668	.70	78. 6. 6	£8. 0. 0 Customs £8. 0. 0 Excise	41.6	49
Reedness	3,884	3,082	1.26	84.11. 7		45.9	36
Skelbrooke	961	1,147	.84	25.16. 8		37.2	44
Skellow	1,143	932	1.23	42. 0. 0		27.2	22
Smeaton, Kirk; and Wentbridge	1,721	1,700	1.01	28. 0. 0		61.5	61
Smeaton, Little	1,092	1,238	.88	25.12. 9		42.6	48
Snaith	3,159	def.	def.	62.19. 4	£8. 0. 0 Excise	50.2	def.
Stapleton	697	1,633	.43	13.16. 2		50.5	118
Sutton and Askern	1,006	1,612	.62	32. 0. 0		31.4	50
Swinefleet	2,569	2,470	1.04	75. 7.10		34.1	33
Tanshelf	1,400	297	4.71	14.10. 0	£12. 0. 0 Excise	96.6	11
Thorpe Audlin	1,798	1,311	1.37	42. 4. 0		42.6	31
Upton	1,322	1,114	1.19	37. 8. 0		35.3	30
Walden Stubbs	1,338	1,272	1.05	36. 9. 6		36.6	35
Whitgift	1,683	1,502	1.12	59. 1. 4		28.5	25
Whitley	1,116	1,842	.60	24.11.10		45.4	75
Womersley	2,927	3,990	.73	64.19. 0		45.1	61
TOTAL	131,334[a]	108,007	1.22				
TOTAL	124,778[b]			2,853. 6. 4	£55. 0. 0 Excise £8. 0. 0 Customs	43.7	
TOTAL		101,981[c]		2,702.16. 8 1/2[d]			37

Notes: [a]Excludes property tax value when acres is def. (defective).
[b]Excludes property tax value when land tax quota is def. or NR (no return).
[c]Excludes acres when land tax quota is def. or NR. [d]Excludes land tax quota when acres is def.

Wapentake Township	1815 property tax	Acres	Property tax: £/acre	Net land tax quota	Deductions from land tax quota Amount	Type	Net ratio: property tax/ land tax	Acres/£1 gross land tax
Skyrack								
Aberford	1,516	1,580	.96	33. 0. 0			45.9	48
Addle and Eccup	3,936	4,890	.80	60. 0. 0			65.6	82
Allerton Bywater	1,779	945	1.88	25. 4. 41/4			70.6	38
Allerton, Chapel	6,107	2,811	2.17	NR			NR	NR
Alwoodley	575	1,510	.38	22. 8. 0			25.7	67
Arthington	3,434	2,266	1.52	58. 8. 0			58.8	39
Austhorpe	1,031	858	1.20	32.15. 0			31.5	26
Baildon	4,724	2,605	1.81	59. 4. 0			79.8	44
Bardsey and Rigton	1,423	2,748	.52	71. 1. 0			20.0	39
Barwick in Elmet, Barnbow, Kiddal, Morwick, Potterton, and Scholes	6,898	6,966	.99	164.16. 9			41.8	42
Bingley	12,596	10,336	1.22	146.17. 0	£3.14. 0	Excise	85.8	69
Bramhope	2,202	1,398	1.58	28. 0. 0			78.6	50
Burley	2,569	3,133	.82	52. 0. 0			49.4	60
Carlton	785	1,288	.61	16.13. 0			47.1	77
Collingham	1,373	2,595	.53	48. 8. 2			28.4	54
Garforth	2,695	1,516	1.78	32.17. 0			82.0	46
Guiseley	2,356	1,554	1.52	47.12. 0	£6. 6. 0	Excise	49.5	29
Harewood	3,837	3,654	1.05	109.17. 0	£8. 0. 0	Excise	34.9	31
Hawksworth and Esholt	3,588	3,154	1.14	77.16. 4			46.1	40
Headingley	10,687	3,183	3.36	NR			NR	NR
Horsforth	5,790	2,801	2.07	75. 5. 6			76.9	37
Ilkley	1,901	3,822	.50	61. 4. 0			31.1	62
Keswick, East	1,584	1,288	1.23	50. 6. 0			31.5	26
Kippax	3,534	1,632	2.16	38. 7. 6	£6. 0. 0	Excise	92.0	37
Leeds (all divisions)	103,435	2,736	37.80	NR			NR	NR
Menston	1,075	1,126	.95	33. 8. 0			32.2	34

Morton, East and West	3,831	3,772	1.02	81.10. 0			47.0	46
Otley	4,805	2,370	2.03	72.16.11	£12. 0. 0	Excise	66.0	28
Parlington	4,382	1,770	2.48	43.17. 0			99.9	40
Pool	1,329	951	1.40	19. 0. 0	£6. 0. 0	Excise	69.9	38
Potter Newton	6,097	1,710	3.56	NR			NR	NR
Rawdon	3,746	1,559	2.40	46.12. 0			80.4	33
Roundhay	2,760	1,482	1.86	61.12. 0			44.8	24
Scarcroft	736	1,073	.68	17. 2. 0			43.0	63
Seacroft	3,924	1,834	2.14	56. 3. 0	£8. 0. 0	Excise	69.9	28
Shadwell	1,392	1,499	.93	40.15. 0			34.2	37
Sturton Grange	558	877	.64	NR			NR	NR
Swillington and Great and Little Preston	5,874	3,664	1.60	72.17. 0			80.6	50
Temple Newsam	5,229	4,086	1.28	103. 7. 8			50.6	40
Thorner	2,591	2,316	1.12	40.17. 4			63.4	57
Thorpe Stapleton	500	294	1.70	NR			NR	NR
Weardley	1,001	874	1.14	26. 0. 0			38.5	34
Wigton	1,114	1,294	.86	29. 8. 0			37.9	44
Wike	1,016	879	1.16	17. 4. 0			59.1	51
Wothersome	206	653	.32	NR			NR	NR
Yeadon	3,776	1,723	2.19	42. 4. 0			89.5	41
TOTAL	246,297	107,075	2.30					
TOTAL	118,707[a]			2,116.14. 6 1/4	£50. 0. 0	Excise	56.1	
TOTAL		94,811[b]		2,116.14. 6 1/4				45

Notes: [a]Excludes property tax value when land tax quota is NR (no return).
[b]Excludes acres when land tax quota is NR.

APPENDIX P.2 (continued) page 586

Wapentake Township	1815 property tax	Acres	Property tax: £/acre	Net land tax quota	Deductions from land tax quota Amount	Type	Net ratio: property tax/ land tax	Acres/£1 gross land tax
Staincliffe								
Addingham	4,708	3,198	1.47	59.12. 8	£5. 6. 8	Excise	78.9	49
Airton	2,056	2,558	.80	27.19. 2			73.6	92
Appletreewick	1,932	7,689	.25	33. 8. 1			57.8	230
Arncliffe	1,541	3,189	.48	24.13. 6			62.4	129
Barden	863	7,338	.12	22.18. 3			37.7	320
Barnoldswick, Brogden, Coates, and Salterforth	7,308	6,306	1.16	81. 5. 6			89.9	78
Bashall Eaves	3,777	3,806	.99	39. 9. 9			95.6	96
Bolton Abbey	1,165	2,071	.56	NR			NR	NR
Bolton by Bowland	6,249	5,941	1.05	59.18. 2	£2. 0. 0	Excise	104.3	96
Bowland Forest, High and Low	6,590	23,464	.28	70. 4. 6			93.8	334
Bracewell	1,941	2,025	.96	26.10.10			73.1	76
Bradford, West	1,964	1,955	1.00	29.16. 1			65.9	66
Bradley, Lower and Upper	2,004	1,951	1.03	48. 9. 0			41.4	40
Broughton and Elslack	4,934	4,148	1.19	95.12. 8			51.6	43
Buckden	4,031	15,981	.25	62. 5. 4			64.8	257
Burnsall and Thorpe sub Montem	1,873	2,962	.63	26.19. 2 3/4			69.5	110
Calton	1,166	1,449	.80	11.12. 2			100.5	125
Carleton	5,591	5,258	1.06	86.12. 2			64.6	61
Coniston, Cold	1,832	1,337	1.37	22.13.11			80.7	59
Conistone and Kilnsey	2,824	8,646	.33	41. 1.10			68.7	210
Cowling	4,196	4,716	.89	49.19. 9			83.9	94
Cracoe	1,393	2,134	.65	23. 4. 4			60.0	92
Draughton	2,482	2,500	.99	46. 8.10			53.5	54
Easington	4,514	9,199	.49	64.16. 6			69.6	142
Embsay and Eastby	3,759	4,460	.84	42. 2. 5			89.3	106

Eshton	1,372	1,111	1.23	22.11. 3 1/4		60.8	49
Farnhill and Cononley	3,050	2,000	1.52	38.11. 3	£6. 0. 0 Excise	79.1	45
Flasby and Winterburn	3,090	4,340	.71	67.11.11		45.7	64
Gargrave	4,996	2,540	1.97	69.12. 9	£6.19. 2 Excise	71.7	33
Giggleswick	5,592	4,338	1.29	84. 5. 6		66.3	51
Gisburn	4,260	1,997	2.13	37.14. 8	£3. 4. 0 Excise	112.8	53
Gisburn Forest	2,257	4,859	.46	24.16.10		90.8	196
Glusburn	1,985	1,525	1.30	38.19. 7		50.9	39
Grassington	3,714	5,801	.64	38.12. 5	£5. 0. 0 Excise	96.2	136
Grindleton	4,906	3,776	1.30	47. 2.10		104.0	80
Halton, East; and Bolton Bridge	1,289	1,076	1.20	58.15. 8		21.9	18
Halton Gill	2,545	7,860	.32	NR		NR	NR
Halton, West	2,075	2,289	.91	25. 2.10 3/4		82.5	91
Hanlith	693	965	.72	12. 3. 6		56.8	79
Hartlington	917	1,352	.68	22.15. 7		40.2	59
Hawkswick	1,229	3,028	.40	21.12. 2		56.9	140
Hebden	1,446	3,583	.40	25.14. 7		56.2	139
Hellifield	2,987	3,401	.88	28.10.10		104.6	119
Hetton and Bordley	2,248	4,636	.48	46.18. 5		47.9	99
Horton	2,631	2,019	1.30	39. 4. 3		67.1	52
Keighley	15,838	10,132	1.56	134. 6. 3	£2. 8. 0 Excise	117.9	74
Kettlewell and Starbotton	3,552	8,412	.42	51.14. 7		68.6	162
Kildwick	1,117	871	1.28	26.13. 4		41.9	33
Kirkby Malhamdale	919	1,145	.80	12.14.10		72.1	90
Langcliffe	2,467	2,552	.97	34. 9. 6		71.5	74
Linton	1,207	1,204	1.00	21. 8. 9		56.3	56
Litton	1,422	3,924	.36	61. 1.10		23.3	64
Malham, East and West	3,022	4,282	.70	43. 4. 9		69.9	99
Malham Moor	3,253	10,978	.30	43. 4. 9		75.2	254
Marton, East and West	4,110	2,805	1.46	109. 2. 9		37.6	26
Middop	1,078	1,161	.93	18.16.10		57.2	62
Mitton	2,602	1,720	1.51	39. 9. 9		65.9	44
Nappa	748	578	1.29	9.12.10		77.5	60
Newsholme	1,218	751	1.62	19. 2. 1		63.8	39
Newton	4,597	5,869	.78	63.12. 2		72.3	92
Newton, Bank	3,306	2,339	1.41	78.16. 1 1/4		42.0	30
Otterburn	862	1,126	.76	18. 7.10		46.8	61

APPENDIX P.2 (continued) page 588

Wapentake Township	1815 property tax	Acres	Property tax: £/acre	Net land tax quota	Deductions from land tax quota Amount	Type	Net ratio: property tax/ land tax	Acres/£1 gross land tax
Staincliffe								
Paythorne	1,686	2,634	.64	35.11. 6			47.4	74
Preston, Long	4,810	3,578	1.34	45.18. 2			104.8	78
Rathmell	2,576	3,424	.75	44.16. 6			57.4	76
Rilston	1,859	3,196	.58	32. 8. 9			57.3	98
Rimington	2,861	3,080	.93	48. 3. 4			59.4	64
Sawley and Tosside	3,327	4,328	.77	28. 2. 2			118.4	154
Scosthorp	794	1,274	.62	17. 9.10			45.4	73
Settle	6,683	4,490	1.49	83.13. 3	£4. 4. 7	Excise	79.9	51
Silsden	5,203	7,060	.74	69.14. 0			74.6	101
Skipton	15,997	4,245	3.77	126. 8. 1	£20. 0. 0	Excise	126.6	29
Slaidburn	3,997	5,182	.77	62. 9.10			64.0	83
Stainforth, Great and Little	3,787	4,558	.83	67. 7. 6			56.2	68
Steeton and Eastburn	3,017	2,065	1.46	48. 5. 0			62.5	43
Stirton and Thorlby	3,427	3,098	1.11	34. 7. 6			99.6	90
Sutton	2,610	2,348	1.11	42.16. 4			61.0	55
Swinden	1,502	1,050	1.43	20.17. 6			71.9	50
Thornton in Craven	6,167	5,434	1.13	86.10. 2			71.3	63
Threshfield	1,375	2,646	.52	24.16. 1			55.4	107
Waddington	2,423	2,073	1.17	29.16. 1			81.3	70
Wigglesworth	2,659	4,288	.62	55.11. 6			47.8	77
TOTAL	262,053	326,677	.80					
TOTAL	258,343[a]			3,639.13. 7	£55. 2. 5	Excise	71.0	
TOTAL		316,746[b]		3,639.13. 7				86

Notes: [a]Excludes property tax value when land tax quota is NR (no return).
[b]Excludes acres when land tax quota is NR.

Wapentake Township	1815 property tax	Acres	Property tax: £/acre	Net land tax quota	Deductions from land tax quota Amount	Type	Net ratio: property tax/ land tax	Acres/£1 gross land tax
Staincross								
Ardsley	2,556	1,259	2.03	42.17. 4			59.6	29
Barnsley	15,029	2,386	6.30	70.14. 8	£30. 0. 0	Excise	212.4	24
Barugh	2,584	1,437	1.80	42. 7. 4	£8. 0. 0	Excise	61.0	28
Bretton, Monk	3,576	2,220	1.61	63.14. 0			56.1	35
Brierley	3,614	2,590	1.40	73.10. 1 1/2			49.2	35
Carlton	2,509	1,978	1.27	55. 0. 8			45.6	36
Cawthorne	2,556	3,708	.69	100.14. 8			25.4	37
Chevet	1,505	839	1.79	16.15. 9			89.6	50
Clayton, West	1,972	1,140	1.73	50. 7. 4			39.2	23
Cudworth, Over	3,046	1,744	1.75	75.10.11 1/2			40.3	23
Cumberworth, High	2,468	1,392	1.77	33.11. 7			73.4	41
Darton	2,638	1,378	1.91	44. 1. 4	£6. 6. 0	Excise	59.9	27
Denby	3,465	2,884	1.20	50. 7. 4			68.8	57
Dodworth	2,568	1,916	1.34	54.16. 3			46.9	35
Gunthwaite	887	952	.93	20.19. 9			42.2	45
Havercroft	850	1,364	.62	25. 7.11			33.5	54
Hemsworth	5,684	4,161	1.37	86.13. 3			65.6	48
Hiendley, South	1,513	1,292	1.17	29. 9.10			51.3	44
Hoyland, High	911	852	1.07	27.15. 5			32.8	31
Hoyland Swaine	1,936	2,024	.96	50. 7. 4			38.4	40
Hunshelf	2,063	2,464	.84	50. 7. 4			41.0	49
Ingbirchworth	1,051	1,104	.95	20.19. 9			50.0	52
Kexbrough	2,553	1,544	1.65	50. 7. 4			50.7	31
Langsett	1,393	4,916	.28	50. 7. 4			27.7	98
Notton	3,648	2,602	1.40	54.16. 3			66.6	47
Oxspring	1,061	1,203	.88	20.19. 9			50.5	57
Penistone	1,509	1,133	1.33	37.14. 0	£6. 0. 0	Excise	40.0	26
Royston	2,006	1,022	1.96	37. 4. 0	£6. 0. 0	Excise	53.9	24
Ryhill	1,638	592	2.77	33.11. 6 1/2			48.8	18
Shafton	926	823	1.12	23.13. 8			39.1	35
Silkstone	2,472	1,497	1.65	57. 0. 8			43.3	26
Stainborough	2,704	1,718	1.57	48.12. 9			55.6	35

APPENDIX P.2 (continued) page 590

Wapentake Township	1815 property tax	Acres	Property tax: £/acre	Net land tax quota	Deductions from land tax quota Amount	Type	Net ratio: property tax/ land tax	Acres/£1 gross land tax
Staincross								
Tankersley	4,610	2,463	1.87	50. 7. 4			91.6	49
Thurgoland	2,398	2,220	1.08	75.11. 3			31.7	29
Thurlstone	3,625	8,118	.45	100.14. 8			36.0	80
Wintersett	1,252	1,065	1.18	33.11. 6½			37.3	32
Woolley	3,701	2,587	1.43	50. 7. 4			73.5	51
Worsborough	6,493	3,778	1.72	100.16. 6			64.4	37
Wortley	4,188	5,616	.74	69.11. 3	£6. 0. 0	Excise	60.2	74
TOTAL	111,158	83,981	1.32	1,981.17. 1	£62. 6. 0	Excise	56.1	41
Strafforth and Tickhill								
Adwick le Street	3,119	1,637	1.90	55. 8. 0			56.3	30
Adwick upon Dearne	1,375	1,142	1.20	52.16. 0			26.0	22
Aldwark and Wheatcroft	NR	298	NR	25. 0. 0			NR	12
Anston, North and South	2,961	3,709	.80	75. 6. 0			39.3	49
Arksey and Bentley	10,067	5,133	1.96	224.10. 4			44.8	23
Armthorpe	2,732	2,924	.93	37. 2. 0			73.6	79
Aston and Aughton	4,012	3,006	1.33	68. 0. 0			59.0	44
Attercliffe and Darnall	5,244	1,297	4.04	88.16. 0	£8. 0. 0	Excise	59.0	13
Auckley and Blaxton	1,781	3,937	.45	NR			NR	NR
Austerfield	2,419	2,780	.87	24.12. 0			98.3	113
Balby and Hexthorpe	3,606	1,613	2.24	NR			NR	NR
Barmbrough	2,423	1,959	1.24	76. 6. 0			31.8	26
Barnby upon Don	3,869	2,306	1.68	85. 1. 4			45.5	27
Bawtry	1,857	259	7.17	58.12. 2	£20. 0. 0	Excise	31.7	3
Bilham	1,026	536	1.91	13.14. 0			74.9	39

Billingley	1,289	862	1.50	37. 8. 0			34.5	23
Bolton upon Dearne	3,427	2,323	1.48	98. 0. 0	£8. 0. 0	Excise	35.0	22
Bradfield, Waldershelf, and Westnall	15,710	38,424	.41	460. 8. 0	£8. 0. 0	Excise	34.1	82
Braithwell	2,432	1,948	1.25	46.16. 0			52.0	42
Bramley	1,629	1,014	1.61	35.12. 8			45.7	28
Brampton Bierlow	1,559	3,224	.48	76.18. 0			20.3	42
Brampton en le Morthen	1,192	1,122	1.06	24. 4. 0			49.2	46
Brampton Ulley	954	934	1.02	24. 4. 0			39.4	38
Brightside Bierlow	16,229	2,820	5.75	112.16. 0			143.9	25
Brinsworth	3,077	1,391	2.21	52.10. 0			58.6	26
Brodsworth, Pickburn, and Scansby	1,784	3,120	.57	46.16. 0			38.1	67
Cadeby	1,434	1,234	1.16	31. 4. 0			46.0	40
Cantley	6,248	5,590	1.12	56. 0. 0			111.6	100
Clayton and Frickley	2,390	1,589	1.50	75. 4. 0			31.8	21
Conisbrough	6,113	4,559	1.34	141. 0. 0			43.4	32
Dalton Magna and Parva	2,251	1,414	1.59	53.10. 0			42.1	26
Darfield	3,709	2,017	1.84	82.16. 0			44.8	24
Denaby	1,693	1,058	1.60	33. 9. 91/4			50.5	32
Dinnington	1,311	1,650	.79	28.16. 0	£8. 0. 0	Excise	45.5	45
Doncaster	28,207	1,690	16.69	NR			NR	NR
Ecclesall Bierlow	19,164	4,343	4.41	104. 8. 7	£16. 0. 0	Excise	183.5	42
Ecclesfield	19,824	11,192	1.77	215.12. 0	£8. 0. 0	Excise	91.9	50
Edlington	2,437	1,758	1.39	22. 7. 5			109.0	79
Firbeck	1,315	1,297	1.01	31.15. 8			41.4	41
Fishlake	4,892	3,909	1.25	92.16. 0			52.7	42
Greasbrough	4,311	2,456	1.76	74. 2. 0			58.2	33
Hallam, Nether	6,995	1,832	3.82	60. 4. 31/4			116.2	30
Hallam, Upper	3,693	6,330	.58	60. 4. 33/4			61.3	105
Hampole and Stubbs Hall	1,427	1,540	.93	23. 4. 0			61.5	66
Handsworth	9,960	3,638	2.74	93. 0. 0	£8. 0. 0	Excise	107.1	36
Harthill	4,976	3,565	1.40	88. 4. 0			56.4	40
Hatfield	12,472	14,293	.87	206.16. 0	£6.10. 0	Excise	60.3	67
Hickleton	1,493	1,061	1.41	31.12. 31/4			47.2	34
Hooton Levett	637	548	1.16	12. 2. 0			52.6	45

APPENDIX P.2 (continued) page 592

Wapentake Township	1815 property tax	Acres	Property tax: £/acre	Net land tax quota	Deductions from land tax quota Amount	Type	Net ratio: property tax/ land tax	Acres/£1 gross land tax
Strafforth and Tickhill								
Hooton Pagnell	2,429	2,002	1.21	66. 4. 4			36.7	30
Hooton Roberts	1,517	1,056	1.44	23. 8. 0			64.8	45
Houghton, Great	2,121	1,648	1.29	72. 0. 0			29.4	23
Houghton, Little	1,104	670	1.65	30.10. 0			36.2	22
Hoyland, Upper	3,256	2,085	1.56	54. 0. 0	£6. 0. 0	"Officer"	60.3	35
Kimberworth	10,770	3,760	2.86	112. 4. 0			96.0	34
Langthwaite and Tilts	735	649	1.13	19. 0. 0			38.7	34
Laughton en le Morthen and Throapham	4,421	4,940	.89	130.16. 0			33.8	38
Letwell	1,194	1,329	.90	28.12. 0			41.7	46
Loversall	2,631	2,172	1.21	NR			NR	NR
Maltby	3,213	4,096	.78	67. 8. 0			47.7	61
Marr	1,542	1,820	.85	22. 2. 0			69.8	82
Melton on the Hill	1,247	1,525	.82	39. 4. 0			31.8	39
Mexborough	2,030	1,292	1.57	55.12. 0			36.5	23
Ravenfield	1,839	1,235	1.49	42. 4. 0			43.6	29
Rawmarsh	4,699	2,578	1.82	76. 4. 0	£8. 0. 0	Excise	61.7	31
Rossington	4,831	3,051	1.58	NR			NR	NR
Rotherham	9,807	1,270	7.72	112. 4. 0	£40. 0. 0	"Officers Out Ride"	87.4	8
Sandall, Kirk	2,583	1,638	1.58	42. 8. 0			60.9	39
Sandall, Long; and Wheatley	3,918	2,482	1.58	NR			NR	NR
Sheffield	75,217	3,028	24.84	308.18. 0			243.5	10
Sprotbrough	4,655	1,973	2.36	73.14. 0			63.2	27
Stainforth and Bramwith	3,989	3,484	1.14	69. 2. 0			57.7	50
Stainton and Hellaby	2,423	2,857	.85	62. 2. 0			39.0	46

Stancell, Wellingley, and Wilsick	1,357	1,200	1.13	44. 4. 0			30.7	27
Stotfold	276	257	1.07	10.12. 0			26.0	24
Swinton	2,337	1,700	1.37	60.16. 0			38.4	28
Sykehouse	4,888	4,281	1.14	91. 4. 0			53.6	47
Thorne	13,705	12,408	1.10	136. 4. 0	£6. 0. 0	Excise	100.6	87
Thorpe in Balne	1,327	1,498	.88	31. 6. 8			42.3	48
Thorpe Salvin	1,414	2,295	.62	32. 7. 0			43.7	71
Thrybergh	2,147	1,318	1.63	52.12. 6			40.8	25
Thurnscoe	1,658	1,672	.99	55. 6. 0			30.0	30
Tickhill	9,160	5,578	1.64	152.16. 0	£10. 0. 0	Excise	59.9	34
Tinsley, Catcliffe, and Orgreave	16,214	2,925	5.54	67.12. 0	£8. 0. 0	Excise	239.8	39
Todwick	1,922	1,808	1.06	36.10. 5			52.6	50
Treeton	2,792	1,632	1.71	60.16. 0			45.9	27
Wadworth	3,507	3,133	1.12	47. 6. 0			74.1	66
Wales	1,321	1,318	1.00	38. 0. 0			34.8	35
Warmsworth	2,471	1,311	1.88	42. 0. 0			58.8	31
Wath upon Dearne	8,736	1,724	5.07	41. 0. 0	£6. 0. 0	Excise	213.1	37
Wentworth	13,354	2,328	5.74	42. 4. 0			316.4	55
Whiston	5,884	3,948	1.49	110.12. 0			53.2	36
Wickersley	1,917	1,273	1.50	29.10. 0	£6. 0. 0	Excise	65.0	36
Wombwell	5,854	3,851	1.52	99.18. 0			58.6	38
Woodsetts and Gildingwells	1,295	1,770	.73	46.12. 0			27.8	38
TOTAL	498,432	279,851[a]	1.78					
TOTAL	453,458[b]			6,331. 9. 8 1/2[c]	£134.10. 0 £6. 0. 0	Excise Officer	71.6	
TOTAL		265,204[d]		6,356. 9. 8 1/2	£40. 0. 0	Officers Out Ride		42

Notes: [a]Excludes acres when property tax value is NR (no return).
[b]Excludes property tax value when land tax quota is NR.
[c]Excludes land tax quota when property tax value is NR.
[d]Excludes acres when land tax value is NR.

APPENDIX P.2 (continued) page 594

Wapentake Township	1815 property tax	Acres	Property tax: £/acre	Net land tax quota	Deductions from land tax quota Amount	Type	Net ratio: property tax/ land tax	Acres/£1 gross land tax
RIDING TOTAL[a]	2,372,072	1,698,682	1.40					
TOTAL[a]	2,129,926			36,154. 9. 9	£727.17. 5	Excise	58.9	
					£8. 0. 0	Customs		
TOTAL[a]		1,631,488		36,288.11.11½	£40. 0. 0	Excise and Customs		45
					£9. 0. 0.	Salary		
					£6. 0. 0.	Officer		
					£40. 0. 0	Officer Out Ride		

Notes: [a]Values are excluded as indicated in wapentake subtotals.
Sources: PP 1818 (82.) XIX, 550-71 (1815 property tax); 6-inch Ordnance Survey maps (acres); land tax duplicates 1781-1783, West Yorkshire Archives, Wakefield. See maps 13, 14, and 15.

APPENDIX P.3

Ratios of 1815 property tax valuations (schedule A) to land tax quota, property tax valuation per acre, and acres per land tax quota; all townships and parishes, City of York and the Ainsty

Wapentake Township	1815 property tax	L.T. gross total	L.T. net total	Gross ratio	Net ratio	Deductions Amount	Deductions Type	Acres	P.T./ acre	Acres/gross L.T. quota
Ainsty										
Acaster Malbis	2,476	171. 1. 0.		14				1,886	1.31	11
Acaster Selby	2,017	90.15. 0.		22				1,573	1.28	17
Acomb	3,279	56.14. 8.		58				1,580	2.08	28
Appleton Roebuck	3,529	96. 4. 4.		37				2,920	1.21	30
Askham Bryan	2,397	63. 6.10.		38				1,894	1.26	30
Askham Richard	1,685	39. 4. 8.		43				980	1.72	25
Bickerton	915	53.14. 2.		17				1,073	.85	20
Bilbrough	2,002	52.15. 8.		38				1,446	1.38	27
Bilton	2,448	62. 6. 0.		39				1,923	1.27	31
Bishopthorpe	1,110	36.11. 6.		30				719	1.54	20
Bolton Percy	3,346	96. 8. 4.		35				2,340	1.43	24
Catterton	(948)	NR		NR				(741)	1.28	NR
Colton	1,630	41. 2. 2.		40				1,206	1.35	29
Copmanthorpe	2,415	80. 4. 0.		30				1,656	1.46	21
Dringhouses	1,551	34.14. 4.		45				778	1.99	22
Healaugh	(4,461)	NR		NR				(2,770)	1.61	NR
Hessay	1,107	30. 0. 0.		37				1,255	.88	42
Holgate	971	23.14.10.		41				298	3.26	12
Hutton Wandesley and Angram	1,518	42. 6. 0.		36				1,749	.87	41
Knapton	1,651	22. 7. 2.		74				870	1.90	39
Marston, Long	2,952	70. 3. 4.		42				2,846	1.04	40
Middlethorpe	1,438	43.16. 8.		33				630	2.28	14
Monkton, Moor	2,838	95. 3. 4.		30				3,067	.92	32
Oxton	1,434	42. 2. 4.		34				658	2.18	16
Poppleton, Nether	1,742	50.19. 4.		34				1,278	1.36	25
Poppleton, Upper	1,652	46.13. 4.		35				1,407	1.17	30
Rufforth	2,998	75. 2. 8.		40				2,464	1.22	33

APPENDIX P.3 (continued) page 596

Wapentake Township	1815 property tax	L.T. gross total	L.T. net total	Gross ratio	Net ratio	Deductions Amount	Deductions Type	Acres	P.T./ acre	Acres/gross L.T. quota
Ainsty										
Steeton	1,382	40. 0. 0.		34				1,141	1.21	28
Thorp Arch	2,029	52.12. 8.		38				1,670	1.22	32
Tockwith	2,168	91. 0. 0.		24				1,814	1.20	20
Walton	1,316	127.10. 6.		10				1,446	.91	11
Wighill	3,410	88. 9.10.		38				2,247	1.52	25
Wilstrop	1,394	49. 0. 3.		28				1,079	1.29	22
SUBTOTAL	62,800	1,966. 4.11		32				47,893	1.31	24
City of York										
All Saints, North Street	(918)	NR		NR				def.	def.	def.
All Saints, Pavement	1,222	104.14. 2.		12				def.	def.	def.
Andrew, St	437	15. 8. 6.		28				def.	def.	def.
Crux, St	1,682	137. 8. 2.		12				def.	def.	def.
Cuthbert, St, with St Helen on the Walls, and All Saints Peaseholme	370	51. 0. 8.		7				def.	def.	def.
Dennis, St	1,117	46. 3.10.		24				def.	def.	def.
Giles, St	1,765	26. 9. 6.		67				def.	def.	def.
Helen, St, Stonegate	2,331	97. 0.10.		24				def.	def.	def.
Holy Trinity, Goodramgate	754	50. 5. 0.		15				def.	def.	def.
Holy Trinity, Kings Court	1,495	103. 4. 2.		14				def.	def.	def.

Holy Trinity, Micklegate	2,271	85.15. 6.	26	def.	def.	def.
John, St, Delpike	526	34. 3.10.	15	def.	def.	def.
John, St, Micklegate	1,331	72.17. 6.	18	def.	def.	def.
Lawrence, St, with St. Nicholas	1,837	51.10.10.	36	def.	def.	def.
Margaret, St, Walmgate	741	29.14. 0.	25	def.	def.	def.
Martins, St, Coney Street	3,019	182. 5. 4.	16	def.	def.	def.
Martin, St, cum Gregory	1,461	84. 7.10.	17	def.	def.	def.
Mary, St, Bishophill Jr.	3,307	116.17. 6.	28	def.	def.	def.
Mary, St, Bishophill Sr.	1,972	64. 4.10.	31	def.	def.	def.
Mary, St, Castlegate	1,651	69.14.10.	24	def.	def.	def.
Maurice, St	1,196	39.15. 2.	30	def.	def.	def.
Michael, St, Le Belfrey	3,769	196.11. 0.	19	def.	def.	def.
Michael, St, Spurriergate	1,513	118. 7.10.	13	def.	def.	def.
Peter, St, the Little	969	50.16. 2.	19	def.	def.	def.
Peter, St, Le Willows	354	7.11.10.	46	def.	def.	def.
Sampson, St	1,536	84.13.10.	18	def.	def.	def.
Saviour, St	1,470	43.10. 2.	34	def.	def.	def.
Wilfred, St	3,355	76.18.10.	44	def.	def.	def.
SUBTOTAL	43,451	2,041.11. 8.	21	1,971	22.51	0.96
City of York and the Ainsty TOTAL	106,251	4,007.16. 7.	26	49,864	2.13	12

Sources: PP 1818 (82.) XIX, 526-9 (1815 property tax); 6-inch Ordnance Survey maps (acres); land tax duplicates, York Archives.

APPENDIX Q.1

Frequency distribution, net ratio of 1815 property tax valuations (schedule A) to land tax quotas, all parishes, Bedfordshire

Numbered columns:

1 = Barford hundred
2 = Biggleswade hundred
3 = Clifton hundred
4 = Flitt hundred
5 = Manshead hundred
6 = Redbornestoke hundred
7 = Stodden hundred
8 = Willey hundred
9 = Wixamtree hundred
10 = Bedford borough

										All cases		Summary	
Ratio	1	2	3	4	5	6	7	8	9	10	N	%	Range	% of cases[a]
0-4					1						1	0.8		
5-9	1		3	3	2		1				10	7.6	0-19	92.2
10-14	5	7	7	5	18	9	11	13	2	1	78	59.1		
15-19	2	4		1	5	5	1	5	5	1	29	22.0		
20-24		2			1		1			2	6	4.6		
25-29		1		1						1	3	2.3	20-39	7.8
30-34								1			1	0.8		
35-39														
40-44														
45-49													40-59	
50-54														
55-59														
60-64														
65-69													60-79	
70-74														
75-79														
80-84														
85-89													80-99	
90-94														
95-99														
100-104														
105-109														
110-114														
115-119													100-149	

120-124													
125-129													
130-134													
135-139													
140-144													
145-149													
150-154													
155-159													
160-164													
165-169													≥ 150
170-174													
175-179													
180-184													
185-189													
190-194													
195-199													
≥ 200													
def.				1							1	0.8	
NR									3		3	2.3	
N	8	14	10	11	27	14	14	19	10	5	132	100.0	
Mean	12	15	10	12	12	14	13	13	14	16	13		
Minimum	8	10	6	6	4	11	8	10	13	14	4		
Maximum	16	27	14	25	23	18	22	32	19	25	32		
Maximum as % of minimum	200	270	233	417	575	164	275	320	146	178	800		

Note: [a]Defective (def.) and no return (NR) cases are excluded from the denominator.
Sources: Land tax duplicates, Bedfordshire Record Office; PP 1818 (82.) XIX (1815 property tax).

APPENDIX Q.2

Frequency distribution, net ratio of 1815 property tax valuations (schedule A) to land tax quotas, all parishes, Cornwall

Numbered columns:

1 = East hundred
2 = Kerrier hundred
3 = Lesnewth hundred
4 = Penwith hundred
5 = Powder hundred
6 = Pydar hundred
7 = Stratton hundred
8 = Trigg hundred
9 = West hundred

										All cases		Summary	
Ratio	1	2	3	4	5	6	7	8	9	N	%	Range	% of cases[a]
0-4													
5-9												0-19	25.9
10-14	4				4	1	6		2	17	8.0		
15-19	8		2	1	5	1	3	1	5	26	12.3		
20-24	8	4	4	1	12	4		3	8	44	20.8		
25-29	8	2	4	5	4	6		1		30	14.2	20-39	62.6
30-34		5	1	1	1	3		4		15	7.1		
35-39	1	5		5	1	2		1		15	7.1		
40-44		2		1						3	1.4		
45-49				1	1					2	0.9	40-59	4.2
50-54													
55-59	1			1						2	0.9		
60-64					1					1	0.5		
65-69												60-79	2.4
70-74		1		1						2	0.9		
75-79				1						1	0.5		
80-84					1					1	0.5		
85-89												80-99	2.4
90-94				2	1					3	1.4		
95-99													
100-104					1					1	0.5		
105-109													
110-114													
115-119					1					1	0.5		

120-124												100-149	1.2
125-129													
130-134													
135-139													
140-144													
145-149													
150-154													
155-159		1								1	0.5		
160-164													
165-169												≥ 150	1.2
170-174													
175-179													
180-184													
185-189													
190-194													
195-199													
≥200				1						1	0.5		
def.	5	7	6	5	9	2	2	2	6	44	20.8		
NR							1		1	2	0.9		
N	35	27	17	26	42	19	12	12	22	212	100.0		
Mean	23	41	23	51	34	27	14	28	19	29			
Minimum	11	22	17	19	10	13	12	16	12	10			
Maximum	57	155	31	226	119	36	18	38	24	226			
Maximum as % of minimum	518	704	182	1,189	1,190	277	150	238	200	2,260			

Note: [a]Defective (def.) and no return (NR) cases are excluded from the denominator.
Sources: Land tax duplicates, Cornwall Record Office; PP 1818 (82.) XIX (1815 property tax).

APPENDIX Q.3
Frequency distribution, net ratio of 1815 property tax valuations (schedule A) to land tax quotas, all townships, Cumberland

Numbered columns:

1 = Allerdale abcve Derwent ward
2 = Allerdale below Derwent ward
3 = Cumberland ward
4 = Eskdale ward
5 = Leath ward
6 = City of Carlisle

Ratio	1	2	3	4	5	6	All cases N	All cases %	Summary Range	Summary % of cases[a]
0-4										
5-9									0-19	
10-14										
15-19										
20-24										
25-29									20-39	0.6
30-34				1			1	0.5		
35-39										
40-44	1			1			2	0.9		
45-49	1						1	0.5	40-59	4.0
50-54	2						2	0.9		
55-59	2						2	0.9		
60-64	2	1					3	1.4		
65-69	3						3	1.4	60-79	6.2
70-74	2						2	0.9		
75-79	1		1		1		3	1.4		
80-84	1	1			2		4	1.9		
85-89	1				1		2	0.9	80-99	9.0
90-94	3			1	2		6	2.8		
95-99	2			1	1		4	1.9		
100-104	3	1			1		5	2.3		
105-109	1				2		3	1.4		
110-114	2		1		1		4	1.9		
115-119	1		1		3		5	2.3	100-149	21.5
120-124			2		2		4	1.9		

125-129			2		2		4	1.9		
130-134	3		1				4	1.9		
135-139	2						2	0.9		
140-144		1		1			2	0.9		
145-149		1		1	3		5	2.3		
150-154	4	2					6	2.8		
155-159		1	3		2		6	2.8		
160-164		1	2				3	1.4		
165-169		1					1	0.5	≥ 150	58.8
170-174		1		1	1		3	1.4		
175-179			2	1			3	1.4		
180-184	3	1	1	1			6	2.8		
185-189		2		1			3	1.4		
190-194		1		1	1		3	1.4		
195-199					2		2	0.9		
200-249	1	9	5	4	6		25	11.7		
250-299	3	5	1	5	1	1	16	7.5		
300-349	1	3		3	1		8	3.7		
350-399	1	2		3			6	2.8		
400-449		2		1			3	1.4		
450-499		1		1			2	0.9		
500-549										
550-599										
600-649					1		1	0.5		
650-699						1	1	0.5		
700-749										
750-799		1					1	0.5		
800-849										
850-899										
900-949				1			1	0.5		
950-999										
≥ 1,000	2			1		1	4	1.9		
def.	6	7	4	4	3	3	27	12.6		
NR		1	3	2	4		10	4.7		
N	54	46	29	36	43	6	214	100.0		

APPENDIX Q.3 (continued) page 604

							All cases		Summary	
Ratio	1	2	3	4	5	6	N	%	Range	% of cases[a]
Mean	170	223	181	240	191	606	199			
Minimum	41	64	75	34	76	296	34			
Maximum	1,346	794	270	1,060	611	1,210	1,346			
Maximum as % of minimum	3,283	1,241	360	3,118	804	409	3,959			

Note: [a]Defective (def.) and no return (NR) cases are excluded from the denominator.
Sources: Land tax duplicates, Cumbria Record Office, Carlisle; PP 1818 (82.) XIX (1815 property tax).

APPENDIX Q.4

Frequency distribution, net ratio of 1815 property tax valuations (schedule A) to land tax quotas, all townships, Herefordshire

Numbered columns:

1 = Broxash hundred
2 = Ewyas Lacy hundred
3 = Greytree hundred
4 = Grimsworth hundred
5 = Huntington hundred
6 = Radlow hundred
7 = Stretford hundred
8 = Webtree hundred
9 = Wigmore hundred
10 = Wolphy hundred
11 = Wormelow hundred, Lower Division
12 = Wormelow hundred, Upper Division
13 = Hereford City

Ratio	1	2	3	4	5	6	7	8	9	10	11	12	13	All cases N	All cases %	Summary Range	Summary % of cases[a]
0-4																	
5-9																0-19	5.4
10-14			1			2					1			4	1.6		
15-19	2		2			1		1				1		7	2.8		
20-24	3		6	3		9	3	4		2	7			37	15.0		
25-29	4	7	3	7		3	4	3		1	4			36	14.6	20-39	54.0
30-34	6	2		2		1	3	4	1	6	4			29	11.7		
35-39	2		1	4		1		5		2	2			17	6.9		
40-44	1		3	3	1		1	3	3	1	3			19	7.7		
45-49	2			1	1		1	6	1	1	3		1	17	6.9	40-59	24.8
50-54	1				2				3	5		1		12	4.9		
55-59									1	1				2	0.8		
60-64		3	1							1				5	2.0		
65-69					1			1						2	0.8	60-79	6.4
70-74				1					1		1			3	1.2		
75-79					1				1		1			3	1.2		
80-84									1					1	0.4		
85-89									1					1	0.4	80-99	1.0
90-94																	
95-99																	
100-104									1					1	0.4		
105-109									2					2	0.8		

APPENDIX Q.4 (continued) page 606

Ratio	1	2	3	4	5	6	7	8	9	10	11	12	13	All cases N	All cases %	Summary Range	Summary % of cases[a]
110-114																100-149	3.0
115-119																	
120-124			1											1	0.4		
125-129					1				1					2	0.8		
130-134																	
135-139																	
140-144																	
145-149																	
150-154							1							1	0.4		
155-159																	
160-164																	
165-169																≥ 150	0.5
170-174																	
175-179																	
180-184																	
185-189																	
190-194																	
195-199																	
≥ 200																	
def.	5		2			1	1	2		4		1		16	6.5		
NR	5		1	5		8	2		4	2		2		29	11.7		
N	31	12	21	26	7	26	16	29	21	26	26	5	1	247	100.0		
Mean	29	32	30	31	67	23	34	33	60	38	28	34	48	33			
Minimum	16	25	12	20	41	11	21	17	33	20	14	19		11			
Maximum	53	63	121	71	125	35	152	65	127	63	75	53		152			
Maximum as % of minimum	331	252	1,008	355	305	318	724	382	385	315	536	279	NA	1,382			

Notes: A few duplicates in some hundreds (e.g. Wigmore) may have higher ratios due to half yearly assessments being entered. Duplicates were sometimes ambiguous (e.g. ''1798 half yearly'' appearing in the heading). Only ''totals'' recorded at the bottom of the duplicate were used, except where such totals were directly and unambiguously designated as half-yearly. Some duplicates in the same hundreds specifically designated their totals as yearly, however, and ratios for such duplicates were at levels comparable to those of the ambiguous duplicates. I have therefore concluded that the ratios are probably correct as computed.

[a]Defective (def.) and no return (NR) cases are excluded from the denominator.

Sources: Land tax duplicates, Hereford and Worcester County Record Office, Hereford; PP 1818 (82.) XIX (1815 property tax).

APPENDIX Q.5

Frequency distribution, net ratio of 1815 property tax valuations (schedule A) to land tax quotas, all parishes, Hertfordshire

Numbered columns:

1 = Braughing hundred
2 = Broadwater hundred
3 = Cashio hundred
4 = Dacorum hundred
5 = Edwinstree hundred
6 = Hertford hundred
7 = Hitchen and Pirton hundred
8 = Odsey hundred
9 = Hertford borough
10 = St. Albans borough and liberty

Ratio	1	2	3	4	5	6	7	8	9	10	All cases N	All cases %	Summary Range	Summary % of cases[a]
0-4														
5-9	2	1		2		2	1	1			9	6.3	0-19	92.3
10-14	10	9	4	3	13	1	2	11		2	55	38.7		
15-19		3	9	9	4	1	5			1	32	22.5		
20-24			3	3				1			7	4.9	20-39	6.7
25-29														
30-34														
35-39														
40-44														
45-49				1							1	0.7	40-59	1.0
50-54														
55-59														
60-64														
65-69													60-79	
70-74														
75-79														
80-84														
85-89													80-99	
90-94														
95-99														
100-104														
105-109														
110-114														
115-119														

120-124													100-149
125-129													
130-134													
135-139													
140-144													
145-149													
150-154													
155-159													
160-164													
165-169													≥ 150
170-174													
175-179													
180-184													
185-189													
190-194													
195-199													
≥ 200													
def.	1	10	1	2		11		1	4		30	21.1	
NR			2	2	1			2		1	8	5.6	
N	13	23	19	22	18	15	8	16	4	4	142	100.0	
Mean	11	13	16	16	13	12	15	11	def.	13	14		
Minimum	9	9	11	7	10	8	8	9		10	7		
Maximum	14	19	21	49	18	16	17	20		18	49		
Maximum as % of minimum	156	211	191	700	180	200	212	222	NA	180	700		

Note: [a]Defective (def.) and no return (NR) cases are excluded from the denominator.
Sources: Land tax duplicates, Hertfordshire Record Office; PP 1818 (82.) XIX (1815 property tax).

APPENDIX Q.6

Frequency distribution, net ratio of 1815 property tax valuations (schedule A) to land tax quotas, all townships, Lancashire

Numbered columns:

1 = Amounderness hundred
2 = Higher Blackburn hundred
3 = Lower Blackburn hundred
4 = Leyland hundred
5 = Lonsdale hundred
6 = Salford hundred
7 = West Derby hundred
8 = Lancaster borough
9 = Liverpool borough
10 = Manchester borough
11 = Wigan borough

Ratio	1	2	3	4	5	6	7	8	9	10	11	All cases N	All cases %	Summary Range	Summary % of cases[a]
0-4															
5-9														0-19	0.5
10-14							2					2	0.5		
15-19															
20-24					1		1					2	0.5		
25-29							1					1	0.2	20-39	1.8
30-34															
35-39	1					1	2					4	0.9		
40-44	1	2				1	2					6	1.4		
45-49		1			1	2	3					7	1.6	40-59	8.4
50-54		3				1	5					9	2.0		
55-59	2	1	1			1	6					11	2.5		
60-64	3	1			1	1	5					11	2.5		
65-69	1	3		1	3	2	6					16	3.6	60-79	16.0
70-74	2	5	1		1	3	6					18	4.1		
75-79	2	3	1	1		7	4					18	4.1		
80-84	1	1		2	2	4	4					14	3.2		
85-89	3	2		1		2	3					11	2.5	80-99	11.9
90-94	2	2	1	1	1	4	2					13	3.0		
95-99	1			1	1	6						9	2.0		
100-104	3	3	2	3	1		2					14	3.2		
105-109	3		2	1	5	7	4					22	5.0		
110-114	1	2	2	1	2	3	4					15	3.4		

115-119	2				3	7	2					14	3.2		
120-124		2	2	2	4	5	3					18	4.1	100-149	34.9
125-129	3			1	2	5	1					12	2.7		
130-134	4		2	2	5	4	1					18	4.1		
135-139	3			1	1	3	1					9	2.0		
140-144	2	1		1	7	1	1					13	3.0		
145-149			1			1	1					3	0.7		
150-154	2		1	2	1	2						8	1.8		
155-159			1	1	1							3	0.7		
160-164	1				1	1					1	4	0.9		
165-169	1		1	2		1	1					6	1.4	≥ 150	26.6
170-174		1		3		2						6	1.4		
175-179			1		4	1						6	1.4		
180-184			1	3	2							6	1.4		
185-189				1	1							2	0.5		
190-194	1			1	3	1						6	1.4		
195-199	1		2	1	2	1						7	1.6		
200-249	5		5	4	5	3				1		23	5.2		
250-299	1		2		1	1						5	1.1		
300-349	3		1		2	1	2	1		1		11	2.5		
350-399	1			1	1	2	1					6	1.4		
400-449				1		1						2	0.5		
450-499	1		1			1	1					4	0.9		
500-549															
550-599															
600-649															
650-699															
700-749															
750-799															
800-849															
850-899															
900-949															
950-999															
≥ 1,000															
def.	2	3	3	1	6	6	13		1			35	8.0		
NR	1	3			1	1	2					8	1.8		
N	60	39	34	40	72	96	92	1	1	2	1	438	100.0		

APPENDIX Q.6 (continued) page 612

												All cases		Summary	
Ratio	1	2	3	4	5	6	7	8	9	10	11	N	%	Range	% of cases[a]
Mean	118	82	181	144	133	127	84	328	def.	317	163	126			
Minimum	35	40	55	67	20	37	13			233		13			
Maximum	482	172	491	403	370	467	481			336		491			
Maximum as % of minimum	1,377	430	893	601	1,850	1,262	3,700	NA	NA	144	NA	3,777			

Note: [a]Defective (def.) and no return (NR) cases are excluded from the denominator.
Sources: Land tax duplicates, Lancashire Record Office; PP 1818 (82.) XIX (1815 property tax).

APPENDIX Q.7

Frequency distribution, net ratio of 1815 property tax valuations (schedule A) to land tax quotas, all townships, Leicestershire

Numbered columns:

1 = East Goscote hundred
2 = Framland hundred
3 = Gartree hundred
4 = Guthlaxton hundred
5 = Sparkenhoe hundred
6 = West Goscote hundred
7 = Leicester borough

								All cases		Summary	
Ratio	1	2	3	4	5	6	7	N	%	Range	% of cases[a]
0-4					1			1	0.3		
5-9					2			2	0.6	0-19	31.6
10-14	5	5	12	3	6	1		32	9.7		
15-19	11	7	17	11	12	1		59	17.9		
20-24	4	5	7	3	7	3		29	8.8		
25-29	3	7	9	5	17	5		46	13.9	20-39	51.8
30-34	11	5	8	11	11	7		53	16.1		
35-39	8	2	3	3	4	6		26	7.9		
40-44	3	4		1	1	9		18	5.4		
45-49	2	3			3	3	1	12	3.6	40-59	13.8
50-54	1	3			1	1		6	1.8		
55-59	3		1			1		5	1.5		
60-64		1				2		3	0.9		
65-69	1							1	0.3	60-79	2.0
70-74					1	1		2	0.6		
75-79											
80-84											
85-89		1				1		2	0.6	80-99	0.7
90-94											
95-99											
100-104											
105-109											
110-114											
115-119											
120-124										100-149	

APPENDIX Q.7 (continued) page 614

Ratio	1	2	3	4	5	6	7	All cases N	All cases %	Summary Range	Summary % of cases[a]
125-129											
130-134											
135-139											
140-144											
145-149											
150-154											
155-159											
160-164											
165-169										≥ 150	
170-174											
175-179											
180-184											
185-189											
190-194											
195-199											
≥ 200											
def.			1	2	5		6	14	4.2		
NR	2	2	1	2	4	8		19	5.8		
N	54	45	59	41	75	49	7	330	100.0		
Mean	26	26	21	24	24	39	46	26			
Minimum	13	11	11	12	2	14		2			
Maximum	68	89	55	44	72	87		89			
Maximum as % of minimum	523	809	500	367	3,600	621	NA	4,450			

Note: [a]Defective (def.) and no return (NR) cases are excluded from the denominator.
Sources: Land tax duplicates, Leicestershire Record Office; PP 1818 (82.) XIX (1815 property tax).

APPENDIX Q.8

Frequency distribution, net ratio of 1815 property tax valuations (schedule A) to land tax quotas, all townships, Lincolnshire, Parts of Holland

Numbered columns:

1 = Elloe hundred
2 = Kirton hundred
3 = Skirbeck hundred

Ratio	1	2	3	All cases N	All cases %	Summary Range	Summary % of cases[a]
0-4							
5-9						0-19	11.1
10-14							
15-19	2	2		4	8.7		
20-24	1	6	4	11	23.9		
25-29	4	2	1	7	15.2	20-39	63.9
30-34	1	3		4	8.7		
35-39			1	1	2.2		
40-44	1		3	4	8.7		
45-49	2			2	4.4	40-59	19.4
50-54			1	1	2.2		
55-59							
60-64	1	1		2	4.4		
65-69						60-79	5.6
70-74							
75-79							
80-84							
85-89						80-99	
90-94							
95-99							
100-104							
105-109							
110-114							
115-119						100-149	
120-124							

APPENDIX Q.8 (continued) page 616

Ratio	1	2	3	All cases N	All cases %	Summary Range	Summary % of cases[a]
125–129							
130–134							
135–139							
140–144							
145–149							
150–154						≥ 150	
155–159							
160–164							
165–169							
170–174							
175–179							
180–184							
185–189							
190–194							
195–199							
≥ 200							
def.	4			4	8.7		
NR	2	4		6	13.0		
N	18	18	10	46	100.0		
Mean	28	24	36	28			
Minimum	15	16	21	15			
Maximum	63	64	51	64			
Maximum as % of Minimum	520	400	243	427			

Note: [a]Defective (def.) and no return (NR) cases are excluded from the denominator.
Sources: Land tax duplicates, Lincolnshire Archives Office; PP 1818 (82.) XIX (1815 property tax).

APPENDIX Q.9

Frequency distribution, net ratio of 1815 property tax valuations (schedule A) to land tax quotas, all townships, Lincolnshire, Parts of Kesteven

Numbered columns:

1 = Aswardhurn hundred
2 = Aveland hundred
3 = Beltisloe hundred, north division
4 = Beltisloe hundred, south division
5 = Boothby Graffo hundred, high division
6 = Boothby Graffo hundred, south division
7 = Flaxwell hundred
8 = Langoe hundred, first division
9 = Langoe hundred, second division
10 = Loveden hundred
11 = Ness hundred
12 = Winnibriggs and Threo hundred
13 = City and Liberty of Lincoln

Ratio	1	2	3	4	5	6	7	8	9	10	11	12	13	All cases N	All cases %	Summary Range	Summary % of cases[a]
0-4																	
5-9				1								1		2	1.0	0-19	30.0
10-14	7	1	2	3	2	1	3			2	1			22	11.3		
15-19	1	7	2	3	1	1	3			8	1			27	13.9		
20-24	1	3	1	1	1	2		1	1	2				13	6.7		
25-29	3	4	1	4	2	1	1	1		4	2	1		24	12.4	20-39	41.8
30-34	3	1	2	1	1	1	2			3	5	3		22	11.3		
35-39	1	1			1	1	1			3	3	1		12	6.2		
40-44	1	1	1		1	2	1	3						10	5.2		
45-49	2			2		1	2			1	1	1		10	5.2	40-59	17.6
50-54	2						3					2		7	3.6		
55-59		1					1			1				3	1.6		
60-64				1	2			2	1	1				7	3.6		
65-69					1	1								2	1.0	60-79	7.1
70-74					1									1	0.5		
75-79							1			1				2	1.0		
80-84								1						1	0.5		
85-89																80-99	2.9
90-94							1	1	1					3	1.6		
95-99		1												1	0.5		
100-104																	
105-109																	

APPENDIX Q.9 (continued) page 618

Ratio	1	2	3	4	5	6	7	8	9	10	11	12	13	All cases N	All cases %	Summary Range	Summary % of cases[a]
110-114																	
115-119																	
120-124																100-149	
125-129																	
130-134																	
135-139																	
140-144																	
145-149																	
150-154																	
155-159																	
160-164																	
165-169																≥ 150	0.6
170-174																	
175-179																	
180-184																	
185-189																	
190-194																	
195-199																	
≥ 200								1						1	0.5		
def.						1			2	1	1			5	2.6		
NR	1						2			8	1	6	1	19	9.8		
N	22	20	9	16	13	12	21	10	5	35	15	15	1	194	100.0		
Mean	25	24	21	18	32	32	30	53	48	25	29	30	NR	27			
Minimum	11	14	11	9	13	14	10	22	22	12	14	9		9			
Maximum	52	97	42	60	74	68	92	548	90	75	47	51		548			
Maximum as % of minimum	473	693	382	667	569	486	920	2,491	409	625	336	567	NA	6,089			

Note: [a]Defective (def.) and no return (NR) cases are excluded from the denominator.
Sources: Land tax duplicates, Lincolnshire Archives Office; PP 1818 (82.) XIX (1815 property tax).

APPENDIX Q.10

Frequency distribution, net ratio of 1815 property tax valuations (schedule A) to land tax quotas, all townships, Lincolnshire, Parts of Lindsey

Numbered columns:

1 = Aslacoe hundred, east division
2 = Aslacoe hundred, west division
3 = Bolingbroke hundred
4 = Bradley Haverstoe hundred
5 = Calceworth hundred
6 = Candleshoe hundred
7 = Corringham hundred
8 = Gartree hundred, north division
9 = Gartree hundred, south division
10 = Hill hundred
11 = Horncastle hundred
12 = Lawress hundred
13 = Louth Eske hundred, marsh division
14 = Louth Eske hundred, wold division
15 = Ludborough hundred
16 = Manley hundred, east division
17 = Manley hundred, north division
18 = Manley hundred, west division
19 = Walshcroft hundred, east division
20 = Walshcroft hundred, west division
21 = Well hundred
22 = Wraggoe hundred, east division
23 = Wraggoe hundred, west division
24 = Yarborough hundred, east division
25 = Yarborough hundred, north division
26 = Yarborough hundred, south division

APPENDIX Q.10 (continued) page 620

Ratio	1	2	3	4	5	6	7	8	9	10	11	12	13	14	15
0–4															
5–9							1								1
10–14	1	1		1	1	2						1		1	
15–19		1	1	3	3	7		3	5	1		7	5	2	1
20–24	1	1	5	10	6	5	3	2	4	4	1	5	2	4	2
25–29	1	1	3	2	7	2	2	3	2	3	1	2	5	7	1
30–34	1	1	4	4	6	2	2	3		2	3	2	1	2	1
35–39	2		2	4	2		2		3	5	1			2	1
40–44	1	1	4	4	3	2	2		2	2	2	1			
45–49	2			1	3		1	1			1	2		2	
50–54	1	3		1			2	1			2	2		1	
55–59	1				1	1	1		1		2			1	
60–64				1		1	1					1			
65–69	1			1											
70–74															
75–79															
80–84	1														
85–89												1			
90–94				1											
95–99														1	
100–104				1											
105–109															
110–114												1			
115–119															
120–124															
125–129															
130–134															
135–139															
140–144															
145–149															
150–154															
155–159												1			
160–164															
165–169															

Ratio	16	17	18	19	20	21	22	23	24	25	26	All cases N	All cases %	Summary Range	Summary % of cases[a]
0-4															
5-9												2	0.5	0-19	17.3
10-14					2	1	2	2				15	3.4		
15-19		1		1	4		2	2	3		1	53	12.1		
20-24				1	1	1	1	4	1	1	2	67	15.3		
25-29		2			1	2	3	3	2	1	1	57	13.0	20-39	53.6
30-34	2		1	2	1	5	3	4	1	4	4	61	14.0		
35-39	1	1	1	1		2			1	1		32	7.3		
40-44	1		1	1			1			1	3	32	7.3		
45-49		3	2		1		1	1	2			23	5.3	40-59	21.0
50-54		2	2									17	3.9		
55-59	1			2			1				1	13	3.0		
60-64			1						1	2		8	1.8		
65-69			2								1	5	1.1	60-79	4.7
70-74				1								1	0.2		
75-79	3		2									5	1.1		
80-84	1								1			3	0.7		
85-89								1				2	0.5	80-99	2.2
90-94	1											2	0.5		
95-99				1								2	0.5		
100-104												1	0.2		
105-109															
110-114												1	0.2		
115-119															
120-124														100-149	0.7
125-129			1									1	0.2		
130-134															
135-139															
140-144															
145-149															
150-154															
155-159												1	0.2		
160-164															
165-169														≥ 150	0.5

APPENDIX Q.10 (continued) page 622

Ratio	1	2	3	4	5	6	7	8	9	10	11	12	13	14	15
170-174															
175-179															
180-184															
185-189															
190-194															
195-199															
≥ 200			1												
def.					1	1	1								1
NR			7	1	2		2			4	2				1
N	13	9	27	35	35	23	20	13	17	21	15	26	13	23	9
Mean	40	29	32	28	26	21	35	26	25	30	41	30	20	34	20
Minimum	14	14	18	13	14	12	9	16	16	18	23	14	17	14	7
Maximum	84	53	594	100	55	63	62	51	58	42	59	158	30	95	38
Maximum as % of minimum	600	378	3,300	769	393	525	689	319	362	233	256	1,128	176	678	543

Lincolnshire county mean net ratio = 29

Ratio	16	17	18	19	20	21	22	23	24	25	26	All cases N	All cases %	Summary Range	Summary % of cases[a]
170–174															
175–179															
180–184															
185–189															
190–194															
195–199															
≥ 200												1	0.2		
def.	1									2		7	1.6		
NR	5			1								25	5.7		
N	16	9	13	11	10	11	14	17	12	12	13	437	100.0		
Mean	56	40	52	38	19	28	24	23	30	38	33	30			
Minimum	33	17	32	17	11	11	14	11	16	22	17	7			
Maximum	90	53	127	96	45	37	56	85	81	62	67	594			
Maximum as % of minimum	273	312	397	565	409	336	400	773	506	282	394	8,486			

Note: [a]Defective (def.) and no return (NR) cases are excluded from the denominator.
Sources: Land tax duplicates, Lincolnshire Archives Office; PP 1818 (82.) XIX (1815 property tax).

APPENDIX Q.11

Frequency distribution, net ratio of 1815 property tax valuations (schedule A) to land tax quotas, all parishes, Norfolk

Numbered columns:

1 = Blofield hundred
2 = Brothercross hundred
3 = Clackclose hundred
4 = Clavering hundred
5 = Depwade hundred
6 = Diss hundred
7 = Earsham hundred
8 = North Erpingham hundred
9 = South Erpingham hundred
10 = Eynesford hundred
11 = East Flegg hundred
12 = West Flegg hundred
13 = Forehoe hundred
14 = Freebridge Lynn hundred
15 = Freebridge Marshland hundred
16 = Gallow hundred
17 = North Greenhoe hundred
18 = South Greenhoe hundred
19 = Grimshoe hundred
20 = Guiltcross hundred
21 = Happing hundred
22 = Henstead hundred
23 = Holt hundred
24 = Humbleyard hundred
25 = Launditch hundred
26 = Loddon hundred
27 = Mitford hundred
28 = Shropham hundred
29 = Smithdon hundred
30 = Taverham hundred
31 = Tunstead hundred
32 = Walsham hundred
33 = Wayland hundred
34 = City of Norwich

Ratio	1	2	3	4	5	6	7	8	9	10	11	12	13	14	15
0-4															
5-9	1									1					
10-14	1		4		5	2	1	7	9	5			5	5	
15-19	6	4	7	9	16	4	9	16	10	12	4	8	12	8	1
20-24	4	3	8	8		4	2	4	8	5	3	4	3	12	4
25-29	3	1	9					3	4	3			2	5	2
30-34	1	1	1	1		1		1	1					1	1
35-39								1						1	1
40-44			1							1					1
45-49															
50-54	1														
55-59															
60-64			2							1				1	
65-69							1								
70-74															
75-79				1									1		
80-84															
85-89	1														
90-94															

95-99															1
100-104															
105-109															
110-114															1
115-119															
120-124															
125-129															
130-134														1	
135-139															
140-144															
145-149															
150-154															
155-159															
160-164															
165-169															
170-174															
175-179															
180-184															
185-189															
190-194															
195-199															
≥ 200															1
def.						3			5	1					2
NR										1	1			1	
N	18	9	32	19	21	14	13	32	37	30	8	12	23	35	15
Mean	22	20	25	20	15	16	18	18	19	19	20	19	20	22	35
Minimum	9	16	13	15	10	10	14	10	10	8	16	15	13	12	18
Maximum	86	30	64	78	19	33	67	35	30	64	23	24	75	130	243
Maximum as % of minimum	956	188	492	520	190	330	478	350	300	800	144	160	577	1,083	1,350

APPENDIX Q.11 (continued) page 626

Ratio	16	17	18	19	20	21	22	23	24	25	26	27	28	29	30
0–4						1									
5–9			1												2
10–14	1	4	3	2	2	2	6	6	7	7	4	3	2		1
15–19	9	5	8	1	3	4	9	5	8	12	7	7	2	2	2
20–24	8	3	3	5	3	8	2	10	2	3	6	8	7	5	8
25–29	5	1	1	2	3	1		3	2	5	2		6	5	1
30–34	3		2	2	1		1	2					1	3	1
35–39	2			2						2				1	1
40–44	2									1					
45–49		1	1												
50–54															1
55–59															1
60–64	1	1													
65–69		1													
70–74															
75–79															
80–84															
85–89				1											
90–94															
95–99															
100–104															
105–109															
110–114															
115–119															
120–124															
125–129			1												
130–134															
135–139															
140–144															
145–149															
150–154													1		
155–159															
160–164															
165–169															

170-174															
175-179															
180-184															
185-189															
190-194															
195-199															
≥ 200															
def.			3	1						2	1			1	
NR													1		
N	31	16	23	16	12	16	18	26	19	32	20	18	20	17	18
Mean	24	20	25	30	24	18	16	19	16	18	19	18	25	26	19
Minimum	11	12	9	13	13	3	10	10	10	10	13	11	11	16	8
Maximum	62	67	128	86	31	28	31	33	27	42	27	24	152	37	58
Maximum as % of minimum	564	558	1,422	662	238	933	310	330	270	420	208	218	1,382	231	725

APPENDIX Q.11 (continued) page 628

Ratio	31	32	33	34	All cases N	All cases %	Summary Range	Summary % of cases[a]
0-4					1	0.2		
5-9					5	0.7	0-19	51.2
10-14		2		1	97	14.4		
15-19	17	3			230	34.0		
20-24	6	4	2		165	24.4		
25-29	3	1	2		75	11.1	20-39	43.5
30-34			4		29	4.3		
35-39			3		14	2.1		
40-44					6	0.9		
45-49					2	0.3	40-59	1.7
50-54					2	0.3		
55-59					1	0.2		
60-64					6	0.9		
65-69					2	0.3	60-79	1.5
70-74								
75-79					2	0.3		
80-84								
85-89					2	0.3	80-99	0.5
90-94								
95-99					1	0.2		
100-104			2		2	0.3		
105-109								
110-114			1		2	0.3		
115-119			1		1	0.2		
120-124							100-149	1.2
125-129					1	0.2		
130-134					1	0.2		
135-139								
140-144			1		1	0.2		
145-149								
150-154					1	0.2		
155-159								
160-164								
165-169							≥ 150	0.3

170–174						
175–179						
180–184						
185–189						
190–194						
195–199						
≥ 200					1	0.2
def.		2			21	3.1
NR					4	0.6
N	26	12	16	1	675	100.0
Mean	20	19	44	11	20	
Minimum	15	12	23		3	
Maximum	26	29	140		243	
Maximum as % of minimum	173	242	609	NA	8,100	

Note: [a]Defective (def.) and no return (NR) cases are excluded from the denominator.
Sources: Land tax duplicates, Norfolk Record Office; PP 1818 (82.) XIX (1815 property tax).

APPENDIX Q.12
Frequency distribution, net ratio of 1815 property tax valuations (schedule A) to land tax quotas, all parishes, Northamptonshire

Numbered columns:

1 = Chipping Warden hundred
2 = Cleley hundred
3 = Corby hundred
4 = Fawsley hundred
5 = Greens Norton hundred
6 = Guilsborough hundred
7 = Hamfordshoe hundred
8 = Higham Ferrers hundred
9 = Huxloe hundred
10 = Kings Sutton hundred
11 = Navisford hundred
12 = Nobottle Grove hundred
13 = Orlingbury hundred
14 = Polebrook hundred
15 = Rothwell hundred
16 = Spelhoe hundred
17 = Towcester hundred
18 = Willibrook hundred
19 = Wymersley hundred
20 = Peterborough Liberty
21 = Northampton borough
22 = Peterborough city

APPENDIX Q.12 (continued) page 630

Ratio	1	2	3	4	5	6	7	8	9	10	11	12	13	14	15
0-4															
5-9			1										1		
10-14		6	6	1	2	2	1	3	2	4		1	5	1	
15-19	2	3	11	6	5	7	2	6	5	3	4	4	4	3	5
20-24	1	2	8	4	4	1	3	1	11	9	1	6	3	1	6
25-29		1	1	4	1	7		1		2	1	7	3	1	5
30-34	2		2	5		1	1		1		1	1		2	3
35-39	2					1				1					1
40-44							1			1					
45-49															2
50-54										1					
55-59															
60-64															
65-69															
70-74															
75-79															
80-84															
85-89															
90-94															
95-99															
100-104															
105-109															
110-114															
115-119															
120-124															
125-129															
130-134															
135-139															
140-144															
145-149															
150-154															
155-159															
160-164															
165-169															

Ratio	16	17	18	19	20	21	22	All cases N	All cases %	Summary Range	Summary % of cases[a]
0-4											
5-9								2	0.6	0-19	44.8
10-14			3	8				45	13.7		
15-19		1	3	4				78	23.7		
20-24	4	2	6	4				77	23.4		
25-29	1	3	1	2				41	12.5	20-39	53.4
30-34	2		1	2				24	7.3		
35-39	1			1				7	2.1		
40-44								2	0.6		
45-49								2	0.6	40-59	1.8
50-54								1	0.3		
55-59											
60-64											
65-69										60-79	
70-74											
75-79											
80-84											
85-89										80-99	
90-94											
95-99											
100-104											
105-109											
110-114											
115-119											
120-124										100-149	
125-129											
130-134											
135-139											
140-144											
145-149											
150-154											
155-159											
160-164											
165-169										≥ 150	

APPENDIX Q.12 (continued) page 632

Ratio	1	2	3	4	5	6	7	8	9	10	11	12	13	14	15
170-174															
175-179															
180-184															
185-189															
190-194															
195-199															
≥ 200															
def.		2		1				2	1	1				1	
NR	2		1					1		1					4
N	9	14	30	21	12	19	8	14	20	23	7	19	16	9	26
Mean	27	16	17	22	19	21	21	17	19	21	20	22	17	17	24
Minimum	15	11	9	11	12	13	14	13	12	10	15	14	8	13	15
Maximum	37	25	33	32	26	37	43	28	31	51	31	32	28	33	48
Maximum as % of minimum	247	227	367	291	217	285	307	215	258	510	207	228	350	254	320

Ratio	16	17	18	19	20	21	22	All cases N	All cases %	Summary Range	Summary % of cases[a]
170–174											
175–179											
180–184											
185–189											
190–194											
195–199											
≥ 200											
def.	1							9	2.7		
NR	1				29	1	1	41	12.5		
N	10	6	14	21	29	1	1	329	100.0		
Mean	27	23	20	19				20			
Minimum	20	15	10	10				8			
Maximum	36	28	33	38				51			
Maximum as % of minimum	180	187	330	380	NA	NA	NA	638			

Note: [a]Defective (def.) and no return (NR) cases are excluded from the denominator.
Sources: Land tax duplicates, Northamptonshire Record Office; PP 1818 (82.) XIX (1815 property tax).

APPENDIX Q.13

Frequency distribution, net ratio of 1815 property tax valuations (schedule A) to land tax quotas, all parishes, Oxfordshire

Numbered columns:

1 = Bampton hundred
2 = Banbury hundred
3 = Binfield hundred
4 = Bloxham hundred
5 = Bullingdon hundred
6 = Chadlington hundred
7 = Dorchester hundred
8 = Ewelme hundred
9 = Langtree hundred
10 = Lewknor hundred
11 = Pirton hundred
12 = Ploughley hundred
13 = Thame hundred
14 = Wootton hundred
15 = Oxford City, Liberty and University

Ratio	1	2	3	4	5	6	7	8
0-4								
5-9	1				1			2
10-14	5	1	2		7	3	3	7
15-19	5	1	2	1	13	9	4	5
20-24	8	3	4	3	4	9	1	1
25-29	9	1		5	6	4		
30-34	1	3		5	3	4		1
35-39		1		3		4		
40-44		1						
45-49								
50-54								
55-59				1				
60-64				1				
65-69								
70-74								
75-79								
80-84								
85-89								
90-94								
95-99								
100-104								
105-109								

								All cases		Summary	
Ratio	9	10	11	12	13	14	15	N	%	Range	% of cases[a]
0-4			1					1	0.4		
5-9		1	1	1		4		11	4.1	0-19	47.6
10-14	6	2		7	5	1		49	18.2		
15-19		6	3	6	1	9	1	66	24.5		
20-24	3			9	1	13		59	21.9		
25-29	1	1		4		7		38	14.1	20-39	48.7
30-34				5		2		24	8.9		
35-39			1					9	3.4		
40-44				1				2	0.7		
45-49				2				2	0.7	40-59	2.6
50-54						1		1	0.4		
55-59						1		2	0.7		
60-64						1		2	0.7		
65-69										60-79	0.8
70-74											
75-79											
80-84											
85-89			1					1	0.4	80-99	0.4
90-94											
95-99											
100-104											
105-109											

APPENDIX Q.13 (continued) page 636

Ratio	1	2	3	4	5	6	7	8
110-114								
115-119								
120-124								
125-129								
130-134								
135-139								
140-144								
145-149								
150-154								
155-159								
160-164								
165-169								
170-174								
175-179								
180-184								
185-189								
190-194								
195-199								
≥ 200								
def.								
NR	1							
N	30	11	8	19	34	33	8	16
Mean	20	27	17	30	18	22	16	14
Minimum	9	12	11	18	9	11	14	7
Maximum	32	42	24	63	33	39	21	32
Maximum as % of minimum	356	350	218	350	367	354	150	457

Ratio	9	10	11	12	13	14	15	All cases N	All cases %	Summary Range	Summary % of cases[a]
110-114											
115-119											
120-124										100-149	
125-129											
130-134											
135-139											
140-144											
145-149											
150-154										≥ 150	
155-159											
160-164											
165-169											
170-174											
175-179											
180-184											
185-189											
190-194											
195-199											
≥ 200											
def.											
NR						1		2	0.7		
N	10	10	7	35	7	40	1	269	100.0		
Mean	15	16	18	22	13	21	19	20			
Minimum	10	7	4	5	10	6		4			
Maximum	27	28	89	48	22	60		89			
Maximum as % of minimum	270	400	2,225	960	220	1,000	NA	2,225			

Note: [a]No return (NR) cases are excluded from the denominator.
Sources: Land tax duplicates, Oxfordshire Record Office; PP 1818 (82.) XIX (1815 property tax).

APPENDIX Q.14

Frequency distribution, net ratio of 1815 property tax valuations (schedule A) to land tax quotas, all townships, Surrey

Numbered columns:

1 = Blackheath hundred, first division
2 = Blackheath hundred, second division
3 = Brixton hundred, east division
4 = Brixton hundred, west division
5 = Copthorne hundred, first division
6 = Copthorne hundred, second division
7 = Effingham hundred
8 = Elmbridge hundred, first division
9 = Elmbridge hundred, second division
10 = Farnham hundred
11 = Godalming hundred, first division
12 = Godalming hundred, second division
13 = Godley hundred, first division
14 = Godley hundred, second division
15 = Kingston hundred, first division
16 = Kingston hundred, second division
17 = Reigate hundred, east division
18 = Reigate hundred, west division
19 = Tandridge hundred, first division
20 = Tandridge hundred, second division
21 = Wallington hundred, first division
22 = Wallington hundred, second division
23 = Woking hundred, first division
24 = Woking hundred, second division
25 = Wotton hundred, first division
26 = Wotton hundred, second division
27 = Guildford borough
28 = Southwark borough

Ratio	1	2	3	4	5	6	7	8	9	10	11	12	13	14	15	16	17	18
0-4																		
5-9		1				1										1		
10-14	4	5			1	2	2			1	2	3	3	1	2		3	4
15-19		1			1	1	1	3	2		3	1	1	1		1	1	3
20-24				1	1	2		1		1			1			2	1	
25-29			1	3		1			1	1					2			1
30-34				1	1										1			
35-39			1	1														
40-44				1														
45-49			1											1				
50-54																		
55-59			1															
60-64																		
65-69																		
70-74			2															
75-79																		
80-84																		
85-89																		
90-94																		
95-99																		

Ratio	19	20	21	22	23	24	25	26	27	28	All cases N	All cases %	Summary Range	Summary % of cases[a]
0-4									1		1	0.7		
5-9							1			1	5	3.4	0-19	58.2
10-14	3	1			2	3	2	1	2	2	49	33.1		
15-19	3				1	4		1		1	30	20.3		
20-24	2	5	3	2	1	1					24	16.2		
25-29		1	1	2							14	9.5	20-39	34.2
30-34			1	1	1					1	7	4.7		
35-39			1	1	1						5	3.4		
40-44											1	0.7		
45-49											2	1.4	40-59	3.4
50-54				1							1	0.7		
55-59											1	0.7		
60-64														
65-69													60-79	1.4
70-74											2	1.4		
75-79														
80-84														
85-89													80-99	
90-94														
95-99														

APPENDIX Q.14 (continued) page 640

Ratio	1	2	3	4	5	6	7	8	9	10	11	12	13	14	15	16	17	18
100-104																		
105-109				1														
110-114																		
115-119													1					
120-124																		
125-129																		
130-134																		
135-139																		
140-144																		
145-149																		
150-154				1														
155-159																		
160-164																		
165-169																		
170-174																		
175-179																		
180-184																		
185-189																		
190-194																		
195-199																		
≥ 200																		
def.			1							1								
NR																		
N	4	7	8	8	4	7	3	4	3	4	5	4	6	3	5	4	5	8
Mean	12	12	60	33	20	15	14	20	19	19	16	13	17	19	20	17	14	15
Minimum	11	8	27	24	11	5	13	16	15	13	12	11	12	10	13	9	11	11
Maximum	12	15	109	150	30	25	15	21	28	27	17	16	116	48	30	20	21	26
Maximum as % of minimum	109	188	404	625	273	500	115	131	187	208	142	145	967	480	231	222	191	236

Ratio	19	20	21	22	23	24	25	26	27	28	All cases N	All cases %	Summary Range	Summary % of cases[a]
100-104					1						1	0.7		
105-109											1	0.7		
110-114														
115-119											1	0.7	100-149	2.0
120-124														
125-129														
130-134														
135-139														
140-144														
145-149														
150-154											1	0.7		
155-159														
160-164														
165-169													≥ 150	0.7
170-174														
175-179														
180-184														
185-189														
190-194														
195-199														
≥ 200														
def.											2	1.4		
NR														
N	8	7	6	7	7	8	3	2	3	5	148	100.0		
Mean	16	19	30	27	22	16	10	14	8	16	25			
Minimum	13	13	20	21	14	13	9	11	2	7	2			
Maximum	20	26	38	54	103	20	11	15	12	31	150			
Maximum as % of minimum	154	200	190	257	736	154	122	136	600	443	7,500			

Note: [a]Defective (def.) cases are excluded from the denominator.
Sources: Land tax duplicates, Surrey Record Office; PP 1818 (82.) XIX (1815 property tax).

APPENDIX Q.15

Frequency distribution, net ratio of 1815 property tax valuations (schedule A) to land tax quotas, all townships, Westmorland

Numbered columns:

1 = East ward
2 = Kendal ward
3 = Lonsdale ward
4 = West ward

Ratio	1	2	3	4	All cases N	All cases %	Summary Range	Summary % of cases[a]
0-4								
5-9							0-19	
10-14								
15-19								
20-24								
25-29							20-39	
30-34								
35-39								
40-44	2	2			4	3.8		
45-49	3				3	2.9	40-59	10.6
50-54		1		2	3	2.9		
55-59								
60-64	4	2			6	5.7		
65-69	4	1		1	6	5.7	60-79	25.5
70-74	4				4	3.8		
75-79	1	4	1	2	8	7.6		
80-84	1			2	3	2.9		
85-89	1	4	1		6	5.7	80-99	20.2
90-94	2	3	1		6	5.7		
95-99	1	2		1	4	3.8		
100-104		1		1	2	1.9		
105-109		1	2	1	4	3.8		
110-114		3			3	2.9		
115-119			2	2	4	3.8		

120-124		1		2	3	2.9	100-149	29.8
125-129	1	3			4	3.8		
130-134		2		1	3	2.9		
135-139	1	1	1		3	2.9		
140-144			1		1	1.0		
145-149	1				1	1.0		
150-154		2			2	1.9		
155-159	1				1	1.0		
160-164			1		1	1.0		
165-169		1			1	1.0	≥ 150	13.8
170-174			1		1	1.0		
175-179		1	1		2	1.9		
180-184								
185-189								
190-194								
195-199		1			1	1.0		
200-249				1	1	1.0		
250-299								
300-349		1			1	1.0		
350-399								
400-449								
450-499								
500-549								
550-599								
600-649								
650-699								
700-749		1			1	1.0		
750-799								
800-849								
850-899								
900-949								
950-999								
≥ 1,000		1			1	1.0		
def.	2	1		6	9	8.6		
NR	1	1			2	1.9		
N	30	41	12	22	105	100.0		

APPENDIX Q.15 (continued) page 644

Ratio	1	2	3	4	All cases		Summary	
					N	%	Range	% of cases[a]
Mean	80	122	126	89	102			
Minimum	41	44	75	52	41			
Maximum	155	1,086	177	216	1,086			
Maximum as % of minimum	378	2,468	236	415	2,649			

Note: [a]Defective (def.) and no return (NR) cases are excluded from the denominator.
Sources: Land tax duplicates, Cumbria Record Office, Kendal; PP 1818 (82.) XIX (1815 property tax).

APPENDIX Q.16

Frequency distribution, net ratio of 1815 property tax valuations (schedule A) to land tax quotas, all tythings, Wiltshire

Numbered columns:

1 = Alderbury hundred
2 = Amesbury hundred
3 = Bradford hundred
4 = Branch and Dole hundred
5 = Calne hundred
6 = Cawdon and Cadworth hundred
7 = Chalk hundred
8 = Chippenham hundred
9 = North Damerham hundred
10 = South Damerham hundred
11 = Downton hundred

12 = Dunworth hundred
13 = Elstub and Everley hundred
14 = Frustfield hundred
15 = Heytesbury hundred
16 = Highworth, Cricklade and Staple hundred
17 = Kingsbridge hundred
18 = Kinwardstone hundred
19 = Malmesbury hundred
20 = Melksham hundred
21 = Mere hundred
22 = Potterne and Cannings hundred

23 = Ramsbury hundred
24 = Selkley hundred
25 = Swanborough hundred
26 = Underditch hundred
27 = Warminster hundred
28 = Westbury hundred
29 = Whorwelsdown hundred
30 = Devizes borough
31 = Marlborough borough
32 = Salisbury city

APPENDIX Q.16 (continued) page 646

Ratio	1	2	3	4	5	6	7	8	9	10	11	12	13	14	15
0-4															
5-9	1												1		
10-14	1			1		2						1			2
15-19	2	6	1	4		4	4	1			1		5	1	2
20-24	4	6	1	2		5	3			1	3	2	5	1	
25-29	2		3	6	4	1	1	2		1	2	2	2		4
30-34					2			2	1				1		3
35-39	1				1	1		2	1	1		3			
40-44									1	1					1
45-49								1				1			
50-54				1	1			1							
55-59															
60-64								2	1						
65-69								3	1						
70-74															
75-79															
80-84															
85-89															
90-94															
95-99															
100-104								1							
105-109															
110-114															
115-119															
120-124															
125-129															
130-134															
135-139															
140-144															
145-149															
150-154															
155-159															
160-164															
165-169															

Ratio	16	17	18	19	20	21	22	23	24	25	26	27	28	29	30
0-4			2												
5-9									2						
10-14		2	1					1	2	1	1			1	
15-19	10	5	2	2	3	1	2	2	7	4					
20-24	4	2	1	3	5	1	3			6		1		2	1
25-29	4	1	6	3		3	1			7	1	5	1	2	
30-34			2	5			2			3		2			
35-39	1			3						2	1	1			
40-44			1	2			1			1		1		1	
45-49				3											
50-54														1	
55-59														1	1
60-64															
65-69															
70-74															
75-79															
80-84															
85-89				1											
90-94															
95-99															
100-104															
105-109															
110-114															
115-119															
120-124															
125-129															
130-134															
135-139															
140-144															
145-149															
150-154															
155-159															
160-164															
165-169															

APPENDIX Q.16 (continued) page 648

Ratio	31	32	All cases N	All cases %	Summary Range	Summary % of cases[a]
0-4			2	0.6		
5-9		2	6	1.8	0-19	32.1
10-14			16	4.9		
15-19			69	21.0		
20-24			62	18.8		
25-29			64	19.4	20-39	57.6
30-34			23	7.0		
35-39			18	5.5		
40-44			10	3.0		
45-49			5	1.5	40-59	7.2
50-54			4	1.2		
55-59			2	0.6		
60-64			3	9.9		
65-69			4	1.2	60-79	2.4
70-74						
75-79						
80-84						
85-89			1	0.3	80-99	0.3
90-94						
95-99						
100-104			1	0.3		
105-109						
110-114						
115-119					100-149	0.3
120-124						
125-129						
130-134						
135-139						
140-144						
145-149						
150-154						
155-159						
160-164						
165-169					≥ 150	

Ratio	1	2	3	4	5	6	7	8	9	10	11	12	13	14	15
170-174															
175-179															
180-184															
185-189															
190-194															
195-199															
≥ 200															
def.		1								1		1			
NR	2	3		2		1		11			1				
N	13	16	5	16	8	14	8	26	5	5	7	10	14	2	12
Mean	18	19	25	23	40	21	22	47	48	30	22	30	22	17	25
Minimum	9	15	16	10	25	14	16	16	30	20	18	14	7	16	10
Maximum	36	24	27	53	53	35	26	102	66	44	26	48	31	22	42
Maximum as % of minimum	400	160	169	530	212	250	162	638	220	220	144	343	443	138	420

APPENDIX Q.16 (continued) page 650

Ratio	16	17	18	19	20	21	22	23	24	25	26	27	28	29	30
170-174															
175-179															
180-184															
185-189															
190-194															
195-199															
≥ 200															
def.		1		4						1					
NR	2		3				1		1					1	
N	21	11	18	26	8	5	10	3	12	25	3	10	1	9	2
Mean	20	17	18	32	21	25	24	14	13	24	25	34	28	25	26
Minimum	15	13	3	16	17	16	16	13	5	14	12	21		10	20
Maximum	37	29	42	87	23	29	40	19	17	40	35	43		56	55
Maximum as % of minimum	247	223	1,400	544	135	181	250	146	340	286	292	205	NA	560	275

			All cases		Summary	
Ratio	31	32	N	%	Range	% of cases[a]
170–174						
175–179						
180–184						
185–189						
190–194						
195–199						
≥ 200						
def.			9	2.7		
NR	2		30	9.1		
N	2	2	329	100.0		
Mean	NR	7	23			
Minimum		6	3			
Maximum		8	102			
Maximum as % of minimum	NA	133	3,400			

Note: [a]Defective (def.) and no return (NR) cases are excluded from the denominator.
Sources: Land tax duplicates, Wiltshire Record Office; PP 1818 (82.) XIX (1815 property tax).

Notes

ABBREVIATIONS

NYCRO North Yorkshire County Record Office
PP Parliamentary Papers

CHAPTER ONE

1 Soltow, "Wealth Distribution in England and Wales." For the debate which followed, see Ginter, "Wealth of Problems"; Wilson, "The Land Tax Problem"; Soltow, "Land Tax Redemption Records."
2 Johnson, *Disappearance of the Small Landowner*. These were the Ford Lectures for that year. For a fuller and balanced account of the early historiography, see especially Mingay's introduction to Gonner, *Common Land and Inclosure* and Mingay, *Enclosure and the Small Farmer*. Much of the ground has more recently been surveyed by Turner in *Enclosures in Britain*, chapter 5. Cf. Douglas, *Land, People & Politics*.
3 Toynbee's *Lectures on the Industrial Revolution in England* were published posthumously in 1884, one year after his death. Useful excerpts are conveniently reprinted in Taylor, ed., *Industrial Revolution in Britain*. Although Toynbee was by no means a Marxist, many of his views may be found in the writings of Marx. More modern views of the agricultural revolution, especially since the 1960s, tend to emphasize its gradual character. See Kerridge, *Agricultural Revolution*, which places primary importance on the developments of the sixteenth and seventeenth centuries, but in a manner which has provoked much controversy. A more judicious view may be found in Chambers and Mingay, *Agricultural Revolution 1750–1880*, where the importance of earlier innovations is acknowledged. The linkages between the agricultural and industrial revolutions continue to define important avenues for research today, partly through the intermediary of

demographic variables such as nutrition, fertility, and age at marriage, but also through economic assumptions regarding transfers of labour and capital and the development of demand curves. The spirit of Toynbean analysis is reflected in the influential essay of Ashton, *Industrial Revolution*, where the industrial revolution is characterized as "a movement," occurring under differing conditions in different countries, and everywhere entailing (among other effects) "a conversion of rural into urban communities and a rise of new social classes" (98).

4 Mantoux, *La révolution industrielle au XVIIIe siècle* was published in Paris in 1905. A newly revised and translated English edition was published in London in 1928. The above quotations are taken from the second revised English edition entitled *Industrial Revolution in the Eighteenth Century*, 136–7, 141n. There was a widespread assumption – or perhaps one should say an implication – in the early literature that in earlier centuries of English history small owner-occupiers, or yeomen, had been widely dispersed throughout the countryside and numerically dominant. It was rarely specified when that golden age of an English peasantry was supposed to have occurred, or for how long, though its decline was most often traced from the close of the fifteenth century. Since quantitative benchmarks for the early period have not been established, and probably cannot be, *rates* of decline cannot really be measured. My own feeling is that if there ever was a golden age – and there may not have been – it was confined to the fifteenth century, when servile tenure became transformed into leasehold and copyhold, and much freehold came into the hands of former villeins in an unusually active land market. See Hilton, *Decline of Serfdom in Medieval England*. To some extent the "decline" discussed in the literature (and everyone agrees that there was one – debate only centres on its degree, timing, and consequences) may be no more than a measurement (vaguely formulated due to a lack of precise statistics) from a high water mark which was itself intrinsically unusual. The situation in the medieval centuries was not a simple one. Joan Thirsk has described a sort of rough homogenization of village landholding structure occurring in the east midlands from Domesday to the thirteenth century, with free tenants increasing in those villages where they previously had scarcely existed and decreasing where they previously had dominated. Thirsk, "Field Systems of the East Midlands," especially 264–5. Whether free tenants under medieval manorial conditions constitute "yeomen" or "owner-occupiers" in a sense comparable to later centuries is another question. I would argue they do not. If not, then any "decline" in "owner" occupation – or even smaller tenancies – since the fifteenth century (if it can be measured) may be no more than a long secular adjustment to the extraordinary transitional conditions of that century, an adjustment in which prices and other economic and demographic factors played their role. Nostalgia for a mythical golden age, however, is misplaced.

5 Johnson, *Disappearance of the Small Landowner*; Gray, "Yeoman Farming in Oxfordshire."
6 See note 1 above.
7 For examples of this work, see especially the essays by Noble, Henstock, and Unwin in *Land and Property*, ed. Turner and Mills.
8 The revisions of the later Stuart period were inaugurated by the 1965 Ford Lectures of Plumb, *Growth of Political Stability in England*. The most comprehensive statement is still found in Holmes, *British Politics in the Age of Anne*. Both emphasized the fundamental importance of the emergence of political parties in this early period, but neither endorsed the older, and then discredited, view of political party continuity following 1714, a view which had been demolished by Namier in his *Structure of Politics* and *England in the Age of the American Revolution*. The continuity of the Whig and Tory parties into the reigns of George I and George II, and perhaps beyond, have been subsequently urged by, among others, Colley, *In Defiance of Oligarchy*; Hill, *Growth of Parliamentary Parties* and *British Parliamentary Parties*.
9 During the early 1960s I uncovered the papers of William Adam of Blair Adam. Adam turned out to be the political manager, or what we would now call the chief whip, of the Whig opposition during the late 1780s and early 1790s. His papers showed that a modern political party organization emerged in England during those years and, in my view, for the first time. See my *Whig Organization* and my article "Financing of the Whig Party Organization." O'Gorman's often cited *Whig Party and the French Revolution* is reasonably sound in narrating the party split but is a grievously misleading guide to organizational developments. His facts and interpretations concerning national organization are repeatedly and grossly inaccurate, and he misses many of the capital points to be found in the Blair Adam papers. The shift to political parties among the borough electorate during the 1780s has recently been argued persuasively and with a massive data base by Phillips, *Electoral Behavior*.
10 This interpretation seems to have originated with Ostrogorski, *Democracy and the Organization of Political Parties*. For the classic later work, see Gash, *Politics in the Age of Peel*. A well-informed summary of nineteenth century developments, and one which takes this classic view, may be found in McKenzie, *British Political Parties*, chapters 1, 4(i), and 5(i).
11 It has begun for example in Cannon, ed., *Whig Ascendancy*.
12 Rudé, *Wilkes and Liberty*.
13 Phillips, *Electoral Behavior*.

CHAPTER TWO

1 For the classic debate regarding the importance of these relatively minor but significant difficulties, see Mingay, "Land Tax Assessments and the Small

Landowner''; Martin, ''Landownership and the Land Tax Returns''; Mingay, ''Letter to the Editor.''

2 These remarks in no way endorse the rash procedures of Davies, ''Small Landowner,'' 276n.: ''Since the assessors were meticulous in their use of titles such as Esqs., Revs., etc., the occupying owners not so described have been included with the occupying owners of the yeoman class, despite the fact that they contributed over £20.'' As Mingay rightly noted in ''Land Tax Assessments and the Small Landowner,'' 383, the assessors were by no means meticulous in their use of titles and status ascriptions. Indeed the names themselves can sometimes be recognized only phonetically, and it is not unusual for a major landowner to be entered without a status ascription or title, especially on smaller holdings. My remarks must therefore be understood to emphasize a considerable knowledge of regional landholding and a prudent use of land tax duplicates for adjacent series of years. The unfortunate consequences of Davies' procedure should also be noted. He almost certainly lumped some of the estates of some of his gentry into ''yeoman'' class intervals, thus deflating the size of his gentry holdings and enlarging his population of yeomen.

3 Mingay, ''Land Tax Assessments and the Small Landowner,'' 387–8, was the first to draw these conclusions forcefully: ''even if the returns were a perfectly clear, consistent and accurate guide, the counting from them of the numbers of owners, and the placing of these owners in various categories according to the acreages which the assessments are supposed to represent, would still result often enough in a picture of landholding remote from reality. The return referred of course to the parish, but in fact it was not very uncommon for even the smaller owners to have land in more than one parish. (Some of the 'absentee ownership' was due to small owners having detached parcels of land let out in other parishes.) Small owners might therefore be on average somewhat larger proprietors than the figures from the returns would suggest. Furthermore, they might more often be much larger *farmers*. The discussion of the increase or decline of small owners never seems to have taken into account the fact that in this period a significant proportion of small owners rented land: although they were only small *owners* of land, they might still be quite substantial *farmers* of land. In the later eighteenth century small owners quite often rented as much or considerably more land than they occupied as owners. ... It is also likely, although here direct evidence is difficult to obtain, that small owners not infrequently rented land in neighbouring parishes, instead of, or perhaps in addition to, land rented in their own parish. ... What is certain is that there was often greater fluidity in the total size of small men's farmland than is sometimes supposed, for the acreage of both their owned and rented land often varied considerably over a period of years. In this context, the apparent shifts in arbitrary categories of small owners, based only on the

acreages of owned land as deduced from the land tax assessments, may not be at all meaningful.'' Martin failed to address this point in his 1966 article responding to Mingay. But in ''Parliamentary Enclosure Movement,'' 28, he briefly made the same point: ''In freehold society ... it was the neighbourhood, rather than the village or parish, which formed the unit of family relations, and sometimes of ownership also,'' adding in a footnote ''This is one of the weaknesses of using Land Tax Returns which has not perhaps received the attention it deserves.'' Hunt, ''Land Tax Assessments,'' 286, conceded the same point but, without offering any grounds, went on to conclude ''This does not mean that the assessments should be discarded altogether as a source of enquiry on the much-debated problem of the 'disappearance of the small landowners.' On the contrary, they remain an essential guide to the moving picture of land distribution in any given village during the period of violent price fluctuations from 1780 to 1830'' even though ''a proportion – perhaps only a small proportion – of both owners and tenants were paying in more than one parish.'' There has still been no serious and sustained attention to this problem reported in the literature. County poll books, which list both the residence and the qualifying freehold for each voter, make it abundantly clear that a very large proportion of both urban and rural landholders, including even labourers, held freeholds in townships outside that in which they resided.

4 Examples to be found among the assessors and collectors of the North Riding in 1830 are reported in appendix G.2. Some townships were held entirely by one or two tenant farmers. Such large holdings would not have been possible without considerable capital. It cannot therefore be assumed that these large tenants lacked the capital to purchase holdings, if suitable holdings had been available and they had desired to do so. Unless it can be shown that the local land market was essentially closed, it must be assumed that economic choice was at work, and the patterns of such choice must inform our explanations of both ''smallholder'' and owner-occupier decline.

5 Mingay, ''Land Tax Assessments and the Small Landowner,'' 383–4, rightly pointed out that ''the frequent inclusion of some names two or three times in the same return (either because an owner pays separately for individual parcels of his land, or because there were in the parish two or more men of the same name) obviously entails some risk of double-counting.'' Martin, ''Landownership and the Land Tax Returns,'' 96–7, acknowledged that problems may arise from ''the frequent inclusion of some names two or three times in the same return because an owner was paying separately for individual parcels of land'' but concluded that such problems ''can easily be coped with, once the student is aware of the dangers.'' Martin's phrasing suggests that he had in mind only multiple entries of the same person, however. He ignored Mingay's further stipulation that multiple persons with the same name may be present.

6 For the classic essays on nominal record linkage see Wrigley, ed., *Identifying People in the Past.*

7 The designation of "Sr" or "Jr" seems to have been employed with some consistency, but numerous exceptions have been found in comparing land tax duplicates with county rate valuations and estate records. Let there be no misunderstanding: Linking within townships will produce some amount of error. The proportion of such errors for any given township would be extremely small, however; and very few townships would be so affected. The error in accepting such designations for linkage seems statistically trivial, and the compensatory gains fully justify such a procedure.

8 Gray, "Yeoman Farming in Oxfordshire," 300–1; Hunt, "Land Tax Assessments," 285; "Landownership and Enclosure" 498.

9 Glebe is not always separately identified as such. Tithe is sometimes specified as having been aggregated into the landed entries of major landowners who are impropriators. The North Riding valuations for the county rate in 1824 also clearly indicate that tithe was often being silently incorporated into numerous tax entries for land within a single township. In other townships tithe entries were separately reported. The land tax duplicates for Rosedale East Side in the later 1820s specifically state that every line entry represents a combined tax on both rent and tithe. Such practices were common, as other duplicates show. In Wiltshire a large number of duplicates list one or more properties as a "parsonage." Since such entries characteristically bear very large tax values (often considerably higher in their proportions to total tax than "tithe" entries in other counties), it is possible that several categories of entry were being mixed. At the very least one can conclude that assessors in general were highly inconsistent in reporting tithe, even within a county. It is in fact uncertain that tithe was always taxed, at least in all its forms. Some degree of incomparability *may* therefore remain even when tithe entries are included in the data base. But incomparabilities probably arise in fewer cases when tithes are included in the analysis.

10 See chapter 5 below for a more extended discussion of the problems entailed by acreage conversions.

11 For an example of long secular comparisons of tax entries grouped by unadjusted class intervals, see Grover's comparisons of tax entries for c. 1702 and c. 1781 in fifteen parishes of Kent and Sussex, "Early Land Tax Assessments Explored," table 6. The tax quotas recorded in that table for several of the parishes are significantly different in the two years. It should also be remembered, of course, that "quotas" and tax entries must be adjusted when the statutory rate differs.

12 Habakkuk, "English Landownership," 9.

CHAPTER THREE

1 The linkage of names between townships for small and middling proprietors and tenants is the only problem discussed in chapter 2 which is not sufficiently resolvable.
2 For a recent example of such a procedure, see Soltow, "Wealth Distribution in England and Wales." I raised preliminary objections to this procedure in "Problems with the Land Tax," 418.
3 Gray, "Yeoman Farming in Oxfordshire," 300, imposed a cutoff at 6s. His object was to eliminate non-agricultural properties from his analysis of owner-occupiers. He was prepared to accept buildings, provided some "land" was attached. He recognized that variations in tax rates and property values could cause some proportion of small cottagers who held a few acres to fall both above and below his cutoff. Gray does not seem to have been equally aware of the dangers of multiple listings per line entry. Nor was he aware that many small to middling occupiers may have been excluded from the land tax duplicates.
4 Mingay, "Land Tax Assessments and the Small Landowner," 383; Martin, "Landownership and the Land Tax Returns," 97; Wilson, "Land Tax and West Derby Hundred," 71. Turner cites an example of the phenomenon at Stoke Mandeville in "Parliamentary Enclosure and Landownership Change in Buckinghamshire," 570.
5 Wilson, "Land Tax and West Derby Hundred," 80–1.
6 See especially Noble, "Physical Development of Country Towns," table 3. See also her conclusion on page 116. Banks has examined the size of holdings for each proprietor in eighty-nine rural parishes of northwest Norfolk, comparing the estimates based on acreage conversions from the 1831 land tax duplicates with estimates derived from the tithe apportionments of c. 1840. She found that the land tax duplicates collectively reported 25 percent fewer proprietors than did the tithe surveys. The missing proprietors were, in an overwhelming proportion of cases, very small holders. Banks' findings are reported in "Parish Landownership," 46, and are discussed in chapter 5 below.
7 Tate, *Domesday of English Enclosure Acts and Awards*, 294–301.
8 Burn, *Justice of the Peace*, 1:438. The county rate, like the poor rate, was "not a charge upon the land, but upon the occupier in respect of the land," ibid, 3:587. The land tax was, by contrast, a charge directly upon the land. Such an observation does not constitute an objection to this analysis, however. The land tax duplicates must be seen as an accounting system for the collection of such charges. So long as the land tax duplicates appear to report all occupiers, and do not employ such entries as "sundry tenants,"

the properties assessed to the land tax should be fully traceable to the county rate through the matching of occupiers. Under such conditions, any occupiers appearing on the county rate but not on the land tax duplicate must constitute a property omitted from the land tax. A major problem was encountered only in Rainton; appendix B.1, col. 1 for this township is thus treated as defective. The reader will notice that appendix B.1 calculates missing *occupiers*. Appendix B.2 calculates missing *properties*, i.e., individual entries in the county rate valuation without aggregating for multiple holdings of a single occupier. The discussion in the following paragraph is based principally on percentages of missing occupiers, since there is some chance that some properties held by a single occupier and shown as separate properties on the county rate valuation have been aggregated into a single occupier entry on the land tax.

9 See especially Wrigley, ed., *Nineteenth Century Society*, 90–105. Payne mentioned missing properties, as well as problems associated with labourers' cottages, in "Property in Land in South Bedfordshire," but failed to pursue the problem systematically. Sheppard, "Inhabited Houses," confirms that houses are sometimes *under*enumerated in the 1801–31 censuses. Underenumeration further strengthens my conclusions.

10 It may be that some proportion of such annotations in the duplicates refer to no more than the value of the holding itself, namely, that it is valued at less than £1 rental. Observe the wording in Burn, *Justice of the Peace*, 3:42 [land tax]: "No poor person shall be charged with, or liable to the pound rate, whose lands, tenements, or hereditaments are not of the full yearly value of 20s. in the whole." But the evidence presented in Payne, ibid, makes it clear that some landlords and larger tenants in some parishes were concerned to exempt poor but rateable cottagers, even in so heavily taxed a county as Bedfordshire (see chapter 15 below for Bedfordshire being the most heavily taxed county in the kingdom for its land).

11 Burn, *Justice of the Peace*, 3:576–7.

12 This statement should not be interpreted to mean that tax values can be totalled across township boundaries in order to compute percentages within regions. Tax values are not comparable between townships, due to differences in ratios of valuation to tax. See especially chapter 14.

13 Gray, "Yeoman Farming in Oxfordshire," 299, noted that "In a few cases lessees for long terms of years are substituted for owners." Since he cited only three parishes, he apparently believed he had successfully identified and eliminated all such cases. Davies, "Small Landowner," 272, was able to find leaseholders in the proprietor column in at least one additional Oxfordshire parish. He noted the frequent appearances of the terms copyholder and leaseholder in the property description columns, and in the end he concluded that these forms of tenure could not be systematically disentangled from freehold in counting "proprietors." He therefore included

them. Mingay, "Land Tax Assessments and the Small Landowner," 383, noted leaseholders as a problem, citing Gray, but neglected Davies' caution regarding copyholders. Mingay also suggested that "it is possible that tenant farmers who paid the land tax as an addition to their rent (instead of deducting it from the rent, as was the usual practice) may have been carelessly returned as owners." I have found no evidence for such a practice among assessors. See my remarks later in this chapter on who paid the tax. Martin, "Landownership and the Land Tax Returns," 97, in responding to Mingay suggested that a use of enclosure awards, parliamentary poll lists, and manorial and other land-owning records "enables the student to go a long way in solving the problems of distinguishing landowners from leaseholders in those few cases where this is not clear." This unsupported and sanguine view is wholly unwarranted. Enclosure awards, along with manorial and estate records, where they survive, will certainly solve some number of problems. But even under the most favourable conditions of survival, such records are not systematic in their geographical coverage. Poll books before 1832 convey no *reliable* information whatever regarding tenure. Nor are only a "few" cases at risk in most counties. The problem lies precisely in our inability to identify all such cases, though enough can be identified to demonstrate the problem is significant. Martin made no mention of copyholders.

14 On tenurial relations in Muker and Arkengarthdale see *Victoria History of York, North Riding*, ed. Page, 1:38, 240–2. Hartley and Ingilby, *Old Hand-Knitters of the Dales*, 22; Fieldhouse and Jennings, *History of Richmond and Swaledale*.

15 Attempts to achieve a more complete annual bookkeeping are discernible in some townships. For example, the town of Whitby regularly entered both the tax for each tenant and the total tax (i.e., the combined tenant entries) of each proprietor. The recording of both sums was clearly unnecessary for tax collection purposes. Such a practice is widely (but not commonly) encountered in the later duplicates.

16 In the eighteenth century it was generally believed that owners bore the burden of the tax. Davies, "Small Landowner," 271–2, pondered the significance of the fact that the pre-1780 returns recorded only a single list of names, without distinguishing between proprietors and tenants. He noted that after 1780 some of the earlier names were entered as proprietors, while others were entered as tenants. He concluded that "the tenant was responsible for the payment of the tax; and that this had greatly influenced the mode of compilation previous to 1780, the assessor having adopted the practice of inserting the name of the payee, whether landlord or tenant, in the one column of the assessment." His evidence therefore suggested that payees included mixtures of both proprietors and tenants. Habakkuk, "English Landownership," 9, lent his considerable authority to the

eighteenth century view, suggesting that on many estates tenants had paid a share of the old parliamentary assessment; some had paid it all. But in the late seventeenth and early eighteenth centuries in Northamptonshire and Bedfordshire "the land tax was in almost all cases paid by the landowner and attempts to shift the incidence on to the tenant failed." Mingay, "Land Tax Assessments and the Small Landowner," 382, shared this view, but more cautiously, citing eighteenth century commentators as evidence that "in the midlands and north it was not very uncommon for the tax to be paid by the tenants without deduction from their rents." Beckett, "Local Custom and the 'New Taxation,' " 116–17, found direct evidence that actual practice varied in Cumberland and perhaps elsewhere, despite local testimony to the contrary. Cf. Beckett, "Land Tax Administration." Direct evidence to support my hypothesis is available in a number of townships. For example, the 1832 duplicate for Crathorne in Langbaurgh wapentake records thirty-three tenants on the lands of Michael Tasburgh. Valuational rents were assigned individually to each tenant, but only a total tax for the entire Tasburgh property was given. The following note was entered at the end of the Tasburgh properties in the property description column: "The above let Land Tax free & paid by Mr. Tasburgh." Comparable examples from other townships could also be cited. But while actual practice undoubtedly varied, and contemporary opinion and modern historians might differ, later eighteenth century law appears to have been quite clear on who technically owed the tax: the tenant. King's Bench found that "With respect to the public, it [the land tax] is a tenant's tax, and consequently where both landlords' and tenants' names are upon the rate, it is prima facie a rating of the tenant." *Rex* v. *Mitcham*, Cald. 276: *S. P. In re St. Lawrence, Winchester*, Cald. 379. *Caldecott's Settlement Cases* reports cases in King's Bench for 17 to 27 Geo. III. The opinion is cited in Harrison, *Analytical Digest*, 3:1892.

17 This is not to argue that the holdings of tenants on multiple tenant estates are "small" but only that they are "smaller" than the combined holdings of their proprietor – an important distinction, as we shall see shortly when we come to discuss recent findings by Dennis Mills.

18 Mills contributed chapter 11 and Grover chapter 12 to *Land and Property*, ed. Turner and Mills. The following account of their views, including quotations and references to tables, is taken from those two essays. It may be that not all surviving pre-1780 duplicates are in single-column format. Grover found that thirteen out of thirty-two surviving c. 1702 duplicates for Hastings Rape in Sussex reported both occupiers and proprietors, while forty-five out of fifty-five 1699 duplicates for St Augustine East division in Kent also did so. But Grover did not indicate whether some entries in these duplicates just happen additionally to indicate proprietors when tenants are listed (as in Mills' table 2), but in single-column format, or whether these

duplicates are fully in the double-column format of later years, where a fuller accounting system of occupancy is clearly present and owner-occupancy can be inferred or ascribed with more confidence. Mills, in his chapter, assures us that *all* duplicates utilized by Grover are in the later double-column format, but this assertion does not conform to Grover's own description of his type-one or type-two duplicates as illustrated in his tables. Mills found only single-column formats in Rutland. The early returns for Birdforth wapentake in the North Riding of Yorkshire, which I have utilized here in chapters 2 and 4, are exclusively in single-column format with only occasional tenure attributions.

19 It is not clear whether Mills' type-one lists *only* contain entries where both tenant and proprietor are given, or whether in addition they contain entries of single names that do not specify tenurial status. But, even if he found no such intermixtures in Rutland, they exist elsewhere. Some of the early single-column duplicates of Birdforth wapentake in the North Riding of Yorkshire contain sporadic entries ascribing tenure or ownership, while the remaining entries in those duplicates give no more than a name. It is by no means certain that the entries giving no more than a name on such duplicates (or some proportion of such entries) are not tenants; nor, if they are all owners, is it clear that they are owner-occupiers.

20 Examples of large tenancies may be found in appendices A, F, and G. If there are any lingering doubts about the inadequacy of Mills' evidence as presented in his table 3, let me put them to rest with these few additional observations. As this volume shall demonstrate over and over again, both tax entries and tax quotas in the land tax duplicates are not comparable between townships in their absolute values, not even in the early eighteenth century. Identical values (say £5) in two different townships do not represent the same amounts of rent or wealth or acres. It would therefore be spurious to submit Mills' mean tax series to more sophisticated analysis, by comparing the distribution to that derived in other counties, for example. The data simply will not sustain more formal statistical routines. Even the more informal observations I have presented have a dubious character, to the extent that they suggest comparisons between the parishes. Nor can I accept the reliability of Mills' parish acreage figures. He derives his acreages from the *Victoria History of the County of Rutland* "on the assumption that parish acreages did not change between 1712 and the end of the nineteenth century." This is a rash assumption indeed. See my analysis of the reliability of acreages in chapter 5. It might be noted that the ratios of tax to acres (such as they are) in his forty-four parishes are ranged on a normal curve from 0.8 to 32, with 19 cases falling below 10 and above 19. Even if the acreage totals were reliable, a distribution such as this provides a very shaky basis for estimating largeness and smallness of holdings from absolute values.

21 Professor Mingay informs me he found evidence on the Kingston estates that in depressed times the tax was paid by the proprietor, but that in good times the proprietor shifted the burden on to the tenant without reducing the rent. I have found that some land tax duplicates also vary over periods of years in reporting, or failing to report, the tax at the level of the tenant on a given estate. Perhaps this reflects the variations in payment responsibilities Mingay encountered.

22 See note 16 above.

CHAPTER FOUR

1 Wilson, "Land Tax and West Derby Hundred," 64–6; Ward, *English Land Tax*, 32–3, 130. Turner briefly reviewed the problem of double assessment in his introduction to *Land and Property*, 3–4. Beckett, "Land Tax Administration," 166, found that Roman Catholics "in practice" were "rarely" double assessed in Cumbria.

2 As late as 1830, I found notations of double assessment in the North Riding upland township of Bowes.

3 For full computations of such ratios throughout the three ridings of Yorkshire, and a discussion of the results, see chapter 14 below, appendices M and P.1–3, and maps 9, 12, and 15.

4 For a full discussion of these ratios, see chapters 13 and 14. Table 4.1 includes only those estates listed at £100 or more annual value in Estcourt and Payne, eds., *English Catholic Nonjurors*, 299–305. Not all Catholic estates were so registered, or at least they do not all appear in that book. The argument does not rest on the completeness of the sample, however. It only requires a number of illustrative examples.

5 See chapters 14 and 15.

6 As we shall see shortly, when we again examine Welwick, the cessation of double assessment might lead to a general revaluation of a township for tax purposes. If an old valuational base was badly out of date, a general revaluation might correct extensive accumulated anomalies and thus cause even the tax on the Catholic properties to rise. Such appears to be precisely the situation Wilson found in Ince Blundell ("Land Tax and West Derby Hundred," 64, 89).

7 The evidence of the land tax duplicates is confirmed by *Victoria History of York, North Riding*, ed. Page, 1:508, which records that the manor and capital messuage of East Ness was released by the Crathorne trustees in 1788 to the use of Thomas Kendall for 2,000 years; and by *Victoria History of York, East Riding*, ed. Allison, 5:142–3, which records the 1796 sale by H.R. Crathorne of Welwick Farm in Welwick Provost manor to Thomas Fewson and of 416 acres of Ploughland manor to Robert Taylor. Welwick Thorpe manor was not sold until 1819. The VCH makes no mention of sales

of smaller parcels. The seat of the family in the eighteenth century appears to have been at East Ness and not on the ancient holdings at Crathorne. Contemporaries referred to the head of the family as Crathorne of East Ness, rather than as Crathorne of Crathorne, which was genealogically more correct.

8 Roebuck, *Yorkshire Baronets*, 57, 171–3, 202, 322. Cf. the evidence given in PP 1828 (550.) IV 20, where the Hunlokes of Derbyshire are described as paying half of their tenants' double assessed land tax.

9 Rack rent for Welwick in 1803 can be computed from PP 1803–04 (175.) XIII 596, col. 3.

10 Evidence before the 1828 select committee suggested that it was the large estates, such as that of the Crathornes in Welwick, which experienced the most severe difficulties in reaching agreements to end double assessment. William Blount, who acted as auditor to several large Catholic landlords, testified on conditions at the end of the eighteenth century: "In parishes where a Roman Catholic possessed or paid a small proportion of the rate, he might certainly obtain partial relief. I have a letter here from Mr. Baylis, the agent of Sir William Jerningham, who in the year 1796 applied to the parish of Painswick in the county of Gloucester, to be relieved of his double tax. He called a meeting of the vestry, and the parishioners consented to abate about one-third, taking upon themselves to make up the payment. Mr. Baylis says in his letter, what is not so much law as matter of feeling, 'I called a parish meeting, and I informed the gentlemen of the parish that Parliament had relieved the Catholics from the double Land Tax, and that Sir William expected to be assessed to the Land Tax in future as other inhabitants of the parish were. To which the gentlemen readily assented, and it was agreed that 2d. in the pound should be added to the then existing rent upon all land, tithe, and houses in the parish, which took off from Sir William about £22 and this was done in a most handsome manner without a dissenting voice, as no man ever lived that was more respected by the parish of Painswick than Sir William Jerningham.' But where he was owner of a large part of a parish he could hardly obtain any; and if he possessed a whole parish since the 38 Geo. 3 c. 60 (the Redemption Act) the commissioners would refuse altogether to give relief." PP 1828 (550.) IV 18. It should also be noted that Welwick did not merely halve the Crathorne tax. Nor should historians *necessarily* do so when adjusting for double assessment entries. The persistence of double assessment may be coupled with a long term failure to revaluate, as in Welwick, in which case a simple reduction by 50 percent would be inappropriate.

11 It is entirely possible that the sudden appearance or disappearance of smallholders in the land tax duplicates at the time of enclosure, so widely reported by students, may to some degree be the result of similar efforts to meet the quota under conditions of radical revaluation.

12 PP 1828 (550.) IV. There is a brief chapter devoted to Roman Catholic double assessment in Bourdin, *Land Tax*, 51–8. The discussion in Bourdin is heavily based on the report of the 1828 select committee and adds little to it. The information in the report is much fuller and should be used in interpreting Bourdin.

13 Burn, *Justice of the Peace*, 4:10–11.

14 Nothing is known about the actual operation of double assessments in the later nineteenth century. The Roman Catholic Relief Act of 1829 made no provision for ending such assessments, and the report of the 1828 select committee makes it clear that double assessments were then still common among those townships or parishes which had held Catholic estates in the earlier eighteenth century. Bourdin, *Land Tax*, 55–8 notes that the proceedings of the 1828 select committee resulted in the passage of 1 & 2 Wm. IVc. 21, in September 1831. That statute provided explicit machinery for the discharging of double assessments. The amount to be discharged was the balance exceeding "the just proportion which would have been charged on the said estates" had the owner not been Roman Catholic at the time of the imposition. Note, however, that so simple an approach would, by the 1830s, have caused new imbalances in the distribution of parish quotas within a division. It may be that the commissioners of taxes would in practice have elected to discharge a sum which would have more precisely fit the land values current within the parish (when the Catholic properties did not comprise the whole) and the hundred division. Lesser adjustments had been characteristic in the 1790s, as we shall see. It may be well to suspend judgment on the actual operation of the 1831 statute until we have direct evidence of how, and to what extent, it was applied. It is possible that the act caused some amount of quota alteration during the years following its passage; but, by that date, double assessment was intrinsically difficult to prove, and especially on those great estates which comprised all or virtually all of the parish in which they lay. The 1828 select committee also heard testimony that Lord Shrewsbury had earlier sought relief from double assessment for his estate at Bampton in Oxfordshire, basing his plea on the 84th clause of 38 Geo. III c. 5. According to Shrewsbury's auditor, the case was taken before King's Bench, seeking a mandamus. The plea was successful, and the commissioners were required to reassess the quotas of the entire hundred. The report leaves the impression that this procedure, and its result, were virtually unique due to the enormous expense.

15 For information on Yorkshire Catholics, in addition to Estcourt and Payne, eds., *English Catholic Nonjurors*, see the works of Aveling, *Post Reformation Catholicism in East Yorkshire*; "Catholic Recusants of the West Riding"; *Northern Catholics*.

16 The Breckenbrough case is not a clear one when considering quotas, however. The reduction on the Smithson property appears in 1699. But the

returns for 1696–98 are not extant. The reduction may therefore have occurred prior to the establishment of quotas, as such, in 1698. Such reductions could easily have been made under a system of direct poundage rates.

17 This conclusion must be understood to be tentative. See Bourdin, *Land Tax*, 55–8, for a discussion of the provisions (but not the practice) of 1 & 2 Wm. IV c. 21, which provided machinery for the end of double assessment. How that machinery was applied, and to what extent, is unknown. Those North Riding duplicates which survive for 1832 show no alterations in the quotas of townships listed in table 4.4. So small an amount of negative evidence, and at so early a date, is inconclusive, however.

18 Aveling, "Catholic Recusants of the West Riding," 258.

19 Indeed double assessment in single proprietor townships is meaningless by the 1790s, after a century of differentially rising land values. Only in a comparative inter-township context could it be meaningful. But quotas in general had long ceased to be comparable (if they ever were) between townships, with respect to wealth. Since this lack of comparability was well known at the time, single proprietor townships had little incentive, or even moral and legal grounds, to seek an end to provisions that had originally been designed as penalties. This realization may have further contributed to the continuance of the old penal quotas in such townships.

CHAPTER FIVE

1 Johnson, *Disappearance of the Small Landowner*.

2 Gray, "Yeoman Farming in Oxfordshire," 300, 303, 305, 306, 308, 309n.

3 Davies, "Small Landowner," 1:287n., 291 (table 7).

4 Chambers, "Enclosure and the Small Landowner," 122n., 126n. It is curious that Chambers did not cite Gray.

5 Hunt, "Landownership and Enclosure," 498–9, 501n. Ten years later Hunt rejected acreage equivalents as unreliable, "Land Tax Assessments," 285–6.

6 Grigg, "Land Tax Returns," 83–8.

7 Mingay, "Land Tax Assessments and the Small Landowner," 384–8.

8 Martin, "Landownership and the Land Tax Returns," 99–103. It should be noted that in one of his five sample parishes, Cubbington, the enclosure award was dated 1768, while the land tax duplicate was for the year 1781. Some of the error may be due to landholding transactions which occurred in the interim.

9 Mingay, "Letter to the Editor," 18.

10 I.e., conversion factors (acreage equivalents), if the statutory rate for the land tax were at 4s. in the pound, as it was by the 1780s.

11 Banks, "Land Tax Assessments in West Norfolk," 42 (table 1). The following comments on her work are based on this article.

12 Mills, *Lord and Peasant*; Obelkevich, *Religion and Rural Society*; Banks, "Open and Close Parishes in Nineteenth-Century England." See also Grigg, "Land Tax Returns."

13 The six Banks intervals, with the percentage of total acres owned by each class as estimated by the tithe survey (T) and by the land tax (LT), are given below. The number of cases is given in parentheses.

	(T)		(LT)	
Owners of 1,000 acres plus	3.7	(69)	3.9	(55)
Owners of 500–999 acres	1.9	(36)	4.1	(58)
Owners of 100–499 acres	7.0	(132)	14.0	(196)
Owners of 10–99 acres	19.0	(351)	35.0	(491)
Owners of 1–9 acres	29.0	(544)	41.0	(584)
Owners of less than 1 acre	40.0	(747)	1.7	(24)

14 Banks incorrectly interprets her Spearman coefficients as though they were Pearson product-moment correlation coefficients. She interprets an earlier set of Spearman coefficients as suggesting that "between eighty and eighty five percent of the variation in one variable can be explained by variation in the other." See for example Blalock, *Social Statistics*, 321, where he explains that neither the Spearman nor the Tau coefficients "can be interpreted in terms of the percentage of variation explained since the notion of variation, as we have been using the term [and as Banks employs it], is meaningless with ordinal scales." Only an intuitive interpretation, noting placement along the +1 to -1 range and comparative differences among different results, can be given.

15 Turner, "Parish Landownership and the Land Tax Assessments in Twelve Buckinghamshire Parishes: a Comparison with Enclosure Awards," *Land and Property* chapter 3. See also his introductory chapter in the same volume, where his endorsement of acreage equivalents is much more guarded.

16 The eight Turner intervals are:

≥ 300 acres	25–49 acres
200–299 acres	10–24 acres
100–199 acres	5–9 acres
50–99 acres	< 5 acres

17 Eden, *State of the Poor*, and Young, *Six Months Tour*, are replete with such references, for example. These sources also contain references to houses being separately and more lightly assessed.

18 Banks, "Land Tax Assessments in West Norfolk." Acres constitute the denominator in computing the acreage equivalent (tax per acre, traditionally computed in shillings, which causes rounding errors, especially among small properties). A 30 percent underestimation of total parish acres will result in a 30 percent inflation of the acreage equivalent, which in turn will cause a 30 percent underestimation of the acreages for each property bundle when

the equivalent is divided into each tax entry. Martin, "Landownership and the Land Tax Returns," 102–3, reported "Total Parish Acreage" as well as "Enclosure Award Acreage" for two of his parishes (Cubbington and Harbury). His "Total Parish Acres" are those reported in the 1831 census. In Cubbington the census acres exceed those of the enclosure award by 112 percent, while in Harbury they exceed by 107 percent. Curiously, Martin based his Cubbington acreage equivalent (0.8s. tax per acre) on the census acres, but in Harbury he computed his equivalent (1.1s.) from the enclosure acres. Such inconsistencies in procedure do not affect rank order within parishes, of course, since the denominator is a constant. Similarly, over- and under-estimations of total parish acreage have no internal rank order effects within a parish. But procedural inconsistencies as well as estimation errors may have considerable impact on class interval analyses and on rank order arrays when the data is gathered across parish boundaries. It is impossible to know how often or to what degree inconsistency has occurred, since studies normally do not report their findings in a way that would permit its detection.

19 In compiling the six-inch Ordnance series I have assigned equal shares of commonable lands to each township specified on the map as enjoying undifferentiated rights. Only a few townships are significantly affected by such allocations, most notably those in Masham parish in Hang East, Middleton parish in Pickering Lythe, and Lastingham parish in Ryedale. In Masham parish, where the commons were equally shared by all its townships, the Census Office obviously assigned a disproportionate share of the parish commons to Masham township; but the combined acres reported in the census for the parish were still only 91 percent of its true acreage. In Middleton parish the township of Hartoft Dale was severely overestimated by the census, but again the combined acreage for the parish was underestimated by the Census Office at 95 percent of its true acreage. In Lastingham parish the township of Rosedale West Side was similarly the only one in the parish to be overestimated, but in this case the Census Office overestimated the parish as a whole by 7 percent. In each of these parishes the proportion of commonable land was large (about 34 percent in Masham and 26 percent in Lastingham, for example). It seems fair to conclude that the Census Office did assign commons, as they certainly should have done, but that they frequently misassigned such lands and characteristically made other errors in estimation while doing so. The identification and assignment of detached areas undoubtedly caused further problems. In Hang West wapentake the two townships of High and Low Abbotside shared extensive upland commons. While one was underestimated at 63 percent and the other was overestimated at 123 percent, the two townships together were reported in the census at 100 percent of their true acreage.

20 PP 1833 XXXVI xxii (Preface, 1831 Census of Population).

21 Robert C. Allen informs me that he has attempted such reconstructions in the South Midlands.

22 By contrast, the northern acreages are very promising indeed for purposes other than conversions of tax values to acres. For example, density studies for the period before 1850, based on the aggregate census and other documentation, can reliably be undertaken at the township level in Lancashire and Yorkshire. In non-northern counties such early nineteenth century studies should only proceed at the hundred or county level, where estimation error tends progressively to become more negligible (appendix C). In the second half of the century, parish and township entries in the census tend to lose comparability for time series, and great care must be taken in determining which units have undergone significant boundary changes. Before mid-century a few boundary changes occurred, but no more than would cause an acceptable number of outliers.

23 Best, *East Yorkshire*, 16.

CHAPTER SIX

1 The early statutes did not prevent the alteration of quotas below the county level; and, as noted during the discussion on Roman Catholic double assessment, township quotas did fluctuate before the middle years of Queen Anne. The annual land tax acts provided mechanisms for altering such quotas by appeal, when it could be demonstrated that the amount of tax thereby collected exceeded the statutory rate on improved rack rent valuation. Literary evidence suggests that virtually no such revisions of township quotas occurred, but no systematic comparisons of early land tax quotas have, to my knowledge, been undertaken. By mid-century, and probably much earlier, the mechanisms for such revisions were no longer operable, since rising rental values had caused the revenues assigned by the fixed quotas to fall well below the statutory rate. I know of no eighteenth century statutory provision for revising the county quotas themselves. Any revision below county level would therefore have required an internal redistribution of quotas to meet the demand on the county. In 1798 the Redemption Act (38 Geo. III c. 60) made the township quotas perpetual. In order to simplify the discussion which follows, the township quotas will be considered and characterized at all times as ossified and unalterable. The early history of the land tax and the imposition of quotas is most fully treated in Ward, *English Land Tax*.

2 The "local poundage rate," as I shall call it, is not to be confused with the nominal or "statutory rate" embedded in the annual land tax statutes. In the later eighteenth and subsequent centuries, the statutory rate was at 4s. in the pound, purportedly on rack rents. Nothing of the kind was actually being imposed on the countryside. The only effect of the statutory rate was to

adjust the quotas themselves, the quota for a 4s. rate being twice that of a 2s. rate. In the discussion that follows, the relationship of rent to tax at the township and other levels will not, except for the statutory rate, normally be expressed as a local poundage rate. Instead it will be expressed as a ratio. A local poundage rate of 1s., for example, will be expressed as a ratio of 20 (20:1 being understood). It should be noted that the values of local poundage rates and of ratios proceed in opposite directions when expressing alterations in tax burden. An alteration which lightens a tax burden would be expressed by a smaller local poundage rate, but the ratio of valuational rent to tax would rise.

3 A further mechanism for adjusting the burden of tax was available to assessors of most local rates. Parish rates, for example, were not governed by quotas. On the contrary their total receipts were continuously altering with demand. Rather than undertake frequent general revaluations, which were expensive when done professionally, many townships levied a fixed system of assessments multiple times per year. I have encountered as many as 220 assessments levied for the poor rate in a single year. This practice of multiple rating was clearly a common one among parishes throughout the country. The land tax, being governed by quotas, was not generally appropriate for multiple ratings. It sometimes happened that the quotas themselves would be expressed in the terminology of a multiple rating, however. The land tax quotas for Cumberland were based on an ancient system of local tax allocation called the "purvey" (see especially Beckett, "Local Custom and the 'New Taxation' "), and, in 1798, the quotas imposed by the 4s. statutory rate were described in the Cumberland duplicates as thirty-seven purveys.

4 It should be noted that "revaluation" can occur in two senses: a general revaluation, which systematically and simultaneously reviews and revises all properties within the township, and a limited revaluation, which revises only a small number of properties. General revaluations were complex and difficult, even if undertaken only by local valuers, and occurred only at intervals. Limited revaluations were virtually incessant, reflecting activity in the land market. For a more complete discussion, see chapter 7 below.

5 Beckett, "Local Custom and the 'New Taxation' "; and his "Westmorland's 'Book of Rates.' "

6 For the bases of local taxation in Lancashire, see Eden, *State of the Poor*, 2:90; Lawton, ed., "Northwich Hundred Poll Tax," i–ix, 1–24; Quintrell, ed., "Proceedings of the Lancashire Justices." For a brief survey of the use of early books of rates in several counties see Beckett, *Local Taxation*, 10–16. Caution must be exercised in associating these books of rates to various forms of taxation, however. Until the late eighteenth century the county rate, for example, never required large collections. Books of rates may therefore have continued to be employed in the collection of these

small tax amounts while, in some counties, other more current valuations may have been developed for the more onerous taxes. The 1739 County Rate Act, in requiring the churchwardens and overseers to pay the county rate out of collections for the poor rate, need not have impeded the use of separate valuations for each of those rates (see Beckett, *Local Taxation*, 10).

7 See chapter 7.

8 William Baldwin was a legal adviser of Lord Fitzwilliam and had been Member of Parliament for Fitzwilliam's pocket borough of Malton from 1795 until June 1798.

9 Lord Fitzwilliam to French Laurence, "Monday night," [10 or 17 Dec. 1798] Box X515/138, Milton MSS, Northamptonshire Record Office.

10 That is, the local poundage rate would tend to stabilize when it was computed against the separate tax entries recorded in the land tax duplicates. Many West Riding duplicates, especially in the industrial districts, record tax entries which lump together the land tax and a local rate. The amount owed for the land tax cannot be distinguished on such duplicates. If the local poundage rate were calculated as a township aggregate against the land tax quota, which is often the "total" recorded at the bottom of the duplicate, the rate would not tend to stabilize as valuational totals rose. I should also remark that I have generally assumed that the West Riding duplicates with lumped tax entries are suitable for analysis to the extent that the lumped entries, while distorted in their absolute magnitudes, are correct (or as correct as a non-lumped duplicate from the same township would be) in their proportional distribution of the tax burden among proprietors and tenants. This assumption may be unwarranted and requires further investigation.

11 Marshall, *Landed Property of England*, 7–8.

12 See for example Eden, *State of the Poor*, 2:8–9, 272; 3:717, 749.

13 See chapters 11 and 15 below. Interesting evidence for the meaning of "rent" and on the process of valuation in the West Riding appears in Bayldon, *Treatise on the Valuation of Property*. Bayldon was a professional valuer operating out of Carlton near Barnsley. He acknowledged the four meanings of rent I have outlined above: full potential annual rental, or gross improved rack rent; the local, informed perception of full rental value, with minimal or no further improvements; actual rents being paid, either gross, or net after taxes and abatements; a percentage of one of the above. Bayldon rejected the first three as inequitable for purposes of tax valuation, and for reasons similar to those I have outlined. He found no objection to percentage reductions, since the general level of valuation is irrelevant. Fairness only requires that a valuation be equitably laid. His own recommendation for determining basic valuational rents was rather more complex: "In rating the land of a township, where the occupiers are chiefly farmers, one way of estimating the average rent different soils are worth, is, by deducting all the

expenses and outgoings of cultivating an acre of the best soil, from the average value of its produce; then deduct 5 per cent. as a reasonable profit for the farmer's exertions, the remainder will probably be the fair annual value. The same may be done by one acre of the worst land in the township, and the intermediate qualities may be fixed by comparison. Due allowance must, at the same time, be made for land lying at a distance from the homestead, and other disadvantages, which vary according to local circumstances. Another plan is, to deduct all the expences of management from the average value of the produce, and then divide the remainder betwixt the landlord and tenant; the one-half for rent, and the other half for interest of the tenant's capital and a maintenance for his family, and profit. In many cases only a trifling difference will be found in the result of these two modes of ascertaining the annual value, they both arrive as near the truth as any method yet discovered." Bayldon, ibid, 54–5. It is unlikely that eighteenth century, non-professional local valuers undertook any such elaborate procedures. In any case, one must accept Bayldon's portrayal of valuation procedures with some reservations, when attempting to determine procedures underlying the land tax. He describes procedures current in the 1830s, and perhaps somewhat earlier, a period when general revaluations and the use of professional valuers were becoming far more common. See also chapter 14 for an examination of the newly devised valuation procedures (on the Lancashire model) which were adopted in the West Riding in the early 1830s.

14 Mingay, "Land Tax Assessments and the Small Landowner," 388.

CHAPTER SEVEN

1 An abridged version of this chapter appeared in *Land and Property*, ed. Turner and Mills, chapter 10.

2 The early history of the land tax is most fully treated in Ward, *English Land Tax*. An excellent account for the later eighteenth century may be found in Binney, *British Public Finance*, 49–60.

3 Alterations did occur in the national statutory rate during the eighteenth century, and such alterations changed the quotas. For example, a 4s. rate would double quotas owed under a 2s. rate. But such alterations in the statutory rate do not constitute revaluation, since the proportional distributions of the burden of the tax were not thereby altered among townships or regions.

4 Beckett, "Local Custom and the 'New Taxation,'" has shown that in at least one county (Cumberland) the 1698 parish quotas were merely those compounded for purveyance in 1617. Much more work needs to be done on the origins and equitability of the 1698 quotas.

5 Studies of the impact of enclosure and of the disappearance of the small

landowner have commonly employed class intervals across townships, although they usually first converted tax values to acreage equivalents. Soltow, "Wealth Distribution in England and Wales," has attempted a statistically more sophisticated use of the land tax values by computing gini coefficients of wealth inequality. For criticisms of that attempt by myself and Wilson, and for Soltow's reply, see *Economic History Review*, 2d ser., 35 (1982), 416–33.

6 Including myself. I noted in my reply to Soltow that, in the North Riding, ratios of total valuational rent (as reported in the land tax duplicates) to total tax per township varied from the statutory ratio of 5:1 to as high as 80:1. Since writing that reply I have found ratios many times higher than 80:1. See chapter 15 below.

7 For the years 1826–32, "rents" are commonly reported on the land tax duplicates throughout the country. In some counties they are widely and regularly reported from the 1780s. In most counties they appear only rarely before 1826, however. In the North Riding they appear before that date in only a scattering of townships, and only irregularly, except in the wapentake of Gilling East where the level of reporting rents is unusually full from an early date. These "rents" must not be construed as actual rents. They should be viewed strictly as the valuational basis for the individual tax assessment, and they must be assumed to depart to some degree from both actual and rack rents unless direct evidence proves the contrary. It can be shown that land tax rents generally fall below contemporary valuations for other purposes (see chapter 13). One should therefore be particularly careful not to assume that ratios of valuational rent (as reported in the duplicates) to tax reveal actual burdens of the tax. By the later eighteenth century actual burdens should in general be considerably lighter than such ratios indicate, and to different degrees within each township. Ratios of 5:1 (which is the 4s. statutory rate) should be viewed with peculiar suspicion. When genuine, they almost certainly result from a long-standing failure to increase the valuational total of the township – although the proportional contributions to that total by individual properties may have changed. They may also be fraudulent, however.

8 Kirby Wiske is a good example. For the ratios, see appendix K.

9 Chambers and Mingay, *The Agricultural Revolution*, 112, 118, 167.

10 The total rentals on the Duncombe of Duncombe Park estates rose by about 130 percent between 1790 and 1815 and then fell off marginally through the 1820s (ZEW IV 5, NYCRO). The Danby estate of Lord Downe increased its rentals by 59 percent during the 1780s, and further increased them by an additional 141 percent during the war years. By 1831 the Danby rentals had fallen off 18 percent. The Downe estate at Liverton underwent no significant increases during the 1780s, but the rents rose 74 percent between 1790 and 1815 and then stabilized during the 1820s (ZDS IV 2/2, NYCRO). The

Cleveland estates of Dundas of Aske approximately doubled its rentals over the war years (ZNK V 3, NYCRO).

11 We saw in chapter 3 that land tax duplicates may, from year to year, erratically omit or exempt cottages or houses and other properties. Such omissions or exemptions constitute revaluation. But the tax amounts assigned such properties are generally quite small, and the effect of the revaluation on the quota may be marginal and have no impact on other properties within the township. The actual total tax collected each year (which is often different than the total recorded at the bottom of the duplicate) normally varies in any case. Balances are either applied to local rates or carried to the following year. The tax values of omitted or exempted properties, being normally small, should also have only a marginal impact, if any, on rent to tax ratios within a township. The data tabulated in appendix F do not generally appear to be due to omissions or exemptions but rather to land transactions.

12 Historians who are tempted to employ land tax "rents" instead of tax values, however, should first determine whether total rents were rising or remaining constant in their townships. Land tax rents should not be construed as actual rents, in any case, and must be assumed to depart from actual and rack rents to some degree. But land tax rents in townships with constant totals should depart from current actual and rack rent values to a greater degree than rents in other townships where totals vary. Such departures introduce further elements of incomparability into inter-township analyses when rents are employed. See also table 10.5.

13 The valuational basis for the poor rate in 1803 can be calculated from PP 1818 XIX 235ff. Eden, *State of the Poor.*

14 Revenue from local rates was also frequently increased by simply collecting multiples of a fixed rate. This third mechanism need not in any given year entail any alteration in valuation or local poundage rate, although over the long run valuations had to be altered for the reasons given above. This mechanism could substantially relieve pressures to revalue for periods of time in those townships where it was employed, to the extent that the land market was stable.

15 The incidence of revaluation revealed in appendix E seems to have peaked in the half decade following passage of the 1798 Redemption Act, when most redemption agreements were completed. But the increase is only a marginal one, and the wapentake level series may be distorted by the meagerness of reporting before 1801. Certainly the frequency and magnitude of revaluation in the two decades before 1801 was substantial. The duplicates of 1798–1801 do contain frequent revisions of names of proprietors, however. The most numerous instances involve transmissions to heirs and appear to reassign responsibility for the tax rather than alter its burden.

16 While there is evidence that revaluations sometimes occurred in association

with enclosures in other regions of Yorkshire, Gilling East was entirely free of enclosures during these years, with a single minor exception: Yafforth Moor, lying within Danby Wiske, Little Langton, Thrintoft and Yafforth townships, was enclosed to the extent of just over four hundred acres in 1790 (Tate, *Domesday of English Enclosure Awards*, 297). The rise in Yafforth valuational rents between 1790 and 1795 might be thus explained, but no other changes can be traced to enclosure.

CHAPTER EIGHT

1 Davies, "Small Landowner," 1:273; Johnson, *Disappearance of the Small Landowner*, 131; Gray, "Yeoman Farming in Oxfordshire," 299; Chambers, "Enclosure and Labour Supply," 108; Mingay, "Land Tax Assessments and the Small Landowner," 382–3; Martin, "Landownership and the Land Tax Returns," 98; Hunt, "Land Tax Assessments," 284–5; Turner, *Land and Property*, ed. Turner and Mills, chapter 1. In Yorkshire it is not unusual to find tax values missing from redeemed entries, even when the owners and occupiers for those properties are recorded. The omission of redeemed entries is in fact a variant of an older problem. The omission of occupiers, or of proprietors, or the inclusion only of some undifferentiated mixture of owners and occupiers, is a common characteristic of duplicates before the later 1780s. See chapter 3. It should be noted that no attempt has been made in this or other chapters to distinguish between "redeemed" and "exonerated" holdings. The distinction is rarely made in the duplicates and is not an important one for the topics under discussion.

2 The tax ceilings for each category could of course be altered by further redemption, which would further adjust the mix between improving and unimproving properties. But such an observation does not affect the argument presented.

3 Changes in tenantry could not be verified in one township, where one of the two entries listed only "tenants" in the occupier column rather than the names of those tenants.

4 All major departures in ratios coincide precisely with major revaluations identified in appendix E. Apparent exceptions are explicable by decreases in (e.g.) redeemed values being counterbalanced by increases in unredeemed values (see appendix F).

5 For a discussion of the 1830 North Riding sample, see chapter 12 below.

CHAPTER NINE

1 For written expressions of these apprehensions, see for example Mingay, "Land Tax Assessments and the Small Landowner," 384, citing Ward and Payne; Hunt, "Land Tax Assessments," 285; Beckett, "Local Custom and

the 'New Taxation,' " 124–5. For an example of the despotic manipulation of tax valuations by an urban magistrate, see *Eighteenth Century Constitution*, ed. Williams, 275.

CHAPTER TEN

1 I have suggested in chapter 3 that such practices may reflect who was responsible for paying the tax, the tenant or the proprietor.
2 The composition of the North Riding sample is discussed in chapter 12. It comprises 41 percent of all townships in the riding, which is all those reporting valuational rent in the duplicates c. 1830.
3 For a discussion of undervaluation of land tax rentals, see chapter 13.
4 By the 1820s and 1830s, as attitudes towards the nature of taxation fundamentally altered in the countryside, valuations by professional land surveyors were becoming more commonplace. The suggestions in this paragraph must be treated with caution. In many cases they may be more logical than empirically well founded.
5 If this conclusion seems reasonable, then it may be unwise to try solving the problems of faulty redeemed tax entries (see chapter 7) by substituting redeemed rentals.

CHAPTER ELEVEN

1 Habakkuk, "English Landownership," 9; Ward, *English Land Tax*, 6–10, whose national estimates have been widely accepted and never superseded; Mingay, "Land Tax Assessments and the Small Landowner," 382; Beckett, "Local Custom and the 'New Taxation' " 115–16. Beckett dates the undervaluation of the northwestern counties to periods well before the Civil War.
2 Eden, *State of the Poor*.
3 Ginter, "A Wealth of Problems," 420–1.

CHAPTER TWELVE

1 Ginter, "A Wealth of Problems."
2 The 1803 poor rate returns for Yorkshire do show that local poundage rates reported at rack rent were almost invariably below the wapentake average, however. The rate reported for Rosedale East Side in 1803, when the township was in long leasehold and not at rack rent, was 3s. 11d. PP 1803–04 (175) XIII 622. By 1830 it was wholly back in the control of the King, the land tax was based on rack rent, and a new general valuation had probably taken place. The 1803 nominal ratio was thus 5.1, while the 1830 ratio was 45.4 – a considerable difference, and scarcely one wholly attributable to changing land values. Valuations at rack rent do cause ratios

to rise, but not necessarily higher than those of other townships with valuations which depart from rack rent.

3 Young, *Six Months Tour*, 3:387–92, 419–20; 4:337–8. Tuke, *General View of Agriculture*, 49. But Tuke had reported the same figures for rents in his first (1794) edition.

4 Both Young and Tuke emphasized the variability of soil quality and of rents over short distances, however. It is precisely this variability, along with the differences in date of reporting, that makes such evidence so difficult to judge.

5 The calculation of valuational rent per acre facilitates a further test of the interactive nature of the land tax mechanisms, which we might note in passing. If it is true that increases in levels of valuational rents required decreases in the local poundage rates, in order to preserve the levels of the receipts imposed by the land tax quotas, then a simple regression should reveal a negative relationship between rent and poundage rate. Such a regression was run on 1810 valuational rent per acre (y), thus to some degree standardizing rent between townships, and ratios of total rent to total tax (x) for each of the twenty-nine townships in Gilling East. The result confirmed the expected relationship. When all twenty-nine cases were considered and included tithe, r equalled .48 and was significant at the .01 level. Tithe was not always identified as such in the 1810 returns; but comparisons with the 1826–32 duplicates, where the nature of the property is regularly specified, made it possible to identify tithe entries in all but three of the 1810 returns. A regression on the remaining twenty-six townships yielded a coefficient of .46 significant at the .02 level. Two of the townships were marked outliers. The rent per acre for Warlaby was clearly too high, as was the ratio for Scorton-Uckerby. After smoothing for these two outliers, coefficients of .70 (including tithes) and .69 (excluding tithes) emerged, both significant at the .01 level. While only half the variation was accounted for, the relationship is clearly a strong one. Indeed it would be disturbing if the relationship were stronger, since the logic outlined in the earlier chapters suggests that other factors should influence the interplay of these two mechanisms. Even more importantly, a perfect correlation would require that rental levels be perfectly correlated with numbers of acres, taking no account of either soil differences or rental practices. While it was useful to introduce an element of standardization into the equation by associating rents with acres, the two variables are most certainly not strongly correlated. A coefficient of .70 is therefore a strong one for so crude a measurement. Note that the Pearson correlation coefficients are positive because ratios rather than local poundage rates were employed in the regression equation.

6 PP 1803–04 (175) XIII. Evidence that poor rate valuations most often exceeded, when they did not equal, land tax valuations may be found, for example, in table 12.5. But evidence to the contrary may be found in appen-

dix I. Both samples are small and unrepresentative of the country as a whole. The evidence does suggest that the poor rate valuations do approach or equal land tax valuations in the majority of cases. But it is not clear whether the 1803 report of poor rate valuations at rack should as a whole overestimate or underestimate the incidence of rack as a basis of the land tax. Given the political purpose for which the report was made, it was in the interest of the townships to report their basis as rack rent. In principle, then, the report should not underestimate poor rate valuations at rack rent. Two factors militate against this conclusion. The enquiry which produced the report does not seem to have uniformly received any indication of valuational basis, suggesting incomplete instructions; and five clerks of the peace replied that their county was generally at rack rent when none, or no more than a mere handful, of their townships reported their basis as at rack (appendix L). The data from the poor law report on the low incidence of poor rate valuations at rack must therefore, taken by itself, be considered more suggestive than conclusive. The small numbers gleaned from the report seem convincing, however, because they are so striking. They will become even more convincing when various valuations are compared in the next chapter.

CHAPTER THIRTEEN

1 Testimony before the select committee on the county rates (PP 1834 [542.] XIV) noted that valuations in some regions were rapidly becoming out of date during these years, but that testimony seems to refer principally to expanding urban centres. The North Riding underwent little enclosure at this time and was never significantly urbanized. Its few important towns, such as Whitby, Scarborough, Malton, or Richmond, are easily isolable and provide useful controls.

2 For the operation and basis of the property tax see especially Hope-Jones, *Income Tax in the Napoleonic Wars*; O'Brien, "British Incomes and Property"; Grigg, "Changing Regional Values." Some of Grigg's comments must be treated with caution. He suggested that county rate valuations of 1815 [sic] and 1840–47 for Holland and Kesteven may be used in measuring regional trends in rent. "As long as urban parishes are excluded, a comparison of rent per acre in 1815 with 1840–47 gives an accurate picture of regional trends in rent during this period" (93). Evidence presented in this chapter and in appendix N would suggest that significant differences may occur in the valuational bases for county rate valuations within the same administrative county in different years. Each valuation may depart from rack rent to varying degrees, thus rendering the different valuations incomparable in their absolute (and perhaps also in their proportionate) values.

3 Beckett, *Local Taxation.*

4 Burn, *Justice of the Peace*, 1:435–6.

5 On 11 April 1825, the North Riding Easter sessions deducted a proportion of the 1814 property tax valuation from the Gilling West quota for the new county rate as an allowance for lead mines, Special Order Book, QSM, NYCRO.

6 This and the following paragraph are principally based on PP 1834 (542.) XIV. The testimony of George Broadrick and a description of the Lancashire method for a general county valuation may be found there. See also Beckett, *Local Taxation*.

7 The following account of the proceedings regarding the county rate in the North Riding 1823–25 is based on its Quarter Sessions Special Order Book, QSM, and on the returns from each township for the county rate valuation in 1824, QFR/1–18, NYCRO. Quotations are either from the Special Order Book at the date indicated or from the return of the township to which reference is made. For the instructions of the clerk of the peace for the West Riding, see PP 1834 (542.) XIV, sec. II, 22.

8 *Victoria History of York: The City of York*, ed. Tillott, 526–7.

9 The committee consisted of Messrs Newton (of Coxwold), Peirse, Dent, Crompton, Monson, Elsley, Blanshard, Fowle, Coore, Robson, and Lord Tyrconnel. The clerk of the peace was to act as clerk to the committee.

10 Note that appendix O.4 cannot by definition produce values in excess of 100.0 percent. The land tax itself reports the highest valuation in eleven townships, and these cases therefore produce percentages of 100.0.

11 See chapter 7.

12 Marshall, *Landed Property of England*, 7–8. See also chapter 6 above.

CHAPTER FOURTEEN

1 In the North Riding the 1815 property tax valuations have generally been employed. Where the 1815 valuations were missing, those for 1814 have replaced them. In the East and West ridings, and in all other counties, the 1815 valuations, the only ones available, have been employed.

2 Lest anyone were to believe they have found here a procedure that would standardize all land tax entries, thereby making them directly comparable across township and county boundaries, it should be remembered that redemption had made such a procedure impossible by 1815. By then the redeemed and unredeemed entries were themselves no longer comparable in the wealth they represented. See chapter 8. The process of redemption had proceeded very far by that date. Since no other reliable systematic series of full valuations is available for an earlier date, no general standardization is possible.

3 Both Langbaurgh and Pickering Lythe wapentakes were divided into East and West divisions for land tax purposes. They have not been so divided in this study.

4 For example Soltow, "Wealth Distribution in England and Wales," 62.
5 Ratios have been computed to one decimal point only in the North and West ridings, where I wished to test my results more precisely. In the East Riding, and in all other counties, the ratios of 1815 valuation to tax quota have been computed to whole numbers.
6 "The church [at Kilnsea], dedicated to St. Helen, is now in a state of dilapidation, and in such a dangerous situation, being near to the cliff, that the inhabitants think it useless to bestow on it any further repairs, expecting from the annual encroachments of the sea, that it will, in a short time, be shaken into the abyss which has already swept away part of the burial ground." Baines, *Directory of the County of York*, 2:360. The fear was not an idle one. Under the village of Owthorne, Baines (ibid, 375) records: "This village, situated on the shore of the German ocean, has suffered much from the encroachments of the sea, which are averaged at, from 1 to 2 1/2 yards annually along the coast. The church, dedicated to St. Peter ... on the night of February 16th, 1816, fell with a most tremendous crash into the bosom of the ocean." The vicar at Owthorne, as that at Kilnsea, appears to have been non-resident.
7 Harris, *Rural Landscape*, 45.
8 See especially Rennie, Broun, and Shirreff, *General View of the Agriculture of the West Riding of Yorkshire*; Brown, *General View of the Agriculture of the West Riding of Yorkshire*; Marshall, *Review and Abstract of the County Reports*, 1:espec. 402–3; Raistrick, *West Riding of Yorkshire*; and Raistrick, *Old Yorkshire Dales*.
9 For example, Phillips, *Electoral Behavior*, employs rents derived from land tax duplicates to calculate the socio-economic characteristics of the Norwich electorate in the late eighteenth century. Norwich had multiple internal parishes.
10 Arden also provides an example of how the profile of a North Riding township can be distorted by my having consistently employed the 1815 property tax valuations instead of whichever valuation was highest. The 1824 overseer's valuation for Arden was 56 percent greater than the 1815 property tax valuation. The value per acre only alters from £.06 to £.09 by adopting the 1824 valuation, however, and remains the lowest value in the riding. Its quota burden is also still a heavy one.

CHAPTER FIFTEEN

1 Ward, *English Land Tax*, 6–10; Habakkuk, "English Landownership," 9; Beckett, "Local Custom and the 'New Taxation' " and "Land Tax Administration," 169; Tait, ed., *Taxation in Salford Hundred*, introduction. Habakkuk contends that contemporaries were of the opinion that in the early eighteenth century "the most distant" border counties paid "not much

above a shilling in the pound'' on a 4s. land tax. Beckett directly cites northern contemporary opinion that the actual rate was about 9d.

2 A search was actually made of 5,744 parishes or townships in these administrative counties, but 513 either had no surviving duplicates that I could locate or they were judged to be defective for the calculation of ratios. The Public Record Office was closed during the period of this research, and its 1798 series was unavailable to me. The research was therefore conducted in county record offices. Since I had found that in some counties the individual land tax entries incorporated and lumped together amounts owed for one or more local rates, the ''quota'' for each township was taken to be the amount recorded at the foot of each duplicate. In the West Riding, where such lumping of the land tax and a local rate occurs, the individual property bundles add to totals which are considerably larger than the ''total'' given at the foot of the duplicate. It is the ''totals'' that approximate the quotas. These totals often vary from year to year, but only marginally. Care was exercised to employ duplicates for 1798 whenever those were available and, in any event, to use duplicates prior to the onset of redemption. In most counties 1798 duplicates were available. The only important exceptions are Kesteven and Lindsey, where the 1830 duplicates seemed of unusually high quality and were well-arranged. When a ''total'' was not recorded at the bottom of a duplicate, that township was treated as ''defective.'' No attempt to add property bundles was undertaken in such townships due to the possibility of aggregations with local rates. Every duplicate was searched for salary and stock-in-trade entries. Such entries were subtracted from the ''totals'' and both gross and net ratios were calculated. Only net ratios are reported in appendix Q.

3 In 1693 the northern Members of Parliament had argued for the imposition of county quotas. They lost that argument, and a direct pound rate was imposed. By 1698, steadily declining receipts forced Parliament to adopt the assessments of 1693 as perpetual county quotas. The House *could in principle* have adopted county quotas which conformed more closely to the economic realities of 1698. But politically that was impossible. It is not that the government could not have won the necessary votes in the House – indeed southern and eastern Members strongly outnumbered those from the northern counties, and many of the southwestern counties were fairly heavily taxed by the quotas. The political problem may be inferred, even without direct evidence: So long as the counties were self-evaluating for tax purposes, it was simply impossible to impose a true valuation – and thereby an equitable quota – upon them. Centralized revaluation was something few men in seventeenth and eighteenth century England would have supported. It was French. It violated the prescriptive freedoms of Englishmen. It was inquisitorial and smacked of excise. The northern counties had under-reported their values in 1693, despite the pound rate. Who could stop them?

But underreporting among northern and some western counties was not wholly undiscriminating. It conformed to ancient and traditional patterns, and it was surely this conformity that made the 1693 county assessments politically acceptable to Parliament as quotas in 1698.

4 See county level maps of population change in seventeenth and eighteenth century England and Wales (based on estimates by Rickman and by Deane and Cole) in Darby, ed., *New Historical Geography of England*, 306–7.

5 In a strict sense, it is too much to say that the distribution of the 1815 burdens was "caused" by the original distribution of the land tax quotas. But the correlation is remarkably strong. Even without converting to logs, r = .74 for all counties of England and Wales when y = county ratios and x = acres per land tax quota in a Pearson regression. The value of r rises to .88 when English counties alone are computed and rises further to .94 when Cumbria and Lancashire are deleted. All three coefficients are significant at the .01 level. These two variables are not nearly so strongly related at the township level, however. The correlation coefficient for the entire North Riding (n = 478), again not converting for logs, is merely .29. But when the more purely vale wapentakes of Allertonshire, Gilling East, and Hallikeld are separately combined (n = 87), r = .74 and is significant at the .01 level. Ratios of North Riding townships are not well correlated with 1815 property tax valuations per acre, and these in turn are poorly correlated with the quotas. Those two pairs are also poorly correlated among counties at the national level. These observations are included only to note that the latter two pairs, unlike ratios and quotas, depart signficantly from one another in their patterns; there can of course be no question of any causal relationship.

6 It must be noted that the Northamptonshire quota, when measured per acre, was 18 percent lighter in its burden than that for Bedfordshire. Habakkuk, "English Landownership," treats the burden in the two counties as though they were equal. Either Habakkuk was general in his remarks and did not intend a precise statement, or the estates he examined misled him regarding general conditions within the two counties, or per acre estimates of burden are subject to substantial error. Any or all of these explanations may be true.

7 If we assume that the real rate in Cumberland at the beginning of the eighteenth century was 1s., then the decline in its burden by 1815 would be 90 percent. The burden of Westmorland would have declined by 80 percent under the same assumption.

8 Ward, *English Land Tax*, 8.

9 Soltow, "Wealth Distribution in England and Wales." For the debate which followed see Ginter, "A Wealth of Problems"; Wilson, "The Land Tax Problem"; Soltow, "Land Tax Redemption Records."

10 Davies compared eight counties within ten class intervals for the years 1780–86 and 1802. Additional tabulations were made in six of those

counties (Cheshire and Oxfordshire were excluded) for 1832. The counties (with their mean 1815 ratios) were Cheshire (37.9), Derbyshire (36.8), Leicestershire (26.8), Lindsey (30), Northamptonshire (19.6), Nottinghamshire (27.0), Oxfordshire (18.2) and Warwickshire (31.0). Davies, "Small Landowner," 276. Johnson, *Disappearance of the Small Landowner*, drew on parishes from nine counties whose 1815 mean ratios ranged from 15.1, in Sussex, to 147.1, in Lancashire.

11 It should be remembered that historians who have engaged in direct comparisons of their results with those of studies completed earlier for other counties have adopted a procedure which is not essentially different than that employed by Davies. Such comparisons are based, either explicitly or implicitly, on a commonly shared definition of "smallness," a definition which is expressed or measured in absolute tax values that take no account of variance in tax burdens.

12 Hadwin, "Medieval Lay Subsidies," has found that assessors for the lay subsidies in the late thirteenth and early fourteenth centuries "were clearly varying their valuations to minimize the impact of increases in the tax fraction demanded, and they differed in the degree to which they did this." The resulting variations in real mean county tax burden were "not of such an extreme kind as to destroy the value of the data altogether, though a reminder of the need for care in using them." A few counties altered their valuations from 50 to 200 percent of their 1334 level, but most counties varied within a much narrower range. If these variations in valuation reflect true ranges of inequalities in mean county tax burdens (such variations may mask further inequalities, though they do confirm that inequalities existed), then county level inequalities in 1815 land tax burdens were considerably more serious among regions at a national level. Unlike Hadwin's county series, rank order is significantly disturbed in 1815. Although Hadwin's data is only sufficiently full at the county level, since he employed the totals reported in the enrolled accounts, the evidence he has been able to assemble has led him to conclude that "there may be serious dangers in using the 1334 data as indicative of the absolute *or relative* wealth of hundreds, wapentakes, or individual townships. The 1334 assessments for these places may well resemble those of Oxfordshire, where tax anomalies had somehow become ingrained in the system" (pp. 209–10, his emphasis). It would seem that the problems I am reporting in the land tax are very ancient ones indeed. What is needed is a much longer secular study than either Hadwin or I have been able to undertake.

13 Frequency distributions and means for the hundreds of each of the fourteen counties additional to Yorkshire may be found in appendix Q. The ratios for those counties are displayed on maps 23 to 39.

14 The reader should be cautioned that the structure of the class intervals in table 15.2 can be misleading. The intervals are not grouped exponentially.

Burdens do not double within each successive group. The lowest intervals include wider variations in burden than do the highest intervals. For example, the burdens of townships falling within the lowest interval of 0–19 can vary by a factor of 19. Burdens in the second interval of 20–39 can vary by a factor of no more than 2. The same caution should be applied to all other similar tables in this study.

15 Information on soils has been gleaned principally from the various *General View of Agriculture* volumes for each county, from Marshall, *Review and Abstract of the County Reports*, and from the Land Utilization Surveys edited by Stamp, *The Land of Britain*.

16 Information on enclosure has been taken from Tate, *Domesday of English Enclosure Acts and Awards*.

17 For the spread of country houses and villas in Hertfordshire, and the development of its land market, see especially L. and J.C.F. Stone, *An Open Elite?*

CHAPTER SIXTEEN

1 Mingay, "Land Tax Assessments and the Small Landowner," 388.

2 It may occur to some historians that, if the real burden of the land tax can be determined for each township in 1815, then adjustments may be made for error, and inter-township comparisons utilizing tax entries may at least be made in that year, and perhaps in others. Unfortunately these conclusions are not warranted. It has generally been assumed that internal revaluations within townships did not occur. I have been able to show that, on the contrary, revaluation within townships was virtually incessant and universal. But because internal revaluation was incessant, ratios of assessed rental value to tax were also subject to constant fluctuation. Thus no inference of error based on 1815 duplicates may be applied to other years, and the 1815 duplicates themselves are not suitable for analysis due to redemption.

3 Mingay, "Land Tax Assessments and the Small Landowner," 387–8.

4 Turner, "Landownership Change in Buckinghamshire." It should be noted that Turner's inclusion of anciently enclosed parishes does not "control" for the objections I am raising.

5 Martin, "Parliamentary Enclosure in Warwickshire," 334.

6 Ibid, 335. It is important to understand that I am not denying that numbers of real turnovers can be counted by means of the land tax. I agree with those who believe property bundles can in general and to a sufficient degree be traced from year to year. Genuine sales and alienations in most townships do appear quickly in the duplicates (transfers among family members, by contrast, are not always quickly recorded), and such alterations constitute a leading feature of the continuous process of internal revaluation. What I am denying is that *all* apparent turnovers are genuine alienations from a family,

or that *all* genuine alienations appear in the duplicates (due to missing smallholders). Turnover *rates* cannot therefore be calculated.

7 As we have seen in chapter 4, small numbers of smallholders commonly appear suddenly in land tax duplicates for the first time immediately following the lifting of double assessment. They then proceed to disappear from the duplicates a few years later. Strictly speaking, these and other similar phenomena cannot be explained. The duplicates rarely provide direct clues to their cause, and I would emphasize that my principal conclusions – which are based on the *fact* and *consequences* of such appearances and disappearances and the widespread incidence of significant smallholder omissions – do not depend on explaining why such phenomena occur. My impression is that the temporary appearance of new smallholders following the lifting of double assessment was a response to the arithmetic difficulties experienced in levying a radically restructured valuation in a manner which would precisely conform with the requirements of a fixed township tax quota. The new valuation may have failed to yield precisely the total amount of tax required without adopting an awkward poundage rate. Some number of smallholders could then have been drawn from a normally untaxed pool to meet the shortfall in the full quota. Within a few years the continuing process of revaluation would permit such smallholders to return to their untaxed status. Why such pools of untaxed smallholders existed in so many townships and on so large a scale remains a mystery, although there are many annotations on the land tax duplicates that "poor" householders were being omitted from the tax. Poverty may not be a general explanation, however. Double assessment and smallholder omissions are discussed at length in chapters 3 and 4. I should also emphasize that I am not suggesting that *all* new appearances in the land tax following *enclosure* were accommodations to the quota. Many may have been drawn from the untaxed pool, but others may have resulted from genuine activity in the land market, the transformation of common rights into freehold, or other obscure factors. We cannot learn the causes, or in what proportion they operated.

8 A percentage, or "rate," can be a crude and misleading statistic. When the number of cases is small, a single case alteration can produce a large percentage difference. Turnover studies sometimes report rates which are for this reason misleading. But an equally serious problem arises when the number of cases is sufficiently large but (1) the cases are disproportionately distributed among the smaller size categories and (2) the smaller size categories are the locus of most change in surname and (3) are also the locus of most data deficiency. There is no doubt that most turnover "rates" are primarily the result of movements among smallholders, who in the larger townships comprise so large a proportion of both the numerator and denominator employed in the calculation.

9 Henstock, "House Repopulation," 127.

10 Turner, "Landownership Change in Buckinghamshire," 567n. and Martin, "Parliamentary Enclosure in Warwickshire," 334, both acknowledge this source of error but dismiss it out of hand as insignificant. It has also not been demonstrated (nor can it be) that all "turnovers" in agrarian townships involve farmers. Many non-occupying owners in particular may hold non-farming occupations. Or, if they are farmers, they may have other farms elsewhere. Such problems cannot generally be solved. Nor should they be discounted or merely dismissed. Cf. my discussion of "residence" in chapter 3.

11 Mingay, "Land Tax Assessments and the Small Landowner," 381. My conclusions should not be interpreted as supporting the views of the Hammonds or of later Marxist historians who have wholly evaded a quantitative examination of the impact of enclosure. They do not win by default. Their work has its own peculiar problems. I view my conclusions as neutral in the debate and as simply reopening the question.

12 Henstock, "House Repopulation." See also chapter 6 (especially pages 115–16) of the same volume, in which Noble expresses sensible reservations regarding the reliability of the land tax for morphological studies at both the aggregate and more detailed levels.

13 Unwin, "The Barnsley Coalfield 1690–1830." Estate records, where available, would be superior to the land tax duplicates for the type of information Unwin seeks. The land tax can be useful in those cases when estate records are not available. But the exploitation of some estate records, even if marginally outside the specific region under study, would enhance the credibility of an analysis from land tax duplicates by providing controls.

14 Soltow, "Wealth Distribution in England and Wales."

15 For a fuller expression of my objections, see Ginter, "A Wealth of Problems." For the cogent objections raised by Wilson, and Soltow's response to us both, see *Economic History Review*, 2d ser., 35 (1982): 422–33.

16 Rudé, "Middlesex Electors;" *Wilkes and Liberty*.

17 Errors arising from inter-township aggregations have probably been reduced by employing valuational rents. But it should also be remembered that valuational rents are probably more subject to intra-township inequalities arising from differential departures of those "rents" from rack rent. See chapter 10. A wiser strategy would therefore employ tax values, and do so parish by parish. Other problems, such as missing smallholders, would remain, however.

18 Phillips, *Electoral Behavior*, chapters 5 and 7.

19 I have for many years experimented with electorate analysis employing the land tax and have reluctantly come to these tentative conclusions: Ingenuity *may perhaps* yet solve the problems I have posed for electoral analysis, or do so sufficiently. Minimally, procedures should in future observe the following guidelines. Analysis should proceed parish by parish within

boroughs and separately among boroughs. Tax values are probably more reliable than rents, but each parish should be inspected in the light of chapter 10. Redeemed land tax values should not be employed after 1798, or at least not many years thereafter. Where possible and appropriate, analyses should be run separately on middling to large values, since these tend to be more reliable. Analyses which include smaller values should allow for large proportions of missing holders in the tax rolls. The analyst should also resist generalizing too firmly about the characteristics of the poorest voters; it is they whose values are most unreliable and who will tend to be missing from his tax documents. No inference should be made regarding the wealth of a voter simply because he fails to appear in a tax document – except that he is probably not a largeholder. Statistics which employ the total numbers of owners or occupiers must be avoided. "Mean" and "median" rentals are not genuine means or medians of the entire population, since many middling to small holders are probably missing. Such statistics, like the raw values from which they are calculated, are not comparable across parish boundaries and should never be employed for inter-parish comparisons. The total numbers of qualified voters cannot be calculated due to problems in nominal record linkage between parishes. It would appear to me that an analyst who proceeded with extreme care along these lines *might* yet produce convincing results employing sophisticated statistical analysis. Procedures should be meticulously and fully described, however. The proof will be in the pudding.

20 Gray, "Yeoman Farming in Oxfordshire," especially the table on p. 302.

21 Davies, "Small Landowner," 279–80, 283. Davies defined four types of parish: those owned by one large landowner; those owned by more than one (how many are allowed is not specified) large (largeness is not defined) landowner; those with no occupying owners; and those with less than six occupying owners. The first two types overlapped the last two, and the four together did not constitute a single continuum. The last two types designated by Davies, which provide counts of occupying owners, are clearly unreliable due to redemption and to underestimation of smallholders. His first two types are important in this respect, however: They demonstrate clearly (even if imprecisely) that the incidence of very large holdings can alter sharply within a space of twenty years or less. Even those parishes within his two samples which had been wholly owned by one largeholder in 1780–86 had declined in number by 10 to 14 percent by 1802. It has become commonplace for historians to acknowledge that such differences can occur, but they then blithely proceed to employ sources such as tithe apportionments in the 1840s, or Bateman and the New Domesday survey in the 1870s, as a basis for generalizations well removed from those sources chronologically. Such generalizations are unwarranted and should cease, *unless* their reliability is argued by a case by case examination of available direct evidence.

22 Mills, *Lord and Peasant*, chapter 4, where he defines his method and reviews the methods and findings of himself and others. Cf. his earlier explanation, which influenced Obelkevich, in "English Villages"; Holderness, " 'Open' and 'Close' Parishes in England."

23 Obelkevich, *Religion and Rural Society*, 12, 30. Obelkevich classified his townships "on the basis of data from local directories and from the Land Tax returns of 1831." The way in which the two sources were permitted to interact is unspecified. The precise nature of his method, and whether it was genuinely systematic, is thereby rendered even more unclear. Unlike Mills' definition, "seats" do not appear to have constituted an element in his definition of "residence."

24 Grigg, *Agricultural Revolution*, 83–4. He alludes to this method in his "Land Tax Returns," 89, but applies it in his book.

25 For the last twenty years I have been experimenting with various modes of constructing landholding classifications for the townships of the three ridings of Yorkshire. I am presently employing the following two alternative schemes. The first scheme is employed when a precise statistical analysis of dispersion and concentration of ownership of real property is the primary objective of analysis. Each of the holdings (i.e., the tax values of property bundles) of the five (if there are that many) largest proprietors (regardless of ascribed rank or status) within each township are entered into a machine readable data base. The largest proprietors are identified by inspection. Nominal record linkage is applied (by inspection and by the use of unique identification codes for each individual proprietor) within each township. The holdings (tax values) of each of the five proprietors as a proprietor and as an occupier are separately recorded and labelled as such. The proprietor of their occupied holdings is identified ("himself" being recorded when he is in occupation of his own property). The total tax values for each sampled proprietor are then totalled by the computer, the tax values as proprietor and as occupier being totalled separately. The total tax owed by the township is then computed by first entering all remaining tax values (omitting entries for salaries of office and stock-in-trade) recorded on the duplicate (without associating those remaining values with specific proprietors or occupiers); the computer then totals the raw entries for a total of tax owed. Tithe, when known, is included in the total but flagged. The "total" recorded at the bottom of the duplicate is also coded, when present; when 1798 duplicates are employed, that total constitutes the statutory land tax quota and can act as a control and supplementary variable. The total tax owed as proprietor of each sampled holder is then computed as a percentage of the total computed tax. The total tax which he owes as occupier is also computed as a percentage of total computed tax. The decision to code the five largest proprietors, rather than some other number, is in part empirically based. In Yorkshire, at least, the significantly large proprietors within each township are

almost invariably less than five in number; and arithmetically the smallest of the five must hold 20 percent or less. The fifth proprietor is therefore quite small (when there are as many as five or more recorded proprietors; often there are fewer). The inclusion of five proprietors thus permits the data base to be built in a maximally flexible manner. Arbitrary decisions regarding the number of "large" proprietors to be incorporated into each "type" of township, or the minimum "size" of their properties, are not built into the data base. The full range of such decisions remains open to the analyst following the completion of the coding. Classification decisions can then be made partially on the basis of exploratory data analysis. More importantly, the analysis may be based directly on a ratio scale of percentages rather than merely on a nominal scale of codes for derived "types." Nominal scales are principally suited to nonparametric forms of statistical analysis, which are inherently less precise and reliable. Ratio scales are open to the full range of mathematical and statistical manipulations. Cluster analysis presently seems most appropriate to me for achieving purely typological constructs within a comparative framework. In order to build a larger pattern of major landholding, I have also included in the data base all smaller proprietor bundles of every individual bearing a rank ascription in the duplicates of "esquire" or higher. I have also included all clerical proprietors, regardless of holding size. Percentages (understood as "wealth" in real property and not as acres) may thereby be compiled within each township for each "large" or titled proprietor in the county. Record linkage of names between townships may then be completed by inspection, confirmed by extensive knowledge of landholding within the county derived from other sources, and undertaken conservatively. The result is a detailed mapping of large estates within the county. Seats and residence are identified from other sources. No attempt is made to achieve aggregative percentages representing the collective "size" of estates across township boundaries. A single, county-level or regional-level percentage for each largeholder is not possible. The resulting analysis and data base is maximally adaptable for analysis in combination with a large array of economic, social, or political variables at regional or higher levels. If the results prove sufficiently satisfactory when published, I shall propose parallel projects elsewhere. The mode of data retrieval within most townships is not inordinately time consuming – although it is arduous. In principle, and with moderate funding, a data base of this type could be built for the whole of England and Wales, preferably for the year 1798. A second, alternative scheme may usefully be employed when the primary focus of research is on the peerage and gentry as such, and on the location and size of their estates, rather than on patterns of dispersion and concentration. Unlike previous attempts, which rely on heraldic literature and contemporary lists, I define what I mean by "gentry" in terms of size of estate. This second scheme therefore entails a prior arbitrary stipulation of a minimum holding size in order that a proprietor, regardless of rank or status ascription, qualify for the data base as a large landowner. My own stipulation has been that a holding is "large" within a township and therefore must be included in the data base if the aggregate tax owed by its owner comprises 20.0 percent or more of the total tax of that township. As in the first scheme, I then add to the data base all smaller properties within the township owned by clergy and by persons bearing the ascription esquire or higher. In both schemes, smaller gentry and clerical holdings of less than 20 percent will be significantly undercounted, since it frequently happens that local assessors fail to assign lesser titles such as "esquire" and even "reverend" to non-resident owners of very small holdings – probably reflecting some local uncertainty regarding their status and identity. The second scheme will also provide data for preliminary estimates of dispersion and the concentration of ownership, but in this case statistical rigour is diminished by omitting holdings of untitled proprietors who are within the top five but who own less than 20 percent of real property value.

26 It is unfortunate that Mills employed 1832 duplicates in Leicestershire. Obelkevich used 1831 duplicates in South Lindsey. Grigg was able to use 1798 duplicates for Holland, but only the 1808 duplicates were available to him in the Lincolnshire Record Office at an early date for Kesteven. All three computed from tax values and not from rents. Gray employed duplicates for 1785. In this respect his results are inherently likely to be more reliable than those of Mills or Obelkevich, or those of Grigg for Kesteven. Cf. the attempts to measure concentration and dispersion of ownership in 1832 (as percentage of land owned by the largest owner and by the four largest owners) by Banks, "Land Tax Assessments in West Norfolk." Broad, "Alternate Husbandry," 82–3, makes an effective use of 1798 duplicates for four hundreds in north Buckinghamshire.

27 There were numerous large Catholic estates registered in Oxfordshire in the eighteenth century. Gray's results are therefore vulnerable in some townships, since they are based on 1785 duplicates, 1785 being well prior to the general movement to lift double assessments. Broad should have been on sounder ground because he employed duplicates for 1798. The selection of 1798 has some disadvantages. Comparisons with 1799 duplicates suggest that many townships were stimulated by the requirements of redemption to revise their returns more strictly – in their individual entries, though not in their valuational totals. Many 1798 duplicates may be somewhat out of date, especially in recording transfers of property within families. But the differences are not usually serious for the types of data bases recommended in note 25 above, nor do the 1798 duplicates appear to be out of date by more than a very few years. The uniform availability of the 1798 duplicates offsets these disadvantages. Substitute years, when employed, should be identified, however.

28 Inter-township nominal record linkage should not be attempted for occupiers, however. The overwhelming proportion of large occupiers, unlike large proprietors, bear no status or other ascriptions in addition to their name. Nor can they be traced in supplementary sources such as Burke's *Landed Gentry*. The confirmation of linkages through parish registers, where available, would be a risky task of truly monumental proportions and it is quite impracticable. No general basis for linkage outside a single township is therefore available. A project analysing tenancy would have to confine itself to very limited objectives discretely within each township. Its measurements would also be subject to significant underestimation, since genuine "farms" often spill over into more than one adjacent township. *Firm* linkages that would aggregate such farms cannot be made at the level of the tenant. The artificial fragmentation of farming patterns caused by the administrative structure of taxation is therefore more serious for tenancy than it is for proprietorship.

29 Walpole was almost toppled by this issue at the height of his political power. See the excellent study by Langford, *Excise Crisis*. For direct evidence that the parliamentary opposition cynically understood the value of a cry of "general excise" in its struggles with the government, see Ginter, ed., *Whig Organization*, 246–9.

Bibliography

MANUSCRIPT SOURCES

BEDFORDSHIRE RECORD OFFICE

Land Tax Duplicates.

CORNWALL RECORD OFFICE

Land Tax Duplicates (microfilm).

CUMBRIA RECORD OFFICE, CARLISLE

Land Tax Duplicates, Cumberland.

CUMBRIA RECORD OFFICE, KENDAL

Land Tax Duplicates, Westmorland.

HEREFORD RECORD OFFICE, HEREFORD

Land Tax Duplicates.

HERTFORDSHIRE RECORD OFFICE

Land Tax Duplicates.

HUMBERSIDE COUNTY RECORD OFFICE

Land Tax Duplicates.

LANCASHIRE RECORD OFFICE

Land Tax Duplicates.

LEICESTERSHIRE RECORD OFFICE

Land Tax Duplicates.

LINCOLNSHIRE ARCHIVES OFFICE

Land Tax Duplicates.

NORFOLK RECORD OFFICE

Land Tax Duplicates.

NORTHAMPTONSHIRE RECORD OFFICE

Fitzwilliam (Milton) MSS.

Land Tax Duplicates.

NORTH YORKSHIRE COUNTY RECORD OFFICE

Ailesbury MSS, ZJX.

Downe (Dawnay) of Danby Castle MSS, ZDS.
Feversham (Duncombe) of Duncombe Park MSS, ZEW.
Hartley of Middleton Tyas MSS, ZKU.
Land Tax Duplicates.
Quarter Sessions Special Order Book, QSM.
Returns of Valuation for the County Rate, 1824–25, QFR.
Zetland (Dundas) of Aske MSS, ZNK.

OXFORDSHIRE COUNTY RECORD OFFICE

Land Tax Duplicates.

SURREY RECORD OFFICE

Land Tax Duplicates.

WEST YORKSHIRE ARCHIVES, WAKEFIELD

Land Tax Duplicates.

WILTSHIRE RECORD OFFICE

Land Tax Duplicates.

YORK ARCHIVES

Land Tax Duplicates.

PARLIAMENTARY PAPERS

PP 1803–04 (175.) XIII Abstract of the Answers and Returns ... Relative to the Expence and Maintenance of the Poor in England.

PP 1812–13 (293.) XII An Account of the Amount of Land Tax Now Assessed upon the Several Counties in England and Wales in Respect of Land; and also, of the Amount of the Same, which has been Redeemed in Each of the Said Counties.

PP 1818 (82.) XIX Abridgement of the Abstract of the Answers and Returns ... Relative to the Expence and Maintenance of the Poor in England.

PP 1822 (502.) XV 1821 Census of Population.

PP 1828 (550.) IV Report from the Select Committee on the Land Tax, as Affecting Roman Catholics.

PP 1831–2 (577.) XLIV An Account of the Latest Valuation of Every Parish, Township or Place ... [for] the County Rates.

PP 1833 (149.) XXXVI–XXXVIII 1831 Census of Population.

PP 1834 (542.) XIV Report from the Select Committee on County Rates.

MONOGRAPHS, ARTICLES, AND OTHER PRINTED SOURCES

Allison, K.J., ed., *The Victoria History of the County of York, East Riding*. Vol. 5. London: Oxford University Press, 1984.

Ashby, A.W. *One Hundred Years of Poor Law Administration in a Warwickshire Village*. Oxford: Clarendon Press, 1912.

Ashton, T.S. *The Industrial Revolution 1760–1830*. London: Oxford University Press, 1948.

Aveling, Hugh. "The Catholic Recusants of the West Riding of Yorkshire 1558–1790." *Proceedings of the Leeds Philosophical and Literary Society, Literary and Historical Section* vol. 10, part 6 (1963): 190–306.

– *Northern Catholics: The Catholic Recusants of the North Riding of Yorkshire 1558–1790*. London: Chapman, 1966.

– *Post Reformation Catholicism in East Yorkshire 1558–1790*. East Yorkshire Local History Society, Local History Series no. 11, 1960.

Bailey, John, and George Culley. *General View of the Agriculture of the County of Cumberland*. London, 1794.

Baines, Edward. *History, Directory & Gazetteer of the County of York*. 2 vols. Leeds, 1822–23.

Banks, Sarah. "Open and Close Parishes in Nineteenth-Century England." Ph.D. diss., University of Reading, 1982.

– "Parish Landownership and the Land Tax Assessments in West Norfolk: A Comparison with the Tithe Surveys." In *Land and Property: The English Land Tax 1692–1832*, edited by Michael Turner and Dennis Mills. Gloucester: Alan Sutton, 1986.

Batchelor, Thomas. *General View of the Agriculture of the County of Bedford*. London, 1808.

Bayldon, J.S. *A Treatise on the Valuation of Property for the Poor's Rate*. 2d ed. London, 1834.

Beckett, John V. "The Decline of the Small Landowner in Eighteenth- and Nineteenth-Century England: Some Regional Considerations." *Agricultural History Review* 30 (1982): 97–111.

– "Land Tax Administration at the Local Level, 1692–1798." In *Land and Property: The English Land Tax 1692–1832*, edited by Michael Turner and Dennis Mills. Gloucester: Alan Sutton, 1986.

– "Land Tax or Excise: The Levying of Taxation in Seventeenth- and Eighteenth-Century England." *English Historical Review* 100 (1985): 285–308.

– "Local Custom and the 'New Taxation' in the Seventeenth and Eighteenth Centuries: The Example of Cumberland." *Northern History* 12 (1976): 105–26.

– *Local Taxation: National Legislation and the Problems of Enforcement*. London: Bedford Square Press for the Standing Conference for Local History, 1980.

– "Westmorland's 'Book of Rates.' " *Transactions of the Cumberland and Westmorland Antiquarian and Archaeological Society* 77 (1977): 127–37.

Beckett, John V., and D.K. Smith. "The Land Tax Returns as a Source for Studying the English Economy in the Eighteenth Century." *Bulletin of the Institute of Historical Research* 54 (1981): 54–61.

Best, S.E.J. *East Yorkshire: A Study in Agricultural Geography*. London: Longmans, Green, 1930.

Binney, J.E.D. *British Public Finance and Administration 1774–92*. Oxford: Clarendon Press, 1958.

Blalock, Hubert M. Jr. *Social Statistics*. New York: McGraw-Hill, 1960.

Bourdin, Mark. *Bourdin's Exposition of the Land Tax*. Edited by Frederick Humphreys and Charles C. Atchison. 4th ed. London: Stevens and Sons, 1894.

Broad, John. "Alternate Husbandry and Permanent Pasture in the Midlands, 1650–1800." *Agricultural History Review* 28 (1980): 77–89.

Brooks, Colin. "Public Finance and Political Stability: The Administration of the Land Tax, 1688–1720." *Historical Journal* 17 (1974): 281–300.

Brown, Robert. *General View of the Agriculture of the West Riding of Yorkshire*. Edinburgh, 1799.

Browning, Andrew, ed. *English Historical Documents 1660–1714*. London: Eyre & Spottiswoode, 1953.

Burn, Richard. *The Justice of the Peace and Parish Officer*. 4 vols. 15th ed. London, 1785.

Cannan, Edwin. *The History of Local Rates in England in Relation to the Proper Distribution of the Burden of Taxation*. 2d ed. London: P.S. King, 1912.

Cannon, John, ed. *The Whig Ascendancy: Colloquies on Hanoverian England*. London: St Martin's Press, 1981.

Chambers, J.D. "Enclosure and Labour Supply in the Industrial Revolution." Reprinted in *Agriculture and Economic Growth in England 1650–1815*, edited by E.L. Jones, 94–127. London: Methuen, 1967.

– "Enclosure and the Small Landowner." *Economic History Review* 1st ser., 10 (1939–40): 118–27.

– "Enclosure and the Small Landowner in Lindsey." *Lincolnshire Historian* 1 (1947): 15–20.

– *Nottinghamshire in the Eighteenth Century: A Study of Life and Labour under the Squirearchy*. 2d ed. London: Frank Cass, 1966.

– *The Vale of Trent, 1670–1800: A Regional Study of Economic Change*. Economic History Review Supplement no. 3 [1957].

Chambers, J.D., and G.E. Mingay. *The Agricultural Revolution 1750–1880*. London: Batsford, 1966.

Clark, John. *General View of the Agriculture of the County of Hereford*. London, 1794.

Colley, Linda. *In Defiance of Oligarchy: The Tory Party 1714–60*. Cambridge: Cambridge University Press, 1982.

Craigie, Captain Patrick George. "Ten Years' Statistics of British Agriculture, 1870–79." *Journal of the Royal Statistical Society* 43 (1880): 275–312.

Darby, H.C., ed. *A New Historical Geography of England.* Cambridge: Cambridge University Press, 1973.

Davies, C. Stella. *The Agricultural History of Cheshire 1750–1850.* Chetham Society, 3d ser. 10 (1960).

Davies, E. "The Small Landowner, 1780–1832, in the Light of the Land Tax Assessments." Reprinted in *Essays in Economic History,* edited by E.M. Carus-Wilson, 1:270–94. London: Edward Arnold, 1954.

Davis, Richard. *General View of the Agriculture of the County of Oxford.* London, 1794.

Davis, Thomas. *General View of the Agriculture of the County of Wilts.* London, 1794.

Denman, D.R., and V.F. Stewart. *Farm Rents: A Comparison of Current and Past Farm Rents in England and Wales.* London: George Allen & Unwin, 1959.

Dickson, R.W. *General View of the Agriculture of Lancashire.* London, 1815.

Donaldson, James. *General View of the Agriculture of the County of Northampton.* Edinburgh, 1794.

Douglas, Roy. *Land, People & Politics: A History of the Land Question in the United Kingdom 1878–1952.* London: Allison & Busby, 1976.

Dowell, Stephen. *A History of Taxation and Taxes in England from the Earliest Times to the Present Day.* 3d ed. 6 vols. London: Frank Cass, 1965.

Duncumb, John. *General View of the Agriculture of the County of Hereford.* London, 1805.

Eden, Sir Frederick Morton. *The State of the Poor.* 3 vols. London, 1797.

Estcourt, Edgar E., and John Orlebar Payne, eds. *The English Catholic Nonjurors of 1715.* London, 1885.

Fieldhouse, R., and B. Jennings. *History of Richmond and Swaledale.* Chichester, 1978.

Fraser, Robert. *General View of the County of Cornwall.* London, 1794.

Gash, Norman. *Politics in the Age of Peel.* London: Longmans, 1953.

Gazetteer of the British Isles. 9th ed. Edinburgh: John Bartholomew & Son, 1966.

Geological Survey Office. Drift maps, Yorkshire.

Gibson, Jeremy, and Dennis Mills, eds. *Land Tax Assessments c.1690–c.1950.* 2d ed. Plymouth: Federation of Family History Societies, 1984.

Ginter, Donald E. "The Financing of the Whig Party Organization 1783–1793." *American Historical Review* 71 (1966): 421–40.

– "The Incidence of Revaluation." In *Land and Property: The English Land Tax 1692–1832,* edited by Michael Turner and Dennis Mills. Gloucester: Alan Sutton, 1986.

– "A Wealth of Problems with the Land Tax." *Economic History Review* 2d ser., 35 (1982): 416–21.

– ed. *Whig Organization in the General Election of 1790*. Berkeley: University of California Press, 1967.

Gray, H.L. "Yeoman Farming in Oxfordshire from the Sixteenth Century to the Nineteenth." *Quarterly Journal of Economics* 24 (1910): 293–326.

Grigg, David B. *The Agricultural Revolution in South Lincolnshire*. Cambridge: Cambridge University Press, 1966.

– "Changing Regional Values During the Agricultural Revolution in South Lincolnshire." *Transactions of the Institute of British Geographers* 30 (1962): 91–103.

– "An Index of Regional Change in English Farming." *Transactions of the Institute of British Geographers* 36 (1965): 55–67.

– "The Land Tax Returns." *Agricultural History Review* 10 (1962): 82–94.

Grover, Richard. "Early Land Tax Assessments Explored: (2) Kent and Sussex." In *Land and Property: The English Land Tax 1692–1832*, edited by Michael Turner and Dennis Mills. Gloucester: Alan Sutton, 1986.

Habakkuk, Sir John. "Economic Functions of English Landowners in the Seventeenth and Eighteenth Centuries." *Explorations in Entrepreneurial History* 6 (1953–54): 92–102.

– "The English Land Market in the Eighteenth Century." In *Britain and the Netherlands*, edited by J.S. Bromley and E.H. Kossmann, 154–73. London: Chatto & Windus, 1960.

– "English Landownership, 1680–1740." *Economic History Review* 1st ser., 10 (1940): 2–17.

– "The Long-Term Rate of Interest and the Price of Land in the Seventeenth Century." *Economic History Review* 2d ser., 5 (1952–53): 26–45.

– "Marriage Settlements in the Eighteenth Century." *Transactions of the Royal Historical Society* 4th ser., 32 (1950): 15–30.

– "The Rise and Fall of English Landed Families, 1600–1800." *Transactions of the Royal Historical Society* 5th ser., 29 (1979): 187–207; 30 (1980): 199–221.

Hadwin, J.F. "The Medieval Lay Subsidies and Economic History." *Economic History Review* 2d ser., 36 (1983): 200–17.

Hammond, J.L., and Barbara Hammond. *The Village Labourer 1760–1832*. New ed. London: Longmans, Green, 1913.

Harris, Alan. *The Rural Landscape of the East Riding of Yorkshire 1700–1850*. London: Oxford University Press, 1961; 2d ed. East Ardsley: S.R. Publishers, 1969.

Harrison, S.B. *An Analytical Digest of All the Reported Cases Determined in the House of Lords, the Several Courts of Common Law, in Banc and at Nisi Prius; and the Court of Bankruptcy: And Also the Crown Cases Reserved, from Mich. Term, 1756, to Mich. Term, 1834* [continued in vol. 4 to Easter Term 1836]. 4 vols. London, 1835–37.

Hartley, Marie, and Joan Ingilby. *The Old Hand-Knitters of the Dales*. Clapham: The Dalesman, 1951.

Henstock, Adrian. "House Repopulation from the Land Tax Assessments in a Derbyshire Market Town, 1780–1825." In *Land and Property: The English Land Tax 1692–1832*, edited by Michael Turner and Dennis Mills. Gloucester: Alan Sutton, 1986.

Hill, B.W. *British Parliamentary Parties 1742–1832*. London: George Allen & Unwin, 1985.

– *The Growth of Parliamentary Parties 1689–1742*. London: George Allen & Unwin, 1976.

Hilton, R.H. *The Decline of Serfdom in Medieval England*. London: Macmillan, for the Economic History Society, 1969.

Holderness, B.A., "The English Land Market in the Eighteenth Century: The Case of Lincolnshire." *Economic History Review* 2d ser., 27 (1974): 557–76.

– " 'Open' and 'Close' Parishes in England in the Eighteenth and Nineteenth Centuries." *Agricultural History Review* 20 (1972): 126–39.

Holmes, Geoffrey. *British Politics in the Age of Anne*. London: Macmillan, 1967.

Holt, John. *General View of the Agriculture of the County of Lancaster*. London, 1795.

Hope-Jones, Arthur. *Income Tax in the Napoleonic Wars*. Cambridge: Cambridge University Press, 1939.

Hughes, John. *Studies in Administration and Finance 1558–1825 with Special Reference to the History of Salt Taxation in England*. Manchester: Manchester University Press, 1934.

Humphrey-Smith, Cecil R., ed. *The Phillimore Atlas and Index of Parish Registers*. Chichester: Phillimore, 1984.

Hunt, H.G. "The Chronology of Parliamentary Enclosure in Leicestershire." *Economic History Review* 2d ser., 10 (1957–58): 265–72.

– "Landownership and Enclosure, 1750–1830." *Economic History Review* 2d ser., 11 (1958–59): 497–505.

– "Land Tax Assessments." *History* 52 (1967): 283–6.

Johnson, Arthur H. *The Disappearance of the Small Landowner*. Ford Lectures, 1909. Oxford: Clarendon Press, 1909.

Kent, Nathaniel. *General View of the Agriculture of the County of Norfolk*. London, 1794.

Kerridge, Eric. *The Agricultural Revolution*. London: George Allen & Unwin, 1967.

Langdale, Thomas. *A Topographical Dictionary of Yorkshire*. 2d ed. Northallerton, 1822.

Langford, Paul. *The Excise Crisis: Society and Politics in the Age of Walpole*. Oxford: Clarendon Press, 1975.

Lawrence, John. *The Modern Land Steward.* 2d ed. London, 1806.

Lawton, G.O., ed. "Northwich Hundred Poll Tax 1660 and Hearth Tax 1664." *The Record Society of Lancashire and Cheshire* 119 (1979).

Leatham, Isaac. *General View of the Agriculture of the East Riding of Yorkshire, and the Ainsty of the City of York.* London, 1794.

McKenzie, R.T. *British Political Parties.* 2d ed. New York: St Martin's Press, 1963.

Malcolm, William, and James and Jacob Malcolm. *General View of the Agriculture of the County of Surrey.* London, 1794.

Mantoux, Paul. *The Industrial Revolution in the Eighteenth Century.* Rev. ed. London: Jonathan Cape, 1961.

Marshall, William. *On the Landed Property of England.* London, 1804.

– *The Review and Abstract of the County Reports to the Board of Agriculture.* 5 vols. York, 1808–17.

– *The Rural Economy of Yorkshire.* 2d ed. 2 vols. London, 1796.

Martin, J.M. "Landownership and the Land Tax Returns." *Agricultural History Review* 14 (1966): 96–103.

– "The Parliamentary Enclosure Movement and Rural Society in Warwickshire." *Agricultural History Review* 15 (1967): 19–39.

– "The Small Landowner and Parliamentary Enclosure in Warwickshire." *Economic History Review* 2d ser., 32 (1979): 328–43.

Mavor, William. *General View of the Agriculture of Berkshire.* London, 1808.

Mills, Dennis R. "Early Land Tax Assessments Explored: (1) Rutland, Cambridgeshire, and Lincolnshire." In *Land and Property: The English Land Tax 1692–1832*, edited by Michael Turner and Dennis Mills. Gloucester: Alan Sutton, 1986.

– "English Villages in the Eighteenth and Nineteenth Centuries: A Sociological Approach." *Amateur* (now *Local*) *Historian* 6 (1965): 271–8.

– *Lord and Peasant in Nineteenth Century Britain.* London: Croom Helm, 1980.

Mingay, G.E. "The Course of Rents in the Age of Malthus." In *Malthus and his Times*, edited by Michael Turner, 85–95. London: St Martin's Press, 1986.

– *Enclosure and the Small Farmer in the Age of the Industrial Revolution.* London: Macmillan, for the Economic History Society, 1968.

– *English Landed Society in the Eighteenth Century.* London: Routledge & Kegan Paul, 1963.

– "Introduction to Second Edition." In *Common Land and Inclosure*, by E.C.K. Gonner, 2d ed. xxxiii–liii. London: Frank Cass, 1966.

– "The Land Tax Assessments and the Small Landowner." *Economic History Review* 2d ser., 17 (1964–65), 381–8.

– "Letter to the Editor." *Agricultural History Review* 15 (1967): 18.

– "The Size of Farms in the Eighteenth Century." *Economic History Review* 2d ser., 14 (1961–62): 469–88.

Monk, John. *General View of the Agriculture of the County of Leicester.* London, 1794.

Namier, Sir Lewis. *England in the Age of the American Revolution.* 2d ed. London: Macmillan, 1961.

– *The Structure of Politics at the Accession of George III.* 2d ed. London: Macmillan, 1957.

Noble, Margaret. "The Land Tax Assessments in the Study of the Physical Development of Country Towns." In *Land and Property: The English Land Tax 1692–1832*, edited by Michael Turner and Dennis Mills. Gloucester: Alan Sutton, 1986.

– "Land-Tax Returns and Urban Development." *Local Historian* 15 (1982): 86–92.

Obelkevich, James. *Religion and Rural Society: South Lindsey 1825–1875.* Oxford: Clarendon Press, 1976.

O'Brien, P.K. "British Incomes and Property in the Early Nineteenth Century." *Economic History Review* 2d ser., 12 (1959–60): 255–67.

O'Gorman, Frank. *The Whig Party and the French Revolution.* London: Macmillan, 1967.

Ordnance Survey Office. Six-inch Ordnance Survey of Yorkshire.

Ostrogorski, Moisei. *Democracy and the Organization of Political Parties.* 1st English ed. 2 vols. London, 1902.

Outhwaite, R.B. "Progress and Backwardness in English Agriculture, 1500–1650." *Economic History Review* 2d ser., 34 (1986): 1–18.

Page, William, ed. *The Victoria History of the County of York, North Riding.* 2 vols. London: Oxford University Press, 1914–23.

Payne, Ernest Oscar. "Property in Land in South Bedfordshire 1750–1832." *Publications of the Bedfordshire Historical Record Society* 23 (1946).

Pearce, William. *General View of the Agriculture in Berkshire.* London, 1794.

Phillips, John A. *Electoral Behavior in Unreformed England: Plumpers, Splitters, and Straights.* Princeton: Princeton University Press, 1982.

Pitt, William. *A General View of the Agriculture of the County of Leicester.* London, 1809.

– *General View of the Agriculture of the County of Northampton.* London, 1809.

Plumb, J.H. *The Growth of Political Stability in England 1675–1725.* London: Macmillan, 1967.

Pringle, Andrew. *General View of the Agriculture of the County of Westmoreland.* Edinburgh, 1794.

Quintrell, B.W., ed. "Proceedings of the Lancashire Justices of the Peace at the Sheriff's Table during Assizes Week, 1578–1694." *The Record Society of Lancashire and Cheshire* 121 (1981).

Raistrick, Arthur. *Old Yorkshire Dales*. Newton Abbot: David and Charles, 1967.

– *West Riding of Yorkshire*. London: Hodder and Stoughton, 1970.

Rennie, Broun, and Shirreff. *General View of the Agriculture of the West Riding of Yorkshire*. London, 1794.

Roebuck, Peter. *Yorkshire Baronets 1640–1760: Families, Estates, and Fortunes*. London: Oxford University Press, 1980.

Rudé, George, "The Middlesex Electors of 1768–1769." *English Historical Review* 75 (1960): 601–17.

– *Wilkes and Liberty: A Social Study of 1763 to 1774*. Oxford: Clarendon Press, 1962.

Sabine, B.E.V. *A History of Income Tax*. London: George Allen & Unwin, 1966.

Seligman, Edwin R.A. *The Income Tax: A Study of the History, Theory, and Practice of Income Taxation at Home and Abroad.* 2d ed. New York: Macmillan, 1914.

Sheppard, June. "Inhabited Houses 1801–51: an Evaluation of Census Figures." *Local Historian* 18 (1988): 106–11.

"The Significance of Land-Tax Assessments: Report of a Conference Held in September 1981." *Local Historian* 15 (1982): 161–5.

Sinclair, Sir John. *The History of the Public Revenue of the British Empire*. 3d ed. 3 vols. London, 1803–04.

Snell, K.D.M. *Annals of the Labouring Poor: Social Change and Agrarian England, 1660–1900*. Cambridge: Cambridge University Press, 1985.

Soltow, Lee. "The Land Tax Redemption Records, 1798–1963." *Economic History Review* 2d ser., 35 (1982): 427–33.

– "Wealth Distribution in England and Wales in 1798." *Economic History Review* 2d ser., 34 (1981): 60–70.

Stamp, Sir Laurence Dudley, ed. *The Land of Britain: The Report of the Land Utilization Survey of Great Britain*. 92 parts. London: Geographical Publications, 1936–46.

Stevenson, William. *General View of the Agriculture of the County of Surrey*. London, 1809.

Stone, Lawrence, and Jeanne C. Fawtier Stone. *An Open Elite? England 1540–1880*. Oxford: Clarendon Press, 1984.

Stone, Thomas. *General View of the Agriculture of the County of Bedford*. London, 1794.

– *General View of the Agriculture of the County of Lincoln*. London, 1794.

Strickland, H.E. *A General View of the Agriculture of the East-Riding of Yorkshire*. York, 1812.

Tait, James. *Taxation in Salford Hundred 1524–1802*. Chetham Society, new ser., 83 (1924).

Tate, W.E. *A Domesday of English Enclosure Acts and Awards.* Edited by M.E. Turner. Reading: The Library, University of Reading, 1978.

Thirsk, Joan. "Agrarian History, 1540–1950." In *The Victoria History of the Counties of England, Leicestershire*, edited by W.G. Hoskins, vol 2, 199–264. London: Oxford University Press, 1954.

– "Field Systems of the East Midlands." In *Studies of Field Systems in the British Isles*, edited by Alan R. H. Baker and Robin A. Butlin, 232–80. Cambridge: Cambridge University Press, 1973.

Thompson, F.M.L. *English Landed Society in the Nineteenth Century.* London: Routledge & Kegan Paul, 1963.

– "The Land Market in the Nineteenth Century." *Oxford Economic Papers* new ser., 9 (1957): 285–308.

Thompson, R.J. "An Inquiry into the Rent of Agricultural Land in England and Wales during the Nineteenth Century." *Journal of the Royal Statistical Society* 70 (1907): 587–616.

Tillott, P.M., ed. *The Victoria History of the County of York: The City of York.* London: Oxford University Press, 1961.

Toynbee, Arnold. *Lectures on the Industrial Revolution in England*, excerpts reprinted in *The Industrial Revolution in Britain*, edited by Philip A.M. Taylor, 1–6. Boston: D.C. Heath, 1958.

Tuke, John. *General View of the Agriculture of the North Riding of Yorkshire.* London, 1794; 2d ed. London, 1800.

Turner, Michael E. *Enclosures in Britain 1750–1830*. London: Macmillan, for the Economic History Society, 1984.

– *English Parliamentary Enclosure: Its Historical Geography and Economic History*. Folkestone: William Dawson, 1980.

– "Parliamentary Enclosure and Landownership Change in Buckinghamshire." *Economic History Review* 2d ser., 28 (1975): 565–81.

Turner, Michael E., and Dennis Mills, eds. *Land and Property: The English Land Tax 1692–1832*. Gloucester: Alan Sutton, 1986.

Unwin, Robert W. "An Industrial Dimension to Land Tax Studies: the Barnsley Coalfield, 1690–1830." In *Land and Property: The English Land Tax 1692–1832*, edited by Michael Turner and Dennis Mills. Gloucester: Alan Sutton, 1986.

– *Search Guide to the English Land Tax*. Wakefield: West Yorkshire County Record Office, 1982.

Walker, D. *General View of the Agriculture of the County of Hertford*. London, 1795.

Ward, W.R. *The English Land Tax in the Eighteenth Century*. London: Oxford University Press, 1953.

Williams, E.N., ed. *The Eighteenth Century Constitution: Documents and Commentary*. Cambridge: Cambridge University Press, 1960.

Wilson, G.J. "The Land Tax and West Derby Hundred 1780–1831." *Transactions of the Historical Society of Lancashire and Cheshire* 4th ser., 129 (1980): 63–91.

– "The Land Tax Problem." *Economic History Review* 2d ser., 35 (1982): 422–6.

Wordie, J.R. "Social Change on the Leveson-Gower Estates, 1714–1832." *Economic History Review* 2d ser., 27 (1974): 593–609.

Worgan, G.B. *General View of the Agriculture of the County of Cornwall.* London, 1811.

Wrigley, E.A., ed. *Identifying People in the Past.* London: Arnold, 1973.

– *Nineteenth Century Society: Essays in the Use of Quantitative Methods for the Study of Social Data.* Cambridge: Cambridge University Press, 1972.

Young, Arthur. *General View of the Agriculture of the County of Norfolk.* London, 1804.

– *General View of the Agriculture of Hertfordshire.* London, 1804.

– *General View of the Agriculture of Lincolnshire.* London, 1813.

– *General View of the Agriculture of Oxfordshire.* London, 1813.

– *A Six Months Tour Through the North of England.* 2d ed. 4 vols. London, 1771.

Yelling, J.A. *Common Field and Enclosure in England 1450–1850.* London: Macmillan, 1977.

Index

Personal and place names in the text are not separately indexed when they are discussed directly in conjunction with a table, map, or appendix. Tables, maps, and appendices are not indexed for their subject or contents.